MOON

Washington State

MARISSA PEDERSEN

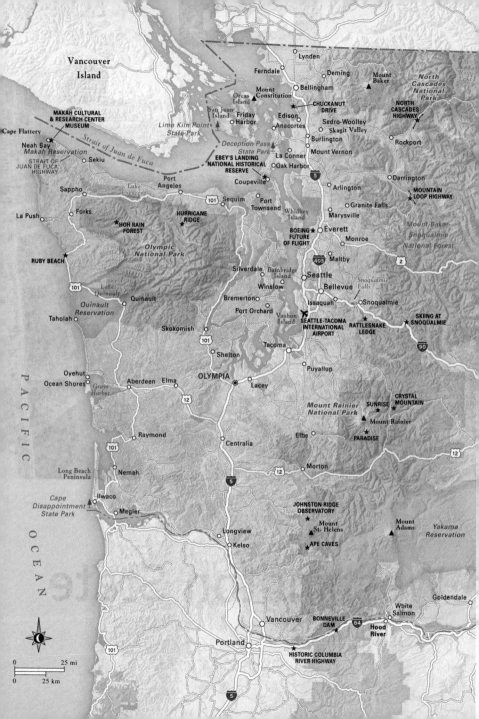

Contents

Hurricane Ridge in Olympic National Park

Washington State

Brimming with enchantment, Washington state is a true spectacle of nature, culture, and adventure. Picture this—snowy mountaintops puncturing the skyline, dense forests veiling hidden waterfalls, vast vineyards stretching under the clear skies, and rugged coastlines kissed by the Pacific, all interspersed with unique towns and cities.

Seattle, distinguished by its skyline bearing the iconic Space Needle, is located in the middle of it all. With a population surpassing 725,000 people, the city hums with life, stirring the senses with vibrant street art, the tantalizing aromas of Pike Place Market, the rhythmic strumming of street musicians, and, of course, the unparalleled taste of its famed coffee. Any local will tell you, in Seattle life isn't just lived—it's savored.

Yet beyond the city lights, Washington whispers an invitation to the great outdoors. Exchange the cityscape for a canvas of stars reflected in the tranquil waters of the Pacific coast. Swap city streets for trails winding through lush, moss-draped rain forests in Olympic National Park. And suddenly, the Emerald City feels like a world away.

Venture into the heart of wine country in the Columbia Gorge, where sprawling vineyards and boutique wineries offer a taste of Washington's finest vintages. Hike the rugged trails of Mount Rainier National Park, where alpine meadows burst with wildflowers in the summer and pristine snow blankets the terrain in winter. Delve into profound Indigenous cultures, take in the sweeping views from Hurricane Ridge, seek majestic whales off the shores of the San Juan Islands. Or simply lose yourself in the wild, untouched landscapes.

Each corner of this state offers a unique slice of its diverse beauty, ensuring that every visit is a new adventure. Washington state isn't just a destination—it's a treasure trove waiting to be discovered.

Rialto Beach

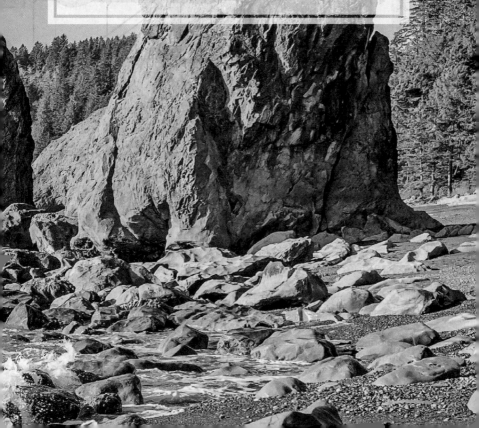

10 TOP
EXPERIENCES

1 Exploring the fresh seafood and unique handicrafts of **Pike Place Market,** one of America's oldest farmers markets (page 46).

4 **Wine-tasting** in top destinations like the Yakima Valley (page 407), Red Mountain (page 417), and Walla Walla (page 419).

5 **Whale-watching** on San Juan Island (page 243).

6 Walking through the lush **Hoh Rain Forest** in Olympic National Park (page 204).

7 Taking a factory tour at the **Boeing Future of Flight** in Everett (page 147).

8 Biking the **Spokane River Centennial Trail** from Spokane to the Idaho border (page 445).

Planning Your Trip

WHERE TO GO

Seattle

Puget Sound and Lake Washington frame Seattle, a city famous for its diverse neighborhoods and landmarks. Visit **Pike Place Market** for local fare and to see the world-famous fish toss, or ride up the **Space Needle** to take in incredible panoramas of the city and surrounding area. The **Seattle Art Museum** and the **Museum of Pop Culture** are world-class cultural institutions, while the trails and beaches of **Discovery Park** or the waters of **Lake Union** are perfect for nature lovers.

Around Seattle

There are several amazing day trips close to Seattle. To the east, you'll find **Snoqualmie Falls** and plenty of hiking trails, or stay a little more local and go wine-tasting in nearby **Woodinville.** To the south, discover energetic **Tacoma,** or venture north to explore picturesque seaside towns like **Edmonds** and **Everett,** home to the Boeing factory. Or drive the **Mountain Loop Highway** for scenic views of Washington's western Cascades. Take a ferry ride to the **Puget Sound islands** of Whidbey, Vashon, or Bainbridge Island to experience small-town life.

Olympic Peninsula

From mild rain forests to rocky shores, the Olympic Peninsula is home to a wide variety of ecosystems. One must-see is **Olympic National Park,** which boasts beautiful beaches, old forests, and majestic mountains in an unspoiled natural setting. Take a stroll around **Rialto Beach**'s sea

view from Mount Storm King, Olympic National Park

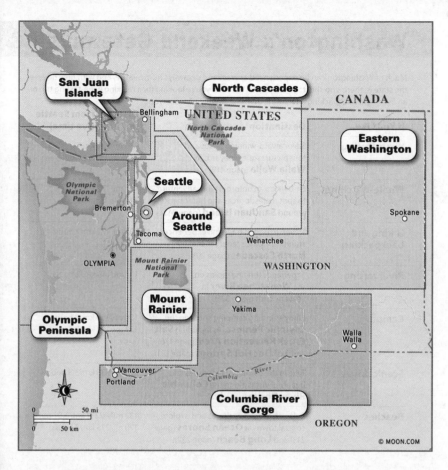

stacks and tidal pools, or wander through moss-draped trees and lush foliage in the **Hoh Rain Forest**. **Port Angeles** and **Forks** are just two of the quaint communities on the peninsula that make great home bases for adventures.

San Juan Islands

The San Juan Islands are a haven for outdoor enthusiasts and wildlife watchers. On **San Juan Island,** you can visit the town of **Friday Harbor,** explore historic sites like Lime Kiln Point State Park, and take a whale-watching tour to see orcas in their natural habitat. **Orcas Island,** the largest of the islands, features Moran State Park with camping opportunities and panoramic views from Mount Constitution, while **Lopez Island** is favored by bikers.

North Cascades

The North Cascades offer some of Washington's most rugged and stunning landscapes. **North Cascades National Park** is a paradise for hikers and climbers, with trails leading to alpine lakes, towering peaks, and pristine wilderness. The scenic **North Cascades Highway** winds through the park with stunning views. The region's small towns, such as **Winthrop** and **Mazama,** are ideal places to fuel up and rest for the night.

Washington's Weekend Getaways

Much of Washington can be experienced as weekend getaways from Seattle, and with how diverse the state is, there's no shortage of options. Whether you're looking for a relaxing wine-tasting trip or an overnight backpacking adventure, there's something for everyone.

If You Like...	Destination	Distance from Seattle (mi/km/drive time)
Wine-tasting	Savor award-winning wines and tour picturesque vineyards in **Walla Walla** (page 419).	260 mi/420 km/ 4 hours 15 minutes
Whale-watching	Embark on an unforgettable adventure to spot majestic orcas and humpbacks around **San Juan Island** (page 243).	107 mi/172 km/ 3 hours 15 minutes
Hiking and backpacking	Traverse rugged trails and experience stunning alpine scenery in the **North Cascades** (page 293).	107 mi/172 km/2 hours
River rafting	Experience thrilling rapids on the **Wenatchee River** in Leavenworth (page 321).	117 mi/188 km/2 hours
Camping	Enjoy stunning camping spots on the **Olympic Peninsula,** including **Salt Creek Recreation Area** (page 176) and **Sol Duc Hot Springs** (page 191).	100 mi/160 km/3 hours 123 mi/198 km/3.5 hours
Scenic drives	Take in the dramatic landscapes and beautiful vistas along the **Columbia River Gorge** (page 388).	210 mi/338 km/3.5 hours
Beaches	Relax on the sandy shores and explore coastal towns at **Ocean Shores** (page 213) and **Long Beach** (page 222).	132 miles/212 km/2.5 hours 170 mi/275 km/3 hours

Mount Rainier

Mount Rainier National Park is a wonderland for hikers, with trails ranging from easy walks through wildflower meadows to strenuous climbs up glaciers. The **Paradise** and **Sunrise** areas are popular for their amazing views and numerous hiking options. The park becomes a haven for cross-country skiers and snowshoers during the winter months. The surrounding towns, like **Ashford** and **Packwood,** provide cozy lodgings. Nearby, **Mount St. Helens** and **Mount Adams** offer additional hiking adventures.

Columbia River Gorge

The Columbia River Gorge, a dramatic canyon cutting through the Cascade Range, has stunning vistas, numerous waterfalls, and many hiking opportunities. Drive along the **Historic Columbia River Highway** to see iconic waterfalls like **Multnomah Falls** and **Bridal Veil Falls.** The town of **Hood River,** known for its vibrant outdoor scene, offers excellent windsurfing and kiteboarding and a charming downtown. Continuing east, you'll find the heart of Washington's wine country in **Walla Walla** and **Yakima Valley.**

Eastern Washington

Eastern Washington, with its vast landscapes and sunny climate, contrasts sharply with the lush western part of the state. **Spokane** is the bustling main city and offers plenty of outdoor recreational opportunities. Discover the **Grand Coulee Dam's** engineering marvel, or see Ice Age remnants at **Sun Lakes-Dry Falls State Park.** Enjoy concerts with a river view at the **Gorge Amphitheatre,** or follow the **Spokane River Centennial Trail,** a paved path ideal for biking and walking.

Mount Rainier National Park

WHEN TO GO

Spring in Washington brings a mix of mild temperatures and increased rainfall, particularly in the western part of the state. While it may rain sporadically throughout the day, sunny skies often appear later. The Cascade Range usually retains snow until late spring, making its lower-elevation hikes more accessible during this season. In the eastern regions, spring sees blooming wildflowers and warmer, drier conditions. There are fewer crowds and beautiful wildflower displays, but also muddy trails and variable weather.

Washington in the **summer** typically means sunshine across the state, with warm, pleasant weather and minimal rain. In central and Eastern Washington, days often reach triple digits (38+°C), with cooler nights providing some relief. The western side, including the Olympic Peninsula and the coast, enjoys warm, pleasant temperatures that rarely exceed the low 80s (28°C). Higher elevations in the Cascade Range and Olympic Mountains might not be completely snow-free until mid-July, with wildflower blooms lasting into August. But with ideal hiking conditions and vibrant wildflower displays, it's also the most popular time of year to visit.

Unfortunately, **wildfires** are becoming more

prevalent in the state and happen mostly **June-October.** These can lead to road closures, hazardous air quality, and evacuations. Always check current conditions before you head outdoors.

Fall in Washington is marked by cooler temperatures and the return of rainfall, especially in the western regions. The foliage in the Cascade Range and around Puget Sound turns vibrant hues of red, orange, and yellow, offering stunning scenic drives and hikes. Eastern Washington experiences a more gradual cooling with less precipitation, making it a pleasant time for apple picking and wine tours.

Washington's **winters** are wet and mild on the western side, with frequent rain and occasional snow in lower elevations. The Cascade Range and Olympic Mountains receive significant snowfall, making them popular destinations for winter sports. In Eastern Washington, winters are colder with more snowfall, and frequent road closures due to snow and ice can make crossing the mountain passes difficult. This makes for excellent conditions for winter sports and fewer crowds in popular tourist areas, but potentially challenging travel conditions.

BEST OF
Washington

This 10-day itinerary covers some of the best things to do in western Washington. You'll explore some of the state's most well-known locations—vibrant Seattle, the serene San Juan Islands, the Olympic Peninsula's untamed beauty, and magnificent vistas of Mount Rainier.

Seattle

Day 1

Start with a visit to iconic **Pike Place Market** to sample fresh seafood and shop for unique handicrafts. Don't miss the **Gum Wall** and the **original Starbucks** store nearby. For lunch, head to **Beecher's Handmade Cheese** for some of their famous mac and cheese. In the afternoon, explore the **Seattle Art Museum,** then rent a bike and ride to **Olympic Sculpture Park.** Return your bike and have a scenic waterfront dinner in Belltown at **Aqua by El Gaucho,** followed by an evening ride on the **Seattle Great Wheel.**

Day 2

Begin your second day with coffee and pastries at **Le Panier,** a French bakery in Pike Place Market. Next head to the **Space Needle** for some of the best views of the city. Take the elevator back down

and walk next door to **Chihuly Garden and Glass** to admire the stunning glass sculptures. Have lunch at **Taylor Shellfish Farms** for fresh oysters. Spend the afternoon at the **Museum of Pop Culture,** exploring exhibits dedicated to music, science fiction, and pop culture. Head back to Pike Place for an Italian meal at **The Pink Door.**

Day 3

In the morning, make your way to Ballard for coffee at **Caffe Umbria.** Afterward, visit the **Ballard Locks** to watch boats pass through the canal and salmon navigate the fish ladder. Stroll through the charming shops in the Ballard area. For lunch, enjoy the vibrant flavors at **La Carta de Oaxaca.**

Spend the afternoon in Fremont exploring quirky art installations, such as the **Fremont Troll.** You can also go to **Gas Works Park** for views of the Seattle skyline. For dinner, try **Ivar's Salmon House,** which offers beautiful views of Lake Union.

San Juan Islands
Day 4
After a cup of coffee at **Storyville Coffee** in Seattle, drive to Anacortes to catch the **ferry** to **San Juan Island.** The drive is about 1.5 hours, and the ferry ride is another 1.5 hours, so factor travel time into your itinerary. Once you get to Friday Harbor, enjoy a burger and fries at **Vic's Drive In.** Spend the afternoon in Friday Harbor exploring local stores like **Griffin Bay Bookstore** and **Arctic Raven Gallery.** Then visit the **San Juan Island National Historical Park,** including the American Camp and English Camp, to learn about the history of the area.

For dinner, visit **Downriggers** to dine with views of the ferry. After dinner, go to **Lime Kiln Point State Park,** see if you can spot any whales, and walk along the trails while enjoying stunning coastal views. Return to your hotel in Friday Harbor on San Juan Island, where you'll stay for two nights.

Day 5
Start your morning at **Rocky Bay Café & Delicatessen,** a local favorite for hearty breakfasts. Join a **whale-watching tour** with a local operator to experience majestic orcas and other marine wildlife. Head to **The Bait Shop** in Friday Harbor for lunch for seafood and stunning waterfront views. In the afternoon, visit **The Farm at Krystal Acres,** where you can meet friendly alpacas and browse the farm store, which sells a variety of ethically produced products made from alpaca wool. Next, enjoy a tasting at **Westcott Bay Cider,** sampling their artisanal ciders made from local apples. For dinner, head to Roche Harbor to dine at **Duck Soup,** then walk around the harbor at sunset.

Olympic Peninsula
Day 6
Before leaving San Juan Island, start your day with a quick breakfast at **Bakery San Juan**

Pike Place Market

Hurricane Ridge in Olympic National Park

in Friday Harbor. Take a morning ferry back to Anacortes and drive 2 hours 45 minutes to **Port Angeles.** Enjoy lunch in Port Angeles at **Downriggers on the Water.** Then start your exploration of **Olympic National Park** at **Hurricane Ridge.** Drive up to this stunning vantage point to enjoy views of the mountains and valleys, and spend the afternoon hiking one of the many trails, such as **High Ridge.** Return to Port Angeles and enjoy dinner at **Next Door GastroPub.** Stay the night in town.

Day 7

In the morning, drive to Neah Bay and learn about the rich heritage of the Makah Tribe at the **Makah Cultural and Research Center.** Then head to nearby **Cape Flattery** for a short hike to the dramatic cliffs overlooking the Pacific Ocean. For lunch, enjoy a meal at **Calvin's Crab House** back in Neah Bay. In the afternoon, make your way to the **Hoh Rain Forest,** one of the most lush and green areas in the Pacific Northwest. Walk the **Hall of Mosses** trail and immerse yourself in the serene beauty of this unique ecosystem. End with dinner in Forks at **Pacific Pizza,** and stay the night in **Forks.**

Day 8

In the morning, grab a bite to eat and coffee from one of the local coffee stands in Forks. Stop at **Kalaloch Beach** to see the famous Tree of Life and enjoy the scenic coastal views as you make your way to **Ocean Shores.** For lunch, try **Bennett's Fish Shack** for some of the best fish and chips in the area. Rent a bike and cruise along Ocean Shores' roads, or visit **Damon Point State Park.** In the evening, dine at **Galway Bay Irish Pub** for Irish food and live music. Stay the night in Ocean Shores.

Mount Rainier

Day 9

After coffee in Ocean Shores, drive the 3 hours to Mount Rainier, stopping in **Olympia** for lunch at **Well 80 Brewhouse.** Continue your journey to Mount Rainier, arriving at **Paradise** in the early afternoon. Spend the afternoon hiking the **Skyline Trail** and stop at **Myrtle Falls** on the way back. In the evening, enjoy dinner at the **Paradise Inn Dining Room** and head to Ashford to stay the night.

Day 10

Start your morning with breakfast at **Paradise Village Restaurant** in Ashford. Drive toward **Mount St. Helens,** which will take 2 hours. Along the way, pause at **Mayfield Lake** for beautiful views and a chance to stretch your legs. For lunch, stop at the **Backwoods Café** at Eco Park Resort near Silver Lake. Visit the **Coldwater Ridge Visitor Center** to learn more about the eruption and the area's recovery. Spend the afternoon exploring the hiking trails, taking in the views of the crater and lava dome. From Mount St. Helens, it's a 3-hour drive back to Seattle, so many people choose to stay the night in **Castle Rock. El Compadre** is a great place for Mexican food in Castle Rock if you stay overnight.

Whale-Watching

Whale-watching is a truly iconic activity in the Pacific Northwest, and Washington boasts no shortage of places to witness these magnificent creatures. Seeing humpback, orca, and gray whales in their own environment is an unforgettable adventure. Even more thrilling are the times of year when these whales migrate. Gray whales travel north **March-May** and migrate south **October-December.** Prime time to watch humpback whales is **May-October,** while orcas are visible all year, with the best sightings **May-September.**

WHALE-WATCHING TOURS

Sign up for one of the numerous whale-watching trips across the state to increase your chances of seeing these fantastic creatures. **Port Townsend** on the Olympic Peninsula offers access to the vast Strait of Juan de Fuca, while **Anacortes** and **Friday Harbor** give direct access to the rich waters around the San Juan Islands. These tours use technology to pinpoint the whales' location, and experienced staff members provide educational information.

WHALE-WATCHING VIEWPOINTS

For those who prefer to stay on land, you have a good chance of spotting whales from the following places.

San Juan Islands

One of the best land-based whale-watching spots is **Lime Kiln Point State Park,** also known as Whale Watch Park, on San Juan Island. Visitors can often see orcas, especially during the summer months. Another great spot on San Juan Island is **San Juan County Park,** which provides fantastic water views where orcas frequently pass by.

Olympic Peninsula

On the Olympic Peninsula, **Cape Flattery** has stunning views of the Pacific Ocean where visi-tors might spot migrating gray whales. **Kalaloch Beach,** located in Olympic National Park, is another excellent spot for whale-watching, particularly during the gray whale migration.

The Strait of Juan de Fuca has great whale-watching locations, such as **Dungeness Spit** near Sequim. The long sand spit provides excellent opportunities for spotting gray whales, particularly in the spring.

Coastal areas like **Westport** are ideal for whale-watching, and gray whales are often sighted there, especially during their migration periods. **La Push,** near the Quileute Indian Reservation, also offers amazing coastal views and opportunities to spot migrating whales.

Whidbey Island

Whidbey Island, with locations like **Langley** and **Possession Point State Park,** offers great viewpoints for whale-watching.

SEALS, SEA LIONS, AND SEA OTTERS

Whales may be Washington's most famous marine animal, but seals, sea lions, and sea otters also call the state's oceans home.

One of the best places to see harbor seals is the San Juan Islands, particularly around **Roche Harbor** and **Friday Harbor,** especially during pupping season in the spring and summer when you can see seal pups resting on the shores. Another excellent spot for seal-watching is the **Edmonds Underwater Park,** where harbor seals often swim close to the shore.

Sea lions are also frequently spotted lounging and fishing around **Port Angeles Harbor,** particularly around the Ediz Hook area.

The best place in Washington to see sea otters is the coastal waters of the Olympic Peninsula. Near **La Push** and the mouth of the **Hoh River** are prime locations for spotting sea otters as they float on their backs in the kelp beds.

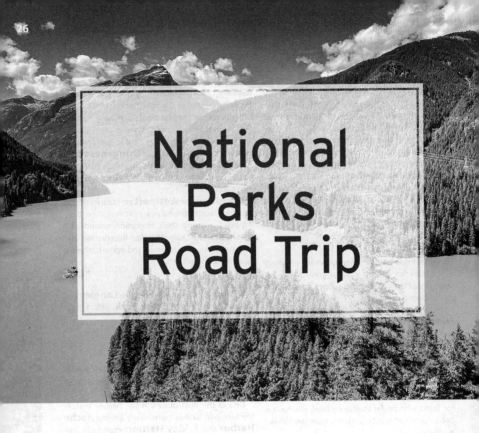

National Parks Road Trip

Washington is lucky enough to have three national parks, each with its own allure. If you have the time, spending a few days in each one is worth it. The best time to go is **July-September,** as all three parks will be open, and your chances of encountering snow are minimal.

Note: Timed reservations are required for entering the Paradise and Sunrise areas of Mount Rainier National Park during high season (for more information, visit recreation.gov).

North Cascades National Park
Day 1
SEATTLE TO NORTH CASCADES
100 mi/160 km/2 hours

From Seattle, make the 2-hour drive northeast via I-5 and Route 20 along the **North Cascades Highway.** Your first stop is in Concrete at the **Lower Baker Dam Overlook** for views of this mighty dam. When you're hungry, take a lunch break at **Annie's Pizza Station,** known for its

freshly made pizzas. After refueling, head to the **Skagit River Bald Eagle Interpretive Center** to spot local birds and have a chance to see bald eagles.

Continue driving to North Cascades National Park. Your base will be in Marblemount, but continue past here for the afternoon. Start with the **Trail of the Cedars,** a short loop hike that takes you over a suspension bridge and through an ancient forest of towering cedar trees. For a

1: Reflection Lakes 2: Ruby Beach

more challenging hike, try **Heather-Maple Pass Loop,** known for its alpine views and wildflower meadows. After a day of hiking, head back to Marblemount and enjoy a hearty dinner at the **Upriver Grill & Taproom.**

Day 2
NORTH CASCADES
114 mi/183 km/2.5 hours

Drive to Newhalem to stock up on food for the day at the **Newhalem General Store.** From Newhalem, head to the **Diablo Lake Overlook** to get stunning photos of the turquoise lake. See more of the lake by going on a **Diablo Lake Boat Tour.**

Enjoy the lunch you packed from Newhalem while taking in the surroundings of Diablo Lake. In the afternoon, drive to the **Blue Lake** trailhead for an easy, rewarding hike that ends at a beautiful lake. Later, make your way to **Washington Pass** at the far edge of the park for more spectacular views of the North Cascades. Return to Marblemount for the night and enjoy dinner at **Mondo's.**

Olympic National Park
Day 3
NORTH CASCADES TO PORT ANGELES
160 mi/260 km/4 hours

Start your morning early and head toward Olympic National Park. To get here, retrace the North Cascades Highway to I-5 then drive south to Edmonds where you'll catch the ferry to Kingston. From Kingston, take Route 104 west towards the Olympic Peninsula. Continue driving until you reach Sequim. Have lunch at the **Oak Table Café.**

Continue to **Lake Crescent** in Olympic National Park and spend the afternoon strolling around the lake's perimeter or go for a hike, such as **Marymere Falls,** an easy hike that leads to a beautiful waterfall. If you're up for something more challenging, head up **Mount Storm King** for incredible panoramic views of the lake.

In the evening, drive to **Port Angeles** and settle in for the night. Enjoy a relaxing dinner at

Fiesta Jalisco, known for its authentic Mexican cuisine.

Day 4
PORT ANGELES TO FORKS
56 mi/90 km/1 hour

In the morning, head toward Neah Bay to visit the **Makah Cultural and Research Center** and learn about the culture of the Makah Tribe. After, enjoy clam chowder at **Warmhouse Restaurant.**

Drive south to the **Hoh Rain Forest,** one of the park's most mystical areas. Stop at the visitor center to learn about the region's ecosystems, and then hike the **Hall of Mosses trail,** a short loop through a forest draped in vibrant mosses and ferns. For a longer hike, check out part of the **Hoh River Trail,** which follows the river deep into the forest.

In the evening, drive to **Forks** and stay overnight. Enjoy burgers and fries at **Sully's Drive-In,** and go on a self-guided *Twilight* tour around town if you have time.

Day 5
FORKS TO LAKE QUINAULT
67 mi/108 km/1 hour 20 minutes

Your last day in Olympic National Park is all about discovering its coastal beauty. Start with a visit to **Rialto Beach** and its dramatic sea stacks, and the **Hole-in-the-Wall hike,** a popular trek that leads to a unique rock formation offering stunning coastal views. After your morning hike, enjoy a fresh seafood lunch at **River's Edge Restaurant.**

In the afternoon, explore the tide pools and sea stacks on **Ruby Beach,** and continue south on US 101 to the iconic **Tree of Life,** a large Sitka spruce precariously perched on a cliff, held in place by its roots.

Continue to Lake Quinault in the southwestern part of the park. To immerse yourself in the lush environment, drive the **Quinault Rain Forest Loop** or hike the **Quinault Loop Trail.** End your day with dinner at **The Salmon House** for baked salmon and a view of the lake.

Regional Cuisine: Seafood 101

Washington is famous for its fresh seafood, particularly Puget Sound oysters, wild salmon, and Dungeness crab. Here are some of the best seafood restaurants across the state. Although some places are more known for a specific item, most serve a variety of seafood dishes, such as oysters on the half shell to fish tacos and rotating catches of the day, so you'll be able to try a bit of everything.

OYSTERS

- **The Walrus and the Carpenter** offers fresh oysters, clams, and seasonal seafood in a cozy Seattle setting (page 94).
- **Taylor Shellfish Farms** is one of the biggest sellers of oysters and other shellfish; you can visit their bright and airy Seattle locations or their waterfront patio along Chuckanut Drive (pages 89 and 271).

SALMON

- **The Salmon House** serves delicious dishes like pan-seared salmon and other sustainable seafood in a rustic setting by Lake Quinault (page 209).
- **Cascade Dining Room at Skamania Lodge** offers Columbia River steelhead and wild-caught salmon in a lush forest setting near the Columbia River Gorge (page 404).
- **Doc's Marina Grill** features fresh, locally sourced seafood, including excellent salmon entrées, with stunning waterfront views on the Olympic Peninsula (page 166).

CRAB

- Choose from fresh crab, prawns, and fish with scenic views of the Columbia River Gorge at **The Chophouse at The Old Warehouse** (page 415).
- As the name implies, **Moby Duck Chowder & Seafood** has famously good chowder, but the real draw for this Olympic Peninsula gem is the Dungeness crab rolls (page 175).

CHOWDER

- **Pike Place Chowder** offers ten different chowders in the famous Pike Place Market (page 86).
- **Duke's Seafood** features award-wining clam chowder with views of the Seattle skyline at their South Lake Union location (page 90).
- **Downriggers** serves chowders and grilled fish with panoramic views of Friday Harbor (page 246).

FISH AND CHIPS

- **The Bait Shop** is a casual, to-go dining experience with fresh, locally caught fish and chips that people take to the nearby benches with views of Friday Harbor (page 246).
- **Alki Spud Fish and Chips** has served British-style fish and chips since 1935—take it to go and enjoy views of Seattle from Alki Beach (page 95).

Above: fresh oysters

Mount Rainier National Park
Day 6
LAKE QUINAULT TO ASHFORD
145 mi/233 km/3 hours

Start with an early-morning departure from Lake Quinault, heading toward Mount Rainier National Park. The drive is approximately 3 hours, and you'll stop at **Rainier BaseCamp Bar & Grill** in Ashford for lunch. This town will be your base, so you could also check into your accommodation before going into the park.

In the afternoon, head to the **Paradise area** of the park and stop at the **Henry M. Jackson Visitor Center** to learn about the park's history, geology, and wildlife. Begin your exploration with a hike on the **Nisqually Vista Trail,** an easy loop with close-up views of Mount Rainier and the Nisqually Glacier. For a second short hike, drive down **Stevens Canyon Road** to reach **Bench and Snow Lakes,** where you'll hike to a lake you can swim in.

Head back toward Ashford and visit **Reflection Lakes** for a few pictures. Stop at **Christine Falls** or one of the many other waterfalls on the way back. Once in Ashford, enjoy dinner at **Copper Creek Inn.**

Day 7
ASHFORD TO SUNRISE
107 mi/172 km/2 hours

Start your day with a quick breakfast at the **Ashford General Store** and embark on a scenic 2-hour drive to the **Sunrise area,** following Stevens Canyon Road and Route 123. If you're up for a hike, make your way to the **Silver Falls trailhead** in the Ohanapecosh area, known for its beautiful waterfall. Continue north to Sunrise, making sure to stop at some of the many viewpoints along **Sunrise Park Road.**

Once you arrive at Sunrise, visit the **Sunrise Visitor Center** to get information on any hikes you're interested in. **Sourdough Ridge Trail** has expansive views of the park's terrain, or hike

to **Mount Fremont Lookout** to visit a historic fire lookout.

Have lunch at **Sunrise Day Lodge** and relax for a bit. You can explore another trail around Sunrise, such as the easy **Sunrise Nature Trail,** or head back toward Ashford. Stop in the **Ohanapecosh area** to hike the **Silver Falls Trail.** Have dinner at **Wildberry** in Ashford.

With More Time
Day 8
MOUNT RAINIER TO MOUNT ST. HELENS
70 mi/113 km/2 hours

Start your day with a scenic 2-hour drive to Mount St. Helens. Make your first stop at the **Mount St. Helens Interpretive Center** at Silver Lake to learn about the history and impact of the eruption. If you're up for a hike, **Hummocks Trail** is an easy one, or **Harry's Ridge** is a longer but rewarding route. **Note:** The Johnston Ridge Observatory is closed until 2027; see www.fs.usda.gov for updates.

End your day by driving to the town of **Castle Rock,** where you can settle in for the night. Enjoy dinner at **Parker's Steakhouse and Brewery.**

Day 9
MOUNT ST. HELENS TO MOUNT ADAMS
136 mi/219 km/2 hours 15 minutes

Set off toward Mount Adams. Your first stop is the **Mount Adams Ranger Station,** where you can learn about the best hiking trails and scenic spots and pick up maps.

For lunch, head into the town of **Trout Lake** and enjoy a filling meal at **Mt. Adams Pizza.** In the afternoon, go on the **Crofton Butte hike,** a moderately challenging trail with views of the surrounding forests and Mount Adams. Return to Trout Lake and dine on sandwiches at the **Station Café.** The return trip to Seattle is roughly 4 hours (250 mi/402 km), so it's worth staying the night at **Trout Lake Valley Inn** and driving back the next day.

Best Hikes in Washington

Washington is a hiker's dream, offering hundreds of diverse trails that cater to all skill levels and interests from a serene coastal beach walk to a challenging alpine wilderness trek. The sheer variety (and beauty) of Washington's hiking trails means there's something for everyone.

Many hikes require a prepaid pass displayed in your car. The **Discover Pass** (www.discoverpass.wa.gov) is required for state parks and recreation lands, while the **Northwest Forest Pass** (www.fs.usda.gov) is needed for national forest trailheads and sites in Washington and Oregon. Both are available as day passes, but if you plan on doing several hikes during your trip, it's worth buying an annual pass to save money. For planning hikes and finding the latest trail conditions, the **Washington Trails Association** (www.wta.org) is an invaluable resource, offering comprehensive trail guides, trip reports, and maps.

Around Seattle

Rattlesnake Ledge
4 MI (6.4 KM), 2 HOURS, EASY/MODERATE
This hike has scenic views of Rattlesnake Lake from above and ends at a ledge with steep drop-offs, perfect for a short adventure.

Mount Si

8 MI (12.9 KM), 5 HOURS, STRENUOUS
A challenging hike with switchbacks through old-growth trees, leading to a clearing with stunning views of the surrounding valley.

Shi Shi Beach

Snow Lake
7.2 MI (11.6 KM), 4 HOURS, MODERATE
Starting from Snoqualmie Pass, the trail features moderate climbing through a talus slope and offers stunning views of Snow Lake.

Ebey's Landing
5.6 MI (9 KM), 2.5 HOURS, EASY/MODERATE
This hike traverses historic sites, wheat fields, and rugged coastal trails, providing panoramic views of the prairie and shoreline.

Olympic Peninsula
Shi Shi Beach and Point of Arches
8 MI (12.9 KM), 4 HOURS, MODERATE
This hike takes you along sandy beaches with bleached logs, sea stacks, and tide pools, ending at the scenic Point of Arches.

Hurricane Hill
3.2 MI (5.1 KM), 1.5 HOURS, EASY/MODERATE
A scenic hike featuring a gradual ascent through shrublands and pine forests, leading to an exposed summit with views of Vancouver Island, Port Angeles, and the Strait of Juan de Fuca.

Sol Duc Falls
1.6 MI (2.6 KM), 1 HOUR, EASY
An easy hike through the forest to Sol Duc Falls, a powerful 48-ft (15-m) waterfall with a picturesque bridge crossing.

Quinault Loop
4 MI (6.4 KM), 2 HOURS, EASY
A loop trail showcasing lush rain forest, ancient fir trees, and highlights like Lake Quinault.

North and Central Cascades
Blue Lake
4.4 MI (7.1 KM), 2.5 HOURS, EASY
This trail features an alpine lake surrounded by granite peaks, wildflower meadows, boardwalks, and views of Cutthroat Peak and Whistler Mountain.

Fun for Families

There are plenty of things to do to entertain kids all over Washington.

SEATTLE

- **Seattle Children's Museum:** This hands-on museum has interactive exhibits such as a pretend grocery store and post office designed for kids to explore, play, and learn (page 53).

- **Seattle Aquarium:** Located on the Seattle waterfront, this aquarium has numerous marine life exhibits and hands-on activities, including touch pools (page 46).

- **Museum of Pop Culture (MoPOP):** This is a fun and interactive museum featuring exhibits on music, science fiction, and pop culture (page 53).

AROUND SEATTLE

- **Price Sculpture Forest:** An outdoor sculpture park with interactive art installations along forested trails on Whidbey Island (page 142).

- **The Outback Kangaroo Farm:** This farm in Arlington offers guided tours and allows visitors to interact with kangaroos, wallabies, and other exotic animals (page 152).

- **Northwest Railway Museum:** This Snoqualmie museum features historic railway artifacts, train rides, and a beautifully restored depot (page 123).

OLYMPIC PENINSULA

- **World Kite Museum:** A museum in Long Beach dedicated to the history and art of kites, featuring interactive exhibits and workshops where you can make your own kite (page 223).

- **Pacific Paradise Park:** A family fun center in Ocean Shores with mini golf, bumper boats, go-karts, and an arcade (page 215).

- **Cape Disappointment Lighthouse:** A short hike in Long Beach takes you to one of the oldest lighthouses on the West Coast (page 221).

SAN JUAN ISLANDS

- **American and English Camps:** These historical sites on San Juan Island have trails, picnic areas, and well-preserved buildings that provide insights into the island's military history, complete with reenactors (page 241).

- **Krystal Acres Alpaca Farm:** Families can meet alpacas and buy alpaca-related gear at this farm on San Juan Island (page 247).

- **Lime Kiln Point State Park:** Known for its whale-watching opportunities, this park offers stunning coastal views and a lighthouse on San Juan Island (page 243).

NORTH CASCADES

- **Sheri's Sweet Shoppe:** A sweets shop with ice cream and candy and an adjacent mini-golf course (page 302).

- **Leavenworth Nutcracker Museum:** A unique museum in Leavenworth featuring an impressive collection of nutcrackers from around the world (page 315).

- **Leavenworth Reindeer Farm:** A fun experience where families can meet and feed reindeer as well as learn about the animals (page 315).

Silver Falls

western hemlock forest, with views of Whitehorse Mountain and Three Fingers, ending at picturesque Lake 22.

Mount Rainier National Park
Skyline Trail Loop
5.5 MI (8.9 KM), 4 HOURS, MODERATE

This loop features a steep climb to Panorama Point, with spectacular views of Mount Rainier, valleys, and mountains, passing through wildflower meadows and by Myrtle Falls.

Naches Peak Loop
3.2 MI (5.1 KM), 1.5 HOURS, EASY/MODERATE

A popular loop hike with views of Mount Rainier and Tipsoo Lake, passing wildflowers in summer and colorful foliage in fall, intersecting with the Pacific Crest Trail.

Silver Falls
3 MI (4.2 KM), 1.5 HOURS, EASY/MODERATE

A shaded loop trail leading along the Ohanapecosh River to the 95-ft Silver Falls, with multiple vantage points of the waterfall.

Bench and Snow Lakes
2.5 MI (4 KM), 1.5 HOURS, EASY

This hike leads to Bench Lake and the beautiful Snow Lake, where visitors often swim, with manageable elevation gains.

Heather-Maple Pass Loop
7.2 MI (11.6 KM), 3.5 HOURS, MODERATE

A scenic loop showcasing summer wildflowers and fall golden larches, with stunning views of Lake Ann, Heather Pass, and Maple Pass.

Colchuck Lake
8 MI (12.9 KM), 4.5 HOURS, STRENUOUS

A challenging hike through forested terrain and across Mountaineer Creek, ending at the dazzling Colchuck Lake with views of Dragontail and Colchuck Peaks.

Lake 22
5.4 MI (8.7 KM), 2.5 HOURS, MODERATE

This trail leads through a red cedar and

Columbia River Gorge and Walla Walla Getaway

While western Washington is beautiful, some of the most scenic spots lie in the Columbia River Gorge and Walla Walla. This itinerary will take you through these regions, showcasing the dramatic cliffs and waterfalls of the Columbia River Gorge, as well as the picturesque vineyards and charming downtown of Walla Walla.

Columbia River Gorge
Day 1
VANCOUVER TO HOOD RIVER
66 mi/106 km/1 hour

Start your day with breakfast in Vancouver at **Relevant Coffee** before driving to Troutdale, Oregon. Stop at the **Depot Rail Museum** to explore the significance of railroads in the area. For lunch, enjoy an Italian meal at **Ristorante di Pompello.**

In the early afternoon, drive the **Historic Columbia River Highway (Route 30)** east toward Hood River, stopping at several beautiful waterfalls along the way, such as **Multnomah Falls** or **Wahkeena Falls.**

Continue east and visit the **Bonneville Dam** to explore the visitor center, see fish ladders, and learn about the dam's history and impact on the region. In the evening, drive to Hood River for dinner at **Solstice** and enjoy wood-fired pizza. End your day with drinks at **Hood River Brewing,** sampling some local craft beers. Stay the night in Hood River at Columbia Gorge Hotel.

Maryhill Stonehenge

Day 2
HOOD RIVER
42 mi/68 km/40 minutes

Start your day with coffee and a light breakfast at **Stoked Roasters + Coffeehouse** in Hood River, enjoying their riverfront location. After breakfast, take a scenic ride on the **Mount Hood Railroad.**

For lunch it's **Golden Goods** in Hood River, then drive to The Dalles and visit the **Fort Dalles Museum** to learn about the area's pioneer history and see one of the oldest structures in the state. Next, explore the **Columbia Gorge Discovery Center** to delve deeper into the natural and cultural history of the region, and take a walk along the paths outside.

End your day with dinner at **Casa El Mirador,** where you'll get a hearty Mexican meal before heading back to your Hood River hotel.

Day 3
HOOD RIVER TO WALLA WALLA
180 mi/290 km/2 hours 45 minutes

Check out of your hotel in Hood River and head

to breakfast at **Cousin's Restaurant & Saloon** in The Dalles. Visit the **Maryhill Stonehenge,** a replica of England's Stonehenge with views of the Columbia River. Afterward, see unique art and historical artifacts at the nearby **Maryhill Museum of Art.**

Continue your journey north to Goldendale, where you'll have lunch at **Pete's Pizza Pub.** Then visit the **Goldendale Observatory** to learn about astronomy and see their giant telescope.

Drive to Walla Walla for the night and enjoy a delicious Italian dinner at **Passatempo Taverna.** Check in to the Eritage Resort, where you'll be staying for the next two nights.

Walla Walla
Day 4
8 mi/13 km/15 minutes

Start your day at **Carte Coffee,** then head to the **Fort Walla Walla Museum,** which replicates a pioneer community from the 19th century. For lunch go to **AK's Mercado,** a trendy spot with street tacos.

Skiing and Snowboarding in Washington

Washington is a huge destination for winter sports enthusiasts, offering some of the best skiing and snowboarding in the Pacific Northwest. Renowned for abundant snowfall and diverse terrain, the state's popular ski resorts offer runs for all skill levels.

MOUNT BAKER

With its deep powder and unprecedented snowfall, Mount Baker is a favored choice for snowboarders and skiers. The region offers both picturesque, well-groomed courses for novices and intermediates and a range of difficult terrain for experienced skiers (page 334).

STEVENS PASS

Stevens Pass has a balanced mix of beginner, intermediate, and advanced runs. It's known for its night skiing and terrain parks (page 318).

SNOQUALMIE PASS

Snoqualmie Pass is a convenient choice, only an hour from Seattle. It features four interconnected ski areas: Alpental, Summit Central, Summit East, and Summit West, and is popular for its night skiing and extensive Nordic trail system (page 126).

CRYSTAL MOUNTAIN

Crystal Mountain, the largest ski resort in Washington, features stunning views of Mount Rainier. The resort offers a variety of runs for all skill levels, and its gondola provides access to the summit for both skiers and sightseers (page 360).

MISSION RIDGE

Mission Ridge, located near Wenatchee, boasts sunny weather and dry powder conditions. The area is known for its long groomed runs and diverse terrain (page 325).

Spend the afternoon wine-tasting in downtown Walla Walla. Begin at **Seven Hills Winery** and watch wine being made and try their Petit Verdot during a tasting. Next, visit **Forgeron Cellars,** located in a historic blacksmith shop, to enjoy wines like cabernet Sauvignon and cabernet Franc. End your day with dinner at **Hattaway's on Alder,** which offers a blend of Northwest and Southern cuisine.

Day 5

19 mi/31 km/35 minutes

Begin your day at the **Whitman Mission National Historic Site** to learn about the history between Native American tribes and European settlers. For lunch, head to **Hop Thief Taphouse and Kitchen,** a self-pour taphouse where you can sample a variety of beers, ciders, and wines, as well as pizza and burgers.

Spend the afternoon wine-tasting in the **Walla Walla Airport District.** Start at **Dunham Cellars,** housed in a restored WWII airplane hangar, and sample their acclaimed Bordeaux-style blend Trutina. Next, visit **Tranche,** known for its picturesque views and array of varietals, including Rhône and Bordeaux blends. Head downtown to enjoy dinner at one of the many restaurants.

With More Time
Yakima

DURATION: 1 DAY

DRIVING TIME: 2 HOURS ONE-WAY

If you have an extra day, Yakima is worth exploring. Popular breweries like **Valley Brewing Co.** and **Wandering Hop Brewery** are part of a thriving local beer scene. For wine-tasting, visit **Naches Heights Vineyard, Freehand Cellars,** and **Treveri Cellars.** Farms and orchards like **Washington Fruit Place** and **Johnson Orchards** are great places to get fresh local produce.

Outdoor enthusiasts can enjoy the **Tieton Nature Trail** and the **Cowiche Canyon Uplands Trail.** Dining options include **Cowiche Canyon Kitchen** for an upscale meal, **Los Hernandez Tamales** for award-winning tamales, and **Miner's Drive-In** for classic burgers and shakes.

Palouse Falls

DURATION: HALF DAY TRIP

DRIVING TIME: 30 MINUTES ONE-WAY

Palouse Falls is an easy excursion from Walla Walla, as it's only an hour north. The park features Washington's official waterfall, which drops 198 ft (60 m) into the Palouse River. The surrounding area offers several hiking trails with stunning views of the falls and the rugged canyon landscape. Pack a picnic to enjoy at the park's designated areas, as there are no nearby restaurants.

Spokane

DURATION: 2 DAYS

DRIVING TIME: 2.5 HOURS ONE-WAY

Riverfront Park is the heart of Spokane, sprawling along the Spokane River, where you can admire **Spokane Falls,** ride the **Numerica SkyRide gondola,** or take a spin on the **Looff Carrousel. Manito Park** features themed gardens, Mirror Pond, and the **Park Bench Café.** The **Northwest Museum of Arts and Culture** houses a vast collection of artifacts and the historic **Campbell House.** Families will enjoy the **Mobius Discovery Center,** an interactive children's museum with hands-on exhibits.

Spokane's vibrant brewery scene includes **Whistle Punk Brewing,** which is known for its rotating tap list of local beer. **Kendall Yards** is great for shopping, with local restaurants and boutique stores. Dining options in Spokane include **Clinkerdagger** for seafood and prime rib, **Baba Spokane** for Middle Eastern-inspired dishes, and **Vieux Carré NOLA Kitchen** for authentic Cajun and Creole dishes.

Seattle

Seattle, often referred to as the Emerald City, is nestled between the sparkling waters of Puget Sound and the rugged Cascade Mountains and renowned for its stunning scenery. But it's the beautiful blend of nature and urban development, with the bustling downtown full of skyscrapers in the center of it all, that makes Seattle so special.

The iconic Space Needle, constructed for the 1962 World's Fair, provides astonishing views of the cityscape and the mountains beyond. But of all the things Seattle is known for, its music scene is one the locals are most proud of. Jazz clubs, rock halls, and opera houses contribute to the city's soundtrack, and live music fills the air practically

Highlights

Look for ★ to find recommended sights, activities, dining, and lodging.

★ **Pike Place Market:** This large, bustling marketplace has a vibrant atmosphere, fresh produce, artisanal goods, and captivating street performances (page 46).

★ **Bill Speidel's Underground Tour:** Discover Seattle's hidden past on a guided tour through the intriguing underground passages of the original city, revealing stories and remnants of its early days (page 47).

★ **Smith Tower:** Once the tallest building west of the Mississippi, Smith Tower offers a historical experience with its Prohibition-era speakeasy and spectacular observatory deck (page 47).

★ **Space Needle:** An iconic symbol of Seattle, the Space Needle features an observation deck and revolving lounge, providing incredible 360-degree views of the city and beyond (page 51).

★ **Washington Park Arboretum and Japanese Garden:** This serene oasis in the city showcases an exquisite collection of plants and a tranquil Japanese garden (page 57).

★ **Gas Works Park:** This unique park, set on a former gas plant, offers panoramic views of Seattle's skyline and blends industrial history with recreational green space (page 59).

★ **Ballard Locks:** Also known as the Hiram M. Chittenden Locks, this engineering marvel connects Puget Sound with Seattle's freshwater lakes, featuring a fish ladder and lush botanical gardens (page 59).

★ **The Museum of Flight:** Aviation enthusiasts can explore a vast collection of aircraft and space artifacts at this world-class museum, including a genuine Concorde and the original Air Force One (page 62).

★ **Alki Beach:** A favorite local getaway, Alki Beach offers sandy shores, stunning views of Puget Sound, and a laid-back vibe perfect for sunbathing, picnicking, and volleyball (page 67).

every night. Whether it's an intimate bar or a large arena, it's easy to immerse yourself in the city's diverse music culture.

From the moment you sip your freshly prepared coffee to the final bite of dessert, Seattle's food scene will wow your taste buds. Pike Place Market, where the aromas of seasonal flowers and seafood come together, highlights the inventive and delicious cuisine that is a hallmark of Seattle. While the city may be famous for Starbucks, the hundreds of local, creative coffee shops throughout the city are the real find.

The landscapes of Seattle are just as dynamic and complex as the city's personality. From biking the Burke-Gilman Trail along the waterfront to kayaking across Puget Sound with Mount Rainier in the background, this place is full of adventure. Each of Seattle's unique neighborhoods, from Capitol Hill's hip vibe to Ballard's historic allure, contributes to the city's character.

ORIENTATION

Seattle is tucked between expansive Lake Washington to the east and glistening Puget Sound to the west. On the north side, you'll find Lake Union and neighborhoods like Ballard and Fremont, while the south is a mix of artist communities and residential areas. The majority of tourist attractions are in the downtown, waterfront, and Seattle Center areas.

I-5 is Seattle's main freeway, cutting north-south through the city. Route 99 parallels it, while I-90 and Route 520 run east-west.

Downtown and the Waterfront: Located in the heart of Seattle, the waterfront and downtown are home to Pike Place Market and the city's most lively sections, with high-rise buildings, upscale shopping, and thriving business districts. Along Elliott Bay's edge is the waterfront, which runs along Alaskan Way and has a charming mix of Puget Sound views, ferry terminals, seafood restaurants, and souvenir shops. Here the downtown streets are straightforward to drive; 1st Avenue starts at the bottom of the hill by the waterfront, and the numbering goes up as you go east to the freeway and beyond to Capitol Hill. You can also use the Link light rail and the bus system to get to other areas, but you may have to transfer to connect neighborhoods that are far from each other.

Pioneer Square and the International District: With its brick streets, Romanesque Revival buildings, and underground passageways from the 1800s, Pioneer Square is the historic core of Seattle, located south of downtown. Art galleries, trendy bars, and high-end lofts have all contributed to the area's recent renaissance, making it a fun mix of new and old. The International District, just east of Pioneer Square, is a gastronomic adventure with a diverse array of restaurants.

Belltown: Just north of Pike Place Market is trendy Belltown, home to numerous art galleries, boutiques, bars, and nightclubs. Urban cool meets ultramodern high-rise residences in this neighborhood, which also has some of the city's best restaurants and music venues.

Queen Anne: Seattle Center, near Lower Queen Anne, is full of tourist attractions, such as the Space Needle and the Pacific Science Center. Going up Queen Anne Avenue, which runs along a steep hill from the Seattle Center, you'll find Upper Queen Anne, which offers picturesque views from Kerry Park and a mix of historical residential homes and small shops and restaurants.

South Lake Union: This neighborhood is a dynamic area just north of downtown that thrives with tech culture, with Amazon's headquarters at its center. Increasing numbers of trendy cafés, restaurants, shops, and outdoor activities line the shores of Lake Union.

Capitol Hill: East of downtown Seattle and up the hill, vibrant Capitol Hill is well known for its lively nightlife and thriving arts and music scenes. The main thoroughfares, Pike

---

Previous: downtown waterfront; Gas Works Park; Space Needle.

Seattle

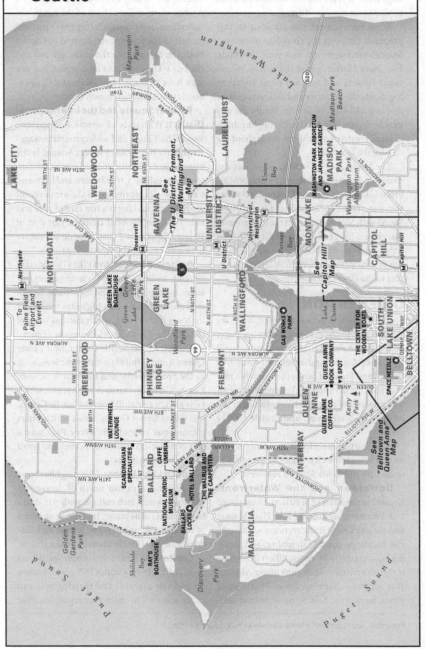

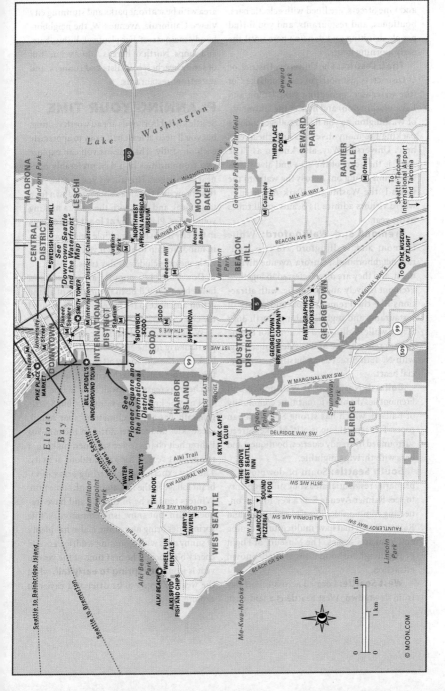

and Pine Streets, are lined with eclectic bars, boutiques, and restaurants, and you'll find people drinking and dancing here until the early morning hours.

The U District: The University District, or U District, is just north of the Montlake Cut (the waterway connecting Lake Union and Lake Washington) and houses the University of Washington, so you'll find college students packing the many dive bars and cheap eats here. University Way, also known as "The Ave," is the heart of the area and always has something going on. Across the water to the south is the Washington Park Arboretum, where visitors admire its beauty at all times of the year.

Fremont and Wallingford: While Fremont and Wallingford are two separate neighborhoods, Aurora Avenue divides them, and they are often referred to together. Fremont is lively and eccentric, with attractions like the Fremont Troll and plenty of restaurants and nightlife along North 36th Street, while Wallingford is known for having a more relaxed vibe and residential setting, with N. 45th Street as its bustling commercial heart.

Ballard: Northwest of Wallingford and Fremont lies the historic maritime community of Ballard, which has strong Scandinavian roots. The central hub is NW Market Street, surrounded by trendy eateries, boutiques, and bars with thriving nightlife.

South Seattle: South of downtown is primarily residential areas but still has plenty to see. Rainier Avenue S. is a key route, connecting communities like Columbia City and Rainier Beach that have multicultural dining and local arts scenes. The Museum of Flight is the neighborhood's most well-known attraction.

West Seattle: Located across Elliott Bay from downtown, West Seattle is a laid-back area with beachfront parks and stunning city views. California Avenue SW, the neighborhood's main street, has plenty of dining, bars, and shops. North of here is Alki Avenue, full of sandy beaches, bicyclists and runners, and waterfront restaurants.

PLANNING YOUR TIME

Seattle's neighborhoods are all worth visiting, but you'll need at least half a day to appreciate each one fully. That means you can explore two communities in a day, preferably ones near each other. This allows you to take your time browsing the area's shops, sit down for a tasty meal, and chat with the barista making your coffee. Plan to stay **at least three days** in the city if you have multiple neighborhoods in mind, and up to a week if you want to visit each one or include any day trips.

Downtown is a popular area to use as a home base—you'll be in the middle of all the action and next to I-5 for easy access around the city.

Weekends are always the busiest time, particularly in the summer when the city is basked in the sun. Many attractions now have timed ticket entries, so buying ahead of time can help decrease your wait time in line.

It may be known as a rainy city, but Seattle generally has a mild climate all year round. Clear skies and temperatures in the mid-70s Fahrenheit characterize summer, making it the perfect season for any outdoor activity. The city experiences a dazzling array of vibrant foliage in the fall, along with some rain. Winters tend to be in the 30s and have frequent rain, but snow isn't common. While spring does bring more rain, it also has plenty of sunny days with blooming wildflowers and cherry blossoms. The best time of the year to visit is from **late spring to early fall,** when the weather tends to be drier and easier to explore.

Itinerary Ideas

DAY 1

1 Start your day in Pioneer Square at **Zeitgeist Coffee.**

2 Join the **Underground Tour** to discover Seattle's hidden past.

3 Savor artisan-cured meats at **Salumi** for lunch.

4 For an afternoon outside, try kayaking on **Lake Union** for city views from the water.

5 End your day enjoying Southwestern-Mexican cuisine at the lively **Cactus** in South Lake Union.

DAY 2

1 Begin with exceptional Italian coffee and pastries at **Caffe Umbria** in Ballard.

2 Visit the **Ballard Locks** and explore the **National Nordic Museum.**

3 Enjoy lunch at **Ray's Boathouse,** featuring fresh, local seafood.

4 For views, head to Queen Anne and journey to the top of the **Space Needle** or join the locals at **Kerry Park.**

5 Dine at **The Pink Door** in Belltown, followed by a cocktail at **Bathtub Gin & Co.**

DAY 3

1 Enjoy French bistro classics at **Café Campagne** in Pike Place Market.

2 Spend the morning walking through **Pike Place Market,** and wander along the shops and attractions on the **waterfront.**

3 Take the **water taxi** from downtown to West Seattle. Have lunch at local favorite **Alki Spud Fish and Chips.**

4 Walk along **Alki Beach,** soaking in the Seattle skyline across the water, before taking the water taxi back to downtown.

5 For dinner, head to Capitol Hill and indulge in the Northern Italian cuisine at **Osteria la Spiga,** and later catch live music at **Neumos.**

Sights

DOWNTOWN AND THE WATERFRONT

TOP EXPERIENCE

★ Pike Place Market

85 Pike St.; 206/682-7453; www.pikeplacemarket.org; 10am-5pm daily; free

Although the Space Needle may be the most iconic of Seattle's landmarks, the historic Pike Place Market is the heart of the city. Originally opened in 1907 as a meeting place for local farmers and customers, the market has expanded into a broad mix of shops, restaurants, and more. Pike Place has stood the test of time, surviving the onslaught of modernization and slated demolitions to become a beloved symbol of Seattle's dedication to community and small business.

Sprawling over 9 acres (3.5 ha) in downtown Seattle, Pike Place Market encompasses multiple buildings and a labyrinth of over 500 stalls, shops, and eateries. Stretching across various levels and alleyways, this vibrant, bustling marketplace buzzes with neon signs, street performers, and everything from freshly caught seafood to bountiful local produce.

Many of Seattle's most recognizable landmarks are in Pike Place Market. The bronze sculpture of **Rachel the Piggy Bank,** a charming mascot and photo opportunity, welcomes guests as they enter the market. Coffee lovers eager to explore the origins of the global coffee giant flock to the **original Starbucks** store, which opened in 1971, just a few minutes away. The market's lower level, the **"Down Under,"** is a labyrinth of unusual and eclectic stores selling anything from antiques to one-of-a-kind handmade items. **Post Alley,** which is close by, is well-known for its lively ambience and the **Gum Wall,** an odd and multicolored mosaic of chewing gum that has evolved into an eccentric icon.

Seattle Aquarium

1483 Alaskan Way, Pier 59; 206/386-4300; www.seattleaquarium.org; 9:30am-6pm daily; $30-40

At the waterfront Seattle Aquarium, visitors are greeted by the captivating Window on Washington Waters, a massive tank replicating the coastal waters of the Pacific Northwest that's teeming with local sealife. Nearby, children can delight in hands-on encounters with sea stars and anemones at the Touch Tank.

The Pacific Coral Reef exhibit highlights the delicate and colorful world of coral ecosystems from around the world. Head outside to see larger animals such as sea otters, harbor seals, sea birds, and salmon. The Underwater Dome has an incredible 360-degree panorama that allows fish and other aquatic species to come right up to and over you. The latest attraction, the Ocean Pavilion, uses cutting-edge digital storytelling to transport visitors into a reef ecosystem of 3,500 species, including rays, coral, and sharks.

Seattle Great Wheel

1301 Alaskan Way, Pier 57, Miners Landing; 206/623-8607; https://seattlegreatwheel.com; 11am-9pm Mon.-Thurs., 10am-10pm Fri.-Sat., 10am-9pm Sun.; $18-50

The Seattle Great Wheel, towering 175 ft (53 m) tall on Pier 57, offers a unique vantage point of the city's skyline and Elliott Bay. This Ferris wheel features 42 fully enclosed glass gondolas, each accommodating up to eight passengers, that provide an intimate viewing experience. Make sure to have your cameras ready during the 15-minute rotation. You'll see more of the city during the day, but the city lights up at night, in addition to the vibrant lights on the Ferris wheel.

Columbia Center and Sky View Observatory

700 4th Ave., Floor 73; 206/386-5151; https://skyviewobservatory.com; noon-6pm daily; $20-38

At 937 ft (286 m), Columbia Center is the

tallest building in Washington state and the second-tallest on the West Coast. Completed in 1985, this striking skyscraper is a prominent feature of Seattle's architectural landscape. The 76 floors house offices, conference spaces, and retail establishments. On the 73rd floor, the Sky View Observatory offers one of the most stunning views in Seattle—a sweeping panorama of the cityscape, Puget Sound, and, on clear days, Mount Rainier. The Observatory also has interactive exhibits, a café and bar, and a gift shop.

Seattle Art Museum

1300 1st Ave.; 206/654-3100; www.seattleartmuseum. org; 10am-5pm Wed.-Sun.

The Seattle Art Museum, known to locals as SAM, has one of the best collections in the state. You can wander through rooms filled with everything from Native American art to modern and contemporary pieces from local artists, in addition to rotating exhibits. The Porcelain Room has a stunning display of intricate ceramics, and the African art collection is popular for its powerful sculptures and masks.

PIONEER SQUARE AND THE INTERNATIONAL DISTRICT

Wing Luke Museum

719 S King St.; 206/623-5124; www.wingluke.org; 10am-5pm Wed.-Mon.; $10-17, under 5 free

The International District is home to the world's only pan-Asian Pacific American community-based museum, the Wing Luke Museum. Artworks by Asian Americans, Native Hawaiians, and Pacific Islanders fill this three-story, 60,000-sq-ft (18,288-sq-m) museum, along with exhibits showing the struggles of early Asian pioneers in Seattle. The museum's Bruce Lee exhibit is highly regarded and gives insight into the life of the legendary martial arts artist from Seattle. The 90-minute guided tour (included with your ticket) offers an interactive experience of the neighborhood's historic sites and businesses.

★ Bill Speidel's Underground Tour

614 1st Ave.; 206/682-4646; www.undergroundtour. com; 10am-6pm daily; $10-22

Seattle has a fascinating history, particularly because large parts of the original city from the 1800s lie underneath the current streets. You'll notice purple skylights in the sidewalks as you walk around Pioneer Square, giving hints of the underground city below. Join Bill Speidel's Underground Tour for a 75-minute tour of the old town, where you'll see original sidewalks and storefronts from after the city rebuilt itself after the Great Fire in 1889. The tour guides are educational and have a reputation for their humor.

★ Smith Tower

506 2nd Ave.; 206/624-0414; www.smithtower.com; 11am-9pm Wed. and Sun., 11am-10pm Thurs.-Sat.; $22

The Smith Tower in Pioneer Square was the tallest building outside New York City when it was constructed in 1914. The museum on the bottom floor showcases artifacts and photographs from the 1900s, then visitors take the golden elevators up to the observatory on the 35th floor. While the views are impressive from the 360-degree outdoor deck that wraps around it, most people spend their time at the Prohibition-era speakeasy **The Observatory Bar** (noon-9pm Wed. and Sun., noon-10pm Thurs.-Sat.; $16-30). Reservations are highly recommended on the weekends and during sunset.

Klondike Gold Rush National Historical Park

319 2nd Ave. S.; 206/220-4240; www.nps.gov; 10am-5pm Wed.-Sun.; free

At the Klondike Gold Rush National Historical Park, exhibits transport visitors back in time by telling riveting tales of the fortune-seekers who left Seattle for the Yukon goldfields. To explain the influence of the Klondike Gold Rush on Seattle's growth, the park showcases in-depth historical accounts, images, and personal anecdotes.

Downtown Seattle and the Waterfront

LE PICHET
THE TASTING ROOM
THE PINK DOOR
PIROSHKY PIROSHKY
LE PANIER
OLD STOVE BREWING
SUR LA TABLE
BEECHER'S CHEESE
INN AT THE MARKET
CAFE CAMPAGNE
SIMPLY SEATTLE
RACHEL'S GINGER BEER
PIKE PLACE MARKET
PIKE PLACE CHOWDER
MADE IN WASHINGTON
SIMPLE LIFE
LAMPLIGHT BOOKS
EARTH WIND & FIRE BOUTIQUE
THE ATHENIAN SEAFOOD RESTAURANT AND BAR
METSKER MAPS
THE CRUMPET SHOP
WORLD SPICE
STORYVILLE COFFEE
LEFT BANK BOOKS
MARKET MAGIC SHOP
VISITOR CENTER
MAXIMILIEN
GREEN TORTOISE HOSTEL SEATTLE
MARKETSPICE
WILD GINGER
PIKE BREWING COMPANY
FOUR SEASONS HOTEL SEATTLE
SEATTLE ART MUSEUM
University Street
ARGOSY CRUISES
SEATTLE AQUARIUM
SEATTLE GREAT WHEEL
YE OLDE CURIOSITY SHOP
ALEXIS ROYAL SONESTA HOTEL SEATTLE
THE METROPOLITAN GRILLE

Pier 62
Pier 59
Pier 58
Pier 57
Pier 56
Pier 55
Pier 54
Piers 50-52

Eliott Bay

To Bainbridge Island
To Bremerton

Ferry Terminal
COLMAN DOCK

ALASKAN WAY
ELLIOTT WAY
WESTERN AVE
1ST AVE
2ND AVE
3RD AVE
STEWART ST
PIKE ST
UNION ST
UNIVERSITY ST
SENECA ST
SPRING ST
MADISON ST
MARION ST
COLUMBIA ST
SR 99 TUNNEL

0   200 yds
0   200 m

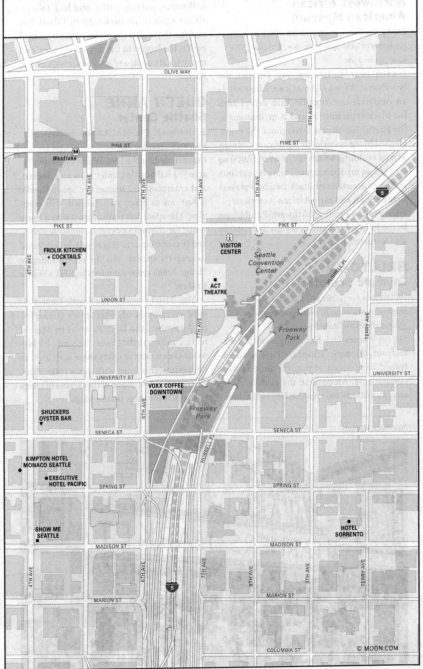

OLIVE WAY

PINE ST   PINE ST

Ⓜ Westlake

5TH AVE   6TH AVE   7TH AVE   8TH AVE   9TH AVE

5

PIKE ST   PIKE ST

4TH AVE

FROLIK KITCHEN
+ COCKTAILS
▼

ⓘ
VISITOR
CENTER

Seattle
Convention
Center

■ ACT
THEATRE

UNION ST

HUBBELL PL

TERRY AVE

Freeway
Park

UNIVERSITY ST   UNIVERSITY ST

VOXX COFFEE
DOWNTOWN
▼

Freeway
Park

SHUCKERS
OYSTER BAR
▼

SENECA ST   SENECA ST

KIMPTON HOTEL
MONACO SEATTLE ●

● EXECUTIVE
HOTEL PACIFIC

SPRING ST   SPRING ST

● HOTEL
SORRENTO

SHOW ME
SEATTLE ■

MADISON ST   MADISON ST

5

MARION ST   MARION ST

COLUMBIA ST

© MOON.COM

Northwest African American Museum

2300 S. Massachusetts St.; 206/518-6000; www. naamnw.org; 10am-5pm Thurs.-Sun.; $10 adult, $5 youth, under 3 free

Located near the International District, the Northwest African American Museum is an important institution that delves into the Black experience in and contributions to the Pacific Northwest throughout the years. Housed in the historically significant Colman School building, which spans over 17,000 sq ft (5,182 sq m), the museum features exhibits on the experiences of Black baseball players in the region and early African American pioneers in the Pacific Northwest. Exhibitions by modern and contemporary Black artists are also featured.

BELLTOWN
Olympic Sculpture Park

2901 Western Ave.; 206/654-3100; www. seattleartmuseum.org; 30 minutes before sunrise-30 minutes after sunset daily; free

Set on 9 acres (3.5 ha) along Seattle's waterfront, Olympic Sculpture Park is an extraordinary blend of natural and creative components. An oasis in the middle of the city, its meticulously planned layout includes sculptures, walking paths, and lush foliage, all set against the backdrop of Elliott Bay and the Olympic Mountains. This beautiful park is the largest in the downtown area, and many locals compare it to an artsy Central Park.

QUEEN ANNE
Seattle Center

305 Harrison St.; 206/684-7200; www.seattlecenter. com; 10am-8pm daily; free

Constructed for the 1962 World's Fair, the 74-acre (30-ha) Seattle Center is an arts, tourist, and entertainment venue; the Space Needle is just one of many structures in this complex. The space has transformed into a lively venue for community events, music festivals, and performing arts. It is regularly renovated to keep its appeal, like the recent Climate Pledge Arena renovation for the NHL's Seattle Kraken.

You'll find events at the Seattle Center almost every weekend, whether it's Winterfest in December, the Irish Festival in March, or live music throughout the year. Its layout makes it easy to enjoy these activities, as the perimeter is lined with quick restaurants where you can sit at one of the dozens of tables and watch the show on the stage.

Pike Place Market

Pioneer Square and the International District

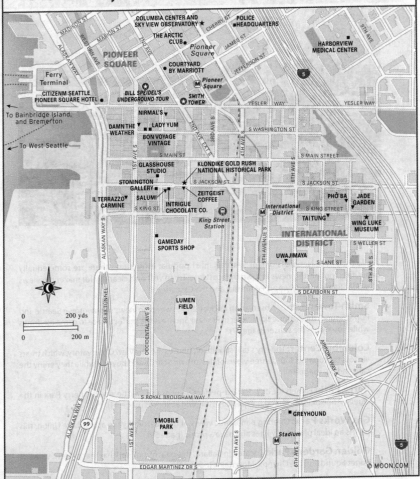

TOP EXPERIENCE

★ Space Needle

400 Broad St.; 206/905-2100; www.spaceneedle.com; 8:30am-10pm Tues.-Wed., 10am-8pm Thurs., 9am-9:30pm Sat., 9am-6pm Sun.; $26-60

If there's one tourist attraction visitors associate with Seattle, it's the Space Needle. This stunning landmark, standing at 605 ft (184 m), has been a symbol of the city since its construction in 1962 for the World's Fair. It was designed with a futuristic vision, featuring a unique flying saucer-like top and an observation deck offering stunning 360-degree views of the Seattle skyline and Mount Rainier (on a sunny day).

The Space Needle has undergone many renovations over the years, including installing a rotating glass floor so guests can have a unique view of their surroundings. It has an outdoor section with glass benches to take "sky-high selfies."

Scenic Views in Seattle

Kerry Park

While the Space Needle is one of Seattle's most popular attractions, there are some equally beautiful, if not better, views in town that cost less. Try to visit on a clear day for maximum views of Mount Rainier, the Olympic Peninsula, and the Cascades.

- **Smith Tower:** With its observation deck offering sweeping views of downtown Seattle and Puget Sound, this historic skyscraper in Pioneer Square is the perfect place to come for drinks while you watch the sunset (page 47).

- **Columbia Center:** The city's tallest building houses the Sky View Observatory, which treats visitors to stunning 360-degree views of downtown Seattle and beyond while they enjoy the café and bar (page 46).

- **Kerry Park:** Famed for its postcard-perfect view of the Seattle skyline, Kerry Park in the Queen Anne neighborhood is especially stunning at sunset (page 64).

- **Gas Works Park:** Offering panoramic views of the Seattle skyline across Lake Union, this park is an ideal place to fly kites and have a picnic (page 59).

- **Golden Gardens Park:** Located in Ballard, this beachfront park has magnificent views of Puget Sound and the Olympic Mountains (page 63).

When you get hungry, head to the **Atmos Café** ($4-10) for light snacks, coffee, beer, and wine. For those who are 21 and over, make a reservation at **The Loupe Lounge** (3pm-7pm Sun.-Mon., 3pm-9pm Thurs.-Sat.; $125/person weekdays, $175/person weekends), where you'll be treated to specially crafted cocktails and set Pacific Northwest-inspired food towers to choose from.

Pacific Science Center

200 2nd Ave. N.; 206/443-2001; https://pacificsciencecenter.org; 10am-5pm Wed.-Sun.; $20-30
Built as part of Seattle's World's Fair, the Pacific Science Center has become a science museum for children of all ages. There's plenty to explore, including the Tropical Butterfly House, where you can walk alongside free-flying butteries, a planetarium for

space lovers, an engaging dinosaur exhibit, and a toddlers-only section for the little ones. While the center is geared toward kids, adults come here at night for the popular laser shows featuring musical themes or a particular artist's soundtrack.

Seattle Children's Museum

305 Harrison St.; 206/441-1768; https:// seattlechildrensmuseum.org; 10am-4:30pm Wed.-Sun.; $14 adult and children, $12 ages 65 and older, under 1 free

The Seattle Children's Museum is the place to let kids' imaginations run wild and pretend to work at any number of jobs—construction worker, eye doctor, postal worker, veterinarian, and many more. The grocery store is complete with shopping carts, groceries on shelves, and a cash register; in the theater, kids can dress up onstage or work behind the scenes to control the lights and sounds. While children of any age can visit, it's geared toward toddlers through early elementary kids.

Chihuly Garden and Glass

305 Harrison St.; 206/753-4940; www. chihulygardenandglass.com; 10am-6pm Mon.-Wed., 10am-6:30pm Thurs., 10am-8pm Fri.-Sun.; $21-60

Chihuly Garden and Glass is in the literal shadow of the Space Needle and full of Dale Chihuly's masterful glasswork. As you make your way through the eight galleries, you'll be captivated by Chihuly's imaginative and colorful glasswork. Just outside the gallery, the stunning Glasshouse feels like a giant greenhouse with views of the Space Needle in the background. The attractions don't end there—stroll through the garden where Chihuly's glass sculptures are thoughtfully integrated among the greenery, creating a magical interplay of art and nature. Night is a particularly fun time to visit, as the illuminated glass artworks transform the garden into a dreamlike space.

Innovative cocktails, beer, wine, and light bites are available at **The Bar at Chihuly Garden and Glass** (10:30am-8pm daily), which is also the only place to see 25 personal

pieces from Chihuly. There are events held here throughout the year, including morning yoga sessions and their famous New Year's Eve party.

Museum of Pop Culture (MoPOP)

325 5th Ave. N.; 206/770-2700; www.mopop.org; 10am-5pm Thurs.-Tues.; $25-30

The Museum of Pop Culture, or MoPOP, is an entertaining tribute to modern popular culture. Called the Experience Music Project when it debuted in 2000, the original museum was dedicated to musical invention and creativity. The name change to MoPOP represents the museum's expanded coverage, including science fiction, video games, fantasy, and all types of pop music. In the Nirvana exhibit, you'll see handwritten song notes from Kurt Cobain, and the Science Fiction and Fantasy Hall of Fame celebrates iconic figures and works in these genres.

SOUTH LAKE UNION
The Center for Wooden Boats

1010 Valley St.; 206/382-2628; www.cwb.org; 10am-4pm Wed.-Sun. winter, noon-7pm Wed.-Fri., 10am-6pm Sat.-Sun. spring, 11am-7pm Mon.-Fri., 10am-6pm Sat.-Sun. summer, Wed.-Sun. 10am-6pm fall; free

The Center for Wooden Boats is a one-of-a-kind maritime museum that honors the Northwest's nautical past and the long tradition of wooden boatbuilding. This interactive museum is a fun place to spend a few hours as you walk around seeing all the details that go into building older and modern wooden boats. The center also offers classes and workshops on sailing and boat building.

Canoes, rowboats, and sailboats are available to rent. The free public sails on Sundays are popular: hour-long boat rides on a first-come, first-served basis (last Sun. each month, Apr.-Oct.).

Seattle Spheres

2111 7th Ave.; www.seattlespheres.com; 10am-6pm first and third Sat. each month; free

Opened in 2018, the Spheres are a botanical and architectural monument, part of

Belltown and Queen Anne

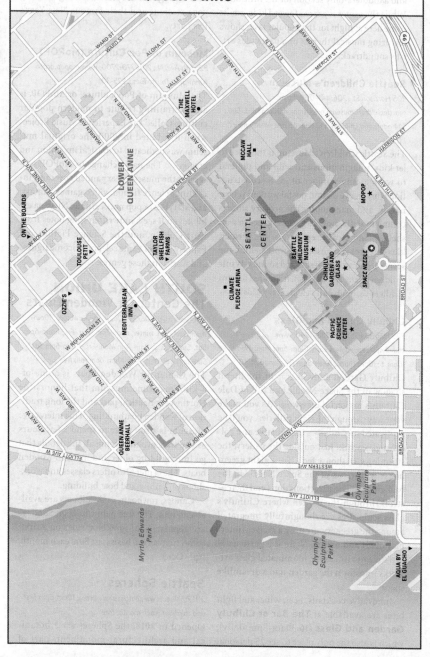

WARD ST
WARD ST
ALOHA ST

99

VALLEY ST

THE MAXWELL HOTEL

ROY ST

QUEEN ANNE AVE N

1ST AVE N

2ND AVE N

WARREN AVE N

3RD AVE N

4TH AVE N

5TH AVE N

TAYLOR AVE N

MERCER ST

MCCAW HALL

W MERCER ST

LOWER QUEEN ANNE

SEATTLE CENTER

MOPOP ★

ON THE BOARDS ▶

W ROY ST

TOULOUSE PETIT ▶

TAYLOR SHELLFISH FARMS ▶

SEATTLE CHILDREN'S MUSEUM ★

CHIHULY GARDEN AND GLASS ★

SPACE NEEDLE ✪

OZZIE'S ▶

MEDITERRANEAN INN ●

CLIMATE PLEDGE ARENA ■

PACIFIC SCIENCE CENTER ★

BROAD ST

W REPUBLICAN ST

W HARRISON ST

1ST AVE N

QUEEN ANNE AVE N

2ND AVE W

3RD AVE W

W THOMAS ST

1ST AVE W

W JOHN ST

QUEEN ANNE BEERHALL ▼

DENNY WAY

BROAD ST

4TH AVE W

ELLIOTT AVE W

WESTERN AVE

Olympic Sculpture Park

ELLIOTT AVE

Myrtle Edwards Park

Olympic Sculpture Park

AQUA BY EL GAUCHO ▶

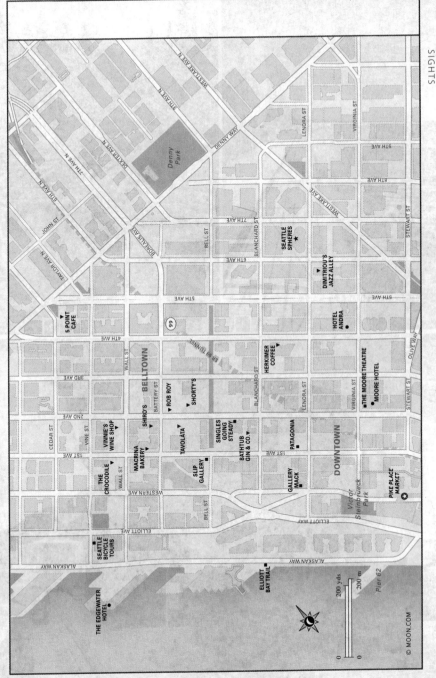

the Amazon campus. These glass-enclosed structures keep the temperature a pleasant 72 degrees Fahrenheit (22°C) with 60 percent humidity during the day, making them perfect for their extensive plant collection. Visitors will love wandering by the elaborate living wall and the majestic 49-ft (15-m) *Ficus rubiginosa*, "Rubi," inside. The only downside is it's hard to get in here—reservations are required and only open up 15 days in advance.

CAPITOL HILL
Seattle Asian Art Museum

1400 E. Prospect St.; 206/654-3210; www. seattleartmuseum.org; 10am-5pm Thurs.-Sun.; $10-18, under 14 free

Located in the middle of Volunteer Park, the Seattle Asian Art Museum is a branch of the Seattle Art Museum. Its art deco building showcases everything from ancient Chinese jade to contemporary Asian art. The range of artwork is impressive, including intricate textiles, delicate ceramics, and vibrant paintings.

Lake View Cemetery

1554 15th Ave. E.; 206/322-1582; www.lakeviewseattle. com; 9am-8pm daily; free

Dozens of people come here each day to see some of its most famous residents: martial arts legend Bruce Lee and his son, Brandon Lee. Each has his own dedicated area, where you can walk right up to the tombstone. It's worth taking a stroll around this cemetery, which has been around since 1872, as you'll see some notable Seattle names from history, such as Arthur Denny, Doc Maynard, and Henry Yesler.

THE U DISTRICT
University of Washington

1410 NE Campus Pkwy; 206/543-2100; www. washington.edu; free

The University of Washington is often bustling with students, but you should still make time to visit if you're in the area—the

---

1: Olympic Sculpture Park 2: Japanese Garden 3: Museum of Pop Culture

campus is among the most picturesque in Washington. If you visit the Quad in the spring, you'll want to check out the cherry blossoms. The campus's beating heart is Red Square, which features its signature redbrick paving. The Suzzallo Library, with its imposing Gothic façade, is located here; it houses the Reading Room, which seems right out of a Harry Potter novel. The Drumheller Fountain is another popular spot—you'll often find students hanging out here on a sunny day.

Burke Museum

4303 Memorial Way NE; 206/543-7907; www. burkemuseum.org; 10am-5pm Tues.-Sun., 10am-8pm last Thurs. each month; $14-22, under 3 free

Founded in 1885, the Burke Museum, also called the Washington State Museum, is the oldest museum in the state. It stands on the University of Washington's Seattle campus and was renovated in 2019 with state-of-the-art exhibits. Among the many geological, biological, and anthropological artifacts are the only authentic dinosaur fossils in Washington. The tribal histories of the Native American people in the Pacific Northwest are also on display.

★ Washington Park Arboretum and Japanese Garden

2300 Arboretum Drive E.; 206/543-8800; https:// botanicgardens.uw.edu; dawn-8pm daily; free

Washington Park Arboretum is a sprawling 230-acre (93-ha) park full of trails perfect for a peaceful stroll or bird-watching. The University of Washington and the City of Seattle work together to manage this beautifully designed urban oasis of diverse habitats and plant collections. Among the Arboretum's themed gardens are the brightly colored Azalea Way and the peaceful, shaded Woodland Garden. There is no bad season to visit; spring is peak bloom, and in fall all the leaves change color and draw in visitors from all over.

Just south of the Washington Park Arboretum is the **Japanese Garden** ($10 adult, $6 ages 6-17 and 65+, under 5 free), a

Capitol Hill

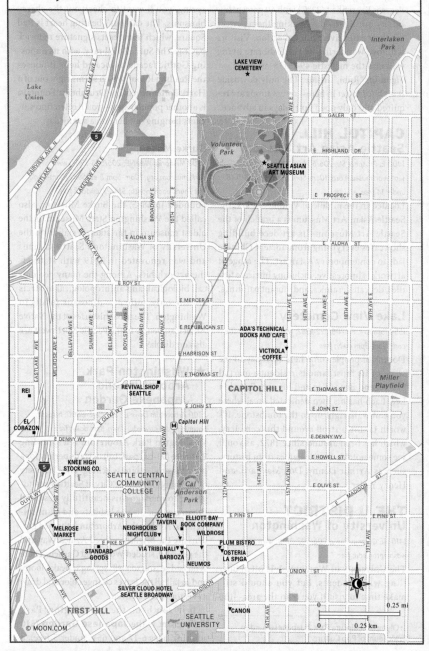

© MOON.COM

carefully planned and executed 3.5-acre (1.4-ha) traditional garden. The area is adorned with Japanese elements such as a koi pond, stone lanterns, and beautifully arched bridges. You'll also pass by a ceremonial entrance, serene rock gardens, expertly tended bonsai displays, and a teahouse.

FREMONT AND WALLINGFORD
Fremont Public Art

between N. 34th St., N. 36th St., Aurora Ave. N., and Evanston Ave. N., Fremont; https://fremont.com

Fremont is known for its distinctive array of public artworks that add character and charm to the neighborhood. The **Fremont Troll** (Steve Badanes, Will Martin, Donna Walter, and Ross Whitehead) (N. 36th St. and Troll Ave. N.) is the most famous: a massive concrete troll clutching a real Volkswagen Beetle that resides under the George Washington Memorial Bridge.

Nearby, you'll find an aluminum sculpture, **Waiting for the Interurban** (Richard Beyer) (N. 34th St. and Fremont Ave. N.), depicting a group of people and a dog waiting for public transportation. You'll often see them colorfully decorated with costumes throughout the year.

Another piece in Fremont's eclectic art scene is the **Statue of Lenin** (Emil Venkov) (Fremont Place N. and N. 36th St.), a thought-provoking work from Slovakia. **The Fremont Rocket** (artist unknown) (Evanston Ave. N. and N. 35th St.), a 53-ft (16-m) tall space-themed sculpture, adds a touch of cosmic flair to the area. When you get to the intersection of Fremont Way North and North 35th Street, look for the **Center of the Universe signpost** (artist unknown), pointing to various fictional and global destinations.

Woodland Park Zoo

5500 Phinney Ave. N. and 750 N. 50th Street; 206/548-2500; www.zoo.org; 9:30am-3pm daily; $10-19

More than 300 different species and 1,000 various animals call the 92-acre (32-ha) Woodland Park Zoo home, and it's won numerous awards over the years. You'll need to spend at least 3 hours walking around to see all the exhibits, including the jaguars and toucans at the Tropical Rain Forest, the snowy owls and gray wolves along the Northern Trail, and the Assam Rhino Reserve.

The zoo hosts special events like WildLanterns every winter, when you can visit after-hours and walk through thousands of colorful light displays, and Brew at the Zoo in the fall, which combines local beer tastings with access to some zoo exhibits.

★ Gas Works Park

2101 N. Northlake Way; 206/684-4075; www.seattle. gov; 6am-10pm daily; free

Gas Works Park is set on the grounds of a former gas plant. Instead of completely clearing the site, the city turned it into a park in 1975, keeping some old structures for a fun, industrial vibe. You can walk around the old plant, and there's a playground nearby for younger kids.

Kite Hill is one of the more popular spots, with its grassy area perfect for flying kites and beautiful views of the Seattle skyline and Lake Union. You'll also find it covered with people on their picnic blankets, enjoying lunch or the sunset in the summertime.

BALLARD
★ Ballard Locks

3015 NW 54th St.; 206/780-2500; https://ballardlocks. org; visitor center 10am-3pm Wed.-Sun.; free

The Ballard Locks, officially known as the Hiram M. Chittenden Locks, were built in 1917 and serve as a gateway between Puget Sound's saltwater and the Ship Canal's freshwater, which flows into Lake Union and Lake Washington. The locks keep the water level between the lakes consistent and are essential for boat navigation. You can walk along the locks and watch boats of all sizes navigate through; it's especially busy in the summer, with a constant stream of yachts, fishing boats, and sometimes even kayaks.

The U District, Fremont, and Wallingford

N 64TH ST
N 63RD ST
N 62ND ST
N 61ST ST
N 60TH ST
N 59TH ST

Green Lake

To Green Lake Boathouse

GREEN LAKE

PHINNEY RIDGE

NW 55TH ST

WOODLAND PARK ZOO ★

Woodland Park

N 65TH ST
N 54TH ST   **KISAKU** ▼
N 53RD ST
N 52ND ST
N 51ST ST

N 50TH ST

N 50TH ST

N 49TH ST
N 48TH ST
N 47TH ST

N 49TH ST
N 48TH ST
N 47TH ST

Meridian Playfield

N 46TH ST
N 45TH ST

ARCHIE MCPHEE ▼

MOLLY MOON'S ▼

N 45TH ST

N 44TH ST

WALLINGFORD

N 44TH ST

N 43RD ST

BOOK LARDER ▼

N 43RD ST

Wallingford Playfield

N 41ST ST
N 40TH ST

N 41ST ST
N 40TH ST

NW 41ST ST
NW 40TH ST
NW BOWDOIN PL

N 40TH ST

FREMONT

● **STAYBRIDGE SUITES SEATTLE - FREMONT**

N 39TH ST

N 39TH ST

N 38TH ST

N 37TH ST

OUTSIDER COMICS ■

THE BACKDOOR ▼

N 36TH ST

HOTEL HOTEL HOSTEL ●

N 35TH ST

FREMONT TROLL ★

N 38TH ST
N 37TH ST
N 36TH ST
N 35TH ST

BROUWER'S CAFE ■

STATUE OF LENIN ★

THE FREMONT ROCKET ★

CENTER OF THE UNIVERSE SIGNPOST ★

SCHILLING CIDER HOUSE ▼

FREMONT BREWING ▼

EVO ●

Fremont Cut

SEATTLE PACIFIC UNIVERSITY

NICKERSON ST

Cheshiahud Lake Union Loop

WAITING FOR THE INTERURBAN ★

Burke Gilman Trail

N 34TH ST

Burke Gilman Trail

N NORTHLAKE WY

W. ETRURIA ST

FLORENTIA ST

N NORTHLAKE WY

David Rodgers Park

QUEEN ANNE

WESTLAKE AVE N

Cheshiahud Lake Union Loop

CANLIS ▼

GAS WORKS PARK ✪

Lake Union

N 64TH ST
N 63RD ST
N 62ND ST
N 61ST ST
N 60TH ST
N 59TH ST

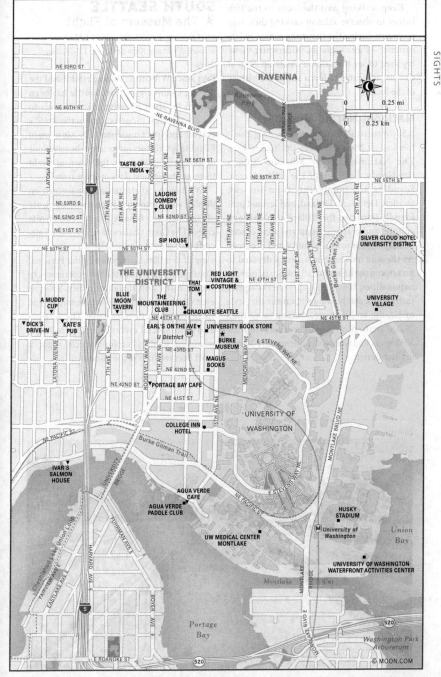

Keep walking past the locks to the fish ladder to observe salmon making their way upstream during the spawning season in late summer—there's also an underwater viewing area to see the salmon closer up. Stop at the visitor center to learn about the history of the locks.

National Nordic Museum

2655 NW Market St.; https://nordicmuseum.org; 10am-5pm Tues.-Sat. (10am-8pm Thurs.); $10-20, under 4 free

The National Nordic Museum honors the Nordic heritage of the Ballard area. Scandinavian immigrants from Norway, Sweden, Denmark, Finland, and Iceland profoundly impacted the Ballard area's history, culture, and craftsmanship and were crucial in shaping the town's identity and progress. As the sole museum in America devoted to presenting the history of all five Scandinavian nationalities, the 57,000-sq-ft (17,374-sq-m-) facility reflects the modern, minimalist style of Nordic architecture. Among more than 77,000 artifacts on display are relics from the Viking era and works of contemporary Nordic art and design.

SOUTH SEATTLE
★ The Museum of Flight

9404 E. Marginal Way South; 206/764-5700; www.museumofflight.org; 10am-5pm daily; $18-26, under 4 free

Ever since William E. Boeing established the Boeing Company in 1916, Seattle has been known for its innovative contributions to the aeronautical industry. One of the world's best air and space museums, The Museum of Flight takes visitors on a comprehensive tour of aviation's past, from the dawn of flight through the earliest days of space travel.

With over 150 aircraft and spacecraft on display, you'll want to plan on spending plenty of time here (fortunately there's two on-site cafés). The Great Gallery has 39 full-sized aircraft and provides a visually stunning overview of aviation history, while the Personal Courage Wing showcases the experiences of World War I and II fighter pilots. You can even climb aboard a space shuttle trainer that spent some time in outer space. The museum also hosts special events like Hops & Props, where guests dress up for a special night of craft beer tastings at the museum.

Ballard Locks

Recreation

PARKS

Discovery Park

3801 Discovery Park Blvd.; 206/684-4075; www.

seattle.gov; 4:30am-11pm daily; free

People often head to Discovery Park in the Magnolia neighborhood when they want urban hiking. The 534-acre (216-ha) park is the biggest public park in the city and has 12 mi (19 km) of hiking trails through a diverse landscape with bluffs, beaches, woodlands, and plains. The historic West Point Lighthouse, Seattle's most westerly point, and the Daybreak Star Cultural Center, a hub for Native American culture, are inside its borders. Discovery Park is renowned for its abundant wildlife, particularly its bird population, with over 270 recorded bird species in the area, and you'll often see harbor seals and California sea lions in the water off the beaches.

Magnuson Park

7400 Sand Point Way NE; 206/684-4075; www.seattle.

gov; 4am-11:30pm daily; free

Magnuson Park on Lake Washington is the easternmost point of Seattle and is packed with people in the summer months. Multiple boat launches make it quick and easy to be on the water on a sunny day. It's also one of the few parks nearby with a dedicated swimming area. Magnuson Park's 350 acres (140 ha) of beautiful scenery includes a 4-mi (6-km) network of walking paths that wind their way along the stunning waterfront and through woodlands and lush meadows.

Volunteer Park

1247 15th Ave. E.; 206/684-4075; www.seattle.gov;

6am-10pm daily; free

Volunteer Park, a tranquil litte spot in north Capitol Hill, is a great place to escape it all. A historic conservatory from 1912, a water tower with an observation deck from 1906, the Volunteer Park Conservatory, and the Seattle Asian Art Museum are just a few of the attractions here. The playground, picnic areas, seasonal pool (11am-8pm daily summer), and open fields are perfect for families. The park also hosts free concerts and outdoor theater events.

Seward Park

5900 Lake Washington Blvd. S.; 206/684-4396; www.

seattle.gov; 6am-10pm daily; free

Spanning more than 300 acres (120 ha) in the south Seattle area, Seward Park is home to a 2.4-mi (3.8-km) biking and walking trail, beaches, old-growth forests with eagles' nests, and multiple boat launches. The baths and ponds were constructed in the early 20th century, and the amphitheater built in 1953 is still used for performances today.

Golden Gardens Park

8498 Seaview Pl. NW; 206/684-4075; www.seattle.

gov; 4am-11pm daily; free

On summer nights, the sandy beach of Golden Gardens Park in Ballard comes alive with hundreds of people enjoying bonfires and watching the sun set over Puget Sound. The park also includes wetlands, hiking trails, picnic and playground areas, and beach volleyball. Although the water is chilly year-round, brave swimmers are often out here during the summer days.

Madison Park Beach

1900 43rd Ave. E.; 206/684-7796; www.seattle.gov;

4am-11:30pm daily; free

On the shore of Lake Washington, Madison Park provides an incredible view across to Mercer Island. The picturesque park sits just south of the I-90 floating bridge, which crosses the lake to connect Seattle and Bellevue. Lifeguards are on duty at the swimming beach in the summer, and the park also has a bathhouse. In addition, the park features two tennis courts, a playground, and a big lawn perfect for picnics.

Kerry Park

211 W. Highland Dr.; www.seattle.gov; 6am-10pm daily; free

Photographers and sightseers adore Kerry Park, one of the most popular photo spots in the city, for its panorama of the Seattle skyline, which includes the Space Needle perfectly framed against distant Mount Rainier. Sunset is the best time of day to visit this park in Queen Anne, since the city lights are even more picturesque against the backdrop of the sky's shifting colors.

BIKING

Seattle residents love their bikes and use them to get around everywhere. The city is slowly installing more bike lanes on streets around town, but parts of Seattle are quite steep, so it's best to have some experience before venturing out on those routes. However, beginner cyclists can still enjoy plenty of flatter biking trails.

Alki Trail

One of the easier routes is West Seattle's Alki Trail, a 4-mi (6-km) round-trip paved route that starts at the Duwamish Head and winds along Alki Beach before ending at the Alki Beach Lighthouse. This is also one of the most scenic biking routes, as it goes along Puget Sound and has views of the Seattle skyline across the way.

Burke-Gilman Trail

The 27-mi (43-km) Burke-Gilman Trail is one of the most popular paths to walk, jog, or bike. The scenic trail follows the northern edge of Lake Union, passes through the University of Washington campus, and continues alongside Lake Washington, providing stunning views and a mix of urban and natural scenery. You'll see locals using it to commute to work and get out for some exercise.

There are numerous places to join the trail. It starts in Ballard at 11th Avenue NW and NW 45th Street and winds its way to Bothell, where it connects with the Sammamish River Trail at Bothell Landing Park.

Elliott Bay Trail

The Elliott Bay Trail is a flat, picturesque waterfront path that stretches around 5 mi (8 km) from Smith Cove Park in the Interbay neighborhood to S. Royal Brougham Way near Lumen Field. It's a beautiful path, and you'll see landmarks such as the Olympic Sculpture Park and Myrtle Edwards Park, with the latter being where many people hop on the trail to do a few miles. You'll pass by the piers on the downtown waterfront and see the Seattle Great Wheel. There isn't a bike rental shop nearby, so you'll need to get your bike elsewhere.

Cheshiahud Lake Union Loop

The Cheshiahud Lake Union Loop is a popular trail around Lake Union that gives you views almost the entire way. You can join this 6-mi (10-km) loop at any point, but many people choose to start and end at Gas Works Park since more parking is available there. You'll whiz by houseboat communities, the Fremont, Westlake, and Eastlake neighborhoods, and attractions such as Lake Union Park and the Museum of History and Industry.

Outfitters
Wheel Fun Rentals

2530 Alki Ave. SW; 206/932-2035; https:// wheelfunrentals.com; 10am-sunset, days vary seasonally; rentals $15-39/hour

When looking for wheels to rent on Alki Beach, Wheel Fun Rentals is the place to go. It has a large selection of options, from modern surreys ideal for families or groups to mountain bikes, beach cruisers, tandems, and electric bikes. For those who forgot their beach gear, the shop even has beach toys and equipment, including essentials like umbrellas and chairs.

Electric & Folding Bikes Northwest

4810 17th Ave. NW; 206/547-4621; www. electricvehiclesnw.com; 11am-6pm daily; rentals $10-25/hour

---

1: Golden Gardens Park 2: kayaking in Lake Union

In Ballard, Electric & Folding Bikes Northwest has mountain, road, and hybrid bikes available for rent; all include a helmet and a lock, so you can get off the nearby Burke-Gilman Trail to stop somewhere for lunch. The shop recommends reserving your bike online to ensure it's available for the day and time you want.

Evo

3500 Stone Way N.; 206/973-4470; www.evo.com; 10am-8pm Mon.-Sat., 10am-7pm Sun.; rentals $50-150/ day

While Evo has expanded around the West Coast, its Fremont location is the flagship store, leaving visitors in awe of how much gear they have available. There are multiple bike rental options, including kids, road, hybrid, mountain, and any accessories you may need with these. It's only a block away from the Cheshiahud Lake Union Loop.

BOATING AND KAYAKING

Between Puget Sound, Lake Union, Lake Washington, and all the smaller lakes in between, Seattle has plenty of places to go boating. You'll find locals on the water at any time of year, but summer is the golden season, when it's not uncommon to drive over the I-5 bridge and see Lake Union packed with hundreds of boats.

Green Lake

Just 5 mi (8 km) north of downtown Seattle is Green Lake. A 3-mi (5-km) paved walking path goes around this calm lake, and you'll often spot dozens of locals picnicking under its many trees. Motorized boats aren't allowed, but paddleboards, pedal boats, and the like are fine. Launch areas around the lake include a dock at the northwest corner by Duck Island, a dock at the northeast corner by East Green Lake Beach, and a dock at the south end.

Green Lake Boathouse

7351 E. Green Lake Dr. N. #5303; 206/527-0171; https:// greenlakeboathouse.com; 9am-5pm daily; rentals $28-31/hour

Part boat rental shop, part coffee shop, Green Lake Boathouse has everything you need to start your morning. Order one of their espresso drinks and then head out on the water with your rental. They have stand-up paddleboards, kayaks, pedal boats, rowboats, and water bikes available.

Lake Union

Lake Union is a favorite spot for boating, thanks to its calm waters, view of the Seattle skyline, and multiple launch points. However, this means there is high traffic during the peak summer season, so being aware of your surroundings and having proper boating skills are necessary—especially because motorized boats are allowed alongside kayaks. The lake is famous for its countless colorful houseboats, which have been featured in films such as *Sleepless in Seattle*.

Launch points include South Lake Union Park (860 Terry Ave. N.) by the Center for Wooden Boats, with a dock best for smaller boats. The northeast end has a launch point for paddleboards and kayaks at Fairview Park (2900 Fairview Ave. E.).

Agua Verde Paddle Club

1307 NE Boat St.; 206/632-1862; https:// aguaverdepaddleclub.com; noon-6pm Mon. and Fri., 10am-6pm Sat.-Sun. winter, 10am-8pm Mon., noon-8pm Tues.-Wed., 10am-8pm Thurs.-Fri., 10am-6pm Sat.-Sun. summer.; rentals $22-40/hour, tours $75-125 pp

The Agua Verde Paddle Club is a top spot for kayak and paddleboard rentals in the area. It operates on a first-come, first-served basis, so get there early. The club also offers a variety of paddling tours, including relaxing sunrise excursions and tours that explore the arboretum, which is a great option if you want some guidance. When you're done, grab a bite to eat at their café next door.

Moss Bay

1001 Fairview Ave. N.; 206/682-2031; www.mossbay.co; 11am-8pm Mon., Wed.-Fri. summer, closed Nov.-Mar.; rentals $24-31/hour

In South Lake Union, Moss Bay rents

paddleboards and kayaks on a first-come, first-served basis, so arriving early in the summer is key. It also provides group tours ($75/person for 2.5 hours) for those interested in a more interactive experience of Lake Union.

Lake Washington

At 34 sq mi (88 sq km), Lake Washington is the second-largest natural lake in the state. It stretches 22 mi (35 km) in length and 3.5 mi (5.5 km) in width, so many people consider this the best lake for boating. Kayaks cruise along the shores, but it's mainly a playground for larger, motorized boats looking to go fast. There are multiple boat launch points here; common ones are Magnuson Park Boat Launch (7400 Sand Point Way NE, Seattle), with multiple lanes and plenty of parking, and Kenmore Boat Launch (17150 68th Ave. NE, Kenmore), further up the west side of the lake but often less crowded.

University of Washington Waterfront Activities Center

3710 Montlake Blvd NE; 206/543-9433; www. washington.edu; hours vary, generally 10am-7pm Wed.-Fri., 9am-8pm Sat.-Sun. in summer, closed Oct.-Mar.; rentals $16-23/hour

The University of Washington Waterfront Activities Center is one of the most affordable places to rent canoes and kayaks by the hour. This location is prime for spotting waterfowl and bald eagles, and you can paddle along the shoreline, explore the small islands in Lake Washington, or go south to the Arboretum and under the Floating Bridge.

★ Alki Beach

In West Seattle, Alki Beach sits on Puget Sound, so launching from here lets experienced boaters go as far south as Tacoma or go north to visit the San Juan Islands and beyond. The Don Armeni Boat Ramp (1222 Harbor Ave. SW) is the easiest place to launch, with multiple boat ramps and paid parking.

Water Taxi

1660 Harbor Avenue SW; https://kingcounty.gov; $2.50-5.75/person each way

For a fun way to get across the water, take a ride on the water taxi that leaves from Seacrest Park in West Seattle and drops you off at Pier 50 in Seattle (801 Alaskan Way). This passenger-only ferry crosses Elliott Bay in just 15 minutes and starts around 6am each morning, going until 7pm weekdays and 11pm weekends.

Alki Kayak Tours

1660 Harbor Ave. SW; 206/935-7669; www.kayakalki. com; 10am-5pm Sat.-Sun.; rentals $25-50/hour, $125-150/day

Alki Kayak Tours offers sit-on-top and sea kayak rentals, both single or double. However, due to the complexity and experience needed with sea kayaks, only people experienced in self-rescue can take them out. You can also rent SUPs with no prior experience ($25/hour).

If you need more confidence, take one of their sea kayak classes ($109 pp) to learn the basics or improve your skills so you'll be ready to go out on your own. Their guided tours ($99-149) are also popular, from daytime tours around West Seattle to sunset sea kayak tours and full moon tours.

SPECTATOR SPORTS
Football
Seahawks

Lumen Field, 800 Occidental Ave. S.; www.lumenfield. com; Sep.-Feb.; $33-530

Two of Seattle's most prized sports teams share the field at Lumen Field—the Seahawks football team (who proudly clinched the Super Bowl title in 2014) and the Sounders soccer team. The Seahawks are the city's treasured NFL team, and their fans have broken multiple noise records during games in the past.

University of Washington Huskies

Husky Stadium, 3800 Montlake Blvd NE; https:// gohuskies.com; Aug.-Nov.; $50-458

For a taste of college football, head down to Husky Stadium, where cheering on the Huskies has been part of Seattle's tradition since 1892. Get there early to see college students and alums alike tailgating in the parking lot. There's a view of Lake Washington from the stands.

Baseball
Mariners
T-Mobile Park, 1250 1st Ave. S.; www.mlb.com; Mar.-Nov.; $19-677

The Seattle Mariners launched in 1977 but played in a fully domed stadium shared with football. T-Mobile Park, their home since 1999, adapts to the city's weather much better with a retractable roof. The stadium is known for its wide range of diverse food and drink options, many of them local vendors. Kids will love the Moose Den playground, where they can release their energy when they need a break.

Those interested in a behind-the-scenes look at the stadium can join a **tour** ($40 pp, under 3 free) when games aren't being played to see the dugout, press box, private suites, and other areas typically closed to the public.

Hockey
Kraken
Climate Pledge Arena, 334 1st Ave. N.; https://climatepledgearena.com; Oct.-Apr.; $68-252

The newest sports team in Seattle is the Kraken, the city's long-awaited NHL team. The Climate Pledge Arena opened in 2021 and was a welcome upgrade from outdated Key Arena. It's the world's first International Living Future Institute Zero Carbon Certified arena and seats up to 17,000 people for hockey games.

Basketball
Storm
Climate Pledge Arena, 334 1st Ave. N.; https://climatepledgearena.com; Oct.-Apr.; $18-120

Although the NBA's Seattle Supersonics left in 2008 (which many locals are still bitter about), the WNBA's Seattle Storm keep the town proud. The Storm have won four championships (2004, 2010, 2018, and 2020) and are an exciting team to watch live.

Soccer
Sounders
Lumen Field, 800 Occidental Ave. S.; www.lumenfield.com; Mar.-Oct.; $33-530

Supporters of the Seattle Sounders gather at Pioneer Square's Occidental Park before every home game for a tradition called the March to the Match. Under the direction of a marching band, fans make their way to Lumen Field in a show of solidarity and team spirit seen nowhere else in Major League Soccer. The team's enthusiastic fan following (the Emerald City Supporters) creates an electric environment during games.

TOURS
Food Tours
One of the hardest parts about visiting Seattle is not being able to try all the food the city's known for, but luckily there are plenty of food tours around the city. Come hungry, as the serving sizes are generous.

Show Me Seattle
https://showmeseattle.com; 206/633-2489; $59-120

Show Me Seattle has several options, including a 2-hour early-bird tour of Pike Place Market, where you'll get to try the best food in the market while having the chance to talk to the vendors before the crowds come.

Boat Tours
Taking a boat tour, which offers a fresh perspective of Seattle, is a great way to get a feel for the city's layout.

Argosy Cruises
Harbor Cruise: 1101 Alaskan Way, Pier 55; Ballard Locks Cruise: Westlake Ave. N. (AGC Marina); www.argosycruises.com; 888/623-1445; $22-54 pp

Argosy Cruises provides a variety of tours, including the famous Harbor Cruise, which follows the waterfront and offers the chance to see the city's most iconic monuments from a new perspective while providing facts about them. Argosy also offers a Locks Cruise, where you can ride through the Ballard Locks and get an up-close look at how they function.

Bike Tours

Biking is a common way to get around Seattle, and it's the quickest way to see some neighborhoods. Many people choose to do a self-tour, but joining a guided tour takes you to areas you wouldn't have explored otherwise.

Seattle Bicycle Tours
11 Vine St. (outside the Vine St. Storage Unit); 206/697-9611; https://seattlebicycletours.com; times vary, daily; $65-185
The Discovery Park Electric Bicycle Tour is a leisurely, 2.5-hour ride along the waterfront, through Magnolia, and to Discovery Park. The Emerald City Standard Bike Tour is slightly more challenging, as you'll use a regular bike and navigate some hills, but you get a deeper look into the city for 3 hours through various neighborhoods.

Nightlife

The nightlife in Seattle depends on which neighborhood you're in and what vibe you're looking for—meaning there's something for everyone. Capitol Hill is the place to be for lively nightlife and a younger crowd, while those looking for a more posh night might try Belltown.

DOWNTOWN AND THE WATERFRONT

Downtown Seattle and the waterfront aren't the places for late nights out due to restaurants closing on the earlier side, but they both give you exceptional views of Elliott Bay and the surrounding area, especially at sunset.

Wine Shops and Brewpubs
Pike Brewing Company
1415 1st Ave.; 206/622-6044; www.pikebrewing.com; 11am-9pm daily
Pike Brewing Company is one of the oldest breweries in the city, opening in 1989 in the heart of Pike Place Market. They have a dozen of their own beers on tap, including the best-selling Pike Kilt Lifter Scotch Style Ale, and plenty of seating options, from the bar to private tables. Ask about their **brewery tour** if you have the time—it's a fascinating look into the brewing process that takes place below the restaurant.

Old Stove Brewing
1901 Western Ave.; 206/602-6120; www.oldstove.com; 11am-9pm daily
On the other end of Pike Place Market is Old Stove Brewing, which gives you views of the waterfront whether you decide to sit inside or are lucky enough to snag an outdoor table in the sun. Their Old Stove Pilsner is a light beer ideal for a sunny day, along with their spicy Hama Hama oysters.

The Tasting Room
1924 Post Alley; 206/770-9463; www. winesofwashington.com; 2pm-8pm Mon.-Thurs., noon-10pm Fri.-Sat., noon-8pm Sun.; $8-18
The Tasting Room brings the wine-country experience to you in their cozy tasting room nestled in Post Alley. They pride themselves on only serving winemaker-owned wineries and have over 60 local wines to try, by the glass or a tasting flight.

Music and Entertainment
The Moore Theatre
1932 2nd Ave.; 206/682-1414; www.stgpresents.org
The Moore Theatre is a historical experience no matter what show you're seeing, as this venue opened in 1907 and is the oldest theater in the city. Inside, you'll find exquisite furnishings from the 1900s, illuminated by delicate chandeliers and soothing

If You're Looking for...

- **Rooftop Bars:** Smith Tower's 35th-floor **Observatory Bar** (page 47) has arguably one of the best views in Seattle, with a 360-degree outdoor deck. **The Mountaineering Club** (page 75) offers views of Lake Union and Lake Washington if you snag a seat outside. **Frolik Kitchen + Cocktails** (1415 5th Ave.; www.frolikseattle.com) is the place to be in the summer, as it has one of the more spacious rooftop bars, complete with fire pits.

- **Live Music:** Head to **Neumos** (page 74) in Capitol Hill or **Tractor Tavern** (page 76) in Ballard for smaller shows featuring up-and-coming bands. You can see bigger bands at **The Moore Theatre** (page 69).

- **Craft Cocktails:** For a well-made cocktail, make a reservation at the tiny speakeasy **Knee High Stocking Co.** (page 72) in Capitol Hill. Belltown's **Rob Roy** (page 70) also has custom cocktails in a cozy setting, and Fremont's **The Backdoor** (462 N. 36th St.), a dimly lit lounge, will make you feel straight out of the 1920s.

Smith Tower Observatory Bar

- **Dive Bars:** The **Waterwheel Lounge** (7034 15th Ave. NW; www.thewaterwheellounge.com) in Ballard isn't near the main strip but makes up for it with its entertaining crowd drinking cheap beers and singing karaoke. The U District's **Blue Moon Tavern** (page 74) is another classic dive bar where you enjoy a tall boy while watching live music.

lighting along with theater seating. Various acts come through here each year, including musicals, big-name musicans, comedians, and more. It's rumored that the theater is haunted, which you can decide for yourself when you visit.

ACT Theatre

700 Union St.; 206/292-7676; https://acttheatre.org; box office noon-5pm Mon.-Fri.

ACT (or A Contemporary Theatre) has been around since 1965 and is housed in the historic Eagles Building in downtown Seattle. With three different stages, they showcase a mix of plays, including reimagined classics and new works by emerging talent.

BELLTOWN

If you're looking for upscale cocktail bars and places you can dress up, Belltown is the place to go.

Bars
Bathtub Gin & Co.

2205 2nd Ave., #310; 206/728-6069; www. bathtubginseattle.com; 5pm-2am daily

You'll feel like you've stepped back into the 1920s when you visit the Prohibition-era cocktail bar Bathtub Gin & Co., and in a way, you have. It's housed in the former boiler room of the Humphrey Building from 1928 and is known for its vast selection of liquors from all over the world. Specialty cocktails include the Zlatan with bubbles, lingonberry cucumber water, honey, and ginger liqueur. No reservations, and seats are limited, so get here early.

Rob Roy

2332 2nd Ave; www.robroyseattle.com; 4pm-2am daily

Stepping off the streets of Belltown and into the dimly lit Rob Roy feels like having cocktails at a good friend's house. Settle down on one of the couches for the most comfortable seats in the bar and order one of their specialty cocktails, like the Desert Star with passionfruit and pineapple or the Jungle Bird with Campari. Enjoy your drinks with live music every Tuesday at 7pm.

Shorty's

2316 2nd Ave.; 206/441-5449; https://shortydog.com; noon-2am daily

Take a break from the upscale bars in Belltown and visit Shorty's, where your inner child will find dozens of pinball games to play. Once you build up an appetite, order the Shorty Dog or any number of other hot dogs and a drink from their full-service bar.

Wine Shops and Brewpubs
Vinnie's Wine Shop

2505 2nd Ave. #103; 206/420-7043; www. vinniesseattle.com; 4pm-midnight Tues.-Sat.

If you're looking for a specific type of wine, chances are good you'll find it at Vinnie's Wine Bar among their collection of hundreds from all over the world. Take advantage of their oyster happy hour Tuesday through Saturday (4pm-5pm), where oysters and caviar are half off.

Music and Entertainment
Dimitriou's Jazz Alley

2033 6th Ave.; 206/441-9729; www.jazzalley.com; shows at 7:30pm and 9:30pm

Dimitriou's Jazz Alley offers a relaxing evening of live jazz music from performers from all over the country. They have two shows each evening, and it's recommended to get there early to enjoy dinner at their restaurant before the performance starts. The stage is the center of attention in this cozy little venue, where only small table lights provide ambient lighting in an otherwise dim setting.

The Crocodile

2505 1st Ave.; 206/420-6351; www.thecrocodile.com; 5pm-2am daily

The Crocodile opened its doors in 1991 and over the years has hosted countless Seattle-based bands as they got their start, including

now-famous musical acts Nirvana and Macklemore. While it tends to book smaller acts, a number of impressive artists stop by here, including the Beastie Boys, Snoop Dogg, and Brandi Carlile. In 2021 the Crocodile moved into a much bigger building that takes up three stories and includes a 300-person venue, a sit-down theater, and a small hotel and restaurant.

QUEEN ANNE

While the U District is the go-to spot for the college crowd, Queen Anne is a close second. It boasts numerous lively bars that attract a younger audience, all conveniently within walking distance of one another.

Bars
Ozzie's

105 W. Mercer St.; 206/284-4618; www.ozziesinseattle. com; 11am-2am daily

Ozzie's, a a self-proclaimed dive bar, is often full of people in their 20s, and it's an ideal place to end the night. You'll find Jell-O shots and cheap cocktails here, fueling a large portion of their crowd, who belt out karaoke all night. For a dive bar, they have an impressively large menu ($9-16) and serve breakfast as well, so you may find yourself here again the morning after.

Wine Shops and Brewpubs
Queen Anne Beerhall

203 W. Thomas St.; 206/420-4326; https:// queenannebeerhall.com; 11am-2am daily

The 7,000-sq-ft (2,134-sq-m) Queen Anne Beerhall follows the typical German beer hall layout, with long wooden tables encouraging you to share and talk with your neighbors. In addition to over two dozen beers on draft, their menu has typical pub food ($12-34) along with European specialties like bratwurst.

Music and Entertainment
McCaw Hall

321 Mercer St.; 206/733-9725; www.mccawhall.com

McCaw Hall is one of Seattle's most exquisite

venues. It boasts a bar, café, and stunning lobbies highlighted by a five-story serpentine glass wall. It's home to the Seattle Opera and Pacific Northwest Ballet and hosts a variety of performances throughout the year, including lectures, concerts, and musicals.

On the Boards

100 W. Roy St.; 206/217-9886; www.ontheboards.org

On the Boards is known for its contemporary performances, which include local and international performers in their shows. You'll walk away entertained and educated; some past shows include the history of Korean theater and interactive Black stories through dance.

SOUTH LAKE UNION

You'll likely run into many Amazon employees celebrating happy hour in South Lake Union, as their campus is right in the heart of plenty of chic eateries and bars. It's a fun mix of business and casual in this area.

Bars
Altitude Sky Lounge

300 Terry Ave. N.; https://altitudeskylounge.com/ seattle; 4pm-11pm Sun.-Thurs., 4pm-midnight Fri.-Sat.

Take the Astra Hotel's elevator 16 stories up to enjoy drinks at Altitude Sky Lounge, a rooftop bar overlooking Lake Union and the Space Needle. While sitting at a fire pit on the outdoor patio is the place to be, the bar's floor-to-ceiling windows still give an impressive view from inside on a rainy day. They have house-crafted cocktails like the Altitude 161 in addition to a full bar and small bites ($16-39). DJs are spinning every Thursday-Saturday night, adding to the fun ambience.

Flatstick Pub

609 Westlake Ave. N.; 206/258-4989; https:// flatstickpub.com; 11am-11pm Tues.-Thurs., 11am-1am Fri.-Sat., 11am-6pm Sun.; $5-10

Grab a putter and play mini golf at Flatstick Pub if you feel like moving while having a beer. They have a fun Pacific Northwest-themed mini golf course and Duffleboard that runs throughout the pizza restaurant ($13-26).

Music and Entertainment
El Corazon

109 Eastlake Ave. E.; 206/262-0482; https:// elcorazonseattle.com

Showcasing metal, punk, and indie bands, El Corazon is one of the smallest musical venues in Seattle, but it's also one of the best places to get up close and intimate with your favorite performers. The inside is a bit gritty and can become sweltering during summertime due to minimal ventilation, but it's a fun way to sweat.

CAPITOL HILL

Night owls and party animals flock to this lively neighborhood, which is always bustling with activity at its array of venues, from underground DJ performances to eccentric dive bars.

Bars
Knee High Stocking Co.

1356 E. Olive Way; 206/979-7049; www. kneehighstocking.com; 6pm-11pm Wed.-Thurs., Sun., 6pm-midnight Fri.-Sat.

Knee High Stocking Co. is one of the original speakeasy bars and is now more popular than ever, with walk-ins being almost impossible on the weekends. Book your reservation in advance and enjoy the specialty craft cocktails in this dimly lit but cozy bar that Anthony Bourdain once visited. They recently added Filipino-style American comfort food ($12-19) to satisfy late-night cravings.

Canon

928 12th Ave.; www.canonseattle.com; 5pm-1am daily

Canon may be one of the pricier cocktail bars, but it's worth it for its vast selection. The bar claims to have the most extensive spirit collection in the country, with over 4,000 different ones, and they have innovative cocktail recipes from all over the world, such as the

---

1: Flatstick Pub 2: The Mountaineering Club

Aviation drink from 1918 and the Bee's Toes from 1937.

Comet Tavern
922 E Pike St.; 206/323-5678; https://thecomettavern. com; 2pm-2am Mon.-Wed., noon-2am Thurs.-Fri., 10am-2am Sat.-Sun.

The Comet Tavern has been around since the 1950s when it was an Irish bar and has changed several times over the decades, but it remains one of the best places to get local beer and a solid meal in Capitol Hill. They're next door to **Lost Lake Café & Lounge** (1505 10th Ave.; 206/323-5678; www.lostlakecafe. com; $12-20)—order anything on the menu, such as sandwiches or burgers, and have it delivered to your table.

Music and Entertainment
Neumos
925 E. Pike St.; www.neumos.com; 4pm-2am daily

Right in the middle of Capitol Hill, Neumo's is a weekend music hot spot. The theater holds 750 people but has hosted some surprisingly popular acts, so be sure to check the schedule and purchase your tickets as soon as they become available. With a balcony, mezzanine, and three bars, the venue's smart layout makes sure no concertgoer will feel too cramped to enjoy the music.

LGBTQ+ Bars and Nightclubs
Neighbours Nightclub
1509 Broadway; 206/420-2958; Facebook @NeighboursNightclub; 9pm-2am Wed.-Thurs. and Sun., 9pm-4am Fri.-Sat.

Neighbors Nightclub is one of the longest-running nightclubs in Seattle and a treasured place among members of the LGBTQ+ community. The club has a vibrant dance scene, frequent drag shows, and themed nights that go into the early morning hours.

Wildrose
1021 E. Pike St.; 206/324-9210; www.thewildrosebar. com; 5pm-11pm Tues.-Thurs., 5pm-2am Fri.-Sat., 4pm-11pm Sun.

Established in 1984, Wildrose is proud to be the oldest lesbian bar in the US and hosts a lively atmosphere with DJs every Friday and Saturday along with plenty of drink specials. There's also plenty to do weekdays with events like Queer Songwriter's Night and Drag Bingo.

Barboza
925 E. Pike St.; www.thebarboza.com; 4pm-2am daily

You can catch a variety of up-and-coming acts nearly every night of the week in underground Barboza, which is below Neumos. With a capacity of just 200, this unfurnished basement provides an intimate setting for live performances, and afterward audiences often get the opportunity to speak with the artists.

THE U DISTRICT
Whether you're a college student or just want to relive your university days, you'll want to visit the U District. You'll find cheap drinks, loud bars, and sticky floors but a fun atmosphere, particularly on game nights.

Bars
Blue Moon Tavern
712 NE 45th St.; 206/675-9116; www. thebluemoonseattle.com; 4pm-2am Mon.-Tues., 3pm-2am Wed.-Sat., 3pm-midnight Sun.

On the outskirts of the U District, the Blue Moon Tavern has been a favorite of college students since 1934. Over the years, it's been everything from a biker bar to a grunge bar, but it now serves a wide range of people, with live music most nights and an art night where artists can bring their sketchbooks.

Earl's on the Ave
4333 University Way NE; 206/525-4493; www. earlsontheave.com; noon-2am daily

Earl's on the Ave is a quintessential college bar near the University of Washington—it's loud and often has long lines, but it has cheap drinks, which is ideal for a college student. It's a fun place to watch sports if you don't mind a bit of noise, as you can cheer on the local team with others.

The Mountaineering Club

4507 Brooklyn Ave. NE; 206/634-2000; www. themountaineeringclub.com; 3pm-10pm Sun.-Mon., 3pm-midnight Tues.-Thurs., 3pm-1am Fri.-Sat.

Located atop the Graduate Hotel, the Mountaineering Club has an inviting atmosphere. If you're lucky enough to get an outdoor seat, you'll have views of the University District and Lake Union, with the downtown skyline in the background, as you sip one of their craft cocktails. A small food menu ($13-26) is also available.

Music and Entertainment
Laughs Comedy Club

5220 Roosevelt Way NE; 206/526-5653; https:// laughscomedyclub.com; 7pm-10pm Wed.-Thurs., 6pm-11pm Fri.-Sat.

You can't help but walk away in a good mood after attending a show at Laughs Comedy Club. It has a mix of newer comedians trying out their material and well-known comedians. Beer, wine, cocktails, and non-alcoholic drinks are available, and there's a small food menu ($9-15) if you get hungry.

FREMONT AND WALLINGFORD

You'll find a handful of laid-back bars in Fremont, many that offer live music on weekends, and numerous restaurants that stay open late to help with the after-bar cravings. Wallingford is a quieter area for nightlife but still has a handful of bars and on the weekends it is often easier to grab a seat here than at some downtown places.

Wine Shops and Brewpubs
Fremont Brewing

1050 N. 34th St.; 206/420-2407; www.fremontbrewing. com; 11am-9pm daily

Fremont Brewing has established itself as one of the larger breweries in the Seattle region, and you'll often find its beers on tap at local bars. The spacious taproom has a large indoor area with tables, couches, and board games, plus the popular outdoor patio. Fremont's beer selection is impressive, with options like the hoppy Lush IPA or the light-bodied Golden Pilsner.

Schilling Cider House

708 N. 34th St.; 206/420-7088; https://schillingcider. com; noon-10pm Sun., 4pm-10pm Mon.-Wed., 4pm-11pm Thurs., noon-11pm Fri.-Sat.

Schilling Cider House is the only cider house in Seattle that serves 100 percent cider, and it has the country's most extensive selection of craft cider. They have over 30 on draft, mainly from cideries around the Pacific Northwest, but also a few international ones. It's best to get a tasting flight—sample several ciders to find your favorite. Kids aren't allowed, but well-behaved dogs are welcome.

Bars
Brouwer's Café

400 N. 35th St.; 206/267-2437; www.brouwerscafe. com; 4pm-9pm Wed.-Thurs., noon-10pm Fri.-Sat., 2pm-7pm Sun.

You'll find beer at any of the bars that line the streets of Fremont, but no other place has 60 beers on tap, in addition to 400 national and international bottles of beer. Brouwer's serves food inspired by Belgium ($12-25) in this spacious warehouse-style restaurant.

Kate's Pub

309 NE 45th St.; 206/547-6832; www.katespub.com; 4pm-midnight Mon.-Tues., 4pm-2am Wed.-Sat.

Kate's Pub in Wallingford has a special event going on almost every night of the week. Stop by for Karaoke Whiskey Wednesday to get half off the whiskey selection, or on Friday for $2 Jell-O shots and a Mario Kart tournament. It has a friendly vibe where you'll likely make new friends by the end of the night. Food ($12-18) includes bar classics like jalapeño poppers and burgers.

BALLARD

Live music venues and a thriving craft beer circuit are the heart of Ballard's vibrant nightlife scene. The neighborhood has a wide choice of restaurants and bars, ranging from casual pubs to classy cocktail lounges, and many are within easy walking distance of one another.

Wine Shops and Brewpubs
Maritime Pacific Brewing Company

1111 NW Ballard Way; 206/782-6181; https:// maritimebrewing.com; 4pm-9pm Tues.-Wed., noon-9pm Thurs. and Sun., noon-10pm Fri.-Sat.

Maritime Brewing has been part of the Ballard brewing scene since 1990. They have high-quality, flavorful beers such as their Drylander Pale Ale with a slight bitterness or their Jolly Roger Christmas Ale, a bold English strong ale. A full food menu ($9-28) has options like burgers or sandwiches, and they even sell their specialty house sauces to take home.

Bars
Percy's & Co.

5233 Ballard Ave. NW; 206/420-3750; https:// percysseattle.com; 5pm-midnight Mon.-Thurs., 3pm-2am Fri.-Sat., 1pm-9pm Sun.

Percy's & Co. in Ballard offers an ideal setting for date night, where you can order apothecary-inspired cocktails and dine on popcorn or charcuterie ($8-28). This intimate bar has inventive cocktails like the Nutty Professor and King Street Station.

The Sloop Tavern

2830 NW Market St.; 206/782-3330; https:// theslooptavern.com; 3pm-11pm Mon.-Tues., 11am-11pm Wed.-Thurs., Sun., 11am-2am Fri.-Sat.

An iconic spot for locals since it opened its doors in 1952, the Sloop Tavern claims to sell more draft Rainier beer than anywhere else in the state. It is also famous as the birthplace of the "Slooper," a 34-ounce super mug filled with cold beer. Traditional pub fare ($6-16) is available, with the crowd-pleaser being the fish and chips.

Music and Entertainment
Tractor Tavern

5213 Ballard Ave. NW; 206/789-3599; https:// tractortavern.com; 8pm-2am daily

After you get dinner and drinks around Ballard, walk over to the Tractor Tavern to watch live music. Although it tends to focus on folk, country, and Americana music, you'll find touring artists of all genres here. The capacity is only a few hundred people, giving each show a cozy feel.

WEST SEATTLE

Although West Seattle is only a short drive across the bridge from downtown Seattle, it has established its own vibe that feels like you're in a different city. There's a large selection of bars and restaurants, particularly along California Avenue.

Bars
The Nook

2206 California Ave. SW, Suite A; 206/420-7414; www. thenookseattle.com; 4pm-midnight Tues.-Thurs. and Sun., 4pm-2am Fri.-Sat.

The Nook has some of the best cocktails in West Seattle and a cozy, intimate setting for meeting friends or going on a date. They always have seasonal cocktails available, so ask about the latest one and grab a seat inside or outside on their small patio to enjoy the sun.

Larry's Tavern

3405 California Ave. SW; 206/453-3009; www. thestedmangroup.com; 4pm-2am daily

For a more casual setting, stop by Larry's Tavern to order a local Seattle beer and play pool or Skee-Ball with friends. They have a full bar and a dozen small bar snacks ($4-14) available for when you get hungry.

Music and Entertainment
Skylark Café & Club

3803 Delridge Way SW; 206/935-2111; www. skylarkcafe.com; 4pm-midnight Mon.-Thurs., 4pm-1am Sat., 10am-3pm Sun.

While Skylark Café has a decent-sized weekday dinner menu ($6-18) and serves brunch on the weekends as well, its nighttime events are what it's known for. Tuesdays are for drag bingo, Wednesdays are for aspiring singers at open mic night, and bands regularly come through on the weekends for live performances.

Festivals and Events

SPRING

Seattle International Film Festival

Multiple locations; 206/464-5830; www.siff.net; May; $65-2,200

The Seattle International Film Festival, or SIFF, draws visitors from worldwide for several weeks in May when it takes over local cinemas with feature-length movies, shorts, documentaries, and animations. This is also the chance to get close to movie stars and directors with premieres, Q&A sessions, workshops, and panel discussions.

SUMMER

Seafair

1455 NW Leary Way, Suite 400; 206/728-0123; www.seafair.org; July-Aug.; free, special event ticket prices vary

A tradition since 1950, Seafair is Seattle's signature summer festival, celebrated over a month with fun activities and events. Some of the most popular ones include the Blue Angels air show during Fleet Week, the lively Pirates Landing, the Seafair Torchlight Parade featuring floats and marching bands, and the spectacular hydroplane racing at the Seafair Cup.

Bumbershoot

Seattle Center, 305 Harrison St.; 323/908-0607; https://bumbershoot.com; Labor Day weekend; $75-130

Bumbershoot marks the unofficial end of summer for most locals and has been a Labor Day weekend tradition since 1971. Under the shadow of the Space Needle at the Seattle Center, thousands of visitors enjoy a variety of musical performances on multiple stages, as well as comedians and art booths showcasing the work of local artists. The festival has gotten some huge names to play over the years, and it's perfect for the last days of summer.

WINTER

Winterfest

Seattle Center, 305 Harrison St.; 206/684-7200; www.seattlecenter.com; late Nov.-late Dec.; free

From the day after Thanksgiving until New Year's Eve, the Seattle Center transforms into

Winterfest at Seattle Center

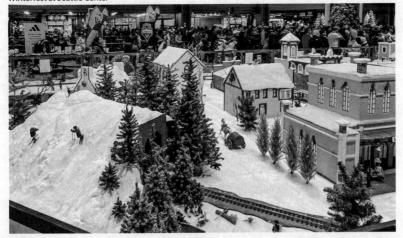

a winter wonderland for Winterfest. Inside the Seattle Center Armory, you'll find a 19th-century model train and village that will captivate kids, while the stage is full of entertaining dances and songs during the weekend. Head outside to the European-inspired Seattle Christmas Market for booths selling local goods and European food and drink, such as bratwurst and mulled wine, visit Santa, and ride the carousel.

Shopping

DOWNTOWN AND THE WATERFRONT
Gifts and Home
Simply Seattle
1600 1st Ave.; 206/485-7325; www.simplyseattle.com; 10am-6pm daily

When you want Seattle souvenirs to commemorate your trip, Simply Seattle has everything you need. The waterfront location on Pier 54 has keychains, mugs, postcards, and plenty of other trinkets, while the Pike Place location (1600 1st Ave.) mainly focuses on Seattle-related clothing, such as shirts, sweatshirts, hats, and more for all the major sports teams.

Ye Olde Curiosity Shop
1001 Alaskan Way, Pier 54; 206/682-5844; www.yeoldecuriosityshop.com; 10am-9pm daily

Ye Olde Curiosity Shop is one of the odder shops along the waterfront, but it always draws visitors due to its name. You never know what you'll find here—anything from a preserved scorpion necklace to a shrunken goat head—but you can guarantee it'll be unique.

Clothing and Jewelry
Simple Life
201 Pine St.; 206/628-7077; https://simplelifeseattle.com; 10am-6pm daily

Simple Life has a beautiful selection of women's boutique clothing in all sizes, and their helpful staff can advise you on putting an entire outfit together. They specialize in selling comfortable, casual clothing with a pop of color.

PIKE PLACE MARKET
Food and Drink
MarketSpice
85 Pike St.; 206/622-6340; https://marketspice.com; 9am-5pm daily

MarketSpice has been selling teas since 1911 and carries a wide range of specialty teas and coffee, but their most popular is the cinnamon orange black tea. Pick up a few boxes, or buy them in bulk to save money.

World Spice
1509 Western Ave.; 206/962-8622; www.worldspice.com; 10am-5pm Wed.-Sun.

You'll love the smell as you walk into World Spice, a vibrant spice bazaar with over 240 types of spices, herbs, and blends. The staff can guide you if you need help deciding, and they also offer free taste tests of some spice blends.

Rachel's Ginger Beer
1530 Post Alley; https://rachelsgingerbeer.com; 10am-7pm Sun.-Thurs., 10am-10pm Fri.-Sat.

Rachel's Ginger Beer has gained a cult following over the years and is found in most local grocery stores, but you'll have plenty more choices of this non-alcoholic drink here. They have everything from blood orange to pink guava, and they can turn it into a cocktail if you want an alcoholic drink.

Beecher's Cheese
1600 Pike Pl.; 206/956-1964; https://beechershandmadecheese.com; 9am-6pm daily

You can't visit Pike Place Market without stopping by Beecher's Cheese. As you walk in, you'll be captivated by watching the cheese being made behind the large windows. Once you're done staring, pick up some of their cheese or stay a little longer and order their famous mac and cheese.

Bookstores
Left Bank Books
92 Pike St. #B; 206/622-0195; www.leftbankbooks.com; 10am-7pm daily

Just before you head into the main section of Pike Place Market, you'll see the quaint Left Bank Books, which has been open since the 1970s. The collectively owned bookshop focuses on radical politics, queer and trans studies, feminism, and more.

Gifts and Home
Sur La Table
84 Pine St.; 206/448-2244; www.surlatable.com; 10am-6pm daily

Sur La Table sells upscale home decor, cookware, and dining items. If the name rings a bell, it's because it's grown into a large chain; this store is the original, established in 1972. It also offer themed cooking nights (sign up in advance on their website), with everything from sushi making to a kids' baking series.

Made in Washington
1530 Post Alley; 206/467-0788; https:// madeinwashington.com, 9am-5pm daily

If you want a specific type of food or drink from Washington or to send it as a gift, you'll likely find it here. Made in Washington sells all local products featuring the best of the state, including smoked salmon, jam, chocolates, coffee, candles, bath salts, and kitchen items.

Market Magic Shop
1501 Pike Pl. #427; 206/624-4271; www. pikeplacemarket.org; 10am-5pm daily

Head to the Down Under section of the market to explore Market Magic Shop, the Pacific Northwest's longest-running magic shop. Children of all ages have been coming here for decades to buy magic cards, jokes and gags, magic books, and more. Stop by Zoltar outside the store to have your fortune told before you leave.

Clothing
Earth Wind & Fire Boutique
1514 Pike Pl. #13; 206/448-2529; www. earthwindandfireboutique.com; 9am-5:30pm daily

Earth Wind & Fire Boutique has everything you need to complete your outfit, from one-of-a-kind handbags to exquisitely handcrafted pieces. The shop takes pride in its unique variety of specialty clothes and caters to a wide range of sizes, from petite to plus-size.

PIONEER SQUARE AND THE INTERNATIONAL DISTRICT
Food and Drink
Lady Yum
116 S. Washington St.; 866/523-9986 ext. 5; https:// ladyyum.com; 10am-10pm daily

Lady Yum has some of the finest macarons in the city, with indulgent flavors like toasted coconut, raspberry chardonnay, and toffee, making your mouth water as soon as you walk in. Keep an eye out for their seasonal flavors, which always introduce one-of-a-kind tastes, and treat yourself to a glass of champagne if you're feeling fancy.

Intrigue Chocolate Co.
157 S. Jackson St.; 206/829-8810; www. intriguechocolate.com; noon-5pm Mon.-Fri., 11am-4pm Sat.-Sun.

Stop here in the heart of Pioneer Square when you're in the mood for rich, smooth chocolate. Intrigue Chocolate makes creative chocolates inspired by the Pacific Northwest, such as a hops and clover honey chocolate or a lavender, coffee, and long pepper bar.

Gifts and Home
Bon Voyage Vintage
110 S. Washington St.; 206/226-5069; https:// bonvoyagevintage.myshopify.com; noon-6pm daily

It's lucky for Bon Voyage Vintage that old styles tend to recycle themselves, as the store has vintage clothing from the 1950s through the 1990s, so you'll want to come here as soon as the next trend starts. This is a fun place to browse and find a unique piece of clothing or jewelry for your collection.

Gameday Sports Shop

540 Occidental Ave. S.; 206/708-1342; https:// officialteamshop.com; 10am-5pm daily

You don't want to be seen around Seattle on game day without wearing the local team, so stop by Gameday Sports Shop across from Lumen Field to get your hat and shirt. Gear can be a bit expensive here, but they always have sales racks, so check those out first.

Art Galleries

With its abundance of galleries showcasing works by regional, national, and international artists, Seattle's Pioneer Square is a hotspot for art enthusiasts. The **First Thursday Art Walk** in this historic district is the longest-running art walk in the country.

Glasshouse Studio

311 Occidental Ave. S.; 206/682-9939; www.glasshouse-studio.com; 10am-3pm Mon., 10am-4pm Tues.-Sat., 11am-4pm Sun.

While Chihuly is the biggest glassblower in

town, Glasshouse Studio is the oldest glass-blowing studio in the city, and possibly more impressive. It has a colorful array of vases, lights, plates, and other glass pieces available.

Stonington Gallery

125 S. Jackson St.; 206/405-4040; https:// stoningtongallery.com; 10am-5pm Tues.-Sat.

Contemporary Northwest Coast and Alaskan masterworks, especially Coast Salish art, are the specialty of Stonington Gallery. Cedar and alder masks, totems, panels, and sculptures fill this art gallery, providing a glimpse into the dynamic Indigenous cultures of the area. Stonington was the first Seattle gallery to dedicate a solo exhibition to Coast Salish cultures.

BELLTOWN
Music
Singles Going Steady

2219 2nd Ave.; 206/441-7396; Facebook @Singles-Going-Steady-Seattle; noon-6pm Tues.-Sat.

Punk and alternative music fans will love Singles Going Steady for its huge selection of secondhand vinyl records and CDs, mainly focused on music from the 1970s through

Lady Yum

the 80s. There's a vast collection of nostalgic memorabilia as well.

Art Galleries

Belltown hosts the Belltown Art Walk every second Friday (6pm-9pm), when galleries in the area stay open late to showcase new exhibits.

Slip Gallery

2301 1st Ave.; www.slipgallery.com; hours vary, typically Thurs.-Sat.

The Slip Gallery features the works of local artists, and it operates entirely on the generosity of its donors. The displays rotate every few weeks, and the gallery offers lessons where you can hone your creative skills (price varies per workshop).

Gallery Mack

2100 Western Ave.; 206/448-1616; www.gallerymack. com; 11am-5pm Wed.-Sat.

Established in 1974, Gallery Mack is widely recognized as one of Seattle's most prestigious art galleries. It features a dynamic assortment of works by well-known and up-and-coming Northwest artists, as well as international and national rising artists, in contemporary fine art and sculpture. You'll find everything from paintings to glass and metal here.

Clothing
Patagonia

2100 1st Ave.; 206/622-9700; www.patagonia.com; 10am-6pm Sun.-Wed., 10am-7pm Thurs.-Sat.

Patagonia is a perfect match for all the nature enthusiasts in Seattle, supplying a huge selection of men's, women's, and children's outdoor clothing that's high-quality. They also have gear such as backpacks, sleeping bags, and camping equipment.

SOUTH LAKE UNION
Outdoor Gear
REI

222 Yale Ave. N.; 206/223-1944; www.rei.com; 9am-9pm Mon.-Sat. 10am-7pm Sun.

Many people go to REI not just to buy outdoor gear but also for the experience of this giant flagship store. You'll be greeted by a massive climbing wall, and you can sign up for classes if you're interested. If you're considering buying a bike, you can take it out on their bike test trail. Everyone who works here is passionate about the outdoors and takes the time to help you find what you need.

CAPITOL HILL
Bookstores
Elliott Bay Book Company

1521 10th Ave.; 206/624-6600; www.elliottbaybook. com; 10am-10pm daily

Locals have been going to Elliott Bay Book Company since 1973 to find their latest read, and with over 150,000 titles, you're guaranteed to walk away with at least one book. This beautiful store is in a converted warehouse full of books in every genre, and their staff is always eager to help you find your next book. There's also a children's area and a café, so you could easily spend a few hours here.

Clothing
Standard Goods

501 E. Pike St.; 206/323-0207; https:// thestandardgoods.com; 11am-7pm daily

Standard Goods is a fun place to get high-quality Pacific Northwest gear, with hats, T-shirts, and sweatshirts with local towns or sayings. It also has an assortment of mugs, stickers, and other items to show your Seattle pride, plus a handful of LGBTQ+ items.

Revival Shop Seattle

233 Broadway E.; 206/395-6414; www. revivalshopseattle.com; 11am-7pm Mon.-Sat., noon-6pm Sun.

Candles, ceramics, and decorative pieces are just a few examples of the locally sourced items at Revival, a charming store that embraces being eco-conscious and sustainable. You'll find unique pieces here from local artists and makers.

Seattle's Bookstore Scene

Elliott Bay Book Company

With almost 50 bookstores, each with its own special appeal, Seattle is a literary paradise. On a rainy day, these bookstores take on an extra charm, offering a cozy haven to choose a new book to read. Seattle's bookstores also serve as lively community centers, with reading areas, cafés, and many literary events throughout the year.

- **Elliott Bay Book Company:** Known for its vast selection and frequent author readings, located in Capitol Hill (page 81).

- **Left Bank Books:** A cooperatively owned bookstore near Pike Place, focusing on anti-authoritarian, anarchist, independent, radical, and small-press titles (page 79).

THE U DISTRICT
Malls
University Village

623 NE University Village St.; 206/523-0622; https:// uvillage.com; 10am-8pm Mon.-Sat., 11am-6pm Sun.

University Village is an upscale, open-air shopping center with dozens of high-end retailers and trendy boutiques. Apple, Sephora, and Pottery Barn are here, as well as dozens of restaurants. Visitors are encouraged to spend more time than just shopping, as there's a covered kids' playground and outdoor events in the summer. Because it's Seattle, you'll also find loaner umbrellas on those days you get caught in the rain while shopping.

Clothing
Red Light Vintage & Costume

4560 University Way NE; 206/545-4044; www. redlightvintage.com; 11am-7pm daily

Seattle loves thrift shopping, and Red Light Vintage & Costume caters to that need. Unlike other thrift shops where you'll find items for 99 cents, they're pickier about what they buy, so you'll pay a bit more but walk away with a high-quality item.

FREMONT AND WALLINGFORD
Archie McPhee

1300 N. 45th St.; 206/297-0240; https:// archiemcpheeseattle.com; 11am-7pm Mon.-Sat., 11am-5pm Sun.

- **University Book Store** (4326 University Way NE; www.ubookstore.com): Operating since 1900, this is one of the oldest and largest independent bookstores in the state, situated in the U District.

- **Magus Books** (1408 NE 42nd St.; www.magusbooksseattle.com): Specializes in used, rare, and well-loved books, a favorite among budget-conscious bibliophiles in the U District.

- **Third Place Books** (5041 Wilson Ave. S.; www.thirdplacebooks.com): Features cozy reading areas and a café, with a robust schedule of community events including book clubs and workshops.

- **Book Larder** (4252 Fremont Ave. N.; https://booklarder.com): A community cookbook store in Fremont that offers cooking classes and events with famous chefs and authors.

- **Ada's Technical Books and Café** (425 15th Ave. E.; www.adasbooks.com): This half-bookstore, half-café in Capitol Hill is nerd heaven where you can find books on anything from computer science to engineering to science fiction.

- **Lamplight Books** (1514 Pike Pl. #14; Facebook @lamplightbooks): Specializes in out-of-print and vintage books, with a good selection of children's, poetry, and philosophy.

- **Metsker Maps** (1511 1st Ave.; www.metskers.com): Offers hundreds of guidebooks, a large selection of maps, and plenty of inspiration.

- **Outsider Comics** (223 N. 36th St.; https://outsidercomics.com): A welcoming LGBTQ+ friendly space in Fremont that has an impressive assortment of comic books from local and independent publishers.

The literary community is also involved with events like the **Seattle Antiquarian Book Fair** (www.seattlebookfair.com; Oct.), an annual gathering of readers and collectors from around the globe who love rare and vintage books.

Pranksters and weird-toy fans will love visiting Archie McPhee, which has some of the strangest pranks and gag gifts you've ever seen. You won't find these anywhere else, whether it's fried chicken candy, Bigfoot toys, or pickle air fresheners. Make sure to visit their free Rubber Chicken Museum.

BALLARD
Music
Sonic Boom Records
2209 NW Market St.; 206/297-2666; www.
sonicboomrecords.com; 11am-7pm daily
Sonic Boom Records plays a big role in Seattle's vibrant music community, with a diverse selection of independent music and new and pre-owned records, CDs, and cassettes. In 1998 the store went from an obscure little record shop to an overnight sensation after hosting the local band Death Cab for Cutie to perform their debut album. The store now routinely has in-house concerts by rising stars, and you never know which famous musicians may drop by to browse the album selection.

Food and Drink
Scandinavian Specialties
6719 15th Ave. NW; 206/784-7020; www.
scanspecialties.com; 10am-5:30pm Mon.-Sat., 10am-
3pm Sun.
You can get a taste of Scandinavia anytime

National Nordic Museum

Ballard's Nordic ancestry dates back to the late 1800s when Seattle transitioned from a rugged frontier town into a thriving city. Scandinavian immigrants, mainly from Sweden and Norway, started moving to the area because of the familiar seaside setting and the promise of employment. Their skills—which included boatbuilding, logging, and fishing—resonated with the abundant natural resources and booming businesses of the Pacific Northwest.

As the Nordic population in Ballard expanded, the core of the city gained the nickname "Little Scandinavia." Many families in Ballard have carried on their maritime and fishing traditions for generations.

- **National Nordic Museum:** Showcases the immigration experience and displays hundreds of artifacts illustrating the impact of Nordic settlers (page 62).

- **Norwegian Constitution Day Parade:** Held annually in May, celebrating Norway's national day with traditional costumes, music, and food (www.17thofmay.org).

- **Ballard SeafoodFest:** Every July, this festival celebrates the community's strong ties to the fishing industry with seafood, live music, and vendor booths (www.seafoodfest.org).

- **Scandinavian Specialties:** A local restaurant and store offering traditional Nordic foods and imported goods (page 83).

- **Viking Days:** An annual July event featuring Nordic crafts, traditional foods, and Viking reenactments (https://nordicmuseum.org).

at Scandinavian Specialties, which has a vast assortment of specialty foods such as Swedish meatballs, pickled herring, and Norwegian cheese. There are also plenty of packaged snacks, coffee, tea, and home goods, in addition to a café offering a small menu of sandwiches and desserts.

Gifts and Home
Good & Well Supply Co.

2108 NW Vernon Pl.; 206/397-3262; https:// goodandwellsupplyco.com; 11am-6pm Mon.-Sat., 10am-5pm Sun.

Good & Well Supply Co. is the place to stock up on clean candles, especially if you like ones with a theme. Many of their candles are based on national parks and do an excellent job of recreating the scents associated with those areas, plus they have shirts, lip balms, and more.

Lucca Great Finds
5332 Ballard Ave. NW; 206/782-7337; www.luccagreat finds.com; 11am-6pm Mon.-Sat., 11am-4pm Sun.

Lucca Great Finds makes buying a gift for someone easy, as they have everything from home goods like candles and incense to art supplies, jewelry, and tea sets, plus garden items in their outdoor section.

Food

Though several cuisines have made Seattle famous, seafood reigns supreme. You'll find fresh catches of the day in many restaurants, all made in different ways by the city's innovative chefs. But you don't have to love fish to eat well. Seattle also has an abundance of Asian cuisines, from pho to dim sum.

DOWNTOWN AND THE WATERFRONT
Coffee
Voxx Coffee Downtown
1200 6th Ave., #150; 206/682-1242; www.voxxseattle. com; 7am-4pm Mon.-Fri.
Conveniently located in the heart of downtown, Voxx Coffee boasts exceptional drinks. All their baristas are trained in creating proper espresso drinks, from extracting shots to the correct texture of milk foam. Enjoy the bright, open setting with views of downtown as you sit with your coffee and pastry or sandwich.

Steak and Seafood
★ The Metropolitan Grille
820 2nd Ave.; 206/624-3287; www. themetropolitangrill.com; 4:30pm-9:30pm daily; $32-195
The Metropolitan Grill may not be the place to go on a budget, but for a celebratory night out, it's well worth the price tag. They claim to have the best steak in town, in addition to plenty of seafood options such as Maine lobster bisque and Dungeness crab and prawn fettucine, all in an elegant setting with

attentive servers. You can save money by going during happy hour (3:30pm-5:30pm Mon.-Fri. in the bar).

Shuckers Oyster Bar
411 University St.; 206/621-1984; www.fairmont.com; 4:40pm-9pm daily; $26-52
Inside the historic Fairmont Olympic Hotel is Shuckers, one of the best oyster bars in the city, which has an old-school feel with wood panels and tables and sleek red chairs. Their specialty is fresh or baked oysters by the dozen, but you can also get a salad or a side of their whipped potatoes.

Pan-Asian
Wild Ginger
1401 3rd Ave.; 206/623-4450; www.wildginger.net; 4pm-8pm Sun.-Thurs., 4pm-9pm Fri.-Sat.; $13-48
After a whirlwind trip through five different countries in the south part of Asia, the Yoders came home and created Wild Ginger as a place where people could get a blend of Asian cuisines in one place. Popular dishes include the fragrant duck and seven flavor beef, and they also have vegetarian options, such as Thai passion tofu. Their downtown location has a sleek, modern feel to it with lounge seating, a bar, and cozy booths.

PIKE PLACE MARKET
French
Le Pichet
1933 1st Ave.; 206/256-1499; www.lepichetseattle.com; 10am-9pm Mon.-Wed., 10am-10pm Fri.-Sun.; $6-20

One of the owners lived and trained as a cook in France, contributing to Le Pichet's unique Parisian café feel. Indulge in pan-roasted duck breast with caramelized fennel or chicken roasted to order with root vegatables. You'll have to call ahead for dinner because they don't take walk-ins during the evenings, and only 32 seats are available.

Café Campagne

1600 Post Alley; 206/728-2233; http://cafecampagne. com; 10am-3pm and 4:30pm-9pm Wed.-Fri., 9am-3pm and 4:30pm-9pm Sat., 9am-3pm and 4:30pm-8pm Sun.; $23-36

Experience joie de vivre dining at the charming Café Campagne, which looks like it's straight out of Paris. They have a menu full of authentic French cuisine, whether you want pan au chocolat and croque monsieur for brunch, or escargots de Bourgogne with your choice of dozens of French wines for dinner.

Maximilien

81A Pike St.; 206/682-7270; www.maximilienrestaurant. com; 4pm-9pm Mon.-Thurs., 11:30am-9pm Fri.-Sun.; $16-42

Maximilien is a great place to get French cuisine, such as foie gras frais or steak frites, in an atmosphere that's a bit more modern. Diners are treated to a stunning view of the Seattle Great Wheel and the waterfront from anywhere in the restaurant, and the outdoor patio is the place to be on warm evenings.

Italian

★ The Pink Door

1919 Post Alley; 206/443-3241; www.thepinkdoor.net; 11:30am-4:40pm, 5pm-10pm Tues.-Sat.; $17-49

As you walk through Post Alley, you'll see a light pink door and a few windows with no name, but this is where you'll find one of the best date nights in town. The Pink Door serves Italian dishes like lasagna and spaghetti and meatballs, but most people come for the entertainment. There's always something going on, from tarot readings to dazzling cabaret dancers to local music. Although they take walk-ins, reservations are

recommended several weeks in advance for the dinner hours.

Seafood

Pike Place Chowder

530 Post Alley; 206/267-2537; www.pikeplacechowder. com; 11am-4:45pm daily; $10-35

Nothing is better on a cold, rainy Seattle day than huddling into Pike Place Chowder and ordering one of their warm, savory chowders. You'll likely find a crowd if you go at lunchtime, as they have something for everyone with about ten different chowders, including gluten-free and vegan options. It's a small, bare-bones place with limited seating, so many people take their chowder to-go.

The Athenian Seafood Restaurant and Bar

1517 Pike Pl.; 206/624-7166; www.athenianseattle.com; 11am-6pm Mon.-Thurs., 11am-7pm Fri., 9am-7pm Sat., 9am-3pm Sun.; $20-39

With its red barstools and diner feel, the Athenian has been around since 1909 and has several claims to fame. It was one of the first restaurants to get a liquor license to serve beer in 1933, making it a popular place back in the day, and it was used for a scene in *Sleepless in Seattle*. Their menu often changes its specials, but items such as wild Gulf prawns and chips and a blackened Swiss bacon burger are usually staples.

Bakeries

Piroshky Piroshky

1908 Pike Pl.; 206/764-1000; https://piroshkybakery. com; 8am-7pm daily; $6-15

You'll know you've found Piroshky Piroshky when you see a line out the door. There's no seating at this tiny bakery, but you'll find plenty of spots nearby around Pike Place Market. The specialty is Russian turnovers with options like potato and cheese or chicken pot pie.

Le Panier

1902 Pike Pl.; 206/441-3669; https://lepanier.com; 7am-5pm daily; $3-26

Le Panier knows how to do French baked goods well, and you'll find savory croissants, brioche, baguettes, and a dozen colorful macarons to choose from. Seating can be limited, so it's best to get it to go and enjoy it as you walk through the market.

The Crumpet Shop

1503 1st Ave.; 206/682-1598; https://thecrumpetshop. com; 7:30am-3pm Wed.-Sun.; $4-10

Start your morning at the Crumpet Shop. It offers savory crumpets topped with things like eggs, English cheese, and ham, and sweet ones with lemon curd or jam. Seating is a bit limited, so take one to go and walk around the market.

PIONEER SQUARE AND THE INTERNATIONAL DISTRICT

Indian

Nirmal's

106 Occidental Ave. S.; 206/683-9701; www. nirmalseattle.com; 11am-2pm Mon.-Fri., 5:30pm-10pm Sat.-Sun.; $18-30

Nirmal's, one of the few Indian restaurants in the area, is housed in a historic terra cotta building in Pioneer Square. You'll find various Mumbai street food and traditional Indian food, with meat, seafood, and vegetarian options, such as spicy paneer makhan masala or slow-roasted Nizami goat curry.

Chinese

Jade Garden

424 7th Ave. S.; 206/622-8181; no website; 9am-9pm daily; $20-30

Jade Garden is the place in the International District to get budget-friendly dim sum. Despite the somewhat outdated exterior, the inside has modern decor with tables big enough to share multiple orders with a group.

Tai Tung

655 S. King St.; 206/622-7372; www.taitungrestaurant. com; 11am-8pm daily; $12-25

Tai Tung is proudly the oldest Chinese restaurant in Seattle and has remained in the family since its opening in 1935. They encourage family-style ordering so you can try multiple dishes, and they have plenty of classics like sweet and sour pork and chow mein.

Vietnamese

Phở Ba

415 7th Ave. S.; 206/621-0532; https://phobaseattle. business.site; 11am-9pm daily; $13-16

Phở Ba serves generous portions of the Vietnamese soup pho at affordable prices and has both beef and vegetarian options. While pho is the main appeal here, you'll also find noodle and steamed rice dishes in this casual restaurant with about a dozen tables.

Hương Bình

1207 S Jackson St. #104; 206/860-3038; no website; 9am-8pm daily; $9-15

Hương Bình has classic Vietnamese dishes such as several dozen types of pho, rice plates, and stir-fried entrees. The interior is basic but has plenty of seating.

Italian

Il Terrazzo Carmine

411 1st Ave. S.; 206/467-7797; www.ilterrazzocarmine. com; 11:30am-3pm Mon.-Fri., 5pm-10pm Mon.-Sat.; $18-64

Treat yourself to one of the best fine-dining restaurants in the city at Il Terrazzo Carmine, with Italian classics like gnocchi sorrentina, fettucini alle vongole, and cioppino. The prized seats are outdoor, where you'll feel like you're in a secret garden with chandeliers above you. There is complimentary valet parking for those dining in.

★ Salumi

404 Occidental Ave. S.; 206/621-8772; https:// salumideli.com; 10am-3pm daily; $14-18

Salumi has created a name for itself over the years as the place to go for hearty sandwiches. While they have their classic salumi sandwich, you'll find Cubanos and meatball subs as well. They also sell salumi sticks and salumi by the quarter-pound you can take home. There's limited seating, so you may fare best by getting your sandwich to go and finding a nearby bench.

Coffee in Seattle

Since the founding of Starbucks at Pike Place Market in 1971, Seattle's been obsessed with coffee. Any local will tell you, however, that the small, independent coffee shops are the place to go for the best coffee. Not only does each one offer a unique experience, whether it's artful latte creations in Capitol Hill or expertly brewed single-origin pour-overs in Ballard, but most also sustainably source and locally roast their beans. They've also become more of gathering places; you'll find locals working out of their local café or meeting with friends to play cards while they enjoy a matcha latte.

Storyville Coffee

- **Storyville Coffee** (Pike Place Market: 94 Pike St., top floor, Suite 34; https://storyville.com): Dedicated to crafting the perfect cup, Storyville Coffee emphasizes high-quality beans and expert roasting to achieve rich, complex flavors. Plus it has one of the nicest views of the market and Puget Sound.

- **Zeitgeist Coffee** (Pioneer Square: 171 S. Jackson St.; www.zeitgeistcoffee.com): With its artsy decor and robust coffee, Zeitgeist in Pioneer Square is a popular gathering spot for artists and locals.

- **Herkimer Coffee** (Belltown: 2101 4th Ave.; https://herkimercoffee.com): With each cup at their three locations, you can taste the premium, artisanal coffee that has become famous for its careful sourcing and roasting.

- **Victrola Coffee** (Capitol Hill: 411 15th Ave. E.; www.victrolacoffee.com): Celebrated for its vintage ambience and skillfully roasted beans, Victrola Coffee's three locations are hubs for coffee enthusiasts.

- **Zoka Coffee** (South Lake Union: 351 Boren Ave. N.; www.zokacoffee.com): They roast their own beans in small batches, and all their locations are spacious and light-filled, which is perfect for socializing.

Creative Contemporary
Damn the Weather

116 1st Ave. S.; 206/946-1283; www.damntheweather. com; 11am-10pm Mon.-Thurs., 11am-11pm Fri.-Sat., 11am- 4pm Sun.; $10-28

Grab a seat at the bar adorned with Pioneer Square's classic brick to try one of the specialty cocktails at Damn the Weather. The food menu is limited but flavorful, with rotating items like seared scallops and burrata.

Markets
Uwajimaya

600 5th Ave. S.; 206/624-6248; www.uwajimaya.com; 8am-8pm

With its humble beginnings selling fishcakes out of a truck in 1928, Uwajimaya has become the go-to spot for Asian food, complete with entire aisles devoted to noodles and tea. From meat and seafood to noodles and obscure delicacies, this market has it all, sourced from all over the world, including Korea, China, Vietnam, and Japan.

BELLTOWN
Pacific Northwest
★ Aqua by El Guacho

2801 Alaskan Way, Pier 70; 206/956-9171; https:// aquabyelgaucho.com; 5pm-9pm Tues.-Fri., 4pm-9pm Sat.; $36-85

Aqua by El Gaucho is at the far northern end of the waterfront area, but it's one of the most impressive restaurants to eat at. Whether in their beautiful lounge or at a coveted spot on their patio, you'll enjoy fresh seafood and meat dishes that always have a seasonal twist, such as wild Alaska black cod with a Korean barbecue glaze. They also have an extensive wine list, in addition to tableside cocktails.

Bakeries
Macrina Bakery

2408 1st Ave.; 206/448-4032; https://macrinabakery. com; 7am-5pm daily; $6-14

You'll notice the name Macrina Bakery all over Seattle, as they supply many local restaurants with their fresh-baked bread. Walking in is a feast for your senses, as you'll be greeted with the smell of fresh pastries and see the dozens of different sweet and savory treats in the display case. Try a warm breakfast sandwich, sourdough bagel, or a grilled cheese sandwich.

Italian
Tavolàta

2323 2nd Ave.; 206/838-8008; https://tavolata.com; 4pm-10pm daily; $25-65

Getting to know your neighbors is encouraged at Tavolata, where they have a large communal table for those feeling chatty, or you can sit at the bar for a more private experience. They have traditional Italian dishes such as bucatini and rigatoni, as well as about a dozen appetizers and a small dessert menu.

Japanese
Shiro's

2401 2nd Ave.; 206/443-9844; https://shiros.com; 4:30pm-9pm daily; $85-140

Shiro's is unique among local sushi places because of its edomae technique, which involves making sushi in the traditional Tokyo fashion using fish caught in the area. You won't need to stress over what to order because they only offer a set course. You can book a table in advance or sit at the sushi bar and observe the skilled chefs in action for a more interactive meal.

QUEEN ANNE
Coffee
Queen Anne Coffee Co.

1811 Queen Anne Ave. N.; 206/566-6788; https:// queenannecoffeeco.com; 7am-5pm daily; $8-12

Head to Queen Anne Coffee Co. on Upper Queen Anne to get your morning coffee and relax outside on their covered patio. This welcoming coffee shop has fun takes on breakfast, such as grilled PB&J, and has salads and sandwiches for lunch in addition to espresso and tea drinks.

Seafood
Taylor Shellfish Farms

124 Republican St.; 206/501-4442; www. taylorshellfishfarms.com; noon-8pm Sun.-Thurs., noon-9pm Fri.-Sat.; $19-63

Taylor Shellfish has become one of the best sellers of oysters and other shellfish over the years, and their bright and airy location just across from Climate Pledge Arena makes it an ideal place to get dinner before an event. Their most popular pick is about a dozen different types of oysters on the half-shell, and they also have crab, geoduck, and prawn options.

Creative Contemporary
★ Canlis

2576 Aurora Ave. N.; 206/283-3313; https://canlis.com; 5pm-midnight Wed.-Sat., 8:30am-11:30pm Sun.; $180

When you have a big occasion to celebrate, Canlis is the place to go, one of the best fine-dining experiences in the city. It sits just south of the Aurora Bridge and provides views of Lake Union while you enjoy a multi-course dining menu, such as sablefish, American Wagyu with rice, and vanilla bean parfait for dessert. This is one of the few restaurants with a strict dress code—men are recommended to wear a sport coat or suit, and women should wear similar dressy attire.

Cajun
Toulouse Petit

601 Queen Anne Ave. N.; 206/432-9069; https://
toulousepetit.com; 10am-midnight Mon.-Fri., 9am-
midnight Sat.-Sun.; $14-42

Toulouse Petit combines Pacific Northwest and Cajun-Creole cuisines, making for some innovative dishes on their extensive menu. Favorites include powdered beignets for the popular weekend brunch, po'boys for lunch, and seafood gumbo or jambalaya for dinner. They're also popular for their twice-daily happy hour (3:30pm-6pm and 10pm-11:30pm). Come at night for the ambience, when dozens of candles light up the dim restaurant.

Diners
5 Spot

1502 Queen Anne Ave. N.; 206/708-6678;
https://5spotseattle.com; 8am-3pm Mon.-Wed., 7am-
3pm Thurs.-Sat.; $13-26

On weekends you'll find a long line of people waiting to get into 5 Spot, where classics like eggs Benedict and waffles are served until 3pm in a colorful, cheerful diner. Solid lunch options include a double bacon cheeseburger, turkey pesto sandwich, and cheese curds.

5 Point Café

415 Cedar St.; 206/448-9991; www.the5pointcafe.com;
24 hours; $15-25

Not to be confused with 5 Spot, the 5 Point Café is one of the most popular places to go after the bars close, as they're open 24 hours and have the motto "Alcoholics serving alcoholics since 1929." This restaurant has earned its place in Seattle history books—having stayed open through Prohibition, the Great Depression, and much more—and it's remained in the family for nearly 100 years. You'll find a boisterous but fun crowd at night, cheap drinks, hearty meals, and plenty of greasy appetizers like deep-fried cheese curds or poutine.

SOUTH LAKE UNION
Southwestern
Cactus

350 Terry Ave. N.; 206/913-2250; www.
cactusrestaurants.com; 11:30am-9:30pm Mon.-Thurs.,
11:30am-10pm Fri., 10am-10pm Sat., 10am-9pm Sun.;
$13-32

Cactus has expanded its locations over the years, but the South Lake Union one is always packed with people celebrating happy hour after work. Their menu mixes Spanish, Mexican, and Southwestern cuisine, where you'll find housemade guacamole and chips, butternut squash enchiladas, and chimichangas. For drinks, fresh margaritas are the specialty, as well as the extensive list of tequila and mezcal.

Seafood
★ Duke's Seafood

1111 Fairview Ave. N.; 206/382-9963; www.
dukesseafood.com; 11am-10pm Sun.-Thurs., 11am-11pm
Fri.-Sat.; $15-44

While Duke's Seafood has several locations around town, you'll have one of the best views from the South Lake Union restaurant. Get here early in the summer to snag an outdoor seat overlooking the lake while you indulge in their award-winning clam chowder, rockfish tacos, or Alaskan salmon. They also have a creative list of Duketails, their own twist on popular cocktail drinks.

Steak
Daniel's Broiler

809 Fairview Pl. N.; 206/621-8262; https://
danielsbroiler.com; happy hour 3pm-5pm daily, dinner
Sat.-Sun. 3pm-9pm; $55-84

For years Daniel's Broiler has been known as one of the best steakhouses in the city, and you'll want to dress well at one of Seattle's fancier restaurants. You'll find over a dozen types of USDA prime steak, including New York, rib eye, and Wagyu. Make sure to come hungry, as they have savory sides like lobster mashed

---

1: appetizers at Agua Verde Café 2: clam chowder at Ivar's Salmon House 3: Aqua by El Guacho

potatoes and crispy brussels sprouts. You'll want to make a weekend reservation several weeks in advance.

CAPITOL HILL
Vegan
Plum Bistro

1429 12th Ave.; 206/838-5333; https://plumbistro.com; 11am-8:30pm Mon., 11am-9pm Tues.-Wed., 11am-9:30pm Thurs.-Fri., 10am-3pm, 4pm-9:30pm Sat., 10am-3pm, 4pm-8:30pm Sun.; $14-33

Vegans have it good in Seattle, and Plum Bistro is the top spot for vegan fine dining. You'll find options like mac and cheese, carne asada, and cheeseburgers, all completely vegan and so flavorful that even a meat eater can be convinced to eat here. The indoor is beautifully decorated with plants on the wall, and the garage-door wall opens up on warm days to let in the breeze.

Markets
Melrose Market

1527 Melrose Ave.; 503/603-4700; https:// melrosemarketseattle.com; 6am-11pm daily

Housed in a historic 1910 building, Melrose Market is the trendy place to shop for groceries in Capitol Hill—freshly baked bread, artisanal cheese, gourmet meats, organic produce, and more. There are also multiple businesses here, including Taylor Shellfish and Glasswing Shop.

Vietnamese
Ba Bar

550 12th Avenue; 206/328-2030; https://babarseattle. com; 10am-midnight; $12-21

Ba Bar serves Vietnamese street food with a twist in a trendy setting, with options like vermicelli noodle dishes and big servings of pho. They have happy hour daily (1pm-5pm), with a handful of their most popular cocktails and appetizers for less than $10. It's a spacious restaurant where you can grab a high-top table with friends or find a seat at the bar for happy hour.

Italian
Osteria la Spiga

1429 12th Ave.; 206/323-8881; www.laspiga.com; 5pm-9pm Tues.-Wed., 5pm-10pm Thurs.-Sat.; $22-39

Osteria la Spiga is a charming restaurant that brings the taste of Italy's Emilia-Romagna region to Seattle. Sit back and enjoy a bottle of Italian wine or a late-night dessert of panna cotta in one of the many comfortable booths, on the patio, or at the center bar. Soups, salads, and savory pasta dishes like gnocchi and tagliatelle are all part of their menu.

★ Via Tribunali

Seattle has plenty of pizza restaurants, but Via Tribunali is one of the few that does authentic Neapolitan pizza right. You won't find greasy pizza overflowing with toppings here, but relatively simple options like the Margherita, where only a few ingredients are needed to bring out the flavor. All pizzas go into their wood-fired brick oven to achieve the perfect level of crispiness, and you'll appreciate their dim, intimate setting with rustic brick walls while you wait.

THE U DISTRICT
Coffee
Sip House

5001 Brooklyn Ave. NE; 206/468-5358; www.siphouse wa.com; 8am-6pm Mon.-Sat., 8am-5pm Sun.; $6-8

Sip House feels like you're in a greenhouse, with its lush green plants and big windows letting light in. They specialize in Vietnamese coffee and have a variety to try, such as Vietnamese iced coffee, matcha latte, and black milk tea. If you're hungry, they offer several pastry and sandwich choices.

Diners
Portage Bay Café

4130 Roosevelt Way NE; 206/547-8230; www. portagebaycafe.com; 8am-1:30pm Mon.-Fri., 8am-2pm Sat.-Sun.; $15-26

Portage Bay Café excels at brunch food, and it's rare to get in without a wait on the weekends. They have good-sized portions of

Dungeness crab Benedict and breakfast sandwiches, but their breakfast bar is the most popular. You'll order a base, such as pancakes or French toast, then go up to the bar to top it off with whipped cream, nuts, and berries to customize it. The restaurant lets in plenty of light on sunny days with its tall ceilings and windows.

Indian
Taste of India

5517 Roosevelt Way NE; 206/590-6460; https://tasteofindiaseattle.com; 11am-9pm Mon.-Sat., 11am-8pm Sun.; $10-22

Taste of India has a large menu full of authentic Indian dishes, such as creamy masalas and spicy vindaloos, catering to both meat-eaters and vegetarians. Their spinach naan, mango pistachio ice cream, and chai all complement the meal well. There's plenty of seating indoors, whether you're at a long table or a cozy booth.

Mexican
★ Agua Verde Café

1303 NE Boat St.; 206/545-8570; www.aguaverdecafe.com; 11am-8:30pm daily; $15-19

Agua Verde Café offers waterfront seating, and it's not uncommon to see people arriving in kayaks from the related Agua Verde Paddle Club below. Mexican dishes such as burritos, enchiladas, quesadillas, and breakfast burritos are reasonably priced. In addition to the main restaurant, they added the Marina Cantina, which features an outdoor bar and food truck open May-September.

Thai
Thai Tom

4543 University Way NE; 206/548-9548; https://thaitomseattle.com; 11:30am-9pm Mon.-Sat., noon-9pm Sun.; $6-10

Thai Tom is small, but it allows you to watch the chefs at work in their open kitchen and is a favorite place to get Thai food in the area. The menu is limited, but you'll find classic options like pad thai and cashew chicken for budget prices.

FREMONT AND WALLINGFORD
Coffee
A Muddy Cup

266 NE 45th St.; 206/245-1015; https://amuddycupcafe.com; 7am-3pm daily

A Muddy Cup feels like you're sitting in a friend's living room, complete with random couches and unique lamps. You'll want to stay awhile in this comfortable setting and order one of their espresso drinks, and perhaps some local, freshly baked pastries.

Seafood
★ Ivar's Salmon House

401 NE Northlake Way; 206/632-0767; www.ivars.com; 11am-8pm Sun.-Thurs., 11am-9pm Fri.-Sat.; $20-50

Ivar's has provided comfort seafood to locals since 1938, whether it's warm clam chowder in the winter or fresh fish and chips in the summer. There are over 20 Ivar's locations in the area, but the Salmon House is unique, set in a beautiful replica of a Northwest Native American longhouse, with views of Lake Union.

Japanese
Kisaku

2101 N. 55th St. Suite 100; 206/545-9050; www.kisaku.com; 11:30am-2pm Mon.-Sat., 5pm-8pm Sun.-Thurs., 4:30pm-8pm Fri.-Sat.; $12-15

If you're craving sushi with, say, octopus, eel, or tuna, Kisaku has you covered with a dozen rolls and nigiri sushi options. Anyone who isn't a fan of raw fish can choose from their udon and yakisoba dishes instead. The best seats in the house are at the sushi bar, where you can watch the chefs prepare your fish.

Burgers
Dick's Drive-In

111 NE 45th St.; 206/632-5125; www.ddir.com; 10:30am-2am daily; $3-5

A long line at Dick's Drive-In is a sure sign that the bars are closing down for the night, as it's where locals have gone for inexpensive burgers, fries, and milkshakes since 1945. The menu is simple, substitutions aren't allowed, and you'll pay for any condiments, but their priciest deluxe burger is only $5. There are now over a dozen locations around the Seattle area, with the original being in Wallingford. As it's just a walk-up window, most people eat in their cars.

Ice Cream

Molly Moon's

2615 NE 46th St.; 206/294-4389; www.mollymoon. com; 11am-10pm Sun.-Thurs., 11am-11pm Fri.-Sat.

Creamy ice cream scoops are guaranteed at Molly Moon's, in flavors like honey lavender and melted chocolate plus seasonal specialties. From the spoons to the cups, they use only compostable materials at their 10 locations, and nearly all the ingredients are sourced locally.

BALLARD

Coffee

Caffè Umbria

5407 Ballard Ave. NW; 206/420-3945; https:// caffeumbria.com; 6:30am-6pm Mon.-Fri., 7am-6pm Sat.-Sun.

Caffè Umbria's Ballard location embraces the European feel of the neighborhood with its mix of tables, high-top bar tables, and patio seating that encourages socializing. In addition to the standard espresso options, they have beer, wine, and baked goods from local bakeries.

Seafood

★ The Walrus and the Carpenter

4743 Ballard Ave. NW; 206/395-9227; https:// thewalrusbar.com; 4pm-10pm daily; $12-29

Since its opening in 2010, The Walrus and the Carpenter has consistently drawn a crowd, but locals agree that the wait is more than justified, especially for the signature oysters on the half shell. Seafood lovers will enjoy the grilled sardines and fried oysters, but those looking for something different can choose from salad or beef tartare. The exposed brick walls and whitewashed wooden beams make for a cozy and welcoming ambience.

Ray's Boathouse

6049 Seaview Ave. NW; 206/789-3770; www.rays.com; 11:30am-9pm daily; $22-52

Ray's Boathouse is set on Shilshole Bay and has one of the best views in Ballard. On the lower level, you'll find the more formal main dining room, and on the upper floor is Ray's Café ($18-54), the perfect place for an appetizer and drink while taking in the view. Popular items include Dungeness crab, freshly shucked oysters, and grilled salmon.

Mexican

La Carta de Oaxaca

5431 Ballard Ave. NW; 206/782-8722; https:// seattlemeetsoaxaca.com; noon-9:30pm Tues.-Thurs., noon-11pm Fri.-Sat.; $14-23

Enjoy the flavors of the Oaxaca region at La Carta de Oaxaca, an upscale Mexican restaurant that serves shrimp tacos, chiles rellenos, tostadas, and more. They also have an extensive tequila and mezcal menu, making this an ideal stop before you hit the nearby bars and nightlife.

Thai

Pestle Rock

2305 NW Market St.; 206/466-6671; https://pestlerock. com; 11:30am-9:30pm Mon.-Thurs., 11:30am-10pm Fri., noon-10pm Sat., noon-9pm Sun.; $12-23

You won't find traditional options like pad thai at Pestle Rock, which makes it stand out. The bold flavors from Northeast Thailand fill this snug restaurant lined with redbrick walls. Try new dishes like stir-fried Thai rice noodles with chicken and Dungeness crab fried rice.

Italian

Stoneburner

5214 Ballard Ave. NW; 206/695-2051; www. stoneburnerseattle.com; 4pm-9pm Wed.-Sat., 10am-3pm, 4pm-9pm Sun.; $17-38

Stoneburner is a beautiful, well-lit restaurant on the lower level of the Hotel Ballard that serves lunch and dinner items including homemade pasta, salads, and wood-fired pizza. They also have a tasty brunch menu featuring items like smoked salmon toast and Dutch baby pancakes.

WEST SEATTLE

Every Sunday along California Avenue, vendors at the popular West Seattle Farmers Market (https://seattlefarmersmarkets.org) sell handcrafted goods and fresh, regional produce.

Coffee
Sound and Fog
4735 40th Ave. SW; www.soundandfog.com; 7am-5:30pm Sun., Tues.-Thurs., 6am-6pm Fri.-Sat.

At Sound and Fog, you'll enjoy a diverse range of roasters and specialty drinks like the aromatic cardamom latte in a sleek, black-and-white, Wi-Fi-free environment. They also have a curated selection of wines and beers for later get-togethers.

Seafood
★ Salty's
1936 Harbor Ave. SW; 206/937-1600; www.saltys.com; 11:30am-3pm Tues.-Fri., 10am-3pm and 4:30pm-9pm Sat.-Sun., 4:30pm-9pm Mon.-Thurs., 4:30pm-9:30pm Fri.; $13-35

While many people search for the restaurant with the best view *in* Seattle, Salty's gives you the most scenic view *of* Seattle from across the water. The specialty is seafood, with options like halibut croquettes, pan-seared scallops, and lobster, with a small menu of salads and meat entrees. With two stories and an outdoor level, plenty of seating is available, although reservations are highly encouraged on the weekends and holidays at one of West Seattle's fancier restaurants.

Alki Spud Fish and Chips
2666 Alki Ave. SW; 206/938-0606; www.alkispud.com; 11am-9pm daily; $15-22

Alki Spud has been around since 1935, when the British-style fish and chips were served out of a garage, and has since expanded to one of the most popular places to eat it in Alki Beach. They make over 600 pounds of french fries and 900 fish orders daily during summer. Indoor seating is sparse, so get your order to go and eat on a nearby bench.

Pan-Asian
Marination Ma Kai
1660 Harbor Ave. SW; 206/328-8226; https://marinationmobile.com; 11am-8pm Mon.-Thurs., 11am-9pm Fri., 9am-9pm Sat., 9am-8pm Sun.; $10-15

Marination Ma Kai has a gorgeous waterfront setting but is also a local favorite for takeout to eat on a bench by Alki Beach. The menu offers a creative fusion of Hawaiian and Korean flavors, featuring delicious options such as kimchi fried rice, Kalbi beef tacos, and shave ice. If you find yourself there on a Monday, you can indulge in their all-day happy hour.

Pizza
Talarico's Pizzeria
4718 California Ave. SW; 206/937-3463; www.talaricospizza.com; noon-midnight Mon.-Thurs., 11am-2am Fri.-Sat., 11am-10pm Sun.; $12-20

You won't leave hungry at Talarico's Pizza, where each pizza slice is 14 inches long. The menu also has a large selection of salads and pastas, and they offer a full bar. It's a great place to watch the local game or get dinner with the family, and their late-night hours combined with weekly events like karaoke and bingo are a fun way to close the night out.

Accommodations

With all the great neighborhoods in Seattle, there's no wrong place to stay. But first consider where most of the attractions you want to see are, and if you'll have a car to reach the farther ones. Most tourists prefer the waterfront and downtown, as many sights are centered there, and it's easy to walk or take public transportation around the area.

DOWNTOWN AND THE WATERFRONT
Under $200
Moore Hotel

1926 2nd Ave.; 206/448-4851; www.moorehotel.com; $155-375

One of the most historic hotels in the city, the Moore Hotel has been welcoming guests since 1907. You'll find 57 modern, restored rooms with a minimalist style and shared bathrooms, with plenty of classic architectural touches to take visitors back in time.

$200-300
Executive Hotel Pacific

400 Spring St.; 206/623-3900; https:// executivehotelseattle.com; $299-339

The Executive Hotel Pacific is in the heart of downtown, so you can walk to dozens of restaurants and stores within minutes. Their 155 rooms have comfortable queen and king beds and family suites for larger groups.

Over $300
Kimpton Hotel Monaco Seattle

1101 4th Ave.; 206/621-1770; www.monaco-seattle.com; $360-500

The award-winning Kimpton Hotel Monaco has unique touches to rooms, such as free yoga mats in each one. Guests are invited to join a social hour every evening to sample wines from nearby wineries, and pets of any size are welcome in the 189 rooms at no additional cost.

Alexis Royal Sonesta Hotel Seattle

1007 1st Ave.; 206/624-4844; www.sonesta.com; $398-460

With its contemporary decor and prime waterfront location, the Alexis Royal Sonesta Hotel is a convenient choice with its 121 rooms and multiple suites. The hotel has a complete gym with a bouldering wall, and guests can also relax with whiskey sampling and look through books at the Bookstore Bar & Café.

PIKE PLACE MARKET
Under $200
Green Tortoise Hostel Seattle

105 Pike St.; 206/340-1222; www.greentortoise.net; $39-55

If you're on a budget, you can't beat staying at Green Tortoise Hostel with 30 bunk rooms. While most options are for a shared room (women-only or co-ed), you'll be right across from Pike Place Market, and it's a great place to meet people if traveling solo. Sheets are included with your stay, and towels are $1.

Over $300
Four Seasons Hotel Seattle

99 Union St.; 206/749-7000; www.fourseasons.com; $900-1,850

The Four Seasons Hotel Seattle has always been one of the most exquisite places to stay in the city, where guests can indulge in a luxurious spa experience or swim in the infinity pool that overlooks the water. Most of its 147 rooms have a view of Puget Sound, and multiple suites are available.

★ Inn at the Market

86 Pine St.; 206/443-3600; www.innatthemarket.com; $390-520

Inn at the Market is the only hotel in Pike Place Market, and in the morning you'll find many guests on the rooftop deck with a cup of coffee, watching the vendors set up. It's worth it to splurge for a room with a view of Puget Sound right from your bed, but any of the 79 rooms make for a convenient stay.

PIONEER SQUARE AND THE INTERNATIONAL DISTRICT

$200-300

citizenM Seattle Pioneer Square Hotel

60 Yesler Way; 206/886-0560; www.citizenm.com; $237-299

Amenities of the citizenM Seattle Pioneer Square Hotel include MoodPad-controlled lighting and XL king-sized beds. While the 216 rooms are on the smaller side, the large lobby area is full of unusual art and has plenty of seating that encourages socializing.

Over $300

Courtyard by Marriott Seattle Downtown/Pioneer Square

612 2nd Ave.; 206/625-1111; www.marriott.com; $409-489

The Courtyard Seattle Downtown/Pioneer Square has 222 modern, spacious rooms, with a bistro, Starbucks, and a convenience store for late-night snacks. There's also an indoor pool and fitness center.

★ The Arctic Club

700 3rd Ave.; 206/776-9090; www.arcticclubhotel.com; $300-417

The Arctic Club was originally a social club for men who profited off the Klondike Gold Rush in the early 1900s; today it is known as one of Seattle's most impressive historic hotels. This stunning hotel stands out for its terra cotta walrus-head sculptures outside and Northern Lights Dome Room inside, where guests dine under stained-glass ceilings. You can upgrade one of its 120 rooms to include a whirlpool tub, or relax at the Polar Bar downstairs.

BELLTOWN

Over $300

★ The Edgewater Hotel

2411 Alaskan Way; 206/792-5959; www.edgewaterhotel.com; $449-540

The Edgewater is the city's only over-water hotel, giving guests unobstructed views of Elliott Bay and the Olympic Mountains. Many of its 223 luxurious rooms feature balconies and gas fireplaces, and an on-site coffee shop, restaurant, and bar are available. Many famous bands have stayed here over the years, including the Beatles, and you can even stay in their exact suite if you have the money.

Hotel Andra

2000 4th Ave.; 206/448-8600; https://hotelandra.com; $392-480

The 123 rooms at Hotel Andra are decorated in a Scandanavian style, which combines modern minimalism with warm Pacific Northwest accents. Two restaurants, Lola (Italian; 7am-9pm Mon.-Fri., 8am-9pm Sat., 8am-8pm Sun.; $17-23) and Assaggio (Greek; 5pm-9pm Tues.-Thurs., 5pm-10pm Fri.-Sat.; $16-52), as well as a state-of-the-art fitness center and spa facilities, are available to guests.

QUEEN ANNE

$200-300

Mediterranean Inn

425 Queen Anne Ave. N.; 206/428-4700; www.mediterranean-inn.com; $269-299

The Mediterranean Inn has 180 guest rooms with courtyard and city views and several with water views. The rooftop balcony is the ideal spot to spend summer evenings, and every suite has a kitchenette.

Over $300

★ The Maxwell Hotel

300 Roy St.; 206/286-0629; www.staypineapple.com; $312-391

The Maxwell Hotel promises guests unmatched comfort with cloud-like European-style duvets, cozy robes, and plush towels in each of its 139 rooms. Enjoy signature pineapple treats and coffee each afternoon, and explore nearby with complimentary bikes.

SOUTH LAKE UNION
$200-300
Silver Cloud Hotel Seattle - Lake Union
1150 Fairview Ave. N.; 206/447-9500; www.silvercloud.com; $269-349

The Silver Cloud Hotel Seattle - Lake Union has 184 spacious rooms with city and lake views and an indoor pool. It also offers complimentary shuttle service to attractions nearby.

Over $300
★ Moxy Seattle Downtown
1016 Republican St.; 206/708-8200; www.marriott.com; $431-449

Moxy Seattle Downtown sets a friendly vibe from the start, where the bar doubles as the check-in area, and each guest receives a free cocktail upon arrival. Their 146 rooms have large windows providing views of South Lake Union, and up to two pets are allowed.

CAPITOL HILL
Over $300
Silver Cloud Hotel Seattle - Broadway
1100 Broadway; 206/325-1400; www.silvercloud.com; $309-329

One of the few hotels in Capitol Hill, Silver Cloud Hotel Seattle - Broadway has 179 rooms and suites and hosts the popular restaurant Jimmy's on Broadway. It offers secure parking for an additional fee.

★ Hotel Sorrento
900 Madison St.; 206/622-6400; www.hotelsorrento.com; $327-417

Hotel Sorrento has welcomed visitors since 1909 with its stunning Italian Renaissance architecture and charming antiques. In addition to white marble bathrooms, each of this hotel's 76 guest rooms and suites features antique furniture, carved wood moldings, and original artwork. Visit the secret speakeasy or relax in the famous Fireside Room to unwind with a drink.

THE U DISTRICT
Under $200
College Inn Hotel
4000 University Way NE; 206/633-4441; www.collegeinnseattle.com; $158-232

Located within a few minutes' walk of the light rail station, the College Inn Hotel provides cost-effective lodging close to the University of Washington. A range of 28 renovated rooms with communal bathrooms and studios with private bathrooms are available.

$200-300
Silver Cloud Hotel Seattle - University District
5036 25th Ave. NE; 206/526-5200; www.silvercloud.com/university; $259-329

The Silver Cloud Hotel Seattle - University District is a popular choice for those who want to shop all day at nearby University Village or cheer on the Huskies at the stadium. The hotel has 179 rooms and an indoor pool, and its **Ag47 Bar & Bistro** (4pm-10pm Tues.-Sat.; $12-18) serves food and refreshments.

Over $300
★ Graduate Seattle
4507 Brooklyn Ave. NE; 206/634-2000; https://graduatehotels.com; $315-345

The Graduate Hotel showcases a whimsical, college-inspired design that pays homage to UW's past in its 158 rooms. In addition to a rooftop bar with water views of downtown Seattle, guests have access to a 24-hour fitness facility.

FREMONT AND WALLINGFORD
Under $200
Hotel Hotel Hostel
3515 Fremont Ave. N.; 206/257-4543; https://hotelhotel.co; $119-219

Hotel Hotel Hostel is a wallet-friendly place to stay when exploring Fremont, with a mix of twin beds with shared bathrooms and king beds with private baths in its 21 rooms. The location makes walking to the numerous restaurants and bars nearby convenient.

Over $300
Staybridge Suites Seattle - Fremont
3926 Aurora Ave. N.; 206/632-1015; www.ihg.com; $338-360

Staybridge Suites Seattle - Fremont is ideal for those having a more extended stay, with 120 rooms including large suites with living areas and kitchens. A complimentary breakfast is offered each morning.

BALLARD
$200-300
Ballard Inn
5300 Ballard Ave. NW; 206/789-5011; www. ballardinnseattle.com; $178-299

The Ballard Inn, once the American-Scandinavian Bank, has been renovated to reflect its original 1902 elegance while incorporating 21st-century amenities. This charming hotel has 16 rooms with options for twin, full, or king beds with shared bathrooms,

and select king rooms featuring private bathrooms.

Over $300
★ Hotel Ballard
5216 Ballard Ave. NW; 206/789-5012; www. hotelballardseattle.com; $475-599

Hotel Ballard stands as the pinnacle of luxury in the neighborhood, offering 29 plush rooms and suites, some featuring cozy fireplaces. Guests have complimentary access to the Olympic Athletic Club and can enjoy dining at two on-site restaurants or relaxing on the rooftop patio.

WEST SEATTLE
Under $200
The Grove West Seattle Inn
3512 SW Alaska St.; 206/937-9920; www. grovewestseattle.com; $161-229

The Grove has 45 simple rooms but is in a convenient location for exploring West Seattle. There's a daily free breakfast and free parking, and you'll love the outdoor deck equipped with a fire pit in the summer.

Information and Services

TOURIST INFORMATION
Stop by one of the three visitor centers to get information on tourist attractions, itinerary recommendations, and maps. You'll find centers at the Seattle Convention Center Arch Building (7th Ave. and Pike St.; 206/461-5888; 9am-5pm), the Seattle Convention Center Summit Building (9th Ave. and Olive Way; 206/461-5865; open during events in the building), and Pike Place Market (1st Ave. and Pike St.; 206/228-7291; 9:30am-5:30pm). You can also go to Visit Seattle's website (www.visitseattle.com) for more information.

SERVICES
Hospitals
Harborview Medical Center
325 9th Ave.; 206/744-3000; www.uwmedicine.org

Harborview is on the edge of downtown and the First Hill neighborhood and caters to trauma patients.

UW Medical Center - Montlake
1959 NE Pacific St.; 206/598-3300; www.uwmedicine. org

The UW Medical Center in Montlake is next to the University of Washington and has an emergency room and a large hospital with a variety of specialty units for long-term stays.

Swedish Cherry Hill
500 17th Ave.; 206/320-2000; www.swedish.org

Swedish Cherry Hill is most convenient to those in east Seattle and has an emergency room along with a 376-room bed hospital.

Police

The Seattle Police's non-emergency line is 206/625-5011 and their website is www. seattle.gov/police. Their main headquarters is at 610 5th Ave., although they have various precincts around town.

Transportation

GETTING THERE

Air

Seattle-Tacoma International Airport (SEA, 17801 International Blvd.; 206/787-3000; www.portseattle.org) is the primary commercial airport for the Seattle area. It's about a 20-minute drive from downtown Seattle (15 mi/24 km) without traffic via I-5.

Paine Field Airport (PAE, 3220 100th Street SW; 425/388-5125; www.painefield. com) serves as a secondary commercial airport for the Seattle area, although it's farther north, in the city of Everett. It's a 20-30-minute drive from downtown Seattle (24 mi/39 km) via I-5.

Airport Transportation

The **Link light rail** (www.soundtransit.org; every 10 minutes 5am-1am Mon.-Sat. and 6am-midnight Sun.) is the quickest and most affordable way to get to downtown Seattle, as there's a station connected to the airport parking garage (follow the signs). It makes over a dozen stops going through downtown and beyond to north Seattle.

While there are no **car rentals** directly at the airport, follow the signs as you exit the airport to take a shuttle to the car rental facility. To get to downtown Seattle, follow signs to I-5 and take the freeway north for about 10 mi (16 km).

Uber and **Lyft** services are available on the 3rd floor of the parking garage as you exit the airport (follow the signs past the taxi stand). Licensed **taxis** are available on the 3rd floor of the parking garage right as you exit the airport.

Train

Amtrak operates several key routes through Seattle, and the **King Street Station** (303 S. Jackson St.; 206/684-2489; www.amtrak.com) in the International District is the primary Amtrak train station. The Coast Starlight route connects Seattle with Los Angeles, the Empire Builder links Seattle to Chicago, going through Spokane, Glacier National Park, and the Rocky Mountains, and the Cascades route goes from Eugene, Oregon, to Vancouver, British Columbia.

The **Sounder train** provides commuter train service through **Sound Transit** (www. soundtransit.org) from Tacoma to Everett, with about a dozen stops in between, including King Street Station for Seattle. However, there are only a few morning and afternoon departures during the weekdays to accommodate commuters, and generally no weekend trains.

Bus

Greyhound services Seattle, and its bus station (503 S. Royal Brougham Way; 800/231-2222; www.greyhound.com) links the town with other major cities, including Portland, Spokane, Vancouver, Boise, and San Francisco. **FlixBus** (www.flixbus.com) provides affordable bus transportation to destinations such as Portland, Vancouver, and Spokane for those on a budget.

Car

From Portland, follow I-5 north for approximately 3 hours (170 mi/275 km) before reaching downtown Seattle.

From Vancouver, British Columbia, follow BC-99 south to the border for about 45 minutes (30 mi/48 km) (valid passports are required) and continue south on I-5 for about 1 hour 45 minutes (110 mi/177 km).

GETTING AROUND

You can use the **ORCA card** (www.myorca. com) to make public transportation in the Puget Sound area easier. The Washington State Ferries, King County Metro buses, the Link light rail, Sounder trains, and other regional public transportation services are compatible with this cashless card. Simply purchase and load up your card with money online or at a Link light rail station, and tap it when boarding buses or light rails. You can also download the **Transit Go Ticket app** (https://kingcounty.gov) to pay for your ticket via your phone and just show the bus driver or transit officer when asked.

Bus

King County Metro Transit (206/553-3000; https://kingcounty.gov/en/dept/metro) is the area's primary public transportation and has several hundred routes. Look up the exact ones you need on their website or download their app. Fares vary depending on age and peak hours, but adult bus fares typically range $2.75-3.25. Reduced fares are available for eligible riders, such as seniors, youths, and those on low incomes. You can transfer to another bus within 2 hours for no charge.

Light Rail

One of the quickest and most effective ways to get around the Seattle area is by using the **Link light rail** (www.soundtransit.org), which lets you bypass the city traffic. The route goes from Angle Lake, just south of Seattle-Tacoma Airport, to as far north as Northgate, with stops including the airport, Westlake Center, Capitol Hill, and University District. Fares range $2.25-3.25 for adults, with discounts available for eligible riders.

While you can get around the city fast with the light rail, the downside is there's only one route, from south to north, so you may need to catch a bus or taxi at your stop to reach your final destination.

Streetcar

Seattle also has a streetcar system to round out the city's extensive network of public transit options. The system's two lines are the **First Hill** and the **South Lake Union.**

The South Lake Union Streetcar runs through the heart of South Lake Union neighborhood, connecting the Westlake Center to the Fred Hutchinson Cancer Research Center, with stops in the neighborhood along the way. The First Hill Streetcar links the International District/Chinatown Station with Capitol Hill, with a handful of stops along the 2.5-mi (4-km) route.

Streetcar fare is $2.25-3.25 for adults, with discounted rates available for low-income riders, qualified kids, and seniors.

Water Taxi

The **West Seattle Water Taxi** (https:// kingcounty.gov) is a scenic way to commute between downtown Seattle (Pier 50, 801 Alaskan Way) and West Seattle (Seacrest Park, 1660 Harbor Ave. SW). The ride takes 15 minutes, and a one-way fare is $5.75. Monday-Friday, the first departure from Seattle is 5:55am, with ferries leaving every 35 minutes until 6:45pm. On weekends, the service runs hourly, 8:30am-6:30pm.

Car

Traffic isn't known for being great in Seattle, and morning and evening rush hours can be a nightmare. That's why many locals rely on public transportation, but sometimes a car is necessary.

Seattle's main freeway for north-south travel is I-5, which goes north to Canada and south to California. Route 99 is the alternative but tends to get just as backed up. Those going east will take I-90 (no toll) or Route 520 (toll bridge using Good To Go! pass) across the floating bridges to reach Bellevue and further east.

You can buy a **Good To Go! pass** online (www.mygoodtogo.com) by registering for an account and connecting a payment method, which will automatically get charged when you cross. If you don't have an account, a camera will take a picture of your license plate and send the bill to the address listed on the registration, but it will be $2 more. Many rental cars have a Good To Go! pass on the dashboard, and the company can keep track of how many times you use it and add it to your total fee at the end.

Parking

Parking in Seattle can be challenging, as much of what's available is street parking (often on a hill). Street parking ranges $0.50-5 per hour, with higher prices typically found downtown and closer to the waterfront. There's usually

a limit of 2-4 hours, so you may need to set a timer to move your car. However, street parking is free on Sundays and most holidays, but always double-check the sign to ensure this is true for your particular spot. Most parking can be paid via a credit card through the **PayByPhone app,** which will let you know how much time you have left. The dozens of covered parking garages around the city are the most convenient for finding a spot quickly. You'll pay more for these, $10-40 depending on how long you're there, but you can often leave your vehicle all day.

Around Seattle

Those looking for a change of scenery have multiple options for great day trips from Seattle.

To the north, a scenic ferry ride brings you to Whidbey Island, the longest island in Washington state. It offers a mix of boutique shops, wineries, and art galleries, plus natural beauty and stunning views of Puget Sound. Science lovers shouldn't miss Everett, home to the Boeing Future of Flight, where visitors can get an inside look at aircraft assembly and marvel at the complexities of modern aerospace engineering. Or drive the Mountain Loop Highway in the Cascade Mountains, where you can take in stunning vistas from plenty of hiking trails.

East of Seattle, the Woodinville area is renowned for its wine country. And the cities of the Eastside offer plenty of shopping and

Highlights

Look for ★ to find recommended sights, activities, dining, and lodging.

★ **Wine-Tasting in Woodinville:** Explore a variety of wineries in Woodinville, known for its wine country and tasting experiences (page 120).

★ **Snoqualmie Falls:** This stunning waterfall is an easy drive from Seattle and one of the easiest waterfalls to visit in the state (page 122).

★ **Hiking Rattlesnake Ledge:** One of the most popular hikes out of Seattle features a 4-mi (6-km) round-trip trail overlooking Rattlesnake Lake (page 123).

★ **Skiing at Snoqualmie:** Snoqualmie Pass is the closest ski area to Seattle and has runs for all levels (page 126).

★ **Ebey's Landing National Historical Reserve:** This reserve showcases a picturesque blend of historical farmlands and natural beauty, with sweeping views over Puget Sound (page 140).

★ **Deception Pass State Park:** Spanning the gap between Whidbey and Fidalgo Islands, Deception Pass Bridge offers stunning views of the surrounding waters and cliffs (page 145).

★ **Boeing Future of Flight:** Take an inside look at the assembly of Boeing aircraft and get a unique perspective on the complexities of modern aerospace engineering (page 147).

★ **Driving the Mountain Loop Highway:** This scenic drive gives you stunning views of the Cascade Mountains, old-growth forests, and access to numerous hiking trails (page 151).

Around Seattle

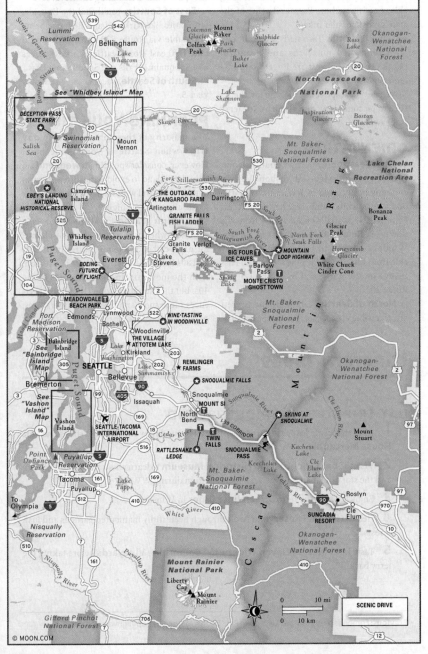

© MOON.COM

restaurants. Further east along the I-90 corridor, you'll find the majestic Snoqualmie Falls, skiing at Snoqualmie Pass, and some of the state's most popular hikes.

South of Seattle, Tacoma is a vibrant city with renowned museums and beautiful parks. And to the west are Puget Sound island getaways.

Whatever escape you're looking for, there's sure to be something an easy drive (or ferry ride) away.

ORIENTATION

West of Seattle are the Puget Sound islands, including Bainbridge and Vashon. Vashon can only be accessed by ferries from Seattle or Tacoma, while Bainbridge has ferry access from Seattle as well as road access from the north via Route 305. Northwest of Seattle, Whidbey Island can be reached by a ferry ride from Mukilteo or via the Deception Pass Bridge on the north end by taking I-5 and Route 20.

North of Seattle, Edmonds and Everett are accessible via I-5. Northeast of Seattle, the

Mountain Loop Highway follows the road of the same name after taking I-5 north.

East of Seattle, you'll find the Eastside, with cities like Kirkland and Bellevue being accessible via Route 520 and I-405. You'll take I-90 east from Seattle to access places like Snoqualmie Falls and Snoqualmie Pass.

South of Seattle, Tacoma can be reached via I-5.

PLANNING YOUR TIME

The majority of these places are easy **day trips** when Seattle is your home base. However, consider spending **a weekend** on Whidbey Island to explore the different parts of this vast island without having to rush back to the city the same night.

The **high season** for all these towns is summer, when you'll have the best chance for dry weather and temperatures in the 70s and 80s Fahrenheit. **Winter** is the low season, with the most rain and temperatures in the 40s. But the Mountain Loop Highway experiences more snow and freezing temperatures, so parts of it will be closed.

Itinerary Ideas

DAY TRIP TO BAINBRIDGE ISLAND

1 After the scenic **ferry ride** from Seattle, start your day by checking out shops like **Salt House Mercantile.**

2 Visit the **Bainbridge Island Historical Museum** to learn about the island's history and the story of Japanese American incarceration during WWII.

3 Enjoy lunch at the retro **Streamliner Diner** in Winslow.

4 Head to **Bloedel Reserve** to stroll through beautifully manicured gardens and lush forests.

5 Taste local wines at **Eleven Winery** and **Bainbridge Vineyards** before taking the ferry back.

Previous: Edmonds ferry at sunset; Deception Pass Bridge; Mountain Loop Highway sign.

DAY TRIP TO WHIDBEY ISLAND

1 Drive up I-5 until you reach **Deception Pass State Park** at the north end of the island. Spend the morning exploring the state park and its iconic bridge.

2 Head south to Coupeville and grab lunch at **The Cove.**

3 Spend the afternoon exploring **Ebey's Landing National Historical Reserve.**

4 Head south to Langely and enjoy a glass at one of the many wineries before grabbing dinner at **Taprom @ Bayview.**

5 Make your way back to Seattle via the the **Clinton-Mukilteo ferry.**

DAY TRIP TO TACOMA

1 Drive south to Tacoma, where you'll begin your morning at the **Museum of Glass.**

2 For lunch, relax on the outdoor patio with a burger at **Katie Downs Waterfront Tavern.**

3 In the afternoon, explore **Point Defiance Park,** including the Fort Nisqually Living History Museum and several beautiful gardens.

4 End your day with dinner at **Boathouse 19,** where you can enjoy clam chowder with views of the Tacoma Narrows Bridge before returning to Seattle.

Puget Sound Islands

Bainbridge and Vashon both have their own charms. Bainbridge is easier to get to from Seattle, especially if you want to walk from downtown and leave your car in the city. But Bainbridge is also a gateway to the north part of the Olympic Peninsula, so you'll need a vehicle if you plan to extend your trip. Vashon is only accessible by ferry, but it's fun to visit if you're looking for a quieter island.

BAINBRIDGE ISLAND

Just a short, scenic ferry trip away from buzzing Seattle, Bainbridge Island is the perfect place to unwind and escape it all. At 10 mi (16 km) long, it has plenty to explore, both in the main town of Winslow, home to galleries, cafés, and specialty shops, and beyond to the nature reserves and vineyards. A half day gives you a taste, but a full day allows you to relax and appreciate Bainbridge Island fully.

Sights

Bainbridge Island Historical Museum

215 Ericksen Ave. NE, Winslow; 206/842-2773; https:// bainbridgehistory.org; 10am-4pm Wed.-Sun.; free

Run entirely by volunteers, the Bainbridge Island Historical Museum showcases the island's history through a collection of artifacts and captivating narratives. One of its most moving displays details the incarceration of Japanese Americans during World War II, shedding light on a pivotal period in the island's past.

Bloedel Reserve

7571 NE Dolphin Dr.; 206/842-7631; https:// bloedelreserve.org; 10am-4pm daily winter, 10am-5pm Tues.-Wed., 10am-6pm Thurs.-Sun. summer; $22 adult, $10 children

Situated on 150 acres (60 ha) at the northern tip of Bainbridge Island, the Bloedel Reserve displays a stunning combination of perfectly manicured gardens and pristine forests. You'll

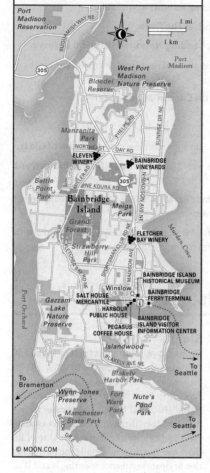

Bainbridge Island

© MOON.COM

There is a mix of in-town tasting rooms and some more remote wineries where you'll have the chance to talk to the owners. These tend to be less crowded than the larger, more popular wineries in Woodinville and Walla Walla, so many people take a day trip here to enjoy a quiet day of wine-tasting. While there isn't a particular variety the island is known for, almost all the vineyards have a mix of reds and whites, so everyone can find a glass they enjoy.

Eleven Winery

7671 NE Day Rd. W.; 206/780-0905; www. elevenwinery.com; noon-8pm daily; tastings $15

Eleven Winery offers a selection of red and white wines, as well as charcuterie and cheese pairings. The small indoor tasting room has a garage-door wall that opens up during warm weather and leads to a relaxed, covered outdoor space. The founder's passion for biking is evident in the details—and cyclists receive half-off tastings. There is a downtown Winslow location (287 Winslow Way E.) for those walking off the ferry.

Bainbridge Vineyards

8989 NE Day Rd.; 206/842-9463; www. bainbridgevineyards.com; 1pm-6pm Thurs.-Sun.; tastings $14

Head north to Bainbridge Vineyards to taste their organic, estate-grown wines in a covered and heated outdoor space. The vineyard welcomes families and dogs, and encourages visitors to check out the horses nearby.

Fletcher Bay Winery

9415 Coppertop Loop NE, Suite 102; 206/780-9463; www.fletcherbaywinery.com; 2pm-8pm Mon.-Thurs., 1pm-8pm Fri., noon-8pm Sat., noon-7pm Sun.; tastings $18-25

Fletcher Bay Winery offers white, red, and dessert wine flights, so there's something for everyone. They have a beautiful indoor tasting room and an outdoor patio with fire pits. There's also a tasting room in downtown Winslow (500 Winslow Way E. #130).

want to take your time walking the paths that go by ponds, meadows, and woodlands, and spring is a perfect time to visit when the flowers are in bloom. It's only a 15-minute (7-mi/11-km) drive north of Winslow on Route 305, the main road through the island.

Wine-Tasting

For a relatively small island, it's impressive that Bainbridge has half a dozen wineries.

Recreation
Grand Forest
9752 Miller Rd. NE; 206/842-2306; https://biparks.org; 7am-8:30pm daily; free

Grand Forest has over 7 mi (11 km) of trails to explore, winding through lush firs, maples, and cedars. Most of the dirt and gravel trails are relatively flat and suitable for beginner hikers and bikers. Private land separates the two halves, Grand Forest West and Grand Forest East, but both have a number of sizable loops with clear signage. The forest is about 4.5 mi north of Winslow.

Fort Ward Park
2241 Pleasant Beach Dr. NE; 206/842-2302; https:// biparks.org; 7am-9pm daily; free

Fort Ward Park is often full of people walking, running, or biking on the paved 1-mi (1.6 km) path that goes through this 137-acre (55-ha) marine park, but you'll also see locals bird-watching, clam digging, and even scuba diving in the underwater park. There is almost a mile (1.6 km) of beach access where you can walk along the shore, and a two-lane boat ramp is available.

Shopping
Salt House Mercantile
119 Winslow Way E., Winslow; 206/780-1606; Instagram @salthousemercantile; 10am-6pm Mon.-Sat., 11am-6pm Sun.

Stop by Salt House Mercantile for all your locally produced Pacific Northwest gear, from pillows that proudly say "Bainbridge Island" to candles, body wash, salts and spices, and dishware. This bright, cheerful store also has fashionable seasonal clothes, from summer dresses to winter sweaters.

Eagle Harbor Book Co.
157 Winslow Way E., Winslow; 206/842-5332; http:// eagleharborbooks.com; 10am-6pm daily

Eagle Harbor Book Co. is the place to go when you're looking for your latest read, whether a used book or one of the newest releases. This independent bookstore also hosts book readings, often with local authors, so check their event calendar.

Food
Pegasus Coffee House
131 Parfitt Way SW, Winslow; 206/317-6914; https:// pegasuscoffee.com; 7am-4pm Mon.-Thurs. and Sun., 7am-8pm Fri.-Sat.

You'll want to stay awhile at Pegasus Coffee House, an ivy-covered building that feels like you're home with comfortable couches and coffee tables throughout. They roast their own coffee and have about a dozen different types if you want to take a bag home.

Streamliner Diner
397 Winslow Way E., Winslow; 206/842-8595; https:// streamlinerdinerbi.com; 7am-3pm Wed.-Sun.; $9-19

The retro Streamliner Diner has been serving Bainbridge for over 40 years. Indulge in breakfast classics like steak and eggs, pancakes, and waffles, or enjoy their lunchtime salads and sandwiches.

Proper Fish
112 Madison Ave. N., Winslow; 206/855-5051; www. properfish.com; 11am-7pm Sun.-Thurs., 11am-8pm Fri.-Sat.; $11-40

Proper Fish specializes in British fish and chips; every fillet is hand-battered and served with a side of mushy peas. You can also get fried oysters or a lobster roll to enjoy at one of their outdoor tables.

Harbour Public House
231 Parfitt Way SW, Winslow; 206/842-0969; www. harbourpub.com; 3pm-9pm Wed.-Thurs., 11am-9pm Fri.-Sat.; $15-28

Orginally housing settlers in the late 1800s, Harbour Public House is the island's most historical place to eat. You'll see glimpses of the past with antiques throughout the restaurant as you dine on dishes like pepper-seared tuna and farro salad or steamed clams.

Information
Stop by the **Bainbridge Island Visitor**

Information Center (395 Winslow Way E.; 206/842-3700; www.visitbainbridgeisland.org; 9am-5pm Mon.-Fri.) to pick up brochures and get ideas for what to do on the island.

Transportation

Many people choose to walk onto the ferry in downtown Seattle and explore Bainbridge by foot. However, you'll want to bring your car on the ferry if you plan on going past the downtown Winslow area.

Ferries

The easiest way to get to Bainbridge Island from Seattle is by ferry at **Pier 52** (801 Alaskan Way; https://wsdot.wa.gov; fares start at $17.50/car and driver, $10/extra passenger or walk-on passenger). Ferries start running around 5:30am daily until 1:35am, and they leave about every 40 minutes. The ferry ride takes approximately 35 minutes and drops you off at the **Bainbridge Ferry Terminal** (270 Olympic Drive SE), only a few minutes from many shops and restaurants. The ferry doesn't accept reservations, so you'll buy your ticket upon arrival.

Car

Alternatively, you can drive onto the island, but it'll take about 2 hours (94 mi/151 km) via I-5 south, Route 16 west, and Route 305 south.

VASHON ISLAND

Vashon Island, just south of Seattle, is a fun day trip thanks to its picturesque scenery and laid-back vibe. The island covers nearly 37 sq mi (96 sq km). The main downtown area in the town of Vashon, about 5 mi (8 km) south of the north-end ferry terminal, has the highest concentration of restaurants, cafés, and shops.

Sights

SAW-Starving Artist Works

9922 SW Bank Rd.; 206/979-4192; Facebook @SawStarvingArtistWorks; noon-4:30pm Wed.-Sat.

About 90 makers and craftspeople from Vashon Island are featured exclusively in Starving Artist Works (SAW) gallery. All the unique pieces are sold on consignment and exclusive to the gallery, including jewelry, ceramics, paintings, photographs, fiber arts, woodworking, glass work, and mixed media.

Northbourne Farm

16530 91st Ave. SW; 314/504-2041; https:// northbourne.farm; 24 hours

There are about a dozen farms around Vashon, but Northbourne Farm stands out for its use of horses to help plow the fields. You can see them at work during the day and stop by their 24/7 stand to buy a wide variety of fruits and vegetables, such as carrots, tomatoes, and berries, as well as eggs and U-pick flowers.

Recreation

Point Robinson Lighthouse

3705 SW Point Robinson Rd.; 206/463-9602; https:// vashonparks.org; 8am-8pm daily; free

The Point Robinson Lighthouse has guided boats since 1885 and is still in operation, although it's been automated since 1978. It sits on 10 acres (4 ha) of shoreline, so many people come to take pictures of the lighthouse and then explore the beach. For a unique experience, two Keepers' Quarters were restored and are now available for rent for overnight stays.

Maury Island Marine Park

SW 244th St.; 206/296-0100; https://kingcounty.gov; 6am-10pm daily; free

Although not technically an island, as it's connected to Vashon, Maury Island Marine Park has over 320 acres (130 ha) and a variety of habitats to explore, including eelgrass beds, a salt marsh, and forests. It's common to see wildlife such as eagles and herons along the 3 mi (5 km) of trails here. Head to the southeast end of Vashon, and follow George Edwards Road to reach Maury Island.

1: Bainbridge Island Historical Museum **2:** Pegasus Coffee

Vashon Island

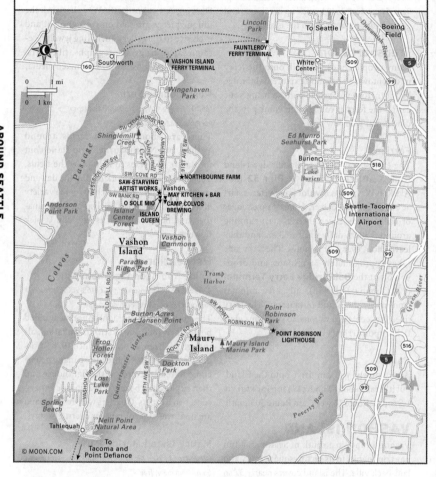

Shinglemill Creek

9924 SW 156th St.; 206/463-2644; https://kingcounty.gov; 7am-10pm; free

An ideal place for a quiet walk through nature, Shinglemill Creek Preserve follows the Shinglemill Creek from Fisher Pond to Fern Cove on Puget Sound. You can walk the 2.5-mi (4-km) trail or join parts of it and watch for spawning salmon in the creek.

Food

Island Queen

17705 Vashon Hwy. SW; 206/463-7777; www.vashoniq.com; 11am-7pm Wed.-Sun.; $8-20

Island Queen is reminiscent of an old-school burger shop—you can get a huge, juicy burger with a side of onion rings for a reasonable price. You'll find it packed in the summer as kids wait in line for a creamy milkshake or scoop of ice cream.

Camp Colvos Brewing

17636 Vashon Hwy. SW; 206/408-7309; https://campcolvos.com; 1pm-8pm daily; $7-15

Camp Colvos Brewing is where you get a cold beer after a day of exploring, such as the light Helles Lager or the Hoppy Pale Ale. They offer a small menu of appetizers like pasties and sliders and have a large outdoor patio to relax on.

May Kitchen + Bar

17614 Vashon Hwy. SW; 206/408-7196; www.maykitchen.com; 4pm-8:30pm Wed.-Thurs., Sun., 4pm-9pm Fri.-Sat.; $12-16

May Kitchen + Bar is a cozy spot that provides traditional Thai cuisine in an intimate setting, using only the freshest ingredients in dishes like tom yum and phad see iew.

O Sole Mio

17607 Vashon Hwy. SW; 206/408-7826; www.osolemiovashon.com; 11am-10pm Thurs.-Sat., 11am-9pm Sun.-Wed.; $17-33

Enjoy New York-style pizza by the slice or the full 18-in pie at the causual pizzeria O Sole Mio. Choose from the classics or go for one of their more unique combos. They also offer an extensive bar with a wide variety of drinks.

Information

You can find out where to eat and what to do on **Explore Vashon Island** (https://explorevashon.com).

Getting There

Vashon Island is surrounded by water with no connecting land or bridges, so the only way to get here is by ferry or private boat. The **Fauntleroy Ferry Terminal** (4829 SW Barton St., Seattle) is the departure point for those traveling from Seattle. Boats depart for Vashon Island about every 45 minutes daily, typically 5am-midnight, though the schedule can change on weekends. The ferry crossing takes approximately 20 minutes.

You can find the ferry schedule online (https://wsdot.com), but you will buy tickets in person at the ferry booth ($15.25/vehicle and driver, $6.75/passenger or walk-on passenger).

The **Point Defiance Ferry Terminal** (5810 N. Pearl St., Tacoma) is the departure point for those traveling from the Tacoma area. A boat departs for Vashon Island about every hour daily, typically 5am-11pm. The ferry crossing takes approximately 15 minutes and brings you to the island's south end.

The ferry schedule is online (https://wsdot.com), and you'll buy tickets in person at the ferry booth ($22.50/vehicle and driver, $6.50/passenger or walk-on passenger).

Getting Around

Having a car on the island is highly recommended, as most places are spread out. However, Vashon Island is served by **King County Metro** bus routes 118 and 119 (https://kingcounty.gov; $2.75 adult, $1 18 and under). On weekdays, buses run around every hour; on weekends, they run less frequently. The ferry terminals are connected to both routes.

Tacoma

Roughly 35 mi (56 km) south of Seattle, Tacoma has a rich cultural heritage and a fascinating industrial background. The historic downtown is experiencing a renaissance thanks to the influx of new stores and restaurants, and Tacoma is becoming more known as a tourist destination while maintaining its own character.

SIGHTS
Museum of Glass

1801 Dock St.; 253/284-4750; www.museumofglass. org; 10am-5pm Wed.-Sun.; $12-20, under 6 free

With over 75,000 sq ft (6,928 sq m) of space, the Museum of Glass hosts a dynamic rotation of exhibitions from international artists, showcasing the versatility and beauty of glass art. Its famous cone-shaped glassblowing hot shop lets guests see the hypnotic process of glassmaking in action.

Point Defiance Zoo and Aquarium

5400 N. Pearl St.; 253/404-3800; www.pdza.org; 9am-3:30pm daily; $7-18

Point Defiance Zoo and Aquarium has over 9,000 specimens representing 367 species from all over the world. Sea otters, seals, and walruses live in the Rocky Shores habitat, which is one of many in the zoo. Other habitats include the Arctic Tundra, the Asian Forest Sanctuary, and the Pacific Seas Aquarium.

LeMay-America's Car Museum

2702 E. D St.; 253/779-8490; www. americascarmuseum.org; 10am-5pm Thurs.-Mon.; $16-22

Harold LeMay's collection, which was once the largest privately owned collection of automobiles, is housed at LeMay-America's Car Museum. This expansive museum has a collection of some 3,000 vehicles, 350 of which are on display at any one moment, including rare and old cars, trucks, and motorcycles from all across the world, along with more contemporary developments and models.

LeMay-America's Car Museum

RECREATION
Parks
Point Defiance Park
5400 N. Pearl St.; 253/404-3980; www.
metroparkstacoma.org; 30 minutes before sunrise-30
minutes after sunset; free

The 760-acre (300-ha) Point Defiance Park is home to several attractions, including the Point Defiance Zoo and Aquarium ($16-26), the Fort Nisqually Living History Museum ($9-13), and a variety of gardens, including the Japanese, Rose, and Rhododendron Gardens (free). There are more than 15 mi (24 km) of hiking paths to explore in the park, as well as the scenic Five Mile Drive and Owen Beach for waterfront activities.

Kayaking
Point Defiance Marina
912 N. Waterfront Dr.; 253/404-3960; www.
metroparkstacoma.org; 6:30am-5:30pm daily; $50-150

The Point Defiance Marina has boat and kayak rentals, a fully stocked tackle shop, boat launches, and moorage. You can also rent fishing poles and cast your line for a variety of fish, including crab and bottom fish, from the piers here.

ENTERTAINMENT AND EVENTS
Tacoma Dome
2727 E. D St.; www.tacomadome.org

Able to hold up to 21,000 people, the Tacoma Dome is one of the world's largest wood-domed structures and plays home to an assortment of events every year, including concerts, sports, and, trade exhibits.

FOOD
Katie Downs Waterfront Tavern
3211 Ruston Way; 253/756-0771; https://katiedowns.
com; 11am-9pm Sun.-Thurs., 11am-10pm Fri.-Sat.; $15-28

Katie Downs Waterfront Tavern is a unique over-the-water restaurant with a fun tavern atmosphere for those who are 21 and older.

It's a favorite spot for enjoying a drink on the outdoor patio or watching sports inside with a burger or pizza.

Hob Nob
716 6th Ave.; 253/272-3200; https://hobnobtacoma.
com; 7am-3pm daily; $15-22

The Hob Nob is known for their hearty breakfasts, including fresh eggs and pancakes, with vegan, vegetarian, and meat lover's dishes. They also serve lunch and dinner with a variety of sandwiches and burgers, and they have a lounge with a full bar.

Boathouse 19
9001 S. 19th St.; 253/565-1919; https://theboathouse19.
com; noon-8pm Mon.-Thurs., noon-9pm Fri.-Sun.;
$14-59

Visit Boathouse 19 for one of the best restaurants with the closest views of the Tacoma Narrows Bridge, while dining on seafood like mahi mahi tacos and clam chowder or salad and burger options. Happy hour is 3pm-6pm weekdays in the bar.

ACCOMMODATIONS
Hotel Murano
1320 Broadway; 253/238-8000; www.
hotelmuranotacoma.com; $112-187

Hotel Murano stands out for its luxury, offering king-sized beds in its 319 rooms and suites ideal for families. It showcases Tacoma's glass art culture with an extensive worldwide collection, displayed throughout the hotel. The hotel is near many popular sights, and it has a sophisticated bar and lounge.

McMenamins Elks Temple
565 Broadway; 253/300-8777; www.mcmenamins.
com; $117-195

McMenamins Elks Temple hosts guests in a restored 1916 building, offering a lively experience with a brewery, tasting room, bars, and the Spanish Ballroom. This unique hotel has 45 colorful king guestrooms decorated with local art.

INFORMATION

Travel Tacoma (1516 Commerce St.; 253/284-3254; www.traveltacoma.com; 10am-4pm Tues.-Fri.) has a visitor center where you can get more information on planning out your trip.

TRANSPORTATION

Tacoma is about 35 mi (56 km) south of Seattle via I-5 and takes 30 minutes to drive without traffic, although it's rare if the route isn't congested.

While multiple bus routes service Seattle to Tacoma, the **FlixBus** (www.flixbus.com) goes directly to Tacoma (drop off at G St. and Puyallup Ave.; $10-20) instead of transferring to another bus and will get you there in about 1 hour 15 minutes, depending on where you get picked up in Seattle. You can also take the **Amtrak** (www.amtrak.com) to arrive in only 45 minutes (drop off at Tacoma Dome Station, 424 E. 25th St.; $12-16).

Eastside

Eastside, the area east of Lake Washington, is composed of three main cities: Bellevue, Kirkland, and Redmond. The first two draw visitors with their waterfront locations and a variety of shopping and dining options, while Redmond, as home of Microsoft and Nintendo, is more for working locals. Just north of here is Woodinville, the most common wine-tasting destination west of the Cascades and a wonderful getaway.

Taking Route 520, or the Floating Bridge, across Lake Washington is the quickest way to reach the Eastside. It's a toll bridge, $1.25-6.50 each way, depending on the time of day and day of the week, with weekends and nights being cheaper. Buying a Good To Go! pass also gives you access to lower rates, and your account will automatically be charged online instead of billed in the mail. Find out more about rates and the pass on the WSDOT website (https://wsdot.wa.gov).

BELLEVUE

Situated on the eastern side of Lake Washington, across from Seattle, Bellevue has lively streets that lead you to a plethora of trendy cafés, posh restaurants, and boutiques. You'll also find over a hundred different stores, ranging from chains to local ones. Even though it's quieter at night, you can still find plenty of chic lounges and bars.

Sights
Bellevue Botanical Garden

12001 Main St.; 425/452-2750; https:// bellevuebotanical.org; 7am-7pm daily; free

The Bellevue Botanical Garden covers 53 acres (21 ha) with diverse ecosystems, including gardens, woodlands, and wetlands, featuring special areas like the Yao Japanese Garden. Visitors can use the interactive What's That Plant? markers to get detailed plant information through their smartphones. If you're looking for a more in-depth experience, there are free docent-led tours on Saturdays and Sundays April-October.

KidsQuest Chidren's Museum

1116 108th Ave. NE; 425/637-8100; www. kidsquestmuseum.org; 9:30am-5pm Tues.-Sat., 11:30am-5pm Sun.; $15

The large KidsQuest Children's Museum has two stories of interactive exhibits that kids of all ages can appreciate, including a climbing structure and water play area. Toddlers will love Tot Orchard, where they can find and sort fruit, and older kids will enjoy shopping and checking out at a realistic grocery store.

Shopping
The Bellevue Collection

575 Bellevue Square; 425/454-8096; https://bellevu collection.com; 10am-9pm Mon.-Sat., 11am-7pm Sun.

Bellevue Square, Lincoln Square, and Bellevue Place make up The Bellevue Collection, a trio of large indoor shopping centers located in the heart of the city. Bellevue Square, the original shopping district that opened in 1946, has more than 200 stores, from national chains to mom-and-pop shops, and a diverse selection of restaurants. Its abundance of inexpensive chain restaurants and apparel businesses contribute to its reputation. Lincoln Square is a haven for entertainment, featuring a movie theater, bowling alley, fine-dining establishments, and the five-star Westin Bellevue Hotel. The smaller Bellevue Place caters to upscale shoppers and is home to the Hyatt Regency Hotel.

Food

Coffeholic House

10000 Main St., Suite 103; 425/590-9916; https:// coffeeholichouse.com; 8am-5pm daily

If you want to try something other than your usual latte, head to Coffeeholic House, which specializes in unique Vietnamese coffee drinks. Try the bold yet sweet tiramisu egg coffee with cocoa powder and egg cream on top, or perhaps the Coffeeholic Dream with cheese foam.

Water Grill

700 Bellevue Way NE; 425/799-2800; www.watergrill. com; 11am-10pm Sun.-Thurs., 11am-11pm Sat.; $31-50

Water Grill has some of the best seafood options in Bellevue, like a raw oyster bar with over a dozen regional oysters to choose from. It focuses mainly on seafood but has a small meat section for those who feel like a steak, and their wine list is extensive. It's in a beautiful setting with a Pacific Northwest-theme, with fish decor and wooden beams throughout.

Monsoon Bellevue

10245 Main St.; 425/635-1112; https:// monsoonrestaurants.com; 11:30am-9pm Mon.-Thurs., 11:30am-9:30pm Fri., 11am-9:30pm Sat., 11am-9pm Sun.; $13-28

Monsoon Bellevue has a menu that features Vietnamese classics, including vermicelli noodle dishes and pho, in an elegant setting. Guests can also enjoy customized cocktails made in the restaurant's full bar.

Gilbert's on Main

10024 Main St.; 425/455-5650; www.gilbertsonmain. com; 8am-3pm daily; $21-28

Step away from the bustle at Bellevue Square and visit Gilbert's on Main in Old Bellevue for massive deli sandwiches you can easily share, such as the cheesy tuna melt. This small but cozy café also serves breakfast, with options like the Danish scramble with tomatoes and Havarti cheese or classic buttermilk pancakes.

Information

Visit Bellevue (www.visitbellevuewa.com) helps you find the best places to eat and drink as well as things to do.

Transportation

To travel from Seattle to Bellevue, you can take either I-90 or Route 520 east across Lake Washington. Both ways take about 15 minutes without traffic, so check which way is faster based on whether it's rush hour.

Multiple bus routes leave from various points in Seattle and can take 30-60 minutes to reach Bellevue. Many buses stop the **Bellevue Transit Center** (10850 NE 6th St.), which puts you within walking distance of many shops and restaurants. The most convenient bus is **Sound Transit** route 550, an express bus with about a dozen stops in downtown Seattle and another dozen around downtown Bellevue (www.soundtransit.org; $1-3.25).

KIRKLAND

Head 5 mi (8 km) north of Bellevue and you'll come across the lakeside town of Kirkland, known for its laid-back vibe and picturesque waterfront views. With an abundance of parks and beaches, Kirkland is a great place to go swimming, boating, or just relaxing and people-watching.

Sights

The Village at Totem Lake

11901 NE Village Plaza; 425/820-9268; www. thevillageattotemlake.com; 10am-9pm Mon.-Sat., 11am-6pm Sun.

The Village at Totem Lake has an extensive selection of shops and restaurants, plus a luxury cinema. You'll find stores such as Snapdoodle Toys and Urban Tread here, and restaurants like Bok a Bok Fried Chicken, Joe's Burgers, and Salt & Straw for when you need a break from shopping.

Beaches

Marina Park

25 Lakeshore Plaza; 425/587-3330; www.kirklandwa. gov; 24 hours; free

Marina Park is a stunning park on Lake Washington with a sandy beach for playing on, plentiful bench seating, and an open-air pavilion that hosts concerts and other events during the summer.

Juanita Beach Park

9703 NE Juanita Dr.; 425/587-3300; www.kirklandwa. gov; sunrise-10pm daily; free

Juanita Beach Park has 1,000 ft (305 m) of Lake Washington shoreline and is a popular place to swim in the summer, thanks to its sandy beaches. There's also a playground, sports courts, and trails to walk on, and the park hosts the Juanita Friday Market during the summer.

Boating and Kayaking

Starting Memorial Day weekend, you'll find hundreds of boaters out each day enjoying the water all summer until late September. There are dozens of launch points along 18-mi (29-km) Lake Washington, so you won't have trouble finding somewhere to get in the water.

Woodmark Waterfront Adventures

1200 Carillon Point; 425/216-2257; www. waterfrontadventures.com; 11am-6:30pm Thurs.-Fri., 11am-8:30pm Sat.-Sun.; $24-299

You can rent boats by the hour at Woodmark Waterfront Adventures, where the variety of watercraft includes boats for up to 12 passengers, wakeboard boats, Jet Skis, single and double kayaks, and stand-up paddleboards. You'll want to make a reservation in advance, as they'll likely be booked up on summer days.

Food

BeachHouse Bar and Grill

6023 Lake Washington Blvd NE; 425/968-5587; https:// beachhouserestaurants.com; 11am-9pm Mon.-Fri., 10am-10pm Sat.-Sun.; $17-34

Located on the waterfront, The BeachHouse Bar and Grill specializes in Northwestern cuisine and has a selection of gourmet burgers, fresh salads, and seafood. Weekend brunches feature favorites like mimosas and buttermilk fried chicken.

203° Fahrenheit Coffee Co.

11901 NE Village Plaza, Suite 171; 425/285-9382; https://203degreesfahrenheit.coffee; 7am-7pm daily; $3-11

In a bright, welcoming setting, 203° Fahrenheit Coffee Co. serves unique coffee drinks such as the Madagascar vanilla latte and the lavender latte. Seattle fogs and matcha lattes are just two of the various noncoffee drinks on the menu, including inventive seasonal drinks.

Carillon Kitchen

2240 Carillon Point; 425/739-6363; www. carillonkitchen.com; 7am-2pm daily; $11-18

For those who are health-conscious, stop by Carillon Kitchen for a light meal that will fuel you up before a day of adventure. They have options like chai seed pudding made with coconut milk for breakfast or chicken sandwiches on local Macrina Bakery bread. There's limited seating, so many people take it to go.

Le Grand Bistro Americain

2220 Carillon Point; 425/828-7778; www.bistrolegrand. com; 11:30am-3pm, 4pm-9pm Mon.-Fri., 10:30am-2pm, 4pm-9pm Sat.-Sun.; $19-55

1: downtown Bellevue **2:** Chateau Ste. Michelle

End your day at one of Kirkland's most scenic waterfront restaurants as you feast on decadent French food, such as French onion soup or boeuf bourguignon. Reservations on the weekends are highly recommended at Le Grand Bistro American, especially if you want one of the highly sought-after window booths to watch the boats pass by.

Information

Explore Kirkland (www.explorekirkland. com) is a great resource for planning your time in the city, with suggested activities and a local events calendar.

Transportation

Kirkland is about 11 mi (18 mi/29 km) from Seattle. The most direct route is Route 520 east across Lake Washington, about 15 minutes with no traffic. An alternative from south Seattle is to take I-90 across the lake and then Route 405 north, but this route tends to have more traffic and can take 20-30 minutes, depending on the time of day.

There is no direct bus from Seattle to Kirkland, but you can take one from Seattle to Bellevue and then catch a different bus from Bellevue to Kirkland (1-1.5 hours). **Sound Transit** (www.soundtransit.org; $1-3.25) route 540 goes from downtown Seattle to Bellevue, and then route 255 stops throughout Kirkland.

WOODINVILLE

The Woodinville area has dozens of wineries. In addition to its thriving wine culture, Woodinville is perfect for a day trip or weekend retreat— boutiques, tasty local restaurants, and picturesque countryside.

★ Wine-Tasting

Since there are dozens of wineries in the area, it's best to pick one area you want to visit and go to a few wineries there. You may be able to walk in for tastings at some of the smaller wineries, but most of the large ones require reservations, especially on the weekends. There is usually a limit of 1-2 hours,

so keep that in mind as well when planning your day out.

The best resource for planning your wine-tasting is **Woodinville Wine Country** (https://woodinvillewinecountry.com), which has all the wineries and districts mapped out on its site. The four main areas are the Hollywood District, Warehouse District, Downtown District, and West Valley District, and they're all different. You'll find fancier wineries in Hollywood, while the West Valley is much more laid-back, with smaller wine-tasting rooms. Downtown has various shops and restaurants in addition to wine, while the Warehouse District has multiple wine-tasting rooms within walking distance of each other and is usually less crowded.

Chateau Ste. Michelle

14111 NE 145th St., Woodinville; 425/488-1133; www.ste-michelle.com; 11am-5pm daily; tasting $30-100
Located on the historic 1912 estate of Frederick Stimson, Chateau Ste. Michelle Winery is known for its expansive grounds and large-scale distribution throughout Washington state. You can walk in to taste their best-selling wines, although reservations are strongly suggested on the weekends, or reserve a spot on a **guided tour** ($55 pp) for a closer look at the winery.

A fun option in the summer is purchasing a bottle of wine and having a picnic on the lawn. The popular **Summer Concert Series,** featuring renowned artists, draws large crowds and often sells out, so buy tickets well in advance. While Chateau Ste. Michelle is one of the more impressive wineries, it tends to get overcrowded in the summer and lacks the personal connections you'll find with owners at smaller wineries.

DeLille Cellars

14300 NE 145th St., Suite 101, Woodinville; 425/489-0544; https://delillecellars.com; 11am-6pm daily; tasting $25
DeLille Cellars wines are characterized by Bordeaux-style blends sourced from esteemed vineyards in the Columbia Valley

and Red Mountain. There are three stories of tasting space, a rooftop terrace, and **The Restaurant** (11:30am-9pm Wed.-Fri., 11am-9pm Sat., 11am-8pm Sun.; $16-54) in what was once the Redhook Brewery building in the Hollywood District.

Alexandria Nicole Cellars

14810 NE 145th St., Woodinville; 425/487-9463; www.
alexandrianicolecellars.com; 11am-5pm Mon. and Wed.-
Sat.; tasting $20-30

Alexandria Nicole Cellars is in the historic Hollywood Schoolhouse building and has a popular outdoor seating area for summer tastings. They have a wide range of wines, including an aromatic Viognier and full-bodied reds.

Biking

Sammamish River Trail

For bikers looking to continue their ride from Seattle, the 10-mi (16-km) Sammamish River Trail connects to the Burke-Gilman Trail and offers an easy, paved road from Blyth Park in Bothell to Marymoor Park in Redmond. This wide path is popular for walking, rollerblading, and biking. However, it can get crowded on the weekends, so it's important to know proper bike etiquette and be aware of your surroundings.

Bothell Ski & Bike

8020 NE Bothell Way, Kenmore; 425/486-3747; www.
bikesale.com; 11am-5pm Mon.-Tues., 11am-6pm Thurs.-
Fri., noon-5pm Sat.-Sun.; $40/day

If you're looking to pick up a bike rental closer to the Sammamish River Trail, head to Bothell Ski & Bike in Kenmore, only a 10-minute drive from Woodinville. This shop is one of the few places in the area that lets you rent bikes for the day, and they're close to the Burke-Gilman Trail, so you can take that to the Eastside.

Food

Hollywood Tavern

14501 Redmond-Woodinville Rd. NE, Woodinville;
425/481-7703; www.thehollywoodtavern.com; 11am-
9pm Sun.-Thurs., 11am-10pm Fri.-Sat.; $15-47

With a rich history dating back to its 1947 opening, the Hollywood Tavern has been a staple in wine country over the years. During the warmer months, you can enjoy live music while dining on burgers and sandwiches, sitting at the bar or a table, or relaxing by the fire pit.

Barking Frog

4580 NE 145th St., Woodinville; 425/424-2999; www.
willowslodge.com; 7am-3pm and 5pm-9pm daily;
$23-58

Inside Willows Lodge, Barking Frog is the go-to spot for locals seeking a celebratory dinner, with reservations necessary due to its popularity. The restaurant uses only the freshest ingredients in its seasonal menu and has an extensive Washington wine list. Relax in the warm glow of the indoor fire pit or at a table to indulge in appetizers such as foie gras and frog leg lollipops and entrées like lamb chops and seafood dishes.

Accommodations

Willows Lodge

14580 NE 145th St., Woodinville; 425/424-3900; www.
willowslodge.com; $299-582

With its idyllic surroundings in nature, the eco-conscious Willows Lodge is the perfect place to unwind after a day of wine-tasting. A combination of rustic elegance and salvaged materials, such as wine cask doors and Douglas fir timbers, define the lodge's architecture. Inside, the 84 guest rooms have fireplaces and soaking tubs, with garden views. The lodge's commitment to farm-to-table cuisine can be seen at its renowned restaurants. Native American artwork, notably that of Haida artist Bill Reid and others from the Northwest, adorns the lodge.

Information

Visit Woodinville (https://visitwoodinville. org) has a comprehensive website on things to do, where to eat, and where to stay.

Transportation

The most direct route from Seattle to Woodinville is taking 520 across Lake

Washington and going north on Route 405, which is about 25 minutes (20 mi/32 km) without traffic.

Various **Sound Transit** (www.sound transit.org) bus routes connect Seattle and Woodinville, but they take an average of 1.5 hours and have several transfers, making it a less feasible option.

I-90 Corridor

The journey from Seattle to the Snoqualmie region and beyond is straightforward, as everything is easily accessed from I-90. Hiking is the main reason people come here, as there are dozens of hikes just off the freeway.

SNOQUALMIE AND NORTH BEND

Only 45 minutes east of Seattle, Snoqualmie and North Bend are easy day trips. While Snoqualmie Falls is the main draw here, both towns have a decent selection of restaurants, breweries, and shopping. The TV show *Twin Peaks* also brought the area fame; many parts of it were shot at buildings that are still around. Snoqualmie and North Bend border each other, so it's easy to go back and forth.

★ Snoqualmie Falls

6501 Railroad Ave.; Snoqualmie; 435/326-2563; www.snoqualmiefalls.com; dawn-dusk daily; free

Standing at 270 ft (82 m), Snoqualmie Falls has gained widespread recognition through its appearances in film and television, most notably in the series *Twin Peaks*, which showcased the falls' mesmerizing presence. It's also one of the few waterfalls you can visit without hiking in, making it popular for travelers of all ages.

In 1898, the world's first underground power plant was constructed at Snoqualmie Falls. This hydroelectric plant, a groundbreaking project for its time, marked a significant step forward in utilizing natural resources for energy production. It harnessed the energy of the falls to provide electricity to nearby towns, contributing to the region's industrialization.

Snoqualmie Falls

Today an ADA-accessible viewing platform allows for close-up views of the falls from the top, making it a popular spot for photography. To see the falls from a different perspective, take the 0.7-mi (1.1-km) path down to the base, where you can walk along the river and get even closer.

At the top is the **Salish Lodge & Spa** (425/888-2556; www.salishlodge.com; $246-489), which *Twin Peaks* fans will recognize as the Great Northern Hotel. You can stay the night at one of their 86 luxurious guestrooms or make a reservation in their dining room for a meal, stop at the coffee shop for pastries and espresso drinks, or visit the gift shop.

Northwest Railway Museum

38625 SE King St.; Snoqualmie; 425/888-3030; https:// trainmuseum.org; 11am, 1pm and 3pm Sat.-Sun. Apr.-Nov.; $28

Another big draw to Snoqualmie is the Northwest Railway Museum, where you can ride a train to the Train Shed Exhibit Hall, which is full of historical freight cars, locomotives, passenger cars, and more. After learning about the history, get back on the train to ride to the top of Snoqualmie Falls before returning to the train station in this 2-hour ride.

Remlinger Farms

32610 NE 32nd St.; Carnation; 425/333-4135; https:// remlingerfarms.com; noon-8pm Thurs., noon-9pm Fri.-Sat., noon-7pm Sun.; $5-7

At Remlinger Farms, 14 mi (23 km) north in Carnation, kids will love visiting the Fun Park to go on the carousel rides, pony rides, slides, and much more. There is also a U-pick farm to take home your own berries or pumpkins, and the family-friendly brewery on-site has live music on the weekends.

Hiking
★ Rattlesnake Ledge

Distance: *4 mi (6.4 km) round-trip*
Duration: *2 hours*
Elevation gain: *1,160 ft (354 m)*
Difficulty: *easy/moderate*
Trailhead: *Rattlesnake Ledge parking lot*

Rattlesnake Ledge is one of the closest hikes to Seattle and has one of the best views, so it's popular year-round with locals. Contrary to the name, you don't have to worry about seeing rattlesnakes here.

Early on, you'll come across a significant moss-laden boulder. As you continue, you'll have views of Rattlesnake Lake from above. At about 2 mi (3.2 km) is a signed junction leading you to Rattlesnake Ledge. While it's an ideal place to rest before turning around, it has steep drop-offs, so children and pets should be kept close. You can also head up to the Middle or Upper Ledge for a different viewpoint and fewer people before returning the way you came.

To get here from North Bend, exit I-90 at exit 32 and turn onto 436th Avenue SE, which is also known as Cedar Falls Road SE. Continue for approximately 4 mi (6.5 km) to the Rattlesnake Lake parking lot, located on the right side.

Twin Falls

Distance: *2.6 mi (4.2 km) round-trip*
Duration: *1 hour*
Elevation gain: *500 ft (150 m)*
Difficulty: *easy*
Trailhead: *Twin Falls parking lot*

This trail parallels to the river, going up a steep hill and down into a swampy area, abundant with skunk cabbage in spring and salmonberries in summer. Cross a bridge to reach the river. The path then ascends again, with switchbacks leading to a stunning view of the Lower Falls. The final stretch involves stairs down to the Big Bridge, which gives you views of the valley below and the Upper Falls, consisting of two waterfalls. Unlike many other hikes in this area, winter is a recommended time to visit, as it's when the falls will be the fullest. However, microspikes may be needed to help with any icy areas.

To get here from North Bend, drive east on I-90 and take exit 34, and make a right turn onto 468th Avenue SE. In about 0.5 mi (0.8 km), turn left onto SE 159th Street and continue for 0.5 mi (0.8 km) to the end of the road, where you'll find the Twin Falls parking lot.

Franklin Falls

Distance: *2 mi (3.2 km) round-trip*
Duration: *1 hour*
Elevation gain: *400 ft (120 m)*
Difficulty: *easy*
Trailhead: *Franklin Falls parking lot*

The trail, featuring gentle inclines and numerous stairs, is an easy hike and good for kids. You'll be in the forest for most of it before coming out to Franklin Falls, which will likely get you wet, depending on how heavy the spray is that day.

To get here from North Bend, travel east on I-90, taking exit 47 for Denny Creek/Tinkham Road. Turn left over the freeway, and at the stop sign make a right onto Forest Road 58. After 0.2 mi (0.3 km), turn left and continue straight for 3 mi until you come to three parking lots.

Mount Si

Distance: *8 mi (12.9 km) round-trip*
Duration: *5 hours*
Elevation gain: *3,150 ft (960 m)*
Difficulty: *strenuous*
Trailhead: *off Mount Si Road*

Mount Si, a favorite among advanced hikers and a training ground for those preparing for Mount Rainier, offers a challenging hike that starts with switchbacks and a steady ascent. The first 1.5 mi is relatively gentle, leading through an area of old-growth trees with a history of surviving fire and logging. Then the trail becomes steeper, and at 3.5 mi (5.6 km), a clearing offers southern views of Mount Rainier on a clear day. This spot is also the unofficial turnaround for most people, and where you'll see dozens having lunch on a sunny day. But this isn't the true summit; the summit is Haystack, but it requires a scramble, and many people skip it for safety reasons.

From North Bend, follow West North Bend Way and SE North Bend Way to SE Mount Si

Road, and continue for 2.4 mi (3.8 km). You'll find the trailhead on your left.

Mailbox Peak

Distance: *9.4 mi (15.1 km) round-trip*
Duration: *6 hours*
Elevation gain: *4,000 ft (1,219 m)*
Difficulty: *moderate/strenuous*
Trailhead: *Mailbox Peak trailhead*

Many locals regard crossing the challenging Mailbox Peak hike off their hiking bucket list as something worthy of bragging rights. The hike to Mailbox Peak starts with bridges and creek crossings in its lower section, followed by switchbacks that climb about 850 ft (259 m) per mile (1.6 km). The switchbacks span about 4 mi (6.5 km) before merging with the old trail at 3,860 ft, leading to the final steep ascent of 960 ft (293 m) over 0.5 mi (0.8 km). The summit has panoramas of the Middle Fork Valley and Mount Rainier. True to the name, there's a mailbox at the peak, so check inside to see what you'll find (kind hikers often leave beer or snacks for others).

From North Bend, take I-90 to exit 34, go north on 468th Avenue SE for 0.5 mi (0.8 km), then turn right on SE Middle Fork Road. Continue for 2 mi (3 km) to a stop sign at SE Dorothy Lake Road. Take a right onto SE Dorothy Lake Road, and shortly after it rejoins Middle Fork Road, watch for the Mailbox Peak trailhead turnoff on your right. The short stretch of paved road leads to the paved parking lot for the trailhead.

Breweries
No Boat Brewing

35214 SE Center St. #2nd, Snoqualmie; 425/292-0702; https://noboatbrewing.com; 3pm-9pm Mon.-Thurs., noon-10pm Fri.-Sat., noon-9pm Sun.

After a hike, head to No Boat Brewing to reward yourself with one of their flagship beers, such as the Bia Hoi Vietnamese Lager or Snoqualmie Maybe Citra Pale Ale. They have daily food trucks that rotate throughout the week and a large outdoor beer garden for enjoying the sun.

Snoqualmie Falls Brewery

*8032 Falls Ave. SE, Snoqualmie; 425/831-2357; https://
fallsbrew.com; noon-8pm Sun.-Mon., 4pm-8pm Tues.-
Thurs., noon-9pm Fri.-Sat.; $14-18*

Snoqualmie Falls Brewery has been around since 1997 and has become the main place to get beer in downtown Snoqualmie. Their two-story indoor seating area is cozy in winter, but head outside when it's dry out to appreciate their large outdoor area and covered bar. They have traditional bar food such as burgers and salads, a kids' menu, and about a dozen beers on tap.

Volition Brewing

*112 W. North Bend Way; North Bend; 425/292-0329;
www.volitionbrewing.com; 3pm-9pm Mon.-Fri., noon-
9pm Sat., noon-8pm Sun.*

Located in downtown North Bend, Volition Brewing is housed in a historical building from the early 1900s. It now serves a variety of beer, from lighter ones like blondes to heavier porters. They also have wine and cider, and their food truck options change daily.

Shopping
North Bend Premium Outlets

*461 South Fork Ave. SW, North Bend; 425/888-4505;
www.premiumoutlets.com; 11am-7pm Mon.-Thurs.,
10am-7pm Fri.-Sat., 11am-6pm Sun.*

Besides hiking, the North Bend Premium Outlets are the prime reason people come from all over to visit the city. You'll find hugely discounted items and clothing at name-brand stores like Under Armour, Pendleton, Levi's, Coach, and more at this giant outlet mall.

Food
Huxdotter Coffee

*101 W. Park St., Suite A, North Bend; https://
huxdottercoffee.com; 7am-7pm daily*

Start your morning at Huxdotter Coffee with breakfast options such as breakfast sandwiches and bagels, or stop by at lunch for various hot and cold sandwiches. In addition to the standard espresso drink options, they have creative ones, such as the Twin Peaks coffee with lavender syrup and honey.

Twede's Café

*137 W. North Bend Way; North Bend; 425/831-5511;
www.twedescafe.com; 9am-7pm daily; $9-23*

Twede's Café is often one of the first stop *Twin Peaks* fans make, as it was the famous Double R Diner in the show. Once you take your pictures of the outside, head inside to find a typical diner menu of pancakes, omelets, sandwiches, and several dozen different types of burgers. They have fun with being in the show with names like "damn fine cup of coffee" for their drip coffee.

Los Cabos North Bend

*580 SW Mount Si Blvd., North Bend; 425/888-5256;
www.loscabos-northbend.com; 11am-9pm Sun.-Thurs.,
11am-9:30pm Fri.-Sat.; $10-19*

This colorful Mexican restaurant is a convenient place to get dinner after a day of shopping at the outlet malls. They have an impressively large menu with everything from burritos to tostadas to quesadillas, and there's also a lounge if you just prefer chips and salsa with a margarita.

The Dining Room at Salish Lodge

*6501 Railroad Ave. #101, Snoqualmie; 425/888-2556;
www.salishlodge.com; 8am-3pm, 5pm-9pm daily;
$38-70*

You won't find a better view in town than when eating at The Dining Room at Salish Lodge & Spa. Reservations are required at the only restaurant that gives you a full view of the roaring Snoqualmie Falls in the background while you dine on fresh, seasonal food such as Washington oysters or Pacific Northwest beef.

Information
North Bend Visitor Information Center

*920 SE Cedar Falls Way, North Bend; 425/888-1211;
https://discovernorthbend.com; 8:30am-4:30pm Mon.-
Thurs., 8:30am-noon Fri.*

Visit the North Bend Visitor Information Center to get maps and recommendations of what to do or where to eat.

Transportation

Snoqualmie is about 35 minutes (30 mi/38 km) east of Seattle, which you can reach by taking I-5 east. Snoqualmie is just west of North Bend, and it's a quick 5-minute (3-mi/5-km) drive from the downtown areas by taking Route 202 east.

SNOQUALMIE PASS

Snoqualmie Pass is only an hour east of Seattle and is the primary way to access the other side of the Cascade Mountains via I-90. It's the closest ski area to Seattle, so winter brings numerous skiers, snowshoers, and cross-country skiers eager to get out in the snow. Once the snow melts, hikers flock to the area for its multitude of hiking trails in the Alpine Lakes Wilderness.

★ Skiing and Snowboarding

Snow typically hits Snoqualmie Pass starting in November and can last well into spring. Parking lots fill up quickly; many locals get to the mountain several hours before the chair lifts open on the weekends, so you'll be wise to follow their lead if you want a parking spot. You'll experience less crowds if you come weekdays.

Summit at Snoqualmie

1001 Route 906, Snoqualmie; 425/434-7669; https:// summitatsnoqualmie.com; 9am-9:30pm daily late Nov.-mid-Apr.; $26-72

There are four distinct skiing areas at Snoqualmie Pass (Alpental, Summit Central, Summit West, and Summit East), with nearly 2,000 acres (800 ha) of skiable terrain, 25 lifts, and the country's most extensive night skiing. The area also features a snow tubing section with over 500 ft (152 m) and 20 lanes, two dedicated terrain parks, and 31 mi (50 km) of Nordic and snowshoe trails.

Daily gear rentals ($35-63) are available for those without equipment, and a repair shop is also on-site for anyone who needs their gear tuned. Private and group lessons ($99-120) are offered daily, and paid lockers are available to store personal items while on the slopes.

Many people bring their own lunch to save money, but there are multiple dining options around the mountain. From coffee shops to quick outdoor meals to a sit-down restaurant and bar, you'll have your choice of eateries.

Hiking

While these hikes are all snow-free by mid- to late summer, snow can linger into June, so microspikes may be necessary. Check each trail's WTA page (www.wta.org) for the most up-to-date trail reports.

Snow Lake

Distance: *7.2 mi (11.6 km) round-trip*
Duration: *4 hours*
Elevation gain: *1,800 ft (550 m)*
Difficulty: *moderate*
Trailhead: *Snow Lake trailhead*

Snow Lake is a popular trailhead for hikers in the region, so get to the parking lot early. After a mile (1.6 km) of moderate climbing, the trail opens up to a talus slope from where you can see Chair Peak. You'll reach a viewpoint overlooking Snow Lake after another switchback ascent, which is a good place to catch your breath. From there, head down the trail to the lakeshore. You'll reach a lakeside inlet where you'll see Roosevelt Peak and an old cabin foundation. Chair Peak's cliffs and waterfalls, occasionally covered with lingering snow, provide picturesque views farther up the trail as it passes the lake's outlet.

Head east on I-90 and take exit 52 (Snoqualmie Pass West). Make a left turn, go north, and pass under the freeway, then take the second right and continue for 1.3 mi until you reach the end of the road, where you'll find the parking lot for the Alpental Ski Area. Cross the parking lot away from the ski area and you'll see a wooden sign for the Snow Lake trailhead.

Gold Creek Pond

Distance: *1 mi (1.6 km) round-trip*
Duration: *30 minutes*
Elevation gain: *10 ft (3 m)*
Difficulty: *easy*
Trailhead: *Gold Creek Pond parking lot*

Gold Creek Pond is one of the easiest hikes in the Snoqualmie Pass area, as the entire loop is almost flat and well-marked. In the summer, the trail is both stroller-friendly and ADA-accessible. Winter is an equally popular time to visit, as it's ideal for snowshoeing while getting a beautiful view of the lake. Many people take advantage of the picnic tables at the start of the trail to enjoy their lunch before going home.

Head east on I-90 and take exit 54, 2 mi (3 km) past the Snoqualmie Pass summit. Turn north and pass under the freeway. Shortly after, turn right onto Forest Road 4832 and continue for 1 mi (1.6 km). Make a left onto Gold Creek Road, and after 0.3 mi (0.5 km), turn left again onto a paved road that leads directly into the Gold Creek Pond parking lot.

Granite Mountain

Distance: 8.6 mi (13.8 km) round-trip
Duration: 5 hours
Elevation gain: 3,800 ft (1,150 m)
Difficulty: moderate/strenuous
Trailhead: Pratt Lake trailhead

Granite Mountain is a challenging hike, with a considerable elevation gain that makes it feel like you're constantly climbing. This isn't without adequate rewards, though—you'll pass through beautiful wildflower meadows and see bear grass in the summer as you make your way uphill. Granite Mountain Lookout sits at the top, which you can explore when it's staffed and open. Note that while this hike can be done in the winter, it passes a large avalanche chute, so it's critical to have the correct equipment and knowledge of how to navigate avalanche terrain.

Head east on I-90 and take exit 47. Turn left, going over the freeway, and at the T intersection, take another left and park at the Pratt Lake trailhead.

Food

All the food is grouped close together at the Pass, so make sure to stop here if you're hungry. Once you go beyond it, you won't find any food until you reach Cle Elum (about 30 mi/48 km east).

The Commonwealth

10 Pass Life Way #1; Snoqualmie; 425/434-0808; www.thepasslife.com; noon-8pm Sun. and Wed.-Thurs., noon-9pm Fri.-Sat.; $12-19

The Commonwealth is a short walk from Summit West and an ideal place to enjoy apres-ski with appetizers like cheese curds and entrées like burgers, sandwiches, and a kids' menu. They also have a full bar, and their long, shared tables give it a European feel where you can't help but chat with your neighbor about their day on the slopes.

Summit Pancake House and Lounge

603 Route 906, Snoqualmie; 425/434-6249; www.summitinnwashington.com; 7am-2pm Mon.-Thurs., 7am-8pm Fri.-Sat., 7am-7pm Sun.; $10-25

The Summit Pancake House is a classic place to eat, as skiers have been coming here for years for an early-morning breakfast before going across the street for a day of skiing. There's classic diner food such as eggs and pancakes, and lunch and dinner options such as burgers and sandwiches, and the place has a classic diner look to it.

Pie for the People NW

741 Route 906, Snoqualmie; 425/518-7799; Facebook @PieforthePeopleNW; 11am-8pm daily; $12-26

Located in the corner of a convenience store, Pie for the People NW is the place to go for a quick slice of New York-style pizza. There are a handful of plastic chairs and tables to sit at, so it's best when you want a cheap meal on the go.

Accommodations

Summit Inn

603 Route 906, Snoqualmie; 425/434-6300; www.summitinnwashington.com; $109-408

Summit Inn is just across the street from The Summit at Snoqualmie, so you can conveniently walk there instead of battling others for parking spots. The 82 rooms are simple but have queen and king bed options, and pet-friendly rooms are available upon request. Guests can enjoy a hot tub and sauna, and a full-service restaurant is next door for breakfast, lunch, and dinner.

Information
Snoqualmie Pass Visitor Center
69802 Route 906, Snoqualmie; 425/434-6111; www. fs.usda.gov; 8:30am-3:30pm Fri.-Sun.

Stop by the Snoqualmie Pass Visitor Center to get information about current conditions regarding skiing in the winter or hiking in the summer.

Edmonds

North of Seattle, Edmonds is a charming waterfront town that hundreds of people pass through each day on their way to the Edmonds-Kingston ferry, but it's worth a stop in itself. As you walk the streets of this historic town, you'll find dozens of locally owned restaurants, stores, and coffee shops, all with their own character. Although nightlife might not go late here, there are a handful of fun bars and wineries.

SIGHTS
Brackett's Landing
50 Railroad Ave.; 425/771-0230; https:// exploreedmonds.com; 6am-10pm daily; free

Brackett's Landing, one of the most-visited spots in town, has the Edmonds-Kingston ferry terminal splitting the north and south sections of the beach. The northern area has a famous underwater park, where scuba divers from all over the state explore the man-made reefs. The southern area is sandier and has a longer stretch to walk along the beach. At low-tide times, you can walk under the ferry dock and spot all kinds of starfish and sea anemones.

Transportation
From Seattle, head east on I-90 for about 52 mi (84 km) to get to Snoqualmie Pass, which takes about 1 hour. Exits 52-54 lead to different parts of the mountain. If you don't have a car, **To The Mountain Shuttle** (206/886-8879; https://tothemountain shuttle.com; $75/person round-trip) makes one daily run that stops in various locations in Seattle, Bellevue, Issaquah, and North Bend before stopping at all four ski areas at Snoqualmie.

Edmonds Museum Summer Market
5th Ave. N. and Bell St.; Facebook @edmondsmuseumsummermarket; 9am-2pm Sat. early May-mid-Oct.; free

Summer Saturdays in Edmonds are bustling with people supporting small businesses by shopping at the famers market, officially the Edmonds Museum Summer Market, where all the vendors make or grow their own items and produce. Over 90 vendors are found here, including those selling fresh fruit and vegetables, honey, popcorn, jewelry, and more.

Edmonds Historical Museum
118 5th Ave. N.; 425/774-0900; https://historicedmonds. org; 1pm-4pm Thurs.-Sat.; $5 adult, $2 student

Founded in 1973 and run by volunteers, the Edmonds Historical Museum is housed in the historic 1910 Carnegie library building and has hundreds of photographs and artifacts of what life used to be like in Edmonds. You'll find an original jail cell, a train room showing how the railroad played a huge part in the town's development, and a Victorian parlor with authentic furniture.

Weekend Getaway: Suncadia Resort

Suncadia Resort

Locals looking for a weekend getaway frequently turn toward **Suncadia Resort** (3600 Suncadia Trail, Cle Elum; 877/220-1438; www.destinationhotels.com; $238-940). Located just east of Snoqualmie Pass, the stunning complex boasts more than 250 rooms spread out across the lodge, inn, and vacation rentals, plus 6,000 acres (2,400 ha) of woodland; guests can easily go hiking, cross-country skiing, or biking.

Suncadia also offers two championship golf courses, indoor and outdoor pools, a sauna, a fitness courses, and personal trainers. Massages, facials, and manicures are just a few of the treatments available at Glade Spring Spa. The resort's abundance of on-site dining options (including bars, coffee shops, and restaurants) makes spending the whole vacation there easy.

Nearby towns of **Roslyn** and **Cle Elum** offer easy excursions, perfect for rounding out your visit. Roslyn was the backdrop for the hit '90s TV series *Northern Exposure* and has a couple of historical musuems for those wanting to dive into Washington's history. Cle Elum is well-known as a destination for outdoor activities, including hikes like the Iron Bear-Teanaway Ridge (6.5 mi/10.5 km round-trip) and fishing on the nearby lakes. Both offer historic downtowns with shops and restaurants—the cherry on top of a weekend getaway.

To get here from Seattle, take I-90 east for about 1.5 hours (83 mi/134 km) to exit 80.

Edmonds City Park

600 3rd Ave. S.; 425/771-0230; www.edmondswa.gov;
7am-9:30pm daily; free

Edmonds City Park hosts a number of events throughout the year, including baseball games in the spring and live musical performances on its outdoor stage. There's also a large playground, a seasonal spray park (Memorial Day-Labor Day), and numerous picnic shelters with grills available for rent.

RECREATION
Hiking
Meadowdale Beach Park

Distance: *2.5 mi (4 km) round-trip*
Duration: *1 hour*
Elevation gain: *425 ft (130 m)*
Difficulty: *easy*
Trailhead: *parking lot at Meadowdale Beach Park (6026 156th St. SW)*

Only 15 minutes north of downtown

Bird-Watching

belted kingfisher

With an estimated 190 bird species passing through Edmonds every year, it is truly a birdwatcher's paradise. You might see the western grebe, Brant goose, bald eagle, great blue heron, and belted kingfisher.

The best time to see birds is **first thing in the morning,** shortly after sunrise, because that's when they start their day. Noon tends to be the least active, then the birds pick up again in the late afternoon and early evening before they settle down for the night. While you can bird-watch throughout the year, **April and May** tend to be the peak seasons.

Bird-watching along the waterfront piers in Edmonds if always a good bet, but here are a few other noteworthy places:

- **Edmonds Marsh** (180 W. Dayton St.) is the most popular. In this 22-acre (9-ha) urban salt-water estuary, you can walk along the boardwalk and observe birds in a quiet setting. Signs along the way let you learn more about the area.

- **Yost Memorial Park** (9535 Bowdoin Way) has easy walking trails that go through one of the only native forests left in the city, and you'll see red alder, western red cedar, and more here. There's also a small playground and a seasonal outdoor pool.

- **Pine Ridge Park** (20330 83rd Ave. W.) is a small forested park with two main out-and-back trails with several small trails branching off them to explore. At the end of each trail, you can either continue walking in a neighborhood or head back the way you came. You'll see plenty of people bird-watching here in the morning, young families walking along the paths, and maybe the native duck family that lives on the small pond.

Edmonds in Meadowdale Beach Park, this hike is nice any time of the year, and it goes through a lush forest and follows a river out to the ocean. A large staircase makes the steepest part of this hike more manageable and easier for families. It's all downhill from the parking lot until you get to the beach, where you'll want to walk around and have a snack break before starting the ascent back up. The parking lot is small; alternative parking is in select spots in the nearby neighborhoods.

1: Brackett's Landing **2:** lobster roll at MARKET

Scuba Diving

Edmonds Underwater Park

Brackett's Landing North, 50 Railroad Ave.; 6am-10pm daily

Established in 1970, Edmonds Underwater Park is a popular 27-acre (11-ha) diving area beside the Edmonds-Kingston Ferry Landing. Renowned as Washington's best underwater park, it draws 25,000 scuba divers yearly to its array of human-made reefs and sunken vessels, interconnected by guide ropes for easy navigation, including the notable 325-ft (100-m) De Lion Dry Dock. The park has restrooms and an outdoor shower.

Underwater Sports

264 Railroad Ave.; 425/771-6322; www. underwatersports.com; 10am-6pm Wed.-Fri., 9am-5pm Sat.-Sun.; various equipment rentals $6-10/day, scuba package $75/day

Located only a few blocks from the Underwater Park, Underwater Sports is the most convenient place to rent any equipment you need. They also offer various scuba classes with friendly instructors, whether you're brand-new or want to add a certification to your skills, such as Enriched Air Nitrox (from $199 pp).

FOOD

Walnut Street Coffee

410 Walnut St.; 425/774-5962; https:// walnutstreetcoffee.com; 6am-6pm Mon.-Fri, 7am-6pm Sat.-Sun.; $4-12

There's always a line of locals waiting to get their morning coffee at Walnut Street Coffee, thanks to the friendly baristas and an inviting atmosphere. They serve a variety of pastries and breakfast burritos sourced from local vendors in a cozy setting with couches, tables, and an outdoor area.

MARKET

508 Main St.; 425/361-4459; www.marketfreshfish. com; 11am-7pm Sun.-Thurs., 11am-8pm Fri.-Sat.; $21-34

You won't get fresher seafood in Edmonds than at MARKET, which regularly sells out of lobster rolls, fish and chips, and chowder.

Order at the window and then grab one of the outdoor tables, which are heated during the winter, and enjoy people-watching in one of the main parts of town.

Salish Sea Brewing

518 Dayton St. #104; 425/582-8474; http:// salishbrewing.com; 11am-10pm daily; $13-17

Salish Sea Brewing is a casual, family-friendly brewpub that makes their own beer, with popular options like the light Honey Golden Ale or hoppy Drop Anchor IPA. They have a good variety of food on their menu, from salads to street tacos to flatbreads, and they always have the latest sports game on TV.

Demetris

101 Main St.; 425/744-9999; www. demetriswoodstonetaverna.com; 11am-9pm Mon.-Thurs., 10am-10pm Fri.-Sat., 11am-9pm Sun.; $14-24

Demetris is thought to have the best view in Edmonds, as you can see the waterfront and ferry from any table in the restaurant, and the train goes right by. They mainly serve tapas, so order a few to split with your party, perhaps flatbread cooked in their woodstone oven, spicy firecracker shrimp, or baked brie.

INFORMATION

Visit the **Explore Edmonds** website (https:// exploreedmonds.com) to learn more about where to eat and what to do.

TRANSPORTATION

Edmonds is about 17 mi (27 km) north of Seattle, about 30 minutes without traffic via I-5.

You can take the E line **bus** from downtown Seattle to the Shoreline Transit Center and then transfer to bus 130 into Edmonds, which will take about 1.5 hours. Buy tickets when you board, and see the schedule online (https://kingcounty.gov). The **Amtrak** train (www.amtrak.com) also has a stop in Edmonds (211 Railroad Ave.), but there are only a few trains per day.

If you're traveling from Edmonds to the

Olympic Peninsula, take the Edmonds-Kingston **ferry** across the water. Ferries run approximately 5:30am-midnight, around every 40 minutes. However, this ferry is first-come, first-served, and lines can be several hours long in the summer if taking your car, so arriving early in the morning is best. The crossing time is 30 minutes and costs $17.50/vehicle and driver and $9.85/passenger.

Whidbey Island

Whidbey Island, the longest in Washington, is nearly 40 mi (64 km) long and beckons with its captivating blend of natural beauty and charming small towns. It feels like a world away from the city as you explore scenic hikes, rolling farmland, and local food.

The island is divided into three distinct sections, each offering its own allure. On the southern end, Langley is the main town, full of boutique shops, wineries, and restaurants. Coupeville and Ebey's Landing Reserve are in the middle and hold most of the island's historic attractions, such as Fort Casey. Oak Harbor is on the northern part of the island, and while it has many chain restaurants and hotels, it's not often a place people stay on a trip since it lacks the charm of the rest of the island. The main draw in this area is Deception Pass State Park north of Oak Harbor.

TRANSPORTATION
Getting There
The best way to experience the full island is to take the Mukilteo-Clinton ferry to the **Clinton Ferry Terminal** (64 S. Ferry Dock Rd.) at the south end of the island, drive up the length to Deception Pass, and take I-5 south back to do a complete loop.

Ferry
The **Mukilteo Ferry Terminal** (910 First St., Mukilteo) is the departure point for those traveling from Mukilteo, and the most popular ferry to take if coming from Seattle. Boats depart for the south end of Whidbey Island to the town of Clinton around 5am-1am about every 30 minutes daily. The ferry crossing takes approximately 20 minutes. Find the ferry schedule online (https://wsdot.com), and purchase tickets in person at the ferry booth ($10.50/vehicle and driver, $6/passenger or walk-on passenger). It's first-come, first-served, so you'll want to get in line early on the weekends or during the summer.

The **Port Townsend Ferry Terminal** (1301 Water St., Port Townsend) is another option if you're coming from the Olympic Peninsula. A boat departs for Coupeville, located on Whidbey Island's west side, less frequently than the Mukilteo ferry, every 2.5 hours roughly 6:30am-10pm. The ferry crossing takes approximately 35 minutes. A reservation is highly recommended on this ferry, especially since it's less frequent. Note that ferry crossings may be canceled in the winter due to high wind or when the tide is too low, so check the schedule for cancellations on the website (https://wsdot.com) before going. The fare is $10.50/vehicle and driver, $6/passenger or walk-on passenger.

Car
To access the island's southern end from Mukilteo, take Route 525 north, which ends at the ferry terminal. The drive from Seattle takes about 35 minutes (26 mi/42 km). To get to the island's north end, follow Route 20 west from Burlington; it takes about 1.5 hours (83 mi/134 km) from Seattle.

Getting Around
Bringing your own car on the ferry is advisable to explore the island, as many parts are spread out. Route 525 is the main road that

Whidbey Island

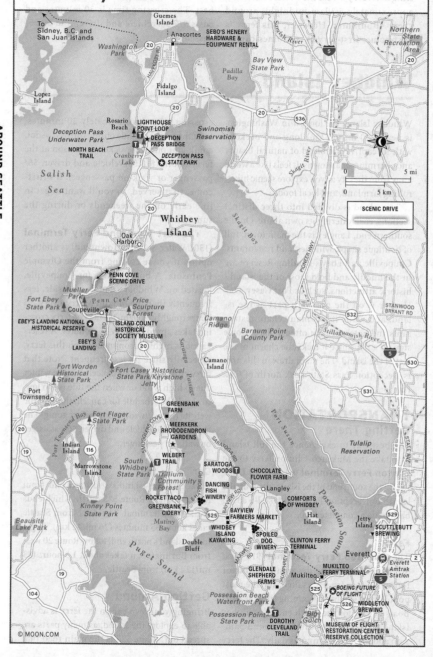

To Sidney, B.C. and San Juan Islands

Guemes Island

Anacortes

SEBO'S HENERY HARDWARE & EQUIPMENT RENTAL

Washington Park

Padilla Bay

Bay View State Park

Northern State Recreation Area

Fidalgo Island

Lopez Island

Rosario Beach

LIGHTHOUSE POINT LOOP

Deception Pass Underwater Park

DECEPTION PASS BRIDGE

NORTH BEACH TRAIL

Cranberry Lake

DECEPTION PASS STATE PARK

Salish Sea

Swinomish Reservation

Skagit River

Samish River

Whidbey Island

Skagit Bay

SCENIC DRIVE

Oak Harbor

PENN COVE SCENIC DRIVE

Mueller Park

Fort Ebey State Park

Penn Cove

Price Sculpture Forest

Coupeville

EBEY'S LANDING NATIONAL HISTORICAL RESERVE

ISLAND COUNTY HISTORICAL SOCIETY MUSEUM

EBEY'S LANDING

Fort Worden Historical State Park

Port Townsend

Fort Casey Historical State Park/Keystone Jetty

Fort Flager State Park

Port Townsend Bay

Indian Island

Marrowstone Island

GREENBANK FARM

MEERKERK RHODODENDRON GARDENS

WILBERT TRAIL

South Whidbey State Park

Trillium Community Forest

SARATOGA WOODS

CHOCOLATE FLOWER FARM

Langley

DANCING FISH WINERY

ROCKET TACO

GREENBANK CIDERY

Kinney Point State Park

Mutiny Bay

BAYVIEW FARMERS MARKET

COMFORTS OF WHIDBEY

Hat Island

WHIDBEY ISLAND KAYAKING

SPOILED DOG WINERY

Beausite Lake Park

Double Bluff

Puget Sound

GLENDALE SHEPHERD FARMS

CLINTON FERRY TERMINAL

Everett

Jetty Island

SCUTTLEBUTT BREWING

Everett Amtrak Station

MUKILTEO FERRY TERMINAL

Mukilteo

BOEING FUTURE OF FLIGHT

Possession Beach Waterfront Park

Possession Point State Park

DOROTHY CLEVELAND TRAIL

Big Gulch

MIDDLETON BREWING

MUSEUM OF FLIGHT RESTORATION CENTER & RESERVE COLLECTION

Camano Ridge

Barnum Point County Park

Camano Island

Saratoga Passage

Port Susan

Tulalip Reservation

Stillaguamish River

Stanwood Bryant Rd

© MOON.COM

starts at the Coupeville ferry terminal and turns into Route 20 halfway across the island.

Island Transit (360/678-7771; www. islandtransit.org) has stops from Clinton to Deception Pass, but they're mainly along Route 525 and Route 20, so you'll miss many major sights on the island if you use only the bus.

LANGLEY AND SOUTHERN WHIDBEY

Southern Whidbey is the most convenient area to visit on a day trip. As you arrive from the ferry, you'll be in the small town of Clinton, which has a few restaurants and stores but not much else.

Langley has become one of the most popular places on the island. Only 7 mi (11 km) from the Clinton ferry landing, this charming area is full of local boutiques and delicious restaurants. It also provides scenic views of Saratoga Passage, where lucky visitors can sometimes spot whales passing through.

Nearby towns of Bayview and Freeland have shops and restaurants for those looking to explore further.

Sights
Langley Whale Center
105 Anthes Ave., Langley; 360/221-7505; www. orcanetwork.org; 11am-4pm Wed.-Sun.; free

This small museum in downtown Langley has exhibits on the whales that pass through the waters of Whidbey Island. You'll learn about both transient and native whales in the area.

Meerkerk Rhododendron Gardens
3531 Meerkerk Ln., Greenbank; 360/678-1912; www. meerkerkgardens.org; 9am-4pm daily; $5, under 16 free

Meerkerk Gardens is one of the more serene places to visit on the island, with 10 acres (4 ha) of display gardens and 43 acres (17 ha) of woodlands with nature trails to explore. April and May are the showiest months, as the gardens are in full bloom, but it's nice anytime. Gardeners will want to check out their nursery to purchase plants to take home, and kids can

stop at the front desk to get a scavenger hunt sheet to make the visit interactive.

Farms
Many of these farms dotting the area are open to visitors, but it's best to call ahead to confirm before you come, particularly during the off-season.

Glendale Shepherd Farms
7616 Glendale Heights Rd., Clinton; 360/593-9935; www.glendaleshepherd.com; 11am-4pm Thurs.-Sun.; free, tours $20

Glendale Shepherd has been in the family for three generations and is known as the place to go for pasture-raised lamb and sheep's milk cheese and yogurt. They're happy to show visitors how their farm works on tours.

Chocolate Flower Farm
5040 Saratoga Rd., Langley; 360/221-2464; www. chocolateflowerfarm.com; 10am-5pm daily; free

Chocolate may not be what you think of when you hear the term "farm," but this nursery grows and sells a variety of flowers that smell like chocolate, including chocolate cosmo plants. Grab a packet of seeds so you can grow your own. The farmstore has an extensive collection of all things chocolate, including body products, candles, jam, and much more.

Greenbank Farm
765 Wonn Rd., Greenbank; 360/222-3797; https:// portoc.org; 11am-5pm daily; free

Greenbank Farm has been around since 1904 and back in the day was the biggest grower of loganberries. It's since expanded from working farms to a café specializing in pies and several specialty shops, on a large property with dog-friendly walking paths. Many people also come for bird-watching; look for herons, eagles, and others.

Wineries and Cideries
Whidbey Island's vineyards are the sole wine-growing area west of the Cascade Mountains in Washington. You'll find variety among

the dozen wineries and wine-tasting shops throughout the island. Cideries are also starting to expand here.

Spoiled Dog Winery

5881 Maxwelton Rd., Langley; 360/661-6226; www. spoileddogwinery.com; 2pm-5pm Fri., noon-5pm Sat.-Sun.; tasting $10

At Spoiled Dog, not only will you be greeted by a cute Australian shepherd, but you'll also have a chance to try their Pinot Noir and chocolate and crackers for a delectable pairing. Sip your wine outside under a heated gazebo and enjoy views of the vineyard.

Comforts of Whidbey

5219 View Rd., Langley; 360/969-2961; www. comfortsofwhidbey.com; 2pm-6pm Fri., noon-6pm Sat.-Sun.; tasting $15

Part winery, part bed-and-breakfast, this beautiful building overlooks the waterfront and has a spacious covered deck for relaxing with wines like Madeleine Angevine and Siegerrebe. There's live music on Sunday afternoons, or you can volunteer to help pick the grape harvest mid-September.

Dancing Fish Winery

1953 Newman Rd., Freeland; 360/632-4190; www. dancingfishvineyards.com; 3pm-6pm Mon., Thurs., noon-7pm Fri.-Sat., noon-6pm Sun.; tasting $15

Indulge at Dancing Fish Vineyards by taking a leisurely stroll around the picturesque grounds, enjoying a game of bocce ball, or relaxing in the tasting room with their delicious rosé or syrah. Thursday nights feature live music.

Greenbank Cidery

5488 S. Freeland Ave., Freeland; 360/627-0382; www. greenbankcidery.com; 3pm-8pm Wed., 3pm-9pm Thurs., noon-9pm Fri.-Sat., noon-8pm Sun.

Greenbank Cidery has a welcoming atmosphere, with its small indoor tasting room and large outdoor area with tables, chairs, lawn games, and a food truck selling hot dogs. And there's about a dozen different ciders to try.

Beaches
Double Bluff

6378 S. Double Bluff Rd., Freeland

When the tide is out at Double Bluff, you can walk the sandy beach for miles. This is also an off-leash park, so you'll find dozens of dogs happily running around.

Hiking
Saratoga Woods

Distance: 5.3 mi (8.5 km) round-trip
Duration: 2.5 hours
Elevation gain: 488 ft (149 m)
Difficulty: easy
Trailhead: 4246 E. Saratoga Rd.

Saratoga Woods is a network of trails, so you can easily make a long or short hike. Loops start at 0.5 mi (0.8 km) long, or the whole perimeter of the property is over 5 mi (8 km). It's a relaxing, heavily forested area, and you'll often find locals walking their dogs here.

Dorothy Cleveland Trail

Distance: 1.1 mi (1.7 km) round-trip
Duration: 1 hour
Elevation gain: 392 ft (119 m)
Difficulty: easy
Trailhead: 8212 Possession Rd., Point Possession Waterfront Park, Clinton

Although this is a shorter hike, you'll gain a good amount of elevation via switchbacks, but your hard work will pay off at the top. Rest here to enjoy views of Puget Sound and possibly even see whales, depending on the time of year.

Wilbert Trail

Distance: 0.8 mi (1.3 km) round-trip
Duration: 30 minutes
Elevation gain: 140 ft (43 m)
Difficulty: easy
Trailhead: South Whidbey State Park

South Whidbey State Park is another network of trails, from short and easy to the full 3.5 mi (5.6 km). The Wilbert Trail takes you through the forest, while others go along the shoreline for a view of Admiralty Inlet. This area is popular with young children, who love taking their time exploring big-leaf maple trees or Douglas firs.

From Clinton, head north on Route 525 for 10 mi (16 km), and turn left onto E. Bush Point Road; at 2 mi (3 km) it turns into Smugglers Cove Road, which you'll follow for 2.5 mi (4 km). Turn left onto Park Road, where you'll see several large parking lots.

Kayaking

The waters of Whidbey Island are sheltered from large waves by Camano Island and the Olympic Peninsula, making it an ideal place to kayak. The only open, and therefore rougher, waters are by Deception Pass. Beginners can stay near the coastline for an easy activity, while advanced kayakers with knowledge of the changing tides and currents can venture out further. There's a high chance you'll see sealife such as harbor seals, and bald eagles are also common in the area.

Possession Beach Waterfront Park

8212 Possession Rd., Clinton; https:// portofsouthwhidbey.com; dawn-dusk

With beach access and a boat launch, Possession Beach is one of the most accessible places to go kayaking. You'll have views of the Clinton-Mukilteo ferry passing by to the north and see larger boats navigating Puget Sound to the south.

Mutiny Bay

Mutiny Bay Boat Launch, 6000 Robinson Rd., Freeland

Head 8 mi (13 km) west of Langely to Freeland to an area that's less crowded but still lets you experience kayaking in Puget Sound. There's a small area for street parking right next to the beach, and you can follow the coast north to explore Mutiny Bay. Advanced kayakers can go all the way up to Bush Point Lighthouse.

Whidbey Island Kayaking

5781 Bayview Rd., Langley; 360/221-0229; www. whidbeyislandkayaking.com; 9am-6pm daily; rentals $55-120, classes $135-400, tours $140-200

Get out on the water with Whidbey Island Kayaking, who can deliver all your gear to

your launch point—everything from single and tandem kayaks to stand-up paddleboards. However, they stress that rentals are for experienced kayakers, so joining one of their kayaking classes is a better option for beginners. You also can join a 4- or 7-hour tour and see the best of Whidbey's coastline with an experienced guide.

Festivals and Events

Bayview Farmers Market

Route 525 and Bayview Rd.; www. bayviewfarmersmarket.com; 10am-2pm Sat. Apr.-Oct

The Bayview Farmers Market is a fun way to spend a Saturday morning, as you can get lunch from a local vendor, listen to live music, and shop. There's an impressive variety of vendors, from fresh-baked bread and pastries to local produce and fresh-cut flowers, and plenty of artists selling their crafts.

Whidbey Island Fair

819 Camano Ave., Langley; 360/221-7950; www. whidbeyislandfair.com; last weekend of July; $12 adult, $6 child, under 5 free

People wait all summer to attend the Whidbey Island Fair, a fun weekend jam-packed with activities to do. You can walk through the barns to see farm animals, see dogs run obstacle courses, and watch various horse shows. They also have classic fair rides for the kids, plenty of fair food, and live music throughout the weekend.

DjangoFest NW

565 Camano Ave., Langley; 360/221-8268; www. djangofest.com; typically last weekend of Sept.; $25-50

Gypsy jazz, as popularized by Django Reinhardt, is the focus of the acclaimed DjangoFest celebration. Attracting Gypsy jazz artists and enthusiasts from all over the globe, this yearly event has ticketed and free performances, workshops, and jam sessions.

Shopping

Sweet Mona's Chocolates

221 2nd St., Ste. 16, Langley; 360/221-5222; https:// sweetmonas.com; 10am-5pm daily

Indulge your sweet tooth at Sweet Mona's, the island's go-to for all things chocolate and dessert. You'll find something for everyone, with toffee, caramels, fudge, chocolate-covered lollipops, and more.

The Star Store

201 First St., Langley; 360/221-5222; www. starstorewhidbey.com; 8am-7pm Mon.-Sat., 8am-6pm Sun.

The Star Store serves as both the downtown area's grocery store and a gift shop. You can stock up on produce, wine, snacks, and frozen meals and then head to the other side of the store for all your clothing needs.

Fair Trade Outfitters

112 Anthes Ave., Langley; 360/221-1696; Facebook @FairTradeOutfitters; 10am-6pm daily

Fair Trade Outfitters specializes in fair-trade items, meaning anyone involved in making the products in this store works in a safe and fair environment. You'll find a variety of women's apparel, including shirts, pants, dresses, jewelry, and home decor and accessories.

Food

Most of the restaurants are centered in Langley, but you can find a handful scattered around Bayview and Freeland as well.

Village Pizzeria

106 1st St., Langley; 360/221-3363; www. villagepizzerialangley.com; noon-7pm Thurs.-Mon.; $20-31

Locals have been coming to Village Pizzeria since 1979 to chow down on New York-style pizza and pasta and enjoy a drink from the full bar. Get here early on the weekend and snag an outdoor table for a picturesque waterfront view.

Taproom @ Bayview

5603 Bayview Rd. Langley; 360/222-2643; https:// taproombayviewcorner.com; noon-9pm Thurs.-Tues., 2pm-8pm Wed.; $14-27

Beer lovers, the Taproom has a dozen local beers on tap that are constantly changing. The left side of the full-service restaurant is an all-ages area with food options such as pub nachos and shrimp tacos and has occasional live music, while the right side is a 21-and-over bar.

Saltwater Fish House & Oyster Bar

113 1st St., Langley; 360/221-5474; http:// saltwaterlangley.com; noon-8:30pm Sun.-Mon. and

Ultra House

Thurs., 3pm-8:30pm Tues.-Wed., noon-9pm Fri.-Sat.;
$16-37

When craving seafood, head to Saltwater Fish House and Oyster Bar for dozens of options. Fresh oysters on the shell is a popular choice, as is the Maine lobster roll, complemented with a large selection of wine and beer. The restaurant is cozy but small, so get there early for a table or sit at the bar for service.

Ultra House

221 2nd St. #9A, Langley; 360/221-4959; https:// ultrahouse.us; 11:30am-3pm, 4:30pm-7:30pm Sun.- Thurs., 11:30am-3pm, 4:30pm-8:30pm Fri.-Sat.; $7-17

Tucked back in the shops of Langley Village is Ultra House, where you'll be served a giant portion of steaming Japanese ramen. They have various proteins, including beef, chicken, seafood, and tofu, as well as imported Japanese beer, sake, and snacks to take home.

Rocket Taco

1594 E. Main St., Freeland; 360/331-0760; https:// rocket-taco.com; 11:30am-7pm Tues.-Sun.; $11-14

Rocket Taco specializes in delicious street tacos with a variety of fillings, including chorizo potato, sweet potato black bean, and fish. In the warmer weather, head to the back to enjoy your meal on the outdoor patio and then enjoy free lawn games.

Accommodations

While the southern part of Whidbey may lack hotels, it makes up for it with dozens of vacation rental options through Airbnb or VRBO.

Saratoga Inn

201 Cascade Ave., Langley; 360/221-5801; www. saratogainnlangley.com; $160-275

At the edge of downtown, Saratoga Inn is a beautiful 16-room hotel with a waterfront view. It's private and intimate, and guests will enjoy a vegetarian breakfast each morning before heading out into the town.

Comforts of Whidbey

5219 View Rd., Langley; 360/969-2961; www. comfortsofwhidbey.com; $195-295

If you prefer to stay in a more remote area, book one of the six rooms at Comforts of Whidbey, where you'll be surrounded by a working farm and vineyard and have access to the winery. Their spacious covered deck is a relaxing place to have coffee and watch the sun rise as you start the day.

Information

Langley Chamber of Commerce & Visitor Center

208 Anthes Ave., Langley; 360/221-6765; https:// visitlangley.com; 11am-4pm Tues.-Sat.

Visit the visitor center to get maps of the area and hear about current activities happening.

WhidbeyHealth Medical Center

101 N. Main St., Coupeville; 360/678-5151; https:// whidbeyhealth.org

WhidbeyHealth has 24-hour care, a birth center, and a variety of inpatient and outpatient services.

Transportation

The southern end of Whidbey Island is best reached by the **Mukilteo-Clinton ferry** (https://wsdot.com). Once on the island, everything is best reached by car. From Clinton, it's a 10-minute (6 mi/10 km) drive via Route 525 and Langley Loop.

Island Transit (360/678-7771; www. islandtransit.org) stops along Route 525, with stops in Freeland and Bayview.

COUPEVILLE AND CENTRAL WHIDBEY

Coupeville is one of Washington's oldest towns, established in 1852 and named after Captain Thomas Coup. Its advantageous waterfront location made it an important trading post, and it quickly became home to numerous farmers and sea captains. Maritime and pioneer history are echoed along the town's historic waterfront, which is bordered by structures dating back to the late 19th century.

Situated in the middle of Whidbey Island, Coupeville is an ideal location if you plan on exploring the historic areas or want a good

Preserving Washington's Forts

Fort Casey Historical State Park

Washington's many forts were significant in the political, military, and economic growth of the state and the surrounding region. These historic locations have been carefully restored over the years, becoming educational spaces where people can learn more about the significance of Washington's military past.

There were about 30 forts in Washington, although only about a dozen are still standing and welcome visitors. Forts are typically free to walk around, and you can often pick up a map to do a self-guided tour. Guided tours may be available in the summer at some of the more popular forts. You can walk around the outside of historic buildings, and some have a museum housed inside one of these structures. The following list comprises some of the most notable forts in the state:

base for exploring the whole of the island. It's the main town in the central part of Whidbey and has a downtown full of restaurants and shops.

Sights
Penn Cove Scenic Drive
Historic Coupeville sits on the southern bank of Penn Cove, and the picturesque Penn Cove Scenic Drive winds its way 20 mi (32 km) north to the island's major settlement, Oak Harbor. You'll pass by stunning vistas on this scenic half-hour tour. As you leave Coupeville on Main Street, travel north toward Front Street onto Madrona Way. Route 20 will lead you along the cove's shore, providing picture-worthy views.

Island County Historical Society Museum
908 NW Alexander St.; 360/678-3310; www. islandhistory.org; 10am-4pm Tues.-Sat., 11am-4pm Sun.; donation

Whidbey Island has a fascinating history, and the Island County Historical Society Museum has worked hard over the years to preserve artifacts from long ago. You'll see dugout canoes from Coast Salish tribes, learn about the early European exploration and settlement of the island, and see how it came to be what it is now.

★ Ebey's Landing National Historical Reserve
162 Cemetery Rd.; 360/678-6084; www.nps.gov; 9am-4pm Mon.-Fri.; free

WHIDBEY ISLAND

- **Fort Casey Historical State Park** (1280 Engle Rd., Coupeville; https://parks.state.wa.us) is a part of the "Triangle of Fire" (along with Fort Worden and Fort Flager), a trio of forts designed to defend Puget Sound. It offers stunning views, historic gun batteries, and the Admiralty Head Lighthouse.

OLYMPIC PENINSULA

- **Fort Worden Historical State Park** (200 Battery Way, Port Townsend; https://parks.state.wa.us) features over 100 historic structures and provides a wide array of recreational opportunities alongside its historical exhibits.

- **Fort Flagler State Park** (10541 Flagler Rd., Nordland; https://parks.state.wa.us) offers historical tours of gun emplacements, barracks, and stunning Puget Sound views as another part of the Triangle of Fire.

VANCOUVER

- **Fort Vancouver National Historic Site** (1501 E. Evergreen Blvd., Vancouver; www.nps.gov) offers a glimpse into the 19th-century fur trading industry and early Pacific Northwest settlement. It has a reconstructed fort, a visitor center, and a museum.

WALLA WALLA

- **Fort Walla Walla Museum** (755 Myra Rd., Walla Walla; www.fortwallawallamuseum.org) may not be a traditional military fort, but Fort Walla Walla Museum is significant for its exhibitions on the military, Native American, and pioneer history of the Walla Walla Valley.

Covering an expansive 27 sq mi (70 sq km), Ebey's Landing is a fascinating combination of natural beauty and historical significance, a living museum of agricultural life in the 19th century. The area was named for Isaac Ebey, an early settler of the island. Immerse yourself in the past and present at this site, where you can see well-preserved buildings and farms, trek along beautiful trails, and see the area's long-standing farming techniques.

Fort Ebey State Park

400 Hill Valley Dr.; 360/678-4636; https://parks.wa.gov; 8am-dusk daily; $10 Discover Pass

The underground chambers and gun emplacements of Fort Ebey State Park date back to the 1940s and are sure to captivate history buffs. At low tide, you can stroll along the beach, and a vast system of bike and walking paths winds through wooded regions and along the cliff.

Fort Casey Historical State Park

1280 Engle Rd.; 360/678-4519; https://parks.wa.gov; 8am-dusk daily; $10 Discover Pass

One of the most famous historical sites to visit in the state is Fort Casey. Built in the late 1800s, it served as a piece of the "Triangle of Fire," a network of fortifications meant to guard the entrance to Puget Sound. The fort, founded in honor of Brigadier General Thomas Lincoln Casey, was an important coastal defense position throughout both

World Wars. Guests can wander through the underground bunkers and antique gun batteries, as well as hike along the bluff, gaining incredible views of the Olympic Mountains and Puget Sound. One of the park's most important landmarks, the Admiralty Head Lighthouse, shows visitors the region's maritime past, and tours are available when the lighthouse is open.

Price Sculpture Forest

678 Parker Rd., Coupeville; https://sculptureforest.org; 8am-7pm daily; free

One of the most unique places to hike on the island is at Price Sculpture Forest, where you'll walk through a short, 0.6-mi (0.9 km) forested loop trail of sculptures of all kinds from local artists. Kids will love going on a mini scavenger hunt here, and you can download the app from their website to hear the artists talk about their pieces to make them come to life even more. There are two loops to choose from – one starts from the parking lot and is mainly flat, and you can add on the second loop with a bit more elevation gain if you want to keep exploring.

Kayaking
Mueller Park

2099-2081 Madrona Way; https://wdfw.wa.gov

The beach access at Mueller Park is an ideal place to launch a kayak. In the calm waters of Penn Cove, you can stay along the shoreline or go deeper out into the water depending on your experience. You're also right next to Captain Whidbey if you want to get a bite to eat after.

Wharf Dog Paddle and Pantry

24 Front St. NW; 360/969-0737; Instagram (@wharfdogpaddle; 11am-5pm Mon.-Tues. and Thurs., 10am-7pm Fri.-Sun.; $25/hour single, $35/hour double

Rent a single or double kayak and launch from Coupeville Wharf to see the historic town from a different viewpoint. It's a peaceful way to spend the morning, with coffee from a nearby shop after.

Diving

Keystone Jetty, or Fort Casey Underwater State Park, is a famous diving site with a wide variety of marine life and intriguing underwater structures such as human-made reefs. However, diving here requires careful planning and safety measures. In order to dive safely in these waters, divers need to schedule their dives around slack tide times, as the currents can be strong and unpredictable.

Due to the ever-changing weather and seasons, as well as the frigid water temperatures, divers need to wear drysuits or thick wetsuits at all times. These challenges make the site suited for more experienced divers.

Fort Casey Underwater State Park/Keystone Jetty

1280 Engle Rd.; 360/678-4519; https://parks.wa.gov; 8am-dusk daily; Discover Pass $10

The brilliant anemones, colorful sea stars, and diverse fish species that call Keystone home provide a spectacular underwater scene that divers can't get enough of. A wide variety of marine life flourishes in the unusual aquatic habitat that abandoned dock pilings provide. The site's wealth of marine life results from its closeness to Admiralty Inlet, making it a dynamic and ever-changing undersea habitat.

Hiking
Ebey's Landing

Distance: *5.6 mi (9 km) round-trip*
Duration: *2.5 hours*
Elevation gain: *260 ft (79 m)*
Difficulty: *easy/moderate*
Trailhead: *Prairie Overlook trailhead*

Where this trail switches from gravel to rough coastal terrain is one of the best views on the entire hike, as you'll be walking along a narrow trail on top of a cliff looking out across the water to the Olympic Peninsula. Follow the loop to go into the woods and end up where you started.

From Coupeville, take a left onto S. Ebey

1: Ebey's Landing National Historical Reserve
2: sculpture by artist Joe Treat in the Price Sculpture Forest

Road and drive about 1.7 mi (2.7 km). You'll come to a sharp right bend, followed by a tight left hairpin curve. As you navigate the hairpin, turn to the left; the trailhead is on the right side. You'll need to display a Discover Pass to park in this area.

Festivals and Events
Musselfest
downtown Coupeville; 360/682-6400; www. coupevillehistoricwaterfront.com; early Mar.; $10-40
Mussel lovers flock to downtown Coupeville each year to see which local restaurant serves the best chowder, as about a dozen are giving out tastings with their unique spin on it, which the crowd then votes on. There's plenty of entertainment as well, including a beer garden with live music and a scavenger hunt for kids.

Whidbey Island Cider Festival
180 Parker Rd.; 360/678-5586; www. whidbeyislandciderfestival.com; late Sept.; $40
While Whidbey is known for its wine, it also does cider well, which is shown off at the annual Whidbey Island Cider Festival. There's a vairety of ciders, beers, and meads to choose from, in addition to nonalcoholic drinks. The festival is complemented by local food, lively music, and activities for kids.

Shopping
A Touch of Dutch European Market
11 Front St. NW #1395; 360/678-7729; ww.atouchofdutch.com; 9am-7pm daily
If you're craving a snack from Sweden, England, the Netherlands, Germany, or Norway, you'll likely find it at A Touch of Dutch. It's a well-stocked store full of European drinks, candies, crackers, decor, and more.

Lavender Wind
15 NW Coveland St. #284; 360/544-4132; www. lavenderwind.com; 10am-5pm Tues.-Sat., noon-5pm Sun.
You'll feel relaxed before walking inside Lavender Wind, as the outside is covered with vibrant purple lavender. You can buy your own plants inside, or stock up on lavender soaps, bath products, candles, teas, and baked goods.

Food
Front Street Grill
20 Front St. NW; 360/682-2551; www.fsgcoupeville. com; 11:30am-8pm Sun.-Thurs., 11:30am-9pm Fri.-Sat.; $18-32
Make a reservation at Front Street Grill to enjoy fresh seafood like Penn Cove mussels with a view of the waterfront. They also have an extensive wine list with selections from all over the world, as well as beer and cocktails.

Toby's Tavern
8 Front St. NW; 360/678-4222; https://tobysuds.com; 11am-8pm Sun.-Thurs., 11am-9pm Fri.-Sat.; $15-30
Take a step back in history at Toby's Tavern, housed in a building from 1890. While it's been many different businesses over the years, it's been the town's tavern since the 1960s and serves fish and chips and burgers for lunch and dinner. Try their own Toby's Parrot Red Ale while you browse the walls covered in memorabilia from the past.

The Cove
26 Front St. NE; 360/632-0922; www. thecoveonpenncove.com; 9am-3pm Fri.-Mon.; $14-16
Start your morning at The Cove with a hearty breakfast sandwich or waffles, or enjoy one of their sandwiches for lunch. They have a variety of vegetarian and gluten-free options as well.

Ciao Food and Wine
701 N. Main St.; 360/678-0800; www.ciao.store; 11:30am-7:30pm Tues.-Sat.; $8-25
Ciao Food & Wine has a delectable Italian menu that includes wood-fired pizza, fresh pasta, seafood, and locally grown produce. Stop by their store to purchase food or wine to take home with you to recreate your meal.

Kapaws Iskreme
21 Front St. NE; 360/678-3637; Facebook @Kapaws-Iskreme; noon-5pm daily Mar.-Oct.

It's easy to find Kapaws Iskreme during the summer months, as there's regularly a line out the door. You can choose from several dozen different flavors of ice cream and get it in a freshly made waffle cone.

Accommodations

Captain Whidbey

2072 W. Capt Whidbey Inn Rd.; 360/678-4097; www. captainwhidbey.com; $186-249

Captain Whidbey is one of the most sought-after places to stay on the island, with its iconic waterfront location and rustic lodge housing its 30 rooms. It dates back to 1907 and has been everything from a boardinghouse to a general store to a post office. The rooms in the original lodge are on the smaller side and have shared bathrooms, but their lagoon rooms or cabins are also available for more privacy.

Tyee Restaurant and Motel

405 S. Main St.; 360/678-6616; https://tyee4u.com; $85-95

The Tyee Restaurant and Motel is a no-frills hotel ideal for an affordable place to call your base, with a queen bed in each of its nine rooms. They have a restaurant and bar on-site, and small dogs are welcome for an additional fee.

Information

Coupeville Chamber of Commerce and Visitor Center

905 NW Alexander St.; 360/678-5434; https:// coupevillechamber.com; 10am-4pm daily

Stop in downtown Coupeville to visit the Chamber, pick up maps, and get more information about the area.

Transportation

There are multiple ways to get to Coupeville, including a ferry from Port Townsend, which is a 35-minute crossing. You can drive from Oak Harbor south to Coupeville in about 15 minutes (11 mi/18 km) via Route 20, or from Clinton in 45 minutes (37 mi/60 km) on Route 525 and Route 20. From Langley to Coupeville is a 35-minute drive (27 mi/43 km) via Route 525 north.

Island Transit (360/678-7771; www. islandtransit.org) has a free route from the Clinton ferry all the way north to Oak Harbor, which stops in Coupeville.

★ DECEPTION PASS STATE PARK

41229 Route 20; 360/675-3767; https://parks.wa.gov; 6:30am-dusk summer, 8am-dusk winter; $10 Discover Pass

The iconic Deception Pass Bridge, which links Whidbey and Fidalgo Islands, is mainly responsible for Deception Pass State Park's status as the state's most-visited park. When Captain George Vancouver first arrived in 1792, he mistakenly believed the region to be a peninsula and named it Deception Pass after he realized it was part of an island.

Deception Pass State Park spans over 4,000 acres (1,600 ha). It has plenty of activities, including hiking on more than 38 mi (61 km) of trails, camping, fishing, swimming, and boating in freshwater and saltwater areas. Kayaking at Deception Pass may sound scenic but is considered dangerous—there's strong tidal currents and unpredictable whirlpools. Cranberry Lake in the park is a popular spot for fishing for rainbow trout, swimming, kayaking, and paddleboarding.

Sights

Deception Pass Bridge

41229 Route 20; https://whidbeycamanoislands.com

The Deception Pass Bridge, completed in 1935, features an outstanding design and stunning views of the canal. Visitors can see the whirlpools and crashing waves 180 ft (55 m) below. The bridge is 976 ft (297 m) long and a vital transportation link, as it's the only way to drive to the island.

To see it up close, park your car in one of the marked spaces off Route 20, then carefully make your way along the bridge's sidewalk. Under the bridge are several unofficial paths you can explore to get a new perspective on the region, but watch out for loose rocks.

Rosario Beach

*Fidalgo Island; 360/675-3767; https://parks.wa.gov/
find-parks/state-parks/deception-pass-state-park;
6:30am-dusk summer, 8am-dusk winter; $10 Discover
Pass*

Rosario Beach features two beaches on either side of a peninsula, boasting tide pools, driftwood-lined shores, and picnic areas amid old-growth trees and wildflower meadows. The beach is also home to a story pole carving that tells the legend of the Maiden of Deception Pass from the Samish tribe.

Hiking

North Beach Trail

Distance: *1.8 mi (2.9 km) round-trip*
Duration: *1 hour*
Elevation gain: *118 ft (39 m)*
Difficulty: *easy*
Trailhead: *Deception Pass State Park*

The North Beach trail starts in a parking lot just south of Deception Pass Bridge and follows the coastline west into a point that gives you views of Lopez Island to the north. You can take a slight detour south to Cranberry Lake or head back the way you came.

Lighthouse Point Loop

Distance: *1.9 mi (3 km) round-trip*
Duration: *1 hour*
Elevation gain: *236 ft (72 m)*
Difficulty: *easy*
Trailhead: *Deception Pass State Park*

Lighthouse Point Loop starts just past the north end of Deception Pass Bridge and heads down the shoreline of Bowman Bay before looping by Lighthouse Point. While there isn't an actual lighthouse here, you'll have a great view of the bridge to the south and multiple points of beach access along the way.

Fishing

Cranberry Lake is the easiest place to fish, and you'll find perch, trout, and bass. The east side of the lake has a fishing pier, and on the northwest side there's a gravel boat launch for nonmotorized boats. You can also fish from the shore or out in a boat by the waters of Deception Pass.

Sebo's Henery Hardware & Equipment Rental

*1102 Commercial Ave., Anacortes; 360/293-4575; www.
doitbest.com/henery-hardware; 7am-7pm Mon.-Fri.,
7am-6pm Sat., 8am-6pm Sun.*

You can get fishing supplies like poles and bait at Sebo's, as well as any gear you might have forgotten, for a day out on the water.

Camping

https://parks.wa.gov; $20/night

If you're lucky enough to get a campsite at Deception Pass State Park, you'll love having amazing views of Deception Pass and the surrounding waters and have an ideal base for the numerous hiking trails. There's a handful of sites north of the bridge by Bowman Bay, but most sites are in the south portion of the park near Cranberry Lake. Many visitors want to camp at Deception Pass in the summer months, so book your campsite well in advance. There are 315 campsites at the park, about one-third with RV hookups.

Getting There

Deception Pass is about an hour north (46 mi/74 km) of the Clinton ferry terminal, via Route 20 north, which becomes Route 525 to the park. From Coupeville, Deception Pass is a 25-minute drive (20 mi/32 km) east via Route 20. From Seattle, it takes about 1 hour 20 minutes (82 mi/132 km) via I-5 north and Route 20 west.

Everett

While Everett isn't often a destination in itself, it's easily accesible from I-5 and an easy trip from Seattle, not to mention a good place to spend part of the day if you're on your way north. Its main claim to fame is the Boeing factory, where you can see actual planes being assembled, but Everett has a beautiful waterfront and quite a few impressive breweries.

SIGHTS

★ Boeing Future of Flight

8415 Paine Field Blvd.; 800/464-1476; www.boeing. com; 8:30am-5:30pm Thurs.-Mon.; $15-38

In the largest building in the world by volume, visitors can learn about the aviation industry at Boeing Future of Flight. Tours of the Boeing assembly factory let you see the complex process of building the 747, 767, 777, and 787 Dreamliner planes. Witness the assembly line process as an airplane goes from raw materials to a finished product.

The center's interactive exhibits dive into the evolution of aviation technology and the past and the future of flight. You can experience flying a variety of aircraft with the help of flight simulators, and learn about the science and engineering that go into flight.

One highlight is the Sky Deck, which offers views of the Boeing assembly plant and the surrounding Paine Field airport. From this vantage point, you can watch planes taking off and landing and see various aircraft being tested.

Jetty Island

Jetty Island Ferry Launch, 522 10th St.; www. snohomishcountywa.gov; Wed.-Sun. July-early Sept.; $3-5

For a fun day trip, pack your beach bags and a picnic, and make a reservation for the ferry to visit Jetty Island, a 2-mi (3-km) strip of land just west of downtown Everett. Kids love to run around its shallow waters, look for sealife, and come back to their picnic blanket for lunch.

Ferries leave every 15-30 minutes from the ferry launch 10am-6:15pm from early July-early September, and the ride takes only 5 minutes. You'll need to book a return ticket ahead of time, which can be done on the same website.

Schack Art Center

2921 Hoyt Ave.; 425/259-5050; www.schack.org; 10am-5pm Tues.-Sat., noon-5pm Sun.; classes $85-360

The Schack Art Center hosts a variety of free events, including exhibitions, workshops, and community outreach activities, all with a focus on social justice, diversity in art, and contemporary art. In its 19,000-sq-ft (1,765-sq-m) building, the center showcases the work of more than 200 local artists in a gallery store and a unique public hot shop for glassblowing. They have a variety of classes open to the public, including block printing, paint and sip, glass fusing, and classes geared toward kids.

ENTERTAINMENT AND EVENTS

Everett's downtown district has flourished in recent years. And since the opening of the Angel of the Winds arena in 2003, it has become a popular place to go for events. However, it's smart to avoid barhopping or walking around after dark, since going out in some parts of town might be unsafe, such as Broadway.

Festivals and Events

Angel of the Winds Arena

2000 Hewitt Ave.; 425/322-2600; www. angelofthewindsarena.com

Angel of the Winds Arena hosts everything from concerts to trade shows throughout the year and can seat up to 10,000 people. There are children's shows and ice skating events here, but it's mainly known for hosting the Everett Silvertips hockey team.

Salty Sea Days

2900 block of Wetmore; 425/258-0700; https://downtowneverettwa.org; 4pm-10pm Fri., noon-10pm Sat., late July; free

Celebrate summer at Salty Sea Days—dance to live music, try out local brews in the beer garden, and taste an assortment of food trucks over two days. There's plenty for kids to do, including games, an inflatable slide, and even a pop-up skate park.

Music at the Marina

3632 Rucker Ave.; www.musicatthemarina.com; 5pm-9pm Thurs. July-Aug.; free

Enjoy summer's warm weather and long days by listening to a new local band each Thursday by the waterfront, and fill up from an assortment of food trucks available.

Breweries and Cideries

Crucible Brewing

909 SE Everett Mall Way; 425/374-7293; www.cruciblebrewing.com; noon-10pm Mon.-Sat., noon-8pm Sun.

Sours and bourbon barrel-aged beer are the specialties of Crucible Brewing, a small-batch brewery known for its excellent beer. The brewery has a laid-back vibe and welcomes children and dogs. Feel free to bring in outside food or enjoy their food trucks on the weekend.

Middleton Brewing

607 SE Everett Mall Way, Suite 27-A; 425/280-9178; Facebook @MiddletonBrews; 2pm-9pm Thurs., 2pm-10pm Fri., 2pm-9pm Sat.-Sun.

Middleton Brewing has been around for over a decade, and it's gained quite a fan base for its beer offerings, such as hazy IPAs and blonde ales. There's also a full food menu with options such as pizza and paninis, so it's an ideal place for dinner with plenty of indoor seating and picnic tables outside.

Scuttlebutt Brewing

1205 Craftsman Way #101; 425/257-9316; https://scuttlebuttbrewing.com; 11am-9pm Sun.-Thurs., 11am-10pm Fri.-Sat.

Located right by the scenic Everett waterfront, Scuttlebutt Brewing's cozy pub is ideal for families and beer enthusiasts alike. The restaurant has 12 unique beer taps in addition to homemade root beer, plus a full menu including hearty burgers, various sandwiches, and fresh seafood options.

Soundbite Cider

909 SE Everett Mall Way, Suite A-175; 425/610-8389; www.soundbitecider.com; 3pm-9pm Wed.-Thurs., 3pm-10pm Fri., 1pm-10pm Sat., 1pm-6pm Sun.

Everett doesn't just do beer well—it also knows how to make quality cider. Visit Soundbite Cider for gluten-free ciders ranging from dry and tart drinks to sweeter, while sitting on a comfortable couch or at a larger table.

SHOPPING

Everett Comics

2831 Wetmore Ave.; 425/252-8181; https://everettcomics.com; 11am-5pm Mon., 11am-6pm Tues., 11am-7pm Wed., 11am-6pm Thurs., 11am-7pm Fri.-Sat., 11am-5pm Sun.

Everett Comics boasts a vast selection of graphic novels, comics, back issues, and more. Established in 1983, this is known as the place to go when you want all things comics, including posters, toys, patches, pins, magic cards, and more.

Burkett's

2617 Colby Ave.; 425/252-2389; www.shopatburketts.com; 11am-5pm Mon.-Fri., 11am-4pm Sat.

Burkett's carries modern men's and women's clothing and accessories, as well as kitchenware, home decor, and children's items in their home store next door.

1: Jetty Island **2:** Crucible Brewing

Aeronautics Mecca

Boeing factory

Nearly 99,000 individuals work for over 900 different companies in the aeronautics industry in the greater Seattle area. Washington state, home to over 112,000 individuals employed by over 1,300 aircraft industries, amplifies this impact. Several aeronautical sights and attractions in the Seattle area offer a fascinating glimpse into the industry's history and innovations for visitors wanting to learn more about this rich aerospace heritage.

- **The Museum of Flight:** This South Seattle museum has a vast collection of exhibits covering flight history and the future (page 62).

- The Museum of Flight also has an offsite facility in Everett, **Museum of Flight Restoration Center and Reserve Collection** (2909 100th St. SW; 206/764-5700; www.museumofflight.org), that is dedicated to restoring aircraft. Call to see if tours are available (note the center may be closed for restoration).

- **Boeing Future of Flight:** One of the main attractions in Everett for aviation lovers, the Boeing Future of Flight features its famous Boeing factory tour (page 147).

FOOD

Capers + Olives

2933 Colby Ave.; 425/322-5280; www.capersandolives.com; 4pm-9pm Mon.-Sat.; $20-46

Capers + Olives offers a seasonally driven Italian menu emphasizing fresh seafood, vegetables, and handcrafted pasta in a small, cozy restaurant. The menu showcases dishes like shishito pepper and burrata for starters and a range of pasta, including paccheri and bucatini.

Buck's American Café

2901 Hewitt Ave.; 425/258-1351; https://bucksamericancafe.com; 11:30am-8:30pm Mon.-Thurs., 11:30am-9pm Fri.-Sat., 11:30am-2pm Sun.; $16-27

Head to Buck's when you're craving classic American appetizers, such as hot artichoke dip or fried cheese ravioli, or enjoy a wide range of salads. Their weekend brunch specials include eggs Benedict and hearty shrimp and grits.

The Irishmen

2923 Colby Ave.; 425/374-5783; https://theirishmen. com; 3pm-2am Mon.-Thurs., noon-2am Fri.-Sun.; $12-25

You're guaranteed to have fun at The Irishmen, where you'll be treated to live music while you sip your pint of beer and eat delicious food such as traditional Irish shepherd's pie and colcannon. You'll feel like you're in a Irish pub, with all the pictures of Ireland and vintage signs that line the walls.

Narrative Coffee

2927 Wetmore Ave.; 425/322-4648; https://narrative. coffee; 7am-2pm Mon.-Fri., 8am-3pm Sat.-Sun. $4-20

Set in a historic, light-filled building from 1921, this charming coffee shop mixes up its coffee every two months by getting different, high-quality coffee from some of the top roasters in the world. They have a full espresso bar with tea, noncaffeinated drinks, and savory pastries.

TRANSPORTATION

Downtown Everett has plenty of paid parking lots and free street parking available around town. It's also walkable if you want to explore the downtown by foot (during daylight hours). Everett Transit provides bus service around the city as well.

Getting There

Everett is right off I-5, and it's a straightforward drive north from Seattle that takes about 30 minutes.

Because it's a larger city, Everett has many public transportation options. **Everett Transit** (3201 Smith Ave.; 425/257-7777; www.everetttransit.org) provides bus service all over the Everett city limits, as well as to park-and-rides where riders can connect to **Sound Transit** buses (888/889-6368; www.soundtransit.org) going to Seattle. **Greyhound** (800/231-2222; www. greyhound.com) and **Amtrak** (800/872-7245; www.amtrak.com) also stop at this station, which can take you as far south as Portland or up north to Vancouver, British Columbia.

Mountain Loop Highway

The Mountain Loop Highway is a beautiful 55-mi (89-km) scenic byway, where you'll pass through lush greenery, drive along calming rivers, and see glimpses of towering mountains. This is easy enough to do as a day trip, perhaps also doing one of the many hikes found off the highway. Numerous campsites are also available, which is a big draw in the summer. While this technically isn't a complete loop, many people start in Granite Falls, follow Mountain Loop Highway to its end at Darrington, and then continue onto Route 530 for 28 mi (45 km) to get back to I-5.

The loop is accessible late spring-fall; Barlow Pass is often snow-covered until late spring. The route has asphalt roads from Verlot to Barlow Pass and from Darrington to White Chuck River Road, with a 14-mi (23-km) one-lane gravel stretch in between.

Wildlife like deer may cross the road, so caution is advised. Facilities such as gas stations are scarce, so prepare accordingly.

★ Driving the Mountain Loop Highway

Start: *Granite Falls*
End: *Darrington*
Driving Distance: *55 mi (89 km)*
Driving Time: *2 hours*

Granite Falls to Verlot

The first segment of the Mountain Loop Highway follows Route 92 from Granite Falls to Verlot, covering approximately 11 mi (18 km) in about 20 minutes. This portion of the journey may not be the most visually stunning, but Granite Falls serves as an important gateway to the splendors of the Mount

Baker-Snoqualmie National Forest that lie just beyond Verlot. It's worth pausing at the **Verlot Public Service Center,** an excellent spot to grab maps, check current weather and trail conditions, and consult with rangers about your hiking plans.

Verlot to Barlow Pass

In the next segment, the scenery dramatically transforms—towering trees, winding roads, and glimpses of fast-flowing rivers found in the Mount Baker-Snoqualmie National Forest. It's about 30 minutes (19 mi/31 km) from Verlot up to Barlow Pass.

Barlow Pass

Barlow Pass serves as a pivotal point on the route, and it's closed seasonally. Check online (www.snohomishcountywa.gov) before heading out to confirm the pass is open. It's a popular starting point for several hiking trails and has a small parking area. Although it's only a mountain pass without a nearby town, it's the general halfway point of this loop, so many people choose to get out and explore one of its hikes.

Barlow Pass to Darrington

This segment down to Darrington trades the dense, forested landscapes for more expansive mountain views, giving you a front-row seat to the towering peaks of the Cascades. The road conditions vary here, with a 14-mi (23-km) one-lane gravel section on Forest Road 20 before returning to asphalt on the remainder of Mountain Loop Highway to Darrington. This part of the loop offers fewer amenities but adds an element of backcountry charm, with a drive time of around 50 minutes (26 mi/42 km).

Darrington to Arlington

Darrington is officially the end of the Mountain Loop Highway, but most people keep driving west on Route 530 to Arlington (30 mi/48 km) to fully complete this loop. The scenery here changes from mountainous terrain to the Skagit Valley's more pastoral

surroundings. The route gets less winding, and farmlands start to appear. Arlington is a wonderful location to stop for a break or restock supplies because it has amenities including gas stations, grocery stores, and food options.

SIGHTS

The Mountain Loop Highway doesn't have many sights to stop at, but the drive itself and the numerous hikes along the way make it worthwhile.

Granite Falls to Verlot
Granite Falls Fish Ladder

10630 Mountain Loop Hwy., Granite Falls; 6am-10pm daily; free

Just off the left side of Mountain Loop Highway about 9 mi (14 km) west of Verlot Public Service Center is the Granite Falls Fish Ladder, where you'll find a small parking lot and start path to the fish ladder. It's a flat, easy walk (0.7-mi/1-km round-trip), and you can take the trail to the lower part of the fish ladder or take the stairs to the middle section to see the fish, such as Chinook, sockeye, and coho.

Darrington to Arlington
The Outback Kangaroo Farm

10030 Route 530 NE, Arlington; 360/403-7474; www. theoutbackkangaroofarm.com; 10am, noon, 2pm, 4pm Thurs.-Sat.; $25 adult, $15 ages 2-12

The 40-minute guided tours at the Outback Kangaroo Farm are fun and informative for all ages. Knowledgeable staff members guide visitors through the many different animal species living on the farm, including kangaroos, wallabies, lemurs, peacocks, and Nigerian dwarf goats.

HIKING
Verlot to Barlow Pass

A Northwest Forest Pass is required for all these hikes.

1: Big Four Ice Caves **2:** South Fork Stillaguamish River **3:** Mount Pilchuck

Mount Pilchuck

Distance: *5.4 mi (8.7 km) round-trip*
Duration: *2.5 hours*
Elevation gain: *2,300 ft (700 m)*
Difficulty: *moderate*
Trailhead: *off Mount Pilchuck Road*

Start at the trailhead and follow the right fork, crossing a stream, to enter Pilchuck State Park (0.2 mi/0.3 km). Signage is minimal, and be prepared for various trail conditions, especially in later sections where traction devices and poles are recommended. At the 1-mi (1.6-km) mark, follow an orange marker left through a boulder field. After exiting the forest, you should see the fire lookout atop the summit; be cautious of false summits. Upon reaching the summit, you'll find a restored fire lookout, originally constructed in 1921, making for the perfect place to take a break. Then head back down, while you enjoy views of miles upon miles of the valley below.

To get here, drive 1 mi (1.6 km) east of the Verlot Public Service Center, go over a bridge, and turn right on Mount Pilchuck Road (Forest Road 42). Continue 7 mi (11 km) to the parking lot.

Lake 22

Distance: *5.4 mi (8.7 km) round-trip*
Duration: *2.5 hours*
Elevation gain: *1,350 ft (412 m)*
Difficulty: *moderate*
Trailhead: *Lake 22 trailhead*

Follow the trail from the trailhead through a red cedar and western hemlock forest, crossing a few small streams. At 0.6 mi (1 km), cross a bridge over 22 Creek. The path emerges onto a talus slope at 1.5 mi (2.4 km), providing a glimpse of Whitehorse Mountain and Three Fingers on clear days. At 2.1 mi (3.4 km), the trail reenters the forest. Skunk cabbage is noticeable in the spring as the landscape becomes more wetland-like. Walk 2.7 mi (4.3 km) through a lush rain forest environment to arrive at the bridge spanning Lake 22's outflow.

The trail is 2 mi (3 km) east of the Verlot Public Service Center; take a right at the Lake 22 trailhead sign.

Big Four Ice Caves

Distance: *2.2 mi (3.5 km) round-trip*
Duration: *1 hour*
Elevation gain: *220 ft (67 m)*
Difficulty: *easy*
Trailhead: *Ice Caves trailhead*

From the trailhead parking lot, follow the paved path to an intersection. To head toward the caves, continue straight and cross the Stillaguamish River via a bridge. Cross Ice Creek and follow a mostly boardwalk trail through the forest. Eventually, views of Big Four Mountain and the caves below will emerge. Despite their allure, avoid entering or climbing the caves because they are unstable and dangerous, as shown by warning signs and a plaque honoring a past victim. The trail ends in a circle of rocks, offering a safe vantage point for admiring the caves and surrounding scenery.

These caverns originate from a persistent snowfield that develops at the base of Big Four Mountain. The snow and ice melt as the weather warms, revealing the ice caves' hollow passageways beneath. Carved out of the snowpack by warm air currents and melting water, the caverns are completely composed of ice and snow.

To get here, drive 14 mi (23 km) east of the Verlot Public Service Center and take a right at the Ice Caves trailhead sign.

Heather Lake

Distance: *4.6 mi (7.4 km) round-trip*
Duration: *2.5 hours*
Elevation gain: *1,034 ft (315 m)*
Difficulty: *moderate*
Trailhead: *Heather Lake trailhead*

Start the hike from the large parking lot, heading left to enter an old second-growth forest filled with switchbacks. Take note of rotting stumps with historic springboard notches once used by loggers. The trail eventually intersects an old logging road before climbing again on a rocky, rooty path that can be wet during high runoff. Upon reaching a clearing, continue through more old-growth forests until the trail levels out, signaling the lake is close. Here, the terrain turns marshy, and a boardwalk offers easier passage. The trail forks at the lake's edge; either direction loops around the lake, offering various scenic and rest spots.

To get here, drive 11 mi (18 km) east of the Verlot Public Service Center and turn right on Mount Pilchuck Road (Forest Road 42). The Heather Lake trailhead sign will be 1.4 mi (2.3 km) ahead on the left.

Barlow Pass

The following hikes start from the same area, the Barlow Pass parking lot. To get here, drive 20 mi (32 km) east of the Verlot Public Service Station and take a left at the Barlow Pass sign.

Barlow Point
Distance: 2.4 mi (3.9 km) round-trip
Duration: 1.5 hour
Elevation gain: 800 ft (244 m)
Difficulty: easy
Trailhead: Barlow Pass trailhead
Starting at the former Forest Service Guard Station, the trail splits early on; the path to the right leads to Barlow Point, and the path to the left leads to part of the old Everett-Monte Cristo railroad grade. These trails eventually reconnect, so you can go up one way and down the other. After passing two signed junctions, go straight to ascend switchbacks through a forest scarred by a 1905 fire. The summit, once the site of a fire lookout (1935-1964), offers panoramic views, making this a great trail for those who want a short hike but a scenic vista at the end.

Monte Cristo Ghost Town
Distance: 8 mi (12.9 km) round-trip
Duration: 4 hours
Elevation gain: 700 ft (213 m)
Difficulty: moderate
Trailhead: Barlow Pass trailhead
In the 1890s, the mining boom led to the rise of Monte Cristo, complete with a railway and over 200 mining claims. Various setbacks led to its decline, and by 1907 mining ceased. Today it's a ghost town with a few remnants such as old wooden buildings and faded signs. Starting from the Barlow Pass trailhead, a 4-mi (6.4 km) hike along a closed, partially eroded road leads to the site. Most of this hike is a flat stroll through the woods, largely shaded until the river, which you cross via a bridge. You'll know you've reached the town when you see the old metal "Welcome to Monte Cristo" sign.

Barlow Pass to Darrington
North Fork Sauk Falls
Distance: 0.4 mi (0.6 km) round-trip
Duration: 30 minutes
Elevation gain: 200 ft (60 m)
Difficulty: easy
Trailhead: North Fork Sauk Falls trailhead
This short trail drops down 200 ft (61 m) to reach a stunning 45-ft (18-m) waterfall. A worthwhile 30-minute detour for those journeying on the Mountain Loop Highway, it offers a chance to stretch your legs or warm up for a longer hike. However, be cautious, as the steps near the waterfall's base can get slippery when wet.

From Darrington, drive for 20 mi (32 km) on Mountain Loop Highway and turn left onto Sloan Creek Road (Forest Road 49) and drive 1 mi (1.6 km) to the trailhead.

Old Sauk River Trail
Distance: 6 mi (9.7 km) round-trip
Duration: 3 hours
Elevation gain: 150 ft (45 m)
Difficulty: moderate
Trailhead: 0.5 mi (0.8 km) east of Clear Creek Bridge, Darrington
Three access points are available for this trail: one at 3.6 mi (5.8 km) from the Darrington intersection, the main trailhead at another 1.8 mi (2.9 km), and a roadside spot near Murphy Creek just a bit further. From the main trailhead, start on a graveled trail to reach a junction for Murphy Creek, a brief scenic detour. Return to the main trail, which becomes a

dirt path near the river. Enjoy moss-covered trees and seasonal flora like trillium, or watch for ospreys and herons, especially in winter. The trail features old-growth stumps from 1930s logging, newer trees sprouting from them, and a wooden bridge with river views. When you reach the end of the trail at the north parking lot, turn around and come to a junction at the graveled trail. If you go left to the lower section of the loop, you'll end where you started, or you can go right through the forest, which takes you to the main parking lot a different way.

FOOD
Granite Falls to Verlot
Playa Bonita

206 E. Stanley St., Granite Falls; 360/691-3152; https:// playabonitarestaurant.com; 11am-9:30pm daily; $8-26

This local Mexican chain features appetizers such as nachos and ceviche and traditional favorite main courses like enchiladas, tacos, and fajitas. Meat, seafood, and vegetarian options as well as specialty dishes such as arroz con pollo and chile colorado are available. This large, colorful restaurant has multiple rooms full of booths as well as a bar area.

Barlow Pass to Darrington
Red Top Tavern

1020 Darrington St., Darrington; 360/436-1590; Facebook @The-Red-Top-Tavern; 11am-midnight Sun.-Thurs., 11am-2am Fri.-Sat.; $12-20

The Red Top Tavern has a roadside dive-bar feel, and you'll likely see locals catching up over a cold beer. There's a small food menu available with options like cheese pizza and nachos with cheese and chili, ideal for those wanting cheap bar food after a day of hiking.

Darrington to Arlington
The Stilly Diner

223 N. Olympic Ave., Arlington; 360/403-8486; www. stillydiner.com; 6am-3pm Wed.-Sun.; $10-20

The menu at Stilly Diner features all the standards of American diner food. Pancakes, omelets, and breakfast sandwiches are available

for the morning crowd. Later in the day, burgers, sandwiches, salads, and hearty main dishes like meatloaf and fish and chips are served in this small but cozy diner.

The Woodstone Kitchen and Bar

7705 204th St. NE, Arlington; 360/322-6943; https:// woodstone.popmenu.com; noon-8pm daily; $8-22

Burgers, tacos, and sandwiches are just some items on The Woodstone's menu in this beautifully decorated space with Pacific Northwest-themed wood carvings throughout. The blackened salmon tacos are a favorite, topped with cabbage and mango salsa. The exceptional Woodstone burger is made up of two 5-ounce beef patties with cheddar, applewood bacon, onion rings, and serrano aioli.

CAMPING
Granite Falls to Verlot
Verlot Campground

Mountain Loop Highway, 11 mi (18 km) east of Granite Falls; 360/386-8214; www.recreation.gov; $30-32

Verlot Campground is an ideal base to explore the many nearby hikes on Mountain Loop Highway. The quiet campground is located near the South Fork Stillaguamish River, which provides easy access to fishing. Reservations for its 26 campsites are required, and drinking water and restrooms are available.

Verlot to Barlow Pass
Red Bridge Campground

Mountain Loop Highway, 20 mi (32 km) east of Granite Falls; 509/932-0242; www.recreation.gov; $25-27

It's easy to spot Red Bridge Campground when coming from Granite Falls—you'll cross a red bridge right before turning into the campsites. This quiet, shaded campground has 15 sites with vault toilets but no running water. It's next to the South Fork Stillaguamish River, which provides a soothing backdrop as you relax in your site or walk along the riverbanks.

Darrington to Arlington
Clear Creek Campground

Mountain Loop Highway, 3 mi (5 km) south of Darrington; 509/932-0242; www.recreation.gov; $30-32

You'll have access to vault toilets, picnic tables, and tent pads at Clear Creek Campground and easy access to the Sauk River. There are 13 sites available, and you might even see Mount Baker from here on a clear day.

INFORMATION
Verlot Public Service Center

33515 Mountain Loop Highway, Granite Falls; 360/691-7791; www.fs.usda.gov; 8am-4pm Mon.-Fri.

The visitor center for outdoor activities like hiking, camping, and more is located at the Verlot Public Service Center. It is the best location to talk to rangers about hiking plans, acquire the most recent weather and route information, and peruse maps.

TRANSPORTATION

From I-5, take exit 194 to US 2 east, Route 204 east, Route 9 north, and follow Route 92 east to Granite Falls. The drive from Seattle to Granite Falls takes about 50 minutes (43 mi/69 km).

Olympic Peninsula

Pristine beaches, ancient forests, and snow- capped mountains make the Olympic Peninsula feel straight out of a fairy tale. Right in the heart of it, Olympic National Park shows off nature's amazing splendor, and you can easily spend days exploring all its different parts.

If you're looking for a peaceful spot, Lake Crescent mirrors the surrounding mountains and sky as you kayak along. For more excitement, hike Hurricane Ridge and marvel at the incredible views of the Olympic Mountains and the Strait of Juan de Fuca, the stretch of water between Washington and Canada.

Step into the lush Hoh Rain Forest, where moss clings to old trees and sunshine streams through a verdant canopy. Or walk along the beach

Highlights

Look for ★ to find recommended sights, activities, dining, and lodging.

★ **Sequim Lavender Farms:** Visit Sequim to immerse yourself in fields of purple blooms in North America's lavender capital (page 167).

★ **Whale-Watching in Port Angeles:** Experience the thrill of spotting orcas and humpback whales in their natural habitat on a boat tour (page 172).

★ **Hurricane Ridge:** With beautiful views of the Olympic Mountains, Hurricane Ridge is full of hiking trails to explore (page 181).

★ **Lake Crescent:** A deep, glacial lake known for its crystal-clear waters, Lake Crescent is ideal for kayaking, fishing, or spending the night (page 186).

★ **Makah Cultural and Research Center:** Take an in-depth look into the heritage and traditions of the Makah Tribe, complete with ancient artifacts and exhibits, in Neah Bay (page 191).

★ **Cape Flattery:** As the northwesternmost point of the contiguous United States, Cape Flattery offers dramatic sea cliffs and ocean views (page 192).

★ **Hoh Rain Forest:** This lush, temperate rain forest is famous for its towering trees and moss-covered grounds (page 204).

★ **Ruby Beach:** With sea stacks and abundant driftwood, Ruby Beach is a rugged coastline ideal for photography or beachcombing (page 206).

© MOON.COM

★ **Ocean Shores:** This popular beach destination has activities ranging from kite flying to horseback riding (page 213).

★ **Cape Disappointment State Park:** Cape Disappointment impresses with its rich history, scenic views, and hiking trails where the Columbia River meets the Pacific Ocean (page 219).

Olympic Peninsula

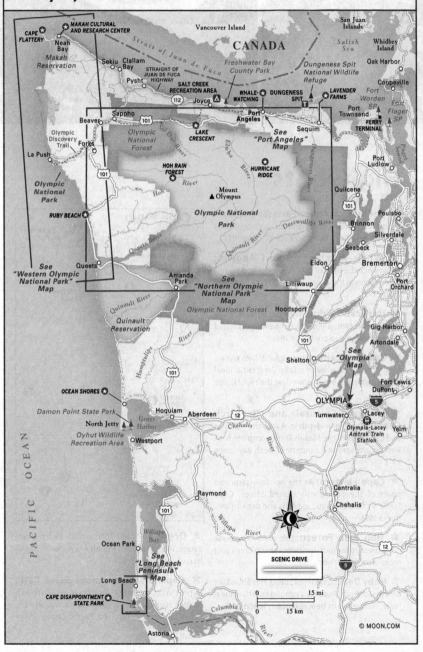

CAPE FLATTERY

MAKAH CULTURAL AND RESEARCH CENTER

Neah Bay

Makah Reservation

Sekiu

Clallam Bay

Pysht

STRAIGHT OF JUAN DE FUCA HIGHWAY

Strait of Juan de Fuca

Vancouver Island

San Juan Islands

CANADA

Freshwater Bay County Park

Dungeness Spit National Wildlife Refuge

Salish Sea

Oak Harbor

Whidbey Island

Coupeville

Fort Worden SP

Port Flager SP

Joyce

SALT CREEK RECREATION AREA

112

WHALE-WATCHING

DUNGENESS SPIT

Port Angeles

LAVENDER FARMS

Sequim

Port Townsend

FERRY TERMINAL

Beaver

Sappho

101

Olympic National Forest

LAKE CRESCENT

See "Port Angeles" Map

Port Ludlow

Olympic Discovery Trail

Forks

La Push

101

HOH RAIN FOREST

Hoh River

HURRICANE RIDGE

Elwha River

Quilcene

101

Poulsbo

Olympic National Park

Mount Olympus

Olympic National Park

Dosewallips River

Brinnon

Silverdale

RUBY BEACH

Queets River

Quinault River

Eldon

Seabeck

Bremerton

Port Orchard

See "Western Olympic National Park" Map

Queets

Amanda Park

See "Northern Olympic National Park" Map

Lilliwaup

Quinault River

Quinault Reservation

Olympic National Forest

Hoodsport

Gig Harbor

Artondale

Humptulips River

101

Shelton

See "Olympia" Map

Fort Lewis

DuPont

OCEAN SHORES

Damon Point State Park

North Jetty

Oyhut Wildlife Recreation Area

Hoquiam

Aberdeen

Grays Harbor

Westport

Chehalis River

12

OLYMPIA

Tumwater

Lacey

Olympia-Lacey Amtrak Train Station

Yelm

PACIFIC OCEAN

Raymond

Willapa Bay

Willapa River

Centralia

Chehalis

5

Ocean Park

See "Long Beach Peninsula" Map

12

SCENIC DRIVE

Long Beach

CAPE DISAPPOINTMENT STATE PARK

Columbia River

Astoria

0   15 mi

0   15 km

© MOON.COM

and look for marine life in the tidal pools as you take in the epic beauty of the Pacific coast.

The southern tip of the Olympic Peninsula is more populated than the rest of its Pacific Ocean coastline, dotted with picturesque seaside communities. Even though the water is usually too chilly to swim in, every year people are drawn to this spot by the sweeping vistas.

ORIENTATION

It's straightforward to get around, as there is one main loop (US 101) around the Olympic Peninsula. This road also takes you to the different sections of Olympic National Park, since you can't drive through the park. Some stretches are isolated, so it's best to fuel up in the bigger towns. Multiple areas of the Peninsula don't have cell phone service, particularly in the interior.

Getting There
Car

From Seattle there are several ways to get to the Olympic Peninsula. If you're starting in the southern section, take I-5 and US 101 and then continue to drive up the coast to reach other parts.

Ferry

Taking your car across the **Seattle-Bainbridge ferry** is the quickest option if you're starting in the northern region of the Olympic Peninsula. The ferry leaves from Pier 52 (801 Alaskan Way) and takes approximately 35 minutes to get across the water. Ferries run about 5:30am-1:35am, departing about every 40 minutes. Fares are $28/vehicle under 14 ft (4 m) plus the driver, and an additional $10/passenger 19-64 years old.

Once the ferry docks at **Bainbridge Ferry Terminal** (270 Olympic Drive SE), you'll head along the east part of the Peninsula by taking Route 305, Route 3, and Route 104. To reach the northern portion, keep traveling north on

US 101. It's about 1.5 hours (73 mi/117 km) to drive from the Bainbridge ferry terminal to Port Angeles.

PLANNING YOUR TIME

Due to its large size, the Olympic Peninsula is impossible to see in one day, nor would you want to try. Although you can take a long day trip from Seattle to certain areas, such as Port Angeles or Olympia, spending at least **2-3 days** covering the entire loop around the Peninsula is best.

If you're exploring the northern part of the Peninsula, Port Angeles is an ideal base for visiting multiple areas without driving too far each day. Forks is a convenient base for traveling along the west side. Some areas, such as Long Beach, aren't close to much else, so they're best visited as a standalone getaway and not used as a base. Olympia is the largest city on the Peninsula (and the state capital) and a convenient stop going to or from Seattle if you're not taking the ferry.

Summer is ideal because by then much of the snow has melted and all the sights are accessible. It's also the least rainy time of year. On the other hand, this is peak season, so make reservations well in advance and be prepared to deal with traffic.

However, don't rule out the spring and fall just because of the rain—you'll still have plenty of dry days, and depending on when you visit, you might see wildflowers and foliage. Just bring a raincoat, and you'll be able to explore the park without the summer crowds.

Although snow is uncommon across most of the Peninsula, winter can bring dense fog that obscures roads, especially on the western side, so exercise caution. You'll also want to check the road conditions for closures because snow does fall in higher elevations, such as Hurricane Ridge. The biggest benefit of visiting in the winter is it's the least crowded time of year; it's possible you'll have many spots you visit all to yourself.

Previous: Hoh Rain Forest; Hurricane Ridge; Lake Crescent.

OLYMPIC PENINSULA

Itinerary Ideas

DAY 1

1 Start in Sequim and get a coffee at **Essence Coffee Roasters.**

2 Head over to **Purple Haze Lavender Farm** for a lavender field experience.

3 Head into Olympic National Park to visit **Lake Crescent** and hike **Marymere Falls.**

4 Go to Port Angeles for dinner at **Next Door GastroPub.**

5 Conclude the day by checking into the **Olympic Inn & Suites** for the night.

DAY 2

1 Begin your morning in Port Angeles with breakfast at **The Great Northern Coffee Bar.**

2 Venture to the **Elwha Klallam Heritage Center** to explore the area's cultural history.

3 Continue on to **Forks** and take a self-guided *Twilight* tour, or stop by the **Forks Timber Museum.** Get lunch at **Sully's Drive-In.**

4 Continue the journey south to **Lake Quinault.** Along the way, stop at **Ruby Beach** to walk along the sand and admire the views.

5 Dine at **The Salmon House** for a taste of local cuisine and stay the night at **Lake Quinault Lodge.**

DAY 3

1 Start your day at Lake Quinault by hiking the **Quinault Loop** and having breakfast at the lodge.

2 Head down to Ocean Shores and visit **Damon Point State Park** for beachcombing and bird-watching at **Oyhut Wildlife Recreation Area.**

3 For lunch, head to **Bennett's Fish Shack.**

4 Continue to Olympia, and explore the **Yashiro Japanese Garden** and the **Capitol Campus,** including the Legislative Building and Governor's Mansion.

5 End your day with dinner at **Olympia Oyster House** and stay overnight at the **Olympia Hotel at Capitol Lake.**

Port Townsend

On the northernmost tip of Washington's Olympic Peninsula, the city of Port Townsend embodies Victorian elegance and has a significant maritime heritage. Established in the middle of the 19th century, its importance as a Customs port of entry for the United States led to its rapid growth. The downtown district has been recognized as a National Historic District, and the Victorian buildings there beautifully maintain the city's past.

Today, Port Townsend is lauded for its vibrant arts scene, one-of-a-kind cultural events, and a wide variety of things to do. While the city isn't in the best location to access Olympic National Park (about 1.5 hours away), it's a destination in its own right.

SIGHTS
Fort Worden Historical State Park

200 Battery Way E.; 360/344-4400; www.parks. wa.gov/511/Fort-Worden; 6:30am-dusk summer, 8:30am-dusk winter, museum 11am-4pm Fri.-Tues. Apr.-Oct., 11am-4pm Sat.-Sun. Nov.-Mar.; $10 Discover Pass

Established in the 1890s, Fort Worden was a military base and a component of the "Triangle of Fire," a group of three forts tasked with preventing naval attacks on Puget Sound. Until 1953, the fort served as a training and coastal defense facility for the United States Army. In 1973, it was repurposed as a state park. Today you can still see Fort Worden's historical significance as a military installation in its museums and preserved buildings.

The Commanding Officer's Quarters Museum lets you experience what it was like to live as an officer's family in the 1900s. For a deeper look at the guns and defenses that kept Puget Sound safe from the end of the 19th century until WWII, stop by the Puget Sound Coast Artillery Museum. You'll also find 12 mi (19 km) of hiking trails winding through the park between the buildings, offering views of the fort's lighthouse and the Sound.

Fort Flagler Historical State Park

10541 Flagler Rd., Nordland; 360/385-1259; www. parks.wa.gov/508/Fort-Flagler; 7am-8pm daily; $10 Discover Pass

The well-preserved military defenses and museum at Fort Flagler Historical State Park on Marrowstone Island are a part of the historic "Triangle of Fire" forts. The park's 1,400 acres (565 ha) have beautiful views of Puget Sound and the surrounding mountains, and camping, bird-watching, cycling, and beachcombing are all popular activities.

Stop by the free museum to see vintage photographs of the fort and items like guns that date back to the fort's military days. When you're hungry, **Beachcomber Café** is open seasonally (11am-4pm Sat.-Sun. Apr., May, and Sept., 11am-4pm daily Memorial Day-Labor Day) and provides coffee, burgers, sandwiches, and grocery and camping supplies. To get to Marrowstone Island, head south on Route 19 from Port Townsend, then head east on Route 116, crossing a bridge to reach the island.

Port Townsend Aero Museum

105 Airport Rd.; 360/379-5244; https://ptaeromuseum. com; 9am-4pm Wed.-Sun.; $12

The Port Townsend Aero Museum specializes in antique and classic aircraft. Learn about the history and science of flight, and explore exhibits that document the development of aviation from the first biplanes to the present day. The youth program is a highlight of the museum—young people actively participate in aircraft restoration and maintenance.

RECREATION
Kayaking

Port Townsend is one of the best places to kayak on the Peninsula, as more experienced kayakers have the chance to challenge themselves with the open waters north of the city,

while beginners are sheltered with calmer waters in **Port Townsend Bay.** You can paddle up and down the coastline to see Fort Worden, Fort Flagler, and the Port Townsend waterfront.

The area near **Marrowstone Island** is a particularly great spot for kayaking. Marine life is plentiful in the area's waters—seals, sea lions, migratory birds, and even the occasional whale. This is also a popular spot for bird-watching. While the waters here are generally calm, paddlers should always watch the weather forecast and the tides to ensure they have a safe trip.

Olympic Kayak Tours & Rentals
501 Harbor Defense Way; 360/453-7135; www. Olympickayaktours.com; rentals $25-45/hour, $10-20/half hour, guided tours $79-119

Olympic Kayak Tours offers tours around Fort Flagler, where naturalists will point out the local sealife and birds during their sea kayak eco-adventure tours. A unique experience available here is bioluminescent night kayaking, allowing paddlers to witness the captivating glow of marine life at night. They have an additional location at **Fort Worden** (501 Harbor Defense Way; 360/453-7135), where you can rent a single or double kayak or stand-up paddleboard.

NIGHTLIFE
Sirens Pub
823 Water St.; 360/379-1100; www.sirenspub.com; noon-midnight Thurs.-Sat., noon-10pm Sun.-Wed.

Sirens Pub has eleven different microbrews on tap, and in the warmer months, the deck is a popular place to unwind. Burgers, pasta, and pizza are just some of the traditional pub fare available.

Port Townsend Brewing Company
330 10th St.; 360/385-9967; www. porttownsendbrewing.com; noon-7pm Mon., 2pm-7pm Tues.-Thurs., noon-8pm Fri.-Sun.

Port Townsend Brewing Company specializes in making 10 distinct ales in-house, complemented by a selection of pub snacks. While they don't serve full meals, guests are welcome to bring their own food. The brewery seasonally features live music in its beer garden and provides a cozy tasting room.

The In Between
823 Water St.; 360/379-2425; https://theinbetweenpt. com; 4pm-10pm Thurs.-Mon.

The In Between has a small menu of appetizers, such as such as deviled eggs and lamb sliders, alongside a variety of specialty cocktails like the Dancing Queen in addition to wine. This makes it a great place to spend happy hour or wind down after a day exploring the town.

SHOPPING
World's End
1020 Water St.; 360/379-6906; Facebook @worldsendporttownsend; 10am-6pm daily

World's End is one of the most captivating shops in the area, as they specialize in steampunk, pirate, Victorian, and nautical-inspired garments, decor, and accessories. You'll have a hard time leaving this store without purchasing a unique item to take with you.

William James Bookseller
829 Water St.; 360/385-7313; https:// williamjamesbookseller.com; 11am-5pm daily

William James Bookseller is a charming independent bookstore that stands out for its carefully curated selection of new and used books, in a wide range of genres, including rare and out-of-print titles.

The Spice & Tea Exchange of Port Townsend
929 Water St.; 360/385-1633; www.spiceandtea.com; 10am-5pm daily

The Spice & Tea Exchange is the place to go if you love tea, as it has over 85 handcrafted seasonings, loose-leaf teas, and fine spices—all hand-mixed in-store—and it's known as one of the best gift shops in town. The staff will

1: lighthouse at Fort Worden Historical State Park
2: downtown Port Townsend

happily help you pick out a unique culinary gift or spices for your next meal.

FOOD

Better Living Through Coffee

100 Tyler St.; 360/385-3388; www.bltcoffee.com; 7:30am-5pm daily; $5-20

Better Living Through Coffee is a colorful coffee shop on the water serving organic, fairtrade, locally roasted drip coffee and espresso, along with organic herbal teas and specialty drinks. They also serve a variety of food options including pastries, quiches, and bagels.

Blue Moose Café

311-B Haines Pl.; 360/385-7339; www.takeout-guide.com/blue-moose-cafe; 7am-2pm Thurs.-Tues.; $4-18

When you're in the mood for breakfast, head to Blue Moose Café, as they serve eggs, pancakes, and more all day in their cozy setting.

Doc's Marina Grill

141 Hudson St.; 360/344-3627; https://docsgrill.com; 11am-9pm Thurs.-Mon.; $14-38

Doc's Marina Grill offers a range of fresh seafood and classic American dishes in a relaxed, maritime-themed atmosphere, complemented by scenic waterfront views. Don't miss their fish tacos topped with chimichurri aioli slaw or prime rib and cheddar sandwich on sourdough.

★ Hillbottom Pie

215 Tyler St.; 360/385-1306; 11am-3pm, 4:30pm-7:30pm Mon.-Fri.; $10-17

When you're craving delicious pizza, head to Hillbottom Pie. They have a dozen different options to choose from in addition to salads and a small dessert menu. While you wait for your pizza, take a seat by the large windows and people-watch, or get a local beer on draft and settle in at the small bar with your meal.

ACCOMMODATIONS

Palace Hotel Port Townsend

1004 Water St.; 360/385-0773; https://palacehotelpt.com; $149-162

Built in 1889, the Palace Hotel is a beautiful historic three-story hotel, offering 26 unique rooms and a central location in downtown Port Townsend. Guests should note that it has no elevator or air-conditioning but provides fans for comfort.

Aladdin Motor Inn

2333 Washington St.; 360/385-3747; www.aladdinmotorinn.com; $89-129

The simple motel boasts 30 rooms with stunning views of Port Townsend Bay, along with the Olympic and Cascade mountains. Guests can choose from a variety of rooms, including those with these impressive water views. There is complimentary on-site parking in a spacious lot.

The Tides Inn & Suites

1807 Water St. #6909; 360/385-0595; tides-inn.com; $169-259

The Tides Inn & Suites is one of the top places to stay thanks to its waterfront location on Port Townsend Bay, and many of the 44 rooms have private decks with ocean views. The rooms are modern and sleek with basic amenities, and select rooms have the option of luxurious additions like a gas fireplace and whirlpool tub.

CAMPING

Fort Townsend Historical State Park

1370 Old Fort Townsend Rd.; 360/385-3595; https://parks.wa.gov/find-parks/state-parks/fort-townsend-historical-state-park; campgrounds closed Oct. 1-Apr. 15; $12-37

Spanning 414 acres (168 ha) with a vast saltwater shoreline, Fort Townsend is a marine camping park rich in military history from the pioneer era. There are 40 campsites available, with showers and restrooms. Visitors can enjoy exploring the forested landscape, including a historic torpedo tower from World War II and a parade lawn lined with interpretive plaques detailing its past.

Fort Worden State Park
Beach Campground
200 Battery Way; 888/226-7688; www.parks.
wa.gov/511/Fort-Worden; $40-45

Fort Worden Historical State Park has over 2 mi (3 km) of beach to explore, and the camping facilities include RV sites, showers, picnic tables, and a boat launch. There are 80 campsites to choose from, with the beach campground sites having full hook-ups and the upper forest area having partial hook-up sites.

INFORMATION
Port Townsend Visitor
Information Center
2409 Jefferson St.; 360/385-2722; https://enjoypt.com;
9am-5pm Mon.-Fri., 10am-4pm Sat., 11am-4pm Sun.

Stop by the visitor center to get information about things to do, including local events, get help with your ferry reservations, and have a personalized itinerary created for your trip.

TRANSPORTATION

To get to Port Townsend from Seattle, you can take the **Edmonds-Kingston ferry** from Edmonds by taking I-5 north to exit 177 and following signs for the Edmonds-Kingston ferry. Once on the Kingston side, you'll then take Route 104 west to Route 19 north until you reach Port Townsend, about a 2-hour (56 mi/90 km) journey in total.

Alternatively, you can take the **Seattle-Bainbridge Island ferry** from Pier 52 and then follow Route 305, Route 3, Route 104, and Route 19 to Port Townsend, which also takes about 2 hours (58 mi/93 km). You'll want to consider the time of day and day of the week you're travelling—ferry waits can be several hours long during the summertime.

Sequim and Port Angeles

Port Angeles and neighboring Sequim are beautiful seaside communities with their own special appeal. Sequim is a charming small town with a downtown district full of shops, cafés, and art galleries. Port Angeles, being closer to the national park, attracts many people who want to explore the area's immense wilderness. The town is a little bigger than Sequim, and it has a more metropolitan vibe with its bustling downtown, numerous dining options, and active waterfront. The two towns are next to each other, so it's easy to go back and forth for sights and activities.

SEQUIM AND THE DUNGENESS VALLEY

Located on the shores of Dungeness Bay and the Dungeness River, Sequim (pronounced "Skwim") is a small town well worth a visit. Before logging and agriculture developed in the late 19th and early 20th centuries, the S'Klallam people called this area home. Due to the rain shadow effect of the Olympic

Mountains, Sequim has a microclimate that makes it one of the sunniest areas in Western Washington. This unusual climate has given rise to the nickname "Sunny Sequim."

★ Lavender Farms

Sequim is also called the "Lavender Capital of North America" because of its many vibrant lavender farms you can spot from the road. Every year, the Sequim Lavender Festival brings in thousands of visitors.

There are over 25 lavender farms to visit, many of which offer U-pick options and tours, and almost all have farm shops to browse. Late spring through early fall is usually the sweet spot for visiting these farms, with July being peak for blooms. You can visit the **Sequim Lavender Experience** (https://sequimlavender.org) for a map of all the farms.

One of the most popular times to visit Sequim is the third weekend of July when the **Sequim Lavender Weekend**

Port Angeles

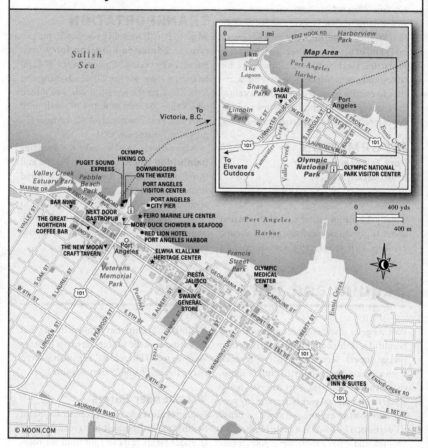

(www.lavenderfestival.com) takes place across the many lavender farms in the area. Each one is free to attend and has different offerings, including live music, interactive arts and crafts, demonstrations, beer gardens, and more.

Purple Haze Lavender Farm

180 Bell Bottom Rd.; 360/809-9615; https://purplehazelavender.com; 10am-5pm Thurs.-Sun.; free

Purple Haze Lavender is a 7-acre (3-ha) farm with U-pick lavender in the summer. It features a gift shop, ice cream stand, and vacation rental farmhouse ($1,200 for two-night min.). The farm also hosts bees and chickens.

In Bloom Lavender Farm

1526 Marine Dr.; 360/461-6464; https://inbloomlavenderfarms.com; 10am-5pm Thurs.-Sun. June-Sept.; free

In Bloom Lavender Farm is one of the oldest commercial lavender farms in the United States, and it produces essential oil and a

---

1: New Dungeness Lighthouse 2: Dungeness Spit 3: lavender farm in Sequim

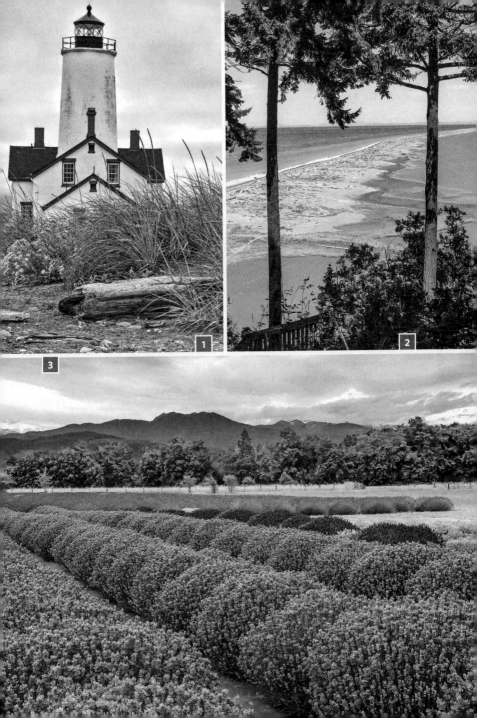

range of lavender-based products on-site in addition to their U-pick farm. They also have a farmhouse available for rent during the summer ($1,000 for two-night min.).

Jardin Du Soleil

3932 Sequim-Dungeness Way; 360/582-1185; www. jardindusoleil.com; 10am–5pm daily Apr.-Sept., 9am–6pm daily July, 10am–4pm Fri.-Sun. Oct.-Dec., closed Jan.-Feb.; free

There's over 10 acres (4 ha) of fragrant lavender fields at Jardin du Soleil, a certified organic lavender farm located on historic land. From late June to August, the farm lets guests pick their own lavender, or they can buy their high-quality organic lavender products.

Hiking
Dungeness Spit

Distance: *11 mi (17.7 km) round-trip*
Duration: *5.5 hours*
Elevation gain: *130 ft (40 m)*
Difficulty: *easy*
Trailhead: *Dungeness National Wildlife Refuge*

The Dungeness Spit National Wildlife Refuge ($3/family) is a popular hiking location. After a short, steep walk through the woods, you'll find yourself on a sandy beach with the New Dungeness Lighthouse at the end of the spit. The majority of this hike is walking along the beach to the lighthouse, after which you'll turn around to return the way you came. In addition to the occasional basking seal, the region is home to hundreds of birds, including black oystercatchers and snowy owls, making it a go-to spot with bird-watchers. It's best to go at low tide so you have more room to walk on the beach, so check the tide charts before you go.

From US 101, turn right at milepost 260 onto Kitchen-Dick Road, which will turn into Lotzgesell Road after 3 mi (5 km). Drive 0.25 mi (0.4 km) and then turn left onto Voice of America Road, which marks the entrance to Dungeness National Wildlife Refuge and Dungeness Recreation Area. Proceed through the county park and campground

until you reach the trailhead 1 mi (1.6 km) down the road.

Food
Essence Coffee Roasters

461 W. Washington St.; 360/683-8206; www.essence coffeeroasters.com; 7am-4pm Tues.-Sat., 7am-noon Mon.; $3-5

This modern coffee shop is a relaxing place to start your day, with espresso options such as cortados and nitro cold brew. They also serve kombucha and cold-pressed juice.

Oak Table Café

292 W. Bell St.; 360/683-2179; https://oaktablecafe. com; 7am-3pm daily; $12-20

This family-run restaurant has been in business for over 40 years and has breakfast options like French-baked omelets and their famous apple pancakes. They also serve lunch with a variety of salads, burgers, and sandwiches. This restaurant is great for groups, as its spacious area has a mix of booths and tables, in addition to large windows that let in light.

Nourish Sequim

101 Provence View Ln.; 360/797-1480; www. nourishsequim.com; 5pm-8pm Thurs.-Sun.; $22-42

Nourish is the place to go for fresh, farm-to-table dining, as their menu constantly changes based on the seasons so they can use the freshest ingredients and source everything locally. Join them for appetizers and a cocktail, or indulge in a three-course prix fixe menu ($72). It feels like you're having dinner with a friend as you walk through the garden to get to the charming red building that offers both indoor and outdoor seating.

Dockside Grill

2577 W. Sequim Bay Rd.; 360/683-7510; www. docksidegrill-sequim.com; 11:30am-4pm Wed-Sun.; $30-60

Treat yourself to waterfront dining at Dockside Grill—all the tables in this Pacific Northwest-themed restaurant have stunning views of Sequim Bay. They offer seasonally updated menus highlighting local organic ingredients and fresh seafood. Start with a signature martini and oysters, enjoy dishes like the cedar planked salmon, and end with a paired dessert.

Tedesco's Italian Fresh

210 W. Washington St.; 360/504-3821; www. tedescosfresh.com; 4pm-8pm Wed-Sat.; $18-40

Tedesco's is a contemporary Italian eatery with a cozy and warm ambience blending traditional favorites like eggplant parmesan and capelli romantica with modern dishes. They also boast a diverse bar with Italian wines, craft cocktails, and a nonalcoholic zero proof menu.

Accommodations
Olympic Railway Inn

24 Old Coyote Way; 206/880-1917; www.pikehg.com/ olympicrailwayinn; $118-205

The Olympic Railway Inn is a fun bed-and-breakfast where guests can choose from several converted train cabooses decorated with various themes, such as Native American artwork or wildflowers. Every caboose has a whirlpool tub and a comfortable mattress, and guests get free breakfast every morning.

PORT ANGELES

Port Angeles is known as the gateway to Olympic National Park. It's an ideal place to base your trip to the northern part of the peninsula, thanks to its buzzing waterfront and a downtown full of shops and restaurants. On clear days, you can look across and spot Vancouver Island, which is just a ferry ride away. Beyond the views, there's plenty to do, from whale-watching and fishing to hiking and biking the trails.

Sights
Feiro Marine Life Center

315 N. Lincoln St.; 360/775-5182; https:// feiromarinelifecenter.org; noon-4pm Thurs.-Mon.; $4-6

Located right on the waterfront, Feiro Marine Life Center is the best place to get up close and

personal with the vibrant marine life of the North Olympic Peninsula. Three touch tanks are full of sea stars and sea cucumbers, and plenty of exhibits show the local sealife, which all lives in water coming from the neighboring Port Angeles Harbor.

Elwha Klallam Heritage Center

401 E. 1st St.; 360/417-8545; www.elwha.org; 8:30am-4pm Mon.-Fri.; free

The Lower Elwha Klallam Tribe is one of three federally recognized S'Klallam tribes and has historically thrived around the Elwha River. This river has greatly impacted their way of life, fishing, and transportation. A vital center for preserving and sharing the rich history, culture, and profound influence of the Elwha Klallam people in the region, the Elwha Klallam Heritage Center emphasizes the tribe's long-lasting connection to the Elwha River, especially through the massive Elwha River restoration project.

Festivals and Events
Dungeness Crab & Seafood Festival

122 N. Lincoln St.; 360/452-6300; www.crabfestival. org; October; free

CrabFest honors Native American traditions with the Lower Elwha Song & Drum Group opening the ceremony up with traditional songs and stories. You'll also find food, drinks, and live music in several settings, including the renowned Crab Dinner at the Crab Central Tent ($25-40/person). In addition to the 5K Fun Run and demonstration by the United States Coast Guard, there are typically over 75 different vendors including arts and crafts, sweets, homemade goods like soaps, and much more.

Tour de Lavender

601 N. Sequim Ave.; 360/775-5395; https:// tourdelavender.com; August; $75

This long-distance bike ride encompasses eight different lavender farms, winding through Sequim and the Dungeness Valley's back roads, the Olympic Mountain foothills, and 30 mi (48 km) on the picturesque

Crabbing 101

crab pots

Thanks to its position on the Strait of Juan de Fuca, Port Angeles offers abundant crabbing opportunities.

SEASONS

Crabbing for Dungeness crab typically occurs in the colder months. The winter season for Dungeness crab is often **from early October to the end of December,** but it varies based on the specific region within Washington and the health of crab populations. Red rock crab, on the other hand, has a more extended season and is less regulated than the Dungeness.

Olympic Discovery Trail, a highlight of the North Olympic Peninsula's scenic bikeways, all in one day.

★ Whale-Watching

Port Angeles, with its proximity to the Strait of Juan de Fuca, is an ideal spot to observe the majestic mammals' annual migrations. After giving birth in Baja California, Mexico, gray whales migrate north to the Arctic to feed March-May. In May-September, you can see the iconic resident orcas, which are black and white and easily recognizable.

To get the most out of the experience, some preparation is necessary. Dressing in layers is essential, as temperatures on the water are cooler than on land, even in the summertime. It's also important to know that whale-watching takes patience, as the tour companies can't always predict when the whales will come. Lastly, while the waters here generally are tame, seasickness can happen when the waters get choppy, so it's smart to take preventative measures so you can enjoy your trip.

If you're lucky and the whales are friendly, you may be able to see them from the shoreline. But your best bet is to book a tour so you have a higher success rate.

It's essential to always check with the **Washington Department of Fish and Wildlife** (WDFW; https://wdfw.wa.gov) for the latest regulations and season dates since these can change.

LICENSES

In Washington, everyone 15 or older needs a **fishing license** (WDFW; https://wdfw.wa.gov; $18-70 residents, $36-125 nonresidents). Licenses for sturgeon, halibut, salmon, steelhead, or Puget Sound Dungeness crab include a catch record card. Buy licenses online at WDFW's website or at local sports stores around Port Angeles.

GEAR

Crabbing essentials include a crab pot or ring, bait, a buoy, and a line.

WHERE TO GO

- **Port Angeles City Pier** (next to Feiro Marine Life Center, 315 N. Lincoln St.; 360/417-4523; www.cityofpa.us; 24 hours; free): The Port Angeles City Pier is an easy place to go crabbing since crabbers can drop their pots from the pier or neighboring boats and into waters where Dungeness and red rock crabs thrive. There are also cleaning stations and plenty of storage space for crabbers' gear at the pier.

- **Freshwater Bay** (2298 Freshwater Bay Rd.; 360/417-2291; www.clallamcountywa.gov): Freshwater Bay is a favored location for crabbing, where crabbers can drop their pots from boats in the bay.

TOURS

Hood Canal Adventures (306146 US 101, Brinnon; 360/301-6310; https://hoodcanaladventures.com; 10am-4pm Thurs.-Mon.; $19-145), on the eastern side of the Olympic Peninsula, offers a kayak crabbing package that comes with everything you need for a day of crabbing in a kayak, which is a great way to try your hand if you don't have your own gear.

Puget Sound Express

115 E. Railroad Ave.; 360/385-5288; www.pugetsoundexpress.com; May-Oct.; $105-135

This 3-4-hour cruise includes both a warm, heated cabin and an outdoor deck. A professional naturalist will educate on everything from whales to puffins as well as the area's history and geography as you go from the San Juan Islands to Victoria, British Columbia, across the Strait of Juan de Fuca.

Freshwater Bay County Park

2298 Freshwater Bay Rd.; 360/417-2291; 24 hours; free

Freshwater Bay County Park has 21 acres (8.5 ha) and 1,500 ft (450 m) of tidelands and is a good place for wildlife-watching, especially orcas and seals. There's also year-round beach access, a boat launch, and picnic spots.

Biking

Olympic Discovery Trail

Port Townsend to La Push; https://olympicdiscoverytrail.org

The Peninsula's Olympic Discovery Trail stretches 135 mi (217 km) from Port Townsend's Victorian charm to the coastal beauty of La Push. Bikers will go along the Port Townsend harbor and the north shore of Lake Crescent and end up at the Pacific Ocean.

This trail has a combination of gravel

and pavement, and while a good portion of it is traffic-free, occasionally you'll be on the highway with cars (check the website's maps). Some people love to do the whole 135 mi (217 km), but you can easily enjoy the trail in shorter sections. For example, the East Trail Segment is only 26 mi (42 km) and goes from Port Angeles, through Sequim, and ends at Blyn. If you want to camp, make a reservation at one of the state parks along the way, such as Sequim Bay State Park or Salt Creek Campground.

Elevate Outdoors

2358 US 101; 360/417-3015; www.elevateoutdoors.us; 10am-3pm daily; tours from $109

Elevate Outdoors provides exciting bike tours for road and gravel cyclists looking for singletrack adventures. Over the course of 3 hours, you will explore the Olympic Discovery Trail's Adventure Route. They also have bike and rack rentals for those who want to go alone.

Elwha eBike Adventures

47 Lower Dam Rd.; 360/457-9024; www. elwhaebikeadventures.com; 9am-5pm daily; bike rentals $65-100, tours $200-250/person

If you're 18 or older, you can rent an e-bike to explore Port Angeles and the surrounding trails. This outfit offers a variety of different bikes and will meet you at certain trails for an additional fee. Guided tours are also available if you'd prefer to have someone show you around.

Kayaking
Port Angeles Harbor

338 W. First St.; 360/457-8527; https://portofpa.com

The Port Angeles Harbor is an ideal area for kayakers to paddle in calm waters and have the chance to see a variety of animals, including seals, sea lions, and even orcas. **Ediz Hook,** a sand spit sheltering the harbor, is just one of the surrounding kayaking spots accessible from the harbor.

Elevate Outdoors

2358 US 101; 360/417-3015; www.elevateoutdoors.us; 10am-3pm daily; tours from $89, SUP rental $64/day

Discover the shoreline of Freshwater Bay and the pristine waters of Lake Crescent with guided kayak tours of 2.5-3.5 hours. Stand-up paddleboards are also available to rent for those who want a solo adventure.

Fishing

Fishing is popular in Port Angeles, and anglers often gravitate toward Ediz Hook for shore fishing. Freshwater Bay and areas around Salt Creek Recreation Area are popular for boat fishing, especially for salmon and halibut.

Chinook salmon is abundant July-September, while coho salmon runs late August-September. Pink salmon makes its appearance in August, but only every odd-numbered year. A fishing license is required for anyone over 15 and can be purchased online through the **Washington Department of Fish and Wildlife** (WDFW; https://wdfw. wa.gov; $18-70 residents, $36-125 nonresidents) or at local sports stores.

All-Ways Fishing

360/374-2052; www.allwaysfishing.com; call for customized price

While All-Ways Fishing is based in Forks and goes all over the northwestern coast, they do some fishing out of Port Angeles. Each trip is customized, so call for an exact quote and let them know what type of fish you want to catch, such as halibut, salmon, or lingcod. Some fish species are located farther out, so you might have to drive a bit to meet the charter.

Swain's General Store

602 E. First St.; 360/452-2357; www.swainsinc.com; 8am-8pm Mon.-Sat., 9am-6pm Sun.

Swain's General Store's slogan is "Slain's has everything," which you'll find true as you browse through the dozens of crab pots, fishing poles, lures, and other fishing gear needed. In case you forgot something, they also have men's and women's clothing and footwear.

Nightlife
Bar N9NE
229 W. First St.; 360/797-1999; Facebook @BarN9NE; 2pm-2am daily; $10-15

There's always something going on at Bar N9NE, from live music to trivia nights, and weekly specials such as Wednesday wing night. They have a full bar and a small food menu including appetizers and pizza options. While it's a hole-in-the-wall dive bar, it has a fun atmosphere for meeting locals.

The New Moon Craft Tavern
130 S. Lincoln St.; 360/452-4471; 3pm-midnight Tues.-Sat., 3pm-10pm Mon.; $10-25

The New Moon Craft Tavern is a lively dive with over 20 beers on tap in addition to a full bar. They bring in local music performers and have open mic nights for aspiring singers.

Food
The Great Northern Coffee Bar
118 W. First St.; 360/797-1658; www. thegreatnortherncoffeebar.com; 7am-4pm Sun.-Thurs. 7am-6pm Fri.-Sat.; $6-16

You can get a hearty breakfast at this coffee shop, with options such as breakfast sandwiches and burritos. Their coffee names will have you smile with drinks like Into the Woods and Campers Delight.

★ Next Door GastroPub
113 W. First St.; 360/504-2613; https:// nextdoorgastropub.com; 11am-10pm Thurs.-Tues.; $10-20

Next Door GastroPub elevates pub cuisine with a menu full of fresh, local ingredients, offering everything from poutine to burgers to fish tacos, paired with a dynamic selection of craft cocktails and local artisan beers on 10 rotating taps. It's a family-friendly spot catering to all seasons, with outdoor seating in the summer and a cozy indoor ambience for colder months.

Fiesta Jalisco
636 E. Front St.; 360/452-3928; Facebook @Fiesta-Jalisco-Port-Angeles; 11am-9pm Mon.-Thurs., 11am-9:30pm Fri.-Sat.; $15-22

Fiesta Jalisco has a vibrant atmosphere with authentic Mexican cuisine, such as fajitas and enchiladas, all crafted with fresh ingredients. Their large portion sizes will leave you full.

Sabai Thai
903 W. 8th St. #5721; 360/452-4505; www. sabaithaiportangeles.com; 4pm-8:30pm Tues.-Thurs., 4pm-9pm Fri.-Sat.; $12-45

Sabai Thai creates a variety of authentic Thai dishes, ranging from crab Rangoon to tom kha or swimming rama, customized to the spice level you prefer. The relaxed setting has a giant fish tank and Thai decor throughout.

Downriggers on the Water
115 E. Railroad Ave., Suite 207; 360/452-2700; www. downriggerspa.com; 11:30am-8pm Sun.-Thurs., 11:30am-9am Fri.-Sat.; $12-43

Famous for its fresh, locally caught seafood, Downriggers on the Water has beautiful harbor views too. Indoor and outdoor seating is available, making this a great place to have a meal while people-watching among the boats and marine life. Don't miss the pan-fried oyster po'boy or the creamy crab and prawn fettuccini.

Moby Duck Chowder & Seafood
222 N. Lincoln St.; 360/912-2835; https:// mobyduckchowder.com; 11am-8pm Tues.-Thurs., 11am-9pm Fri.-Sat., 11am-8pm Sun.; $15-42

It's no surprise there are plenty of places to get seafood in town, given its proximity to the ocean, and Moby Duck Chowder & Seafood has plenty of fresh-caught fish in its welcoming setting with a giant fishing ship mural on the wall. Try the Dungeness crab roll served on a buttery brioche bun, or have a bowl of their famous Moby Duck chowder.

Accommodations

Red Lion Hotel Port Angeles Harbor

221 N. Lincoln St.; 360/452-9215; www.redlion.com; $157-179

The Red Lion Hotel Port Angeles Harbor is located on the waterfront and features a restaurant and bar. Thanks to its convenient position on the harbor, guests can easily reach the Vancouver Island ferry terminals. Its sleek 187 rooms have comfortable queen- and king-sized beds, and the hotel has a fitness center and outdoor pool.

Olympic Inn & Suites

1510 E. Front St.; 360/452-4015; www. olympicinnandsuites.net; $75-195

The Olympic Inn and Suites in Port Angeles has 109 rooms, including some equipped with a kitchen with a microwave, refrigerator, and stovetop so you can make your own meals. There is also a seasonal outdoor pool. While it's more of a basic, no-frills hotel, it's an affordable place to stay while still being in downtown Port Angeles.

Juan de Fuca Cottages

182 Marine Dr.; 360/683-4433; https://juandefuca. com; $177-269

There are 13 different charming homes to choose from at Juan de Fuca Cottages, all with stunning views of the lake or nearby mountains, and several of them include full kitchens. You'll find everything from a 2-person suite to a large house with a deck that fits 16 people, making it ideal for large groups. A private beach is available for guests to use as well.

Camping

Salt Creek Recreation Area

3506 Camp Hayden Rd.; 360/928-3441; www.clallam countywa.gov; 6am-10pm May-Sept., 7am-9pm Oct.; $30

Sand volleyball courts, horseshoe pits, hiking trails, a basketball court, and a large playing field are just some of the features that can be found at Salt Creek Recreation Area. It has 92 campsites, some reservable in advance and some first-come, first-served.

Information and Services

Port Angeles Visitor Center

21 E. Railroad Ave.; 360/452-2363; www.portangeles. org; 10am-4pm Mon.-Fri., 10am-3pm Sat., 10am-1pm Sun.

The Port Angeles Visitor Center is one of the busiest visitors centers in the state. You can ask volunteers about your travel plans and get maps of the area.

Olympic National Park Visitor Center

3002 Mt. Angeles Rd.; 360/565-3130; www.nps.gov; 9am-4pm daily

Stop by the Olympic National Park Visitor Center to get tips on which hikes to do, how to best plan your day, and learn more about the park through its exhibits. They also have a gift shop for souvenirs.

Olympic Medical Center

939 Caroline St.; 360/417-7000; www.olympicmedical. org

Olympic Medical Center is the main hospital in the Port Angeles area. It has an emergency room, birth center, and is a Level III trauma center.

Transportation

Car

Port Angeles can be reached from Seattle by heading south on I-5 and then taking Route 16, Route 3, Route 104, and then US 101 north into Port Angeles (138 mi/222 km, 3 hours). To reach Port Angeles from Port Townsend, take Route 20 west to US 101, then US 101 into Port Angeles. It takes about 1 hour (47 mi/76 km) to get there.

Ferry

You can also reach Port Angeles by driving I-5 north and Route 104 from Seattle west to Edmonds (17 mi/27 km) and taking the Edmonds ferry to Kingston, and then continuing on Route 104 until it turns into US 101 to Port Angeles (61 mi/98 km). The trip takes about 2.5 hours in total.

Greyhound buses picking up from various locations in downtown Seattle stop at the Port

Northern Olympic National Park

If people have time to visit only one area of
Olympic National Park, the northern section
is usually it. It's easiest to access via Port
Angeles and has the popular Hurricane Ridge
area, as well as the park's two hot springs,
mountains, lakes, and plenty of wildlife. The
main visitor center for the park is also here,
so you can get plenty of helpful information
before venturing out.

PARK INFORMATION
Planning Your Time
It's easy to visit a couple of sights within the
same section of the park in one day. For example, if you're in the northern section, you can
visit Hurricane Ridge in the morning to hike
and then take the 1-hour drive over to Lake
Crescent to kayak in the afternoon. But it's
best to avoid going between sections within
a day—the Northern, Western, and Eastern
portions are hours apart, and the driving time
adds up.

If you'd prefer to join a tour, you can go
with **Olympic Hiking Co.** (115 E. Railroad
Ave., Port Angeles; 360/457-2259; www.
hikeolympic.com; $110), who will take you on
an all-day tour of Sol Duc, Lake Crescent, and
Hurricane Ridge. They also offer tours to the
Hoh Rain Forest and Rialto Beach.

Areas
The northern section has four different areas,
but they are not connected. That means you'll
need to go to one area and retrace the way you
came before heading into another part of the
park.

Hurricane Ridge: In the summer, this
area becomes a hiker's paradise due to its
many trails and abundance of wildlife viewing opportunities. When winter rolls around,

it becomes a snow sports wonderland with the
Hurricane Ridge Ski and Snowboard Area.
Access this area via the Heart O' the Hills
Entrance Station on Hurricane Ridge Road.

Elwha River Valley: A prime example of
the ecological restoration achieved with the
effective dismantling of the Elwha and Glines
Canyon Dams is the Elwha River Valley.
Olympic Hot Springs and West Elwha are just
two of the popular hiking trails here. Access
this area via the Elwha Entrance Station on
Olympic Hot Springs Road.

Lake Crescent: Glaciers formed Lake
Crescent, which is perfect for kayaking and
fishing due to its deep and clear waters. The
historic Lake Crescent Lodge adds to the allure, an ideal place to eat at or stay overnight. Access this area via US Highway 101,
about 20 mi (32 km) west of Port Angeles.
There is no entrance station, but you will
still be expected to display a national parks
pass, which can be obtained online or at
the Olympic National Park Visitor Center
in Port Angeles.

Sol Duc River Valley: The area is well-
known for its salmon runs and the therapeu-
tic Sol Duc Hot Springs. There are a handful
of hikes here as well, including Sol Duc Falls.
Access this area via the Sol Duc Entrance
Station on Sol Duc Hot Springs Road.

Seasons and Weather
Summer is by far the best time to visit the
park—flowers are blooming everywhere, and
there's little rain, making it ideal for camping and hiking. Since this is the peak season,
everything is open, from visitor centers to
lodging and restaurants. The downside is that
everyone else also agrees it's the prime time to
go, so you'll be fighting for parking spots on

Northern Olympic National Park

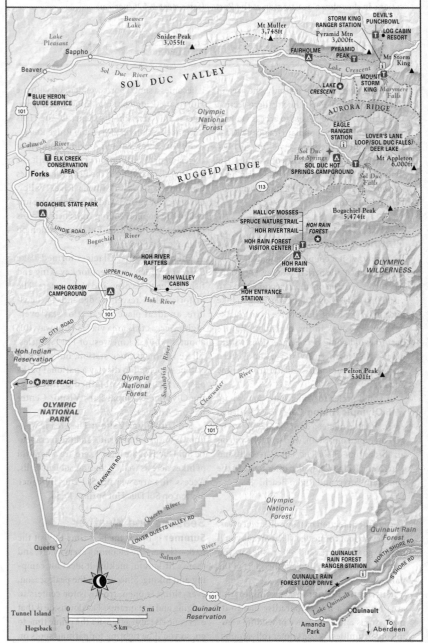

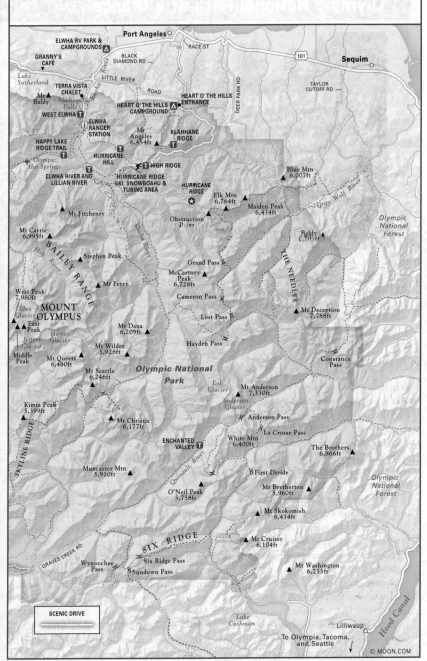

Port Angeles

Sequim

ELWHA RV PARK & CAMPGROUNDS

GRANNY'S CAFÉ

Lake Sutherland

BLACK DIAMOND RD

LITTLE RIVER

RACE ST

101

DEER PARK RD

TAYLOR CUTOFF RD

TERRA VISTA CHALET

Mt Baldy

Madison Falls

WEST ELWHA

ELWHA RANGER STATION

ROAD

HEART O' THE HILLS ENTRANCE

HEART O' THE HILLS CAMPGROUND

HAPPY LAKE RIDGE TRAIL

Olympic Hot Springs

HURRICANE HILL

ELWHA RIVER AND LILLIAN RIVER

Mt Angeles 6,454ft

KLAHHANE RIDGE

HIGH RIDGE

HURRICANE RIDGE SKI, SNOWBOARD & TUBING AREA

HURRICANE RIDGE

Blue Mtn 6,007ft

Gray Wolf River

Mt Fitzhenry

Obstruction Point

Elk Mtn 6,764ft

Maiden Peak 6,434ft

Olympic National Forest

Mt Carrie 6,995ft

BAILEY RANGE

Hoh River

Stephen Peak

Mt Ferry

Grand Pass

McCartney Peak 6,728ft

THE NEEDLES

Buckhorn 6,701ft

West Peak 7,980ft

MOUNT OLYMPUS

Blue Glacier

East Peak

Jeffers Glacier

Humes Glacier

Cameron Pass

Lost Pass

Mt Deception 7,788ft

Middle Peak

Mt Queets 6,480ft

Mt Dana 6,209ft

Mt Wilder 5,928ft

Hayden Pass

Constance Pass

Mt Seattle 6,246ft

Olympic National Park

Eel Glacier

Mt Anderson 7,330ft

Kimta Peak 5,399ft

SKYLINE RIDGE

Mt Christie 6,177ft

Anderson Glacier

Anderson Pass

La Crosse Pass

The Brothers 6,866ft

ENCHANTED VALLEY

White Mtn 6,400ft

Muncaster Mtn 5,910ft

Quinault River

First Divide

Olympic National Forest

O'Neil Peak 5,758ft

Mt Bretherton 5,960ft

Mt Skokomish 6,434ft

SIX RIDGE

Mt Cruiser 6,104ft

Mt Washington 6,255ft

GRAVES CREEK RD

Wynoochee Pass

Six Ridge Pass

Sundown Pass

SCENIC DRIVE

Lake Cushman

Lilliwaup

Hood Canal

To Olympia, Tacoma, and Seattle

© MOON.COM

Olympic National Park at a Glance

Olympic National Park Visitor Center

The ancient rain forests, rocky shores, and snowcapped mountains of Olympic National Park make it seem like you're in a storybook. In the northern section, relax on the picturesque shores of Lake Crescent or ascend Hurricane Ridge for stunning views of the Olympic Mountains and even Canada. The western section is home to the beautiful, moss-covered Hoh Rain Forest, and if you travel further west to the wild Pacific coast, you'll find waves crashing against rocky shores and aquatic life abounding in tidal pools. With activities such as hiking through alpine meadows

summer weekends. The best bet is to go weekdays or get into the park early. Summer is the warmest season, with average temperatures ranging from 50-70°F (10-21°C).

In **fall,** temperatures gradually decrease, averaging between 40-55°F (4-13°C). You'll see beautiful foliage, and if you can stand a little rain, you will have more of the park to yourself. The same goes for **spring**—you'll probably get some drizzle, but you won't be fighting crowds for parking at trailheads, and you'll also have the chance to see some vibrant wildflowers. Spring sees temperatures rising to about 45-55°F (7-13°C).

Winter is the least popular time to visit. During winter, temperatures typically range from 35-45°F (2-7°C). There are still plenty of areas to explore, but don't expect much in the way of services, as many resorts and visitor centers will be closed until the spring. Before

setting out on a snowshoe trek, check the local route conditions, and be wary of the powerful winds, tides, and surges that winter brings to the coastline. If traveling to Hurricane Ridge, all vehicles must carry tire chains above the Heart O' the Hills entrance station November 1-April 1.

Fees

Entrance fees are $30/vehicle, $25/motorcycle, or $15/hiker or biker, and the fee is good for seven days. Most entrances have a ranger booth where you stop and pay the fee before proceeding. If you get there before the ranger arrives, you can pay at the booth on the way out.

Food and Accommodations

Food is somewhat limited in the park, with the exception of the restaurants at Lake Crescent

adorned with wildflowers, unwinding in Sol Duc Hot Springs, and stargazing under the park's perfect night sky, Olympic National Park is one of the most spectacular parks in Washington.

Navigating this park is very different compared to other national parks. Olympic is divided into standalone sections. Rather than driving through it to reach the different areas, you can only return the way you came, travel on the highway for a bit, then enter the next section. Luckily, your entrance fee covers seven days of exploration.

- **Park website:** www.nps.gov/olym

- **Entrance fee:** $30/vehicle, $25/motorcycle, $15/walk-in, or America the Beautiful Pass ($79 for all national parks for one year; purchase at any visitor center or entrance booth)

- **Main visitor center:** Olympic National Park Visitor Center (3002 Mt. Angeles Rd.; 360/565-3130; www.nps.gov; 9am-4pm daily)

- **Main Regions:** Northern (Hurricane Ridge, Elwha River Valley, Lake Crescent, Sol Duc River Valley), Western (Hoh Rain Forest, Kalaloch, Lake Quinault and Quinault Rain Forest)

- **Hotel and park activity reservations:** www.olympicnationalparks.com

- **Campsite reservations:** www.recreation.gov

- **Permits:** Permits are required for overnight camping and can be obtained from recreation.gov through the Olympic National Park Wilderness Permit page or through the Wilderness Information Center at 360/565-3100 ($8/person/night plus $6 reservation fee per permit).

- **Gas:** There is no gas within the park. There are two gas stations close to each other at Lake Quinault, or fuel up in surrounding cities such as Port Angeles or Forks.

- **High season:** June-Sept.

Lodge and Sol Duc Hot Springs Resort. It's best to bring your own food with you, and you'll be nearby Port Angeles and its plentiful grocery stores and restaurants.

Due to limited accommodations in the park, booking your rooms months in advance is necessary if you plan on visiting during the summer. The same goes for campsites—some campgrounds have a small number of sites, so reserve those well in advance.

★ HURRICANE RIDGE

Hurricane Ridge is one of the most-visited spots in the park, thanks to its stunning views and easy-access hikes. Situated just 17 mi (27 km) south of Port Angeles, the area is easily accessible by car, and the drive up to the ridge is scenic, winding through forests and offering views of the Olympic Mountains. On the way, stop at **Heart O' the Hills Entrance**

Station to pay the entrance fee. Once at the ridge, visitors are greeted with views of the park's rugged mountain terrain, green valleys, and, on clear days, a view of the Strait of Juan de Fuca and even Canada.

Visitor Centers and Ranger Stations
Hurricane Ridge Visitor Center
3002 Mt. Angeles Rd.; 360/565-3130; www.nps.gov
Hurricane Ridge is open, but the visitor center burned down in 2023 and has no estimated rebuilding date. You'll pass through the Heart o' the Hills entrance station to pay your park fee before continuing to Hurricane Ridge. Portable toilets, water, and information services are available at Hurricane Ridge.

Hiking
Keep an eye out for wildlife on the trail,

including deer, black bears, and a variety of bird species.

Klahhane Ridge

Distance: 5 mi (8 km) round-trip
Duration: 2.5 hours
Elevation gain: 1,700 ft (520 m)
Difficulty: moderate
Trailhead: Switchback Trail parking lot off Hurricane Ridge Road

Klahhane Ridge is accessible by four different routes, with the most direct one being Switchback Trail off Hurricane Ridge Road. You'll quickly gain 1,500 ft (450 m) in only 1.5 mi (2.5 km) as the steep climb goes through subalpine forests and open meadows. In summer you'll be rewarded with wildflowers like lupine and glacier lilies—and possible mountain goat sightings—as well as views of the surrounding valley and mountains. When you're ready, head back the way you came.

High Ridge

Distance: 0.8 mi (1.3 km) round-trip
Duration: 30 minutes
Elevation gain: 213 ft (65 m)
Difficulty: easy
Trailhead: Hurricane Ridge Visitor Center parking lot

Starting as a paved path before transitioning to dirt, this easy loop trail is often taken by people looking to connect longer hikes. It merges with the Sunrise Trail that goes to Klahhane Ridge Trail for those seeking a more challenging trek. Early on, the trail forks, but both routes lead to the top and are collectively known as the High Ridge Trail.

Hurricane Hill

Distance: 3.2 mi (5.1 km) round-trip
Duration: 1.5 hours
Elevation gain: 650 ft (200 m)
Difficulty: easy/moderate
Trailhead: main parking area for Hurricane Ridge

A peaceful walk through shrublands and pine

1: Hurricane Ridge 2: Madison Falls 3: Lake Crescent

forests sets the stage for the gradual ascent via three wide switchbacks to a summit. Along the way, you'll see signs that describe the landscape's peaks, nearby cities, and the history of fires. The trail winds up to Hurricane Hill, becoming steeper as you ascend, eventually leading to an exposed summit. Sit back and enjoy the view of Vancouver Island, Port Angeles, and the Strait of Juan de Fuca from the peak before returning the way you came.

Winter Sports

With 20 mi (32 km) of trails, Hurricane Ridge is a popular spot for **snowshoeing** and **cross-country skiing.** There's a variety of unmarked trails to explore, and novice skiers will find beginner-friendly terrain in the level meadows situated above the **Hurricane Ridge Visitor Center.** The region has a number of bowls and slopes that backcountry skiers can enjoy, but navigation skills are important, as they aren't groomed or marked.

Accessing Hurricane Ridge Road in winter can be tricky. Assuming favorable weather and road conditions, the road opens at 9am Fridays through Sundays and certain holidays, and 4pm is the cutoff for anyone going through the entrance station. All vehicles must exit the park by 5pm to avoid spending the night behind the gates. Tire chains are required for all vehicles, including those with four-wheel drive.

Gear rental isn't currently available here due to the lodge fire, so bring your own or rent in Port Angeles.

Snowshoeing

Once there is enough snow, you can join a **ranger-led snowshoe walk** (1:30pm Sat.-Sun.). Snowshoes and instructions are included, and these 1.5-hour treks cover less than a mile (1.6 km) and ascend 130 ft (40 m) in elevation. The walk is limited to the first 15 people who show up at 1pm at the visitor contact station in the Hurricane Ridge parking area. To verify if the walks are still taking place, you can call 360/565-3130.

Hurricane Ridge Ski, Snowboard, and Tubing Area

Hurricane Ridge Rd. just before the visitor center; 360/565-3130; www.hurricaneridge.com; 10am-4pm Sat.-Sun. mid Dec.-late Mar.; $25-57

Operated by the Hurricane Ridge Winter Sports Club, this is a family-friendly ski destination. It features two rope tows, a tubing park, and a poma lift. Lessons ($70-99) in skiing, snowboarding, and snowshoeing are available for individuals aged four and older. Equipment rental is not currently available due to the lodge fire.

Camping
Heart O' the Hills Campground

2823 S. Oak St.; 360/565-3131; www.nps.gov; year-round; $24

Heart O' the Hills Campground is set in an old-growth forest and operates on a first-come, first-served basis. There are 97 sites, flush toilets, and potable water. The campground accommodates RVs, although there is no dump station. In summer there are ranger-led programs.

Transportation

Hurricane Ridge is a 40-minute drive from Port Angeles. From US 101 in Port Angeles, head south on Race Street, then make a slight right onto Hurricane Ridge Road, which you follow to the Hurricane Ridge parking lot (17 mi/27 km).

ELWHA RIVER VALLEY

One of America's largest ecological restoration projects, the Elwha River today flows freely from its mountain headwaters to the Strait of Juan de Fuca. Dams constructed in the early 1900s to generate hydroelectric power were blocking the river for more than a century and causing severe damage to ecosystems. Salmon populations were hit the hardest because the dams cut off their migration routes.

The Elwha Dam was demolished in 2011 and the Glines Canyon Dam in 2014—the biggest dam removal project in American history. Since the Elwha River reestablished its connection to the sea, many fish and other aquatic species have been able to return to their original spawning locations, reviving the river's ecosystem.

Elwha River Valley offers fewer sights than the other areas, so you might do a hike or two here before moving on. Access this area via the Elwha River Valley entrance station on Olympic Hot Springs Road. Note: Car traffic is currently prohibited past the Madison Falls parking lot due to a road washout caused by flooding, and there is no estimated reopening date.

Visitor Centers and Ranger Stations
Elwha Ranger Station

Olympic Hot Springs Rd.; www.nps.gov

Stop by the Elwha Ranger Station to pick up permits and get information about the Elwha Valley in general. Restrooms are also available.

Sights
Madison Falls

Madison Falls is one of the easiest waterfalls in the park to see with minimal effort, as it's a very short walk (0.1 mi/0.2 km) on a paved trail through a forest. To get here from Port Angeles, head west on US 101 for 6 mi (10 km), and turn left onto Olympic Hot Springs Road and continue for 2 mi (3 km). The parking lot for Madison Falls is on the left.

Hiking
Olympic Hot Springs

A number of hot springs can be found spread out along the Olympic Hot Springs Trail. Some of the pools are close together and others are more remote; you might see guests enjoying the hot springs in swimwear and others in nothing at all. Checking the water temperature is a must when venturing into the hot springs; different pools reach temperatures, up to 118°F (48°C). Also, these hot springs may have fecal coliform bacteria since the National Park Service doesn't maintain them.

The road washout has made the journey to these springs longer than before—it's now close to 20 mi (32 km) round-trip—but the extra effort is well worth it. The trail can be accessed from Madison Creek Falls trailhead. Visit nps.gov for current road conditions.

Elwha River and Lillian River

Distance: *13.5 mi (21.7 km) round-trip*

Duration: *7 hours*

Elevation gain: *1,200 ft (365 m)*

Difficulty: *moderate*

Trailhead: *Whiskey Bend Trailhead*

This well-maintained trail takes you through the quiet forest and along the beautiful Lillian River, so it's a good hike to enjoy some peace and quiet. Initially flat, the trail begins a gentle climb, surrounded by lush mosses and dense foliage. At 1.8 mi (2.9 km) is a three-way junction and a historic log cabin. Continue straight. The trail eventually opens to a sunny, rocky area with madrone trees, then descends to the base of Idaho Falls, which is a stunning place to stop for pictures as you feel the cool mist on your face. At 3 mi (4.8 km) is the turn-off for Lillian River. The quieter and more secluded Lillian River trail stretches for another 3.5 mi (5.6 km) to its endpoint at the banks of the river, where you can return the way you came.

To reach Whiskey Bend Trailhead, travel west on US 101 to Olympic Hot Springs Road, then turn left and proceed for 4 mi (6.5 km) to Whiskey Bend Road. Follow Whiskey Bend Road for an additional 4 mi (6.5 km) to the trailhead. Note: Due to a washout, Olympic Hot Springs Road is closed to vehicle traffic. However, hikers and bikers can still reach the trail by traveling 6 mi (10 km) one-way on the closed road, starting from the Madison Falls parking area.

West Elwha

Distance: *7 mi (11.2 km) round-trip*

Duration: *4 hours*

Elevation gain: *1,400 ft (425 m)*

Difficulty: *moderate*

Trailhead: *End of Herrick Road*

Hiking the West Elwha Trail evokes echoes of the past, when it was a primary pack train route for transporting supplies to the historic Olympic Hot Springs Resort, before the era of automobiles. This trail skirts private property before entering the lush, green expanse of the national park. Along the way, hikers can enjoy views of the Elwha River and picturesque side creeks. The trail ends at the site of the former Altair Campground, which the river has since reclaimed.

From the junction of US 101 and Route 112, head west on US 101 for 3.9 mi (6.3 km), then turn left onto Herrick Road. The trailhead is at the end of Herrick Road, which has a parking capacity of about 3 cars.

Backpacking

Happy Lake Ridge Trail

Distance: *30 mi (48 km) round-trip*

Duration: *3-4 days*

Elevation gain: *9,650 ft (2,940 m)*

Difficulty: *strenuous*

Trailhead: *Madison Falls trailhead*

The trail ascends to Happy Lake, reaching a reliable water source at 0.25 mi (0.4 km). After climbing 3 mi (5 km) to a ridge at 4,500 ft (1,370 m), enjoy views of the Elwha Valley and nearby mountains. At 5.8 mi (9.3 km), a side trail descends to Happy Lake, suitable for a day hike turnaround or camping. The trail then offers vistas of the Strait of Juan de Fuca and Mount Olympus before continuing at 8.3 mi (13.4 km) toward Boulder Lake, with an overlook of Boulder Peak. Descend 500 ft to Boulder Lake's campsites, then follow the Boulder Lake Trail for 2.9 mi (4.7 km) to a junction, turning left toward Boulder Creek Campground and a side trail to Olympic Hot Springs. This is another good spot to set up camp if you're backpacking. Note that Happy Lake Ridge has limited water sources; refill at the lakes. Head back the way you came.

Note: Due to the road washout, you'll need to park at Madison Falls and hike or bike 8 mi (13 km) to the Happy Lake trailhead. From Port Angeles, follow US 101 west for about 10 mi (16 km), then turn left onto Olympic

Hot Springs Road, just before the bridge over the Elwha River. Follow Olympic Hot Springs Road to the park entrance gate, and park at the Madison Falls trailhead.

Accommodations
Terra Vista Chalet

907 Herrick Rd.; 360/406-5490; https:// terravistachalet.com; $109-347

At Terra Vista Chalet, each of the four rooms is a relaxing experience in itself and features a fireplace, balcony, and custom lighting. It's a beautiful place to relax and enjoy the Elwha River Valley views out the massive windows in the shared grand living room.

Elwha RV Park & Campgrounds

47 Lower Dam Rd.; 360/452-7054; https:// elwhadamrvpark.com; $49-82

Elwha RV Park & Campgrounds caters to tent campers and RV owners. The tent sites offer essential amenities like picnic tables and fire pits, situated close to restrooms and showers. RV sites have full hookups, and Wi-Fi is available throughout the park.

Transportation

From Port Angeles, head west on US 101 for about 10 mi (16 km), then turn left onto Olympic Hot Springs Road. This scenic drive takes you directly into the Elwha River Valley. While it's only about 10 mi (16 km), it's narrow and windy, so allow at least 30 minutes to safely drive it.

Note: Olympic Hot Springs Road is closed at Madison Falls trailhead due to the road washout. For the latest status update, visit the NPS website.

★ LAKE CRESCENT

Formed by glaciers, Lake Crescent is one of the deepest lakes in Washington and is famous for its crystal-clear waters and dazzling scenery. Many people come here for beautiful hikes, kayaking trips, and fishing. As if the lake's captivating beauty weren't enough, the historic Lake Crescent Lodge, a landmark resort building, has been welcoming guests since 1916 and is worth an overnight stay.

Access this area via US 101. There is no entrance station, but you still be expected to display a national parks pass which can be obtained online.

Visitor Centers and Ranger Stations
Storm King Ranger Station

Lake Crescent Rd., Marymere Falls trailhead; 360/928-3380; www.nps.gov

The ranger station is located right at the Marymere Falls and Mount Storm King parking lot, so it's an ideal place to check on the trail conditions for these two hikes.

Hiking
Marymere Falls

Distance: *1.8 mi (2.9 km) round-trip*
Duration: *1 hour*
Elevation gain: *500 ft (150 m)*
Difficulty: *easy*
Trailhead: *Storm King Ranger Station*

Marymere Falls is one of the most popular trails in the park, as it's doable for most skill levels. The flat trail goes through a forest, over a bridge, and then up a small hill with waterfalls on the other side.

To get here, travel 20 mi west from Port Angeles on US 101, and at milepost 228, turn right into the well-signed parking area for Lake Crescent and Marymere Falls. Proceed to Storm King Ranger Station and park there.

Mount Storm King

Distance: *4 mi (6.4 km) round-trip*
Duration: *2.5 hours*
Elevation gain: *2,065 ft (630 m)*
Difficulty: *moderate*
Trailhead: *Storm King Ranger Station*

The trail to Mount Storm King begins at the Marymere Falls trailhead and is flat until the signed left turn for Mount Storm King. You'll get glimpses of the valley below, and after 1.3 mi (2.1 km) the trail turns into a steeper, more difficult, unmaintained one. Unmaintained ropes are there to help you reach the top, but be sure to know your limits. While it's a challenging hike, the views make everything worth it. As you stand on a rocky outcropping, you can see for miles down glistening Lake Crescent, and lush Barnes Creek Valley is spread out below you in an iconic vista.

To get here, head west for 20 mi (32 km) on US 101 from Port Angeles, turn at milepost 228, and follow signs for Marymere Falls, which shares the parking lot and trailhead with Mount Storm King.

Pyramid Peak
Distance: 6.8 mi (10.9 km) round-trip
Duration: 4 hours
Elevation gain: 2,750 ft (840 m)
Difficulty: strenuous
Trailhead: 3 mi (5 km) off of Highway 101 on North Shore Road

On this mostly shaded hike through old-growth forest, you'll cut laterally across a tricky 100-yard slope around 2 mi (3.2 km) in. Use caution (and hiking poles) as this area is prone to slides. Past the slide, the trail ascends via switchbacks to a plateau. The final stretch leads to a former WWII lookout at the top, which is fun to look around and photograph. As you have your snack, take in the glimpses of Lake Crescent and the much smaller Lake Sutherland below you

To get here, travel west on US 101 from Port Angeles and, at Lake Crescent's end, turn northeast onto Camp David Jr. Road after milepost 221. Follow North Shore Road for 3 mi; the first half is paved and the second crushed rock. Keep an eye out for a yellow pedestrian crossing sign at the 3-mi (4.8-km) mark.

Devil's Punchbowl via Spruce Railroad Trail
Distance: 2.4 mi (3.9 km) round-trip
Duration: 1.5 hours
Elevation gain: 137 ft (42 m)
Difficulty: easy
Trailhead: Spruce Railroad trailhead

If you're looking to cool off after a hike, Devil's Punchbowl is the perfect swimming hole. This easy hike tends to get fairly crowded during the summer due to the stunning blue color of this pocket of water, so get here early if you can. The trail follows a flat path through the woods along Lake Crescent and ends up at a bridge, where you'll find the aquamarine Devil's Punchbowl glistening in the sun. Make sure to take your pictures here, as it's the most scenic part of the whole trail and possibly of Lake Crescent.

To get here from Port Angeles, head west on US 101 for 14 mi (23 km), turn right on E. Beach Road, proceed for 3 mi (5 km), then turn left to stay on this road for 1 mi (1.6 km) to the Spruce Railroad trailhead.

Boating and Fishing
With calm, crystal-clear waters, Lake Crescent is a popular fishing and boating destination. This lake is home to two rare fish species, the Crescenti and the Beardslee trout, found only here. During fishing season, which usually runs May-October, you can also find kokanee salmon. However, fishing is only catch and release, so don't plan on keeping any. Lake Crescent Lodge offers first-come, first-served kayak, canoe, and paddleboard rentals (8am-3pm; $20-55 boat rentals, $5-12 fishing rods). Rentals are available for half-day or full-day periods, and summer is quite busy here, so it's recommended to get here early.

Food and Accommodations
Granny's Café
235471 US 101; 360/928-3266; https://grannyscafe.net; 11am-7pm Thurs.-Mon.; $12-19
The menu at Granny's Café features locally sourced natural beef burgers, salads, and sandwiches, complemented by their renowned homemade desserts. Be sure to try their pies, which pair perfectly with their famous soft-serve ice cream. As the name indicates, it feels like you're in your grandmother's kitchen in this small but cozy restaurant with basic chairs, tables, and antiques lining the walls.

Lake Crescent Lodge
416 Lake Crescent Rd.; 888/896-3818; www.olympicnationalparks.com; $173-368

One of the more sought-after places to stay in the park is Lake Crescent Lodge, which sits right on the edge of the lake and takes you back in time with its historic 1915 building. There are 55 cozy rooms, including some with patios or balconies and views of the lake. There are also 10 cottages available. The **Lake Crescent Lodge Dining Room** (7:30am-10:30am, 11:30am-2:30pm, 5pm-9pm daily summer, reduced winter hours; $9-30) offers a variety of locally sourced options, such as the house-made Olympic clam chowder or the Olympic pub burger topped with three-peppercorn aioli. Dinner reservations are recommended in the summer.

Log Cabin Resort

3183 E. Beach Rd.; 888/896-3818; www.olympicnationalparks.com; late May-early Oct.; $104-294

On the other side of Lake Crescent is Log Cabin Resort, which has 24 different rooms, including lakeside chalets, lodge rooms, and two-bedroom cabins, some with kitchenettes. There are also tent camping and full-hookup RV sites available.

Fairholme Campground

west side of Lake Cresent off Camp David Jr. Rd.; 360/565-3130; www.recreation.gov; Apr.-Sept.; $24

Fairholme Campground has 84 campsites, featuring walk-in lakeside options in addition to reserved sites. Food storage lockers are available at some sites, and drinking water is available throughout the campground. There are no hookups, but RV facilities include a water fill station and a septic dump station near the campground's boat launch.

Transportation

Lake Crescent is about 17 mi (27 km) from Port Angeles and runs along US 101, and it takes about 20 minutes to reach the eastern part of the lake from Port Angeles. Clallam Transit accesses the east and west corners of Lake Crescent via Route 14, which leaves from the **Gateway Transit Center** in Port Angeles (123 E. Front St.; 360/452-4511; www.clallamtransit.com; $10, under 18 free). There is very little public transportation in the park, so this is one of the few places you can reach without a car.

SOL DUC RIVER VALLEY

The Sol Duc River Valley is in a dense temperate rain forest with old-growth trees like Douglas firs and western hemlocks, creating a canopy over a lush undergrowth that has an almost mystical feel when you walk through it. Known for its Sol Duc Hot Springs, the area has been a visitor attraction for centuries, from a sacred Indigenous site to a five-star hotel in the 1920s to the contemporary resort you see today.

The valley is also famous for its salmon runs, visible at the Salmon Cascades, and is popular among anglers for coho and Chinook salmon and steelhead trout. While it's a bit out of the way to get here, hikers love the more remote trails, including paths leading to the scenic Sol Duc Falls. Access this area via Sol Duc entrance station on Sol Duc Road.

Visitor Centers and Ranger Stations
Eagle Ranger Station

Sol Duc Rd.; 360/327-3534; www.nps.gov

This station is only staffed intermittently, but you can call the park's main number to find out information.

Sol Duc Hot Springs

12076 Sol Duc Hot Springs Rd.; 888/896-3818; www.olympicnationalparks.com; 8am-7:30pm daily Mar.-Oct.; $12-18 guest pass

Enjoy the restorative powers of the area's historic hot springs while taking in incredible views. Sol Duc Hot Springs Resort features three mineral hot spring pools (water temperatures 99-104°F/37-40°C) and one freshwater pool (50-85°F/10-30°C). Sessions are limited to 1.5 hours, and reservations are made in person on a first-come, first-served basis. There is also a restaurant and gift shop on-site.

The spring water, which begins as rain and

melting snow in the Olympic Mountains, filters through sedimentary rocks, mixing with gases from volcanic rocks before surfacing. Originating from the Quileute language, the name *Sol Duc* means "sparkling waters." Native Americans held the location in high regard for its curative powers, and in 1912 lumber magnate Michael Earles turned it into a tourist attraction. In 1938 it became part of Olympic National Park, guaranteeing its preservation.

Hiking

The following hikes all start in the same parking lot. In fact, they all start from Sol Duc Falls Trail and branch off at around 0.8 mi (1.3 km). To get here from Port Angeles, take US 101 west for 27 mi (44 km), turn left on Sol Duc Hot Springs Road, and continue for 14 mi (23 km) until the road ends at the trailhead parking lot.

Sol Duc Falls

Distance: *1.6 mi (2.6 km) round-trip*
Duration: *1 hour*
Elevation gain: *200 ft (60 m)*
Difficulty: *easy*
Trailhead: *Sol Duc Falls trailhead*

While it takes a bit to get here from US 101, the drive is more than worth it. You'll have an easy, relatively flat hike through the forest and over a bridge to end up at the powerful Sol Duc Falls, which cascades down 48 ft (15 m). Don't just stop at the main bridge—continue on to get views from all angles.

Lover's Lane Loop

Distance: *5.8 mi (9.3 km) round-trip*
Duration: *3 hours*
Elevation gain: *480 ft (145 m)*
Difficulty: *moderate*
Trailhead: *Sol Duc Falls trailhead*

Lover's Lane Trail runs alongside the Sol Duc River, linking the Sol Duc campground, the falls, and the resort. The initial mile (1.6 km) is easy and scenic, and further along the trail inclines, leading through an ancient forest of Douglas firs and hemlocks. You then ascend toward Sol Duc Falls and finish the loop by following a trail on the river's other side back to the starting point.

Deer Lake

Distance: *8 mi (12.9 km) round-trip*
Duration: *4.5 hours*
Elevation gain: *1,650 ft (500 m)*
Difficulty: *moderate*
Trailhead: *Sol Duc Falls trailhead*

Start on the trail to Sol Duc Falls, passing the Lover's Lane Trail junction as you ascend to Deer Lake. Deer Lake comprises two adjacent lakes, one significantly smaller. The trail to the lake follows Canyon Creek, featuring several waterfalls ideal for a break. At Deer Lake, you can rest and head back, or continue around the lake for first-come, first-served campsites for an overnight stay.

Rafting

OP Raft Co.

360/640-8109; https://opraftco.com; mid-Oct.-early May; $150/person

You can navigate the exciting rapids of the Sol Duc River, which offers 30 mi (48 km) of rough wilderness access where the river goes through a dense forest that you wouldn't otherwise be able to drive to or have a hard time hiking through. The tour guide provides all the necessary equipment and will teach you about the fauna and flora in the surrounding forests as you go through them.

Fishing

Anglers from across the globe travel to cast their lines in the Sol Duc River for its abundant, varied fish populations. Notoriously difficult rapids, however, make this a pretty tough river to fish. Unless you have a lot of experience, it's best to go with a guide.

Blue Heron Guide Service

950 S Forks Ave., Forks; 360/640-0447; www.blueheronguideservice.com; $550-700/group

You can join a guided fishing trip almost any time of the year: in the fall for hatchery coho salmon and wild kings, in the winter for wild

steelhead, and in the summer for sockeye, coho salmon, and cutthroat trout. Its difficult topography, with steep banks and big rocks, makes the river ideal for Spey fishing, but it's also great for gear fishing and fly fishing.

Food
The Springs Restaurant
12076 Sol Duc Hot Springs Rd., Sol Duc Hot Springs Resort; 888/896-3818; www.olympicnationalparks.com; 7:30am-10am, noon-2:30pm, 5pm-8pm daily; $14-26

In between hiking or soaking in the hot springs, you'll have plenty of food choices at this basic but satisfying restaurant, such as French toast and omelets for breakfast and burgers and salads for lunch and dinner.

Accommodations and Camping
Sol Duc Hot Springs Resort
12076 Sol Duc Hot Springs Rd.; 888/896-3818; www. olympicnationalparks.com; Mar.-Oct.; $194-246

The resort offers a range of cabins that can fit up to four people, some of which have fully equipped kitchens. With three bedrooms, two bathrooms, and several living areas, the Riverside Suite is perfect for larger parties looking for a roomy and comfortable stay.

Sol Duc Hot Springs Resort Campground
12076 Sol Duc Hot Springs Rd.; 888/896-3818; www. recreation.gov; Mar.-Oct.; $33-55

The RV campground has 17 gravel sites for vehicles 26-36 ft (8-11 m); no pull-through options are available. The campground also has 81 standard non-electric camping sites, but there isn't much privacy. Animal-proof food lockers are available for rent and required in this area.

Transportation
To get to the Sol Duc area of the park from Port Angeles, drive about 30 mi (48 km) west on US 101 and turn off onto Sol Duc Hot Springs Road.

Northwestern Peninsula

The northwestern part of the Olympic Peninsula is by far the most remote area, but that doesn't mean it's not worth visiting. You'll be greeted with scenic ocean views and glimpses of Vancouver Island in Canada as you drive west on Route 112 toward Neah Bay. Cape Flattery, the northwesternmost point in the contiguous United States, alone is worth a visit, even if it's short.

NEAH BAY
Located on the Makah Reservation, Neah Bay signifies that you've reached the far northwest corner of the Olympic Peninsula. You'll have some incredible views of the Strait of Juan de Fuca from here, as most of

the town is flat and looks over to Vancouver Island. At only 2 sq mi (5 sq km), the town is small but is the spot to stop if you want to visit Cape Flattery, as you'll need to buy your permit in town.

Sights and Recreation
★ **Makah Cultural and Research Center**
1880 Bayview Ave.; 360/645-2711; https:// makahmuseum.com; 10am-5pm daily; $10

The Makah Tribe created the Makah Cultural and Research Center to showcase their deep connection to their ancestral lands and the sea, as well as their rich heritage. The **museum** here is a major draw for tourists, providing an insight into the Makah's lasting impact through an impressive collection of artifacts, historical displays, and works of

1: Sol Duc Falls 2: Cape Flattery 3: Makah Cultural and Research Center

Strait of Juan de Fuca Highway

Start: Port Angeles
End: Neah Bay
Driving Distance: 61 mi (98 km)
Driving Time: 1.5-2 hours

Route 112, also known as the Strait of Juan de Fuca Highway, is a scenic drive that is a destination in its own right due to its stunning coastal views and access to natural attractions. Starting from US 101 near Port Angeles, the highway stretches approximately 61 mi (98 km) westward to Neah Bay, and the drive typically takes 1.5-2 hours, depending on stops and traffic.

This route is renowned for its breathtaking views of the Strait of Juan de Fuca, with the water on one side and the lush forests of the Olympic Peninsula on the other. This drive takes you through beaches, dense forests, and small towns, and on clear days, you're able to see across the water to Canada. There are numerous places to stop to explore the water or take pictures.

Parts of this drive are quite windy, and sections through the forest are largely unlit, so it's best to do this drive during the day when there's plenty of visibility.

art. From incredible displays of traditional weaving to ancient tools and ceremonial relics, it showcases the tribe's artifacts from various archaeological sites including the Ozette Archaeological Site.

The museum is part of a larger facility that includes preservation offices and education departments, highlighting its role as a vital resource for the Makah community. A gift shop is available here, and it's also the place where you purchase Cape Flattery permits. The center offers **guided tours** (1.5-2 hours; $70/person) of the museum. They also offer tours ($35-80/person) to Cape Flattery, local beaches, and local village sites if you want to explore the area more with a knowledgeable tribe member.

★ Cape Flattery

As the farthest northwestern point in the continental United States, Cape Flattery is one of the region's most popular places to visit. It's characterized by spectacular cliffs, sea caves, and abundant marine and bird life, not to mention spectacular views of the Pacific Ocean, the Strait of Juan de Fuca, and Tatoosh Island. Natural forces have sculpted the terrain into something nearly otherworldly,

giving the impression of being on the very edge of the world.

The cape is part of the Makah Reservation, and visitors are required to obtain a recreational use **permit** ($20/vehicle, valid for the calendar year) from the Makah Tribe, a measure that helps protect and maintain this culturally and environmentally significant area. These permits are available for purchase at various locations in Neah Bay, including the Makah Cultural and Research Center. The path to Cape Flattery is a fairly easy 0.75-mi (1.2 km) trail, a combination of dirt paths and a boardwalk that winds its way through the forest to a collection of wooden platforms. These lookout points provide stunning vistas, so take your time to take pictures and appreciate the sights here.

To get here from Neah Bay, head west and turn left on Cape Flattery Road at the edge of town. Follow this for 8 mi (13 km) until you reach the parking lot (follow signs for Cape Flattery).

Shi Shi Beach and Point of Arches

Distance: 8 mi (12.9 km) round-trip
Duration: 4 hours
Elevation gain: 200 ft (60 m)

Difficulty: *moderate*
Trailhead: *Fish Hatchery Road*

Shi Shi Beach is a beautiful destination for day hikers and backpackers alike. Restored pathways wind between clear-cuts and groves of Sitka spruce for the first mile (1.6 km) of this journey, which begins near a fish hatchery. A sharp drop onto the beach at the end of the second mile tends to be muddy.

But Shi Shi Beach is well worth the effort—a stretch of sand dotted with bleached logs, views of waves slamming against offshore stacks, and eagles and seagulls. Beach and forest campsites are available throughout the 1.3-mi (2.1-km) beach walk leading to Petroleum Creek. A mile (1.6 km) of rocky sea stacks with colorful tide pools and marine wildlife makes Point of Arches one of the hike's highlights.

Visitors to Shi Shi Beach need **two permits:** the Makah Recreation Pass, available in Neah Bay, and an Olympic National Park wilderness permit, obtainable in Port Angeles or Lake Quinault. Overnight camping is available first-come, first-serve, and all food must be stored in bear canisters.

To get here from Neah Bay, turn left onto Cape Flattery Road and continue for 2.5 mi (4 km), then make another left onto Hobuck Road. Follow this road for 4.3 mi (7 km), keeping an eye out for signs directing you to the fish hatchery, which will lead you to the trailhead and day-use parking area. If you plan to stay overnight, you'll need to park approximately 0.6 mi (1 km) away at a designated private home ($10/day, cash). Be sure to pay for each day you intend to park there.

Festivals and Events
Makah Days

various locations in Neah Bay; https://makah.com; last weekend of Aug.; free

Makah Days is a lively event where the members of Makah Tribe of Neah Bay reunite to honor their ancient culture and to commemorate the anniversary of becoming US citizens. The event is open to all, including neighboring tribes and First Nations from Vancouver Island. The event celebrates the first raising of the American flag in Neah Bay (August 26, 1913) and the establishment of Makah citizenship and voting rights (June 2, 1924), as well as the tribe's contributions to major American conflicts. Activities include traditional dancing, war canoe races, a grand parade, fireworks, salmon bakes, a street fair with Native and contemporary arts and crafts, and the coronation of Makah Royalty during a talent show.

Food
Warmhouse Restaurant

1471 Bayview Ave.; 360/645-2077; Facebook @NeahBayWarmhouseRestaurant; 6am-7pm Tues.-Fri., 6am-8pm Sat, Mon; $13-25

The Warmhouse is known for its burgers, seafood (like fresh fish and clam chowder), and salads, along with breakfast options. It's also a top spot to watch the sunset over the bay, offering a beautiful backdrop to enjoy a meal.

Linda's Woodfired Kitchen

1110 Bayview Ave.; 360/643-2697; Facebook @LindasWoodFiredFood49; 1:30pm-9pm Thurs.-Mon.; $12-25

The casual and cozy Linda's Wood Fired Kitchen is the place to go for pizza and has unique toppings like pulled pork. They also offer cheese bread, hot wings, lasagna, meatball subs, and desserts like their famous cinnamon rolls.

★ Calvin's Crab House

160 Bayview Ave.; 360/374-5630; Facebook @Calvin'sCrabHouse; 11am-6pm Tues.-Sat.; $10-16

You'll love the seafood options at the family-run Calvin's Crab House, whether you go with the crab bisque or fish and chips. They also have a bakery with daily espresso drink specials and pastries such as doughnuts and cookies. The inside is small, so most people take their food across the road to the Adirondack chairs set up overlooking the water.

Accommodations and Camping

Most people visit Neah Bay as a day trip from their base in either Forks or Port Angeles, but there are a couple of options for those looking to stay the night.

Hobuck Beach Resort

2726 Makah Passage; 360/645-2339; https:// hobuckbeachresort.com; tents and RVs $25-50, cabins $305-409

The resort is divided along Hobuck Beach into two different sections. The north end features 10 cabins and a designated area for up to 300 tent campers, while the south end has 16 cabins and 10 RV sites. Facilities include a meadow for tent/dry camping and full RV hookups. RV and tent sites are available on a first-come, first-served basis.

Cape Resort

1510 Bayview Ave.; 360/645-2250; https://cape-resort. com; tents and RVs $25-40, cabins $120-230

The cabins at Cape Resort can sleep up to four people and come with a queen-sized bed, a set of twin bunk beds, and a covered patio. The resort has 39 RV sites, some of which are pull-throughs, and others are nestled among the trees for shade. In addition, there are dedicated grassy places under the trees for tent camping.

Information and Services
Neah Bay Chamber of Commerce

1081 Bay View Ave; 360/645-3474; www.neahbaywa. com; 10am-4pm Tues.-Sat. summer, 10am-2pm Tues.-Sat. winter

The Neah Bay Chamber of Commerce is a helpful place to find out about nearby attractions, restaurants, and permits needed for hikes or camping.

Transportation

Neah Bay is about 1 hour 45 minutes (70 mi/113 km) from Port Angeles. Take US 101 west for 14 mi (23 km), then turn onto Route 112 west for approximately 60 mi (100 km).

From Forks, the drive to Neah Bay is around 1 hour (50 mi/80 km). Head north on US 101, and follow Route 113 north to Route 112 west to Neah Bay.

LAKE OZETTE

Lake Ozette is one of the largest natural lakes in the state and is popular for fishing and camping. But most people come here to hike the Ozette Triangle Trail, a 9-mi (14.5-km) round-trip hike that goes out to the Pacific Coast, down the coastline, and back into the forest.

Hiking
Cape Alava Loop (Ozette Triangle)

Distance: *9.4 mi (15.1-km) round-trip*
Duration: *5 hours*
Elevation gain: *100 ft (30 m)*
Difficulty: *moderate*
Trailhead: *Ozette Triangle Coastal trailhead, near the Ozette Ranger Station on Lake Ozette Road*

The Cape Alava Loop, also known as the Ozette Triangle, is one of the most popular hikes on the Washington coast. It has two starting points: Cape Alava to the north or Sand Point to the south. Both are about 3 mi (5 km) long and end up on the beach on the Pacific Ocean. At this point, you can either head back into the forest the way you came (for a total of 6 mi/10 km round-trip) or go the 3 mi (5 km) on the beach to the opposite trail to make a total of about 9 mi (15 km) round-trip.

If you choose to walk along the beach, keep an eye out for the ancient Makah petroglyphs at Wedding Rocks. They make for great photos, but make sure not to touch them so as not to alter them at all. In addition, take into account that while the beach is flat, it can take quite a bit of time to do these 3 mi (5 km) since you may be navigating around deep pockets of water. You'll need to look at tide charts and ensure you have plenty of time to do this stretch when the tide is out; otherwise, you'll be rushed for time and get stuck.

Fishing

Lake Ozette is a popular fishing spot for many fish species, including largemouth bass, kokanee, coastal cutthroat trout, yellow perch, and northern pikeminnow. The season runs April 30-October 31. The National Park Service has certain fishing regulations, such as the ban on using two poles, and artificial lures with barbless single-point hooks are required. Fishers can cast from the shoreline or boats with no license needed, and boat launches are found at the Lake Ozette campground and Swan Bay.

Ozette Kayak Rentals

101 Barber Rd., Clallam Bay; 971-226-8435; https://ozettekayakrentals.com; 9am-7pm Wed.-Sat., 10am-6pm Sun.; $15/hour or $75/day

There are no kayak rentals at Ozette Lake, so stop by Ozette Kayak Rentals on your way down to pick up a kayak for the day. If you don't have a car rack, they can also deliver your kayak to the lake ($15). They only have a handful of kayaks available, so call in advance to try to reserve one.

Accommodations and Camping

Lost Resort

20860 Hoko-Ozette Rd.; 360/963-2899; www.lostresort.net; Apr.-Oct.; $30/night camping; $110/night cabins

Priding itself on being the westernmost lodging point in the contiguous United States, Lost Resort offers 30 campsites and three cabins (although pets are not allowed at either). The campsites have fire pits and picnic tables and are for up to four people, while the cabins sleep four and have full electricity, a double bed, and a bunk bed.

Cape Alava

21 mi (34 km) on Ozette Lake Road, just past Ozette Ranger Station; 360/565-3130; www.recreation.gov; $14

You need a permit in advance to camp here, which you can purchase online (www.recreation.gov) for $8/person/night plus a $6 permit fee, but the actual campsites are first-come, first-served once you arrive at the beach. Bear canisters are required, as the forest and beach by the campsites are frequented by bears as well as other critters. The campsite is right off the beach, so bring reinforcement to make your tent strong enough to resist any afternoon wind. Otherwise, it's a beautiful place to call base for the night, and many hikers choose to hike down the coast and back to their car via the Sand Point Trail to complete the Ozette Triangle.

Information and Services

Stop at the **Ozette Ranger Station** at the end of Hoko Ozette Road June-September to get information about hiking conditions. It isn't always staffed, so call the main visitor center (360/565-3130) if no one's there.

Transportation

From Neah Bay, take Route 112 east and Hozo Ozette Road until you reach the Ozette Ranger Station, which will take about an hour.

From Forks, it takes about 1 hour 15 minutes to get to Ozette Lake, which you reach by taking Route 113 north, continuing onto Route 112 west, and turning left onto Hoko Ozette Road to arrive at the ranger station.

Forks and La Push

Forks is the main town on the western part of the peninsula, where you'll find the most options for lodging, restaurants, and gas, making it a great place to base yourself. It's also a welcome break from the forested stretch of US 101 that doesn't have a ton to see. Just north of Forks, La Push is a much smaller area on the Quileute Indian Reservation but has some beautiful beaches, including the popular Rialto Beach.

FORKS

Founded near the turn of the 20th century, Forks rose to prominence as a center of the lumber industry thanks to the Olympic Peninsula's rich flora and fauna. While the town's economy has changed throughout the years, it's managed to keep its strong sense of community. More recently, the area got put on the map by the *Twilight* film and book franchises, which were set in town. Since then, Forks has become a tourist destination for fans looking to experience the setting for their favorite vampire and werewolf stories, and there's now a museum, a scavenger hunt of filming locations, and even a festival dedicated to the series.

Sights
Forever Twilight in Forks Collection
11 N. Forks Ave.; 360/374-2531; https://forkswa.com; noon-4pm Fri.-Sat. Sept.-May, noon-4pm Thurs.-Mon., 2pm-4pm Tues.-Wed. May-Sept.; free
Twilight lovers will want to stop here for the huge collection of props and clothing from the movie. There are also plenty of photo ops next to pieces used in famous scenes.

John's Beachcombing Museum
143 Andersonville Ave.; 360/640-0320; https://forkswa.com; 10am-5pm daily; $5
This quirky little museum is the result of one local's hard work collecting everything that's

washed up on the shores over the decades and creating art from it. The owner is quite friendly and always excited to tell you where certain items are from, including some from Japan.

Forks Timber Museum
1421 S. Forks Ave.; 360/374-9663; https://forkstimbermuseum.org; 10am-5pm Mon.-Sat., 11am-4pm Sun. May-Sept., 10am-4pm Mon.-Sat., 11am-4pm Sun. Oct.-Apr.; $3
Forks was known as the Logging Capital of the World after a 1970s logging boom, and that history is now celebrated at the Forks Timber Museum. This log cabin highlights the region's history in homesteading, farming, and logging, and showcases a logging camp bunkhouse and steam donkey.

Tours
Twilight Tours In Forks
130 Spartan Ave.; 360/374-5634; $30
Many spots in town feature props from the movie or serve as inspiration for it, so you'll need a few hours to go on a tour with Twilight Tours in Forks (or grab a map to do a self-guided one) and go around to see areas in both Forks and La Push and take pictures of them. Bella's truck and the high school sign from the movie are among the fan favorites.

Fishing
Piscatorial Pursuits
866/347-4232; www.piscatorialpursuits.com; Oct.-May; $375/person
Whether you want to fish for fall salmon or spring chinook, join this fishing tour bright and early to visit one of the many rivers in the area with an experienced guide. They'll meet you at either your lodging or a local breakfast spot and have all the transportation and gear arranged for an all-day fishing trip.

Hiking

Elk Creek Conservation Area

Distance: 2.5 mi (4 km) round-trip
Duration: 1 hour
Elevation gain: none
Difficulty: easy
Trailhead: from Forks, east 2 mi (3 km) on Calawah Way to parking area

This interpretive route follows what was once a logging road through a mossy forest along Elk Creek, which looks like an old-growth rain forest. Attractions include "The Sisters" trees and a wide variety of fish in the creek, including coho, steelhead, and salmon.

Food

Blakeslee's Bar and Grill

1222 S Forks Ave.; 360/374-5003; Facebook @bbgforkswa; 11am-10pm Tues.-Thurs., 11am-midnight Fri.-Sat., 11am-9pm Sun.; $11-30

This casual bar and grill is the local place to go for a drink, as they have a full bar in addition to a thorough menu with pub food like nachos and burgers. Kids are allowed until 3pm, and there are plenty of adults-only events throughout the night for entertainment, making it a fun environment.

Pacific Pizza

870 S. Forks Ave.; 360/374-2626; https://pacificpizza. four-food.com; 11am-9pm Sun.-Thurs., 11am-10pm Fri.-Sat.; $11-30

Come hungry to Pacific Pizza, as it's an ideal place to split one of their gourmet pizzas or get your own panini or grinder in addition to salad and pasta. While the service may be a bit slow, it's a casual place with plenty of seating.

★ Sully's Drive-In

220 N. Forks Ave.; 360/374-5075; 11am-8pm Wed.-Sat., 11am-3pm Tues.; $2-10

Sully's Drive-In is the place to go for burgers and has been serving locals for decades. They have over a dozen different burgers to choose from, in addition to corn dogs, chicken strips, and fries. While it's no longer a drive-in where food is brought to your car, it still has the fun

feel of one, whether you sit at a booth inside or a picnic table outside.

D&K BBQ

275 N. Forks Ave.; 210/683-5357; noon-5:30pm Fri.-Mon.; $9-22

When you're craving barbecue, head to the bright-red D&K BBQ food truck for some of their signature meats like ribs or brisket slow-cooked and marinated. Make sure to add a few sides like coleslaw, baked beans, and creamed corn.

Accommodations

You'll find the biggest cluster of hotels on the western peninsula in Forks, making it a good home base.

Miller Tree Inn Bed-and-Breakfast

654 E. Division St.; 360/374-6806; www.millertreeinn. com; $180-225, 2-night min.

This is a favorite among *Twilight* fans because it's dubbed the "Cullen House" based on the author's description of the Cullen family home. The three-story historic farmhouse has 8 rooms, including a couple of suites, and is just a few minutes from the downtown area. Breakfast options rotate but include dishes like parmesan baked eggs and avocado toast.

Forks Motel

351 S. Forks Ave.; 360/374-6243; www.forksmotel.com; $111-498

This 73-room motel features a variety of amenities such as family Jacuzzi suites, wheelchair-accessible rooms, and pet-friendly rooms. Guests can cool down in the summer in the enclosed outdoor pool.

Bogachiel State Park

185983 US 101; 360/374-6356; www.parks.wa.gov/478/ Bogachiel; 8am-dusk daily; free

This state park is full of hiking trails to explore and provides access to the Bogachiel River. There are also 36 campsites, including a handful of RV sites, available with a reservation.

Information and Services
Forks Chamber of Commerce
1411 S. Forks Ave.; 360/374-2531; https://forkswa.com; 10am-5pm Mon.-Sat., 10am-4pm Sun.

You'll spot the Chamber of Commerce easily after a large "Welcome to Forks" sign, and Bella's red truck from *Twilight* sits right outside the building. The friendly staff here will answer questions about things to do in town and can provide a free *Twilight* map to go on your own self-guided tour.

Forks Community Hospital
530 Bogachiel Way; 360/374-6271; www.forkshospital.org

Forks Community Hospital's emergency room is a Level IV trauma center, so it's equipped to stabilize any severe conditions before sending them to Seattle.

Transportation
US 101 goes right through Forks, making it easy to find. Forks is 1 hour 15 minutes (66 mi/106 km) from Lake Quinault and a little over an hour (56 mi/90 km) south of Port Angeles. To get to Forks from Neah Bay, it's about an hour (49 mi/79 km), and you'll follow Route 112 east to US 101 south.

Clallam Transit services Forks via Route 14 and goes up to Port Angeles from **Forks Transit Center** (144 East E. St., Forks; 360/452-4511; www.clallamtransit.com).

LA PUSH AREA
La Push is about 20 minutes from Forks and is on the Quileute Reservation. Some of the most famous beaches on the western part of the peninsula are found here, and most are reachable by an easy walk or short hike through the woods.

The area has also grown in popularity due to *Twilight*, as Jacob Black, one of the main characters, was fictionally part of the tribe who live on this land. Many fans come here to visit the beaches he supposedly walked on (although they were actually filmed in Oregon).

Beaches
The La Push area is known for its beaches. Remember to consult the tide tables when walking along the beach so you don't get stuck.

Rialto Beach
Mora Rd.; www.nps.gov; free

Easily the most popular in the area, Rialto Beach is an easy 200-ft (60-m) walk from the parking lot. It's famous for its views of **Hole-in-the-Wall,** a natural sea-carved arch that you can only access during low tide. The vast, driftwood-strewn beachfront, extraordinary sea stacks, and marine life-rich tide pools are further highlights. For a unique camping experience, you can camp between Ellen Creek and Hole-in-the-Wall by calling for a **Wilderness Camping Permit** (360/565-3130) in advance. Pets are not allowed, and you can use only driftwood for fires.

To get here from La Push, head east on Route 110 toward Forks, and take a left on Mora Road, driving 5 mi (8 km) west until you end at the parking lot.

First Beach
Ocean Front Dr.; www.wta.org; free

First Beach is one of the easiest to get to, as you can park in Quileute Oceanside Resort's parking lot. This is a popular place for surfers, so go early in the morning to watch them catch the first waves. You'll also notice a large island—James Island used to have a fortified village on it, and then it became the burial site for local tribal chiefs.

Second Beach
Ocean Front Dr.; www.wta.org; free

The 2-mi (3.2-km) trail from the parking area to the beach goes down through a forested area, crossing a portion of the reservation before beginning switchback stairs. Keep your eye out for some unique landmarks, including an upturned tree and a cabinet tree filled with

1: Hole-in-the-Wall at Rialto Beach 2: Second Beach 3: Forks welcome sign

keepsakes. Once you reach the beach, dramatic sea stacks and a natural arch provide stunning views. To get here, drive 1 mi (1.6 km) south past First Beach on Ocean Front Drive. Look for a parking with a sign for the trail.

Third Beach

Ocean Front Dr.; www.wta.org; free

Two miles (3 km) south past First Beach, you'll see a parking lot for about 20 cars that marks the trailhead for Third Beach. You'll walk through a wide, graveled path with majestic hemlocks before dropping off sharply to the beach in this 3.6-mi (5.8-km) round-trip hike. The drop down can be precarious when there's been recent heavy rain. Once you get over the driftwood, spend some time walking the shore and looking closely at the cliffs for a narrow but tall waterfall cascading into the ocean.

Surfing

La Push is a popular destination for surfers of all experience levels. Since the waves surge over sandy bottoms, the beach breaks here are more forgiving for beginners. But outside the summer months, the area's frigid water requires surfers to wear wetsuits, booties, and sometimes hoods and gloves. You can surf any time of the year, but beware that winter storms often bring much larger and more powerful waves.

La Push Surf Adventures

meets at First Beach; 425/241-5941; www. lapushsurfadventures.com; lessons $160-200/person, rental package $120/day

If you've ever wanted to learn to surf, now's your chance with La Push Surf Adventures. They offer private or group lessons as well as wetsuit and board rentals, so you'll be out in the water and standing up in no time.

Festivals and Events

Quileute Days

La Push; 360/452-8552; https://quileutenation.org; July; free

Quileute Days is a lively weekend festival that celebrates the unique culture of the Quileute

Tribe. Traditional salmon bakes, colorful dancing and songs honoring their heritage, and competitive games of softball and horseshoes are just a few of the highlights of this event.

Food and Accommodations

River's Edge Restaurant

41 Main St.; 360/374-0777; https://forkswa.com; 8am-8pm daily; $10-15

River's Edge Restaurant is the only restaurant in La Push and offers breakfast through dinner, all with a view of the nearby ocean. Try the chicken fried steak and eggs for breakfast, or later the River's Edge Chop Salad or black and blue steak skewers.

Quileute Oceanside Resort

330 Ocean Front Dr.; 360/374-5267; https:// quileuteoceanside.com; cabins and motel rooms $248-380, camping $30-55

Eighteen oceanfront cabins, two motel rooms, 10 camper cabins, a campground, and 28 full-service RV sites are just some of the options for lodging at the Quileute Oceanside Resort. Located at a short distance from First Beach, this hotel features rooms decorated in a traditional Native American style and equipped with full or mini kitchens.

Three Rivers Resort

7764 La Push Rd.; 360/374-5300; www.3riversresort. net; cabins $109-409, camping $30-45

Three Rivers Resort has nine cabins, 30 campsites, and nine RV hookups, and you'll find one of the few restaurants and convenience stores in the area here. The menu of **Three Rivers Restaurant** (11am-7pm daily; $5-22) is extensive and features dishes like the "World Famous River Burger" and delicious milkshakes.

Mora Campground

3283 Mora Rd.; 360/565-3130 (staffed seasonally), 360/565-3056 (general info year-round); www. recreation.gov; $24

Mora Campground has 94 campsites, with potable water and flush toilets available. Each site has a fire ring with a grate and a picnic table, and while there are no electrical hookups, an RV dump station is accessible in the summer ($10). The campground is also only 2 mi (3 km) from Rialto Beach.

Information
Quileute Tribe
The Quileute Tribe's website (https://quileutenation.org) has plenty of helpful information about La Push, its history, and things to do.

Mora Ranger Station
3283 Mora Rd.; 360/374-5460; www.nps.gov; open intermittently in summer

Stop at the Mora Ranger Station to get information about local hikes and beach visits,

get permits for camping, and check out bear canisters.

Transportation
La Push is about 20 minutes (15 mi/24 km) west of Forks via US 101 north and Route 110/La Push Road. Clallam Transit's Route 15 runs from the **Forks Transit Center** (144 East E St., Forks; 360/452-4511; www.clallamtransit.com) to the main part of La Push free of charge, and the ride is about 25 minutes. However, La Push itself doesn't have much unless you plan on bringing your own picnic to the beach, so having your own car is more convenient if you want to explore other areas from here.

Western Olympic National Park

Countless visitors head to the western portion of Olympic National Park each year to see the Hoh Rain Forest. It's one of the most fascinating and easily accessible rain forests in North America and a prime example of the lush vegetation that characterizes the region.

But the western side of Olympic National Park has many other scenic wonders. The Pacific Ocean carves out sea stacks and tidal pools along this stretch of coastline, which visitors can explore on the driftwood-strewn beaches of Kalaloch. And Lake Quinault is a hiker's paradise and a perfect getaway for those looking to get on the water.

PARK INFORMATION
Planning Your Time
It's best to pick a few areas per day when in this region, as the driving time can add up. You could start your day hiking the Hoh Rain Forest, then spend the afternoon on Ruby Beach. Similarly, you could spend one morning exploring the Quinault Rain Forest and the afternoon walking along the beaches of Kalaloch.

Areas
The western section of the park has several distinct areas, all with their own appeal.

The **Hoh Rain Forest** is one of the park's most famous attractions, known for its old-growth temperate rain forest. Hiking trails, including the popular Hall of Mosses and Spruce Nature Trail, give visitors the chance to explore the lush greenery, with towering trees, mosses, and ferns that thrive in the heavy annual rainfall. Access this area via the Hoh Entrance Station on Upper Hoh Road.

Kalaloch has a rugged coastline and half a dozen beaches, including the picturesque Ruby Beach. Visitors love walking among the dramatic sea stacks and tide pools that reveal a microcosm of marine life during low tide. It's a prime location for beachcombing, birdwatching, and camping by the ocean. Access this area via US Highway 101, about 35 mi (56 km) south of Forks. There is no entrance station, but you will still be expected to display a national parks pass, which can be obtained online or at the Kalaloch Ranger Station.

The **Quinault Rain Forest** is an impressive introduction to the park's magnificent

Western Olympic National Park

rain forests, and **Lake Quinault** is its gateway. Among the things to do at this glacial lake are fishing, boating, and exploring the many hiking paths around the verdant, deep rain forest that is home to some of the biggest tree species on earth. The area is co-managed by the Quinault Indian Nation and the National Park Service. Access this area via South Shore Road or North Shore Road off US Highway 101. There is no entrance station, but you will still be expected to display a national parks pass, which can be obtained online or at the Quinault Ranger Station.

Seasons and Weather

Each season offers unique experiences. Although summer is ideal for most of the park's attractions, the Quinault Rain Forest is best experienced in the second half of spring or the beginning of summer. At this time of year, the verdant underbrush and thick foliage are the most impressive since everything is in bloom, adding an extra splash of green to the landscape.

Summer tends to be the most popular time of year and will be the most pleasant time to visit the beach, but the roads and trails will be more crowded in general.

Fall crowds decrease some, and it's an excellent time to see the fall foliage around the park, particularly Lake Quinault. While the west side of the park doesn't see much snow in the **winter,** and heavy rains can shut down some of the smaller roads. Many of the restaurants, campsites, and accommodations may also be closed during this time. The Hoh Rain Forest visitor center is also closed January-March, so you'll need to plan your hikes ahead of time.

Fees

All visitors must purchase a park pass to enter, either at the ranger booth at each entrance or online at the NPS website. One pass is $30 for

1: mossy tree in the Hoh Rain Forest 2: Hall of Mosses

a vehicle, covers all occupants in the car, and is good for up to seven days. Motorcycles are $25/person, and hikers and bikers are $15/person.

Food and Accommodations

The two main places to stay on this side of the park are **Lake Quinault Lodge** and **Kalaloch Lodge.** Both have on-site restaurants and make for a good home base.

There are also several campsites to choose from. Gatton Creek Campground only has 5 walk-in tent sites ($25/night), so your chances of getting a spot are better on weekdays. Willaby Campground has 19 campsites for tents and RVs (reservations www.recreation.gov; $25/night). Falls Creek Campground has 21 sites for tents and RVs and 10 walk-in sites (reservations www.recreation.gov; $25/night).

TOP EXPERIENCE

★ HOH RAIN FOREST

The Hoh Rain Forest is a stunning ecosystem—a lush understory of mosses and ferns, and a majestic canopy of trees such as Sitka spruce, Douglas fir, and western red cedar. Rainfall totals in this old forest average 12-14 ft (3.6-4 m) per year, making it an exceptionally verdant and diverse ecology. The Hoh is relatively isolated compared to other parts of the park, but its hypnotic beauty, as well as the sense of solitude you'll find, make the trip there well worth the effort.

Access this portion of the park via the Hoh Entrance Station, 12 mi (19 km) east of US 101 on Upper Hoh Road.

Visitor Centers and Ranger Stations

Hoh Rain Forest Visitor Center

18113 Upper Hoh Rd.; 360/565-3000; www.nps.gov/olym; 10am-4:30pm daily summer, closed Jan.-Feb., limited hours Fri.-Sun. Mar.-May and Sept.-Dec.
Stop here to learn about the three hiking trails in the area, get a national park passport stamp, and visit their small bookstore.

Hiking

There are only three hiking trails in this area, and you can easily do two of them on the same day. The visitor center serves as the starting point for all three trailheads, which then fork off into separate trails with clear signs.

Hall of Mosses

Distance: *0.8 mi (1.3 km) round-trip*
Duration: *30 minutes*
Elevation gain: *100 ft (60 m)*
Difficulty: *easy*
Trailhead: *Hoh Rain Forest Visitor Center*
Hall of Mosses is easily the most popular trail in the Hoh Rain Forest, if not the entire national park. There's a slight hill to climb at the start, and then you'll be wandering through a flat loop, admiring all the moss hanging off the giant trees and reading educational signs about what you're seeing. Because this is such a short trail, many visitors tack on the Spruce Nature Trail to explore the rain forest more.

Spruce Nature Trail

Distance: *1.2 mi (1.9 km) round-trip*
Duration: *1 hour*
Elevation gain: *230 ft (70 m)*
Difficulty: *easy*
Trailhead: *Hoh Rain Forest Visitor Center*
This loop trail goes along the Hoh River and Taft Creek, through a combination of old- and new-growth forests. It's a peaceful walk that's family-friendly, with the sound of the rushing river in the background. As you make your way along the route, look for wildlife that frequent the area, such as deer, elk, and even bald eagles.

Hoh River Trail

Distance: *up to 36 mi (58 km) round-trip*
Duration: *up to 15 hours*
Elevation gain: *up to 3,700 ft (1,125 m)*
Difficulty: *moderate-difficult*
Trailhead: *Hoh Rain Forest Visitor Center*
If you want a longer hike, join the Hoh River Trail for as far as you'd like. Most of the trail is an easy, flat hike where you'll likely see wildlife along the way, and if you continue

on to the end, you'll start to climb until you see Mount Olympus. Many camping spots are available along the trail, but you'll need a backpacking permit, and likely reservations, in advance. Just over 5 mi (8 km) into the trail lies Five Mile Island, where many hikers choose to turn around after a lunch break.

Climbing

Mount Olympus, the highest summit in the Olympic Mountains, stands at an impressive 7,980 ft (2,432 m). To reach the peak, you'll have to overcome a number of obstacles, including an elevation gain of more than 5,000 ft (1,525 m). It's one of just seven "Ultra" summits in Washington with a prominence of over 5,000 ft (1,525 m).

Getting to the top of Mount Olympus is no easy feat and calls for expert mountaineering abilities. Due to the peak's location in a dangerous area, the lengthy nature of the paths leading up to it, and the unpredictability of the weather, the success rate of summit attempts is low. The Hoh River Trail through the rain forest is the most common route up the mountain. At higher elevations on Mount Olympus, where six active glaciers can be found, the annual precipitation ranges 141-165 inches.

Given these factors, a walk up Mount Olympus is not for inexperienced hikers. Technical mountaineering knowledge, the ability to navigate in adverse conditions, and thorough planning are all essential.

Mountain Madness
9249 17th Ave. SW, Seattle; 206/937-8389; https:// mountainmadness.com; $2,850
For those looking for a guide-led climb, check out Mountain Madness.

Kayaking and Rafting
Hoh River Rafters
4883 Upper Hoh Rd., Forks; 360/683-9867; www. hohriverrafters.com; 9am and 2pm daily Mar.-Sept.; $120/person
Floating through deltas and valleys on the Hoh River is a relaxing experience that's great

for beginners because you just have to follow paddle commands. In the summer, rafters can experience the upper Hoh River and its Class II rapids while passing through a temperate rain forest and witnessing the wild river's wildlife, tall trees, and natural dynamics.

Accommodations and Camping

This is one of the more remote areas, so you won't have as many accommodation options as the other parts of the park. Forks is the most convenient gateway town to stay in with multiple options, and it's about 45 minutes away from the Hoh Rain Forest via US 101.

Hoh Valley Cabins
5843 Upper Hoh Rd.; 360/640-2074; www. hohvalleycabins.com; $290-370
These simple cabins have a queen bed and sofa bed, a fully equipped kitchenette, and space to enjoy outside. With only four cabins, you'll get plenty of solitude here and may even spot some wildlife walking through.

Hoh Rain Forest Campground
18113 Upper Hoh Rd.; 360/565-3130; www.recreation. gov; May-Sept.; $24
There are 72 tent and RV campsites available at Hoh Campground, each with its own fire ring and picnic table. Food storage lockers and drinking water are available, but no RV hookups.

Hoh Oxbow Campground
US 101 milepost 176/177; 360/565-3005; www.nps.gov, www.dnr.wa.gov; $10 Discover Pass
Located just outside the park boundaries and close to US 101, this eight-site campground is a good choice if others are full. Due to its small size, your best chance of getting a site is in the off-season, and there are only a few RV sites available.

Transportation
Whether you're coming from the north or south, the only way to get to the Hoh Rain Forest is by taking US 101 to Upper Hoh Road.

From there, it's an 18-mi (29-km) drive to the parking lot for the visitor center and hikes. It takes about 2 hours (90 mi/145 km) from Port Angeles or less than an hour (30 mi/50 km) from Forks.

KALALOCH

Kalaloch is a quieter area that some people may be tempted to drive through, but it's worth stopping at one of the many beaches along US 101. This scenic area runs between the Quinault and Hoh Reservations on the Pacific coast. Several prominent beaches, such as Ruby Beach with its sea stacks and tidal pools, are easily accessible, and the area has a stunning, rugged coastline. People are drawn here for the beaches, tidal pools, and abundant bird and marine life.

Kalaloch is also home to the **Tree of Life,** an extraordinary Sitka spruce that clings to life, its roots hanging over an erosion-carved hole, yet still thrives along the coastal bluff. It can be accessed from Kalaloch Campground.

Access this area via US 101. There is no entrance station, but you still be expected to display a national parks pass which can be obtained online.

Visitor Centers and Ranger Stations
Kalaloch Ranger Station
156954 US 101; 360/962-2283; www.nps.gov/ places/000/kalaloch-ranger-station.htm; hours vary summer and spring, closed fall and winter
You can find out about beaches to visit on the coast, what to do in Forks, and how to attend guided talks in the summer.

Beaches
The Kalaloch area boasts eight beaches. They're numbered 1-6, with Beaches 1 and 2 located south of the Kalaloch Campground and Beaches 3-6 to the north. The other two beaches are named: South Beach at the very southern end, and Ruby Beach at the north. These beaches are easily accessible from US 101, with most having prominent signs.

★ Ruby Beach
www.nps.gov; $30 Olympic National Park entrance pass
Ruby Beach is about 7 mi (11 km) north of Kalaloch Campground, and a large sign marks where you'll turn off US 101. It's about a 0.25-mi (0.4-km) hike downhill to reach the beach, where you'll have 6 mi (10 km) of shoreline to explore. The area is known for its sea stacks, unique driftwood, and unique rock formations. If you get here at low tide, you'll have the chance to explore starfish and other sealife in the tide pools. The dramatic and rugged landscape makes Ruby Beach a popular destination for photographers, especially at sunset.

South Beach
www.nps.gov; $30 Olympic National Park entrance pass
South Beach is about 10 mi (16 km) north of Ruby Beach, and the first beach you'll encounter on US 101 as you enter Olympic National Park. There is a campground here, and visitors can stop in the parking lot to take the short walk to the beach. South Beach offers stunning panoramic views and direct beach access from its location on a hill overlooking the Pacific Ocean.

Food and Accommodations
The only restaurant is located at Kalaloch Lodge, so you'll want to stock up on food at **Queets Trading Post** (402 Jackson Heights Dr.) south of this area. Otherwise, pick up supplies north in Forks or south in Aberdeen, depending on which way you're coming from.

Kalaloch Lodge
157151 US 101; 866/662-9928; www.thekalalochlodge. com; $274-332
Kalaloch Lodge features a variety of housing options, including the central Main Lodge with 64 rooms, ocean-view Bluff Cabins, and numerous cabins perfect for families or couples. There's also the Seacrest House, where

---

1: Ruby Beach 2: sea stars in a tide pool found in Kalaloch 3: Lake Quinault 4: Lake Quinault Lodge

every room has its own balcony or patio with a view of the Pacific. It also features a gift shop and activities throughout the year. The on-site **Creekside Restaurant** (8am-10am and 5pm-8pm daily; $10-25) is the sole dining option in the area. The impressive menu focuses on locally sourced ingredients, with options like smoked salmon dip, crab mac and cheese, and elk burgers.

South Beach Campground

US 101, 10 mi (16 km) north of Ruby Beach; 360/565-3130; www.recreation.gov; May-Oct.; $20

South Beach Campground has 50 campsites available on a first-come, first-served basis. There's room for tents as well as RVs and trailers, although keep in mind that most sites don't have shade.

Kalaloch Campground

US 101; 360/565-3130; www.nps.gov; year-round; $24/ night

Half a mile (0.8 km) north of Kalaloch Lodge, Kalaloch Campground has 160 campsites and is near one of the most popular beaches in the area. A short staircase leads to various beaches, tide pools, hiking trails, and the famous Tree of Life. There is also an amphitheater where a ranger leads an evening program throughout the year.

Transportation

Kalaloch is 40 minutes (35 mi/56 km) from Forks via US 101 north, 1 hour 45 minutes (90 mi/145 km) from Port Angeles via US 101 north, and a little over 2 hours (117 mi/188 km) away from Olympia by taking US 101 south, US 12 east, and Route 8 east.

LAKE QUINAULT AND QUINAULT RAIN FOREST

Though less renowned than its northern neighbor, Lake Crescent, Lake Quinault is a beauty worth visiting. The area is home to the rustic Lake Quinault Lodge and boasts the world's largest Sitka spruce tree. Most of Lake Quinault and its enchanting rain forest are part of Olympic National Park, but its southwestern portion resides within the Quinault Reservation. This blend of natural beauty and cultural heritage enriches the visitor's experience, offering not just a glimpse into one of North America's most spectacular rain forests but also an opportunity to appreciate the area's rich cultural history. The park also offers a variety of easy hiking trails, perfect for exploring the serene and lush surroundings. Access this area via US 101. There is no entrance station, but you still be expected to display a national parks pass which can be obtained online.

Visitor Centers and Ranger Stations
Quinault Rain Forest Ranger Station

902 North Shore Rd.; 360/288-2444; www.nps.gov; Memorial Day-late Sept., call for hours

Stop at the Quinault Rain Forest Ranger Station to find out about hikes in the area and get information about fishing on the lake.

Quinault Rain Forest Loop Drive

An easy way to experience the rain forest is through the Quinault Rain Forest Loop Drive. This gorgeous drive travels 31 mi (50 km) around Lake Quinault, entering Olympic National Park via the Quinault River and returning along the opposite side of the lake. This is a loop route, so start on the western side of Lake Quinault off US 101 and go either way. There are plenty of places to break up the roughly 2-hour drive. Among these are hiking trails that lead through a verdant rain forest, waterfalls along the way, and plenty of potential wildlife spotting.

Hiking
Quinault Loop

Distance: *4 mi (6.4 km) round-trip*
Duration: *2 hours*
Elevation gain: *360 ft (110 m)*
Difficulty: *easy*
Trailhead: *parking lot just north of Lake Quinault Lodge*

On the Quinault Loop, you can go from lush

rain forest to tall, ancient fir trees without ever leaving the forest. This loop provides a fantastic perspective of the Olympic temperate rain forest and Quinault Lake, with 1.3 mi (2 km) along the lake's south bank and 2.7 mi (4 km) into the forest. Highlights include Cascade Falls, Cedar Bog, and an educational nature trail.

Enchanted Valley

Distance: *27.8 mi (44.7 km) round-trip*
Elevation gain: *3,700 ft (1,125 m)*
Difficulty: *strenuous*
Trailhead: *Graves Creek trailhead*

Enchanted Valley is best done as an overnight backpacking trip, which you'll need to get a permit for in advance (www.recreation.gov). There are 12 campsites in total by Pyrites Creek, about 10 mi (16 km) into the trail. Otherwise, you can join for parts of it as it winds through the forest and waterfalls. Bears are frequent visitors in the backcountry area, so be prepared with bear spray and store your food properly. If you want to do a portion of this trail, hike 2.5 mi (4 km) to Pony Bridge, enjoy the river view, and then head back the way you came.

To get here from US 101, follow South Shore Road along the south end of Lake Quinault and drive for 13.5 mi (22 km). At the junction at Quinault River Bridge, turn right, then it's 6 mi (10 km) to the trailhead.

Boating and Fishing

Lake Quinault is popular for its fishing and boating, but there are rules. Trout fishing is only permitted in the summer on Lake Quinault, whereas steelhead fishing is permitted mid-February-mid-April. Fishing for salmon is prohibited in the lake itself, but legal in the lower Quinault River with a **licensed guide.** Anyone interested in fishing should check with the Lake Quinault Lodge front desk for information regarding local fishing guide services and regulations, as the area encompasses both US Forest Service and Tribal property. A Quinault Indian Nation Fishing Permit is necessary for fishing on

the lake. Stop at the **Quinault Wilderness Information Office** (353 S. Shore Rd.; 360/288-0232; www.nps.gov; 8am-3pm Thurs.-Sat. late May-late Oct.) to find out about fishing and boating regulations and get the necessary permits.

Lake Quinault Lodge

345 S. Shore Rd.; 888/896-3818; www. olympicnationalparks.com; 9am-4pm daily Memorial Day-late June, 9am-noon, 1pm-4pm daily July-Sept.; rentals $45/half day, boat cruise $35-50

Canoes, kayaks, and stand-up paddleboards are available for day use from Lake Quinault Lodge. There are also boat cruises that guests can take to see the lake at different times of day, including sunrise, afternoon, and sunset.

Food

You have a few food options here, but the open hours and days may be limited, particularly in the winter.

The Salmon House

516 S. Shore Rd. in the Rain Forest Resort Village; 360/288-4307; www.rainforestresort.com; 3pm-9pm daily; $10-29

As the name indicates, The Salmon House specializes in salmon dishes, particularly their smoked salmon that's smoked over an alder wood fire. They also have steak, pasta, salads, and more. This beautiful wooden building has comfortable table seating, or you can grab a place at the bar while you look out onto Lake Quinault.

Dino's Pizza and Grill

8 River Dr.; 360/288-0555; noon-9pm daily; $15-23

Dino's is a no-frills place where you can get a burger or pizza as well as beer on draft as a quick stop on your trip.

Accommodations and Camping

Lake Quinault Lodge

345 S. Shore Rd.; 888/896-3818; www. olympicnationalparks.com/lodging/lake-quinault-lodge; $142-316

This rustic lodge from 1926 is a cozy place to stay and the ideal base for relaxing by the lake, fishing, or exploring the rain forest. Amenities include an arcade room and an indoor swimming pool, and guests have their choice of 92 rooms, some of which feature views of the lake, fireplaces, or private balconies.

Rain Forest Resort Village

516 S. Shore Rd.; 360/288-2535; www.rainforestresort. com; $160-215

You'll have multiple accommodations to choose from at the Rain Forest Resort Village, including parkside suites, fireplace cabins, the Village Inn with 16 rooms, and an RV campground. They also have an on-site restaurant, The Salmon House, and a general store on-site for any small needs.

Falls Creek Campground

3 mi (5 km) from US 101 on S. Shore Rd., just past Pacific Ranger District office; 360/288-2525; www. recreation.gov; $25

The campsite offers 31 spots for tents, trailers, and RVs up to 16 ft without hookups. Sites vary between wooded areas and open spaces, with many offering lake views.

Transportation

Lake Quinault is 2.5 hours (123 mi/198 km) south of Port Angeles via US 101 north (43 mi/69 km) or 1 hour north of Aberdeen via US 101 south. **Jefferson Transit** provides bus service from Quinault Rain Forest Visitor Information Center (6084 US-101, Amanda Park; free) next to Lake Quinault up to Forks.

Grays Harbor and Vicinity

Named after Captain Robert Gray's 1792 expedition to the area, Grays Harbor is a county surrounding the body of water with the same name. Ocean Shores is to the north, Aberdeen in the middle, and Westport to the south. It's full of historical significance, and ocean views are almost everywhere you look.

To the east sits the city of Aberdeen, which has a rich timber industry heritage and is famous as the birthplace of Nirvana's Kurt Cobain. In the north, you'll find Ocean Shores, a coastal city that many consider the perfect vacation destination with its long sandy beaches. The town offers various outdoor activities, from horseback riding on the beach to flying kites along the coast.

Heading south, you'll arrive in the town of Westport, set on a narrow peninsula between the Pacific Ocean and Grays Harbor. This area is a true haven for fishing enthusiasts and surfers, many of whom come from far away for these experiences. Its marina is the largest on the outer coast of the Pacific

Northwest and always has something going on with boats coming and going.

ABERDEEN AND HOQUIAM

Aberdeen's slogan, "Come As You Are," is a reference to a famous Nirvana song. Kurt Cobain grew up here, and the city proudly displays that around town. Although Aberdeen isn't often a destination, it is the last major city you'll drive through before heading out to the coast, so it's an ideal place to stock up on food and gas.

Sights
Grays Harbor Historical Seaport

500 N. Custer St.; 360/532-8611; https://historical seaport.org; 9am-6pm Wed.-Fri, 9am-1pm Sat.; free

Grays Harbor Historical Seaport is home to the *Lady Washington* and the *Hawaiian Chieftain*, two replicas of tall ships from the 18th century. These ships travel along the Pacific Ocean coastline throughout the year, so check their website to see where they're

Kurt Cobain's Hometown

Aberdeen was an important influence on Kurt Cobain's music and art throughout his formative years, as it was his hometown and where he got his start. Known for his raw emotion and insightful songs, the late Nirvana vocalist is memorialized in his hometown at various sites.

- At the outside of Cobain's **childhood house** (1210 E. 1st St.), you'll often find flower bouquets from adoring fans.

- A more personal connection to Cobain's legacy can be found at the nearby Kurt Cobain Memorial Park, also known as **Kurt Cobain Landing.** A guitar monument and a plaque honoring his legacy can be found in a park near the **Young Street Bridge** over the Wishkah River. The bridge is mentioned in the Nirvana song "Something in the Way," and it's widely thought that Cobain spent a significant portion of time underneath the bridge during his turbulent childhood. It's now one of the most famous spots for Nirvana fans to visit and spend time reflecting on his life.

- If you make the trip to Seattle, you can visit the address where Kurt Cobain formerly lived (171 Lake Washington Blvd. E.). The house is privately owned and off-limits to the public, but supporters still pay their respects at nearby Viretta Park. The park seats are covered in Cobain memorials and graffiti, and people come from far and wide to pay their respects, leave flowers and candles, and take pictures.

currently located and try to book a sailing on them.

Lady Washington

500 N. Custer St.; 360/280-3980; https:// historicalseaport.org; 1pm tour available if ship is in port; $49-72

The *Lady Washington* is a replica tall ship that serves as a floating museum and educational vessel. Known for its distinctive appearance, it has appeared in various films and TV shows including *Pirates of the Caribbean: The Curse of the Black Pearl*. The ship travels throughout the year, but when in port it offers dockside tours in Aberdeen and brunch and family cruises with an educational program.

Polson Museum

1611 Riverside Ave.; 360/533-5862; www. polsonmuseum.org; 11am-4pm Wed.-Sat., noon-4pm Sun.; $5

The Polson Museum showcases the history of Grays Harbor County and works to preserve it. The wood industry, Native American history, and local culture are just a few of the topics covered by the museum's displays and artifacts.

Food

Tinderbox Coffee Roasters

113 E. Wishkah St.; 360/743-9046; Instagram @tinderboxroasters; 7am-4pm daily

Tinderbox has an inviting vibe and is the place where locals go to grab their morning coffee. The seasonal espresso drink menu is always changing, and there's plenty of breakfast sandwiches and other food options.

Billy's Bar & Grill

322 E. Heron St.; 360/533-7144; https://billysaberdeen. com; 9am-9pm daily; $13-20

Billy's Bar & Grill is in a historic building from the 1900s and even has a bar that's rumored to be haunted. It's an affordable place to get quick eats like pancakes, sandwiches, and burgers.

La Salvadoreña Restaurant

122 N. H St.; 360/532-8747; https://la-salvadorena. square.site; 10am-8pm Mon.-Thurs., 10am-9am Fri.-Sat., 10am-6pm Sun.; $7-15

La Salvadoreña is a quaint place to get authentic Salvadoran food, such as pupusas, fried plantains, and pastelitos, as well as burritos and fajitas.

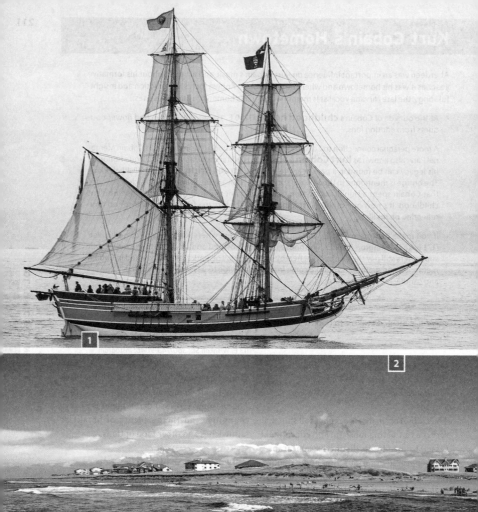

Lighthouse Drive-In

*2121 Simpson Ave.; 360/533-4841; https://
lighthousedrivein.com; 10:30am-8pm daily; $8-11*

You can't miss the Lighthouse Drive-In with its replica lighthouse attached to its small restaurant. This is the place to get hearty burgers, fries, and a milkshake.

Accommodations
A Harbor View Inn

111 W. 11th St.; 360/533-7996; www.aharborview.com; $129-199

Set in a 1905 Colonial Revival-style home, A Harbor View Inn has four rooms with picturesque views of Grays Harbor and historic downtown Aberdeen, complete with Victorian-era furnishings, king-size beds, and private baths.

Best Western Plus Aberdeen

701 E. Heron St.; 360/537-7460; www.bestwestern. com; $157-184

The renovated Best Western boasts the unique feature of having the only pool in town, and they have 158 rooms to choose from. Guests can also enjoy a complimentary breakfast.

Information and Services
Greater Grays Harbor

506 Duffy St.; 360/532-1924; https://graysharbor.org; 8am 5pm Mon.-Fri.

Greater Grays Harbor is a convenient place to stop and get information about nearby attractions.

Grays Harbor Community Hospital

915 Anderson Dr.; 360/537-4130; www.ghcares.org

Grays Harbor Community Hospital has an emergency room, is a Level III trauma center, and has more than a dozen different specialty departments if you need to be referred.

Transportation

From Olympia, take Route 8 west to US 12 west. It's about a 1-hour drive (50 mi/80 km) from Olympia or 2 hours from Seattle.

1: *Lady Washington* 2: Ocean Shores

Grays Harbor Transit (360/532-2770; www.ghtransit.com) has buses available around Aberdeen and Hoquiam and goes up to Lake Quinault as well.

★ OCEAN SHORES

Ocean Shores is a popular Grays Harbor destination, known for its 6-mi-long (9.6-km) peninsula on the Washington coast. Despite the region's reputation for wind and rain throughout the year, that doesn't stop people from visiting in the summer months to fly kites and ride bikes around town.

Beaches

There are 6 mi (10 km) of beaches to enjoy in Ocean Shores, so you won't have a problem finding somewhere to go.

North Jetty

1581 E. Ocean Shores Blvd. SW; https://waparks.org

North Jetty is the southernmost point of Ocean Shores and looks into Grays Harbor; across the water you can see the town of Westport. Carefully climb the large rocks and watch massive waves come in, which is particularly fun on a stormy day.

Damon Point State Park

Grays Harbor County; https://stateparks.com; 8am-5pm daily

Damon Point has a 1-mi (1.6 km) strip of beach, so it's ideal for hiking and spotting wildlife. Make sure you look down too, as it's a great area for finding sea glass.

Horseback Riding

Horseback riding in Ocean Shores is a popular activity, as it's a scenic way to take in views of the beach and Pacific Ocean.

Chenois Creek Horse Rentals

*491 Damon Rd.; 360/533-5591; https://
chenoiscreekhorserentals.com; 10am-5pm Sat.-Sun.; $25*

The guided horseback rides go for about an hour and are suitable for riders of all ages and experience levels. Riders must be at least 6

Razor Clam Digging

digging for razor clams

If you've ever wanted to see where clams come from, now's your chance with razor clam digging in Ocean Shores.

This all-ages activity is fairly easy to do and only requires a clam gun (a specialized tool for digging up clams) or shovel, a container to put your clams in, and a valid clam license. All you have to do is walk along the shore at low tide looking for small, roughly dime-sized holes, and then carefully dig down to where the clam is buried beneath.

You'll find many people digging in the **fall and winter,** often equipped with lanterns or flashlights for nighttime digging. It's also important to stay safe by **monitoring tide schedules,** avoiding incoming tides, dressing warmly, and wearing waterproof boots.

There are multiple beach access points in Ocean Shores for clamming enthusiasts, such as Damon Point and Ocean City State Park, which are renowned for their clam populations.

The **Washington Department of Fish and Wildlife** (https://wdfw.wa.gov; 360/902-2200) sets the digging schedule and provides valuable information about the tides and daily catch limits, so check with them before heading out. The WDFW also monitors dangerous marine toxin levels and will shut down certain beaches if necessary. You can secure a shellfish permit from either authorized vendors such as Buck Electric Ace Hardware (641 Point Brown Ave. NW; 360/289-2888) or online.

years old, 48 in tall, and under 240 pounds. There are 30 horses available for beach rides, and you'll be given a saddle and instructions from professionals on how to safely guide your horse down the beach as part of a large group.

Kite Flying

Ocean Shores is an ideal location for kite flying due to its wide sandy beaches along the Pacific Ocean, with miles of space for flying kites. You'll find people on the beach trying their hand at flying kites throughout the year, but spring is the best time, when winds are at their peak. There's also kite shops and festivals to encourage people to get involved.

Ocean Shores Kites

172 W. Chance a La Mer NW; 360/289-4103; www. oceanshoreskites.com; 10am-5pm daily; $17-219

Ocean Shores Kites has dozens of different kites to choose from and caters to everyone from beginners to advanced flyers. There are also plenty of fun beach toys, such as Frisbees and spinners.

Bikes and Mopeds

Bikes and mopeds are convenient ways to get around the area, and you'll see people riding them throughout town.

Electric Beach Bike Rentals

172 W. Chance a La Mer NW, no. 1; 360/593-7441; www. electricbeachbikerentals.com; 9am-5pm Sat., 9am-4pm Mon.-Fri. and Sun.; $30-45/hour

Electric Beach Bike Rentals is the place to get your bikes in Ocean Shores. They have electric beach bikes and tandem bikes, as well as trailers for dogs and kids.

Bird-Watching

Bird-watching in Ocean Shores is a popular year-round activity, thanks to the area's numerous avian scenes and the beautiful Pacific Ocean backdrop. It's a good place to see the Olympic gull, which lives there year-round, and other gulls like the Heermann's gull and the California gull that only visit during certain times of the year. Other species, such as sanderlings, brown pelicans, and sandpipers, join the party during migration.

Oyhut Wildlife Recreation Area

4686 Wishkah Rd.; 360/533-5676; https://wdfw. wa.gov; $10 Discover Pass

The Oyhut Wildlife Recreation Area has over 600 acres (240 ha) to explore and is ideal for bird-watchers due to how quiet the area is. Its wetlands and estuaries are home to a wide variety of animals like birds, reptiles, and fish, and it's one of the four remaining nesting sites in Washington for the western snowy plover, a bird that is currently threatened.

Entertainment and Events
Pacific Paradise Park

767 Minard Ave. NW; 360/289-9537; www. pacificparadisepark.com; 10am-8pm Sun.-Thurs., 10am-9pm Fri., 10am-10pm Sat.; $17-30

Families will love stopping at Pacific Paradise Park to enjoy mini golf and bumper boats on sunny days. If it's raining, head inside to play at their arcade or try their Lazermaze activity.

Shopping
Sharky's

695 Ocean Shores Blvd NW; 360/289-4462; Facebook @SharkysOceanShores; 9:30am-7:30pm daily

Sharky's is the place to stock up on all your Ocean Shores souvenirs and any beach items you may have forgotten, such as swimsuits or shoes. It's easy to spot, as the entrance is a giant great white shark's mouth, which is also fun for photo shoots.

Food
★ Galway Bay

880 Point Brown Ave. NE; 360/289-2300; www. galwaybayirishpub.com; 11am-8pm Sun.-Thurs., 11am-9pm Fri.-Sat.; $10-30

Galway Bay makes you feel like you walked straight into a pub in Ireland, with authentic food like corned beef hash and Guinness on draft. Try to time your visit with one of their live bands to enjoy music with your meal, and stop at their gift shop next door to buy souvenirs and food imported from Ireland.

Bennett's Fish Shack

105 W. Chance a La Mer Blvd.; 360/289-2847; www. bennettsfishshacks.com; 11am-8:30pm Sun.-Thurs., 11am-9:30pm Fri.-Sat.; $15-27

Stop at Bennett's Fish Shack to enjoy fresh, local seafood such as crab cakes and oyster shooters. They also have a full bar, and it's a relaxing atmosphere to watch the game on one of their TVs.

Our Place Restaurant

676 Ocean Shores Blvd. NW; 360/940-7314; Facebook @ourplaceos; 8am-12:30pm Mon. and Thurs., 7am-1:30pm Fri.-Sun.; $10-25

Come to Our Place to get a hearty breakfast at a casual diner before heading out for a day of exploring. You'll have plenty of options from eggs Benedict to breakfast burritos.

Peppermint Parlor

748 Point Brown Ave. NE; 360/289-0572; https://
playtimefamilyfun.com; 10am-9pm Sun.-Thurs., 10am-
10pm Fri.-Sat.; $5-25

Nothing completes a trip to the beach
like a scoop of homemade ice cream, and
Peppermint Parlor has dozens of flavors available. They also have soft pretzels, doughnuts,
and other treats.

Accommodations and Camping

Lighthouse Suites Inn

491 Damon Rd.; 360/289-2311; www.
lighthousesuitesinn.com; $99-119

Lighthouse Suites Inn is close to the beach
and has many pet-friendly rooms. Some
rooms have an ocean view or are Jacuzzi
suites. The rooms are modern and sleek, and
you'll know you're at the right place when you
see the large lighthouse replica at the front
of the hotel.

Quinault Beach Resort and Casino

78 Route 115; 888/461-2214; https://
quinaultbeachresort.com; $139-219

While having a casino on the beach may seem
odd, Quinault Beach Resort and Casino is one
of the most popular places to stay. In addition
to their casino, they have multiple restaurants
on-site, and all guests have private beach access via a boardwalk from the resort. Many
of their 158 rooms have ocean views, and it's
worth the upgrade to get one.

Shilo Inns Ocean Shores

707 Ocean Shores Blvd. NW; 360/289-4600; www.
shiloinns.com; $129-179

Shilo Inns has 113 deluxe suites, all with private balconies perfect for enjoying stunning
sunsets. The lobby showcases a 3,000-gallon
aquarium, and guests have access to a pool
and a hot tub.

Ocean City State Park

148 Route 115; 360/289-3553; https://parks.wa.gov;
8am-dusk daily; $20-37

Camping is an option for those interested,
but be aware that winds can get pretty high
in this area, so you'll need to bring the right
equipment for tent camping. The campground has 149 standard sites, as well as 29
full-hookup sites, and coin-operated showers are available.

Information

Ocean Shores Visitor Information Center

120 W. Chance a La Mer NW; 360/289-9586; https://
toursmoceanshores.com; 10am-2pm Thurs.-Tues.

Stop at the visitor center when you get into
town to get maps of the area and information
on activities.

Transportation

Ocean Shores is about 2.5 hours from Seattle
(approximately 130 mi/210 km). You'll take
I-5 south through Olympia and then US
101 north, Route 8 west, and US 12 west to
Aberdeen. From there, continue on to Route
109 north and turn left on Route 115 north.
If you're coming straight from Aberdeen, it's
about a 30-minute drive.

Grays Harbor Transit provides free
bus service around the Ocean Shores area
with pickups at the **Ocean Shores Transit
Center** (165 W. Chance a La Mer NW, Ocean
Shores; 360/532-2770; www.ghtransit.com)
and to Aberdeen from the **Aberdeen Transit
Station** (101 S. G St. Aberdeen; 360/532-2770;
www.ghtransit.com), with about a dozen trips
per day.

WESTPORT

Westport is a mecca for deep-sea fishing lovers, and visitors come from far and wide to
take part in a trip. You can pick from a number of charters, all of which offer the chance to
catch everything from salmon to tuna, as well
as the comfort of having your gear provided
and catch cleaned for you.

Westport is also home to some of the best
surfing areas in the state. There are plenty of
places to rent surfboards and wetsuits, but sitting on the beach with a cup of coffee in hand
and watching the experts in action is also fun.

In addition, there are a number of state parks in the region from which you can get to the coast via a network of paths.

Beaches

Westport Light State Park

1595 W. Ocean Ave.; https://parks.wa.gov; 8am-10pm daily summer, 8am-6pm daily winter

Westport Light State Park has over 560 acres (225 ha) and 1,200 ft (365 m) of shoreline to explore. The day-use park is popular for activities including saltwater fishing, crabbing, surfing, beach exploring, and clamming. The park also features an ADA-accessible concrete boardwalk trail for strolling along the shore.

Fishing

Westport's most popular activity is deep-sea fishing, thanks to the expansive ocean that lies just next to the narrow peninsula. However, fishing in the Pacific's deep waters requires expertise and experience due to the ocean's unpredictability. That's why it's best to hire a local charter boat; there are many to choose from in the area. Charters come with not only all the gear and bait you'll need but also experienced captains and crews who are familiar with the area's weather, fish habits, and the best fishing techniques.

That said, you don't have to go out on a boat for all types of fishing—you can go jetty fishing, surf fishing, and onshore fishing. Any outfitter will be happy to tell you more about the different types and find the best one for you.

Westport Charters

2411 Westhaven Dr.; 360/268-0900; https:// westportcharters.com; 9am-4pm daily; $250-425/ person

Westport Charters has a variety of charters to choose from and caters to beginners as well as advanced fishers. They'll help you pick the best charter for you, and you could catch halibut, ling cod, rockfish, salmon, and more, depending on the season.

Pacific Bluewater Sportfishing

326 Lamb St.; 253/350-8502; https:// pacificbluewatersportfishing.com; 5:30am-5pm Thurs.-Sat., 6:30am-5pm Sun.; $375-545/person

This charter company only allows up to six people, so there's plenty of room to fish without feeling crowded while having a full 360-degree fishing space. They also have Ocean-Tamer bean bags for a comfortable ride there, and the boat's bow flare is designed to minimize how wet passengers get while riding out to the ocean.

Gold Rush Charters

Float 8, Westhaven Dr.; 360/260-9300; www. goldrushcharters.com

Gold Rush Charters offers a variety of fishing excursions, and it's recommended to book several months in advance, as they book up quickly. Their boat has twin, non-smoking, and eco-friendly John Deere diesel engines, meaning the boat is quieter and more efficient, minimizing travel time.

Surfing

The waves in Westport are some of the best and most dependable in the Pacific Northwest, and the town's three main surf breaks welcome surfers of all skill levels. The Jetty at **Westport Light State Park** (1595 W. Ocean Ave.; 360/268-9717; https:// parks.wa.gov; 8am-8pm daily summer, 8am-6pm daily winter) claims the most reliable, consistent waves in Washington State, with conditions suitable for all skill levels and an all-sand bottom great for beginners.

Steepwater Surf

316 Montesano St.; 360/268-5527; https:// steepwatersurf.com; 10am-5pm Mon.-Fri., 9am-5pm Sat.-Sun.; rentals $39-51, lessons $115

Steepwater Surf is the go-to destination for fast and efficient surf rentals, boasting a 10-minute turnaround from renting to being on the waves. They offer wetsuit and board rentals, and they also have group surf lessons available.

BigFoot Surf

2700 Jetty Haul Rd.; 360/515-7969; https://bigfootsurf.com; $169-249

At Westport Light State Park, BigFoot Surf School's knowledgeable instructors give surf classes to students of all skill levels. They offer both private and semi-private classes.

Whale-Watching

During the months of March-May, the California gray whale makes its epic trek from Baja California to the Arctic feeding grounds, making for fantastic whale-watching in Westport. The 23,000 whales that make up this migration are well-known for their playful demeanor around boats and dramatic breaches. Seeing these gray whales, which were nearly wiped out in the 1850s but have now recovered to historical population levels, is a must if you visit Westport. They can grow to a length of 47 ft and a weight of 70,000 pounds.

While you have the best chance of seeing whales out at sea, they do come near the shore at times. **Westport Light State Park** is a great place, as you can walk along the beach or go out on **Westport Jetty** to (hopefully) see whales.

Ocean Sportfishing Charters

2549 Westhaven Dr.; 360/268-1000; www.openoceansportfishing.com; Mar.-Apr.; $400/boat

Ocean Sportfishing Charters offers customized whale-watching tours March-April as the gray whales migrate through the area. These 2.5-hour tours take up to six people out into the Pacific Ocean to see these magnificent creatures breaching in the water. Harbor tours offered March-September give you an overview of the area while your guide points out other native sealife like seals.

Food

Knotty Pine Tavern

201 E. Dock St.; 360/268-0591; Facebook @KnottyPineatTheWestportDocks; 8am-midnight daily; $11-30

You'll find yourself sitting among locals finished with a day of work at this cozy tavern. It's a great place to grab pub food while watching sports or listening to live music.

★ Blue Buoy

2323 Westhaven Dr.; 360/268-7065; Facebook @bluebuoyrestaurant; 8am-2pm Mon.-Fri., 8am-3pm Sat., 8am-2:30pm Sun.; $11-20

Start your morning at Blue Buoy with a filling Dungeness crab omelet, or try their famous clam chowder during lunchtime. This diner by the water has no shortage of seafood menu options.

Blackbeard's Brewing Company

700 W. Ocean Ave.; 360/268-7662; https://blackbeardsbrewing.com; 12:30pm-7:30pm Thurs. and Sun., 12:30pm-8pm Fri.-Sat., 3pm-7:30pm Mon.; $13-20

Blackbeard's Brewing Company is the perfect place to end an evening, as they have about a dozen beers on tap and a food menu, including pizza. There's also an outdoor beer garden to enjoy on those sunny days.

Accommodations and Camping

The Westport Inn

2501 Nyhus St. N.; 360/268-0111; https://westportinnhotel.com; $99-199

The Westport Inn has 41 various rooms, including queen and king rooms with ocean views, one-bedroom suites, and even a three-bedroom apartment. Three cabins are also available that sleep 4-12 people.

LOGE Westport

1416 S. Montesano St.; 360/980-8088; www.logecamps.com; $109

If you don't already have plans to get outside, LOGE Westport encourages it with their surfer-themed rooms, surfboard racks, and wetsuits, surfboards, and kayak rentals available. Enjoy their café when you're done for the day and sit by the outdoor fire pit at night.

Twin Harbors State Park

3120 Route 105; 360/268-9717; www.parks.wa.gov; year-round; $48-79

Twin Harbors State Park features a variety of camping options, including standard and full-hookup sites, but with space limits for bigger RVs. A campfire and grill are available, but no running water or electricity is available. Rustic huts and yurts that are heated for the winter are also available, and some even allow pets.

Information

Stop by the **Westport/Grayland Visitor Information Center** (2985 S. Montesano St.; 360/268-9422; www.experiencewestport.com) to find out where to go and how to spend your time here.

Transportation

Westport is about 2.5 hours (130 mi/210 km) from Seattle and can be reached by taking I-5 south to Olympia, US 101 north, Route 8 west, and US 12 west to Aberdeen. From there, get on Route 105 south, turning right on Montesano Street South.

Although you can see Westport across the harbor when you're in Ocean Shores, it takes about an hour (44 mi/71 km) to drive around. From Ocean Shores, take Route 109 south through Aberdeen, and follow Route 105 south to get on the other side of the water headed toward Westport before turning right on Montesano Street.

It's only a 25-minute drive (21 mi/34 km) to Westport from Aberdeen; take Route 105 south most of the way before turning right on Montesano Street.

Long Beach Peninsula

Located in southwestern Washington, the Long Beach Peninsula has 28 mi (45 km) of sandy coastline ideal for kite flying, clam digging, and leisurely strolls. Cape Disappointment State Park, where the Columbia River empties into the Pacific Ocean, is a historic site rich in significance to the Lewis and Clark expedition. The small towns of the peninsula make for good coastal getaways.

★ CAPE DISAPPOINTMENT STATE PARK

244 Robert Gray Dr.; 360/642-3078; www.parks. wa.gov; 6:30am-dusk daily; $10 Discover Pass

Cape Disappointment State Park is at the meeting point of the Columbia River and the Pacific Ocean, making it home to both saltwater and freshwater ecosystems. In addition to two old lighthouses, the area is home to verdant old-growth forests, excellent fishing sites, and a rough shoreline. The park is ideal for camping, fishing, boating, and exploring the shore. Many pathways allow visitors to hike through the park and discover its rich history and beautiful landscape.

Native American tribes lived here before European explorers and the Lewis and Clark expedition found it. The park's somewhat melancholy name comes from Captain John Meares, an English explorer who failed to cross the river bar in 1788 and named the area to reflect his frustration. It was Lewis and Clark who put Cape Disappointment on the map when they arrived in 1805, completing their westward journey to find the Pacific Ocean. The area served as a military installation in the late 19th and early 20th centuries, with the remains of old fortifications still visible today.

Lewis and Clark Interpretive Center

244 Robert Gray Dr.; 360/642-3029; www.parks. wa.gov; 10am-5pm daily Apr.-Oct., 10am-5pm Wed.-Sun. Nov.-Mar; $5 adult, $2.50 children, under 6 free

On the cliffs of Cape Disappointment State Park sits the Lewis and Clark Interpretive Center, which links the intriguing marine and

Long Beach Peninsula

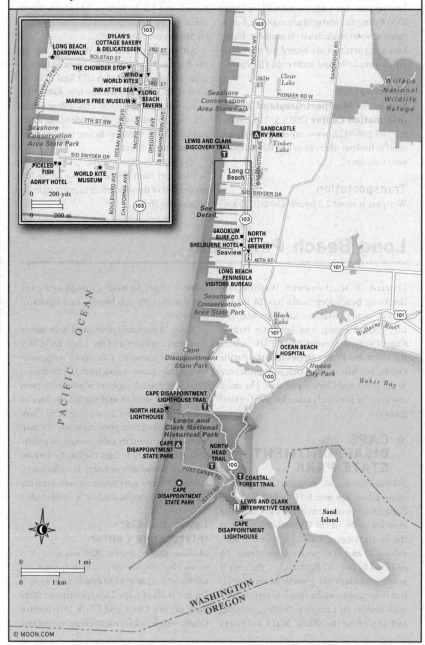

© MOON.COM

military feats of the Chinook tribe, the Lewis and Clark expedition, and other related stories. Attractive displays, authentic artifacts—including a first-order Fresnel lens—and an intriguing short film await you at the center. There are amazing views of the Pacific Ocean and the Columbia River from the covered observation deck.

Lighthouses
Cape Disappointment Lighthouse

Cape Disappointment Lighthouse Trail; dawn-dusk daily; free

Built in 1856, the Cape Disappointment Lighthouse is among the West Coast's oldest lighthouses. Its primary purpose was to aid sailors in going through the treacherous waters around the mouth of the Columbia River, often known as the "Graveyard of the Pacific." You can reach the lighthouse after a short, easy climb along the Cape Disappointment Trail.

North Head Lighthouse

North Head Trail; www.parks.wa.gov; 11am-3pm daily May-Sept.; $3 adults, free ages 7-17, under 7 not allowed

Built in 1898, the North Head Lighthouse served as a beacon for mariners approaching from the north. It was constructed to mitigate the rising number of shipwrecks along the Peninsula, as the Cape Disappointment light was not visible to those coming from the north. Standing 65 ft (20 m) tall, this lighthouse is set on solid basalt and towers more than 190 ft (58 m) above sea level. When the lighthouse is staffed, volunteers will let you climb to the top for an even better view.

Hiking
North Head Trail

Distance: *3.6 mi (5.8 km) round-trip*
Duration: *1.5 hours*
Elevation gain: *420 ft (128 m)*
Difficulty: *easy*
Trailhead: *From Long Beach, head south on North Head Road toward Cape Disappointment State Park. Take a right on North Head Lighthouse Road until you reach the parking area.*

The trail travels through a meadow and a forest. As you go deeper into the woods and pass creeks, the wide route gets narrower, and you'll be surrounded by mossy wood and young hemlocks. At the end of the trail is a steep, muddy descent to a road that takes you to the beach or back to the ranger station.

Cape Disappointment State Park

Cape Disappointment Lighthouse Trail

Distance: *0.6 mi (1 km) round-trip*
Duration: *20 minutes*
Elevation gain: *150 ft (45 m)*
Difficulty: *easy*
Trailhead: *From Long Beach, head south on North Head Road toward Cape Disappointment State Park. Take a right on Fort Canby Road until you reach the parking lot for the Cape Disappointment Lighthouse.*

This is the easiest trail in the park when you want to see a stunning lighthouse, as it's only a quick walk to the ocean, where the Cape Disappointment Lighthouse sits. Though short, the trail can be muddy, so bring appropriate footwear.

Coastal Forest Trail

Distance: *1.4 mi (2.6 km) round-trip*
Duration: *1 hour*
Elevation gain: *260 ft (79 m)*
Difficulty: *Easy*
Trailhead: *Proceed down Fort Canby Road after taking the 100 spur past the North Head Lighthouse turnoff. At a four-way intersection, turn left, and then immediately turn left again onto a gravel parking lot to reach the trailhead.*

Depending on how far you choose to go, the Coastal Forest Loop can be a 0.5-mi (0.8-km) or a 1.5-mi (2.4-km) walk. Insights about forest ecology, nurse logs, and plant succession can be found on trailside signs. Keep an ear out for soaring bald eagles, and look out for local newts. The trail connects to Maya Lin's Confluence Project, a sculpture monument to the Chinook people who lived in the area before the Lewis and Clark expedition.

Camping

There are about a dozen RV campgrounds scattered around Long Beach, but Cape Disappointment State Park is the main place to go for tent camping.

Cape Disappointment State Park

244 Robert Gray Dr.; www.parks.wa.gov; $30-79
Cape Disappointment has about 250 different campsites to choose from that include electricity, running water, and a boat ramp. Sites are dispersed throughout the park, so there are plenty of options, whether you want to be close to the shore or near Lake O'Neil. For those seeking a bit more luxury, the park also offers cottages and yurts with all the essentials included. Booking in advance is highly recommended during the busy summer months.

Transportation

Cape Disappointment is approximately 3 hours (170 mi/275 km) from Seattle via I-5 and US 101, and 2 hours 15 minutes (110 mi/175 km) from Portland via US 30. From Westport, Cape Disappointment is about 1 hour 45 minutes (80 mi/130 km) away, via Route 105 and US 101.

LONG BEACH AND SEAVIEW

Long Beach and Seaview have the area's largest selection of lodging and dining, so they're popular places to stay. Long Beach in particular is known for having the country's longest drivable beach and delicious seafood.

Sights and Beaches

While Long Beach may be small, with a population of about 1,700, it's the largest town around. The main draw here are the miles of beaches to explore. Most people spend their days there, and then come into town to explore the museum and restaurants.

The Beach

Long Beach boasts a 28-mi (45-km) stretch of drivable coastline, making it the longest contiguous beach in the country. While driving is generally permitted from Long Beach to Oysterville, some areas are off-limits to protect local ecosystems. See the Beach Safety and Driving page of the town's website (www.visitlongbeachpeninsula.com) to learn more. The beach is known for its annual International Kite Festival and the traditional razor clam digging.

It's important to note that, while tempting, swimming is never recommended at the beaches due to the strong current.

World Kite Museum

303 Sid Snyder Dr., Long Beach; 360/642-4020; www.worldkitemuseum.com; 11am-4pm daily, closed weekends Apr. 21-June 15 and Sept. 12-Oct. 30; $6 adult, $4 children

In the late 1980s, a group of kite enthusiasts got together with the idea of opening a museum devoted solely to the hobby, and by 1990 they were able to open the World Kite Museum, thanks to a large contribution of international kites. The museum features over 1,500 kites from 26 different nations and hosts various educational events, making it a top center for kite history. Visitors can make their own kite to fly on the beach in the arts and crafts area upstairs.

Marsh's Free Museum

409 Pacific Ave., Long Beach; 360/642-2188; www. marshsfreemuseum.com; 10am-5pm Sun.-Thurs., 10am-6pm Fri.-Sat.; free

One of the more unusual places to visit in the area, Marsh's Free Museum is great when you need a break from the beach. The building is famous for its bizarre collection of exhibits, everything from antique taxidermy and arcade games to the popular Jake the Alligator Man, a half-man, half-alligator. Stop at the gift shop to pick up seashells, odd trinkets, and other assorted items.

Hiking

Lewis and Clark Discovery Trail

Distance: *16.4 mi (26.4 km) round-trip*
Duration: *8 hours*
Elevation gain: *15 ft (5 m)*
Difficulty: *easy*
Trailhead: *Beards Hollow in Ilwaco and the Breakers (210 26th St. NW) in Long Beach*

Most people don't aim to complete the entire 16-mi (26-km) Lewis and Clark Discovery Trail, which stretches from Ilwaco to Long Beach. Instead, they opt for sections of the trail that appeal to them. Starting at Beard's Hollow overlook, the path goes through coastal forests and swamps, leading you to Long Beach. Along your walk, you'll encounter scenic boardwalks, landmarks like a gray whale skeleton, and a weathered tree marking the end of Clark's northern journey. It's mostly paved the entire way and is one of the few trails in the area that welcomes bikers.

The one downside to this trail is most of the ocean views are blocked, so the Long Beach Boardwalk alongside the Discovery Trail can give you elevated views of the water.

Surfing

Skookum Surf Co.

1216 48th St., Seaview; 360/358-7873; www. skookumsurf.com; 10am-4pm daily June-Sept.

If you're looking to surf on the beach, Skookum Surf Co. is the go-to spot for surfboard rentals.

Kite Flying

Wind World

115 Pacific Ave. S., Long Beach; 360/642-5483; 10am-5pm daily

For kite flying on the beach, Wind World offers a wide selection of beginner to advanced kites.

Food

★ Pickled Fish

409 Sid Snyder Dr., Long Beach; 360/642-2344; www. pickledfishrestaurant.com; 3pm-10pm Mon.-Thurs., 8am-1pm Sat.-Sun., 3pm-11pm Fri.-Sat.; $11-37

One of the best views in town for dinner is at the Pickled Fish, set in the Adrift Hotel. This 4th-floor restaurant overlooks the Pacific Ocean, and menu highlights include Dungeness crab cakes, fried oysters, Waygu cheeseburgers, and mac and cheese. You'll often find live music here on the weekends.

Long Beach Tavern

305 Pacific Ave. S., Long Beach; 360/642-3235; https:// longbeachtavern.com; 2pm-8pm Thurs.-Mon.; $10-25

Long Beach Tavern has been around since the

1960s and is still a fun place to grab a quick bite to eat in a pub atmosphere where you'll be among the locals. They have a variety of pub food, such as oyster shooters, burgers, and pizza.

The Chowder Stop

203 Bolstad Ave.; 360/777-3749; Facebook @The-Chowder-Stop; noon-7pm Tues.-Fri., noon-8pm Sat., noon-7pm Sun.; $10-18

The nautical-themed Chowder Stop is perfect for those cold winter days in Long Beach, as they have their signature chowder to warm you up as well as their chowder fries. They also have paninis, cod fish and chips, and salads available.

North Jetty Brewery

4200 Pacific Way, Seaview; 360/642-4234; https://northjettybrew.com; noon-7pm Mon.-Tues., noon-9pm Wed., noon-10pm Thurs.-Sat., noon-9pm Sun.; $8-10

North Jetty Brewery is the spot when you want a pint of beer, as they have 18 different ones on tap. Children are allowed until 7pm daily, and it's a lively atmosphere with various events like bingo and trivia going on during the week.

Dylan's Cottage Bakery & Delicatessen

118 Pacific Ave. S., Long Beach; 360/642-4441; https://cottagebakerylongbeach.com; 4am-5pm daily; $5-14

Doughnuts, pastries, soups, and sandwiches are all prepared from scratch at Dylan's Cottage Bakery & Delicatessen, making it a popular place to satisfy your sweet tooth first thing in the morning. A fun option is getting the food to go and bringing it to the beach for a picnic, as indoor seating is limited.

Accommodations

Adrift Hotel

409 Sid Snyder Dr., Long Beach; 360/642-2311; www.adrifthotel.com; $107-248

The Adrift Hotel is conveniently located near the beach, with many of its 80 rooms offering a view of the ocean and the beach itself

being reachable in a few minutes on foot. A heated saline pool, a barrel sauna, and a full spa are all available at the Pool House. Next door you'll find Adrift Distillers, where you can get dollar spirit tastings.

Inn at the Sea

115 3rd St. SW; 360/642-3714; https://innatthesea.com; $79-198

Inn at the Sea is centrally located in downtown Long Beach and minutes from the beach. The inn has a light grab-and-go breakfast and 43 rooms, including ocean-view ones and larger suites with living areas.

Shelburne Hotel

4415 Pacific Way; 360/642-2442; https://shelburnehotelwa.com; $105-236

Built in 1896, the Shelburne Hotel is Washington state's longest continuously operating hotel, featuring updated Victorian interiors with community spaces like a parlor and a room for games. The hotel offers 18 rooms, including ones with balconies or claw tubs, and houses the famous Shelburne Pub for local dining using fresh ingredients.

Sandcastle RV Park

1100 Pacific Ave. N., Long Beach; 360/642-2174; www.sandcastlerv.com; $45

Sandcastle RV Park has 38 full hookup sites with free Wi-Fi and expanded cable TV. The pet-friendly park features amenities like a 24-hour laundromat and a fish/clam cleaning station. A beach trail is just across the street, and the town center is an easy 10 blocks away.

Information and Services

Long Beach Peninsula Visitors Bureau

3914 Pacific Way, Seaview; 800/451-2542; www.visitlongbeachpeninsula.com; 9am-6pm Mon.-Sat., 10am-6pm Sun.

Stop by the visitor center to get maps of the area and recommendations of what to do, where to go, and local hikes.

Ocean Beach Hospital

174 1st Ave. N., Ilwaco; 360/642.3181; www.
oceanbeachhospital.com

Ocean Beach Hospital services the Long Beach Peninsula area with a 24/7 emergency room and various medical clinics.

Transportation

Long Beach is 3 hours 15 minutes (170 mi/285 km) from Seattle via I-5 and US 101, and 2.5 hours (110 mi/175 km) from Portland via US 30. Cape Disappointment is only 5 mi (8 km) south of Long Beach, via US 101 and Route 100.

Olympia

With its strategic location on Puget Sound, Olympia has long benefited economically, even before it was named the state capital in 1889. During the 19th-century gold rush, Olympia played a crucial role in supplying miners; its early economy was based on maritime trade, forestry, and agriculture.

As the state capital, the city is home to a considerable number of government employees, and you'll often find political activists outside of the capitol, marching with others for their cause.

Olympia also has a thriving cultural scene, with a more laid-back vibe than Seattle. You'll find many locals hanging out at coffee shops or browsing the farmers market.

SIGHTS
Capitol Campus

A variety of historic buildings can be found on the Capitol Campus, including the majestic Legislative Building, featuring one of the country's tallest masonry domes. The Governor's Mansion, the Office of the Superintendent of Public Instruction, and the Temple of Justice are also located here. Beautiful gardens, memorials, and monuments surround these structures; two examples are the Winged Victory Monument and the World War II Memorial. Besides serving as a hub for state administration, the campus is also a popular tourist destination due to its rich history and stunning architecture.

Legislative Building

416 Sid Snyder Ave. SW; 360/902-8880; www.
olympiawa.gov; 7:30am-5pm Mon.-Fri., 11am-4pm
Sat.-Sun.; free

The Legislative Building was finished in 1928 and boasts Tiffany chandeliers and marble from five different countries, along with the tallest freestanding masonry dome in North America. Free and open to the public every day, tours include the Rotunda, State Reception Room, North Foyer, and Legislative Galleries. The 50-minute tours depart on a first-come, first-served basis from the Tour Information Desk on the 2nd floor, next to the main entrance. Tours run hourly 10am-3pm on weekdays and every half hour 11:30am-2:30pm on weekends.

Governor's Mansion

504 15th Ave. SE; 360/902-8880; https://
wagovmansion.org; call for tours, free tours only on
select Wed.

The impressive Governor's Mansion is only open once a week, if that, so call in advance to get a reservation. Each tour takes up to 25 people, and you'll have a chance to visit the different rooms in this Georgian-style mansion from 1908.

Hands On Children's Museum

414 Jefferson St. NE; 360/956-0818; www.hocm.org;
9am-5pm Mon.-Sat., 10am-5pm Sun.; $16.95, senior
and military discounts available

With over 300,000 annual visitors, Hands On is undoubtedly the area's most-visited children's museum. With over 150 interactive exhibits between the two indoor levels and large outdoor space, kids will love the exhibits, such as a construction zone, a two-story cargo ship, and exploring a pretend forest.

Olympia

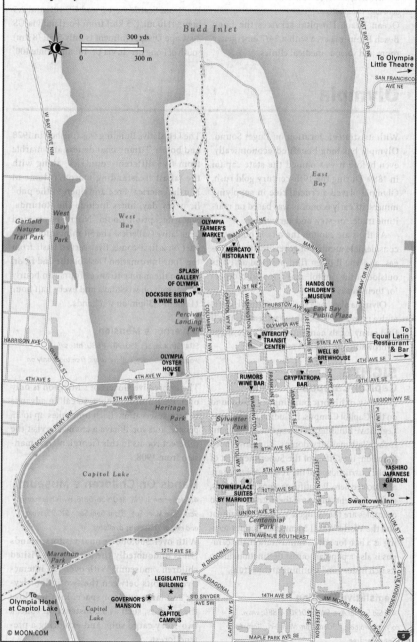

Budd Inlet

0 — 300 yds
0 — 300 m

To Olympia
Little Theatre

SAN FRANCISCO
AVE NE

East
Bay

EAST BAY DR NE

Garfield
Nature
Trail Park

West
Bay
Park

West
Bay

W BAY DRIVE NW

MARKET ST NE

MARINE DR NE

OLYMPIA FARMER'S MARKET

MERCATO RISTORANTE

SPLASH GALLERY OF OLYMPIA

DOCKSIDE BISTRO & WINE BAR

HANDS ON CHILDREN'S MUSEUM

A ST NE

WASHINGTON ST NE

CAPITOL WY N.

THURSTON AVE NE

JEFFERSON ST NE

East Bay Public Plaza

EAST BAY DR NE

Percival
Landing
Park

COLUMBIA ST NW

OLYMPIA AVE

STATE AVE NE

To Equal Latin Restaurant & Bar

HARRISON AVE

OLYMPIC ST

INTERCITY TRANSIT CENTER

WELL 80 BREWHOUSE

CHERRY ST SE

4TH AVE SE

OLYMPIA OYSTER HOUSE

4TH AVE W

4TH AVE S

5TH AVE SW

RUMORS WINE BAR

CRYPTATROPA BAR

FRANKLIN ST SE

ADAMS ST SE

5TH AVE SE

LEGION WY SE

PLUM ST SE

DESCHUTES PKWY SW

Heritage
Park

Sylvester
Park

CAPITOL WY S

8TH AVE SE

Capitol Lake

9TH AVE SE

JEFFERSON ST SE

YASHIRO JAPANESE GARDEN

TOWNEPLACE SUITES BY MARRIOTT

10TH AVE SE

To Swantown Inn

UNION AVE SE

Centennial
Park

11TH AVENUE SOUTHEAST

PLUM ST SE

Marathon
Park

12TH AVE SE

N DIAGONAL

To
Olympia Hotel
at Capitol Lake

Capitol
Lake

LEGISLATIVE BUILDING

GOVERNOR'S MANSION

CAPITOL CAMPUS

SID SNYDER AVE SW

S DIAGONAL

CAPITOL WY S

14TH AVE SE

JIM MOORE MEMORIAL PKWY

JEFFERSON ST SE

HENDERSON BLVD SE

MAPLE PARK AVE SE

© MOON.COM

5

Yashiro Japanese Garden

1010 Plum St. SE; 360/753-8380; www.olympiawa.gov; dawn to dusk daily; free

The Yashiro Japanese Garden is a beautiful place to see the city's connection with its sister city, Yashiro, Japan. This garden's calming water features, bamboo grove, and pond are typical of traditional Japanese gardens.

NIGHTLIFE

Washington's capital has a compact downtown area that makes visiting pubs, bars, and music venues easy. Plenty of the restaurants and bars stay open late for those looking for night on the town. Art galleries and theaters also host exhibits and late-night events on occasion.

Well 80 Brewhouse

514 4th Ave. E.; 360/915-6653; https://well80.com; 11:30am-10pm Sun.-Thurs., 11:30am-11pm Fri.-Sat.; $10-25

Well 80 Brewhouse stands out among the other pubs in town. It's built on an artesian well and proudly uses this pure water to brew all its beer. Try a brewhouse pretzel with pineapple habanero sauce, or get a seared ahi sandwich with cucumber wasabi aioli. This family-friendly pub has a fun atmosphere with trivia nights and a large indoor area with tables and bar seating.

Olympia Little Theatre

1925 Miller Ave. NE; 360/786-9484; https:// olympialittletheater.org; 7:25pm Thurs.-Sat., 1:55pm Sun.; $10-16

If you love community theater, stop by the Olympia Little Theater to see a variety of independent plays, with everything from comedies to mysteries. It's the oldest theater in town and one of the oldest in the state; they've hosted performances here since 1939.

Cryptatropa Bar

421 4th Ave. E; 360/754-3867; www.thecryptbar.com; 4pm-2am daily

Bathed in a pink glow, The Crypt is a queer-inclusive space that often showcases live music, theater, and comedy at night. It's known for a wide genre of music, entertainment like drag shows, and specialty cocktails.

Rumors Wine Bar

430 Washington St. SE; 360/705-9970; www. rumorswinebar.com; 5pm-9pm Tues.-Thurs., 4pm-10pm Fri.-Sat., noon-3pm Sun.

Whether you want to do a wine-tasting or split a bottle with friends, Rumors is the place to go

the Legislative Building on the Capitol Campus

with a diverse selection of wine from around the world. It's a cozy place downtown to enjoy a drink and have a small snack.

FOOD

Most of Olympia's restaurants are in the downtown area, so you don't have to go far to get a bite to eat. The year-round **farmers market** (700 Capitol Way N.; 360/352-9096; www.olympiafarmersmarket.com; 10am-3pm Thurs.-Sun. Apr.-Oct., reduced winter hours) has a good selection local produce, goods, and artisanal food.

Olympia Oyster House

320 4th Ave. W.; 360/753-7000; www. olympiaoysterhouse.com; 11am-8pm Sun.-Thurs., 11am-9pm Fri.-Sat.; $15-26

Located in the original Olympia Oyster Company building from 1859, the Olympia Oyster House is one of the most popular waterfront restaurants in the area. Diners can enjoy eating on the outside patio on the bay and listening to live music May-September. The menu is seafood-heavy, with options like lobster, halibut, and salmon, as well as steak and salads.

Mercato Ristorante

111 Market St. NE; 360/528-3663; www. mercatoristorante.com; 11am-9pm Mon.-Fri., 10am-9pm Sat.-Sun.; $9-25

If you want authentic Italian food created from scratch, come to Mercato Ristorante. The menu has a large selection including pizza, antipasti like cured meats and artisan cheese, and pasta dishes like penne and ravioli that are prepared in-house. The sleek interior makes it an upscale dining experience, and outside is a small patio.

★ Dockside Bistro & Wine Bar

501 Columbia St. NW; 360/956-1928; www. docksidebistro.com; 5pm-8pm Tues.-Wed., noon-2pm, 5pm-8pm Thurs.-Sat.; $12-40

The relaxing Dockside Bistro specializes in Northwest fusion cuisine, blending European and Southeast Asian influences. Their small menu prioritizes locally sourced ingredients and has unique dishes such as pistachio-encrusted seasonal whitefish with gnocchi and elk ribeye wrapped with applewood smoked bacon. Make a reservation in advance to get a table by the window overlooking the water.

Equal Latin Restaurant & Bar

520 4th Ave. E; 360/819-4817; https://equal-latin-restaurant-bar.business.site; 10:30am-10pm Mon.-Thurs., 10:30am-midnight Fri., 10:30am-11pm Sat., 10:30am-9pm Sun.; $15-22

Stop at Equal Latin for a delicious brunch, such as Spanish-style eggs or huevos rancheros, or indulge in their carnitas sandwich or deep-fried burrito for a meal later in the day. It has a casual atmosphere with high ceilings and ample natural light.

ACCOMMODATIONS

Olympia Hotel at Capitol Lake

2300 Evergreen Park Dr. SW; 360/943-4000; www.ihg. com; $98-140

This pet-friendly hotel is a comfortable place to stay, with 193 accommodations that feature stunning views of Capitol Lake. Guests can start their day with an espresso drink from the hotel's coffee shop before checking out nearby stores.

TownePlace Suites by Marriott

900 Capitol Way S.; 360/753-8770; www.marriott. com; $116-233

TownePlace Suites by Marriott has everything you need for a comfortable stay, including a free breakfast, and is only a few minutes' walk to downtown. There are 72 rooms to choose from, including queen and king beds and suites with kitchenettes.

Swantown Inn

1431 11th Ave. SE; 360/753-9123; www.swantowninn. com; $299-359

The Swantown Inn is a bed-and-breakfast in a historic mansion built in the Queen Anne and Eastlake styles in 1887. There are four guestrooms, a suite, and a cottage available, and despite their age, they still have modern conveniences like individually controlled heating and air-conditioning.

INFORMATION AND SERVICES

Experience Olympia (360/763-5656; www.experienceolympia.com; 10am-5pm Mon.-Fri.) has an extensive website as well as a live hotline you can call weekdays to get help planning your trip.

Providence St. Peter Hospital

413 Lilly Rd. NE; 360/491-9480; www.providence.org
Providence St. Peter Hospital has an emergency room, a well-regarded family medicine residency program, and a Level III trauma center.

TRANSPORTATION
Getting There

Olympia is about an hour drive from Seattle (60 mi/100 km) by taking I-5 south. From Long Beach, it's 2 hours to Olympia on US 101 north.

Greyhound buses at the Intercity Transit Center in Olympia (205 Franklin St. NE; 360/786-1881; www.intercitytransit.com) connect to Tacoma, Portland, and Seattle. Tickets are $14-16/person, and there are several buses per day.

The **Amtrak** train stops in Olympia at the Olympia-Lacey Amtrak Train Station (6600 Yelm Highway SE, Lacey; 800/872-7245; www.amtrak.com). This will get you there faster, with an average travel time of 1 hour 20 minutes from Seattle, and trains leave about every 2 hours ($17-47/person). However, the station is in Lacey, which is about 15 minutes from the center of Olympia. You'll need to take a taxi or the 93 bus through Intercity Transit (30-minute ride) to reach downtown Olympia.

Getting Around

Intercity Transit (205 Franklin St. NE; 360/786-1881; www.intercitytransit.com; free) provides free daily bus services throughout the city.

San Juan Islands

When you want to get away from it all, head to the San Juan Islands. You'll feel yourself instantly relax on the ferry ride over, gliding through the calm waters as you make your way to one of the scenic islands. Once there, you're on island time—take a peaceful stroll along the beach, or look for orcas along the shore at your leisure.

While there are over 170 named islands in the San Juan Islands, only a handful are inhabited. The Washington State Ferries serves San Juan, Orcas, Lopez, and Shaw Islands, the only ones you can bring your car to. San Juan, Orcas, and Lopez are the most common to visit, with multiple places to stay.

For further relaxation, head to Lime Kiln Point State Park on San Juan Island, where you can spot orcas from the shore or walk along

Highlights

Look for ★ to find recommended sights, activities, dining, and lodging.

© MOON.COM

★ Whale-Watching on San Juan Island: See these beautiful creatures playing in their natural habitats, one of the area's top activities (page 243).

★ Kayaking Around Orcas Island: Find hidden coves and see the diverse wildlife up close while navigating the waters around Orcas Island (page 254).

★ Hiking Mount Constitution: Drive or hike to the top of Orcas Island as you enjoy the highest peak in the San Juan Islands (page 256).

★ Biking Lopez Island: Lopez Island is a

favorite destination for bikers, offering tranquil routes through charming villages and pastoral landscapes (page 263).

★ Skagit Valley Tulip Festival: This annual festival transforms Skagit Valley into a colorful mosaic of blooming tulips, attracting visitors globally with its stunning floral displays (page 266).

★ Chuckanut Drive: This scenic route winds along the Puget Sound and Chuckanut Bay coastline, providing stunning peekaboo views of the San Juan Islands through a forested landscape (page 270).

hiking trails. For a more adventurous escape, kayak around Orcas Island, discovering secret coves and abundant wildlife, or bike across Lopez Island and soak in the scenery at your own pace.

East of the San Juan Islands, Skagit Valley is a gorgeous region full of farmlands and valleys. The Skagit Valley Tulip Festival brings tourists from across the world to see the valley transformed into a brilliant tapestry of flowering tulips each spring. Head north and drive along Chuckanut Drive, a scenic route that winds along the water overlooking the San Juan Islands and Canada. Continue north and you'll reach Bellingham, a city full of outdoor activities and urban charm.

ORIENTATION

The San Juan Islands and North Puget Sound region are located in the northwest corner of Washington state. Nestled between Seattle to the south and Vancouver Island to the north, this area is easily accessible via ferries, yet its tranquil islands feel worlds away. Anacortes, where you catch the ferry to the San Juan Islands, is reached via I-5 and Route 20. The Skagit Valley is to the east, just off I-5.

PLANNING YOUR TIME

Spend **at least one night on each island** you visit. Given the ferry time, spending several days on each island lets you fully appreciate everything it offers without rushing. Many people spend a week island hopping. You could base yourself at Friday Harbor on San Juan Island and see the other islands on day trips for the most convenient option. Skagit Valley is easy enough to see with a one-night stay, and then you can head north to Bellingham or west to Anacortes.

During the peak summer season, lodging can be limited in the San Juan Islands, so you may not get your choice of hotel or ferry time if you take a spontaneous trip here.

The weather on the San Juan Islands is mild all year. Winter is the low season, when they experience more rain and temperatures hovering around 40°F (4°C). Spring brings mild weather in the 50s°F (10-15°C) with some rain showers, while fall has cooler weather in the 50s-60s°F (10-15 °C) but sunny days. **Summer** is the high season, when temperatures get in the high 70s.

TRANSPORTATION

San Juan, Orcas, and Lopez Islands are accessible by the **Washington State Ferries** (https://wsdot.wa.gov; $10-40). There are about a dozen ferry runs daily 4am-midnight. Cars are allowed on all these ferries, as are walk-ons and bikers.

Although a few walk-up spots are available, reservations are highly recommended—and required during the busy summer months. It's important to note that you need to book your ferry round-trip; otherwise, you might get stuck on the island for an extra night.

Ferries depart from Anacortes, and the journey is 1-1.5 hours long, depending on how many islands your particular ferry stops at, as San Juan Island is the last destination. Every route is different, so confirm the one you're on is stopping at the island you need. You need to arrive at least 30 minutes early to check in, get your spot in line, and have enough time to load onto the ferry. Unless there are weather issues, ferries tend to leave right on time.

Each of the main islands has a central road, making all the sights easily accessible by car.

Previous: Friday Harbor; Skagit Valley Tulip Festival; hiking Mount Constitution.

Itinerary Ideas

This weekend getaway has you visiting San Juan and Orcas Islands, based in Friday Harbor on San Juan the first two nights and then on Orcas Island the third night.

DAY 1

1 Take an early ferry to San Juan Island and start your day with breakfast at the **Rocky Bay Café & Delicatessen.**

2 Spend the morning on a kayaking tour with **San Juan Kayak Expeditions.**

3 Afterwards, enjoy fresh seafood for lunch at **Downriggers.**

4 Explore **San Juan Island National Historical Park,** visiting both the American and English Camps.

5 Dine at **Vic's Drive In** for a classic American dinner. Stay overnight at the **Discovery Inn.**

DAY 2

1 Start the day with a visit to **Krystal Acres Alpaca Farm.**

2 Enjoy lunch at **The Bait Shop.**

3 Indulge in local wine-tasting at **San Juan Vineyard.**

4 Visit **Lime Kiln Point State Park** and its lighthouse, and look for whales from the shore.

5 Experience fine dining at **Duck Soup** and visit **Cease & Desist** for a nightcap.

DAY 3

1 Take a ferry to Orcas Island and start with breakfast at **Island Skillet.**

2 Explore **Moran State Park** and drive or hike up **Mount Constitution.**

3 Have lunch at **Island Pie.**

4 Spend the afternoon relaxing on the beach at **Obstruction Pass State Park.**

5 Dine at **Inn at Ship Bay** for a gourmet experience. Stay overnight at **Smuggler's Villa Resort.**

San Juan Islands

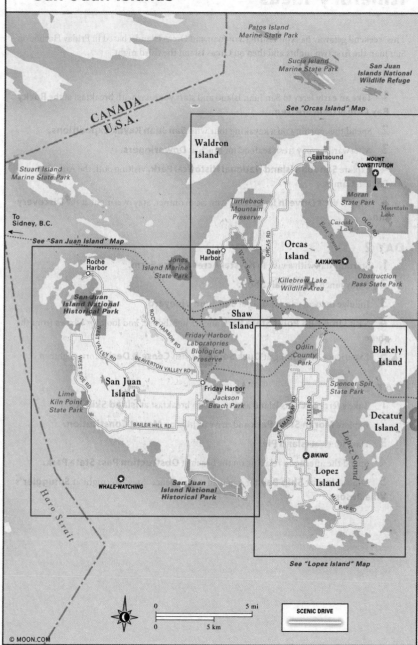

Patos Island
Marine State Park

Sucia Island
Marine State Park

San Juan
Islands National
Wildlife Refuge

See "Orcas Island" Map

CANADA
U.S.A.

Stuart Island
Marine State Park

To
Sidney, B.C.

See "San Juan Island" Map

Roche
Harbor

San Juan
Island National
Historical Park

ROCHE HARBOR RD

WEST VALLEY RD

WEST SIDE RD

BEAVERTON VALLEY RD

Lime
Kiln Point
State Park

San Juan
Island

Friday Harbor
Jackson
Beach Park

BAILER HILL RD

WHALE-WATCHING

San Juan
Island National
Historical Park

Haro Strait

Waldron
Island

Eastsound

MOUNT
CONSTITUTION

Turtleback
Mountain
Preserve

Moran
State Park

Mountain
Lake

Cascade
Lake

East Sound

OLGA RD

ORCAS RD

Deer
Harbor

Jones
Island Marine
State Park

West Sound

Orcas
Island

KAYAKING

Killebrew Lake
Wildlife Area

Obstruction
Pass State Park

Shaw
Island

Friday Harbor
Laboratories
Biological
Preserve

Odlin
County
Park

Blakely
Island

Spencer Spit
State Park

FISHERMAN BAY RD

CENTER RD

Decatur
Island

Lopez Sound

BIKING

Lopez
Island

MUD BAY RD

See "Lopez Island" Map

0   5 mi

0   5 km

SCENIC DRIVE

© MOON.COM

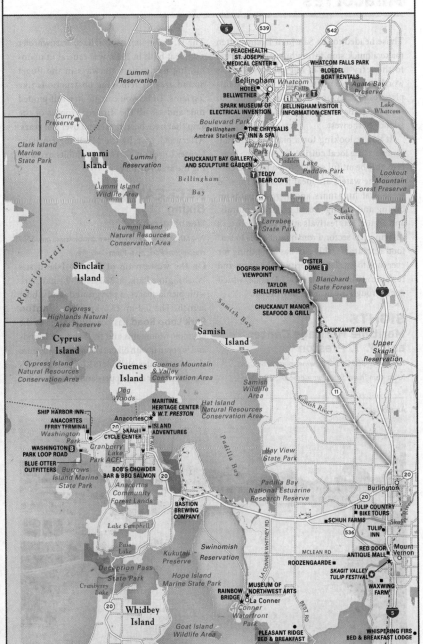

Anacortes

Those headed to the San Juan Islands often make a quick stop through Anacortes to get to the ferry terminal, but the city itself is worth a visit. No matter where you are in this picturesque city on Fidalgo Island, you can see Fidalgo Bay to the east and the San Juan Islands to the west.

If you're looking for a place to unwind, sample some local cuisine, or get some exercise, this beautiful seaside town has you covered. The waters are ideal for kayaking and whale-watching tours, and there are paths for biking and hiking. Local galleries, murals, and annual arts festivals attest to Anacortes's thriving arts sector. From quaint cafés to seafood restaurants, this city has something for everyone to eat. The majority of the shops and restaurants line Commercial Avenue, which goes through the heart of downtown.

SIGHTS
Maritime Heritage Center and *W. T. Preston*

703 R Ave.; 360/293-1915; www.anacorteswa.gov; 10am-4pm Thurs.-Sat., 11am-4pm Sun.; $3-5

The *W. T. Preston*, a specialized sternwheeler snagboat built in 1929, was crucial in maintaining navigable waterways in the Puget Sound area by removing obstructions like log jams. Today you can go on a self-guided tour and see all the different rooms of the ship that have been preserved over the years. Afterward, stop by the Maritime Heritage Center to see artifacts and exhibits explaining the area's history.

RECREATION
Biking
Washington Park

904 6th St.; 360/293-1918; www.anacorteswa.gov/560/ Washington-Park; 6am-10pm daily; free

On the western tip of Fidalgo Island sits Washington Park, a 220-acre (90-ha) park with picnic spaces, a playground, and a boat launch. The 2.2-mi (3.5-km) **Washington Park Loop Road** has beautiful vistas of the Olympic Mountains and the San Juan Islands and is popular with bikers and hikers. There are also 68 campsites available ($30-37/night), so it's a good spot for day trippers and campers alike.

Anacortes

Skagit Cycle Center

1620 Commercial Ave.; 360/588-8776; www.
skagitcyclecenter.com; 10am-6pm Tues.-Sat.; $20-65/3
hours

Skagit Cycle Center has a variety of bikes to rent for the day, including e-bikes, hybrid, gravel, and kid bikes. You can also pick up any accessory you may need, such as a trailer for kids, pets, or cargo, and a car rack.

Kayaking

Anacortes is an ideal place to kayak because it caters to all levels. You can paddle in the calmer, protected waters of Fidalgo Bay to the east, or head west to the open waters toward the San Juan Islands.

Blue Otter Outfitters

2009 Skyline Way #1; 360/488-4247; www.blueotter.
com; 9am-5pm daily; $39-119

If you already know your way around a kayak, Blue Otter Outfitters has plenty to rent for the day. Choose from single, tandem, sit-on-top, or sea kayaks, or rent a stand-up paddleboard.

Whale-Watching

Island Adventures

Sante Marina, Dock A, 712 Seafarer's Way; 360/293-2428; https://island-adventures.com; 10am, 11am, 3:30pm daily Feb.-Nov.; $59-119/person

Island Adventures prides itself on having one of the highest success rates of seeing whales. Tours range 4-5 hours and give you a chance to see gray, humpback, orca, and minke whales.

SHOPPING

Scott Milo Gallery

420 Commercial Ave.; 360/293-6938; www.scottmilo.
com; 11am-5pm Tues.-Sat.; free

Scott Milo Gallery hosts a variety of art throughout the year, including oils, acrylics, and photography from local artists. It also has permanent exhibits, including fused glass, sculptures, jewelry, and metalwork.

MoonWater Arts and Joanie Schwartz Glass

702 Commercial Ave.; 360/298-9074; www.
joanieschwartzglass.com; 11am-5pm Tues.-Sun.

You'll find a variety of handmade artwork from local female artists at MoonWater Arts, including garden decorations and decor for the home. Next door, Joanie Schwartz hosts fused glass classes (from $85/person), including for beginners and children, all with different themes.

FESTIVALS AND EVENTS

Anacortes Arts Festival

www.anacortesartsfestival.com; first weekend of Aug.;
free

The Anacortes Arts Festival is a fun weekend full of over 230 artists' booths, where you'll find everything from hand-drawn greeting cards to oil paintings for purchase. There are also two stages for live music, a kids' area, a wine bar, and a beer garden.

Oyster Run

https://oysterrun.org; 4th Sun. in Sept.; free

The Oyster Run is a motorcycle rally that has been going strong since 1981, with an increasing number of bikers yearly, sometimes totaling 20,000. Riders choose their own routes, making pit stops at biker-friendly restaurants and bars listed on the event's website before meeting in downtown Anacortes. Once there, motorcyclists and spectators can enjoy food vendors, live music, and a vibrant atmosphere.

FOOD

Gere-a-Deli

502 Commercial Ave.; 360/293-7383; https://gereadeli.
com; 9am-4pm Tues.-Sat.; $5-12

Gere-a-Deli is the place to go for lunch, as they have a huge selection of both cold and hot deli sandwiches as well as salads. It gets busy, so go early if you want a seat or order ahead for takeout.

Bob's Chowder Bar & BBQ Salmon

3320 Commercial Ave.; 360/299-8000; www. bobschowder.com; 11am-8pm Thurs.-Sun.; $17-26

You can't stop in Anacortes without visiting Bob's Chowder Bar in its bright-red building. The restaurant boasts award-winning clam chowder in addition to a variety of seafood items like oyster burgers and fish and chips.

Brown Lantern

412 Commercial Ave.; 360/293-2544; www. thebrownlanternalehouse.com; 11am-midnight Mon.- Sat., 9am-midnight Sun.; $12-21

Visit a bit of history at the Brown Lantern, established in 1933 and the longest-standing bar in Anacortes. It's known for its happy hour, burgers, sandwiches, and extensive drink menu. It also has live music every weekend and features a beer garden and heated patio.

Secret Cove

209 T Ave.; 360/982-2008; www.secretcoveanacortes. com; 11:30am-8pm Tues.-Thurs. and Sun., 11:30am-8:30pm Fri.-Sat.; $19-25

Secret Cove has some of the best waterfront dining in Anacortes. From its outdoor patio or cozy indoor seating, you can view Guemes Island across the water. Choose from options like the ultimate crab sandwich on sourdough bread or the crispy cod fish and chips.

ACCOMMODATIONS

Ship Harbor Inn

5316 Ferry Terminal Rd.; 360/293-5177; https:// shipharborinn.com; $109-339

You'll have a relaxing stay at the Ship Harbor Inn, which is within walking distance of the San Juan Islands ferries and provides views of the Rosario Strait and Guemes Channel from all 30 rooms. It's set on 6 acres (2.5 ha) of land, and guests often see wildlife here.

Marina Inn

3300 Commercial Ave.; 360/293-1100; www. marinainnwa.com; $95-115

Marina Inn offers a range of 52 guest rooms, including queen rooms and king rooms with whirlpool tubs. It's located on the main street in Anacortes, so you're within walking distance of multiple restaurants.

Majestic Inn & Spa

419 Commercial Ave.; 360/299-1400; www. majesticinnandspa.com; $146-232

Treat yourself to a stay at Majestic Inn & Spa, an 1890 boutique hotel in the center of downtown with comfortable 52 rooms. Enjoy happy hour from their outdoor rooftop lounge, or get a massage in their award-winning spa.

TRANSPORTATION

Getting There

Anacortes is about 1.5 hours (85 mi/137 km) north of Seattle. To get here and to the **ferry terminal** (2100 Ferry Terminal Rd.) for the San Juan Islands, take I-5 north to exit 230, and head west on Route 20, which ends at the ferry terminal. There are multiple signs along the way to confirm you're on the correct route to the ferry.

Getting Around

Skagit Transit (www.skagittransit.org) provides bus service in and around Anacortes, with routes going as far as Mount Vernon, La Conner, and Burlington.

San Juan Island

The most popular San Juan Island, and the one with the greatest variety of attractions, is San Juan Island itself. It's easy enough to visit on a long day trip, but with so much to do, many people come here for a weekend.

Friday Harbor is on the eastern side of San Juan Island and serves as the primary entry point for many visitors; it's connected to the mainland and other islands in the archipelago through regular ferry services. Friday Harbor is the island's commercial hub and home to numerous restaurants, shops, galleries, and museums. The town's small size makes it perfect for exploring on foot, and its picturesque marina adds to its charm.

Roche Harbor, the second-largest region on San Juan Island, is on the island's northwest shore. Its defining characteristics are the stunning resort and marina structures from the late 1800s and early 1900s. Roche Harbor is a more luxurious alternative to Friday Harbor, with five-star hotels, gourmet restaurants, and unique shops.

Although you can walk on the ferry, bringing your vehicle is advisable unless you only do activities in Friday Harbor. San Juan Island is large, and it's hard to reach other places outside the downtown area without a car. However, some hotels offer shuttles, so it's worth asking about their coverage when deciding.

Getting There

The ferry is the most common way to get here, from Anacortes to the **Friday Harbor ferry landing** (91 Front St. S.). You can also take a seaplane from various locations around the state to Friday Harbor, but this is more expensive and leaves you without a car to explore.

Getting Around

The most common way of getting around the island is driving, as public transportation doesn't service most areas. Unless you only plan on staying within Friday Harbor, you'll want a car so you can travel the full length of the island.

Car

San Juan Island is well connected, with West Valley Road and West Side Road going around the western part of the island, and Bailer Hill Road connecting the south. To get from Friday Harbor to Roche Harbor, you'll take Roche Harbor Road across the north part of the island.

M & W Auto (725 Spring St.; 360/378-2886; www.sanjuanauto.com) provides a car rental service if you don't have your own vehicle on the island.

Public Transportation

San Juan Transit (www.sanjuantransit.com; $8-20) provides daily bus service year-round around the island that makes stops at many popular attractions, such as Lime Kiln and American and English Camps.

San Juan Taxi and Tours (202 Harmony Ln. #7068; 360/378-3550) provides taxi service around the island and transports large groups.

FRIDAY HARBOR

Friday Harbor is considered San Juan Island's downtown, and Spring Street runs through the heart of it. The area is lined with quaint, historic buildings that now house restaurants and shops.

Sights

The Whale Museum

62 First St. N.; 360/378-4710; https://whalemuseum. org; 10am-4pm daily; $10

Before embarking on a whale-watching tour, stop by the fascinating Whale Museum to learn about the specific pods living in the region. You'll see the family trees of resident

San Juan Island

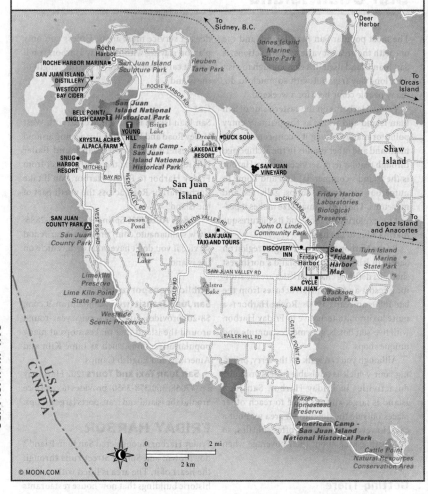

orcas and marvel at whale skeletons that show just how mighty these creatures are.

San Juan Historical Museum

405 Price St.; 360-378-3949; www.sjmuseum.org; 11am-2pm Tues.-Fri.; $5-10

If you want to know what life was like on the island in the early 1900s, visit the San Juan Historical Museum. You'll see dozens of pictures and artifacts in their numerous displays

and visit multiple historic buildings on-site, such as the original farm.

San Juan Islands Museum of Art

540 Spring St.; 360-370-5050; www.sjima.org; 11am-5pm Fri.-Mon.; $10 nonmembers

You'll find unique art from all over the region at the San Juan Islands Museum of Art, including sculptures, photographs, paintings, and other exhibits from local artists.

Friday Harbor

Which Island to Visit?

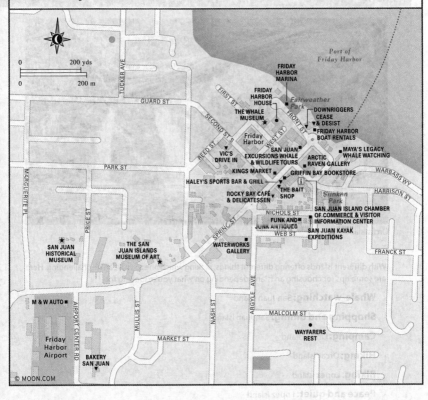

San Juan Island National Historical Park

360/378-2240; www.nps.gov; 10am-3pm Thurs.-Mon.; free

San Juan Island National Historical Park was established in 1966 and is a magnificent monument to the amicable settlement of the Pig War. In 1859, the United States and Britain were fighting over which country San Juan Island belonged to and almost went to war over the slaughter of a pig. It ultimately ended up getting resolved, and San Juan Island became part of the United States. Each country's camp remains here, which you can see in two different sections, and each has its respective visitor center. The park also has reenactors in costume who bring history to life, which adds to the experience.

American Camp, on the island's southernmost point, incorporates elements of the original Hudson's Bay Company farm. Heritage and ecology come together at this site, which has three well-preserved American military structures and is home to the endangered island marble butterfly in its grassland habitat. Several hiking routes and beachside locations are also available to explore. American Camp is 6 mi (10 km) south of Friday Harbor on Cattle Point Road.

English Camp is on the island's northwest coast at Garrison Bay, closer to Roche Harbor. A blockhouse, barracks, and commissary are

Which Island to Visit?

Orcas Island

With different islands offering different things, picking which one to visit can be challenging. Here are some tips for choosing an island depending on what you're looking for:

- **Whale-watching:** San Juan Island
- **Shopping and dining:** San Juan Island
- **Camping:** Orcas Island
- **Hiking:** Orcas Island
- **Biking:** Lopez Island
- **Peace and quiet:** Lopez Island

among the notable remnants of the British occupation. Park rangers in English Camp raise and lower the Union Jack every day, which is unusual in any non-diplomatic American context. English Camp is 9 mi (14 km) northwest of Friday Harbor via Beaverton Valley Road and West Valley Road.

Wineries
San Juan Vineyard
3136 Roche Harbor Rd.; 360/378-9463; www. sanjuanvineyard.com; 1pm-5pm Fri.-Sat.; tasting $10
Most people don't expect to find a vineyard on the island, but San Juan Vineyard makes

award-winning, estate-grown Madeleine Angevine and Siegerrebe wines in a remodeled 1895 schoolhouse. If you're there during a summer weekend, stop by on Saturday evening for their summer music series.

Nightlife
Cease & Desist
10 Front St., Suite #105; 360/726-3705; Instagram @fridayharborbeer; 3pm-10pm Sun.-Thurs., 3pm-11pm Fri.-Sat.
You'll have no problem finding a beer you like at Cease & Desist, which has over a dozen rotating beers ranging from hazy IPAs to light

pilsners. Grab a table outside and watch the ferries come in, as they're one of the closest bars to the waterfront.

Haley's Sports Bar & Grill

175 Spring St.; 360/378-4434; Facebook @Haleys-Sports-Bar-and-Grill; 11am-9pm daily; $13-24

Get a late-night dinner at Haley's Sports Bar & Grill, which has burgers, salads, and appetizers. It's one of the best places to watch sports on the island, and you'll likely mingle with the locals for hometown games.

Shopping

Most of the shopping is found along the blocks closest to the ferry landing, with Spring Street having a large concentration of shops.

Funk and Junk Antiques

85 Nicholas St.; 360/378-9551; Facebook @Funk-and-Junk-Antiques; 9am-5pm Fri.-Sat., 9am-2pm Sun.

Funk & Junk Antiques has been selling unique treasures since 1984. You'll find items from musical instruments to garden equipment and everything in between.

WaterWorks Gallery

315 Argyle Ave.; 360/378-3060; www.waterworksgallery.com; noon-5pm Wed.-Sun.

WaterWorks sells a variety of jewelry and contemporary and classic artwork, including sculptures and paintings. It features artists from the San Juan Islands and around the Pacific Northwest.

Arctic Raven Gallery

130 First St. S.; 360/378-3433; https://arcticravengalleryfridayharbor.com; 1pm-5pm Fri.-Mon., 1pm-5:30pm Thurs.

Arctic Raven Gallery specializes in bone, stone, and ivory sculptures and prints by the Inupiat, Inuit, and Yup'ik tribes of the Pacific Northwest.

Griffin Bay Bookstore

155 Spring St.; 360/378-5511; www.griffinbaybook.com; 10am-6pm Wed.-Sat., 10am-4pm Sun.-Tues.

Griffin Bay Bookstore has been a staple in Friday Harbor for almost 50 years, and it continues to supply the area with new reads as well as hard-to-find titles. Their friendly staff is always ready to help you find what you're looking for in this cozy store.

TOP EXPERIENCE

★ Whale-Watching

The San Juan Islands are one of the best places in the world to see whales in their natural habitat in the Salish Sea, which is the water that includes Puget Sound, the San Juan Islands, and north into Canada. While orcas (also known as "killer whales") are the most common sightings, other whale species, such as humpbacks, minke whales, and even gray whales, are occasionally visible. Resident orcas can be seen throughout the year; the highest concentration of whales and other sealife occurs **March-October.**

The San Juan Islands provide several excellent spots on land where you can observe whales if you get there at the right time. **Lime Kiln Point State Park,** often known as "Whale Watch Park," and **San Juan Island National Historical Park** are great places to try your luck.

The best way to see whales up close, however, is to take a whale-watching cruise. Licensed naturalists will take you to the most likely spots to see whales and teach you about the sealife you encounter.

Lime Kiln Point State Park

1567 West Side Rd.; 360/378-2044; https://parks.wa.gov; 7:30am-8pm daily; $10 Discover Pass

Lime Kiln Point State Park is the best spot on the island to spot whales and porpoises from dry land, thanks to its location on the western side and proximity to the Haro Strait; you can even see across the water to Canada on a clear day. There's a sign that says when the most recent whale spotting was, and you can often talk to a staff member to see if they know where the whales might be headed next. While you're there, check out the lighthouse from 1919, and stop by the interpretive center

May-September to learn about the history of lime mining. The park is about 9 mi (14 km) from Friday Harbor via Bailer Hill Road.

San Juan Excursions
Whale & Wildlife Tours
40 Spring St.; 360/378-6636; www.watchwhales.com; Apr.-Oct.; $125 adult, $115 youth, $95 infant

Have a chance to see whales up close on a 3-hour tour that looks for not only orcas but bald eagles, sea lions, seals, porpoises, and more on this converted search and rescue vessel. They even promise a free return trip if you don't see orcas while on the water.

Maya's Legacy Whale Watching
14 Cannery Landing; 360/378-7996; https:// sanjuanislandwhalewatch.com; June-Oct. daily; $199 299

With nearly 30 years of experience in the industry, Maya's Legacy Whale Watching is known for its small-group tours that allow passengers to have more one-on-one time with the knowledgeable guides. You have the option to join a half-day excursion or a full 8-hour cruise on the water.

Kayaking
While you can kayak all around San Juan Island, the west coast has the best opportunities. The water is deeper and wider here, so you're likely to spot more wildlife.

San Juan Kayak Expeditions
25 Nichols St.; 360/378-4436; https://sanjuankayak. com; May-Sept.; tours from $99, rentals $200/day

San Juan Kayak Expeditions offers four different tours—half- and full-day tours around Lime Kiln looking for whales along Haro Strait with views of Vancouver Island, tours in the calmer Griffin Bay searching for harbor seals during the day, and scenic sunset kayak tours. You can also rent a double kayak for the day if you want to explore on your own.

1: orca off San Juan Island **2:** Lime Kiln Point State Park

San Juan County Park
50 San Juan Park Dr.; 360/378-8420; www.sanjuanco. com; 7am-9:30pm daily; $7 day launch pass

San Juan County Park is an ideal place for kayakers of all skill levels to go out on their own. Beginners will feel comfortable in the protected Smallpox Bay, while more advanced paddlers may want to go out further in the Haro Strait or along the island's coastline.

Biking
Biking on San Juan Island is a leisurely way to get around, with miles of roads to explore. You can follow the **main loop** around the island by going counterclockwise from Friday Harbor; head north on Roche Harbor Road toward Roche Harbor, then take West Valley Road south until you reach West Side Road, which hugs the island's western coastline. It merges into Bailer Hill Road to go east, and then Douglas Road leads back into Friday Harbor. This complete loop is about 35 mi (56 km) and includes some moderate elevation gains.

For a more detailed bike route map along with mileage and elevation gains, visit www.visitsanjuans.com to plan out your route.

Cycle San Juan
845 Argyle Ave.; 360/797-5787; https://cyclesanjuan. com; 8am-8pm daily; rentals $20-65/day, tours from $200/person

Cycle San Juan offers bike rentals and guided bike tours around San Juan Island, and riders can pick up bikes from the shop or have them delivered for a small fee. They have a handful of guided tours that run for about 4 hours and visit various parts of the island, or they can do a private, customized bike tour for an additional cost.

Boating
There are plenty of birds, whales, and seals to see while boating near San Juan Island, making it a boater's paradise. The island also serves as a jumping-off point for excursions to neighboring islands around the Salish

Sea, making it easy to do day trips. The island's two main marinas are **Friday Harbor Marina** (204 Front St.) and **Roche Harbor** (248 Reuben Memorial Dr.).

Friday Harbor Boat Rentals

10 Front St.; 360/317-5578; www.fridayharborboatrental.com; 9am-6pm Sun.-Wed., 9am-8pm Fri.-Sat.; rentals $300-950, charters $650-950

Hire a chartered boat from Friday Harbor Boat Rentals and enjoy a relaxing day on the water exploring nearby islands with your own personalized itinerary. They also have boats you can rent, but you must have boating experience and pass a safety test to prove you can navigate the waters.

Food

Rocky Bay Café & Delicatessen

225 Spring St.; 360/378-5051; Facebook @TheRockyBay; 7am-3pm daily; $11-30

Start your morning with a hearty omelet or eggs Benedict at Rocky Bay Café & Delicatessen, where you can pass the time looking at the colorful murals. They also serve lunch with options like burgers and sandwiches.

Bakery San Juan

775 Mullis St.; 360/378-5810; www.bakerysanjuan.com; 8am-5pm Mon.-Fri.; $9-27

You'll smell the heavenly scent of freshly baked sourdough drifting through Bakery San Juan when you walk in, and you can get a loaf of bread or a variety of pastries to take on the go. They also offer single slices and whole sourdough pizzas, sandwiches, and a selection of European wine and beer.

Downriggers

10 Front St.; 360/378-2700; www.downriggerssanjuan.com; 11am-9pm Mon.-Sat., 11am-8:30pm Sun.; $13-25

Set right on the port, Downriggers has one of the best views in Friday Harbor. Watch ferries come and go as you sip your craft cocktail and enjoy seafood with a twist, such as a salmon Reuben and spicy prawn mac and cheese.

The Bait Shop

175 Spring St.; 360/379-7444; Facebook @TheBaitShopFridayHarbor; 11am-5pm Sun.-Wed., 11am-7pm Fri.-Sat.; $13-25

The Bait Shop has a small interior, so people often take their tasty fish and chips to go and sit on one of the benches in Friday Harbor.

Friday Harbor ferry landing

You can also choose from clam chowder, fish tacos, or fish sandwiches.

Vic's Drive In

25 2nd St. S.; 360/378-8427; https://vicsdrivein.com; 7am-7pm daily; $9-20

Vic's Drive In has been around since 1958, and while the menu has changed since then, it still feels nostalgic to walk in and order a burger and fries. A handful of tables are inside, but many people eat in their car to recreate the old-school drive-in feeling.

Kings Market

160 Spring St.; 360/378-4505; www.kings-market.com; 7:30am-9pm daily

Many visitors stay in a vacation rental and head to Kings Market to stock up on fresh produce, high-quality meats, frozen meals, and beer and wine at this grocery store that's larger than you'd expect for an island shop.

Accommodations

Discovery Inn

1016 Guard St.; 360/378-2000; www.discoveryinn.com; $159-179

Discovery Inn is only a few blocks from the harbor, making it easy to walk to restaurants or shops. In addition to 20 aesthetically pleasing rooms, they have a quiet lawn area to play games or barbecue.

Wayfarers Rest

35 Malcolm St.; 360/610-9562; https://direct-book. com/properties/WayfarersRestDirect; $191

This hostel is an affordable way to visit the island if you're on a budget, and it has shared, fully equipped kitchens if you feel like staying in and cooking. There's a mix of private rooms and suites with their own bathrooms and shared dorm rooms and bathrooms. They also rent bicycles to guests so you can explore the town on wheels.

Friday Harbor House

130 West St. #101; 360/378-8455; www. fridayharborhouse.com; $219-690

One of the most luxurious places you can stay

on the island is Friday Harbor House, which overlooks the harbor and is in the heart of the downtown area. All 24 rooms have a gas fireplace, king bed, and jetted tub, and select rooms have balconies.

Information

Stop by the **San Juan Island Chamber of Commerce and Visitor Information Center** (165 First Street S.; 360/378-5240; www.visitsanjuans.com; 10am-4pm daily) to pick up brochures and maps about the island.

ROCHE HARBOR

Roche Harbor is a small, picturesque community known for its more upscale accommodations and marina. It's a quieter area than Friday Harbor. The main street, Roche Harbor Road, leads all the way from Friday Harbor to Roche Harbor Marina. Roche Harbor is approximately 10 mi (16 km) northwest of Friday Harbor.

Sights

Krystal Acres Alpaca Farm

3501 West Valley Rd.; 360/378-0606; www. krystalacres.com; 11am-4pm Wed.-Sat. and Mon.; free

As you drive through the west part of the island, you'll find the 40-acre (16-ha) family-run farm known as The Farm at Krystal Acres, where you can get your daily dose of cuteness from the resident alpacas. Learn about alpacas as you stroll through the farm and observe them. There's also a store that sells products spun from alpaca fiber, which is sustainable, eco-friendly, and exceptionally soft. You'll find everything from knitwear and home goods to toys and gifts.

Wineries and Distilleries

Westcott Bay Cider

12 Anderson Ln.; 360/472-1532; www.westcottbaycider. com; 1pm-4pm Sat.-Sun.

Celebrated for its wide variety of cider apples gathered from a small orchard, Westcott Bay Cider is the second-oldest ciderworks in Washington. They offer a variety of flavors from extremely dry to medium sweet and give free tastings so you can decide which one you want.

San Juan Island Distillery

12 Anderson Ln.; 360/472-1532; www. sanjuanislanddistillery.com; 1pm-4pm Sat.

San Juan Island Distillery shares the building with Westcott Bay Cider, so you can do a taste tour of the island without going far. The distillery has 14 different gins and their famous apple brandy. You can sample a few of each for free or get a premium cocktail made with their alcohol.

Hiking

Young Hill

Distance: *2.2 mi (3.5 km) round-trip*
Duration: *1 hour*
Elevation gain: *587 ft (179 m)*
Difficulty: *easy*
Trailhead: *Young Hill trailhead*

The hike up Young Hill initially climbs gradually before becoming steeper as it nears the summit. Along the way, hikers pass Pacific madrone trees and can take a short detour to the English Camp cemetery, a memorial to seven Royal Marines who died in the 1860s. The hike's summit at 1 mi (1.6 km) provides even more impressive views of the Salish Sea and surrounding islands.

From Roche Harbor, head south on Roche Harbor Road for 1.5 mi (2.4 km). Turn right onto West Valley Road and continue for 1 mi (1.6 km) to find the trailhead on your left. There's limited parking, so you may need to park at English Camp across the road and walk to the trailhead.

Bell Point and English Camp

Distance: *1.7 mi (2.7 km) round-trip*
Duration: *1 hour*
Elevation gain: *50 ft (15 m)*
Difficulty: *easy*
Trailhead: *English Camp in San Juan Island Historical Park*

A short trail leads to the Parade Grounds, where hikers can stop at the visitor center in the barracks to get detailed maps and information. After looking at the historic buildings, walk across the grounds to Bell Point Trail, marked by old-growth madrones. The loop trail goes through a forested area and a grassy wetland and hugs the coast along Garrison Bay before returning to English Camp.

From Roche Harbor, head south on Roche Harbor Road for 1.3 mi (2 km). Turn right onto West Valley Road and continue for 1.3 mi (2 km), then turn left at the English Camp sign and park in the parking lot. From there, cross through the camp to join the Bell Point trail.

Boating

Roche Harbor Marina (248 Reuben Memorial Dr.; 360/378-2080; www.roche harbor.com) welcomes boats of all sizes, from dinghies to yachts. It has a fuel dock, a well-stocked store, and full-service repair facilities. There's also a handful of stores and restaurants, making it a popular stop among boaters.

San Juan Outfitters

248 Reuben Memorial Dr.; 360/378-1962; 8am-4pm daily mid-May-early Sept.; rentals $25-30/hour, tours $119-145/person

Based out of the marina, San Juan Outfitters rents sea and sit-on-top kayaks and stand-up paddleboards. They also have a handful of 3-hour tours around the island, including a bioluminescent and sunset tour.

Shopping

Gifts & Glass

Roche Harbor Resort, Studio 9; 360/317-3042; https:// giftsandglass.com; 10am-4pm daily June-Sept.

Gifts & Glass has beautiful glass artwork for sale, including handmade jewelry, vases of all sizes, and dried flowers set in glass. They also have unique items such as beaded serving utensils.

Louella's Gifts & Memories

248 Reuben Memorial Dr.; 360/370-7732; www.
rocheharbor.com; 10am-5pm daily

Louella's Gifts is the place to stock up on souvenirs, as they have Pacific Northwest-themed posters, mugs, stickers, and patches. They also have children's toys, loungewear, clothing, books, and more.

Food

Duck Soup

50 Duck Soup Ln.; 360/378-4878; www.
ducksoupsanjuans.com; 4pm-9pm Fri.-Sun.; $27-50

Duck Soup, set in a charming, rustic building overlooking Dream Lake, is one of the best places for fine dining on the island. Enjoy an entrée such as smoked lamb rack, duck breast, or filet mignon, and pair it with a specialty cocktail.

McMillin's Dining Room

248 Reuben Memorial Dr.; 360/378-5757; www.
rocheharbor.com; 5pm-10pm daily; $35-70

McMillin's Dining Room in the Roche Harbor Resort is a fine-dining establishment with white linen tablecloths overlooking the marina. The menu offers options like hazelnut-crusted halibut and chicken wrapped in prosciutto.

Lime Kiln Café

248 Reuben Memorial Dr.; 360/378 9892; www.
rocheharbor.com; 7am-4pm daily; $16-20

This charming waterfront café at Roche Harbor Resort is known for its freshly made doughnuts, but it also has an impressive breakfast and lunch menu. Consider a chili verde-smothered omelet with slow-roasted pork carnitas or a buttermilk fried chicken sandwich.

Accommodations

Roche Harbor Resort

248 Reuben Memorial Dr.; 360/378-9820; www.
rocheharbor.com; $230-520

Roche Harbor Resort, also known as Hotel de

Haro, is one of the most scenic places to stay. Most of the 20 rooms have a view of Roche Harbor or the garden area. Guests also have access to the only heated outdoor swimming pool on the island and access to the **Afterglow Spa** (360/378-9888; 10am-5pm Wed.-Sun.).

Snug Harbor Resort

1997 Mitchell Bay Rd.; 360/378-4762; https://
snugresort.client.innroad.com; $229-549

Located 7 mi (11 km) south of Roche Harbor, Snug Harbor Resort is the perfect place to unwind, with 17 waterfront suites, tastefully rustic decor, and incredible views of Mitchell Bay. A private marina is available for guests, as well as free use of canoes, paddleboards, and bicycles.

Lakedale

4313 Roche Harbor Rd.; 360/378-2350; www.lakedale.
com; $189-529

Located 5 mi (8 km) south of Roche Harbor on 82 acres (33 ha), peaceful Lakedale is surrounded by three freshwater lakes. Guests can choose from various accommodations, including about a dozen lodge rooms, seven yurts with hot tubs, 24 cabins that welcome dogs, an Airstream trailer, several dozen tent campsites, and six RV sites. The area is a paradise for outdoor activities like fishing, swimming, and boating.

Camping

San Juan County Park

15 San Juan Park Rd.; 360/378-2992; www.
visitsanjuans.com; $45

Popular among campers, San Juan County Park is located on the island's western shore and features rocky outcrops and shingle beaches with views of the wide Haro Strait and, beyond that, Vancouver Island. Park amenities include restrooms, a picnic pavilion, places to grill, potable water, picnic tables, access to a beach, and a boat launch. There are 26 campsites to choose from, which you'll need to reserve in advance.

Orcas Island

Known as the "Gem of the San Juan Islands," Orcas Island is easily recognizable by its horseshoe shape. This island is perfect for camping, hiking, or kayaking due to its lush, wooded landscape. It's also home the highest point in the archipelago, Mount Constitution, which offers stunning views of Vancouver Island and the Gulf Islands in Canada.

When you arrive at the ferry terminal on Orcas, you'll be in a small area called Orcas Village, but you won't want to linger here due to its limited amenities. The main towns are Deer Harbor to the west and the larger Eastsound to the north.

It only takes 45 minutes to go all the way from the west side to the east side of the island, so it's easy to have a home base in one area and drive to others during the day.

Getting There

The most conventional way to get to Orcas Island is to take the **ferry** (8368 Orcas Rd.; https://wsdot.com) from Anacortes, which has multiple ferries per day. Seaplanes are also available from Seattle for a more expensive but faster trip.

Kenmore Air

950 Westlake Ave. N., Seattle; 866/435-9524; https:// kenmoreair.com; flight times vary; $169/person each way

Kenmore Air has a convenient dock on Seattle's Lake Union where you can leave your car and be on Orcas Island in only 50 minutes. It drops you off right at Rosario Resort. Be sure to book your return flight as well.

Getting Around

Orcas Island has limited public transportation and the ferry terminal isn't walkable to any other areas of the island, so you'll need a car to get around.

Deer Harbor Road connects the island's west side and ends up running parallel to

Orcas Road, which leads from the ferry terminal to Eastsound and slowly winds through forests, farms, and lakes. Olga Road runs along the east side of the island.

Orcas Island Rental Car (360/376-7433; no address; 9am-5pm Mon.-Sat., noon-5pm Sun.) offers daily rentals and has cars, sedans, SUVs, convertibles, and shuttle vans that they'll deliver to you anywhere on the island free of charge.

If you just need to get from the ferry to Eastsound, book a spot on **Orcas Shuttle** (206/279-7575; www.orcashuttle.com; $19-45/person) for an affordable way to get into town. They also have a day pass available, which can get you to different spots around the island upon request.

DEER HARBOR

Deer Harbor is set on a harbor, and lodging and food options are limited and spread out. It's an ideal base if you want to relax, have a scenic view from your accommodation, and are looking for a quieter area. The marina has the most activity, with several restaurants and hotels.

Whale-Watching
Deer Harbor Charters

5164 Deer Harbor Rd.; 360/376-5989; www. deerharborcharters.com; year-round; $69-125

Since 1988, family-owned Deer Harbor Charters has offered 3-4 hour whale-watching tours from Rosario Village or Deer Harbor Marina, with a "no whale, come again for free" policy, and provides blankets and binoculars onboard.

Boating
Deer Harbor Marina

5164 Deer Harbor Rd.; 360/376-3037; www. deerharbormarina.com; 9am-5pm daily

Deer Harbor provides moorage for guests throughout the year, with a variety of

Orcas Island

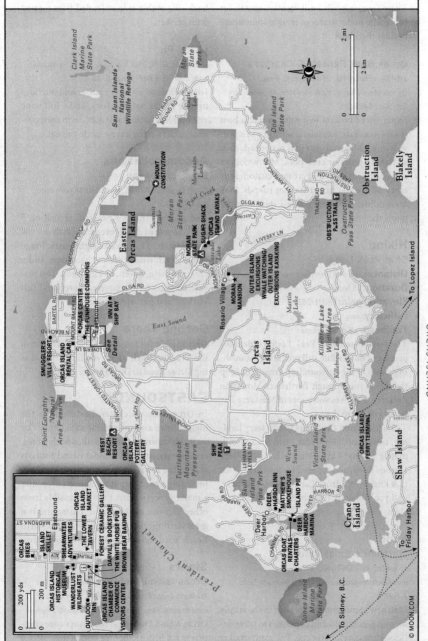

© MOON.COM

amenities at the marina, including a seasonal pool, a small convenience store, and showers. There are also newly built vacation rentals for those who prefer to stay overnight somewhere besides their boat.

Orcas Boat Rentals & Charters

5164 Deer Harbor Rd.; 360/376-7616; www. orcasboatrentals.com; 9am-6pm Mon.-Fri., 9am-5pm Sat.-Sun.; $425-575

Experienced boaters will want to rent a boat from Orcas Boat Rentals, where they can provide any additional gear you may need, such as fishing poles or crab pots. Many visitors also choose to relax and create a custom itinerary, where you can visit other islands, look for wildlife, and more while a staff member pilots the boat.

Hiking

Ship Peak Loop

Distance: *3 mi (4.8 km) round-trip*
Duration: *1.5 hours*
Elevation gain: *860 ft (262 m)*
Difficulty: *easy*
Trailhead: *off Wildrose Lane*

The less-visited Ship Peak Loop is ideal for peace and quiet while still providing astonishing views of the surrounding area. This loop trail takes you through Turtleback Mountain Preserve and gives you views of Massacre Bay when you get to the top.

Starting from the Orcas Island ferry landing, travel north on Orcas Road for approximately 2.5 mi (4 km). Make a left onto Deer Harbor Road, and proceed for another 2.4 mi (3.8 km) to Wildrose Lane. Turn right here, and you'll shortly find the trailhead on your right.

Food

Matthew's Smokehouse

75 Inn Ln.; 360/376-1040; https:// matthewssmokehouse.com; 4pm-8pm Thurs.-Sun.; $17-23

Matthew's Smokehouse has been in the family for two generations and continues to serve delicious homestyle barbecue. The giant smoker is outside the large green house. Sit indoors or at the tables outside and enjoy your baby back ribs with a side of loaded fries topped with brisket.

Island Pie

11 Jack and Jill Pl.; 360/376-2505; https://myislandpie. com; noon-9pm Wed.-Sun.; $12-25

Island Pie is set on Deer Harbor and provides unique pizzas, salads, pasta, and a full wine and beer list. Grab a table outside on their covered deck to enjoy a view while you eat.

Accommodations

Deer Harbor Inn

33 Inn Ln.; 360/376-4110; www.deerharborinn.com; $199-319

Deer Harbor Inn is a peaceful retreat on 5 acres (2 ha) of apple orchards with a view of the water. The inn has eight rustic lodge rooms, each with a private bathroom and a choice of twin, queen, or king beds. Two private cottages have a covered porch and full kitchen, and pets are allowed.

Getting There

Deer Harbor is 13 minutes (7 mi/11 km) from the ferry terminal, which you'll reach by taking Orcas Road to Deer Harbor Road.

EASTSOUND

In Orcas Island's center, Eastsound is the biggest town and the central social hub. The walkable downtown area is filled with stores, restaurants, and cafés. Most island tourists stay in the town for its convenient services, including a hardware store, a food co-op, and a major grocery store. Easily accessible from other sections of the island, Eastsound is a great starting point for exploration, and North Beach Road runs through its downtown area.

Sights

Orcas Island Historical Museum

181 North Beach Rd.; 360/376-4849; www.orcas museums.org; 11am-3pm Wed.-Sat.; $5 adult, $4 youth

Orcas Island Historical Museum's core comprises six historic homes donated by island residents in the mid-20th century. Volunteers meticulously relocated and renovated the cabins, and more than a century after their construction, these buildings still house the varied tales of the island's pioneers and Indigenous people. With an enormous collection of over 6,000 items, including relics, documents, and photos, the museum stands out on the island for its focus on tangible history.

The Funhouse Commons

30 Pea Patch Ln.; 360/376-7177; www.
funhousecommons.org; price varies by program
The Funhouse Commons is an entertaining place to stop if you have kids. It began as a children's science museum and soon became a primary gathering place for the island's young people. This youth-focused community learning center has a variety of programs, for babies up to 18 years old, and visitors can feel free to drop in on the playgroups and programs.

Nightlife
The Lower Tavern

46 Prune Alley; 360/376-4848; www.lowertavern.com;
11am-11pm daily; $13-20
If you're looking for a nightcap, stop by The Lower Tavern for a large selection of drinks and late-night appetizers. There's plenty of

entertainment here, such as playing pool, listening to live music, or watching the game on TV.

Performing Arts
Orcas Center

917 Mt. Baker Rd.; 360/376-2281; https://orcascenter.
org; 11am-3pm Tues.-Fri.; price varies by event
Orcas Center is the island's primary venue for community theater and performing arts. It hosts dance, music, drama, visual art, and performance art events with island-based and touring artists. The center has a beautiful foyer, a main stage theater that can accommodate 216 guests, a black-box theater that can accommodate 75, and several community rooms that transform into art galleries and other uses.

Shopping
Orcas Island Pottery Gallery

338 Old Pottery Rd.; 360/376-2813; www.
orcasislandpottery.com; 10am-4pm Tues.-Sat., 11am-
4pm Sun.
Open since 1945, Orcas Island Pottery is the Pacific Northwest's oldest pottery studio and is located away from the main town on the appropriately named Old Pottery Road, overlooking the water. You'll walk through a

Eastsound

beautiful garden lined with pottery from various artists and see even more inside the main building. There's even a treehouse for kids.

Forest Ceramic Gallery

344 Main St.; 608/445-8280; www.forestceramic.com; 10am-5pm Fri.-Mon.

You'll find beautiful ceramic pieces at Forest Ceramic Company, where each piece is unique with its own colorful structure and pattern. They sell ceramic plates, bowls, tumblers, teacups, vases, and more.

Darvill's Bookstore

296 Main St.; 360/376-2135; https://darvillsbookstore. indielite.org; 9am-5pm Mon.-Sat., 9am-4pm Sun.

Visit Darvill's Bookstore to choose from hundreds of classic, fiction, and nonfiction books, as well as puzzles and games. This cozy bookshop even has a coffee bar that invites you to stay and read your latest find.

Wanderlust + Wildhearts

123 North Beach Rd.; https://wanderlustandwildhearts. com; 11am-4pm Sun.-Mon. and Wed.-Thurs., 11am-5pm Fri., 10:30am-5pm Sat.

Wanderlust + Wildhearts is a fun place to shop for sustainably produced items like handmade jewelry, clothing, and other unique souvenirs to take home. You'll also find many items specific to Orcas Island to remind you of your time here.

Whale-Watching
Outer Island Excursions

1608 Rosario Rd.; 360/376-3711; www.outerislandx. com; Mar.-Nov.; $70-109

Travel around the San Juan Islands on an exciting whale-watching expedition in search of minke, gray, humpback, and orca whales. You can opt for a trip that focuses solely on orcas, or you can have a trained naturalist point out seals, sea lions, porpoises, bald eagles, and more. Tours last 3-5 hours.

★ Kayaking

Orcas Island is a favorite destination for kayakers—in the open ocean for advanced kayakers, or protected sounds for beginners. If you plan on going farther out, guides are the best way to familiarize yourself with the water. Many people choose rentals and stick closer to the shore. Popular kayaking spots include launching from Deer Harbor Marina, Orcas Village, Eastsound, and North Beach. If you want calmer water, head to Moran State Park to kayak on Cascade Lake or Mountain Lake.

Shearwater Adventures

138 N. Beach Rd.; 360/376-4699; https:// shearwaterkayaks.com; Apr.-Sept.; $99-125

A 5-hour kayak tour of Deer Harbor and the Wasp Islands is one of several excursions offered by Shearwater. You can also go on a one-of-a-kind nighttime paddle to take in the ocean's glowing wonders with the captivating bioluminescence trip, or choose the Spring Wildflower Experience, which takes you to an island in a nature preserve.

Outer Island Excursions Kayaking

414 N. Beach Rd.; 360/376-3711; www.outerislandx. com/kayaking; 9am-8pm daily; tours $40-275, rentals $40-75/day

From the 4-hour Point Doughty kayak tour on Orcas Island's north shore to the shorter sunset kayaking trip, Outer Island Excursions offers tours for all skill levels. You can even explore remote Sucia Island, which they'll take you to via boat. You can also rent single or double kayaks for 4 hours or the day, and for an extra $40, they'll deliver the kayak.

Skateboarding
Orcas Island Skatepark

699 Mt. Baker Rd.; https://orcasparkandrec.org; 8am to dusk daily; free

Constructed in 2002, the Orcas Island Skatepark is a renowned creation; people come from around the world to skate here. It features a giant bowl as well as various obstacles to skate over and around.

Biking

Orcas Island has quite a few hills and windy

roads, making biking on the streets here challenging but thrilling. Many people ride their bikes right off the ferry and continue up the main road to Eastsound or head to Moran State Park. To get to Eastsound from the ferry terminal, head north on Orcas Road for 8 mi (13 km) until you reach downtown Eastsound. To ride to Moran State Park, you'll follow the same route, continue east past Eastsound on Crescent Beach Drive, and head south on Olga Road for a total of 13 mi (21 km).

Orcas Bikes

414 North Beach Rd.; 360/820-8282; www.orcasbikes. com; 8:30am-5pm daily; rentals $40-70, tours $80-125

Rent your own electric bike at Orcas Bikes and head out around the island after getting a map of the area. If you prefer a bit more guidance, join one of their bike tours and enjoy views of the area as well as lunch at Buck Bay Shellfish Farm.

Food
Island Skillet

325 Prune Alley; 360/376-3984; Facebook @IslandSkillet; 8am-1pm Wed.-Sun.; $7-14

Island Skillet is the place to go for a hearty breakfast, whether you're craving pancakes, omelets, or a breakfast burrito. They have a small lunch menu if you're in the mood for burgers or sandwiches, all in their charming house with plenty of outdoor seating options.

Brown Bear Baking

29 North Beach Rd. #1966; 360/855-7456; www. brownbearbaking.com; 8am-4pm Fri.-Mon.; $6-13

Brown Bear Baking isn't your average bakery—you'll find a line here almost any day of the week, as visitors and locals alike wait for croissants, quiches, and croque monsieurs. Grab an espresso drink, as they use local favorite Victrola coffee in their drinks.

Inn at Ship Bay

326 Olga Rd.; 360/376-5886; www.innatshipbay.com; 5pm-8pm Thurs.-Sun.; $26-38

For some of the best fine dining on Orcas, make a reservation at the Inn at Ship Bay. They pride themselves on using local ingredients and changing their menu with the seasons, so you'll always have a unique gourmet meal, whether it's steak, scallops, or a vegetarian dish.

Orcas Island Market

469 Market St.; 360/376-6000; www. orcasislandmarket.com; 7am-9pm daily

What started as a small grocery store in 1897 is now the central place to shop on Orcas, and they've added to their services over the decades. In addition to fresh produce, a bakery, a deli, and a meat department, you'll also find a coffee house and a taproom.

The White Horse Pub

246 Main St.; 360/376-7827; Facebook @theWhiteHorsePubEastsound; 11:30am-10pm Sun.-Thurs., 11:30am-11pm Fri.-Sat.; $16-26

This family-friendly Irish pub and restaurant has authentic food such as Guinness stew, fish and chips, and imported beer and cider to enjoy. They also have one of the best views in Eastsound, with large windows overlooking the water.

Accommodations
Outlook Inn

171 Main St.; 360/376-2200; www.outlookinn.com; $197-332

You'll love relaxing at Outlook Inn, where guests can choose from 40 various rooms, including ones with private balconies, water views, gas fireplaces, and heated bathroom floors. It's one of the few hotels right downtown, so there's quick access to restaurants and shops.

Smuggler's Villa Resort

54 Hunt Rd.; 360/376-2297; https://smuggler.com; $225-395

Smuggler's Villa is convenient for families or large groups, as they have ten spacious (1,200 sq ft/112 sq m) townhomes with multiple bathrooms and bedrooms, laundry machines, and full kitchens. You'll also enjoy an outdoor deck with a barbecue and a shared outdoor pool.

Camping

You have plenty of spots on Orcas to choose from for camping, but reservations fill up quickly in the summer. It's best to book your spot in the late winter or spring if you want specific dates.

West Beach Resort

190 Waterfront Way; 360/376-2240; www. westbeachresort.com; $52-479

West Beach Resort has 19 waterfront cabins to rent, but also has 11 tent campsites and 10 RV sites with picnic tables and fire pits. Alternatively, you can choose to go "glamping" with one of their 9 tent cabins that come with a queen bed and futon, outdoor deck, and grill.

Information

Stop by the **Orcas Island Chamber of Commerce Visitors Center** (65 North Beach Rd.; 360/376-2273; https://orcasisland chamber.com; 10am-2pm Wed.-Sat.) to find out the best places to eat and learn about hiking in the area.

Getting There

Eastsound is a 15-minute drive (9 mi/15 km) from the ferry terminal; take Orcas Road north until you reach downtown Eastsound.

EASTERN ORCAS ISLAND

Traveling along Olga Road on the eastern side of Orcas takes you farther away from civilization—you spend extended periods without seeing any towns or stores. If you're in the mood for solitude, this is the spot for you. Because Moran State Park occupies a significant portion of this area, it's also a popular destination for outdoor enthusiasts.

Moran State Park

3572 Olga Rd.; 360/376-2326; https://parks.wa.gov; 6:30am-dusk summer daily, 8am-dusk winter daily; $10 Discover Pass

Moran State Park covers the majority of the east part of the island and is where most outdoor activities happen. Visitors can explore its numerous trails to bike, horseback ride, hike, and camp. Mount Constitution is the most challenging trail for hikers.

There are also five lakes here, with Mountain and Cascade Lakes being the most notable. These are often filled with people kayaking or fishing during the summer. You can fish on both Cascade and Mountain Lakes, which are stocked with rainbow trout, kokanee, and coastal cutthroat.

★ Mount Constitution

Distance: *6.7 mi (10.8 km) round-trip*
Duration: *3.5 hours*
Elevation gain: *1,500 ft (457 m)*
Difficulty: *moderate*
Trailhead: *Mountain Lake group camp*

At 1.3 mi (2.1 km) into this loop, you'll come to a junction with a detour to Little Summit, which is about 0.3 mi (0.5 km) each way. Continue to Summit Lake, about 2.3 mi (3.7 km) into your hike. Although the trail begins relatively flat, elevation gradually increases toward the end due to the steep switchbacks. Keep climbing until you reach the top of Mount Constitution.

A historic stone tower, constructed in the 1930s by the Civilian Conservation Corps, stands at the top of Mount Constitution. As a lookout point, it gives you a view of Canada, the Cascade Mountains, and the San Juan Islands on clear days. When you're done, head downhill to a fork in the path that takes you either to Twin Lakes or the main trail, both of which bring you full circle to Mountain Lake, where you started.

You can also drive all the way to the top via Mount Constitution Road (15 minutes/5 mi/8 km from Olga Rd.), or you can have someone

---

1: Moran State Park **2:** Obstruction Pass State Park

in your group pick you up at the top to cut the hike in half. There's a parking lot, restrooms, and a seasonal gift shop (11am-4pm daily summer) at the top.

To get here from downtown Eastsound, take a right onto Main Street, which becomes Crescent Beach Dri ve. At the four-way crossroads, turn right onto Olga Road. After you pass the park entrance, make a left to stay on Mount Constitution Road. At the next Y intersection, stay to the right and proceed to the trailhead.

Orcas Adventures

3786 Olga Rd.; 360/375-1460; www.orcasadventures. com; noon-4pm Fri., 10am-4pm Sat., 10am-3pm Sun.; rentals $21-29/hour

Orcas Adventures rents everything you need to spend a day out on Cascade Lake: stand-up paddleboards, kayaks, canoes, rowboats, and paddleboats by the hour or the day. It's first-come, first-served, so get here early. Stop by the **Sugar Shack** (360/375-1460; 10am-5pm daily; $4-15) for ice cream, drinks, and sandwiches.

Camping

3572 Olga Rd.; 888/226-7688; https://parks.wa.gov; $27-37

Moran State Park has over 120 tent campsites available, as well as a handful of hiker/biker campsites. About a dozen showers are distributed around the park, and the first firewood vending machine in Washington state parks is at the Midway Camp loop. You can choose from North End, Midway, South End, Mountain Lake, and Primitive Area sites.

Rosario Village

1400 Rosario Rd.; 360/376-2222; www.rosariovillage. com

The Rosario Village is a beautiful resort that sits on the isolated waterfront area of Rosario, and many guests stay here the entire weekend without leaving. Even if you're not staying overnight, you can make a reservation at the on-site restaurant, visit the historic Moran

Mansion from the early 1900s, and make an appointment at the spa.

Rosario Village ($179-269) is the most sought-after place to stay on the island, as it's in a secluded location on Rosario Point and even has its own boat dock for those who take their boat here or fly in via seaplane. You can easily stay here the whole weekend without leaving the resort, and many do. The resort features 107 guest rooms and suites, all of which have patios or decks and many with waterfront views.

Moran Mansion

www.rosariovillage.com; 8am-8pm daily; free

Open daily for self-guided tours, the Moran Mansion at Rosario Village is a tribute to Robert Moran, who came to Seattle in 1875 and founded The Moran Bros. Company shipyard, which was instrumental in constructing the *USS Nebraska* in 1902 and became the city's largest employer. Visitors will see Robert's extraordinary home and artifacts, such as the Music Room, with its 1900 Steinway grand piano and 1913 Aeolian pipe organ, and the unusual hearths inspired by his naval past and interest in the arts. Attractive gardens and walkways line the outside.

The Mansion Restaurant

1400 Rosario Rd.; 360/376-2222; www.rosariovillage. com; 8am-9pm daily; $18-42

The Mansion Restaurant has some of the best fine-dining options on the island, including seared New York strip steak and pan-seared king salmon with mushroom risotto. You can sit by the window for waterfront dining or on one of the couches if you're there for drinks and appetizers.

Obstruction Pass State Park

860 Trailhead Rd.; 360/902-8844; https://parks. wa.gov; 8am-7pm Wed.-Mon., 7am-6:30pm Tues.; $10 Discover Pass

Obstruction Pass State Park is one of the only public beaches on the island, and its calm waters make it suitable for visitors of all ages to explore. Many people pack a picnic and enjoy it at a table in the park or on a blanket on the beach. The park is a 17-minute (7-mi/11-km) drive from Rosario Village, on Olga Road south to Obstruction Pass Road.

Obstruction Pass State Park Trail
Distance: *1.9 mi (3.1 km) round-trip*
Duration: *1 hour*
Elevation gain: *305 ft (93 m)*
Difficulty: *easy*
Trailhead: *Trailhead Road parking lot*

This loop trail leads to a remote beach, and you may feel like you have it to yourself, depending when you go. The trail begins through the forest and then comes out by the water, where you have the option to take a smaller path down to the beach. Multiple interpretive signs along the way explain what you're looking at, so take the time to read through each one.

From Obstruction Pass Road, turn onto Trailhead Road, which ends up at the trailhead parking lot.

Lopez Island

Lopez Island is the third-largest of the San Juan Islands and has a relaxing atmosphere that stands out in the archipelago. The island was named after Gonzalo López de Haro, a Spanish naval officer who charted the Pacific Northwest waters. Over the years, it has transformed from a farming and fishing community into one of the most laid-back islands, known for its friendly "Lopez Wave" that all locals give.

Lopez is a biker's paradise too—rolling hills, flat terrain, and minimal traffic. The island's 15-mi (24-km) length is full of farms, forests, and quiet bays, and it has some of the most beautiful beaches in the San Juans. Visitors also love charming Lopez Village, the only village on the island and considered the main downtown area. While the ferry landing is on the other side, it's only an 8-minute drive (4 mi/6.5 km) to Lopez Village.

Getting There
To get to Lopez Island, take the **Washington State Ferry** (2100 Ferry Terminal Rd.; 206/464-6400; www.wsdot.com) from Anacortes. The journey takes about 50 minutes, and the **Lopez Ferry Terminal** (259 Ferry Rd.) is the first stop, after which the ferry goes on to Orcas and San Juan.

Getting Around
Driving and biking are the main ways to get around the island. The ferry terminal has no restaurants or shops, so you'll need to go 4 mi (6.5 km) to Lopez Village via Ferry Road and Fisherman Bay Road to reach them. There is no public transportation on Lopez Island, but you can call **Lopez Island Taxi and Tours** (360/324-8227; https://lopezislandtaxiandtours.com; $40-80) in advance to reserve a taxi pick-up from the ferry.

SIGHTS
Lopez Island Historical Museum
28 Washburn Pl.; 360/468-2049; https://lopezmuseum. org; 11am-4:30pm Sat.-Sun.; free

Stop by the Lopez Island Historical Museum to learn about the island's history, read stories from settlers long ago, and see historic pictures, artifacts, and documents. They also have several rotating exhibits, model boats, and a kids' corner.

Farms
Lopez is full of small, family-run farms, which adds to the island's appeal. Hours vary depending on the availability of the staff as well as the season, but many farms are happy to give you a tour if you call in advance.

Lopez Island

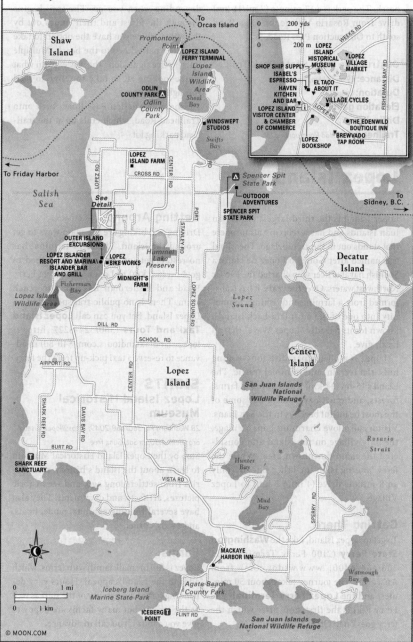

Map labels:

Shaw Island

To Orcas Island

Promontory Point

LOPEZ ISLAND FERRY TERMINAL

Lopez Island Wildlife Area

ODLIN COUNTY PARK

Odlin County Park

Shoal Bay

WINDSWEPT STUDIOS

Swifts Bay

LOPEZ ISLAND FARM

CROSS RD

CENTER RD

LOPEZ RD

PORT RD

To Friday Harbor

Salish Sea

See Detail

Spencer Spit State Park

OUTDOOR ADVENTURES

SPENCER SPIT STATE PARK

STANLEY RD

OUTER ISLAND EXCURSIONS

LOPEZ ISLANDER RESORT AND MARINA ISLANDER BAR AND GRILL

LOPEZ BIKE WORKS

MIDNIGHT'S FARM

Hummel Lake Preserve

Fisherman Bay

Lopez Island Wildlife Area

LOPEZ SOUND RD

Lopez Sound

Decatur Island

To Sidney, B.C.

DILL RD

SCHOOL RD

AIRPORT RD

CENTER RD

Lopez Island

Center Island

San Juan Islands National Wildlife Refuge

Rosario Strait

SHARK REEF RD

DAVIS BAY RD

BURT RD

SHARK REEF SANCTUARY

Hunter Bay

VISTA RD

Mud Bay

SPERRY RD

MACKAYE HARBOR INN

Agate Beach County Park

Iceberg Island Marine State Park

ICEBERG POINT

FLINT RD

Watmough Bay

San Juan Islands National Wildlife Refuge

0   1 mi

0   1 km

© MOON.COM

Detail inset labels:

0   200 yds

0   200 m

WEEKS RD

LOPEZ ISLAND HISTORICAL MUSEUM

LOPEZ VILLAGE MARKET

SHOP SHIP SUPPLY

ISABEL'S ESPRESSO

HAVEN KITCHEN AND BAR

EL TACO ABOUT IT

VILLAGE CYCLES

LOPEZ ISLAND VISITOR CENTER & CHAMBER OF COMMERCE

THE EDENWILD BOUTIQUE INN

BREWVADO TAP ROOM

LOPEZ BOOKSHOP

LOPEZ RD

FISHERMAN BAY RD

Lopez Island Farm

193 Cross Rd.; 360/468-4620; www.lopezislandfarm.
com; call for hours

Lopez Island Farm prides itself on providing pork, beef, and lamb from grass-fed, pasture-raised animals, and you can pick up your own to take home when you stop by their store. The friendly owners are also happy to tell visitors more about how their farm works. The farm is 1 mi (1.6 km) north of Lopez Island via Fisherman Bay Road.

Midnight's Farm

3042 Center Rd.; 360/468-3269; www.midnightsfarm.
com; 9am-8pm daily

Midnight's Farm is well known for its premium pig and beef production, as well as for making high-quality compost and wood chips from discarded yard materials, wood, and agricultural by-products. They also rent out a small vacation home ($150-225/night) and run a public yoga studio. The farm is 2 mi (3 km) south of the town via Hummel Lake Road and Center Road.

BEACHES

Spencer Spit State Park

521 Bakerview Rd.; 360/468-2251; https://parks.wa.gov;
8am-9pm daily; $10 Discover Pass

Spencer Spit State Park is a 138-acre (56-ha) marine park popular for camping (37 sites; $27-37) and day trips to its lagoon-enclosing sand spit. It's one of the only state parks in the San Juans that you can drive to and is known for clamming and crabbing. The park is 3 mi (5 km) east of Lopez Village via Fisherman Bay Road and Cross Road.

Odlin County Park

148 Odlin Park Rd.; 360/378-8420; www.sanjuanco.
com; free to visit, $10 overnight parking

There are few sandy beaches in the San Juan Islands, so the quarter-mile (0.4 km) of sand at Odlin County Park makes it a favorite among locals who want to sunbathe and kids who want to play on the beach. There are also hiking trails, 30 campsites ($35), and a

boat launch available. The park is 3 mi (5 km) north of Lopez Village via Fisherman Bay Road and Ferry Road.

Watmough Bay

Watmough Head Rd.; 360/378-4402; www.lopeztrails.
org/watmough-chadwick-colville; free

The clear waters of Watmough Bay make it yet another peaceful spot to visit. Enjoy a picnic, lying in the sun, and beachcombing on the bay's pebble-strewn beach. The beach is easily accessible by a short trail from the parking area. Once in the bay, paddleboarders and kayakers will love the calm waters, and as the weather warms up, you can also snorkel and swim. The bay is 11 mi (18 km) south of Lopez Village via Center Road and Mud Bay Road.

Agate Beach County Park

Mackaye Harbor Rd.; 360/378-8420; www.
visitsanjuans.com; 6am-9pm daily; free

Located on the island's south side, Agate Beach County Park is easily accessible right off the road, contrary to most of Lopez's other beaches. The park is particularly famous for the agate stones scattered along its shoreline, which attract daily beachcombers. The area also offers a long stretch of sand, where driftwood and lush forests meet the cliffs. The park is 10 mi (16 km) south of Lopez Village via Center Road and Mud Bay Road.

RECREATION
Whale-Watching
Outer Islands Excursions

meets at the dock in front of Lopez Islander Resort
and Marina (2864 Fisherman Bay Rd.); 360/376-3711;
https://outerislandx.rezgo.com; 11:45am May-Sept.;
$89-129

Tours with Outer Island Excursions have a 95 percent chance of seeing a variety of whales, including grays, orcas, minkes, and humpbacks, depending on the time of year. Their boat only holds a few dozen guests at a time, has bathrooms on board, and has a heated cabin.

Hiking

Shark Reef Sanctuary

Distance: 1 mi (1.6 km) round-trip

Duration: 30 minutes

Elevation gain: 40 ft (12 m)

Difficulty: easy

Trailhead: off Shark Reef Road

Contrary to the name, you won't find any sharks at Shark Reef Sanctuary, but a short stroll through a forest takes you to a stunning rocky area where you'll likely spot seals, if not whales. You can continue on the trail and along a boardwalk to finish the loop.

To get here from the ferry landing, head south on Ferry Road for 2 mi (3 km). Turn left onto Center Road and continue for around 5 mi (8 km). Take a right onto Fisherman Bay Road and follow it for 1 mi (1.6 km), then turn left onto Davis Bay Road. After 1 mi (1.6 km), veer right onto Burt Road, and left onto Shark Reef Road to the parking on the right side.

Iceberg Point

Distance: 3 mi (4.8 km) round-trip

Duration: 1.5 hours

Elevation gain: 50 ft (15 m)

Difficulty: easy

Trailhead: 138 Flint Road

Iceberg Point is a beautiful spot visitors can access via a flat loop hike through meadows and forests before emerging at a rocky area with water views. On sunny days, you can spot the Olympic Peninsula and even Mount Rainier far in the distance, and seals and whales are common sightings here.

Kayaking

There are plenty of places to launch a kayak on Lopez Island, with Odlin County Park and Spencer Spit State Park being the more common ones.

Outdoor Adventures

Spencer Spit State Park Rd.; 425/883-9039; www. outdooradventurecenter.com; 11am-7pm daily early

May-early Sept.; tour $120, $10 Discover Pass to park, rentals $45-75

Join Outdoor Adventures at Spencer Spit State Park to head out on the water with a fiberglass sea kayak that even beginners can quickly learn to use. The 3-hour tour goes along Lopez's coastline, with an experienced team member narrating the scenery. They also rent sea kayaks and stand-up paddleboards for the day.

★ Biking

Lopez Island's relatively flat terrain, unlike the other islands, makes it a favorite for biking enthusiasts. This gentle landscape allows riders of all levels to explore at a relaxed pace, from the coastal views you'll have for most of the way to the pastoral charm of rolling farmland and grazing sheep. There's no set route; many bikers enjoy riding on the island's main roads.

To do a clockwise loop from the ferry terminal, head south on Ferry Road to Center Road and across the middle of the island before taking a right on Fisherman Bay Road, which connects with Ferry Road as you follow it north. If you need help creating a route, stop at a local bike shop for assistance.

Lopez Bike Works

2847 Fisherman Bay Rd.; 360/468-2847; www. lopezkayaks.com; 10am-5pm daily; $10-35/day

Lopez Bike Works makes it easy to rent a bike for a few hours, or the entire day for an adventure. Their staff is happy to recommend routes based on your experience and how far you want to go.

Village Cycles

214 Lopez Rd.; 360/468-4013; https://villagecycles.net; 10am-4pm Wed.-Sat.; $48-72/day

Village Cycles has a variety of bikes to rent for the day, including electric, hybrid, and drop-bar performance bikes, and they highly recommend making reservations in advance. Hourly rentals may be available on a walk-in basis only. They also have kid bike trailers so the whole family can ride.

1: Spencer Spit State Park **2:** Watmough Bay

NIGHTLIFE

Islander Bar and Grill

2864 Fisherman Bay Rd.; 360/468-2234; https://lopezfun.com; 11am-9pm; $16-40

Islander Bar and Grill is a fun place to spend the evening. It has a lively tiki lounge where you can get a cocktail while singing karaoke or listening to live music. The food menu includes fresh seafood, salads, and burgers, and you can sit outdoors on the deck overlooking the water.

Brewvado Tap Room

135 Lopez Rd., Suite B; 360/228-8214; www.lopezislandbrewingco.rocks; 1pm-8pm Thurs., 1pm-7pm Fri.-Sat., 1pm-5pm Sun.

Brewvado Tap Room is the only brewery on the island, and you'll find a selection of beer on tap from Lopez Island Brewing Company as well as guest taps, cider, wine, and nonalcoholic drinks. It's a fun place to spend an hour or two with an extensive choice of card and board games to pick from, and outside food is encouraged.

FESTIVALS AND EVENTS

Tour de Lopez

360/468-4664; https://lopezisland.com; last Sat. of Apr.; free to watch, $30-50 to participate

On the scenic Tour de Lopez bike ride, you can pick from multiple routes (3-31 mi/5-50 km) from leisurely flats to hilly challenges. Registration includes the ride and refueling snacks along the way, and the postcelebration has a buffet lunch, beer garden, and live music.

SHOPPING

Lopez Bookshop

211 Lopez Rd.; 360/468-2132; www.lopezbookshop.com; 10am-5pm Mon.-Sat., 10am-4pm Sun.

Stop by Lopez Bookshop to get lost in their large selection of new and used books, from recent best-selling novels to more unique books. The friendly staff is always happy to help you find what you want, so don't hesitate to ask.

Windswept Studios

783 Port Stanley Rd.; 360/472-0468; www.windsweptstudios.com; 11am-5pm daily

You won't want to head home without a painting from Windswept Studio, where you'll find dozens of beautiful pastels depicting everything from country life to city scenes. The artist, Steven Hill, regularly hosts pastel workshops if you want to try your hand at a painting.

Shop Ship Supply

308 Lopez Rd.; https://shopshipsupply.com; 10am-3pm Thurs.-Sat.

The owners' backgrounds—growing up near and on the ocean, but not having fashionable and sturdy women's clothing—inspired them to open Shop Ship Supply. They've now expanded to durable clothing, jewelry, accessories, and home goods.

FOOD

Isabel's Espresso

308 Lopez Rd.; 360/468-4114; http://isabelsespresso.com; 7am-3pm daily

Stop by Isabel's Espresso to get your morning coffee, then grab a table outside or walk around by the water. The shop is small but has a full espresso bar, tea options, and baked goods.

Haven Kitchen and Bar

9 Old Post Rd.; 360/468-3272; www.lopezhaven.com; 5pm-8pm Thurs.-Sat.; $16-34

Haven Kitchen and Bar has a delicious selection of options like Dungeness crab cakes, fresh salads, and pizza. You'll love having a beach view with your dinner, which you can enjoy with a decadent dessert such as chocolate gateau. Reservations recommended.

El Taco 'Bout It

308 Lopez Rd.; 360/429-9942; www.eltaboutit.com; 10:30am-2:30pm Fri.-Sun.; $5-13

For a fun twist on dining, visit the El Taco 'Bout It food truck in Lopez Village. Their small but delicious menu includes burritos, tacos, quesadillas, and tortas with your choice of protein.

Lopez Village Market
162 Weeks Rd.; 360/468-2266; http:// lopezvillagemarket.com; 7:30am-7:30pm daily

You might be pleasantly surprised to find a full-service grocery store on the island. Lopez Village Market has meat, seafood, produce, bulk foods, flowers, a deli, and a bakery. It also sells kegs, camping supplies, bundled wood, and bagged ice.

ACCOMMODATIONS

Those looking to camp can find sites at Spencer Spit State Park and Odlin County Park.

The Edenwild Boutique Inn
132 Lopez Rd.; 360/468-3238; https://theedenwild.com; $125-189

The Edenwild is a charming hotel located in an old house that's within walking distance of the water and shops and restaurants in Lopez Village. The ten rooms have fireplaces and soaking tubs, and a garden cottage is also available to rent.

MacKaye Harbor Inn
949 Mackaye Harbor Rd.; 360/468-2253; www. mackayeharborinn.com; $275-525

Staying at MacKaye Harbor Inn is an intimate experience, as they only have five rooms, and you'll join the other guests for a freshly made breakfast each morning at this bed-and-breakfast. You can also rent out the entire inn for a fairly affordable price if you have a large group. From Lopez Village, it's a 17-minute drive (9 mi/15 km) via Center Road, Mackaye Harbor Road, and Mud Bay Road.

Lopez Islander Resort and Marina
2864 Fisherman Bay Rd.; 360/468-2233; https:// lopezfun.com; $159-179

Lopez Islander Resort and Marina has a variety of accommodations, including 29 hotel rooms, four vacation rentals, a handful of tent sites, and an area for RVs to park. Regardless of where you stay, you can access the whirlpool room, laundry facilities, fitness center, and heated pool.

INFORMATION

The **Lopez Island Visitor Center & Chamber of Commerce** (265 Lopez Rd.; 360/468-4664; https://lopezisland.com; 11am-3pm daily) can help you plan out your trip when you stop by their office, and they also have an extensive website for more information.

Skagit Valley

The scenic Skagit Valley unfolds before your eyes as you cruise along the freeway. Looking east, you'll see the magnificent Cascade Mountains. To the west, you can make out the tranquil Puget Sound and the faraway San Juan Islands. In between, the valley bottom is a mosaic of colorful flower fields and verdant farmlands.

Mount Vernon is the region's main city, with a historic riverfront and vibrant downtown area. To the west lies La Conner, which is a quiet waterside town full of charming stores, restaurants, and art galleries. Head north and drive along Chuckanut Drive, a scenic route connecting the Skagit Valley to Bellingham. This road winds along the edge of the Chuckanut Mountains, offering stunning views of Samish Bay and the surrounding islands. Once you reach Bellingham, you can explore its charming downtown and the beautiful waterfront area.

I-5 is the main route that connects these cities, and some like Mount Vernon and Bellingham are directly off the exits.

MOUNT VERNON AND VICINITY

Mount Vernon was established as a trading post on the banks of the Skagit River in the mid-19th century. It grew into an important agricultural center thanks to the Skagit Valley's fertile soil. Today Mount Vernon is a dynamic city with a downtown area full of shops, restaurants, and long stretches of road made for biking.

Farms, Gardens, and Nurseries

Due to its rich soil and moderate climate, Skagit Valley is well-known as a prime location for farming and gardening. The Indigenous Coast Salish people farmed the region long before European settlers also saw its agricultural potential in the late 1800s and established farms. Many agricultural products, particularly tulips, have brought the valley fame; thousands of people visit the Skagit Valley Tulip Festival each spring.

A number of farms are open year-round, their offerings changing with the seasons. The tulip farms tend to stay open even when it's not tulip season, as they sell local produce, jam, ciders, and other products throughout the year. They are all free to visit, and sometimes a staff member will give you a tour if they have the time.

RoozenGaarde

15867 Beaver Marsh Rd.; 360/424-8531; www.tulips. com; 10am-6pm Mon.-Sat., 11am-4pm Sun.; $15

With a sprawling 25-acre (10-ha) field of tulips, RoozenGaarde has blossomed into one of the country's most expansive tulip farms. The Roozen family adds special touches to their land, like an authentic Dutch windmill imported from the Netherlands, and they have dozens of bulbs to choose from to take home.

Schuh Farms

15565 Route 536; 360/424-6982; https:// schuhfarmswa.com; 9am-6pm daily; free

What started as a small berry farm in the 1970s has become a family-run U-pick

farm that sells corn and pumpkins in the fall and provides fresh-cut trees and handmade wreaths during the holiday season. They also have a store where you can purchase freshly made pies, jams, and flower bouquets.

Waxwing Farm

16665 Britt Rd.; 360/961-0744; https://waxwingfarmllc. com; 10am-5pm Wed. and Sat.; free

A certified organic vegetable farm, Waxwing Farm grows a wide range of vegetables according to the seasons. Salad greens, herbs, peas, radishes, and summer squash are available in the spring and early summer. In the latter half of summer, you can get tomatoes, eggplant, and peppers; in the fall, it's seasonal favorites like winter squash, daikon radishes, and leafy greens. This is an honor-system farmstand, where you pick out what you want from their shelves and pay via cash or check in their safebox.

Festivals and Events
★ Skagit Valley Tulip Festival

360/428-5959; https://tulipfestival.org; Apr.; $15

No other festival in the area is as popular as the Skagit Valley Tulip Festival, when the tulip fields comes to life in a vibrant sea of color for the month of April. Thousands of people from across the state flock to the area to see the millions of tulips displayed across acres of fields, take stunning pictures, go on tractor rides, and attend lively festivals during this month.

Weekends are very crowded, so it's best to go first thing in the morning or on the weekdays if your schedule allows. Otherwise parking can be a nightmare as the streets around the tulip fields get congested. Many fields have up-to-date websites, so you can check their cameras to see if the tulips are in full bloom yet.

Biking

Skagit Valley's flat terrain and minimal traffic on the rural roads make it popular for biking. The valley's network of roads lets bikers roll through farmlands, along rivers, and near the coast. There are several fun biking events to participate in, such as the **Skagit Spring Classic** (www.skagitbicycleclub.org) and the **Tulip Pedal** (www.pnwexploration.com), which occur in the spring.

The **Padilla Bay Shore Trail** is an excellent choice for a shorter, more leisurely ride. Starting at Bay View State Park, follow Bayview Edison Road along the shoreline of Padilla Bay. This route offers beautiful views of the nearby estuary and its abundant bird life. The trail is relatively flat and accessible, and you can turn back the way you came once you get in enough mileage.

Skagit Cycle Center

1704 S. Burlington Blvd.; 360/757-7910; www. skagitcyclecenter.com; 10am-6:30pm Mon.-Sat., noon-5pm Sun.; $85-150/day

Skagit Cycle Center has gravel bikes and regular and electric mountain bikes to rent for the day. They can also provide a car rack if you need help transporting your bike.

Bird-Watching

The area is a popular destination for bird-watchers due to the abundance of migratory species, not to mention bald eagles.

Padilla Bay National Estuarine Research Reserve

10441 Bayview Edison Rd.; 360/428-1558; www. padillabay.gov; 10am-4pm Wed.-Sat.; free

Stop by Padilla Bay National Estuarine Research Reserve to learn more about the birds in the area and see an aquarium full of native sealife. This is one of the best bird-watching spots in Mount Vernon—you can walk out to the water to spot avian species of all kinds. While the building is only open on select days, you can park in the parking lot at any time to bird-watch.

Shopping
Red Door Antique Mall

111 Freeway Dr.; 360/419-0811; Facebook @The-Red-Door-Antique-Mall; 10am-5pm Mon.-Sat., noon-4pm Sun.

You'll easily see the Red Door Antique Mall, with its large redbrick exterior. Inside, you'll find a huge variety of antique items, from children's toys to vintage signs and decor to comic books and teacups.

Easton's Books

701 S. 1st St.; 360/336-2066; www.eastonsbooks.com; 10:30am-5:30pm Mon.-Sat., noon-5pm Sun.

This family-run store has been open since 1976 and has a vast selection of used books in every genre. They also have rare, out-of-print, and collectible books, so ask their staff if you're looking for something specific.

Food
Calico Cupboard Café & Bakery

121-B Freeway Dr.; 360/336-3107; www. calicocupboardcafe.com; 7:30am-3pm Mon.-Fri., 7:30am-3:30pm Sat.-Sun.

You'll want to go early to get a spot at the popular Calico Cupboard Café and Bakery, where locals line up for the hearty Skagit Hash breakfast or get a savory cinnamon roll to go. There's also a lunch menu with options like fresh salads.

Il Granaio Authentic Italian Restaurant

100 W. Montgomery St., Suite #110; 360/419-0674; www.granaio.com; 11am-8pm Mon.-Thurs., 11am-9pm Fri., noon-9pm Sat., noon-8pm Sun.; $20-30

Housed in the Old Town Grainery Building from the 1940s, Il Granaio is a cozy place to enjoy authentic Italian dishes such as spaghetti carbonara and gnocchi gorgonzola.

Skagit River Brewery

404 S. 3rd St.; 360/336-2884; www.skagitbrew.com; 11am-8pm Sun.-Thurs., 11am-9pm Fri.-Sat.; $15-24

With over 24 beers on tap, Skagit River Brewing is the place to go for a quick drink at happy hour or pub food like burgers and pizza for dinner. This spacious restaurant is family-friendly and is known for its signature smoked meats.

Skagit Valley Food Co-Op

202 S. 1st St.; 360/336-9777; www.skagitfoodcoop.com;
7am-9pm daily

There's no better place to shop for fresh, local food than Skagit Valley Food Co-op with its meats, seafood, produce, cheese, and more. Head upstairs to the Mercantile to buy organic clothing, books, art supplies, handmade jewelry, and other gifts.

Accommodations
Tulip Inn

2200 Freeway Dr.; 360/428-5969; www.tulipinn.net;
$80-125

Tulip Inn is a small, affordable hotel near I-5 and plenty of restaurants, making it a convenient stay. They provide the basic amenities in their 40 guestrooms with queen or king beds, and select rooms have full kitchenettes.

Whispering Firs Bed & Breakfast Lodge

19357 Kanako Ln.; 360/428-1990; www.whisperingfirs.
com; $85-125

At Whispering Firs, guests can indulge in activities such as hiking, fishing, swimming in private lakes, and games like volleyball and mini-golf croquet. Enjoy a home-cooked breakfast every morning, relax on your private deck in one of the two rooms, or head to the hot tub.

Information and Services

The **Mount Vernon Chamber of Commerce & Visitor Information Center** (301 W. Kincaid St.; 360/428-8547; www.mountvernonchamber.com; 10am-4pm Mon.-Fri., 10am-2pm Sat.-Sun.) can help you plan out your time and let you know of any seasonal activities and events.

Skagit Valley Hospital (300 Hospital Pkwy.; 360/424-4111; www.skagitregional health.org) has a 24-hour emergency room, 137 beds, and a family birth center.

Transportation

Mount Vernon is about 60 mi (100 km) north of Seattle and takes around 1 hour 15 minutes to reach via I-5.

Thanks to its prime location just off I-5, Mount Vernon has multiple public transportation options. **Skagit Transit** (105 E. Kincaid St.; 360/757-4433; www.skagittransit. org) provides bus service throughout the region, including around Mount Vernon and out to areas like La Conner. **Greyhound** (www.greyhound.com) and **Amtrak** (www. amtrak.com) also stop in Mount Vernon at the **Skagit Transportation Center** (105 E. Kincaid St.).

LA CONNER

La Conner was founded in the late 1800s as a bustling trade and fishing hub on the Swinomish Channel. It's now a place to have a quiet weekend away, walking among the scenic waterfront and historic buildings and enjoying the vibrant arts scene.

Sights
Conner Waterfront Park

intersection of Sherman St. and Maple Ave., just north
of the park

One of the best views of the town is from Conner Waterfront Park. While it's a small park, the picnic tables are a good place to have lunch, and kids will love going down the fish slide.

Pioneer Park

1200 S. 4th St.

Pioneer Park has less than a mile (1.6 km) of trails, but it's a nice walk through a forested area by the **Rainbow Bridge.** One path leads you through the woods up a small hill that will bring you right underneath the Rainbow Bridge, where you can easily take a detour to walk across the iconic bridge.

Museum of Northwest Arts

121 1st St.; 360/466-4446; www.monamuseum.org;
10am-5pm Tues.-Sat., noon-5pm Sun.-Mon.; free

One of the main attractions is the Museum of Northwest Arts, which has two stories of art from Pacific Northwest artists. They have an engaging permanent collection and rotating ones, and there's a large gift shop to purchase art and other souvenirs.

Shopping
Handmade La Conner
106 1st St., Suite D; 360/214-2415; www.handmadelaconner.com; 10am-6pm daily
You'll want to stock up on the handmade home care and body products here, as they have simple, aesthetically pleasing labels and use clean ingredients. They have hair care, candles, bath products, body lotions, baby items, and even outdoor products like bug spray.

La Conner Seaside Gallery
101 N. 1st St.; 360/466-5141; https://shoplaconner.com; 9am-6pm Mon.-Fri.; free
You'll find beautiful oil paintings here depicting the vibrant tulips of Skagit Valley as well as other scenes from around the area. There's also photography to purchase to complete your collection.

Expressions Art Gallery
705 1st St.; 360/466-1911; www.expressionsfineartgallery.com; 10am-5pm Tues.-Fri., 11am-4:30pm Sun.-Mon.
Expressions Art Gallery offers a variety of art to decorate your home with, including paints, bronze sculptures, glasswork, and woodwork. But their specialty is colorful glass in the form of garden decor, vases, and even lamps.

Food
Stompin' Grounds Coffee Co.
603 Morris St.; 360/399-1079; Facebook @StompinGroundsCoffee; 5:30am-6pm daily; $4-12
Stompin' Grounds Coffee Co. is more than just a place to grab a coffee—it's a hangout. The friendly baristas will converse with you while the locals hang out around the tables both inside and out on the patio. In addition

to great espresso options, they have a small gift shop featuring art, jewelry, and more from local artists.

La Conner Brewing Co.
117 1st St.; 360/466-1415; www.laconnerbrewery.com; 11:30am-8pm Sun.-Thurs., 11:30am-9pm Fri.-Sat.; $11-22
You'll have a hard time finding a seat on weekend nights at La Conner Brewing Co., as locals and visitors alike sit down to sample some of the 16 beers on tap. This small-batch brewery also has a full menu, including wood-fired pizza, burgers, and salads.

La Conner Waterfront Café
28 1st St.; 360/466-1579; https://waterfrontcafelaconner.com; 11:30am-3pm Sun.-Fri., 11:30am-7pm Sat.; $17-25
The Waterfront Cafe boasts one of the best waterfront views in La Conner, with a large outdoor deck as well as indoor seating with a view. They're known for some of the best fish and chips in the region, and the Captain's Plate lets you try a little of everything.

The Oyster & Thistle
205 Washington St.; 360/766-6179; https://theoysterandthistle.com; noon-8pm Fri.-Mon., 3pm-8pm Thurs.; $19-55
The Oyster & Thistle has a rustic feel to it, but don't let that fool you—it's one of the top places in town for fine dining. You'll want to try one of the many oyster dishes, all prepared differently, and save room for a decadent dessert.

Accommodations
La Conner Channel Lodge
205 N. 1st St.; 360/466-1500; www.laconnerchannellodge.com; $159-309
La Conner Channel Lodge is the premier place to stay in town, as it's the only waterfront hotel in the area. There are 39 rooms to choose from, including water views, rooms with Jacuzzis, and suites for families or larger groups.

☆ Chuckanut Drive

view from Chuckanut Drive

One of the most scenic drives in the state is Chuckanut Drive, also known as Route 11. This byway stretches 22 mi (35 km) between Burlington and Bellingham, passing through farmlands before winding north along the cliffs. It was initially a gravel road, created in 1896. It became part of the Pacific Highway from California to Canada before a larger road was built inland, making this an alternate route.

The La Conner Inn

107 S. Second St.; 360/466-3101; www.thelaconnerinn.com; $159-189

The La Conner Inn is within walking distance of most of the shops and restaurants in town. It offers the basic amenities in its 28 rooms, and guests can enjoy a complimentary breakfast each morning.

Information

The **La Conner Chamber of Commerce** (210 Morris St.; 360/466-4778) is open at select times to help visitors, but the best way to reach them is by calling or emailing info@laconnerchamber.com with any questions.

Transportation

La Conner is about 1 hour 15 minutes (67 mi/108 km) northwest of Seattle. Take I-5 north, get off at exit 221 on I-5, and head west on Fir Island Road for 6 mi (10 km). Take a left on Chilberg Road and follow it for 1 mi (1.6 km) until you reach La Conner.

Skagit Transit (www.skagittransit.org) provides bus service between La Conner and Mount Vernon. The bus ride is approximately 26 minutes long ($1/person).

BELLINGHAM

At the end of Chuckanut Drive, Bellingham is worth spending the day exploring. It's home to Western Washington University and has a casual, laid-back vibe. It's also a haven for beer lovers, with almost 20 breweries in the area and growing each year.

There are many places to stop along Chuckanut Drive. The following, from south to north, are some of the most popular.

- **MP 9: Chuckanut Manor Seafood & Grill** (3056 Chuckanut Dr.; 360/766-6191; www.chuckanutmanor.com; $28-55): A quaint restaurant north of the Samish flats known for its prime views and fresh seafood

- **MP 10: Oyster Dome:** A popular hiking spot leading to fabulous views of Samish Bay

- **MP 10: The Oyster Bar** (2578 Chuckanut Dr.; 360/766-6185; www.theoysterbar.net; $42-82): A fine-dining restaurant known for its oysters and seasonal menu, perched along a cliff

- **MP 10: Taylor Shellfish Farms** (2182 Chuckanut Dr.; 360/766-6002; www.taylorshellfishfarms.com; $38-60): A famous family-owned shellfish farm offering a variety of seafood options and waterfront dining

- **MP 12: Dogfish Point** (1221 Chuckanut Dr.): Scenic lookout with sweeping views of Samish Bay and the San Juan Islands

- **MP 13: Larrabee State Park** (245 Chuckanut Dr.; 360/676-2093; https://parks.wa.gov): Washington's first state park, with hiking trails, 8,100 ft (2.5 km) of shoreline, tide pools, fishing lakes, and good bird-watching

- **MP 18: Chuckanut Bay Gallery and Sculpture Garden** (700 Chuckanut Dr. N.; 360/734-4885; https://chuckanutbaygallery.com): A local gallery and outdoor sculpture garden showcasing Northwest artists

- **MP 19: Fairhaven Park** (107 Chuckanut Dr. N.; 360/778-7100; https://cob.org): Final stop before Bellingham, with tennis courts, playgrounds, and trails

Sights

SPARK Museum of Electrical Invention

1312 Bay St.; 360/738-3886; www.sparkmuseum.org; 11am-5pm Wed.-Sun.; $6-10

Two private collections of electrical and radio gadgets amassed by Bellingham residents formed the foundation of the SPARK Museum of Electrical Invention. The MegaZapper Tesla coil is one of many unique relics on display, which span the 1600s to the 1940s. This extensive collection covers the whole spectrum of electrical experimentation in science and the golden age of radio.

Boulevard Park

470 Bayview Dr.; 360/778-8000; https://cob.org; 6am-10pm daily; free

Boulevard Park has stunning waterfront views, walking trails, and a boardwalk that extends over Bellingham Bay. The park also features picnic areas, a playground, and a coffee shop.

Hiking

Whatcom Falls Park

Distance: 4 mi (6.4 km) round-trip
Duration: 1.5 hours
Elevation gain: 50 ft (15 m)
Difficulty: easy
Trailhead: 1401 Electric Avenue

Whatcom Falls Park is an easy hike that's a combination of several small trails, so you can walk only one or combine them for the full mileage. You'll see a beautiful stone bridge over the river almost immediately. Once you cross the bridge, you'll see the 20-ft (6 m) Whatcom Falls going over basalt rock. Take your time to get some pictures, and then continue to explore the rest of the park.

Teddy Bear Cove

Distance: *1.8 mi (2.9 km) round-trip*
Duration: *1 hour*
Elevation gain: *164 ft (50 m)*
Difficulty: *easy*
Trailhead: *Teddy Bear Cove parking lot*

You'll zigzag down through the forest before reaching railroad tracks. Cross them to reach Teddy Bear Cove, where you'll have views of Chuckanut Bay and the surrounding islands. Walk around the quarter-mile (0.4 km) of shoreline and notice industrial tile and brick fragments from an early-1900s brick factory.

Fragrance Lake

Distance: *4 mi (6.4 km) round-trip*
Duration: *2 hours*
Elevation gain: *1,260 ft (385 m)*
Difficulty: *easy/moderate*
Trailhead: *291 Chuckanut Drive, Larrabee State Park*

This trail in Larrabee State Park leads steadily uphill for 1 mi (1.6 km) before you get a break. The trail starts to climb again, and at the next intersection, turn left to reach Fragrance Lake. You can add on a 0.6-mi (1 km) loop hike to walk along the shore to find a quiet picnic spot or get different viewpoints. When you're rested, return the way you came.

Kayaking

You'll have 30 sq mi (78 sq km) to kayak on **Bellingham Bay,** with a backdrop of the city and Mount Baker. The area generally has calm conditions so it's good for beginner kayakers, as well as experienced ones who want to go out further.

Bloedel Boat Rentals

2200 Electric Ave.; 360/398-5801; https://bloedelboatrentals.com; 11am-6pm daily mid-June-Labor Day, noon-6pm weekends and holidays Labor Day-Oct.; $25-40/hour

Rent a stand-up paddleboard, single or double kayak, canoe (expert paddlers only), or pedal boat for two or three people at Bloedel Boat Rentals and explore Lake Whatcom at your leisure. Stop at the concession stand for ice cream, drinks, and snacks afterward.

Shopping
Black Noise Records

1230 Bay St.; 360/325-7808; www.blacknoiserecords.com; 11am-7pm Wed.-Sun

Black Noise Records is an independent record store in downtown Bellingham that sells a wide selection of vinyl records and cassette tapes. The store's genres range from indie to jazz to international music.

MW Soapworks

1310 Commercial St.; 360/746-7129; https://mwsoapworks.com; noon-6pm Tues.-Sat.

This woman- and queer-owned store focuses on plant-based skincare that uses local ingredients as much as possible. It sells soap, lip balms, skincare, bath products, and more.

Festivals & Events
Bellingham Beer Week

various breweries; www.bellinghambeerweek.com; end of Apr.

Brewery tours, tastings, and limited releases are just a few of the highlights of Bellingham Beer Week, an 11-day celebration of the city's flourishing craft beer culture. Along with sponsoring events like food pairings with nearby restaurants, some breweries work together to craft one-of-a-kind beers just for the occasion. This week is a great chance for beer lovers to sample some of the many unique brews Bellingham offers.

Ski to Sea

360/746-8861; https://skitosea.com; Sun. of Memorial Day weekend

The Ski to Sea is an annual multisport team relay that's been held since 1973. Teams of 3-8 racers compete in seven sports: cross-country skiing, downhill skiing/snowboarding, running, road biking, canoeing, cyclocross biking, and sea kayaking. The course starts

---

1: downtown Bellingham **2:** Whatcom Falls Park

at Mount Baker, goes down the mountain through many small towns, and finishes at Marine Park in Bellingham.

Breweries
Twin Sisters Brewing Company
500 Carolina St.; 360/922-6700; www. twinsistersbrewing.com; 11:30am-8pm Sun. and Wed.- Thurs., 11:30am-9pm Fri.-Sat.; $13-23

Twin Sisters is one of the larger breweries, with huge floor-to-ceiling windows in its building and ample patio space with umbrellas outside. They have over a dozen beers to try, such as the refreshing Full Circle American Lager or the hoppy Precursor Pale. If you get hungry, they have options like a chipotle black bean burger and blackened salmon tacos.

Stones Throw
1009 Larrabee Ave.; 360/362-5058; www. stonesthrowbrewery.com; noon-9pm daily

This pet- and kid-friendly brewery has a cozy feel to it, whether you're tasting inside the small house or outside on the deck. Their beers have fun names, such as On Your Left Hefe and Happy Valley Hazy IPA.

Boundary Bay Brewery & Bistro
1107 Railroad Ave.; 360/647-5593; www.bbaybrewery. com; 11am-9pm Sun.-Thurs., 11am-10pm Fri.-Sat.; $16-32

You can't go wrong with Boundary Bay Brewery & Bistro, one of the city's longest-standing breweries. The family-friendly pub has an extensive menu with options like burgers, seafood, salads, and over a dozen beers.

Food
Mount Bakery Café
1217 Harris Ave.; 360/778-1261; www.mountbakery.com; 8am-2pm daily; $13-24

One of the most popular places for breakfast is Mount Bakery Café, which has downtown Bellingham and Fairhaven locations. Fill up with hearty breakfast sandwiches or eggs Benedict or enjoy one of their savory crepes.

Jalapeños
501 W. Holly St.; 360/671-3099; www.jalapenos-wa. com; 11am-10pm Sun.-Thurs., 11am-10:30pm Fri.-Sat.; $20-29

Come hungry to Jalapeños, as the generous portions are perfect for sharing in an energetic atmosphere. Enjoy dishes like the chile verde burrito or chipotle enchiladas, and don't miss their famous Big Mama margarita.

Accommodations
Hotel Bellwether
1 Bellwether Way; 360/392-3100; https:// hotelbellwether.com; $229-379

Hotel Bellwether is a luxury boutique hotel on Bellingham Bay, featuring 66 beautiful rooms that make the most of natural light and offer a mix of mountain views and waterfront options. Book the Lighthouse Suite, a three-story, 900-sq-ft (84-sq-m) standalone suite, for a unique stay. They have an on-site pub (3pm-9pm) and the **Lighthouse Grill** (7am-9pm daily; $21-49) with options like omelet lorraine for breakfast or scallops and soba noodles for dinner.

Hotel Leo
1224 Cornwall Ave.; 360/746-9097; www.thehotelleo. com; $229-399

Originally the site of the Leopold Hotel, Hotel Leo combines historic charm with modern comfort, featuring 40 rooms: modern rooms in the new building, and historical ones in the original 1883 building. Located in the heart of downtown Bellingham, the hotel is home to **Amendment 21** (4pm-10pm Tues.-Thurs., 4pm-midnight Fri.-Sat.), a Prohibition-era cocktail bar. They also have a social lounge, pool table, library, and theater.

Information and Services
Bellingham Visitor Information Center
904 Potter St.; 360/671-3990; www.bellingham.org; call for hours

Stop by the visitor center or call them with any questions about planning your trip.

PeaceHealth St. Joseph Medical Center

2901 Squalicum Pkwy.; 360/734-5400; www. peacehealth.org

PeaceHealth St. Joseph Medical Center has an emergency room, cardiovascular center, and childbirth center.

Getting There

To get to Bellingham from La Conner, it's a 45-minute drive (35 mi/56 km) by taking Laconner Whitney Road north, Route 20 east, and I-5 north.

Amtrak (www.amtrak.com) and **Greyhound** (www.greyhound.com) stop at the same location in Bellingham (401 Harris Ave.).

Getting Around

Driving is the best way to get around Bellingham if you plan on exploring outside the city limits.

Whatcom Transit Authority (360/676-7433; www.ridewta.com; $1-2/ride) provides bus service throughout the city and has a large station in downtown Bellingham (205 E. Magnolia St.).

North Cascades

Although it's not as visited as the other national parks in Washington, North Cascades National Park is just as captivating with its dramatic scenery. As you drive the North Cascades Highway, you'll be in awe of the park's sharp mountain peaks, lush forests, and clear lakes. It's hard to drive straight through the park without feeling called to stop and take dozens of photos, as the landscape is unlike any other in the state.

The area is a hiker's paradise. Heather-Maple Pass Loop gives stunning views of the region; the pristine Blue Lake Trail leads to a lake of the same name, where a swim can feel great on a hot day.

The park is also a great place to camp. These peaceful campsites offer nothing but the sound of nature, making them ideal for establishing a

Highlights

Look for ★ to find recommended sights, activities, dining, and lodging.

★ **Driving the North Cascades Highway:** This spectacular drive takes you through North Cascades National Park, passing by rugged mountains and lush valleys (page 282).

★ **Ross Lake:** This serene North Cascades lake is ideal for fishing, kayaking, and hiking during the warmer months (page 293).

★ **Hiking Blue Lake:** A moderately easy hike rewards you with views of crystal-clear Blue Lake and larches in the fall (page 295).

★ **Shafer Historical Museum:** This outdoor museum showcases artifacts from Winthrop's history, a must-visit for history buffs (page 301).

★ **Cross-Country Skiing the Methow Valley:** The Methow Valley is renowned for its pristine trails, with both challenging and beginner-friendly routes (page 304).

★ **Stehekin:** Take a peaceful ferry ride to this remote village at the north end of Lake Chelan to disconnect from the world in nature (page 312).

★ **Bavarian Beer Gardens in Leavenworth:** Immerse yourself in Leavenworth's Bavarian charm while enjoying local craft beers in the town's festive beer gardens (page 315).

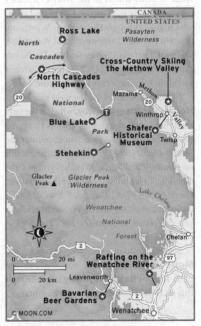

★ **Rafting on the Wenatchee River:** With its varying levels of rapids, the Wenatchee River provides a thrilling rafting experience for all skill levels (page 321).

base camp for the following day's adventures. Kayaking is the perfect activity for Ross Lake's pristine blue waters. Paddle around its serene surface and marvel at the mountains mirrored in the water.

The national park is the main attraction, but there are many other beautiful places to visit in the region. East of the park, the Methow Valley becomes a picturesque snowscape in the winter, ideal for cross-country skiing across its serene terrain. In the summer, you'll find unlimited water activities to enjoy on expansive Lake Chelan. Further south, the German-themed town of Leavenworth is full of restaurants and shops, while Wenatchee is the perfect place to go apple picking and hiking.

ORIENTATION

North Cascades National Park is about 3 hours from Seattle, making it a day trip or a stop en route to other towns in the North Cascades region. This is part of the **Cascade Loop,** which goes through the park to Winthrop, down to Chelan, Leavenworth, and Wenatchee, and back west via US 2 to Seattle. The North Cascades Highway and US 2 are the main roads on this loop and are easy to get around on.

Many people start on the west side of the **North Cascades Highway,** which is the only road that goes through the park. As you come out on the park's east side, you encounter the Methow Valley and Winthrop. Heading south on Route 20 and Route 153 takes you to Lake Chelan. To reach Leavenworth, continue south on US 97 ALT and US 2 west. You'll backtrack on US 2 east to Wenatchee, where you can return to Seattle via US 2 or I-90 to complete the loop.

Separate from the main loop in this region, **Mount Baker** is located northwest of the park. **Mount Baker Highway** runs through this section before ending at the mountain.

PLANNING YOUR TIME

While a scenic drive along the North Cascades Highway could be completed in an afternoon, you'll need at least **several days** to dive deeper into outdoor adventures. Destinations like Stehekin and the Methow Valley alone require more time to get to and need at least an overnight stay. Plan at least **one week** to see the entire region so you're not rushed. Summer is the best time of year to visit, when all roads are open and most hikes are snow-free. This is also when all the stores and restaurants will be open, as opposed to the winter when many are closed or have limited hours.

Winthrop is an ideal base for exploring North Cascades National Park, as it's only about 30 minutes east. If you're looking for plenty of options for lodging, shops, and restaurants, Chelan and Leavenworth are the places to go. But both towns can get exceptionally crowded during the summer and the holidays, so you may want to visit at other times to avoid long waits and traffic.

Heavy snowfall closes parts of the North Cascades Highway during winter and spring, and US 2 can intermittently close if Stevens Pass has too much snow. Winter visits require extra planning, and driving times will be longer. The WSDOT website (https://wsdot.com) provides live conditions on many roads around the state, so check it before you head out on your trip.

SAFETY

Car break-ins are on the rise at trailheads. Always make sure you take anything of value with you, and ensure your car has nothing in it that would tempt theft. An empty-looking car is the safest one—even charging cords might make someone think electronics are hiding nearby.

Previous: North Cascades Highway; Shafer Historical Museum; Blue Lake.

Itinerary Ideas

DAY 1

1 Spend your morning driving the North Cascades Highway. Stop for breakfast at **5B's Bakery & Eatery.**

2 Enter into North Cascades National Park and take in the views at **Diablo Lake Overlook.**

3 Hike **Blue Lake** and enjoy a rest break at the lake.

4 Leaving the park, make your way to Winthrop for dinner at **Old Schoolhouse Brewery.**

5 Check into **Sun Mountain Lodge** for the night.

DAY 2

1 Visit **Blue Star Coffee Roasters** in Twisp for coffee and breakfast before heading down Route 20 to Chelan.

2 Drive the short **Manson Scenic Loop** to take in the best views of the area.

3 Have lunch at **Local Myth Pizza** in Chelan.

4 Enjoy an afternoon of wine-tasting at **Vin du Lac** and **Tsillan Cellars.**

5 Check into **Campbell's Resort** for the evening and have dinner at their on-site restaurant.

DAY 3

1 Head down US 97 Alt to Wenatchee, stopping at **Rocky Reach Dam** along the way.

2 Enjoy lunch at **Pybus Public Market** and walk along the river or explore downtown shops.

3 Make the half-hour drive to Leavenworth and spend the afternoon with reindeer at the **Leavenworth Reindeer Farm.**

4 Visit one of the Bavarian beer gardens, such **München Haus,** for a dinner of German sausages and beer.

5 Stay the night at the **Sleeping Lady Resort.**

North Cascades

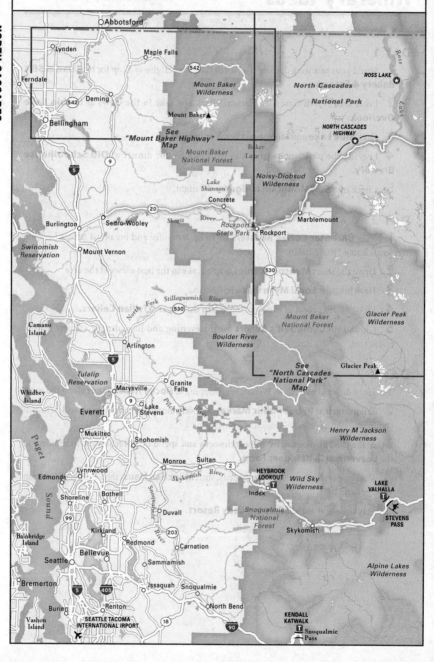

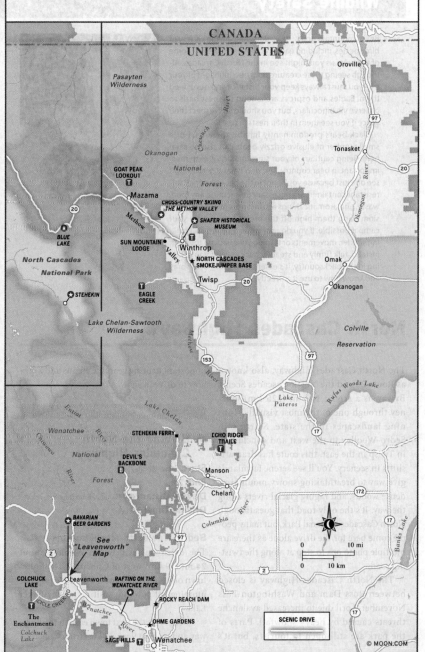

SCENIC DRIVE

© MOON.COM

Wildlife Safety

Bears, mountain goats, mule deer, and a wide variety of bird species, including eagles and ospreys, are just some of the animals you might see in the North Cascades. Although seeing these creatures can be a highlight of your trip, you must always keep your distance and never feed them. Eagles and ospreys are among the best birds to observe via binoculars, but you should still respect their space if you see them in their nests in trees.

Black bears predominantly inhabit the area, but a small number of elusive grizzly bears can also be seen here. Being cautious of your surroundings is extremely important in bear country, and don't assume you won't see one just because you're not in the backcountry. Bear-resistant containers are necessary for securing any food, waste, and aromatic things against potential bear intrusion. Hang them high off the ground away from your camp if possible. If you do encounter a bear, avoid making sudden movements or turning your back on the bear; instead, talk firmly and steadily back away. If you're hiking in the backcountry, it's essential to bring bear spray and know how to use it correctly.

black bear

North Cascades Highway

The North Cascades Highway, also known as Route 20 and the North Cascades Scenic Byway, is a scenic 140-mi (225-km) journey through one of the most visually stunning landscapes in the state. Starting in Sedro-Woolley in the west and concluding in Twisp in the east, this route has dramatic shifts in scenery. You'll see serene farmlands give way to breathtaking snowy mountains, dense woods, and raging glacial rivers along the way. It's the only road that goes through North Cascades National Park, but many people come here for the drive alone as there are multiple photo ops to stop at along the twisting road.

The North Cascades Highway is closed between Ross Dam and Washington Pass November-April due to increased avalanche threats caused by heavy snowfall. Parts of the park are still open to tourists, but it's

important to bring gear like chains and know how to drive in snow.

TOP EXPERIENCE

★ Driving the North Cascades Highway

Start: Sedro-Woolley

End: Twisp

Driving Distance: 140 mi/225 km (one-way)

Driving Time: 3 hours

Sedro-Wooley to Marblemount

The drive starts in Sedro-Wooley, about 24 mi (39 km) west of Concrete. This quiet town offers a few restaurants and is a popular jumping-off point for visiting nearby Baker Lake.

Rockport is the next town east on the highway and is about 9 mi (14 km) from Concrete.

Although it offers limited services, Rockport is well-known for its eagle-watching opportunities and proximity to the Skagit River.

From Rockport, it's 8 mi (13 km) to Marblemount, the last town before entering North Cascades National Park. Marblemount is the "gateway" to the park and an essential stop if you need gas or supplies. It also hosts the **Wilderness Information Center** (7280 Ranger Station Rd.; 360/854-7245; www.nps.gov/noca; 7am-11:30am and 12:30pm-4pm daily May-Oct.), where visitors can obtain trail maps and permits. You'll find a handful of restaurants here before entering the park, which has no dining options available.

North Cascades National Park (Marblemount to Mazama)

Once you head east of Marblemount, you're officially in the park boundaries. This 74-mi (119-km) trip to Mazama slowly ascends and curves around the mountains in the area. Take your time, as some curves are tight. You'll pass some of the park's most famous features, such as the turquoise waters of Diablo Lake, and can stop at the overlook for photos and a bathroom break.

Continue east and you'll drive by Ross Lake, an equally stunning lake popular with kayakers. The road curves up again until you reach Washington Pass, the highest point on the highway, which is another ideal stop for photos and the restroom. From here, the road slowly starts to descend, and you'll get into more farmland as you make your way out of the park and into Mazama.

SIGHTS AND RECREATION
Around Concrete
Lower Baker Dam Overlook
7163 Baker River Rd., Concrete

For a unique look at Baker Dam, stop at the Lower Baker Dam Overlook to see how the water is controlled flowing from Lake Shannon into the Baker River. A small, unofficial pull-off area is available to park in.

Baker Lake

Baker Lake is a tranquil outdoor destination 13 mi (21 km) north of Concrete, accessible via Burpee Hill Road. There's plenty to do here, including fishing and swimming, and hikers will find an abundance of trails around the lake. Baker River Trail is popular as it's a flat, 5-mi (8-km) round-trip stroll that follows the lake's shores and is great for families. The East Bank Baker Lake Trail is a good option for a more demanding hike, at 9 mi (14.5 km) round-trip with a moderate ascent but stunning lake views at the top.

Panorama Point, Horseshoe Cove, and Park Creek Campsite are just a few campgrounds surrounding the lake. You'll want to make reservations in advance.

Around Rockport
Skagit River Bald Eagle Interpretive Center
52804 Rockport Park Rd., Rockport; 360/853-7626; https://skagiteagle.org; 10am-4pm Sat.-Sun.; free

The Skagit River Bald Eagle Interpretive Center provides guided nature walks, educational programs, and the opportunity to spot bald eagles, particularly during winter when they flock to the Skagit River to feed on salmon.

Rockport State Park
51905 Route 20, Rockport; 360/853-8461; www.parks. wa.gov/574/Rockport; 8am-6pm daily; $10 Discover Pass

Rockport State Park is about 8 mi (13 km) from Concrete, covers 632 acres (256 ha), and has more than 5 mi (8 km) of trails. An easy hike is the Evergreen Trail, a 3-mi (5-km) trail through old-growth forest, or head out on the 4-mi (6.5-km) Sauk Mountain Trail. The park is also ideal for bird-watching and wildlife viewing.

North Cascade Kayaks
52925 Railroad Ave., Rockport; https:// northcascadekayaks.com; info@northcascadekayaks. com; $75-150 per day

North Cascade Kayaks in Rockport rents

Hiking the PCT

Pacific Crest Trail sign

The Pacific Crest Trail (PCT) is an incredible 2,650 mi (4,265 km) long and one of the most brag-worthy hikes to do. It begins at the Mexican border in California, and ends near the Canadian border in British Columbia. Hikers usually need around five months to complete the trail, which passes through the varied landscapes of Washington, Oregon, and California. The North Cascades provide some of the most spectacular terrain along the trail, with saw-toothed peaks and verdant valleys.

NORTH CASCADES

- **Tatie Peak and Grasshopper Pass:** Beginning at Hart's Pass, this picturesque 9.5-mi

kayaks and stand-up paddleboards, and the Colonial Creek Boat Launch on Diablo Lake makes for an ideal launching point.

FOOD
Around Concrete
Annie's Pizza Station

44568 Route 20, Concrete; 360/853-7227; www. anniespizzastation.net; 11am-9pm Tues.-Sat.; $13-25

Annie's Pizza Station is a family-run restaurant in a converted gas station, serving up pizza options like Chuck's Diesel with pepperoni and Canadian bacon or the vegetarian Annie's Unleaded—the names are clever nods to the building's history. Fresh

bread, salads, and homemade lasagnas are also available.

5B's Bakery & Eatery

45597 Main St., Concrete; 360/853-8700; https://5bsbakery.com; 9am-4pm Thurs.-Mon.; $5-8

Gluten-free doesn't have to mean flavor-free, and 5B's Bakery is delicious proof of that. Start your day off right with one of their cinnamon rolls, and swing by for a mini pot pie at lunchtime. 5B's is a go-to for both sweet snacks and hearty lunches, with a wide selection of buns, quick breads, and cookies at their casual restaurant with both indoor and limited outdoor seating.

(15.3-km) round-trip trail ascends Grasshopper Pass across summer meadows teeming with wildflowers. When you reach Tatie Peak, the scenery opens up, and you can see the mountains and the Methow Valley from every direction.

- **Cutthroat Pass:** The 10-mi (16-km) hike begins in a thick forest and continues into areas with creeks and waterfalls to listen to. The trail levels off as it makes its way northward back across the valley after traversing it and conquering a succession of switchbacks. As you get closer to the pass, the landscape opens up into a high alpine panorama, with huckleberry plants and granite boulders dotting the landscape.

- **Howard Lake:** If you're looking for an easy way to experience the PCT, get on the 3.3-mi (5.3-km) round-trip Howard Lake Trail, where you'll follow ponderosa trees through the forests, switchback your way up a hill, then follow signs for McGregor Mountain to meet Howard Lake just below it.

STEVENS PASS

- **Lake Valhalla:** Whether it's summer or fall hiking or winter snowshoeing, the 7-mi (11-km) round-trip trek to Lake Valhalla is a beautiful one year-round. The trail starts its moderate ascent between Mounts Lichtenberg and McCausland on the way to Union Gap. It continues down to the lakeshore, covered with wildflowers in the spring, berries in the summer, and brilliant fall foliage.

SNOQUALMIE PASS

- **Kendall Katwalk:** A relatively quick part of the PCT to get to from Seattle is the 12-mi (19-km) Kendall Katwalk hike. You'll cross streams, hike through old-growth forests, and pass through hillside meadows carpeted with wildflowers. The end has rough and exposed terrain, but you'll have views of Mount Rainier and Red Mountain.

ACCOMMODATIONS AND CAMPING
Around Concrete
Panorama Point Campground

19 mi (31 km) off Baker Lake Hwy.; 530/932-0242; www.recreation.gov; mid-May to mid-Sept.; $35-37

Situated on Baker Lake's western shore, Panorama Point Campground has nine campsites for tent and RV camping. There are picnic tables, vault toilets, and water available to campers.

Horseshoe Cove Campground

2 mi down Horseshoe Cove Rd.; 530/932-0242; www. recreation.gov; mid-May-mid-Sept.; $35-37

Horseshoe Cove Campground is in a shaded area on the southern part of Baker Lake. It has 39 campsites with drinking water, a sandy beach, a boat ramp, and firewood available.

Park Creek Campsite

18 mi (30 km) off Baker Lake Hwy. to Forest Road 1144; 530/932-0242; www.recreation.gov; mid-May-mid-Sept.; $30

Park Creek Campground is on the western side of Baker Lake and has 12 campsites for tent and RV camping. It also has vault toilets and campfire rings with grills.

Around Rockport
Glacier Peak Resort

*58468 Clark Cabin Rd.; 360/708-3005; https://
glacierpeakresortandwinery.com; camping $29-35/
night, cabin $139-189/night*

Glacier Peak Resort has an assortment of lodge rooms, tent and RV campsites, and cabins around their property. They also have a wine-tasting at their on-site winery (5pm Fri.-Sat., 11am-2pm Sun.) and a restaurant (breakfast-dinner, $13-19) with options like the Western burger with barbecue sauce or chicken strips and fries.

TRANSPORTATION

Sedro-Wooley is 1 hour 15 minutes (72 mi/116 km) north of Seattle; take I-5 to exit 232 and then head east on Cook Road for 5 mi (8 km) before reaching Sedro-Wooley and continuing east to Highway 20.

North Cascades National Park

North Cascades National Park, often called the "American Alps," is a magnificent natural haven spanning 1,100 sq mi (2,850 sq km). Its 300-plus glaciers covering the snowy peaks is more than any park in the United States outside Alaska. The park's alpine lakes and roaring waterfalls receive their meltwater from these glaciers. From vast, flower-filled meadows to deep, old forests, the park's scenery changes as you ascend and descend the along the winding North Cascades Highway.

There are plenty of hikes and overnight backpacking excursions—but also plenty of photo stops for those who don't feel like exerting themselves as much. Fishing, canoeing, and kayaking fans will love the rivers and lakes, so it's a park where you can make your own adventure.

Unlike the other national parks in Washington, there is no fee to enter. However, visitors need to stock up before arriving at the park, as no restaurants or gas stations exist here.

VISITING NORTH CASCADES NATIONAL PARK
Orientation
Marblemount

Marblemount is the first town you'll encounter on the west side, right before you enter the park boundaries. Restaurants and gas are available here, and not in the park. Cascade River Road, a roughly 9 mi (14.5 km) out-and-back gravel road, leaves from Marblemount and brings you several popular hiking trails. You can access Cascade River Road by crossing the Cascade River Road Bridge instead of continuing east on North Cascades Highway. The road goes for 23 mi (37 km) until it reaches the trailhead for Cascade Pass, where it ends.

Newhalem

As you continue west, you'll pass through Newhalem, home to several campgrounds, the Skagit Information Center, which has a bathroom and water refill station, and the Skagit General Store.

North Cascades Highway

The North Cascades Highway is the only road through the park. You'll find many pullout stops for photos and numerous trailheads. All the major sights are accessed from this road. Note: The road closes seasonally, typically early November-late May.

Diablo Lake

Diablo Lake, near milepost 132 on the North Cascades Highway, is one of the most recognizable sights in the park. Its overlook has a large parking lot complete with bathrooms, but some people may want to spend more time here hiking around the lake.

Ross Lake

Just a few miles east of Diablo Lake near

milepost 134, Ross Lake is another stunning lake that stretches 20 mi (32 km) long and reaches the Canadian border. It's home to multiple hiking trails, Ross Lake Resort, and opportunities to kayak or canoe.

North Cascades National Park Backcountry

The North Cascades National Park backcountry is a hiker's dream. High mountain ridges are mixed with valleys and deep gorges. It offers plenty of challenging trails that can only be reached on foot and remote campsites. You also have a chance to jump on the **PCT** for a taste of this challenging trail.

East of the Park

Washington Pass is the highest point along the North Cascades Highway, at an elevation of 5,477 ft (1,669 m), and the last place in the park to stop for photos before starting your descent east into Methow Valley. You'll find multiple vantage points and interpretive signs about the area's geology at this stop at milepost 162.

As you exit the park's boundaries, you'll enter the Methow Valley and see the first signs of civilization again in **Mazama.** Although it's a small town, Mazama packs quite a punch when it comes to the conveniences available. It's a welcome sight to many visitors to North Cascades National Park after going through the largely isolated section of the park. Mazama has a surprising variety of amenities, such as dining options, a highly rated general store, a gas station, and a number of places to stay. Mazama is right off the North Cascades Highway, 18 mi (29 km) east of Washington Pass and 14 mi (23 km) west of Winthrop.

Stehekin and Lake Chelan National Recreation Area

Unlike the rest of the park, Stehekin isn't connected by a road and can only be accessed by foot or boat. Most people take one of the passenger ferries from Chelan to Stehekin at the northern point of the lake. However, adventurers can go on the 23-mi (37-km) hike from the park's Cascade Pass to High Bridge, where a shuttle transports them into town. That said, it's one of the most remote areas in Lake Chelan National Recreational Area and well worth the journey.

Visitor Centers
North Cascades Visitor Center

376 Newhalem St., Marblemount; 206/386-4495; www. nps.gov; varies, typically 9am-5pm mid-May-late Oct.

Before exploring the park, stop at the North Cascades Visitor Center to learn more about the wildlife and terrain and talk to park rangers about current trail conditions. Souvenirs and maps are available in the small gift shop, plus a theater to watch a short film about the area.

Wilderness Information Center

7280 Ranger Station Rd., Marblemount; 360/854-7245; www.nps.gov; varies, typically 7am-11:30am and 12:30pm-4pm mid-May-late Oct.

The Wilderness Information Center serves as the main backcountry permit office for North Cascades National Park and adjacent recreation areas. Backcountry permits are available even when the center is closed during the winter through an outdoor self-issue station.

Scenic Drives
North Cascades Highway from Newhalem to Washington Pass

The section of the North Cascades Highway that winds its way through the park has many stops along the way that are well worth making. Incredible views of Diablo Lake, with its turquoise waters and craggy mountains, make Diablo Lake Overlook the most popular spot in the park. The Ross Dam trail leads to a historic dam nestled in a beautiful forest. Closer to the end of the drive to Rainy Pass, you can choose between two popular routes: the Rainy Lake and Heather-Maple Loop hikes. Finally, don't forget to stop at the Liberty Bell Mountain viewpoint on the route to Washington Pass, the highway's highest point, where you'll be treated

North Cascades National Park

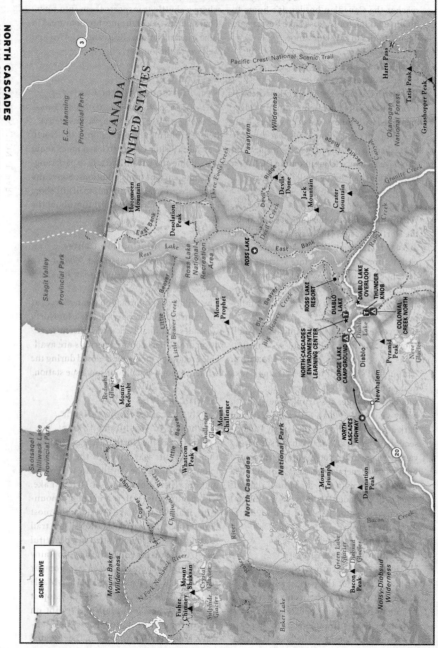

Fire Lookouts

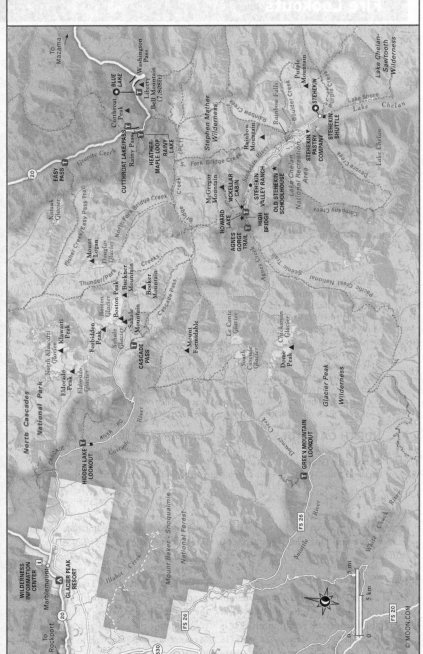

Fire Lookouts

Kelly Butte Lookout

Fire lookouts in the mountains of Washington state provide more than spectacular vistas; they are also windows into the past and places of quiet reflection. These structures were once used to watch for wildfires but are now popular with hikers and history buffs.

Although there's a handful of fire lookouts in Washington you can drive directly to, most require a hike. Some are closed to the public, but others are open during the day when a staff member is present. There are also plenty you can spend the night at, but it's often first-come, first-served, so you'll need to get there early and have a backup camping plan if it's already occupied.

All offer panoramic views of the surrounding evergreen groves, alpine meadows, and glacier lakes. Even though their purpose has changed, lookouts are still recognized as icons of the Pacific Northwest's wild terrain and long history of firefighting. The state has almost 100 fire lookouts, but this list highlights some of the best ones. You can search online at WTA.org by region to find a particular fire lookout, which will have the same trail name as the lookout.

NORTH CASCADES

Park Butte Lookout

Located 22 mi (35 km) from Route 20's milepost 82, Park Butte Lookout is a favorite of hikers who

to beautiful views on a clear day. This drive is 42 mi (68 km) long and takes about 50 minutes.

Harts Pass

Harts Pass makes for a thrilling mountain road trip. At 6,100 ft (1,860 m), it is one of the highest places in Washington that is accessible by car. The drive is 22.5 mi (36 km) from Mazama to Harts Pass, where you turn back the way you came. You pass through the old ghost towns of Chancellor and Barron along the way. A short climb from Harts Pass brings you to the 7,488-ft-high (2,282-m) Slate Peak Lookout, with its panoramic vistas of the North Cascades and the Methow Valley below. While the drive is outside the park in the gateway town of Mazama, it's close enough to add to your itinerary.

want a close-up view of Mount Baker's glaciers. Hikers on this 7.5-mi (12.1-km) out-and-back journey cross streams and pass through fields of wildflowers. The lookout has overnight camping available, but it is first-come, first-served.

Goat Peak Lookout

Goat Peak Lookout, built in 1929, is one of Washington state's oldest fire lookouts. Though no longer staffed, it offers sweeping views and a window into the early conservation efforts in the North Cascades. This 3.7-mi (6-km) round-trip trail in Mazama gains its 1,400 ft (425 m) of elevation in a short period of time, but it's worth it for the views.

Green Mountain Lookout

At an altitude of 6,500 ft (1,980 m), Green Mountain Lookout provides spectacular panoramas of Glacier Peak and the surrounding forest. It was built in 1933 and was instrumental in detecting fires and as an airplane warning post during World War II; today it's on the National Register of Historic Sites. Although overnight stays are prohibited, it is nevertheless a popular destination for hikers seeking a challenging 3,300-ft (1,006-m) elevation increase in a 8.5-mi (13.7-km) round-trip.

CENTRAL CASCADES

Heybrook Lookout

Because of its proximity to Seattle and relatively easy ascent, Heybrook Lookout stands out among Washington's fire lookouts. It is a good option for families and hikers of varied abilities because of its short distance (2.6 mi/4.2 km round-trip) and moderate elevation gain (850 ft/260 m). The summit's lookout tower provides panoramic views of Mount Index, Mount Persis, and, on particularly clear days, the Olympic Mountains to the west.

MOUNT RAINIER

Mount Fremont Lookout

Hikers who want to photograph the night sky or sunrise over the park flock to the Mount Fremont Lookout in the Sunrise area of Mount Rainier National Park. At an elevation of 7,200 ft (2,200 m), the overlook offers one of the most intimate and magnificent perspectives of Mount Rainier, and the 5.6-mi (9-km) round-trip climb passes wildflower meadows and glacial rivers along the way.

Kelly Butte Lookout

Just outside Mount Rainier National Park's borders, Kelly Butte Lookout (3.4-mi/5.4-km round-trip) provides a magnificent vista of the mountain. The trail's endpoint is at an elevation of 5,409 ft (1,649 m), and the peak comes to life in the summer with bear grass and luscious huckleberries.

SIGHTS
Around Newhalem
Trail of the Cedars

Park at the end of Main Street in Newhalem and head toward the suspension bridge for a 0.3-mi (0.5-km) round-trip loop. The middle of the loop is the old Newhalem Powerhouse, where you can peek in the windows to see remnants of it. Well maintained and with no elevation gain, this trail is wheelchair-accessible and kid-friendly.

Diablo Lake

With its surreal turquoise waters colored by glacial silt, Diablo Lake is one of the most photographed spots in the North Cascades. Visitors can quickly stop at the **Diablo Lake Overlook** off the North Cascades Highway

(milepost 132) to get pictures or head down below to explore it more. Hikers can head to the North Cascades Institute parking lot to find the trailhead for the 7.6-mi (12.2-km) round-trip Diablo Lake Trail alongside the lake. Visitors who want to take a dip can access a swimming area at the Colonial Creek Campgrounds.

To get here, take the North Cascades Highway to Diablo Dam Road (milepost 127.5), turn north, and park at the end of the road in the designated parking lot.

North Cascades Environmental Learning Center

1940 Diablo Dam Rd., Rockport; 360/854-2599; https://ncascades.org; 8:30am-4:30pm Mon.-Fri.

On the north side of the lake is North Cascades Environmental Learning Center, an immersive educational hub with interactive, hands-on learning experiences about the local environment, ecology, and conservation efforts. One popular experience is Base Camp, where visitors stay overnight at the lodge and pick from activities such as bird-watching, guided hiking, and stargazing ($85-210/night based on accommodations).

Diablo Lake Boat Tours

1940 Diablo Dam Rd., Rockport; 360/854-2589; https://ncascades.org/signup/programs/skagit-tours; 11:30am and 2:30pm Thurs.-Mon., July-Sept.; $30-45

See the North Cascades in a new light on one of Diablo Lake's boat tours while listening to intriguing stories of the area's early settlers and the massive efforts to build the Skagit River Hydroelectric Project dams in this undeveloped region. The tour takes a little over an hour, and advance reservations are required.

The glacial waters of Diablo Lake are a stunning shade of turquoise, and as your boat cruises across the lake, you'll see amazing views of snowcapped mountains, secluded islands, and gushing waterfalls. An organic boxed lunch from the North Cascades Environmental Learning Center is included to round out the experience.

★ Ross Lake

Ross Lake is only accessible by hiking from Ross Dam trailhead at milepost 134 on the North Cascades Highway. Stretching about 23 mi (37 km) and crossing the Canadian border at its northern end, the lake's clear waters draw kayakers, canoeists, and anglers. Hikers can join parts of nearby trails, such as the Big Beaver Trail and the East Bank Ross Lake Trail, and see more of the lake up close. Near the south end of the lake is Ross Lake Resort. To get there you'll need to take a short boat ride from the bottom of the Ross Dam Trail, as the resort doesn't have road access, adding to its secluded charm.

East of the Park
Washington Pass

One of the best views of the North Cascades Highway is from Washington Pass. A short, paved path leads to an overlook point looking at Liberty Bell Mountain and onto the far eastern section of the highway, where the winding road starts to descend into the Methow Valley.

HIKING

The vast network of hiking trails in North Cascades National Park has major appeal for hikers of all skill levels. This park is a paradise for anyone who wants to explore areas you can't see from the road, with trails ranging from the easy Blue Lake Trail to those that cross the strenuous Pacific Crest Trail. There are also challenging backcountry trips for those looking for more remote locations.

Along Cascade River Road
Hidden Lake Lookout

Distance: *8 mi (12.9 km) round-trip*
Duration: *5 hours*
Elevation gain: *3,300 ft (1,000 m)*
Difficulty: *strenuous*
Trailhead: *Hidden Lake trailhead*

Hidden Lake Lookout Trail has many different

1: North Cascades Highway 2: Baker Dam
3: Cascade Pass 4: Ross Lake

landscapes to explore, from dense forests to alpine meadows and, finally, to rocky granite peaks. Built in 1932, Hidden Lake Lookout still stands on the hill overlooking the North Cascades. From here, you can see a number of peaks, including Eldorado, Mount Baker, and Mount Shuksan. Overnight stays at the fire lookout are allowed on a first-come, first-served basis.

To get here from Marblemount, take Cascade River Road for 10 mi (16 km) until reaching Forest Road 1540, which has a sign for Hidden Lake trail. Drive up a rocky road for 5 mi (8 km) until the road ends at the trailhead.

Cascade Pass

Distance: 7 mi (11.3 km) round-trip
Duration: 3.5 hours
Elevation gain: 1,800 ft (550 m)
Difficulty: strenuous
Trailhead: Cascade Pass Trail trailhead

Cascade Pass climbs just 1,800 ft (550 m) in 3.6 mi (5.8 km) and passes old-growth trees with glimpses of the towering Johannesburg Mountain. The hike itself features over 30 switchbacks, revealing views of glaciers and peaks like Eldorado. After the final switchback, it's a 1-mi (1.6-km) straight path to Cascade Pass. The trail moves from forest to open slopes and crosses a rockfield before reaching the pass. A post points toward Stehekin, a remote community 30 mi (48 km) away at the head of Lake Chelan. Reaching the pass, hikers are greeted with sweeping vistas of valleys, mountains, and possibly local wildlife like marmots, deer, and bears.

From Marblemount, take Cascade River Road until it reaches the end (about 23 mi/37 km), which is the parking lot for the Cascade Pass Trail.

Diablo Lake
Diablo Lake Trail

Distance: 7.6 mi (12.2 km) round-trip
Duration: 3.5 hours
Elevation gain: 1,400 ft (425 m)
Difficulty: moderate

Trailhead: North Cascades Environmental Learning Center parking lot

The Diablo Lake Trail is one of the few hikes accessible year-round and is particularly good to do in late spring when other trails still have snow on them. The route passes through a mature forest and across a few streams that are prone to flooding. The Diablo Lake Overlook at 1.5 mi (2.4 km) is a short out-and-back detour that has spectacular views of the surrounding mountains. After descending to a suspension bridge close to Ross Dam, you walk by a beautiful gorge with waterfalls as high as 700 ft (215 m). This is an avalanche zone in winter and spring, so take extra precautions.

From Marblemount, drive 22 mi (35 km) east, take a left onto Diablo Dam Road, and proceed 1 mi (1.6 km) to the trailhead.

Thunder Knob

Distance: 3.6 mi (5.8 km) round-trip
Duration: 2 hours
Elevation gain: 635 ft (195 m)
Difficulty: easy
Trailhead: Colonial Creek North Campground

The Thunder Knob route in the North Cascades is a short but rewarding climb, ideal for families or beginners. Starting at a clearly marked trailhead in the campground, hikers follow a succession of bridges across Colonial Creek (which are closed in winter). The trail switches from a wet, mossy hemlock and salal woodland to a drier lodgepole pine area. Have a break at a lookout over Colonial Peak, and then stroll over a beautiful marsh. After you reach Thunder Knob, you will be rewarded with stunning views of Diablo Lake, whose turquoise waters are the result of glacial silt, and the historic Diablo Dam.

Drive 25 mi (40 km) east from Marblemount on the North Cascades Highway, and turn left at the Colonial Creek North Campground sign.

East of the Park
Easy Pass

Distance: 7 mi (11.2 km) round-trip

Duration: *4 hours*

Elevation gain: *2,800 ft (850 m)*

Difficulty: *moderate*

Trailhead: *Easy Pass trailhead (between Milepost 151 and 152)*

The hike to Easy Pass is not as simple as its name suggests, but it's well worth the effort. The trail begins in a wooded area, leading you across a log bridge over Granite Creek. After gaining some altitude, you come to Easy Pass Creek, which requires careful navigation. Pass over some talus and switchbacks, and then emerge onto a rocky alpine meadow. The pass offers views of nearby mountains, including Golden Horn and Fisher Peak. The trail provides little shade, so water and sun protection are especially necessary.

To get here, drive east from Marblemount on the North Cascades Highway for 45 mi (72 km), and turn at the Easy Pass sign after milepost 151.

Heather-Maple Loop

Distance: *7.2 mi (11.6 km) round-trip*

Duration: *3.5 hours*

Elevation gain: *2,020 ft (616 m)*

Difficulty: *moderate*

Trailhead: *Rainy Pass trailhead*

Heather-Maple Pass Loop transforms from a haven of summer wildflowers to a vibrant display of golden larches in the fall, making it a popular hike. Hikers often opt to do the loop clockwise, tackling the more challenging sections first. The trail first leads to the stunning glacial cirque known as Lake Ann, and from Heather Pass, there are optional branches to Lewis Lake and Wing Lake. The trail then climbs to Maple Pass, offering lovely vistas of the North Cascades, before descending gradually through a forested area, returning to the starting point.

To get here, drive 50 mi (80 km) east from Marblemount on the North Cascades Highway and turn right at the Rainy Pass trailhead sign. Follow the sign for Heather-Maple Loop once in the parking lot.

Rainy Lake

Distance: *2 mi (3.2 km) round-trip*

Duration: *1 hour*

Elevation gain: *70 ft (21 m)*

Difficulty: *easy*

Trailhead: *Rainy Pass trailhead*

Wheelchair users can skip the tougher mountain climb and go right to the lakeside viewpoint via the paved, 1-mi (1.6-km) Rainy Lake trail. From this vantage point, you can observe fish swimming in the lake's crystal-clear water and the surrounding mountains. Be aware the parking lot is shared with the popular Heather-Maple Loop hike, so get here early on the weekends.

To get here, drive 50 mi (80 km) east from Marblemount on the North Cascades Highway and turn right at the Rainy Pass trailhead sign.

★ Blue Lake

Distance: *4.4 mi (7.1 km) round-trip*

Duration: *2.5 hours*

Elevation gain: *1,050 ft (320 m)*

Difficulty: *easy*

Trailhead: *Blue Lake trailhead*

Blue Lake is a must-see, a gorgeous alpine lake with granite peaks surrounding it. Hikers will cross boardwalks and a forested area, see a wildflower-filled meadow, and possibly even spot climbers making their way to Early Winters Spire. As the trail winds its way to the lake, there's stunning views of Cutthroat Peak and Whistler Mountain. Check out an old log cabin, take in the scenery from the lakeside, and even brave the water for a swim.

To get here, drive 42 mi (68 km) east from Newhalem on the North Cascades Highway and look for the trailhead sign on the right.

BACKPACKING

A backcountry permit is required for all overnight stays while backpacking in North Cascades National Park and can be obtained from the Wilderness Information Center in Marblemount. Trailhead parking in the nearby national forest also requires the purchase of a Northwest Forest Pass. Around 140 approved campsites with level tent pads, water access, and pit or composting toilets are spread out across the park along the route networks.

Camping off the beaten path is allowed, but only if you stay at least a mile (1.6 km) away from sanctioned camps and half a mile (0.8 km) from any trail. Stay away from alpine meadows, water sources, and fragile plants when setting your camp. North Cascades off-trail hiking is notoriously difficult due to the region's steep and densely forested topography, so it's essential to be properly prepared before going on a backpacking trip. If you need a permit or a pass, make sure to get them well in advance of the season, as permits are popular and sell out quickly.

Along Cascade River Road
Cascade Pass to Sahale Glacier
Distance: 11.8 mi (19 km) round-trip
Duration: 8 hours
Elevation gain: 3,940 ft (1,200 m)
Difficulty: strenuous
Trailhead: Cascade Pass Trail trailhead

Cascade Pass is a well-traveled day hike that can connect to other hikes for a longer backpacking trip, such as the scenic Sahale Arm trail that ends at the Sahale Glacier. It's full of wildflowers during the summer and vibrant foliage in the fall. On clear days, you can see Mount Rainier from the Sahale Arm Trail, which is a longer trail with more demanding terrain. Even in July, icy stretches may call for an ice axe. Some people turn around at this point, but spending the night to rest is desirable to others. Backcountry permits are offered first-come, first-served and are required for camping at Sahale Glacier Camp and the surrounding campgrounds in Cascade Pass.

To get here from Marblemount, take Cascade River Road until it reaches the end (about 23 mi/27 km), which is the parking lot for the Cascade Pass trail.

Diablo Lake
Fourth of July Pass
Distance: 11.2 mi (18 km) round-trip
Duration: 6 hours
Elevation gain: 2,400 ft (730 m)
Difficulty: strenuous
Trailhead: Colonial Creek Campground

There are two ways to reach Fourth of July Pass: via Thunder Creek or Panther Creek Trails. Thunder Creek provides stunning scenery along a creek for 2 mi (3.2 km) before a steep 2.5-mi (4-km), 2,000-ft (600-m) climb to Fourth of July Camp. From there, it's less than 1 mi (1.6 km) to the pass. Ideal for backpacking, some camp spots offer fantastic views of surrounding peaks. The best way to experience the trail is a one-way traverse, which requires one car at Colonial Creek Campground and one at the Panther Creek parking area by milepost 138. It requires more planning, but you'll get even more stunning views of the area instead of coming back the way you came.

To get here from Marblemount, head east on the North Cascades Highway for 24 mi (39 km) and turn right at Colonial Creek Campground. The trailhead is 0.5 mi (0.8 km) down the road by the amphitheater.

KAYAKING AND BOATING

Summer is the perfect time to explore Diablo Lake and Ross Lake—the water is refreshingly cold after the hot weather. These lakes are ideal for a variety of water sports, including kayaking, fishing, and boating. Given the park's isolated location, guests should be prepared to either bring their own equipment or arrange for rentals elsewhere.

Diablo Lake

Motorized and nonmotorized boats, such as canoes and kayaks, are allowed on Diablo Lake. Colonial Creek Campground has a boat launch and plenty of parking. Diablo Lake is also a great spot for fishing, with species like rainbow trout and kokanee.

Ross Lake

Ross Lake is also open to both motorized and nonmotorized watercraft, and many people choose to rent a kayak or canoe from Ross Lake Resort. However, getting your own boat here is a bit trickier, as the main boat launches are on the Canadian side. Fishing is also popular here during the summer and fall, with rainbow trout being sought after.

Rentals

If you want to avoid hauling your canoe or kayak 1 mi (1.6 km) down the Ross Lake trail or figuring out how to get a motorboat on the lake, make it easy by renting from Ross Lake Resort. You can request your preferred boat and date in advance on their website (www.rosslakeresort.com).

FOOD

Food options in the North Cascades are limited, especially as you venture deeper into the region. Marblemount serves as the last outpost with restaurants, offering a few local spots where you can grab a meal. Past that point, your choices become even more restricted. The small community of Newhalem has a general store, but it operates with limited

hours, making it unreliable for last-minute meal planning.

It's also important to note that Marblemount and Newhalem's food service availability changes with the seasons. Outside the busy tourist season, many businesses either shut down or operate on limited hours. Because of these limitations, it is essential that you bring your own food while venturing into the North Cascades.

Marblemount
Mondo Restaurant

60102 Route 20; 360/873-2111; Facebook @MondosRestaurant; 9:30am-9pm Fri. Tues., 8am-9pm Wed., 11am-9pm Thurs.; $13-20

Mondo is set in a large log cabin with an older feel, with aged wooden chairs and tables. The menu has dozens of beers on draft and options like a bison burrito with melted cheese or cod and chips.

Upriver Grill & Taproom

60084 Route 20; 360/873-4221; www.uprivergrill.com; 11am-8:30pm Thurs.-Sat., 8am-8pm Sun.; $17-26

Stop at the Upriver Grill & Taproom after a day exploring the park and choose from options like a Caprese panini or salmon pasta in a creamy Alfredo sauce. You'll have plenty

Mazama Store

of places to sit between the large indoor area with big windows and local art on the walls or the outdoor patio.

Around Newhalem
Skagit General Store

502 Newhalem St., Rockport; 206/386-4489; 7am-6pm daily

The Skagit General Store is the last place to purchase snacks until Mazama, so it has a higher price on most items. It's also known to close randomly, so it's best not to rely on them being open and to bring food with you instead.

Mazama
Mazama Store

50 Lost River Rd., Mazama, 509/996-2855; www.themazamastore.com; 7am-6pm daily

The Mazama Store is easily the most popular spot in the area—it's the first store available after North Cascades National Park. They have a variety of gourmet groceries, packaged snacks and meals, and outdoor gear. Head outside to visit their coffee shop that sells fresh pastries, bread, and espresso drinks. It's a popular hangout area for both locals and Pacific Crest Trail hikers.

Mazama Public House

516 Goat Creek Rd., Mazama; 509/519-4321; https://oldschoolhousebrewery.com/visit/mazama-public-house; 3pm-9pm Mon.-Thurs., noon-10pm Fri.-Sat., noon-9pm Sun.; $9-18

Mazama Public House is a great place to unwind after a day of exploring. The pub has a covered patio, an outdoor fire pit, and views of Goat Peak, at a location near the Mazama trailhead. It offers a variety of food, like sandwiches and salads, in addition to the beers and ciders brewed by Old Schoolhouse Brewery.

ACCOMMODATIONS

North Cascades National Park has very few places to stay, so planning ahead is crucial for visitors. There is only one resort in the park, and it fills up quickly during the high season. Besides the resort, camping is your best bet

for spending the night in the park. Resort and campground bookings often need to be made months in advance.

Marblemount
North Cascades Inn

60117 Route 20; 360/661-8990; http://northcascadesinn.com; $109-270

The North Cascades Inn is located in a restored cedarwood structure that dates back to 1889 and was formerly a lumberjack's quarters. The building has since been transformed into 15 mountain-themed rooms. Some rooms have private bathrooms, others have shared ones, and the beds range from twin to king.

Ross Lake
Ross Lake Resort

503 Diablo St., Rockport; 206/486-3751; www.rosslakeresort.com; mid-June-Oct.; $255-460

Ross Lake Resort was created from a 1952 floating logging camp and is now a highly sought-after accommodation, as it's the only resort in the national park. There's no direct road access, but there are two ways to reach it. Option 1: Park at milepost 134 on Route 20, hike 1 mi (1.6 km) down to the lake, and take an on-demand shuttle across the lake (8am-8pm June-Oct.; $4/person). You'll see a wooden telephone pole with a phone on it, which you'll call the resort from. Option 2: Use the **Diablo/Seattle City Light Ferry** (https://seattle.gov; 10:30am and 2pm daily; $5-10/one-way) from Diablo Dam; reservations are required, which the resort can make for you. The resort has 15 floating cabins that are fully furnished, but you'll need to bring your own food as there's no restaurant or store on-site. Children under 4 stay free.

Mazama
The Inn at Mazama

15 Country Rd., Mazama; 509/996-2681; www.innmazama.com; $150-175

The Inn at Mazama is housed in a large, rustic log cabin that has 18 rooms with private bathrooms, TVs, and a queen or king bed. Some

Larch Season in the North Cascades

While Washington state has hikes to do year-round, no other time of the year is like what locals refer to as "Larch Madness." Late September–mid-October, deciduous larch trees transform their needles from a vibrant green to a brilliant golden hue, offering a stunning contrast against the backdrop of evergreen forests and rugged mountain peaks. The exact time of year these colors change varies, so keep an eye on the WTA's **website** (www.wta.org) for individual hikes and read the trail reports from other hikers.

larches at Goat Peak Lookout

BLUE LAKE

Easily the most popular trail in the North Cascades, Blue Lake is a family-friendly trail at 4.4 mi (7.1 km) round-trip and an elevation gain of 1,000 ft (300 m). Larches tend to be seen closer to the lake, and during their prime, they surround the lake in a brilliant yellow color that contrasts with the lake's vibrant blue. To get here, drive 42 mi (68 km) east of Newhalem and look for the Blue Lake Trail sign on the right side of North Cascades Highway.

HEATHER-MAPLE LOOP

Intermediate hikers will love this more challenging 7-mi (11-km) loop hike, which has an elevation gain of 2,000 ft (600 m) but is more than worth the trek for the views of Lake Ann below and the surrounding North Cascades. To get here, drive 50 mi (80 km) east of Marblemount and look for the Rainy Pass Trail sign on the right side of the North Cascades Highway. A trailhead sign in the parking lot indicates the Heather-Maple Loop.

GOAT PEAK LOOKOUT

Many people drive past Goat Peak Lookout on their way to Winthrop without realizing it, but it's worth exploring for the abundance of larches you'll hike through to get to the top. At only 3.7 mi (6 km) round-trip but 1,400 ft (425 m) in elevation gain, this is a steep hike to get to the lookout. While the fire lookout is closed to the public, there are plenty of areas to rest at the top and enjoy the views. From Route 20 in Mazama, turn onto Lost River Road and head east on Goat Creek Road for 1.8 mi (2.9 km) to the intersection with Forest Road 52. Make a left onto Forest Road 52, proceed for 2.6 mi (4.2 km), and turn left onto Forest Road 5225. Continue for 6.2 mi (10 km), make a right onto Forest Road 200, and drive 2.9 mi (4.7 km) to reach the trailhead at the end of the road.

CUTTHROAT LAKE/PASS

Cutthroat Lake is about 0.5 mi (0.8 km) west of Washington Pass, and a well-marked sign for Cutthroat Lake Trailhead indicates where to turn. Go up the road for 1 mi (1.6 km), ending at a parking lot. There are two options for hikes here; the first is the short Cutthroat Lake, a leisurely stroll at 3.8 mi (6.1 km) round-trip and only 400 ft (120 m) of elevation gain. For a longer hike, you can continue to Cutthroat Pass, which is a total of 10 mi (16 km) round-trip.

rooms also include Jacuzzi tubs, gas stoves, and mini-refrigerators. The rooms have no TVs, stereos, or phones to maintain the establishment's peaceful atmosphere.

CAMPING

Despite its limited lodging options, North Cascades National Park excels in its variety of camping options. The park boasts nearly 140 designated campsites complete with tent pads, toilets, and water access, but a backcountry permit is required for all overnight stays. These permits can be in high demand, especially during peak seasons. Generally, campgrounds are open seasonally late spring-early autumn, with varying fees.

Around Newhalem
Newhalem Creek Campground
14 mi (23 km) east of Marblemount, North Cascades Highway milepost 120; 206/386-4495; www.nps.gov; late May-mid-Sept.; $24

Newhalem Creek Campground is a peaceful, wooded campground by the Skagit River that offers 103 total sites for tents and RVs and provides flush toilets but no showers.

Goodell Creek Campground
15 mi (24 km) east of Marblemount, North Cascades Highway milepost 119; 360/854-7200; www.recreation. gov; late May-mid-Sept.; $20

The Trail of the Cedars, River Loop Trail, and Rock Shelter Trail are all easily accessible from Goodell Creek Campground via a connected trail. There is also a raft launch and fishing spots in the creek and river. Black bears and other wildlife often visit this area, so keep all food in locked containers away from the campsites.

Diablo Lake
Gorge Lake Campground
20 mi (32 km) east of Marblemount, North Cascades Highway milepost 126; 360/854-7200; www.recreation. gov; late May to mid-Sept.; $20

Gorge Lake Campground is on a bank with a view of Gorge Lake and has eight primitive sites with no water or services. Campers must bring their own water and pack out all trash, though vault toilets are available. The campground also provides an opportunity for fishing on Gorge Lake.

Colonial Creek North Campground
10 mi (16 km) east of Newhalem, North Cascades Highway milepost 130; 360/854-7200; www.nps.gov; late May-mid-Sept.; $24

Colonial Creek North Campsite is set on Diablo Lake and has a total of 41 campsites, each with a campfire ring and picnic table. The campground also provides drinking water, toilets, and garbage disposal. Hikers can easily access nearby trails such as Thunder Knob Trail and Thunder Creek Trail from the campground.

TRANSPORTATION
Car

The main road into the park is the North Cascades Highway (Route 20). Newhalem is approximately 125 mi (200 km) from Seattle. Take I-5 north to Route 20 east. The drive usually takes 2.5-3 hours, depending on traffic and road conditions. Route 20 is the only road that goes through the park.

The Methow Valley

The Methow Valley, located on the North Cascades' eastern border, is a picturesque rural area with stunning natural scenery.

Mazama, Winthrop, and Twisp are the three main towns that make up the region. Mazama is the closest to the park, and thousands flock here yearly to enjoy the extensive trail systems in both summer and winter. Winthrop takes pride in its Western-themed buildings and is the most common place to stay due to its selection of restaurants, shops, and more. Despite its modest size, Twisp is a bustling community with abundant arts and culture.

Although the area is a popular summer destination, it's also bustling in winter. Cross-country skiers visit when the snow falls, transforming the landscape into a winter paradise with perfectly groomed Nordic paths.

WINTHROP

Winthrop is one of the state's more unique destinations because it transports visitors to the Old West. As soon as you enter the town, you'll notice the old-timey wooden signs and boardwalks, rustic homes, and Western-style storefronts. The town is a favorite vacation spot for families, outdoor lovers, and history buffs because of its historic attractions such as the Shafer Museum; hiking, snowshoeing, and cross-country skiing opportunities; and numerous restaurants.

Sights
★ Shafer Historical Museum

285 Castle Ave.; 509/380-9911; www.shafermuseum. org; 10am-5pm daily; donation-based, suggested $5 adult

While many of Winthrop's stores are Old West-themed replicas, the Shafer Historical Museum provides a genuine glimpse into the past. Just up the steps from Riverside Avenue, you'll find a time warp to the early 1900s, complete with vintage homes, structures, and

relics. The museum houses a wide variety of objects, from historic farming tools and furniture to an original cabin from 1897 and a 1902 doctor's buggy, showcasing the era's medical practices.

Riverside Avenue

Riverside Avenue is the main part of Winthrop, capturing its Western allure with creaky wooden boardwalks and rustic facades. Visitors don't have to go far to find what they need here; the street has a handful of restaurants, shops, and lodging options. Sheri's Sweet Shoppe is a popular stop for ice cream and mini golf, and Three Fingered Jack's Saloon has the atmosphere of an old-timey watering hole. Stop at the Cascades Outdoor Store if you need to stock up for your outdoor adventures.

North Cascades Smokejumper Base

23 Airport Rd.; 509/997-9750; www.fs.usda.gov; 11am-3pm daily; free

Smokejumping, a dangerous but efficient way of fighting wildfires in inaccessible locations, was developed in the Methow Valley in 1939 when the first SR-10 Stinson airplane was used for experimental jumps by the Forest Service. The North Cascades Smokejumper Base is now an essential center for this specialist firefighting tactic, which is utilized to keep forests in central and western Washington from being destroyed. During the active summer months, visitors can take a tour of the facility and get a firsthand look at this innovative method of fighting wildfires.

Winthrop National Fish Hatchery

453B Twin Lakes Rd.; 509/996-2424; www.fws.gov/ fish-hatchery/winthrop; 8am-3:30pm daily; free

The Winthrop National Fish Hatchery plays a key role in breeding salmon and trout to maintain the local ecosystem. Steelhead,

Winthrop's Wild West Theme

Winthrop

Gold finds in the Methow Valley attracted a flood of prospectors and settlers in the late 19th century, marking the beginning of Winthrop's history. The valley was once home to Native peoples but is now a major mining, ranching, and timber center. The town, named for Theodore Winthrop, a 19th-century traveler and writer, saw another major transformation in the 1970s.

In 1972, Route 20 across the North Cascades was nearing completion, and business owners and city officials in Winthrop saw an opportunity to attract tourists by giving the city a Western makeover. It worked, and the town quickly became a tourist destination.

To experience the best of Winthrop's Wild West today, look no further than the creaky boardwalks and historic facades of **Riverside Avenue.** You'll find places like **Three Fingered Jack's Saloon,** which has a swinging saloon door, and **Miss Kitty's Old Time Photo Parlor,** where you use old Western props to recreate scenes from back in the day.

spring Chinook, and coho salmon are all raised at the hatchery and released into the waterway, and a building with a viewing glass is used to lodge returning adults from May until the end of August. In the summer, guests can learn about the fishes' extraordinary voyage to the Pacific Ocean, which is 574 river mi away (924 km).

Shopping
Sheri's Sweet Shoppe
207 Riverside Ave.; 509/996-3834; www. sherissweetshoppe.com; 9am-5pm daily
Sheri's Sweet Shoppe features a charming Old West facade with a rustic wooden exterior and outdoor patio. It sells a vast variety of sweets,

including fudge, homemade ice cream, and candies, and there's also an espresso stand on-site.

Cascades Outdoor Store
222 Riverside Ave.; 509/996-3480; https:// cascadesoutdoorstore.com; 9:30am-5:30pm daily
Outdoor enthusiasts will find a large selection of outdoor apparel, footwear, and gear at Cascades Outdoor Store, perfect for sports like trail running, skiing, and hiking. They also rent snowshoes and cross-country skis and can recommend good hikes in the area.

1: Methow River 2: cross-country skiing in Methow Valley

Hiking

Winthrop has a variety of hikes around the area, with the Sun Mountain network of trails being the most popular. There are various loops here where you can choose to do anything from a 1-mi (1.6-km) hike to longer treks. The region is also a good base for more challenging hikes nearby.

Kraule-Sunnyside Trail

Distance: *2.5 mi (4 km) round-trip*
Duration: *1 hour*
Elevation gain: *300 ft (90 m)*
Difficulty: *easy*
Trailhead: *Kraule trailhead or Sunnyside trailhead*

This easy trail is a loop that shares a trailhead and branches off with Kraule Trail on one side and Sunnyside Trail on the other, so pick either one and connect with the other at the midway point of the circle. It provides stunning views of Winthrop and the surrounding mountains, and wildflowers are often abundant in the spring months.

Turn off Route 20 from Winthrop onto Twin Lakes Road. Follow the signs for Sun Mountain Lodge for 9 mi (14 km) before reaching the end of the road, where the trailhead parking lot is.

Pearrygin Lake Loop

Distance: *6 mi (9.7 km) round-trip*
Duration: *3 hours*
Elevation gain: *364 ft (111 m)*
Difficulty: *moderate*
Trailhead: *From Winthrop, north on Riverside Avenue, right on Bear Creek Road, then 1 mi (1.6 km) to the Pearrygin Lake State Park sign*

Pearrygin Lake is a popular place to swim and float during the summer months, but it also makes an ideal walk. Start at any point on the lake to do the full loop on this unpaved trail and get views of the area from all angles.

★ Cross-Country Skiing

The Methow Valley is widely regarded as one of the best places to go Nordic skiing in North America, and the region caters to cross-country skiers of all skill levels with its 120 mi (195 km) of groomed courses that wind through woods, open valleys, and along the Methow River.

Methow Trails

21 Horizon Flat Rd.; 509/996-3287; https://methowtrails.org

The Methow Community Trail is 18 mi (29 km) one-way and goes through the four major sections of the Methow Trails system: Mazama, Winthrop, Sun Mountain, and Cub Creek. The trail starts in Mazama by the Mazama Store and ends in downtown Winthrop. Beautiful scenery, a suspension bridge over the Methow River, and a variety of lodges are all part of this trail system that encompasses 120 mi (195 km), and for a unique experience you can ski from hut to hut with Rendezvous Huts. Methow Valley Ski School & Rentals and Winthrop Mountain Sports are just two of the companies in the area that offer equipment rentals.

Rendezvous Huts

Cub Creek Trailhead; 509/429-3644; www.rendezvoushuts.com; $130-195

Ski into one of five cozy wooden huts with Rendezvous Huts, which is on the trail system that gets groomed nightly in the winter. All huts can sleep up to 10 people, have pots, pans, dishes, and utensils provided, and have a stove with an oven. For an extra $95 each way, a staff member will haul your gear, food, and water up for you.

Methow Valley Ski School & Rentals

42 Lost River Rd.; 509/996-3744; www.mvskischool.com; 9am-5pm daily; rentals $10-30/day, lessons $50-140/day

Methow Valley Ski School & Rentals has rented high-quality snowshoes and cross-country skis for over 45 years. Lessons range from 30 minutes to 2 hours, depending on how much instruction you need.

Winthrop Mountain Sports

257 Riverside Ave.; 509/996-2886; www.winthropmountainsports.com; 9:30am-6pm Mon.-Fri.,

9am-6pm Sat., 9am-5pm Sun.; rentals $19-39, lessons $70

Winthrop Mountain Sports provides everything you need for cross-country skiing, including skis, poles, boots, and bindings. They also have hiking poles and boots for purchase. Additionally, they give cross-country skiing lessons, both individually and in groups.

Food

Carlos1800 Mexican Grill and Cantina

149 Riverside Ave.; 509/996-2245; https://carlos1800. com; noon-9pm Thurs.-Sat., noon-8pm Sun. Mon., $18-29

Carlos1800 claims to have the best carne asada tacos and is a convenient place to get lunch or dinner in the middle of shopping on Riverside Avenue. In addition to enchiladas, burritos, and fajitas, they have a selection of Yucatecan cuisine as well pollo mole and panuchos made with slow-roasted pork.

★ Old Schoolhouse Brewery

155 Riverside Ave.; 509/996-3183; www. oldschoolhousebrewery.com; 3pm-8pm Mon. and Wed.-Thurs., noon-9pm Fri.-Sun.

No visit to Winthrop is complete without stopping at Old Schoolhouse Brewery, a local brewery housed in an old schoolhouse. It has a wide variety of beers on tap and a menu full of hearty pub food, including burgers, nachos, and hand-crafted pizzas. In the warmer months, the patio near the river attracts a large crowd, and in the evenings there is typically live music.

Rocking Horse Bakery

265 Riverside Ave.; 509/996-4241; www. rockinghorsebakery.com; 7am-2pm Wed.-Sun.

It's not uncommon to see a line forming outside Rocking Horse Bakery in the morning as locals and visitors alike eagerly wait for their daily fix of fresh cinnamon rolls and coffee. This famous bakery is a comforting start to many people's days, giving them a chance to fuel up before heading out to explore the town.

Three Fingered Jack's Saloon

176 Riverside Ave.; 509/996-2411; www.3fingeredjacks. com; 7am-11pm daily; $15-30

Established in 1891, Three Fingered Jack's Saloon boasts that it is Washington state's oldest legal saloon. The swinging door into the bar area adds to the establishment's genuine Wild West ambience. Many customers settle in with a drink to watch sports on TV. The restaurant side is family-friendly and has options including burgers, fries, and pizza.

Accommodations

Hotel Rio Vista

285 Riverside Ave.; 509/996-3535; https://hotelriovista. com; $189-224

Hotel Rio Vista has a prime downtown location with private riverside decks in each of its 29 rooms overlooking the Methow and Chewuch Rivers. Guests can unwind in a spacious hot tub at the end of the day.

★ Sun Mountain Lodge

604 Patterson Lake Rd.; 509/996-2211; www. sunmountainlodge.com; $210-330

Located atop Sun Mountain, Sun Mountain Lodge is the epitome of luxury lodgings, providing stunning views of the surrounding Methow Valley from its 112 guestrooms. Relax in the hot tubs after a day of sightseeing, or indulge in a spa treatment. Active guests can enjoy the mountain's wide trail system before retiring to one of the lodge's beautiful, rustic rooms.

Information

Winthrop Chamber of Commerce Visitor Center

202 Riverside Ave.; 509/996-2125; https:// winthropwashington.com; 10am-4pm daily

Stop by the visitor center to get advice on itinerary planning and pick up brochures, maps, or souvenirs.

Transportation

Winthrop is a destination that requires some planning to reach, as no public transportation is available to get here. In the summer months, the most straightforward route is via the North Cascades Highway, 14 mi (23 km) east of Mazama. However, this is closed during the winter, so visitors need to take US 2 to US 97, connect with Route 153, and take Route 20 into Winthrop.

TWISP

The small town of Twisp (9 mi/14 km south of Winthrop) may not have as many shops or restaurants as its larger neighbor, but it more than makes up for that with its thriving art scene. The abundance of art galleries, art walks, and live theater make this area a unique place to stop. It's also home to the famous Blue Star Coffee Roasters; people come to the town just to buy coffee beans.

Sights

TwispWorks

502 S. Glover St.; 509/997-3300; https://twispworks. org; 9am-4pm Mon.-Fri.; free

The US Forest Service originally bought TwispWorks, a 6.4-acre (2.6-ha) campus, for the management of forests and wildlife. Over the years, it grew into a community hub that includes the offices of local artists in addition to public events, workshops, and classes. The campus also hosts the Methow Valley Interpretive Center, where visitors can learn about the natural and cultural history of the area. In addition, many art studios are open on the weekend for tours.

The Confluence: Art In Twisp

104 S. Glover St.; 509/997-2787; www. confluencegallery.org; 10am-5pm Tues.-Sat.; free

The Confluence was established in 1988 and has since become an important cultural landmark in Twisp by displaying the work of Okanogan County artists in seven rotating exhibitions each year. In addition to perusing a well-appointed gallery, visitors can purchase items such as unique textiles, ceramics, jewelry, and more.

Hiking

Lookout Mountain Lookout

Distance: 2.6 mi (4.2 km) round-trip
Duration: 1.5 hours
Elevation gain: 1,100 ft (335 m)
Difficulty: strenuous
Trailhead: Lookout Mountain Lookout trailhead

This relatively short but steep trek passes through the unique ponderosa woods of northern Washington. Expansive vistas of the Methow and Okanogan Valleys and Hoodoo Peak to the west can be enjoyed as the moderate trail begins to gain elevation. This hike ends at an old 60-ft (18-m) lookout tower with 360-degree views, making the ascent worthwhile.

To get here from Twisp, turn off Route 20 onto W. 2nd Avenue and then onto Lookout Mountain Road for 5 mi (8 km) until reaching the trailhead.

Eagle Creek

Distance: 14.6 mi (23.5 km) round-trip
Duration: 10 hours
Elevation gain: 4,250 ft (1,295 m)
Difficulty: strenuous
Trailhead: on Forest Road 4420-080

Those looking for a longer hike will enjoy the Eagle Creek Trail, which leads to the less-traversed Lake Chelan-Sawtooth Wilderness. At 1.5 mi (2.4 km), a junction leads to Oval Creek Trail, but continue straight to go to Eagle Creek. At 5 mi (8 km), you come upon another detour that takes you to Silver Lake, but once again head straight to stay on Eagle Creek Trail. The 6-mi (9.7-km) mark reveals a meadow basin and subalpine trees, followed by a final stretch to a pass with views of Glacier Peak at 7,710 ft (2,350 m). Due to the long mileage, this is best enjoyed as an overnight backpacking trip in the backcountry.

To get here, drive west on Twisp River Road, join Forest Road 44 at 12.5 mi (20 km), continue for 1.5 mi (2.4 km), and take a left after the bridge past War Creek Campground. Turn left at Forest Road 4420, continue 0.5 mi (0.8 km), take a right on Forest Road

4420-080, and find the trailhead at the end of the road.

Food
Blue Star Coffee Roasters
1240 E. Methow Valley Hwy.; 509/997-2583; www. bluestarcoffeeroasters.com; 8am-2pm Mon.-Sat.
You can't stop in Twisp without visiting Blue Star, and some people come here for this sole purpose. It's won multiple awards for its coffee beans over the years, so make sure to grab a few bags to go. While waiting for your espresso drink, peek inside the glass doors next to the café to watch the huge vats the beans are roasted in.

Cinnamon Twisp Bakery
116 Glover St. N.; 509/997-5030; https:// cinnamontwispbakery.com; 7am-3pm Wed.-Mon.
Cinnamon Twisp Bakery has a fame similar to Blue Star's—people around the Methow Valley make the morning trek here to get their cinnamon twist pastry. The bakery also has a variety of freshly made bagels, breads, soups, sandwiches, and salads, as well as coffee drinks.

La Fonda Lopez
102 Methow Valley Hwy.; 509/997-0247; Facebook @lafondalopeztwisp; noon-8pm Mon.-Sat.; $15-22
La Fonda Lopez is the place to go when you have a craving for Mexican food, with a menu of enchiladas, nachos, and tamales, as well as nontraditional cuisine such as pasta and curry. This roadside restaurant has ample seating inside with local photography lining the walls and a covered outdoor area.

Tappi
201 S. Glover St.; 509/997-3345; Facebook @tappitwisp; 5pm-9pm Thurs.-Mon.; $10-20

Come to Tappi after a day of exploring to enjoy dishes like a Bolognese with house-made rigatoni and tomato and beef sauce or the Argentina pizza with mozzarella and oregano. The restaurant has a cozy feel, and you can watch your pizza cook in their wood-fired oven.

Accommodations
Twisp River Suites
140 Twisp Ave.; 855/784-8328; www.twispriversuites. com; $159-289
Twisp River Suites is only one block away from the downtown area, making it convenient to walk into town for dinner, or you can choose to make your meals in your fully equipped kitchen. Many of the 16 rooms have private porches overlooking the Twisp River and spa-grade baths, and breakfast is included.

Methow Suites Bed & Breakfast
620 Moody Ln.; 509/997-5970; https://methowsuites. com; $125
This two-bedroom bed-and-breakfast is a quiet, intimate place to stay, with private decks, a fire pit for roasting s'mores, and an extensive breakfast for guests each morning.

Information
Twisp Visitor Center
201 Route 20; 509/997-2020; www.twispwa.com; 9am-5pm Mon. Sat
Stop by the Twisp Visitor Center to get maps of the surrounding area and find out about local events and activities.

Transportation
To get to Twisp, head south from Winthrop for about 9 mi (14 km) via Route 20. From Chelan, take US 97 and Route 152 north for 52 mi (84 km), about an hour.

Lake Chelan

At 1,486 ft (453 m) deep, Lake Chelan is the third-deepest lake in the United States and a remarkable 51 mi (82 km) in length. Its turquoise waters surrounded by wild, rugged mountains make an alluring playground for outdoor adventurers. Boating, paddleboarding, and kayaking are popular pastimes, while some visitors just enjoy lounging on sandy beaches and floating in the shallow areas.

Yet the area isn't just for those interested in water sports; it's also a wine lover's paradise. Vineyards thrive in the unique environment that Lake Chelan provides, and the wines that result are both distinctive and of excellent quality.

CHELAN AND VICINITY

Scenic Drives

Manson Scenic Loop

Chelan's neighbor, Manson, has a beautiful 12-mi (19-km) scenic loop that takes you through wooded areas and along the lake, with spectacular panoramas and plenty of wineries along the way. From Manson, head west on Lakeshore Drive to Summit Boulevard, continue north to Loop Avenue, and then east to Wapato Lake Road and finally south on Swartout Road. The loop only takes about 30 minutes, but you'll want to extend your time in this area, as there are dozens of scenic places to stop along the way.

Chelan Butte

Climbing sharply into the highlands above Lake Chelan, Chelan Butte Lookout is another scenic drive that gives you views of the opposite side of the lake. From downtown Chelan, head south on US 97 Alt, take a left on S. Millard Street, and then continue on to Chelan Butte Road for 8 mi (13 km) until the road ends. There are multiple places to pull

off along the way, including Chelan Butte Hang Glider Takeoff and Chelan Butte State Wildlife Area.

Wine-Tasting

Grapes thrive in Lake Chean's climate because of the abundance of sunny days, chilly nights, and extended growing seasons. Some of the most well-known varietals from this area are Syrah, merlot, and chardonnay, but pinot gris and pinot noir are also grown here.

At most vineyards, reservations are highly recommended and often required during the busy summer months. But you may be able to walk in at some of the smaller vineyards. Note that many wineries are open seasonally, so check the hours if you visit during the winter or spring.

Vin du Lac

105 Route 150, Chelan; 509/682-2882; https://vindulac. com; noon-8pm daily; tasting $10
Vin du Lac is ideal for wine-tasting on a sunny day with its spacious outdoor patio overlooking the lake. They have a variety of red and white varietals, as well as a bistro for small bites.

Tsillan Cellars

38/5 US 97 Alt, Chelan; 509/682-9463; https:// tsillancellars.com; noon-8pm daily; tasting $10
With its 135 acres (55 ha) of vineyards and buildings made of Tuscan stone columns, Tsillan (pronounced "Chelan") Cellars gives the impression that you've entered Tuscany. A tasting room is available, but most people choose to combine wine with dinner in their restaurant overlooking the lake.

Benson Vineyards

754 Winesap Ave., Manson, 509/687-0313; https:// bensonvineyards.com; 11am-5pm daily; tasting $20
Benson Vineyards prides itself on being a 100 percent estate winery, meaning all wines are

---

1: Cinnamon Twisp Bakery 2: Chelan Riverwalk Park
3: Vin du Lac winery 4: Lakeview Drive In

made from grapes grown on-site, and the entire bottling process is done there. They often host live music in the evenings to enjoy alongside their wine-tastings.

Nefarious Cellars

495 S. Lakeshore Rd., Chelan; 509/682-9505; https://nefariouscellars.com; noon-5pm Fri.-Tues.; tasting $10

The family-friendly Nefarious Cellars has award-winning wine and a spacious lawn area where kids can get out their energy while parents relax with a glass of Syrah.

Hiking

Echo Ridge Trails

Echo Ridge is a network of 25 mi (40 km) of trails that can be used year-round, such as for cross-country skiing and snowshoeing in the winter and mountain biking, hiking, and horseback riding in the summer. It has everything from challenging trails to family-friendly strolls, all with great views of the lake below.

To get here from Chelan, drive west on Route 150 for 1.5 mi (2.5 km). After 9 mi (14 km), take a right onto Boyd Road and look for signs leading to the Echo Ridge Nordic Ski Area.

Chelan Riverwalk Park

Distance: 1 mi (1.6 km) round-trip
Duration: 30 minutes
Elevation gain: none
Difficulty: easy
Trailhead: 117 E. Wapato Ave., Chelan

The Chelan Riverwalk Loop, located in the heart of Chelan, is a great alternative to driving to farther hikes. Picnic places, fishing sites, and shaded benches are scattered along the wheelchair-accessible paved loop that winds near the Chelan River and some of Lake Chelan.

Boating

Thanks to its warm weather and miles of water, Lake Chelan is a popular destination for

a wide variety of water sports, including waterskiing, wakeboarding, kayaking, paddleboarding, fishing, and Jet Skiing. Many rental shops are available in the area, but you'll want to reserve your equipment in advance during the summer. You can hire a company to charter your boat or drive the boat yourself with a valid boater's education card.

Shoreline Watercraft & Boat Rental

407 W. Manson Hwy., Chelan; 509/682-1515; https://shorelinewatercraft.com; 7:30am-10pm daily; $155-695 boat, $75-380 Jet Ski

Shoreline offers boat, Jet Ski, and paddleboat rentals, and with five locations around town, it's easy to pick up water equipment.

LakeRider Sports

409 W. Manson Hwy., Chelan; 509/433-0463; https://lakeridersportschelan.com; 10am-5pm Wed.-Sun.; $40-150

LakeRider has single and double kayaks for rent, as well as stand-up paddleboards. They can also help with bike repairs, as well as ski and snowboard tuning and waxing during the winter months.

Biking

Devil's Backbone

At 11.7 mi (18.9 km) one-way and an elevation gain of 4,368 ft (1,331 m), Devil's Backbone is great for experienced bikers who want a challenge. But you can also take this trail to shorter routes, such as Story Mountain, 1.3 mi (2.1 km) into the course, or Angle Peak, 8.4 mi (13.5 km) into the route.

Chelan Electric Bikes

204 E. Wapato Ave., Chelan; 509/683-2125; https://chelanelectricbikes.com; 10:30am-4:30pm Sun.-Thurs., 10:30am-4:30pm Fri.-Sat.; $70-90

A fun way to see Chelan is through a bike tour, and Chelan Electric Bikes offers both a winery tour and one that goes on the trails in the mountains, depending on the biking experience you're looking for.

Water Parks

Slidewaters

102 Waterslide Dr., Chelan; 509/682-5751; www.
slidewaters.com; 10am-7pm Memorial Day-Labor Day;
$27-36

Slidewaters is great for kids of all ages, as they can cool off in the lazy river, go down one of the many waterslides, learn to surf, warm up in the hot tub, go to the tot-friendly spray park, or even play sand volleyball. It's only a few minutes from downtown Chelan.

Food

Local Myth Pizza

122 S. Emerson St., Chelan; 509/682-2911; https://
localmythpizza.com; 11:30am-8pm Tues.-Sat.; $13-22

Local Myth Pizza specializes in hand-rolled pizzas, calzones, fresh salads, and desserts. Enjoy a selection of local beers and wine with your meal on the bright red stools, or opt for take-and-bake pizzas if your lodging has a kitchen.

★ Lakeview Drive In

323 W. Manson Hwy., Chelan; 509/682-5322; www.
lakeviewdrivein.com; 11am-8pm daily spring and
summer; $6-12

Lakeview Drive In has been a Chelan landmark known for burgers, fries, and milkshakes since 1957, where people still order a bucket of fries with their famous Mack's Seasoning Salt. There's no indoor seating, so once you place your order, grab a picnic table outdoors and enjoy the lake views.

Tin Lilly

229 E. Woodin Ave., Chelan; 509/888-8101; www.
tinlillychelan.com; 11:30am-8pm Wed.-Sun.; $12-21

Doubling as both a stylish restaurant and a bar, Tin Lilly has a wide variety of options ranging from sandwiches to salads to steak. It also has an extensive liquor menu and TVs at the bar if you want to watch the game.

Fonda Oaxaqueña

127 E. Johnson Ave., Chelan; 509/888-9681; www.
fondaoaxaquena.com; 11am-8pm; $11-30

Fonda Oaxaqueña is the place to get authentic Mexican food, and this colorful restaurant specializes in southern Mexican dishes like mole and tlayuda, in addition to items such as enchiladas and fajitas.

Accommodations

★ Campbell's Resort

104 W. Woodin Ave., Chelan; 509/682-2561; https://
campbellsresort.com; $174-439

One of the most popular places to stay is Campbell's Resort, as there is over 1,800 ft (550 m) of private beach for guests to enjoy and it's conveniently located in the downtown area. All 170 rooms have a private balcony or patio to enjoy views of the lake.

Apple Inn Motel

1002 E. Woodin Ave., Chelan; 509/682-4044; https://
appleinnmotel.com; $89-119

This family-friendly motel provides an affordable place to stay while still being near many Chelan attractions. There are 41 rooms available and kitchen suites with an oven and stove for those looking to eat some meals in.

Lakeside Lodge & Suites

2312 W. Woodin Ave., Chelan; 509/682-4396; www.
lakesidelodgeandsuites.com; $159-209

Lakeside Lodge & Suites offers indoor and outdoor pools, hot tubs, and a complimentary breakfast. It's also one of the few hotels in the area that allows pets in its 93 rooms, and you'll have views of Lake Chelan from the balconies.

Information

Lake Chelan Visitor Center

216 E. Woodin Ave., Chelan; 509/682-3503; www.
lakechelan.com; 9am-5pm Mon.-Fri., 10pm-4pm
Sat.-Sun.

Stop by the visitor center to grab brochures on wine-tasting and outdoor activities and get maps of the area.

Transportation

Chelan is approximately 94 mi (150 km) from Winthrop, reached via US 97 Alt and Route 20. Chelan is about 180 mi (290 km) from

Seattle, and you can get there via I-90 and US 97 Alt or US 2 and US 97 Alt.

★ STEHEKIN

Located at the far northern end of Lake Chelan, Stehekin is one of the most remote towns you can visit in the North Cascades, accessible only by boat, floatplane, or rigorous hiking trails. Its remoteness is part of its allure, as it's about 50 mi (80 km) from the bustling areas of Chelan. From exploring the many hiking trails to viewing a cascading waterfall, it's hard not to reconnect with nature when you're here. With no cell phone service, many visitors find the isolation refreshing—a rare chance to unplug and unwind.

Sights

Golden West Visitor Center

509/699-2080; www.nps.gov; 11am-4pm daily

Golden West Visitor Center is a quick walk to the right of the ferry landing and offers plenty of exhibits on how Stehekin came to be, a short film, a small gift shop, and the chance to talk to rangers regarding your hiking plans.

McKellar Cabin

next to the post office at 31 Defacto Ln.; www.nps.gov

Visit McKellar Cabin to learn about the area's

past through its rustic 1930s log cabin, which belonged to an early settler. Take the short 15-minute loop past the cabin that passes by educational signs regarding the flora in the area, and end up at the post office.

Old Skehekin Schoolhouse

Stehekin Valley Rd., mile 3.4; www.nps.gov

The Old Stehekin Schoolhouse is a preserved one-room schoolhouse built in 1921 that served the Stehekin community until 1988. Among the antique furniture are the original desks and a chalkboard. Guests are welcome to visit the schoolhouse during the summer months when staff is on duty. Inside, you'll find a woodstove and a historic globe and maps that you are welcome to peruse.

Hiking

Rainbow Falls Mist Trail

Distance: *0.25 mi (0.4 km)*
Duration: *15 minutes*
Elevation gain: *30 ft (9 m)*
Difficulty: *easy*
Trailhead: *Rainbow Falls trailhead*

This easy trail takes you to a 312-ft (95-m) waterfall that sprays mist everywhere, as the name indicates. That means the trail can be slippery, particularly the steps up to the viewing platform.

remote village of Stehekin

Backpacking to Stehekin

CHELAN LAKESHORE TRAIL

If you want to reach Stehekin the long way, you can hike the 17-mi (27-km) **Chelan Lakeshore Trail** on the east side of Lake Chelan. You'll take the **Stehekin ferry** (17100 S. Lakeshore Rd., Chelan; 509/669-5045; https://stehekinferry.com; $39 adult, $20 child, under 3 free; daily May 6-Oct. 10, daily Oct. 16-Apr. 30 winter) from Field's Point or Chelan and request to be dropped off at Prince Creek. It is recommended to spend at least one or two nights camping on the trail, which reaches 4,030 ft (1,228 m) in elevation, on the way to Stehekin. Once you see the Golden West Visitor Center, you'll walk down the hill and be in Stehkein. You can return to where you started by reserving the Stehekin ferry for whichever morning you wish to leave.

CAMPING

Camping at **Cascade Creek** is popular since it provides a steady supply of water. **Moore Point Campground,** which is also a potential ferry drop-off location for those who prefer shorter hikes, is another great place to camp. These campsites are available first come, first-served, so it's a good idea to keep backup sites in mind.

Agnes Gorge Trail

Distance: 5.5 mi (8.9 km)
Duration: 2.5 hours
Elevation gain: 300 ft (90 m)
Difficulty: easy/moderate
Trailhead: Agnes Gorge trailhead from High Bridge

High Bridge is the last place the Stehekin shuttle stops before returning to the lake. Some people like to visit the bridge itself, where salmon can be seen during the late summer months, while others head out on the Agnes Gorge Trail. The Agnes Gorge Trail has stunning vistas of the gorge and 8,115-ft (2,473-m) Agnes Mountain, which dominates it. Hikers get their first glimpse of Agnes Gorge as they go through a forest that eventually opens onto a mountainside. Those hiking in the late summer or early fall might see huckleberries scattered throughout the slopes. Eventually you reach a river, perfect for a refreshing dip.

Biking

Stehekin has no traffic lights and limited car traffic, so biking is a fun option to explore the area. Stehekin Valley Road stretches 13 mi (21 km) from the ferry landing to a few miles past High Bridge. Bikes aren't allowed past Car Wash Falls, so they'll have to return at this point.

Discovery Bikes

1 Stehekin Valley Rd.; 509/6824584; https://stehekindiscoverybikes.com; 8am-5pm; $5-30

Discovery Bikes is a family-owned business that offers hourly and daily bike rentals. Their inventory includes comfortable cruiser-style mountain bikes, hard-tail mountain bikes, a variety of e-bikes, children's cycles, and child carriers.

Food
Stehekin Valley Ranch

9 Mile, Stehekin Valley Rd.; 509/682-4677; https://stehekinvalleyranch.com; 7am-9am, noon-1pm, 5:30pm-6:45pm daily; $26-32

At Stehekin Valley Ranch, diners sit at long wooden tables and are encouraged to talk to the other guests. Blueberry pancakes are on the breakfast menu, and there's daily dinner specials such as barbecue chicken and ribs. You'll need to make your reservation in advance by calling or stopping by in person.

Stehekin Pastry Co.

200 ft (60 m) SW of bakery; 509/682-7742; https://stehekinpastry.com; 7:30am-4pm daily May-Oct.; $3-16

The bakery is in a charming, rustic building that's a welcome relief to PCT hikers craving one of their legendary giant cinnamon rolls on the way into Stehekin for an overnight stay. There's also a variety of pastries, quiches, sandwiches, and a full espresso bar that you can enjoy indoors or outside at their picnic tables.

Accommodations
North Cascades Lodge at Stehekin

1 Stehekin Valley Rd.; 855/685-4167; https:// lodgeatstehekin.com; $254-309

North Cascades Lodge at Stehekin is in a picturesque setting right next to the ferry dock overlooking the lake. It has a variety of lodging options, including 27 standard rooms in the lodge as well as cabins with kitchens. There's a restaurant on-site that's open seasonally and serves breakfast, lunch, and dinner, as well as the General Store at the Lodge, which sells prepackaged snacks, meals, and souvenirs.

Purple Point Campground

0.3 mi (0.5 km) south of Stehekin Landing; 509/699-2080; www.recreation.gov; $20

The paved road leading to Purple Point Campground is only eight minutes away from the pier at Stehekin Landing. This small, shaded campground has six campsites, each with a picnic table and fire pit. The campground has drinking water, restrooms with flush toilets, and trash cans, but campers are asked to pack out their own trash if possible.

Transportation

Getting here requires some planning, and reservations are required for the ferries, which are the most common way to visit Stehekin.

Ferry

The **Lady of the Lake ferry** (1418 W. Woodin Ave., Chelan; 509/682-4584; https:// ladyofthelake.com; $25-43 one-way) leaves from downtown Chelan and has multiple options: a leisurely 4-hour ride with multiple stops around the lake, and several express

ferries that take 1.5-2.5 hours from Chelan to Stehekin.

Your best option for a day trip here is to catch the 8am **Lady Liberty ferry** from downtown Chelan, arrive in Stehekin at 9:30am, and get the last ferry of the day that leaves Stehekin at 3:30pm and returns to Chelan at 5pm. This allows six full hours to explore the town.

The other option is to take the **Stehekin Ferry** (Field's Point Landing, 17100 S. Lakeshore Rd., Chelan; 509/669-5045; https:// stehekinferry.com; $20-39) from Field's Point Landing on the west side of the lake, a 2.5-hour ride. One ferry per day leaves at 1pm and arrives at Stehekin at 2:45pm, and the return ferry the next day leaves Stehekin at 10:40am and arrives back at Field's Point Landing at 12:25pm.

While the ferries run throughout the year and some accommodations stay open in the winter, it's important to note that the majority of the food options close from late fall until spring, so late spring through mid-fall are ideal times to visit Stehekin to experience the full range of what it has.

Field's Point Landing has a large parking lot next to the ferry dock ($7/night, $35/week). Parking at the Chelan ferry dock is free for the day in front of the company's office. If you stay overnight, you'll park in a fenced lot across from the pier ($11/day, $66/week).

Stehekin Shuttle

Stehekin Landing; 888/682-4584; https://stehekin.com; weekends Apr.-June, daily July-Sept., first bus 8am, last bus 2:45pm; $5-10

The Stehekin Shuttle is the easiest way to get around without hiking for miles. It starts at Stehekin Landing, makes several stops in between, such as the Stehekin Pastry Company, Stehekin Valley Ranch, and Rainbow Falls, and ends at High Bridge, before going back the way it came. Reservations, which can be made online, are highly recommended during the summer months. Once you get dropped off, ask the shuttle driver when the next bus is coming so you can plan accordingly.

Leavenworth

As travelers wind through the mountainous terrain, they are often struck with awe when a quaint town reminiscent of Germany suddenly appears. This is Leavenworth, famous for its Bavarian-style architecture and alpine setting—features strategically developed in the early 1960s to rejuvenate a declining local economy once reliant on the Great Northern Railway and timber industries.

Today Leavenworth's tourism-centric initiatives have made it a year-round destination. Winter draws crowds for skiing and snowboarding, while the warmer seasons offer outdoor activities such as hiking, rock climbing, and water sports like white-water rafting and tubing. Additionally, the town hosts a variety of seasonal festivals, most notably the annual Christmas Lighting Festival in December and Oktoberfest in the fall. Due to the high demand during these times, booking hotel accommodations months in advance and making restaurant reservations to avoid long waits is highly recommended.

SIGHTS
Leavenworth Reindeer Farm
10395 Chumstick Hwy.; 509/885-3021; www.leavenworthreindeer.com; 10am-4pm Fri.-Mon.; $25-40
Just a mile (1.6 km) from downtown Leavenworth is the Leavenworth Reindeer Farm, a unique chance to get inside the reindeer enclosure and even feed them. Tours are required to visit, and the holidays bring themed ones, such as the *Frozen* characters visiting or Santa coming for Christmas in July.

Leavenworth Nutcracker Museum
735 Front St.; 509/548-4573; www.nutcrackermuseum.com; 11am-5pm daily; $5
Nutcrackers are everywhere in this Bavarian town, and the Nutcracker Museum lets you view over 9,000 nutcrackers from 50 different countries in one spot. Visit the gift shop afterward to purchase your own nutcracker to take home.

Waterfront Park
adjacent to 347 Division St.; https://cityofleavenworth.com; 6am-10pm daily
After grabbing coffee from a local shop, enjoy strolling the flat, paved trails of Waterfront Park along the Wenatchee River, just down the hill from the town's center. Summer is a common time to walk and spot wildlife, but snowshoers also come here during the snowy months.

★ BAVARIAN BEER GARDENS
Bavaria is known for is its beer gardens, and Leavenworth made sure to have numerous ones in town to make it feel like an authentic German experience. With a handful to choose from, each with a Bavarian theme, it's easy to spend a few hours here in the afternoon.

Sausage Garten
636 Front St.; 509/888-4959; www.viscontis.com; 11am-8pm Sun.-Thurs., 11am-9pm Fri.-Sat.; $8-13
This outdoor restaurant serves up bratwurst, currywurst, and even vegetarian sausage, making it ideal for a fast bite to eat. To complete the meal, have a German beer and German potato salad. It's one of the smaller beer gardens, but it has a covered area with long tables where you can overlook Front Street and people-watch.

München Haus
709 Front St.; 509/548-1158; www.munchenhaus.com; 11am-9pm Mon.-Thurs., 11am-10pm Fri.-Sun.; $8-11
To feel like you're in a Bavarian beer garden, step inside the München Haus. It has a range of Bavarian sausages cooked over an open grill and also serves German and Northwest brews, along with local wines. Place your order at the outdoor counter, and then find your seat at

Leavenworth

0   100 yds

0   100 m

CEDAR ST

BURKE AVENUE

To Leavenworth Reindeer Farm and Osprey Rafting

BIRCH ST

LEAVENWORTH RANGER STATION ℹ

12TH ST

CENTRAL AVE

PRICE AVE

SUMMIT AVE

ASH ST

FRONT ST

EVANS ST

LEAVENWORTH CHAMBER OF COMMERCE & VISITOR CENTER ℹ

WHITMAN ST

FRONT ST

DIVISION ST

COMMERCIAL ST

10TH ST

COMMERCIAL ST

THE TAFFY SHOP ■

9TH ST

BAVARIAN LODGE

SOUTH ■

KRIS KRINGL ■

EDELWEISS WEG

Front Street Park

THE ■ BUBBLERY

RHEIN HAUS ▼

ANDREAS KELLER ▼

2

FRONT ST

MOUNTAIN MODERN SUPPLY

To Icicle Village Resort and Icicle Creek Trailhead

▼ SAUSAGE GARTEN

★ LEAVENWORTH NUTCRACKER MUSEUM

8TH ST

9TH ST

THE DANISH BAKERY ▼

MÜNCHEN HAUS ▼

CASCADE MEDICAL ■

MAIN ST

Waterfront Park

To Sleeping Lady Resort

Waterfront Park

Blackbird Island

Trout Unlimited Park

© MOON.COM

one of the many large tables outside that are partially shaded by the nearby buildings.

Rhein Haus

707 US 2, Unit F; 509/642-6615; www.rhleavenworth. com; 11am-7:30pm Sun.-Thurs., 11am-9:30pm Fri.-Sat.; $15-36

Rhein Haus is the largest beer garden in town and is great for groups. The spacious outdoor area has umbrella-covered tables, plus there's seating indoors. It's also pet-friendly if you like bringing your well-behaved dog to a beer garden.

FESTIVALS AND EVENTS

Maifest

Front St.; https://leavenworth.org/maifest; mid-May; free

Experience authentic Bavarian culture at the two-week-long Maifest celebration. Music of the Alps features AlpenFolk's traditional yodeling and the iconic sounds of the Leavenworth Alphorns. There's also plenty of Maipole dancing, grand marches in traditional attire, and various Bavarian music, from accordion to polka.

Oktoberfest

Front St.; https://leavenworth.org/oktoberfest; first three weekends in Oct.; $10-20

The most lively Oktoberfest in the state takes place in Leavenworth, with thousands of people trying out German food and beer all weekend. You can participate in unique events like pretzel tossing and stein-holding contests, dress up in traditional German attire, and listen to live Bavarian music.

Winter Karneval

Front St.; https://leavenworth.org/winterkarneval; weekends in Jan.; free

The party isn't over in Leavenworth once the New Year comes—they keep the holiday lights on all January during Winter Karneval. You'll also see a fireworks display and ice carvings, and be able to participate in winter snow sports nearby.

SHOPPING

Mountain Modern Supply

827 Front St.; 509/548-4858; Facebook @MountainModernSupply; 9:30am-7pm Mon.-Thurs., 9:30am-9pm Fri.-Sat., 9am-9pm Sun.

Mountain Modern Supply is the perfect place to buy a Pacific Northwest-themed gift, whether you're looking for a Washington hiking sweatshirt or prefer a Leavenworth coffee mug. The store has an assortment of hats, clothing, bags, home decor, and much more, most with a picture or phrase related to Washington proudly on it.

The Bubblery

220 9th St., Suite K; 509/548-4591; www.thebubblery. com; 11am-4pm Sun.-Tues., 10am-5pm Wed.-Thurs., 10am-6pm Fri.-Sat.

The Bubblery's clean skincare products include moisturizing body oil, soothing bath salts or bath bombs, and shampoo bars. All products are made with only natural ingredients, and the helpful staff is happy to match the right products for your skin's needs.

The Taffy Shop

900 Front St.; 509/548-4857; www. leavenworthtaffyshop.com; 11am-5pm daily

Satisfy your sweet tooth at The Taffy Shop, where you can grab a paper bag and fill it with dozens of different handmade taffies. They specialize in candy from decades ago, so you may find your old favorites in their collection.

Kris Kringl

907 Front St.; 509/548-6867; www.kriskringl.com; 10am-6pm daily

It's Christmas every day at Kris Kringl, which carries hundreds of different holiday items, including Christmas villages, ornaments, figurines, and more.

RECREATION
Hiking

Leavenworth is surrounded by prime mountain hiking. Stop at the **Leavenworth Ranger Station** (600 Sherbourne St.; 509/548-2550; 8am-4:30pm Mon.-Fri.) to get

Skiing Stevens Pass

Stevens Pass

Skiers and snowboarders flock to **Stevens Pass** (93001 US 2, Skykomish; 206/812-7844; www. stevenspass.com; 9am-4pm Sun.-Thurs., 9am-10pm Fri.-Sat.; tickets $79-139, lessons $129-159), only 40 minutes west of Leavenworth, for its 1,100 acres (445 ha) of groomed slopes. The resort offers excellent conditions for winter sports enthusiasts, with an average annual snowfall of 460 in. This mountain has everything from easy green runs to advanced black diamonds and even terrain parks for freestylers and snowboarders. A day lodge serving food and beverages, ski and snowboard rentals, and lessons for skiers and snowboarders of all ages and abilities are available.

In the summer, Stevens Pass becomes a mountain bike paradise. The chairlift takes riders up the mountain, and they navigate down the hill. **Stevens Pass Bike Park** has trails ranging from easy flow trails to more challenging downhill courses, so there's something for everyone.

ideas for which trails to go on and check hiking conditions in the area.

Icicle Creek

Distance: *3.2 mi (5.1 km) round-trip*
Duration: *1.5 hours*
Elevation gain: *258 ft (79 m)*
Difficulty: *easy*
Trailhead: *Icicle Creek*

This short, flat trail goes through the forest alongside Icicle Creek, leading to a meeting point with French Creek, where two campsites are available. Watch for horses, who share the path here. It leads to beautiful views of the creek for only a small amount of effort, and the end makes for a relaxing place to rest while listening to the babbling creek.

Head west on US 2, take a left on Icicle Road, and drive for 2 mi (3 km), continuing onto Icicle Creek Road for an additional 6.5 mi (10.5 km). Go straight on Forest Road 7600 for just over 8 mi (13 km) and find the trailhead at the end of the road.

Colchuck Lake

Distance: *8 mi round-trip*
Duration: *4.5 hours*
Elevation gain: *2,280 ft (695 m)*
Difficulty: *strenuous*
Trailhead: *Stuart Lake*

1: Leavenworth Nutcracker Museum 2: German beer at Sausage Garten 3: The Taffy Shop 4: The Danish Bakery

One of the most sought-after overnight hikes in Leavenworth is Colchuck Lake, which is part of The Enchantments, a 36-mi (58-km) round-trip strenuous hike through some of the most beautiful parts of the Cascades. You can only camp in this area by winning a lottery (which takes place in February), so most people settle for doing a day hike to Colchuck Lake.

The Colchuck Lake Trail takes hikers across a log bridge at Mountaineer Creek and through a forest on a mixture of flat and steep terrain. After making the final ascent, you're rewarded with a view of the beautiful Colchuck Lake, framed by Dragontail and Colchuck Peaks. People often go to the lake for a swim or a picnic and then head back.

From Leavenworth, turn left from US 2 onto Icicle Creek Road and drive 8.4 mi (13.5 km); turn left onto Forest Road 7601 and follow the uneven 3.7-mi (6-km) road to the parking lot. The road is closed November-May.

★ Rafting and Floating

Rafting season in Leavenworth typically begins in the spring and continues through late summer, depending on water levels. Most people head to the Wenatchee River for its variety of Class II and III rapids, which allow beginners and experienced rafters to enjoy it. Guided rafting tours are generally recommended, as local guides know essential factors such as how to read the water speed, where the turns are, and safety.

In May and June the water tends to be at its highest, due to the melting snow from the nearby mountains, and late summer is ideal for those who want calmer waters.

Floating can be done independently, or companies also rent floats and drop you off at calmer points on the Wenatchee or Icicle River then meet you at the pick-up point. This is the easier option unless you have two cars available for the drop-off and pick-up points.

Leavenworth Outdoor Center
997 Main St.; 509/548-8823; https:// leavenworthoutdoorcenter.com; July-Labor Day; $25-38

The **Icicle River** is a calm, easy-to-navigate river ideal for a laid-back trip for beginners or families. The water tends to be more relaxed with no rapids, so many people go tubing here or on a gentle rafting tour.

Alpine Adventures
201 Riverside Dr., Cashmere; 360/863-6505; https:// alpineadventures.com/wenatchee-river-whitewater-rafting; Apr.-Aug.; $94/person

If you prefer the thrill of white-water rapids, the **Wenatchee River** is the place to go. At the state's most popular white-water rafting spot, you'll work with others to paddle the raft down the river as your guide navigates you through the waves.

Osprey Rafting
10576 US 2; 509/548-6800; https://ospreyrafting.com; $30-60/person

Osprey Rafting offers various trips, including a 3.5-hour trip through the rapids early in the season and a more gentle family rafting session later in the summer. They also have a short floating trip available from Happy Wave Beach.

Blue Sky Outfitters
201 Riverside Dr., Cashmere; 800/228-7238; www. blueskyoutfitters.com, May-July; $85-105/person

Join the Wenatchee Express for a thrilling, 3-hour ride down the Wenatchee River through Class III rapids. If traveling with a group, you might want to book their private rafting option for a unique experience.

FOOD
Andreas Keller
829 Front St.; 509/548-6000; www. andreaskellerrestaurant.com; 11:30am-8pm Sun.-Thurs., 11:30am-9pm Fri., 11:30am-9:30pm Sat.; $11-30

Andreas Keller is one of the most popular

1: Wenatchee River 2: downtown Leavenworth

restaurants in the town, with its German decor, frequent live music, and a wide range of authentic food on the menu. Choose from bratwurst, schnitzel, spätzle, and more.

South

913 Front St.; 509/888-4328; https://southrestaurants. com; 11am-9pm Sun.-Thurs., 11am-10pm Fri.-Sat.; $11-30

South has a modern take on Latin American fare and prides itself on its homemade salsa that compliments its food. Grab a seat outside in the back to feel like you're eating in a private garden.

The Danish Bakery

731 Front St.; 509/548-7514; 9am-5pm Mon.-Thurs., 9am-8pm Fri.-Sat., 9am-6pm Sun.; $2-10

You'll notice the line out the door at The Danish Bakery right when it opens, and for good reason. They have fresh, warm European pastries, including strudels, danishes, and pretzels, plus coffee options. Take your pastry to go and find a seat on a bench around town.

ACCOMMODATIONS

Bavarian Lodge

810 US 2; 888/717-7878; https://bavarianlodge.com; $178-263

The Bavarian Lodge is one of the most convenient places to stay, with its 90 rooms right across from the main part of town. It has a beautiful Bavarian-style facade, free breakfast, and the rustic Woodsman Pub on-site for drinks and food.

Sleeping Lady Resort

7375 Icicle Rd.; 509/548-6344; www.sleepinglady.com; $208-255

Sleeping Lady Resort lets you relax and recharge, only 10 minutes from town. It's on a quiet, wooded property where you'll enjoy staying in one of the 58 modern cabin rooms and have access to their spa, restaurant, pool, hot tub, bar, and game room.

INFORMATION AND SERVICES

Leavenworth Chamber of Commerce & Visitor Center

940 US 2, Suite B; 509/548-5807; https://leavenworth. org; 9am-6pm daily

Stop by the visitor center to pick up brochures about local tours and get maps of the area.

Cascade Medical

817 Commercial St.; 509/548-5815; https:// cascademedical.org

Cascade Medical is conveniently located in downtown Leavenworth and has a 24-hour emergency department and a family practice clinic.

TRANSPORTATION

It takes a little over 2 hours from Seattle to Leavenworth via US 2 through Stevens Pass, or you can get here from I-90, US 97, and then US 2. If you don't have a car, an **Amtrak** (303 S. Jackson St., Seattle; www.amtrak.com/ stations/sea; from $41) train from King Street Station in Seattle takes about 3.5 hours to arrive in Leavenworth.

Wenatchee

Located on the Columbia River, Wenatchee is more than just a stop on the way to or from other destinations in the state. The city is known as the "Apple Capital of the World," and it's become a haven for outdoor enthusiasts who've discovered the abundance of trails for hiking and mountains for skiing that surround the city.

If you're a fan of beer, you'll love Wenatchee. The city's breweries have gained notoriety for their extensive beer and food menus. Much more than a pit stop, the city has many parks and an active brewery scene that make it well worth exploring.

SIGHTS
Ohme Gardens

3327 Ohme Rd.; 509/662-5785; www.ohmegardens. org; 9am-6pm Apr.-Oct.; $8

In 1929 the Ohme family began renovating a rocky outcrop with a view of the Cascade Mountains into a beautiful garden. It was originally the family's private oasis, but the locals convinced them to open up their property to the public. Visitors can now stroll through the stunning gardens, which feature a number of waterfalls and ponds.

Wenatchee Valley Museum and Cultural Center

127 S. Mission St.; 509/888-6240; www. wenatcheevalleymuseum.org; 10am-4pm Tues.-Sat.; $5

From 11,500-year-old relics to the first trans-Pacific airplane that landed in 1931, the Wenatchee Valley Museum provides a comprehensive look at the history of the mid-Columbia Valley. In the children's section, Coyote's Corner, kids can enjoy imaginative play and hands-on learning, while adults can learn about the historic Great Northern Railway through a reproduction of the raiload.

Rocky Reach Dam

5000 US 97 Alt; 509/663-7522; www.chelanpud.org; 9:30am-5pm Tues.-Sun.; free

One of the first places you'll pass on the drive down from Chelan is Rocky Reach Dam, which is worth a stop for a close-up view of the dam and to learn from dozens of different

Columbia River

The Apple Capital of the World

Wenatchee welcome sign

Wenatchee has earned the title "Apple Capital of the World" for its significant contributions to the international apple market. Apples of all shapes and sizes, including red delicious, golden delicious, gala, Fuji, and Honeycrisp, thrive in the region's perfect combination of rich volcanic soil, ample Columbia River water, and a climate characterized by chilly winters and warm summers. Due mainly to this fertile region, Washington state is now the United States' preeminent apple grower. The Wenatchee Valley Museum and other local institutions have extensive displays devoted to the business sector.

The **Wenatchee State Apple Blossom Festival** (www.appleblossom.org; spring) is only one of many celebrations held annually in the area to pay tribute to the fruit and its cultural significance.

STEMILT RETAIL STORE

3615 US 97 Alt; 509/663-7848; www.stemilt.com; 9am-6pm daily
The Stemilt Retail Store is a convenient place to pick up fresh apples, cherries, pears, and other locally grown fruits without having to go to the orchards. They also claim to serve the city's largest scoops of ice cream.

STUTZMAN RANCH

2226 Easy St.; 509/667-1664; www.thestutzmanranch.com; 9am-3:30pm daily June-Sept.; $5 min. for U-pick
Pick your own fruit at Stutzman Ranch, where they have everything from cherries in the spring to pears, apples, and grapes in the late summer. Their website lists exactly what fruit is in season and when, as well as when they run out, so it's best to check before planning your visit.

displays inside its interactive museum. There's also a café available with small bites.

RECREATION
Hiking
Sage Hills
Distance: 5.5 mi (8.9 km) round-trip
Duration: 2.5 hours
Elevation gain: 650 ft (200 m)
Difficulty: easy/moderate
Trailhead: Sage Hills Gateway Trail trailhead

Adjacent to the popular Horse Lake Reserve, Sage Hills has trails for hiking, horseback riding, and mountain biking with panoramic views of the Columbia River, Wenatchee Valley, and North Cascades. Spring is the most colorful time to visit, as the hills explode with vibrant wildflowers like Indian paintbrush, sage, arrowleaf balsamroot, and purple lupine. This is part of a network of trails, so you can make the hike as short or long as you want.

To access Sage Hills via the Gateway Trail, drive uphill on 5th Street, veering left onto Number One Canyon Road after 0.7 mi (1.1 km). Continue for 0.4 mi (0.6 km) to a small gravel pullout that fits 7-8 cars, then walk 0.2 mi (0.3 km) north to the trail. If the lot is full, park in the designated areas on 5th Street, east of N. Surry Avenue, and walk to the trailhead.

Skiing
Mission Ridge
7500 Mission Ridge Rd.; 509/663-6543; www.missionridge.com; 10am-4pm Sat.-Sun.; $43-97

Mission Ridge Ski Resort is a winter sports paradise with 36 unique runs, four lifts, and a reputation for dry snow and plenty of sunshine. Skiers of all skill levels can enjoy the varying difficulty levels on the runs, and ski rentals and lessons are available. Its proximity to downtown Wenatchee makes it an easy day trip.

BREWERIES
Wenatchee has developed into a hub for innovative craft brewing. Its breweries produce a diverse range of beers, from hop-forward IPAs to heavy stouts, by making use of locally accessible ingredients and regional flavors like apple-infused ales or seasonal fresh-hop beers.

Wenatchee Valley Brewing Co.
108 E. Island View St.; 509/881-4529; www.wenatcheevalleybrewing.com; 11:30am-9pm Sun.-Thurs., 11:30am-10pm Fri.-Sat.

Wenatchee Valley Brewing Co. has over a dozen beers on tap at any given time and also a full food menu. They make use of their large patio space that's both dog- and kid-friendly.

Badger Mountain Brewing
1 Orondo Ave.; 509/888-2234; Facebook (@badgermountainbrewing) 3pm-9pm Mon.-Fri., 11:30am-10pm Sat.-Sun.

With over 20 different taps, including their own beer, guest beers, and cider, Badger Mountain Brewing is the largest craft brewery in Wenatchee. It has a cozy indoor space with events like trivia throughout the week.

Saddle Rock Pub & Brewery
25 N. Wenatchee Ave.; 509/888-4790; www.saddlerockbrewery.com; 11am-9pm Mon.-Thurs., 11am-10pm Fri.-Sat.

Saddle Rock Pub & Brewery has a dozen beers and ciders on tap as well as local wine and bottled beer. They also pride themselves on the homemade dough for their pizzas.

The Taproom by Hellbent Brewing
7 N. Worthen St., Suite W8; 509/888-4528; https://taproomby.hellbentbrewingcompany.com; 11am-9pm daily

The Taproom by Hellbent Brewing is located inside Pybus Public Market. It has 20 different beers and ciders on tap, as well as a large wine list and full bar. With a full menu, it's an ideal place to grab a bite to eat after shopping at the market.

FOOD
McGlinn's Public House
111 Orondo Ave.; 509/663-9073; www.mcglinns.com; 11am-10pm Mon.-Fri.; 8am-10pm Sat.-Sun.; $11-32

McGlinn's Public House is housed in a historic building from 1922 and has a scenic

outdoor patio to enjoy during the dry months. They have a variety of pizzas, burgers, and salads that they source locally.

Visconti's Italian Restaurant

1737 N. Wenatchee Ave.; 509/662-5013; www.viscontis. com; 3pm-9pm Sun.-Thurs., 3pm-10pm Fri.-Sat.; $14-28

Visconti's Italian Restaurant is the place to go for an authentic Italian dining experience, with plenty of delicious pasta and antipasti options. It has a cozy ambience, perfect for dinner or happy hour.

Pybus Public Market

3 N. Worthen St.; 509/888-3900; https://pybuspublicmarket.org, 8am-10pm daily

Pybus Public Market is similar to an indoor farmer's market. You can find specialty shops like Mike's Meats for high-quality meats and The Cheesemonger's Store for artisanal cheeses. There are a few restaurants there as well, such as Fire (509/888-4347; www.viscontis.com; 11am-9pm daily), known for its gourmet wood-fired pizzas, and Ice (509/888-4423; www.viscontis.com; 9am-9pm Thurs.-Tues., 11am-9pm Wed.), which serves crepes, ice cream, and espresso. Other local businesses here include a taproom and a coffee shop.

ACCOMMODATIONS

Coast Wenatchee Center Hotel

201 N. Wenatchee Ave.; 509/662-1234; www. coasthotels.com; $113-263

The Coast Wenatchee Center Hotel may be known as a business hotel, but it's an affordable and convenient spot for any visitor—right on the Columbia River and within walking distance of downtown. They offer 147 comfortable rooms and suites with living rooms for those who need more space.

Avid Hotel Wenatchee

1640 N. Wenatchee Ave.; 509/663-8115; www.ihg.com; $97-105

The Avid Hotel Wenatchee provides free breakfast, has a 24-hour store for any last-minute needs, and allows dogs for an additional fee in its modern, sleek hotel. You'll have a comfortable sleep in one of its 95 rooms with sound-reducing headboards and high-quality mattresses.

TRANSPORTATION

Wenatchee is only 23 mi (37 km) east of Leavenworth via US 2 to Route 285. From Seattle, Wenatchee is about 2.5 hours by taking I-90 to Route 970 and US 97.

Mount Baker Highway

Mount Baker is a prominent landmark in Washington state, rising to a height of 10,781 ft (3,286 m) and providing spectacular views across much of the Puget Sound area on a clear day. The mountain is a year-round mecca for adventurers, presenting world-class skiing and snowboarding in the winter and extensive hiking paths with alpine lakes and lush forests in the summer.

Visitors should be aware that few services are available along the Mount Baker Highway, with only a handful of small towns present.

1: Wenatchee Valley Brewing Co. 2: Pybus Public Market

Driving Mount Baker Highway

Start: Bellingham
End: Artist Point
Driving Distance: 57 mi (92 km) one-way
Driving Time: 1.5 hours one-way

Mount Baker Highway, also known as Route 542, is a scenic route that starts in Bellingham and ends at Artist Point on Mount Baker. The drive passes through many small towns and offers opportunities to pull over for hikes or waterfalls. While the road remains open throughout the year, the area gets heavy winter snow, and chains are required November 1-April 1.

Mount Baker Highway

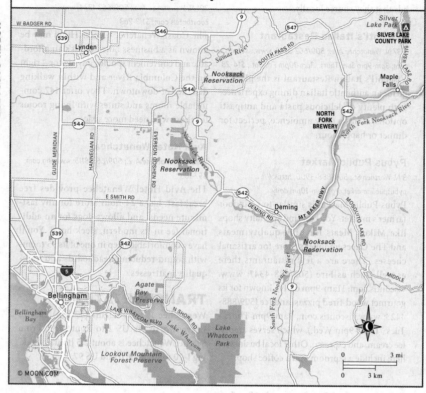

W BADGER RD

9

547

Silver
Lake Park

SILVER LAKE
COUNTY PARK

546

539

Lynden

SOUTH PASS RD

Sumas River

Maple
Falls

544

9

Nooksack
Reservation

NORTH
FORK
BREWERY

542

544

GUIDE MERIDIAN

HANNEGAN RD

EVERSON GOSHEN RD

Nooksack River

Nooksack
Reservation

North Fork Nooksack River

E SMITH RD

542

539

542

Agate
Bay
Preserve

Bellingham

Bellingham
Bay

LAKE WHATCOM BLVD

N SHORE RD

Lake Whatcom

Lookout Mountain
Forest Preserve

DEMING RD

Deming

MT BAKER HWY

Nooksack
Reservation

MOSQUITO LAKE RD

MIDDLE

South Fork Nooksack River

Lake
Whatcom
Park

© MOON.COM

0   3 mi

0   3 km

Bellingham to Glacier

The drive from Bellingham to Glacier takes about 50 minutes (36 mi/58 km), starting in the city and gradually transitioning into farmland and then the mountains as you ascend the Mount Baker Highway. Following the course of the Nooksack River, you enter the Mount Baker-Snoqualmie National Forest, where the scenery becomes even more striking with dense forests, towering evergreens, and glimpses of the snowcapped peaks of the Cascade Range.

As you approach Glacier, the elevation begins to rise, and the air becomes cooler and crisper. The road winds more as you enter the foothills of Mount Baker, and on clear days you might catch your first glimpses

of Mount Baker's majestic snow-covered summit.

Glacier to Mount Baker

The drive from Glacier to the top of Mount Baker at Artist Point takes about 50 minutes (24 mi/39 km). As you leave Glacier behind, the road climbs steadily, with increasingly dramatic scenery unfolding with each mile. The dense forests start to thin out, revealing more expansive mountain views as you wind your way up the mountain. The route includes several scenic pullouts where you can stop to take in stunning vistas of the surrounding mountains and valleys. Near the final stretch, the road passes by the Mt. Baker Ski Area, a popular winter destination.

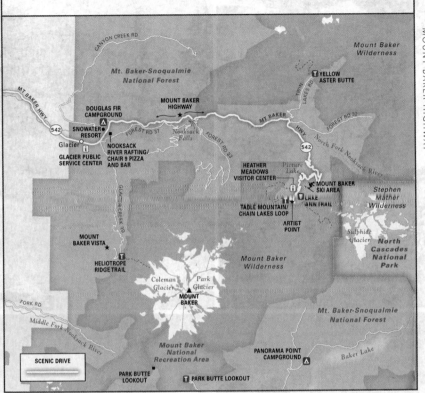

The drive ends at Artist Point, offering incredible views of Mount Shuksan and the North Cascades.

Mount Baker

Mount Baker is a popular spot for thrill-seekers all year round due to the abundance of outdoor activities it offers. Winter sports enthusiasts go to Mt. Baker Ski Area for skiing and snowboarding, and snowshoers go to Artist Point. In the summer, Artist Point is a popular meeting place for hikers and a junction for several other trails. Hikers can choose from easy strolls such as Picture Lake or more strenuous routes to landmarks like Park Butte Lookout.

SIGHTS
Mount Baker Vista

One of the first major stops along the Mount Baker Highway is Mount Baker Vista, which has one of the best views of the mountain. To get here, drive 1 mi (1.6 km) east of the Glacier Public Service Center and turn onto Glacier Creek Road/Forest Road 39. The gravel road heads south for approximately 9 mi (14 km) and ends in the parking lot for Mount Baker Vista.

Nooksack Falls

Continue traveling for 16 mi (26 km) and you'll come upon Nooksack Falls, a stunning waterfall. Take Wells Creek Road off the

Mount Baker Highway, and continue on the gravel road for 1 mi (1.6 km). The observation deck is a short walk from the parking lot. In the spring, as the snow on Mount Baker melts and runs into the river below, the river creates a beautiful waterfall. Unfortunately, the falls have taken lives in the past, so a barrier is there as a caution to visitors to be careful, yet it doesn't take away from the majesty of the falls.

Those looking to stretch their legs further can head out on the nearby Heliotrope Ridge Trail, providing even closer mountain views.

Picture Lake

Picture Lake is a brief but well-visited stop due to its tranquil waters that produce a mirror-like reflection that's particularly beautiful at sunrise and sunset. A flat, paved loop trail (0.5 mi/0.8 km) circles the lake 3 mi (5 km) north of Artist Point, providing several vantage points for it and Mount Baker. The region is particularly colorful in the summer with a profusion of wildflowers, and the autumn season is enhanced by beautiful foliage. Visitors will find plenty of parking along the loop road. Picture Lake is 14 mi (23 km) east of Nooksack Falls on Mount Baker Highway.

Artist Point

Continue on Mount Baker Highway for 3 mi (5 km) to its end at Artist Point. This area is the crowning jewel at the end of the Mount Baker Highway, the grand finale of a scenic drive. Situated at an elevation of approximately 5,100 ft (1,550 m), this viewpoint has panoramic vistas of Mount Baker, Mount Shuksan, and the surrounding Cascade Range.

In the summer, hikers can set out from Artist Point and access routes that lead through subalpine woods, pass fields of wildflowers, and give up-close views of glaciers. There are trails for every level of hiker, from short, family-friendly loops to longer, more challenging routes. Autumn is also a popular

season due to the abundance of vibrant red and yellow leaves.

The first snowfall often occurs in October, closing the route to Artist Point until the snow melts in July. In winter, the only way to reach the area is by snowshoeing or skiing the final 2.7 mi (4.3 km) of the Mount Baker Highway to Artist Point parking lot.

HIKING

The diversity of Mount Baker's routes more than makes up for the mountain's shorter hiking season (late spring-early fall). Hikers will find a variety of trails, from beginner hikes that go past glistening alpine lakes to strenuous ascents rewarded with astonishing views. Parking at most trailheads requires a Northwest Forest Pass ($5/day or $30/year), which gives pass holders access to all national forest land in both Washington and Oregon. Purchase it online (www.discovernw.org/annual-northwest-forest-pass) or at the Glacier Public Service Center (10091 Mount Baker Hwy., Glacier; 360/599-9572).

Heliotrope Ridge Trail

Distance: 5.5 mi (8.9 km)
Duration: 3 hours
Elevation gain: 1,400 ft (425 m)
Difficulty: moderate
Trailhead: Heliotrope Ridge trailhead

Hikers can enjoy gradual ascents on this well-kept trail while going under a canopy of tall trees and across bridged rivers, occasionally catching glimpses of Mount Baker. During the summer, the trail is carpeted with wildflowers; in the fall, you'll have a chance to pick ripe huckleberries.

After 2 mi (3.2 km), you come across a campsite that was once Kulshan Cabin, which the Mount Baker Club built in 1925. Just after that, you come to a fork; take a left to stay on the Heliotrope Ridge Trail. Be careful and use hiking poles as you approach Heliotrope Creek, the most substantial water crossing on the hike.

On the other side of Heliotrope Creek, a short meadow walk leads to Heliotrope Ridge, adjacent to the Coleman Glacier's

---

1: Nooksack Falls 2: Artist Point 3: Mount Baker Highway

lateral moraine. Here, you'll be rewarded with close-up views of the glacier and Mount Baker towering above. Remember to stay on the trail and avoid venturing onto the glacier, tempting as it may be. When you're done resting, head back the way you came.

From Glacier, turn right on Glacier Creek Road/Forest Road 39 and continue for 8 mi (13 km). Take a left on Forest Road 39, and you'll see the trailhead on your left in 0.3 mi (0.5 km).

Yellow Aster Butte

Distance: 7.5 mi (12.1 km) round-trip
Duration: 3.5 hours
Elevation gain: 2,550 ft (777 m)
Difficulty: moderate
Trailhead: 12 mi (19 km) east of Glacier Public Service Center off Mount Baker Highway, go left on Twin Lakes Road (Forest Road 2065) for 4.5 mi (7 km) to the parking area

The Yellow Aster Butte trail is popular for its sweeping wildflower meadows and vibrant fall colors. The trail gains 1,500 ft (457 m) in less than 1.5 mi (2.4 km), eventually opening up to meadows rich in flora like Indian paintbrush and lupine. Views include Mount Baker and Larrabee, as well as peaks in Canada. The trail splits 1.5 mi (2.4 km) in, with the left path continuing to Yellow Aster Butte and the right taking a detour to Tomyhoi Lake. The hike flattens out for about 2 mi (3 km) before reaching an unsigned junction; head right for either camping or summiting Yellow Aster Butte.

Lake Ann Trail

Distance: 8.2 mi (13.2 km) round-trip
Duration: 4.5 hours
Elevation gain: 2,150 ft (655 m)
Difficulty: moderate/strenuous
Trailhead: Mount Baker Highway, 1 mi (1.6 km) east of Artist Point

Starting just below Artist Point from a paved lot, the Lake Ann Trail descends through a subalpine forest and opens up into an alpine basin. The route traverses rocky, root-filled terrains, boulder fields, and meadows, offering intermittent views of Mount Baker and

Mount Shuksan. The trail culminates at a saddle overlooking Lake Ann, set against the stunning backdrop of Mount Shuksan's west face. Camping is restricted to areas 2 mi (3 km) from the trailhead May 15-November 14. Late-season hiking is advised, as snow can persist into August.

Table Mountain

Distance: 2.6 mi (4.2 km) round-trip
Duration: 1.5 hours
Elevation gain: 725 ft (220 m)
Difficulty: moderate
Trailhead: Artist Point (end of Mount Baker Highway)

The trail starts as a gravel path, features an early switchback, and winds through unique rock formations before quickly ascending toward Table Mountain. Heather Meadows can be seen from a side trail after a 400-ft (122-m) ascent, and several forks off the main route lead to different vantage spots along the tabletop. At 1.2 mi (1.9 km) in, Mount Baker and Ptarmigan Ridge become visible, and at 1.3 mi (2 km) are two small tarns with clear Mount Shuksan views. Due to its steep and hazardous terrain, a trek up Table Mountain isn't advisable for young children or pets.

Chain Lakes Loop

Distance: 6.5 mi (10.5 km) round-trip
Duration: 3.5 hours
Elevation gain: 1,820 ft (555 m)
Difficulty: moderate
Trailhead: Artist Point parking lot (end of Mount Baker Highway) or Austin Pass/Heather Meadows, between mileposts 55 and 56 near Heather Meadows Visitor Center

There are multiple starting points for this loop hike. Austin Pass offers a less-crowded alternative to Artist Point, usually with more parking available. Most people hike the loop counterclockwise to get one of the hardest parts out of the way first. After a steep initial descent via the Wild Goose Trail, the trail leads hikers past multiple lakes and up

---

1: Yellow Aster Butte 2: Wake 'N Bakery 3: Mount Baker

to Herman Saddle, with panoramic views of Mount Baker, Mount Shuksan, and other peaks in the North Cascades. After the saddle, walk through meadows to reach Hayes and Iceberg Lakes, with optional detours for swimming or resting. The final stretch loops back to the starting point, offering more stunning vistas along the way.

RIVER RAFTING

The Nooksack River, which originates from Mount Shuksan and Mount Baker, is popular for river rafting. Once the snow melts, the river levels rise, making late spring and early summer prime rafting months. The Nooksack features rapids from Class I to Class IV, making it suitable for both novice and expert rafters. Self-guided rafting is possible for expert paddlers, but excursions are recommended for people who are beginners or unfamiliar with the river.

Nooksack River Rafting

*509/668-7238; https://riverrider.com/nooksack_river.
php; 9am and 1pm daily, June-Aug.; $65-95*

Nooksack River Rafting is an ideal way for beginners to experience rafting. The 9-mi (14-km) ride includes navigating a steep gorge combined with more relaxed stretches. Groups meet at Chair 9 Pizza and Restaurant (10459 Mount Baker Hwy., Glacier).

SKIING

In the summer, hikers swarm to the Mount Baker region to take advantage of the trails, but the peak also draws a sizable number of winter visitors, thanks to the mountain's reputation for consistently falling snow. Skiers and snowboarders from all over the world visit for its steep slopes and deep snow.

Mt. Baker Ski Area

milepost 52 for White Salmon entry, milepost 55 for Heather Meadows entry, Mount Baker Hwy., Deming; 360/734-6771; www.mtbaker.us; White Salmon 9am-3:30pm daily, Heather Meadows 9:30am-3:30pm Sat.-Sun., Nov.-Apr.; $38-91/day

Mt. Baker Ski Area is a must-visit destination for skiing enthusiasts, offering some of the best and most consistent snowfall in the Pacific Northwest. Approximately 24 percent of the runs are designated as beginner, 45 percent as intermediate, and 31 percent as advanced or expert. The ski area features eight quad chairs and two handle tows, plus multiple day lodges with dining options, a bar, a ski school, and ski and snowboard gear rentals. However, overnight lodging is not available.

White Salmon and Heather Meadows are the two ski areas within Mt. Baker. The White Salmon section offers a variety of runs for intermediate and advanced skiers, as well as steep inclines and tree runs. Heather Meadows is more ideal for beginners. Groomed slopes, moguls, and open bowls make up the varied terrain that caters to skiers and snowboarders of all abilities. Exact opening dates vary annually based on the amount of snowfall received.

Rentals
Glacier Ski Shop

9966 Mount Baker Hwy., Glacier; 360/599-1943; www.glacierskishop.com; 8am-5pm Mon.-Fri., 7:30am-5:30pm Sat.-Sun.

This rental shop is conveniently located on the way to Mount Baker. The standard package for both skis and snowboards starts at $49/day, with premium packages at $59, and cross-country skis, snowshoes, and backcountry kits are also available. Their Facebook page (@glacierskishop) provides the most current opening days and hours, which vary each year depending on snow.

FESTIVALS AND EVENTS

Set against the backdrop of one of Washington's most recognizable mountains, the festivals held at Mount Baker are almost as well-known as the mountain's legendary skiing and draw locals and tourists alike.

Legendary Banked Slalom

Mt. Baker Ski Area, Mount Baker Hwy., Deming; https://lbs.mtbaker.us; mid-Feb.; free to spectate

Since 1985, Mt. Baker has hosted the

Legendary Banked Slalom, a renowned yearly snowboarding competition that takes place over three days every February. This is regarded as the forerunner to boardercross and has crowned some renowned snowboarders. Initially having only 19 finishers, the competition has grown and now hosts about 385 racers each day, including amateurs, professionals, and skiers from other countries.

Raven's Edge Dual Slalom

Mt. Baker Ski Area, Mount Baker Hwy., Deming; www. mtbaker.us/the-mountain/upcoming-events/ravens-edge; mid-Apr.; free to spectate, $25 to participate

The Komo Kulshan Ski Club's long-running dual slalom race is an annual tradition that takes place over two days and serves as a competitive gathering as well as a fundraiser. The event is open to all ages and levels of skiing experience and raises money for the club's mission of giving disadvantaged children the chance to go skiing. Participants can choose from skiing, snowboarding, or telemarking.

Mt. Baker Film Fest

104 N. Commercial St., Bellingham; www.mtbaker.us/ the-mountain/upcoming-events/film-fest; Oct.; $10

The Mt. Baker Film Fest has served as a platform for independent filmmakers to showcase their ski and snowboard films to the community since 1999. Held at the historic Mount Baker Theatre, this one-night event features two showings of top films from previous seasons in the Mt. Baker Ski Area.

FOOD

Food is somewhat limited on the Mount Baker Highway, with a few options available along the way, including in small towns like Deming and Glacier. It's best to bring food with you if driving past these towns, as no amenities are available east of Glacier.

North Fork Brewery

6186 Mt. Baker Hwy., Deming; 360/599-2337; www. northforkbrewery.com; 3pm-8pm Thurs.-Mon.; $7-23

North Fork Brewery serves up local beer alongside customizable pizzas. Specializing

in British ales, barrel-aged Belgian-style sours, and lagers, the brewery offers a diverse drink menu. Food options extend beyond pizza to include salads, grinders, and more. During warmer months, visitors can enjoy an outdoor beer garden.

Chair 9 Pizza and Bar

10459 Mount Baker Hwy., Glacier; 360/599-2511; www.chair9.com; noon-close Mon.-Thurs., 11am-close Fri.-Sun.; $10-23

This family-friendly restaurant has a large selection of pizzas, steaks, burgers, and more, as well as a bar for those looking to enjoy apres-ski. It has a fun, casual vibe—an old chair lift sitting outside the entrance, old lining the walls inside, and people excitedly talking about their day's adventures.

Wake 'N Bakery

6903 Bourne St., Glacier; 360/599-1658; www. wakenbakeryglacier.com; 7am-5pm daily summer and winter, 7am-2pm daily fall and spring; $5-15

Wake 'n Bakery has an espresso bar featuring certified organic and fair-trade coffee, plus a variety of breakfast and lunch options, including muffins, scones, breakfast burritos, sandwiches, and soups. It's housed in a large wooden house where you'll find seating, but most people choose one of the many lawn chairs on the covered porch or around the lawn.

ACCOMMODATIONS

Lodging is scattered along the Mount Baker Highway, so consider where you want to spend the most time before picking accommodations. Glacier is a convenient place to stay, whether you're hiking around Mount Baker or skiing it.

Mt. Baker Lodging

7425 Mount Baker Hwy., Maple Falls; 800/709-7669; https://mtbakerlodging.com; $375-1,100

Almost 90 privately owned, self-catered vacation homes in the area are available for rent from Mt. Baker Lodging. The choices range from large cabins that can accommodate groups to condos perfect for couples. In addition, many of the properties welcome pets.

Snowater Resort

10500 Mount Baker Hwy., Deming; 360/599-2724; www.snowater.org; $189-260

A 20-acre (8-ha) forest surrounds the gated enclave of 174 apartments known as the Snowater Condominiums. These are privately owned units and timeshares, many of which have private decks with views of the river or mountains. The complex's two heated indoor swimming pools, two Jacuzzis, a sauna, a fitness center, and several sports courts are accessible through the property's three connected buildings.

CAMPING

Silver Lake County Park

9006 Silver Lake Rd., Maple Falls; 360/778-5850; www.whatcomcounty.us; mid-Apr.-Oct.; $30-72

Silver Lake Park provides three separate campgrounds—Maple Creek Campground (48 sites), Red Mountain Campground (55 sites), and Cedar Campground (15 sites)—as well as a range of activities like boating, fishing, and boat rentals. Cedar Campground is tents only, while the other two are RV-friendly and include water and electricity hookups. Reservations are strongly recommended. The park office rents out a variety of watercraft, including rowboats, canoes, two-seat kayaks, pedal boats, and stand-up paddleboards, during the summer months. Boat rentals start at $20 for 2 hours, and half-day and full-day rentals are available.

Douglas Fir Campground

2 mi (3 km) east of Glacier on Mount Baker Hwy.; 360/386-8214; www.recreation.gov; May-Sept.; $30-32

The 29 standard campsites at Douglas Fir Campground can accommodate both tents and RVs. Many sites are in different forest areas, while others are along riverbanks. A Civilian Conservation Crew-built historical picnic area can also be reserved. Vault toilets, drinking water, and individual sites with picnic tables, fire rings, and tent pads are available. You'll want to make a reservation in advance, especially for the summer months.

INFORMATION

Glacier Public Service Center

10091 Mount Baker Hwy., Glacier; 360/599-9572; www.fs.usda.gov; 9am-3pm Sat.-Sun. spring and fall, 8am-4:30pm daily summer

Outdoors, the Glacier Public Service Center provides visitors with 24-hour self-service information, restrooms, picnic tables, and seasonal access to staffed ranger services. Books, maps, and passes to federal parks and other recreational areas are also available for sale when the center is staffed.

Heather Meadows Visitor Center

Mount Baker Hwy., milepost 56, Deming; www.fs.usda.gov; 10am-4pm daily mid-July-late Sept.

Originally built as a ski warming hut in 1940, the visitor center now serves as a place to inquire about trail conditions and nearby places to visit from staffed rangers who are available seasonally.

TRANSPORTATION

Mount Baker Highway (Route 542) serves as the sole access point to the Mount Baker area. From Bellingham, the drive takes approximately 1.5 hours (57 mi/90 km); those coming from Seattle can expect a 2.5-hour drive (130 mi/210 km). From Seattle, take I-5 north for 89 mi (143 km) to exit 255 for Route 542/E. Sunset Drive. Follow Route 542/Route 9, which turns into Mount Baker Highway. Route 542 is only 1 mi (1.6 km) northeast of downtown Bellingham.

Baker Bus

https://bakerbus.org; Nov.-Apr.; $20/person

For those who would rather not drive, the Baker Bus provides transportation from Bellingham to the Mt. Baker Ski Resort. The service is only available on weekends and holidays during the ski season, and it's a great method to get to the slopes. The schedule and pick-up locations occasionally change, so check their website for the most updated information.

Mount Rainier

As the largest glaciated summit in the contiguous United States and the headwaters of five significant rivers, the majestic 14,410-ft (4,392-m) active stratovolcano known as Mount Rainier stands tall and proud in Mount Rainier National Park, one of the most popular tourist attractions in the state. Ancient forests cover the lower slopes, and subalpine meadows with wildflowers surround the icy volcano, making it a photographer's dream. Parts of the mountain are open throughout the year, meaning visitors can explore this beauty in all seasons.

On clear days in Seattle, magnificent Mount Rainier is an iconic part of the city's skyline. When its snowy peak is visible, locals often

Highlights

Look for ★ to find recommended sights, activities, dining, and lodging.

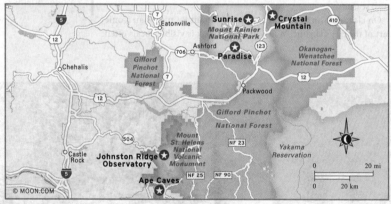

★ **Paradise Area, Mount Rainier National Park:** The Paradise area is ideal for hiking, especially on the Skyline Trail to witness the seasonal wildflowers that pop up (page 354).

★ **Sunrise Area, Mount Rainier National Park:** Visit the highest point in the park accessible by car for hikes, such as the trek to the Mount Fremont fire lookout at sunrise or sunset (page 358).

★ **Crystal Mountain:** Enjoy skiing and snowboarding in the winter and hiking in the summer on this massive mountain (page 360).

★ **Johnston Ridge Observatory:** This observatory has stunning views of the Mount St. Helens blast zone, plus educational exhibits (page 371).

★ **Ape Caves:** Go underground and explore one of the longest lava tubes in North America near Mount St. Helens (page 372).

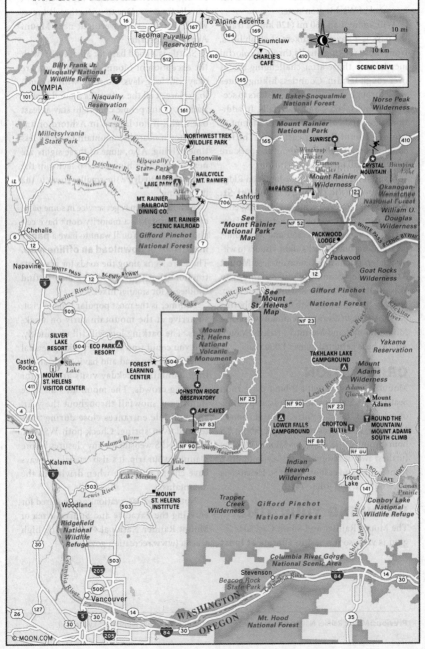

Mount Rainier

To Alpine Ascents

Tacoma
Puyallup Reservation

Enumclaw

CHARLIE'S CAFÉ

SCENIC DRIVE

Billy Frank Jr. Nisqually National Wildlife Refuge

OLYMPIA

Nisqually Reservation

Mt. Baker-Snoqualmie National Forest

Norse Peak Wilderness

Mount Rainier National Park

SUNRISE

Winthrop Glacier

Emmons Glacier

CRYSTAL MOUNTAIN

Bumping Lake

Millersylvania State Park

Deschutes River

NORTHWEST TREK WILDLIFE PARK

Eatonville

Mount Rainier Wilderness

PARADISE

Okanogan-Wenatchee National Forest

William O. Douglas Wilderness

Skookumchuck River

Nisqually State Park

ALDER LAKE PARK

RAILCYCLE MT. RAINIER

Ashford

Alder Lake

See "Mount Rainier National Park" Map

NF 52

WHITE PASS SCENIC BYWAY

Chehalis

MT. RAINIER RAILROAD DINING CO.

MT. RAINIER SCENIC RAILROAD

Gifford Pinchot National Forest

PACKWOOD LODGE

Packwood

Goat Rocks Wilderness

Napavine

WHITE PASS SCENIC BYWAY

Cowlitz River

Riffe Lake

Cowlitz River

See "Mount St. Helens" Map

NF 23

Gifford Pinchot National Forest

Klickitat River

SILVER LAKE RESORT

ECO PARK RESORT

Mount St. Helens National Volcanic Monument

FOREST LEARNING CENTER

JOHNSTON RIDGE OBSERVATORY

TAKHLAKH LAKE CAMPGROUND

Yakama Reservation

Mount Adams Wilderness

Adams Glacier

Mount Adams

Castle Rock

Silver Lake

MOUNT ST. HELENS VISITOR CENTER

Lewis River

NF 25

APE CAVES

NF 83

NF 90

LOWER FALLS CAMPGROUND

NF 23

CROFTON BUTTE

NF 88

ROUND THE MOUNTAIN/ MOUNT ADAMS SOUTH CLIMB

NF 60

Kalama River

Kalama

Swift Reservoir

Yale Lake

Lake Merwin

Indian Heaven Wilderness

Trout Lake

TROUT LAKE HWY

Camas Prairie

Lewis River

MOUNT ST. HELENS INSTITUTE

Trapper Creek Wilderness

Gifford Pinchot National Forest

Conboy Lake National Wildlife Refuge

Woodland

Ridgefield National Wildlife Refuge

White Salmon River

Columbia River Gorge National Scenic Area

Stevenson

Beacon Rock State Park

Columbia River

Vancouver

WASHINGTON
OREGON

Mt. Hood National Forest

© MOON.COM

0   10 mi
0   10 km

N

remark "the mountain is out today" as a way of talking about the weather, and it's become a symbol of Washington state.

With more than 260 mi (420 km) of trails, the park is a haven for hikers of all abilities, from those seeking strolls through colorful meadows to those after challenging routes over rough terrain. Countless hiking routes wind through the park, taking visitors to scenic overlooks, lakes, and waterfalls. In addition, thousands of mountaineers attempt to summit Mount Rainier each year. The few campsites scattered throughout the park are perfect but fill up quickly.

South of the mountain, the Johnston Ridge Observatory tells the story of **Mount St. Helens** and its 1980 eruption, offering educational insights into volcanic activity and unsurpassed views of the crater and lava dome. Surrounding hiking paths allow visitors to witness the eruption's devastation up close. **Mount Adams,** the second-highest mountain in Washington state and located further southeast, tends to be less crowded than its neighboring peaks. Although it's an active stratovolcano like Mount Rainier and Mount St. Helens, Mount Adams hasn't erupted in over 1,000 years.

ORIENTATION

Mount Rainier is about a 2-hour drive from Seattle via I-5 and various roads, depending on which of the four entrances you choose. Mount St. Helens is south of there, about 3.5 hours from Seattle via I-5 and Route 504. The furthest away is Mount Adams, a 4-hour drive from Seattle and east of Mount St. Helens, via I-5, Route 14, and Route 141.

PLANNING YOUR TIME

The Mount Rainier and South Cascades region is vast, so it's best to allocate **at least one day to explore each major part,** as Mount Rainier and Mount St. Helens will be full-day trips. Due to its further distance, you'll want to stay overnight near Mount Adams if exploring.

Seattle is a good base for all of these (with the exception of Mount Adams) if you are okay with long days. However, with so much to explore at all the entrances around Mount Rainier, many people choose to stay at least one night, if not longer, in Ashford or another town near the mountain to spend less time driving. Also, none of these sights are next to the main highways, so factor in the time it takes to drive the smaller roads to the mountains.

Although you may get service in some parts of the mountains, a majority don't have cell phone coverage. You'll want to have a **paper map** handy or **download an offline map.** There are signs along the roads for major attractions, but you will need a map to find trailheads for smaller hikes.

Summer is the most popular time to visit, so arrive at the mountain early on weekends. The parking lots will fill up quickly, and you could find yourself parking several miles down the road and having to walk up the mountain. Weekday visits are best for avoiding crowds. The mountains all have significant snowfall throughout the year, and multiple entrances close during winter and even spring. Check both WSDOT and the NPS website for any closures before planning your trip. It's also crucial to always have chains with you when driving in the mountains.

Note: Timed reservations are required for entering the Paradise and Sunrise Area of Mount Rainier National Park during high season (www.recreation.gov).

Previous: Mount Rainier National Park; Mount St. Helens sign; Myrtle Falls along the Skyline Trail.

Itinerary Ideas

This itinerary is ideal for a weekend at Mount Rainier—spend the first day exploring Longmire and Paradise and the second day at Sunrise.

DAY 1

1 Begin your day at Longmire by stocking up on snacks at the **Longmire General Store** and exploring the nearby **Longmire Museum** to learn about the park's history.

2 Walk the **Trail of the Shadows,** an easy hike looping around Longmire, and then head to the stunning **Christine Falls** a short drive away.

3 For lunch, stop at the **Paradise Inn Dining Room** and visit the **Henry M. Jackson Visitor Center** to talk to rangers about hiking conditions or get recommendations.

4 Spend the afternoon hiking the scenic **Nisqually Vista Trail** or the more challenging **Skyline Trail.** Afterward, drive down to **Reflection Lakes** to see mirror-like reflections of Mount Rainier.

5 Leave the park for dinner at **Rainier BaseCamp Bar & Grill** and stay overnight at **Paradise Village Hotel.**

DAY 2

1 After breakfast at the **Paradise Village Restaurant,** drive to the **Sunrise area,** on the opposite side from Paradise.

2 Hike the **Sunrise Nature Trail** or the **Sourdough Ridge Trail,** both of which have opportunities to spot wildlife.

3 For lunch, head to the **Sunrise Day Lodge** to enjoy a casual meal and fill up your water bottles.

4 In the afternoon, explore the **Berkeley Park Trail** or the **Mount Fremont Lookout** for more adventurous hiking options.

5 Exit the park and have dinner at **The Mint.** Then either return to Seattle or stay in Enumclaw at **GuestHouse Enumclaw.**

Park Information

ENTRANCES

Nisqually, Stevens Canyon, and White River are the three main entrances to Mount Rainier National Park. The **Nisqually Entrance,** located in the southwestern part of the park, is open year-round and gives visitors access to Paradise and Longmire. The **White River Entrance,** which is in the northern part of the park and is usually open late June-early October, provides access to the Sunrise area. You can access the Ohanapecosh area and Stevens Canyon Road via the **Stevens Canyon Entrance** in the southeast, which is usually open late spring-early fall.

Located in the park's northwest corner,

Mount Rainier National Park

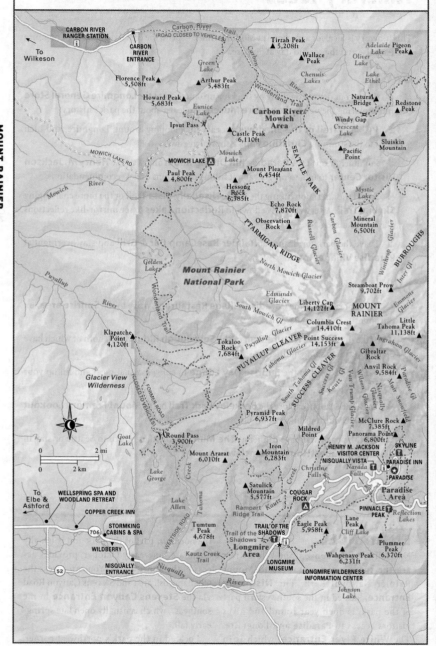

the Carbon River Entrance lea bike and
pedestrian only gateway that leads to the

Mt. Baker - Snoqualmie National Forest

Scarface
6,108ft
Lake
Eleanor

Slide Mountain
6,339ft

White River

410

SOURDOUGH MOUNTAINS

Marcus
Peak
6,962ft

Brown Peak
6,322ft

CRYSTAL
MOUNTAIN

Skyscraper
Mountain
7,078ft

Forest
Lake

SUNRISE
NATURE TRAIL
SOURDOUGH
RIDGE

SUNRISE RIDGE

Clover
Lake

Pacific Crest National Scenic Trail

MATHER MEMORIAL PARKWAY

MOUNT FREMONT
LOOKOUT

BERKELEY PARK

Sunrise
Area

Dege Peak
7,008ft

WHITE RIVER
ENTRANCE/
WILDERNESS
INFORMATION
CENTER

MOUNTAIN

SUNRISE

SUNRISE DAY LODGE

SUNRISE VISITOR
CENTER

Shadow
Lake

Crystal
Lake

Placer
Lake

410

Baker
Point

WHITE
RIVER

White River

410

American River

Deadwood
Lakes

MATHER MEMORIAL PARKWAY

GOAT ISLAND MOUNTAIN

NACHES PEAK LOOP

SHEEP LAKE AND
SOURDOUGH GAP

Chinook Pass
5,432ft

Dewey
Lake

Wenatchee
National
Forest

Fryingpan
Glacier

Sarvant Glaciers

Tamanos
Mountain
6,790ft

GOVERNORS RIDGE

Owyhigh
Lakes

Ghost
Lake

Cayuse
Pass
4,694ft

Swamp
Lake

Panhandle
Gap
6,800ft

Barrier
Peak
6,514ft

Whitman Glacier

Wonderland Trail

Mount Rainier
National Park

123

Seymour Peak
6,337ft

Pacific Crest National Scenic Trail

American
Lake

Cougar
Lake

Double Peak
6,199ft

Ohanapecosh River

Shriner
Peak
5,834ft

Cowlitz
Glacier

Cowlitz Rocks
7,450ft

COWLITZ DIVIDE

Chinook Creek

SHRINER
PEAK

Fan Lake

Bald Rock
5,411ft

Crag
Lake

STEVENS

Marsh
Lakes

CANYON

Grove of the
Patriarchs
Trail

Three
Lakes

Carlton Creek

Bench Lake

Snow
Lake

Stevens
Peak
6,510ft

ROAD

Muddy Fork Cowlitz River

GROVE OF THE
PATRIARCHS

Ohanapecosh
Area

STEVENS CANYON
ENTRANCE

OHANAPECOSH
VISITOR CENTER

SILVER FALLS

OHANAPECOSH
CAMPGROUND

Blue
Lake

Jug
Lake

Gifford Pinchot
National Forest

Ohanapecosh River

123

To
Packwood

© MOON.COM

the **Carbon River Entrance** is a biker and pedestrian-only gateway that leads to the peaceful Carbon River and Mowich Lake. There is a small parking area here where visitors can leave their vehicles before heading by foot or bike into the area.

AREAS

Mount Rainier National Park is divided into five main areas: **Longmire** in the southwest, **Paradise** in the south, **Sunrise** in the northeast, **Ohanapecosh** in the southeast, and **Carbon River/Mowich** in the northwest.

When all roads are open in the summer, you can access the entrances to all regions of Mount Rainier National Park in a big loop. However, it does take awhile to go into each section, exit, and then return to the main road.

Longmire

With its museum, historic inn, and multiple trails, the park's southwest historic area, Longmire, provides year-round attractions.

Paradise

Spectacular wildflower meadows and heavy snowfall make Paradise ideal for sports like hiking and snowshoeing.

Sunrise

With stunning panoramic views and an extensive network of trails through alpine environments, Sunrise is the highest point reachable by vehicle.

Ohanapecosh

Ohanapecosh is known for its serene Ohanapecosh River and old-growth forests; it has a more moderate climate and sights like the Grove of the Patriarchs.

Carbon River/Mowich

The temperate rain forest setting of Carbon River/Mowich in the northwest creates verdant pathways and beautiful scenery.

FEES AND RESERVATIONS

Mount Rainier National Park's entrances are typically staffed during daylight hours, but staffing may extend earlier or later depending on the day. Visitors planning to enter the park outside these hours should either purchase a pass online (www.recreation.gov) in advance or stop at the ranger booth to buy one as they exit the park. The entry fee is $30/vehicle, $15/person on on foot or bike, and $25/motorcycle, and the pass is valid for seven consecutive days.

Mount Rainier National Park has witnessed a 40 percent surge in tourists since 2014, leading to congestion and ecological damage. As a reponse, the park implemented a trial **timed admission reservation system** in 2024 to reduce crowding, wait times, and the damage that overcrowding does to trails. Timed entrance reservations are required for entering the Paradise area 7am-3pm **late May-early September.** The Sunrise area requires timed admission reservations 7am-3pm **early July-early September.** Outside these dates, no reservations are required. The reservation period also does not apply to those who enter before 7am or after 3pm. A timed admission reservation is not necessary for pedestrians and bikers. Reservations can be made on recreation. gov up to three months in advance. A vehicle or motorcycle reservation costs $2. Visitors can enter within a 2-hour window of their entry time and can reenter later with no extra fee. Tickets are likely to sell out in advance, so your best bet is to be online and ready to go as soon as the first block of entries are released 90 days in advance. If tickets are sold out for you desired date, additional entries are released at 7pm the night before.

SEASONS AND WEATHER

In most areas of the park, **spring** still has snow, which doesn't tend to melt until July, but you'll have warmer temperatures than

Winter in the Park

Although many roads in Mount Rainier shut down as soon as the first snowfall starts in October or November and don't reopen until May or June, the Paradise area welcomes the snow and remains open throughout the year. In fact, it gets more snow than any other recorded area on earth—an average of 643 in (16.3 m) per year. Visitors should check the NPS website for any current closures before heading out.

There are a few things to keep in mind when visiting during the winter:

- **Road Closures:** Paradise Road, the road from Longmore to Paradise, is only open on the weekends during the winter, and it shuts down entirely if conditions are too poor. You can check for any closures on the road status page on the NPS website. It's also recommended to look at the webcams to see what conditions are like. The gate to this road closes every night, so you'll need to be past it before 5pm.

winter at Mount Rainier

- **Tire Chains:** All drivers are required to carry tire chains and show proof of them in the vehicle November 1-May 1, regardless of what kind of car you have or the day's weather conditions. If you don't have your own chains, Whittaker Mountaineering (30027 Route 706 E., Ashford; 360/569-2142; https://whittakermountaineering.com) has tire chains available to rent.

- **Ranger Check-In:** Always check with a ranger first at the Longmire Information Center or Jackson Visitor Center to find out about any avalanche hazards in the region or areas you should avoid while winter hiking, snowshoeing, or skiing. Rangers can also check that you have the proper winter gear.

the winter. The park sees its highest volume of visitors during **summer** (70-90°F/21-32°C) between the end of June and the beginning of September, when temperatures rise and most trails, roads, and facilities are open to the public. Cooler temperatures and vibrant foliage are hallmarks of **fall** (50-60°F/10-16°C). As the months pass, precipitation increases and temperatures drop, with the first snowfall often seen in October.

Cold temperatures, particularly at higher elevations, can dip below freezing during **winter,** and snow closes most of the park. Sunrise Park Road is typically the first entrance to close as soon as winter starts (often late September or early October in the mountains) due to its high elevation. Route 410 may stay open a bit longer, but a large portion also tends to shut down completely by November and doesn't reopen until May. However, access to Crystal Mountain remains open throughout the winter season. In the winter, Longmire and Paradise are generally the only areas accessible by road, as the other areas, including Ohanapecosh and Carbon River/Mowich, close due to heavy snow.

FOOD AND ACCOMMODATIONS

There are several places to eat for those who don't bring their own lunch. The restaurant at the National Park Inn in Longmire serves breakfast, lunch, and dinner year-round. The Longmire General Store is right next door and sells food, camping gear, gifts, and trinkets.

The Paradise Inn in Paradise has a

restaurant and café open May-early October for breakfast, lunch, and dinner. Those in a hurry can grab a bite or a hot beverage at the café. Paradise Camp Deli, a cafeteria-style eatery at the Jackson Visitor Center, is open every day May-early October and on weekends and holidays throughout the winter.

Located in the Sunrise area, the Sunrise Day Lodge offers a variety of lighter meal alternatives at its snack bar during the busiest summer months of July-September.

BACKCOUNTRY HIKING AND CAMPING

The park employs a permit system to control the number of campers and climbers, aiming to preserve the natural environment. The system covers designated campsites, off-trail camping zones, and distinct areas for backpacking and climbing activities.

Obtaining a **wilderness camping permit** is mandatory year-round and can be done in person at any park wilderness information center or visitor center. Advance reservations are available online for peak season, June-September. Backpackers can pick up their permits at the Longmire Museum. In the off-season, October-May, permits are available at the Carbon River Ranger Station and the Longmire Museum.

An early-access lottery system is available for highly sought-after trails like the **Wonderland Trail** and popular climbing routes, opening in February each year on recreation.gov. Applicants can secure their preferred itinerary before the general reservation begins on April 25. This lottery system is handy for getting reservations for June 1-October 10, when the demand is highest.

CLIMBING

Mount Rainier beckons thousands of climbers to its challenging slopes annually. With over twenty diverse climbing routes and opportunities for ski descents, adventurers can start their journey from one of **four primary trailheads:** Paradise, Westside Road, White River, or Mowich Lake. Climbing Mount

Rainier requires top-notch physical fitness and meticulous preparation due to the 10 mi (16 km) of hiking and more than 9,000 ft (2,750 m) of vertical gain. Expertise in advanced glacier navigation and ropework is essential for climbers on both the ascent and descent of the peak.

Climbers must buy an annual climbing fee ($68), which covers the entire calendar year and can be purchased in advance online. In addition, for those planning to climb or travel above 10,000 ft (3,050 m), **climbing permits** are required. These permits also cover wilderness camping for the duration of the climb. Climbers can self-register at Paradise Wilderness Information Center. For those seeking professional guidance, climbing instruction, or tailored summit climbs, organizations such as **Alpine Ascents International** (109 W. Mercer St., Seattle; 206/378-1927; www.alpineascents.com), **International Mountain Guides** (31111 Route 706, Ashford; www.mountainguides. com; 360/569-2609), and **RMI Expeditions** (30027 Route 706, Ashford; 888/892-5462; www.rmiguides.com) offer assistance.

INFORMATION AND SERVICES

Mount Rainier National Park has several helpful visitor centers around the area. The Henry M. Jackson Visitor Center, located in Paradise, is the main center and open year-round, though with reduced hours during winter.

Note that there is no gasoline in the park, so fill up before you enter. Cell phone service in the area is limited, so it's best to assume you won't have any and make plans accordingly.

Longmire
Longmire Museum
Paradise Road, 10 mi (16 km) east of Ashford; Longmire; 360/569-6650; https://visitrainier.com; 9am-5pm daily July-Sept., 9am-4:30pm daily Oct.-Dec.; free

Longmire Museum, near the southwest

1: Mount Rainier National Park **2:** Longmire Museum

Wildlife Safety

bears

Mount Rainier National Park is home to many different wildlife species, but the mountain lion and black bear are the ones to be most aware of. Bear sightings are more common than mountain lion sightings, and although attacks are rare, it's essential to know how to act if you encounter one.

Never feed a black bear, either purposely or by accidentally leaving food out. If you see a cub, back away immediately, as its mother is likely nearby. If a bear shows signs of irritation, such as making loud noises or stomping its feet, do not run—speak to the bear in a loud voice, and slowly back away while remaining facing it.

Mountain lions, also known as cougars or pumas, tend to avoid confrontation and not be seen, as they stalk their prey from a distance. If you encounter one, don't run or turn your back; instead, gather in a group, make yourself appear larger, and make noise. If attacked, fight back vigorously, aiming to hit the head, and use any available objects as weapons. Protecting your head and neck is crucial. These guidelines are essential for a safe experience in the park amid these powerful animals.

entrance, is open daily year-round and has historical exhibits about the park. Rangers are on hand to answer any questions you have about nearby trails or road conditions.

Longmire Wilderness Information Center

Longmire Rd., Ashford; 360/569-6650; www.nps.gov; 7:30am-5pm daily late May-Sept., 9am-4pm Fri.-Sun. and Mon. holidays Jan.-late May

Stop here to pick up your backpacking permits, or stop at the Longmire Museum if the Wilderness Information Center is closed.

Paradise
Henry M. Jackson Visitor Center

Paradise Rd. E., Ashford; 360/569-6571; www.nps.gov; 9am-5:30pm daily July-early Sept., 10am-4pm Sat.-Sun. winter, generally Oct.-May

The park's main visitor center is the Henry M. Jackson Memorial Visitor Center, which is open year-round and is a vital resource for visitors. It offers extensive information about the park, including displays about the cultural and ecological history of Mount Rainier, suggestions for hiking trails, and safety tips. An information desk with helpful park rangers on staff, a gift shop, and a cafeteria are also here. A water bottle filling station and restrooms are available.

Paradise Wilderness Information Center

52419 Paradise Rd. E., Ashford; www.nps.gov; 360/569-6641; call for hours, late May-early Sept.

Stop here to get information on hikes and permits for climbing and backpacking.

Sunrise
White River Wilderness Information Center

70002 Route 410, Enumclaw; www.nps.gov; 360/569-6670; 7:30am-5pm daily late May-mid-Oct.

Stop here just past the White River entrance to get information on hiking conditions and for your climbing and camping permits on the east and north sides of the mountain.

Sunrise Visitor Center

Sunrise Park Rd., Ashford; 360/569-2211; www.nps.gov; 9am-5pm daily early July-mid-Sept.

The Sunrise Visitor Center, situated in the park's northeastern corner, offers stunning views and exhibits but is open seasonally, typically July-mid-September. It has exhibits about the surrounding mountains, a small gift shop, and rangers available to give hiking advice.

Ohanapecosh
Ohanapecosh Visitor Center

Route 123, Randle; 360/569-2211; www.nps.gov; 9am-5pm daily late June-mid-Sept.

The Ohanapecosh Visitor Center, found in the park's southeast region, provides insights into the park's old-growth forest and is also open seasonally, usually late June-mid-September. Learn about the nearby trails and get help building an itinerary from a ranger.

Carbon River/Mowich
Carbon River Ranger Station

35415 Fairfax Forest Reserve Rd. E., Carbonado; 360/829-9639; www.nps.gov; call for hours, open year-round

Visit the ranger station to get the status on trails nearby.

Longmire Area

There are multiple entrances to Mount Rainier National Park, but **Nisqually Entrance** is most popular due to its proximity to the Paradise area and being the closest to I-5. Nisqually is also the only entrance open throughout the winter and provides access to Longmire. The towns in this area aren't destinations in themselves, but they provide convenient bases for a few days of exploring Mount Rainier.

Longmire, in the park's southwestern area and 7 mi (11 km) east of the Nisqually Entrance, was the original headquarters after Mount Rainier National Park was established in 1899. James Longmire had built his homestead here, and the region soon became famous as a resort with rooms for rent and mineral springs. The park's headquarters is now in Ashford and not open to visitors, but the 1916 Longmire building is now a museum where visitors can experience life as it was in the past.

To get here, follow Route 706 east through Ashford to reach the Nisqually Entrance, pay your entrance fee, and continue onto Paradise Road to Longmire. Park in the large parking lot at the visitor center while you explore the area.

Ashford is the main town people stay in because it is the closest to the Nisqually Entrance to reach Longmire and Paradise. Ashford doesn't have many sights or recreation of its own, but it's the best nearby base, with numerous options for restaurants and lodging. It's also one of the last areas where you'll get cell phone service before heading into the park, although it can be spotty. The last gas station for a while is here too, so it's smart to fill up before entering the park.

If you're willing to travel a bit further to save money, you might choose **Eatonville** as your base. It's about 20 mi (32 km) west of Ashford and 32 mi (51 km) from Longmire. There are some good sights here, so you can also explore the town on the way back from a day at Mount Rainier.

SIGHTS
In the Park
Longmire Museum

Paradise Rd., 10 mi (16 km) east of Ashford, Longmire; 360/569-6650; https://visitrainier.com; 9am-5pm daily July-Sept., 9am-4:30pm daily Oct.-Dec.; free

The Longmire Museum is one of the oldest national park museums in the country and has displays and photographs showcasing the area's history and development. Rangers are on staff to answer any questions about nearby trails or road conditions.

Christine Falls

One of the park's most popular waterfalls is the 69-ft (21-m) Christine Falls, whose overlook is easily accessible from Paradise Valley Road. However, there is limited parking on the side of the road, so it's best to come here early in the day or later at night. From the Longmire Museum, drive 4.5 mi (7 km) east on Paradise Valley Road, where you'll see the bridge for Christine Falls and several small parking areas on the side of the road. Cross the road to join the short trail, where you'll follow a set of stairs to the overlook.

Eatonville
RailCycle Mt. Rainier

13203 Alder Mashel Connection Rd. E., Eatonville; 253/900-7245; https://railcycle.com; 10am-7:30pm Mon.-Fri., 8:15am-8:30pm Sat.-Sun.; $89-164

For a fun way to spend the afternoon, book a spot on RailCycle Mt. Rainier to pedal a rail bike down a railroad. A group of people works together to propel themselves down the

tracks. All ages are welcome, and you'll pass by forests and rivers and views of the mountain as you explore the area.

Mt. Rainier Scenic Railroad

54124 Mountain Hwy. E., Elbe; 253/900-7245; https:// mtrainierrailroad.com; 9am-4pm Mon.-Fri.; $36-95

In nearby Elbe, you can book a 12-mi (19-km) train ride on the Mt. Rainier Scenic Railroad. Chose a seat in either the historic Pullman cars or open-air cars and enjoy views of the forests, rivers, and mountains. There are various themed events you can join, such as brunch trains, beer, wine, and whiskey trains, and Halloween and Christmas trains.

Northwest Trek Wildlife Park

11610 Trek Dr. E., Eatonville; 360/832-6117; www.nwtrek. org; 9:30am-3pm Fri.-Sat.; $10-22

While animal sightings aren't always guaranteed at Mount Rainier, they are at Northwest Trek Wildlife Park. Guests can marvel at over 100 animals native to the Pacific Northwest, including bison, mountain goats, and caribou, from the comfort of your vehicle on a unique drive-through tour. The park also features forested walking trails for up-close encounters with bears, bald eagles, and river otters. Kids will love the nature-themed playground, and visitors of all ages will walk away more educated on the wildlife they saw.

HIKING
In the Park
Trail of the Shadows

Distance: *0.7 mi (1.1 km) round-trip*
Duration: *30 minutes*
Elevation gain: *20 ft (7 m)*
Difficulty: *easy*
Trailhead: *across the road from Longmire main parking lot*

Trail of the Shadows is a good beginner trail, as it's easy to find, right across from the Longmire visitor center, and is one of the shortest loops in the park. You'll pass by small hot springs and a replica of an old cabin from when this area was populated.

Hiking the Wonderland Trail

Wonderland Trail

Distance: *93 mi*
Duration: *10-14 days*
Elevation gain: *22,000 ft (6,700 m)*
Difficulty: *strenuous*
Trailheads: *Longmire, Sunrise, or Mowich Lake*

If you're looking for a challenge, the Wonderland Trail goes around the entire base of Mount Rainier and takes you through all the different terrain the mountain offers. As you make your way up the trail, you'll see alpine meadows teeming with wildflowers, dazzling glacial rivers, and dense old-growth forests. Various points along the trail provide stunning views of Mount Rainier. Although you're not summitting the mountain, you'll encounter various elevation gains and losses, adding to the journey's toughness.

There is no designated starting point for the Wonderland Trail, so hikers start their journey at various locations along the loop. The time it takes to complete the trail varies widely among hikers, so it's essential to know your physical limits and plan your itinerary accordingly.

Over a dozen campsites are available along the Wonderland Trail, typically spaced 3-4 mi (4-6 km) apart. Each campsite usually has fewer than 10 spots, so planning and securing a permit in advance is essential. Sites fill up quickly in the summer, so pay attention to when recreation.gov opens up sites in the winter. Visit www.nps.gov to see the full list of campsites on the Wonderland Trail. You can also apply for the lottery in the winter, which gives select people first choice before campsites open up to the public.

WINTER SPORTS

Longmire is a popular area for snowshoeing. It's recommended to stop at the ranger station or visitor center first to tell the staff about your plans. They'll let you know about any closed trails or potential avalanche danger. The trails from the Longmire Museum have the same names, such as Trail of the Shadows and Kautz Creek. Maps are available at the Longmire Museum with routes and distances.

FOOD

As with most areas of the park, dining is limited in Longmire and hours vary seasonally, so check ahead on the NPS website to confirm if they're open.

In the Park

National Park Inn Dining Room

*47009 Paradise Rd. E., Ashford; 855/755-2275; https://
mtrainierguestservices.com; 7am-11am, noon-3:30pm,
4:30pm-7pm Mon.-Thurs., 7am-11am, noon-3:30pm,
4:30pm-8pm Fri.-Sun.; $12-30*

The National Park Inn dining room is attached to the hotel and serves options like the Lodge Breakfast with eggs and potatoes or bourbon buffalo meatloaf in a rustic setting. Hours are seasonal during the winter, so it's best to have a backup plan if they're closed.

Longmire General Store

*47009 Paradise Rd. E, Ashford; 855/755-2275; https://
mtrainierguestservices.com; 10am-5pm Sun.-Thurs.,
8:30am-6pm Fri., Sat., and holidays Jan.-June and
Sept.-Jan., 9am-7pm daily June-Sept.*

The Longmire General Store is one of the few places in the park you can count on to be open no matter the season. It's a popular place to stock up on snacks, hiking gear, sunscreen, bug spray, firewood, winter clothes, and more. You can also rent snowshoes and cross-country skis here.

Ashford

While Ashford has numerous food options, it's best to grab something to go on your way into the park or stop here for dinner on your way out. If you leave the park, you'll have to wait in line to reenter at the Nisqually Entrance, even if you already paid your entrance fee. During the summer, it's not uncommon for the wait to be an hour minimum.

★ Rainier BaseCamp Bar & Grill

*30027 Route 706; 360/569-2727; https://
rainierbasecampgrill.com; noon-7pm daily summer,
noon-7pm Fri.-Sun. winter; $10-27*

In the summertime, you'll find Rainier BaseCamp Bar & Grill packed in the afternoons no matter what day you're there. Many hikers end their day here with a cold beer and sharing a pizza. There's a large outdoor area with plenty of picnic benches and chairs, and they'll even pack any of their sandwiches into a trail lunch for you.

Wildberry

*7718 Route 706; 360/569-2277; www.rainierwildberry.
com; noon-7:30pm Mon., noon-8pm Wed.-Sun. May-
Oct.; $11-18*

Wildberry has a mix of American cuisine and some Sherpa Himalayan dishes, such as Himalayan Sherpa stew or pork momo dumplings, which aren't otherwise found in the area but reflect the owner's background. The owner is just as interesting as the food—he holds the world speed record on Mount Everest and has summited it over a dozen times, as well as many other major peaks worldwide. There's spacious seating both indoors and outdoors.

Paradise Village Restaurant

*31811 Route 706; 360/255-0070; www.
paradisevillagelodge.com; 8am-9pm daily; $12-38*

Indulge in Ukrainian food at Paradise Village Restaurant, with its unique selection of vegetarian and meat pierogi, soups and salads, and dishes like gnocchi, in a European-style building. If you prefer something quick, you'll enjoy the selection of Eastern European baked goods.

Ashford General Store

*30402 Route 706; 360/569-2377; https://visitrainier.
com; 7am-11pm daily (winter hours may be reduced)*

Visitors who forgot a few items for their trip will breathe a sigh of relief to see everything Ashford General Store sells, including snacks, quick meals, beer, wine, firewood, hardware, and more. This is particularly helpful for those whose accommodations have a kitchen.

Eatonville

Bruno's Family Restaurant and Bar

*204 Center St. E.; 360/832-7866; www.eatbrunos.com;
8am-9pm Sun.-Thurs., 8am-10pm Fri.-Sat.; $12-26*

Named after the owner's dog, this canine-themed restaurant is a great place to fill up on soup, sandwiches, and steak after a day of exploring. They also have a full bar and TVs around to watch when you're ready to relax.

Mill Haus Cider Co.

*303 Center St. E.; 253/487-7065; www.drinkmillhaus.
com; 4pm-8pm Wed., 4pm-9pm Thurs., noon-9pm Fri.-
Sat., noon-8pm Sun.; $12-15*

Mill Haus Cider Co. has a welcoming space that encourages people to connect over fire pits and games of cornhole. They have small bites like sliders and flatbreads and about half a dozen ciders on tap.

Puerto Vallarta

*220 Center St. E.; 360/832-4033; https://
puertovallartarestaurantes.com; 11am-8pm Sun.-Thurs.,
11am-9pm Fri.-Sat.; $16-27*

Stop by Puerto Vallarta for lunch to fill up on all-you-can-eat tacos (11am-2pm Mon.-Fri.), or come for half-off appetizers in their lounge in the afternoon. You'll find a selection of quesadillas, enchiladas, fajitas, and more on their menu.

★ Mt. Rainier Railroad Dining Co.

*54106 Mountain Hwy. E.; 360/569-2505; www.rrdiner.
com; 11am-6pm daily; $16-28*

If you've never dined on a train before, now's your chance at the Mt. Rainier Railroad Dining Co. The restaurant is set on a historic train and offers a variety of breakfast, lunch, and dinner items, such as homemade lasagna or a pork roast dinner.

ACCOMMODATIONS

As is the case with other places in the park, lodging is limited and should be booked months in advance, as it tends to sell out by the spring.

In the Park
National Park Inn

*47009 Paradise Rd. E., Ashford; 855/755-2275; https://
mtrainierguestservices.com; $192-397*

Serving guests since 1906, the rustic National Park Inn has kept its historic charm. Choose from 25 guest rooms, where you'll enjoy nature without internet or cell phone service and be able to join activities like afternoon tea. All rooms are on the 2nd floor and can be reached by stairs; the restaurant is on the first floor.

Cougar Rock Campground

*next to Cougar Rock Ranger Station, 48627 Paradise
Rd. E, Ashford; 360/569-6626; www.recreation.gov;
$20*

In a forested area next to the Nisqually River 2 mi (3 km) east of the Longmire Museum, Cougar Rock is the closest campground to the Paradise area, so it books up far in advance. The 173 campsites have access to flush toilets and drinking water.

Ashford
Paradise Village Hotel

*31811 Route 706; 360/255-0070; www.
paradisevillagelodge.com; $124-265*

Paradise Village Hotel is a relaxing place to stay after spending the days outdoors, as visitors can soak in the hot tub heated by an open fire or steam in the wood-fired sauna (additional fees apply). There's a mix of five rooms available, including queen, king, and family rooms and two cabins.

★ Copper Creek Inn

*35707 Route 706; 360/569-2326; https://
coppercreekinn.com; $148-440*

Set in 11 acres (4.5 ha) of lush forest, Copper Creek Inn offers nine cabins, some beside the creek and some with views of expansive meadows. Each cabin has a hot tub and a plush bed, and outdoor amenities such as fire pits, barbecue areas, picnic sites by the stream, and areas to play are available to guests. The inn itself is a large red building that sleeps up to 10, has a large living room with a fireplace and a full kitchen, and is only rented to groups.

Wellspring Spa and Woodland Retreat

*54922 Kernahan Rd. E.; 360/569-2799; https://
wellspringspa.com; $185-225*

When you need to rest and recharge, book one of the 14 charming log cabins at Wellspring Spa, where it feels like you're on your own retreat in the woods. Large groups can book the entire Tatoosh Lodge that sleeps up to 12 people. They have a spa on-site, and you can also book their massage therapist to meet you at the spa or in your room. Some cabins have hot tub and sauna access.

Stormking Cabins & Spa

37311 Route 706; 360/569-2964; https://stormkingspa. com; $240-300

If it's peace and quiet you're after, Stormking Cabins & Spa has just five luxury cabins on the property, each with a private deck, gas log fireplace, and hot tub. There' no spa on-site, but guests can book massages at their spa center five minutes away (425/319-9588; $150-300).

Eatonville
Mill Village Motel

210 Center St. E.; 360/832-3200; www.elodging.net; $149-174

Mill Village Motel is a no-frills motel that offers 32 rooms with queen and king beds and is an affordable place to call your base for the weekend. It's in downtown Eatonville and within walking distance to a handful of restaurants and stores.

★ Paradise Area

The most popular spot on Mount Rainier is Paradise, which was appropriately named by James Longmire's daughter-in-law Virinda in the late 1800s. The awe-inspiring beauty of the place made her cry out, "Oh, what a paradise!" during her first visit.

The drive to Paradise requires you to go through Longmire first, which is the gateway into the park. From Longmire, you wind your way up Paradise Road through dense forests and by waterfalls on the side of the road, all while keeping an eye out for wildlife. At the end of the road, you'll find the **Henry M. Jackson Memorial Visitor Center** (also known as the Paradise Visitor Center) on one side and Paradise Inn on the opposite side. In the summer, when the park is busiest with visitors, it transforms into a beautiful

Alder Lake Park

50324 School Rd.; 360/569-2778; www.mytpu.org/ community-environment/parks-recreation/alder-lake- park; $25-42

Located about 10 mi (16 km) south of Eatonville, Alder Lake Park has four campgrounds: Main, Osprey, Elk Plain, and Rocky Point. Various camping options are available in the park, including 62 tent sites, 74 sites with water and electricity, and 35 sites with full hookups.

TRANSPORTATION

Eatonville is 1.5 hours (65 mi/100 km) from Seattle, reached by taking I-5 south to exit 127 for Route 512 toward Puyallup, then Route 7 and Route 161 south. The drive from Eatonville to Ashford takes about 25 minutes (20 mi/32 km); take Alder Cutoff Road east for 7 mi (11 km), turn left on Route 7 south for 5 mi (8 km), then Route 706 east for 8 mi (13 km). It takes 45 minutes (24 mi/39 km) to reach Paradise from Ashford by taking Route 706 and Paradise Road east.

wonderland. Every year, the mountain and its surroundings are decorated with an explosion of wildflowers, painting the environment in a kaleidoscope of color and attracting an endless stream of visitors.

SIGHTS
In the Park
Narada Falls

Paradise Rd.; www.nps.gov

Narada Falls is an easy roadside waterfall to spot on the way from Longmire to Paradise, 15 mi (24 km) east of the Nisqually Entrance. Many people choose to walk only a few feet from their car to peer down the 168-ft (51-m) waterfall, but a short (0.2 mi/0.3 km one-way)

1: Reflection Lakes **2:** Mt. Rainier Railroad Dining Co.

but steep walk to the bottom gives you the best views.

Reflection Lakes

Stevens Canyon Rd., 1.3 mi (2 km) east of Paradise Rd., Ashford; www.nps.gov; June-Sept.

It's not uncommon to find dozens of amateur and professional photographers catching an early sunrise at Reflection Lakes, one of the park's most-photographed sights. Wildflowers are everywhere you look during peak summer, framing Mount Rainier perfectly in the background. While the lake may be beautiful, it's closed to swimming, fishing, and boating to protect its ecosystems. Parking can be tight, as most of the parking lot is shared with the Pinnacle Peak Trail. Note that Stevens Canyon Road closes in the winter, but you can snowshoe here from the Narada Falls parking lot.

HIKING
In the Park

A number of trails start from the Paradise Visitor Center Parking lot, so keep an eye out for signs to make sure you're on the right path. It's also a good idea to grab a map from the visitor center.

Nisqually Vista Trail

Distance: *1.1 mi (1.7 km) round-trip*
Duration: *30 minutes*
Elevation gain: *200 ft (60 m)*
Difficulty: *easy*
Trailhead: *Paradise Visitor Center, up the stone stairs and follow signs*

This is a loop trail, so you can go either way. It's an easy, paved hike with stunning views of Mount Rainier, and you'll want to take your time reading signs about the Nisqually Glacier, which has significantly melted over the years but is still visible.

Skyline Trail

Distance: *5.5 mi (8.9 km) round-trip*
Duration: *4 hours*
Elevation gain: *1,450 ft (440 m)*
Difficulty: *moderate*
Trailhead: *Paradise Visitor Center, up the stone stairs and follow signs*

Skyline is a loop trail, but most people choose to do it clockwise for the best views of Mount Rainier. After a steep climb from the start, you'll come to a scenic rest spot at Panorama Point, where you can catch your breath and take in the views of the surrounding valleys and mountains. You'll slowly start to descend, passing through a meadow, and go by the popular Myrtle Falls before completing the loop.

Pinnacle Peak

Distance: *2.9 mi (4.7 km) round-trip*
Duration: *3 hours*
Elevation gain: *1,584 ft (483 m)*
Difficulty: *moderate*
Trailhead: *Reflection Lakes*

Pinnacle Peak may be short, but you gain elevation quickly, making it deceivingly challenging. However, the views you'll get of the surrounding mountains and valleys are more than worth it.

To get here from the Paradise parking lot, head west on Paradise Road for 2 mi (3 km), turn left on Steven Canyons Road, and follow it for 1.5 mi (2.5 km) to the parking area for Reflection Lakes. Across the road you'll see the trailhead sign and a set of stairs leading into the forest.

Bench and Snow Lakes

Distance: *2.5 mi (4 km) round-trip*
Duration: *1.5 hours*
Elevation gain: *610 ft (186 m)*
Difficulty: *easy*
Trailhead: *Snow Lake parking lot*

Bench and Snow Lakes are some of the prettiest and most accessible lakes in the area. That means they're often crowded, so it's advisable to go early in the morning. You'll first come across Bench Lake, a nice place to take a break but not as impressive as Snow Lake. Continue to Snow Lake, where you'll find many people taking a dip in the calm, blue water on hot summer days. Beware—bugs can be nasty here as they, too, want to cool off, so bug spray is advised. The elevation gain is distributed across ups and downs throughout the hike, making it feel manageable.

To get here from the Paradise parking lot, head west on Paradise Road for 2 mi (3 km), turn left on Steven Canyons Road, and follow it for 3 mi (5 km) to the Snow Lake sign and a small parking lot on the right. If this is full, cars can park carefully along Stevens Canyon Road. The trail starts from the west side of the parking lot.

WINTER SPORTS

Although much of the park shuts down in the winter, snowshoeing is a popular activity you can do throughout the season. Longmire and Paradise are the most common areas to go, and it's recommended to stop at the ranger station or visitor center first to tell the staff about your plans. They'll let you know about any closed trails or potential avalanche danger.

Panorama Point via Skyline Trail and Narada Falls to Reflection Lakes are some of the best snowshoe trails.

Whittaker Mountaineering

30027 Route 706 E., Ashford; 360/569-2142; https://whittakermountaineering.com; 8am-5pm daily

You can rent everything you need for a day out on the mountain here, including insulated parkas, climbing pants, gloves, boots, microspikes, snowshoes, and more. They also have technical gear such as warm-weather sleeping bags and avalanche transceivers.

FOOD AND ACCOMMODATIONS
In the Park
★ Paradise Inn

52807 Paradise Rd. E., Ashford; 855/755-2275; https://mtrainierguestservices.com; mid-May-late Sept.; $299-367

Paradise Inn has been called one of the "Great Lodges of the West" due to its historic charm, with handcrafted furniture and giant stone fireplaces, and is the most convenient place to stay in the area—it's right at the base of all the hiking trails in the Paradise section. The lodge has 121 modest guestrooms with shared bathrooms and no TVs or Wi-Fi. However, cell service does work in select areas of the lodge. An annex was constructed behind the lodge to accommodate the growing number of visitors, and it has four floors with rooms with private bathrooms.

Paradise Inn Dining Room

52807 Paradise Rd. E.; Ashford; 855/755-2275; https://mtrainierquestservices.com; 7am-9:00am, 5:30pm-8:30pm daily May-Sept.; $12-30

Located inside the inn, the Paradise Inn Dining Room is the perfect place to relax for dinner after a day of hiking around the mountain. The cozy restaurant serves a variety of seafood, meat, and vegetarian dishes for lunch and dinner, such as grilled salmon with asparagus or seared duck breast, and they also have breakfast for early risers. Reservations are highly recommended during peak season.

Paradise Camp Deli

52415 Paradise Rd. E., Ashford; 360/569-2211; www.nps.gov; 11am-4:45pm May-June, 11am-5:45pm June-Oct., 10:30am-3pm Sat.-Sun. and holidays winter; $12-30

Stop by the Paradise Camp Deli in the Jackson Visitor Center for a quick bite. It has plenty of casual meals, such as slices of pizza, hot dogs, hot meals, ice cream, and coffee. Many hikers choose to buy a sandwich to take on the trail with them.

TRANSPORTATION

It's 11 mi (18 km) to get to Paradise from Longmire via Paradise Road east.

★ Sunrise Area

Sunrise is one of the park's most beautiful areas, yet also one of the least accessible, as it's generally only open late June-late September. Visitors are well aware of this, so you'll find the parking lot packed almost every day from early morning until dusk. At an elevation of 6,400 ft (1,950 m), it's also the highest point in the park you can reach via car.

Use the **White River Entrance** off Route 410 to get here, and enjoy the 14-mi (23-km) drive up to Sunrise via Sunrise Park Road, with plenty of places to stop along the way for pictures. This road ends at the parking lot for the Sunrise Visitor Center and day lodge, and is the base for the majority of hikes in this area.

Enumclaw is the gateway to Mount Rainier, a common stop for visitors headed to the Sunrise area. With a population of almost 13,000, it's a sizeable town compared to others around the mountain, with the biggest variety of stores and restaurants.

On the way from Enumclaw to the Sunrise area, you'll pass **Crystal Mountain,** which is the biggest ski resort in the state and has winter sports and summer hiking in addition to lodging and restaurants. If you drive a few miles east of Sunrise on Route 410, you'll reach **Chinook Pass,** which has numerous trailheads.

HIKING

There are many hikes in this area, and most of them start from the Sunrise parking lot, so pick up a map at the visitor center and have the ranger show you which trail you want to follow.

In the Park
Sunrise Nature Trail
Distance: 1.5 mi (2.4 km) round-trip
Duration: 1 hour
Elevation gain: 300 ft (90 m)

Difficulty: easy
Trailhead: Sunrise parking lot, northwest corner

The Sunrise Nature Trail is ideal when you want a short stroll that still provides picturesque views. The start of this route connects to other hikes, but look for the Nature Trail sign on the right, and follow that to go through a colorful meadow of wildflowers that are at their peak in August. Even though it's short, bring plenty of water because it's largely unshaded.

Sourdough Ridge
Distance: 2.5 mi (4 km) round-trip
Duration: 1.5 hours
Elevation gain: 400 ft (120 m)
Difficulty: easy/moderate
Trailhead: Sunrise parking lot

From the Sunrise parking lot, walk past the restrooms and lodge to climb a set of stairs. At the T intersection (0.5 mi/0.8 km), make a left to begin the Sourdough Ridge Trail. Sourdough Ridge gains a good amount of elevation right from the start, but it levels out so you can take a break before you proceed. This trail acts as a connector to many others, including Mount Fremont Lookout and Berkeley Park, if you want to add extra miles to your trek. Many people choose to go straight until they reach Frozen Lake, take a few pictures, and then go back the way they came.

Mount Fremont Lookout
Distance: 5.6 mi (9 km) round-trip
Duration: 3 hours
Elevation gain: 1,200 ft (365 m)
Difficulty: easy/moderate
Trailhead: Sunrise parking lot

Mount Fremont Lookout is a popular place to catch the sunrise or stay late to see the stars, as the views from the top are stunning. Follow the Sourdough Ridge Trail just past Frozen Lake, and then take a right to head uphill.

After a steep 1.3-mi (2-km) climb, you reach the two-story 1934 fire lookout. Relax and enjoy your surroundings.

Berkeley Park

Distance: *7.7 mi (12.4 km) round-trip*
Duration: *4 hours*
Elevation gain: *1,700 ft (520 m)*
Difficulty: *moderate*
Trailhead: *Sunrise parking lot*

If wildlife sightings are your goal, you'll have a good chance of achieving it at Berkeley Park. It's common to see marmots, pikas, and sometimes black bears (be sure you keep your dis tance). This route starts on the Sourdough Ridge Trail, so you'll be among others until the crowds start to thin out past Frozen Lake. You'll intersect the Wonderland Trail and begin to descend, which is the beginning of Berkeley Park, notable for its vibrant green grass and wildflowers.

Chinook Pass

Both of these hikes are seasonal, with summer being full of wildflowers and fall having plenty of vibrant foliage. Hikers can't access them at other times of the year when Route 410 is closed.

Naches Peak Loop

Distance: *3.2 mi (5.1 km) round-trip*
Duration: *1.5 hours*
Elevation gain: *600 ft (185 m)*
Difficulty: *easy/moderate*
Trailhead: *Tipsoo Lake parking lot*

Naches Peak Loop is the most popular hike in this area, so you'll need to get here early in the summer. It's a loop hike that goes through the forest, over Route 410, and crosses paths with part of the Pacific Crest Trail, so it's not uncommon to see PCT hikers as they journey north. You can do this hike either way, but clockwise is recommended to get the best views of Mount Rainier and Tipsoo Lake. During the summer, you'll spot wildflowers surrounding the trail, while the fall brings beautiful colors to the foliage.

To get here from the Enumclaw ranger station, head east on Route 410 for approximately 44 mi (70 km). Park at the Tipsoo Lake parking area, located about 0.5 mi (0.8 km) west of Chinook Pass.

Sheep Lake and Sourdough Gap

Distance: *6 mi (9.7 km) round-trip*
Duration: *3 hours*
Elevation gain: *1,100 ft (335 m)*
Difficulty: *easy/moderate*
Trailhead: *Pacific Crest Trail parking lot, Route 410*

The trail starts out following the highway for a bit before dipping into the woods, where it remains largely covered until reaching Sheep Lake at 1.8 mi (2.9 km). Many people with kids choose to stop here, have a picnic lunch, and then return back to the car. However, the views at Sourdough Gap are worth continuing on, and after a steep 1.4-mi (2.3-km) climb to the top, you'll have gorgeous views of the whole area, including Mount Rainier, Mount St. Helens, and Mount Adams on a sunny day.

To get here from Enumclaw, go east on Route 410 for approximately 50 mi (80 km) until you reach Chinook Pass. Look for the Pacific Crest Trail parking lot on the left side of the road, 0.2 mi (0.3 km) past the pass.

WINTER SPORTS
Crystal Mountain

33914 Crystal Mountain Blvd.; 833/279-7895; www. crystalmountainresort.com; 9am-4pm Mon.-Thurs., 8:30am-8pm Fri.-Sat., 8:30am-4pm Sun.; $65-199

Crystal Mountain is the largest ski resort in Washington and boasts an impressive 11 lifts accessing 2,600 acres (1,050 ha) of skiable terrain. The resort features over 80 runs, attracting skiers seeking both beginner and challenging slopes, and gets an average annual snowfall of over 400 in (10 m). The resort offers ski and snowboard lessons, along with gear rental services. Weekends tend to be packed here, so the resort requires parking reservations in advance to help manage the traffic.

☆ Crystal Mountain: Washington's Largest Ski Resort

Crystal Mountain

Locals and tourists alike descend upon **Crystal Mountain** (33914 Crystal Mountain Blvd., Crystal Mountain; 833/279-7895; www.crystalmountainresort.com; 9am-4pm Mon.-Thurs., 8:30am-8pm Fri.-Sat., 8:30am-4pm Sun.; $65-199) in the winter to enjoy the slopes of the state's largest ski resort. It's a winter wonderland for skiing, snowboarding, or snowshoeing, with more than 2,600 acres (1,050 ha) of skiable terrain and routes suitable for all abilities, featuring stunning views of Mount Rainier.

Summertime is just as popular at Crystal Mountain; after the snow melts, the trails become ideal for hikers and mountain bikers. Popular trails include the 6-mi (10-km) Crystal Mountain Loop trail, which connects with other trails for longer hikes. Bikers will love the 14-mi (23-km) loop that goes up and down the hill, connecting Silver Creek Trail and Crystal Mountain Trail. There's also a disc golf course on the mountain.

The one-of-a-kind **gondola** at Crystal Mountain is a must-see, and the only one in Washington. The gondola ride takes passengers on a picturesque ascent of 2,500 ft (760 m) to the peak in about 12 minutes. It runs year-round, serving both winter skiers and summertime sightseers. After reaching the top, visitors can dine at the Summit House Restaurant or ride the gondola back down to the base.

FOOD AND ACCOMMODATIONS

Crystal Mountain has a variety of restaurants, including **Summit House, Snorting Elk,** and **Alpine Inn,** all of which have a laid-back, European ski vibe. There are also a handful of places to stay on the mountain, including the three **Crystal Mountain hotels** and the **Crystal Chalets,** making it easy to start your first run in the morning.

FOOD

In the Park

Sunrise Day Lodge

Sunrise Park Rd., Ashford; 360/663-2574; www.nps. gov; 9am-4pm July-Sept.; $5-10

The Sunrise Day Lodge was built in 1931 with the intention of becoming a hotel, but that never happened, and it's remained a place for hikers to get a quick meal. It serves sandwiches, hot dogs, soup, ice cream, grab-and-go snacks, and beer.

Crystal Mountain

★ Summit House Restaurant

33914 Crystal Mountain Blvd., Crystal Mountain; 833/279-7895; www.crystalmountainresort.com; 10am-3:30pm Mon.-Thurs., 10am-4:30pm Fri. and Sun., 10am-3pm Sat.; $10-29

Take the gondola up to the top of Crystal Mountain to eat at Summit House Restaurant, the highest dining experience in the state. You'll have views of the surrounding mountains while warming up with soup or filling up on halibut and chips.

Snorting Elk

33818 Crystal Mountain Blvd.; 360/663-7798; www. crystalhotels.com; noon-8pm daily; $8-25

The Snorting Elk, an Austrian-inspired ski bar, offers a European ambience with 18 taps featuring locally brewed beers (the unique Snorting Elk Frost is their signature). Cozy up by the roaring fire and enjoy food like heaping servings of nachos and hot soups.

Alpine Inn Restaurant

33818 Crystal Mountain Blvd.; 360/663-2262; www. crystalhotels.com; 7am-10am daily, 11am-8pm Sun.-Thurs., 5pm-9pm Fri.-Sat. and holidays; $15-30

Guests can enjoy a variety of dishes such as Hungarian goulash or wienerschnitzel at the Alpine Inn Restaurant. Their menu varies with the season so they can use fresh ingredients, and seating is available in both the outdoor area and cozy indoor dining section.

Enumclaw

The Local Coffee House

1616 Cole St.; 360/625-0600; Facebook @thelocalenumclaw; 8am-6pm Mon.-Thurs., 8am-7pm Fri.-Sat., 8am-5pm Sun.

You'll feel like you've stepped into someone's home when you visit The Local Coffee House, as it's filled with comfortable couches and inviting round tables. There's an extensive espresso and tea menu and plenty of baked goods to choose from. The back of the café serves as a general store where you can pick up candles, homemade gifts, jewelry, and more.

The Mint

1608 Cole St.; 360/284-2517; www.thehistoricmint. com; 11am-9pm Sun.-Thurs., 11am-10pm Fri.-Sat.; $13-30

Housed in a historic building dating back to 1906, The Mint offers choices including burgers, nachos, salads, and more, as well as over a dozen local beers on tap.

Charlie's Café

1335 Roosevelt Ave. E.; 360/825-5191; Facebook @CharliesCafeEnumclaw; 6am-2pm daily; $13-18

Charlie's Café, easily recognizable by its vibrant red exterior, offers over a dozen sandwich varieties along with chicken, seafood, salads, and a breakfast menu. With its friendly service and efficient turnaround, the café ensures you can enjoy a satisfying meal and promptly continue your day.

★ Pie Goddess

1100 Griffin Ave.; 360/625-8568; Facebook @thePieGoddessEnumclaw; 11am-7pm daily; $5-35

A trip to The Pie Goddess is mandatory for pie lovers. There are many different pie flavors to choose from at this to-go counter, whether you're craving something warm and savory like shepherd's pie or something sweet like a cream, fruit, chocolate, or a specialty pie.

ACCOMMODATIONS

In the Park

White River Campground

360/569-2211; www.nps.gov; June-Sept.; $20

White River Campground is the closest place to stay in Sunrise, as it's only 5 mi (8 km) past the White River Entrance. But, at 4,440 ft (1,340 m), it's only open for a few months before the snow returns again. It has 88 first-come, first-served campsites, and you'll pay via the recreation.gov mobile app once you claim your spot, so download it in advance. The campgrounds have multiple restrooms but no showers.

Crystal Mountain

★ Crystal Mountain Hotels

Crystal Mountain Blvd.; 360/663-2262; www.crystalhotels.com; $480-1,115

All three of the hotels that make up the Crystal Mountain Hotels are next to each other surrounding the parking lot, within a five-minute stroll of the gondola. The **Alpine Inn** (33818 Crystal Mountain Blvd.) is a Bavarian-style hotel located next to a restaurant and bar, while The **Village Inn** (33723 Crystal Mountain Blvd.) has rooms that are suitable for guests traveling with pets. Many visitors love the cozy lobby at the **Quicksilver Lodge** (33914 Crystal Mountain Blvd.), complete with a big stone fireplace, sofas, and rockers.

Crystal Chalets

33613 Crystal Mountain Blvd.; 360/663-2628; https://crystalchalets.net; $239-459

Crystal Chalets condos are all individually owned, meaning each of the 37 one-bedroom condos has its own style. They all have a balcony, full kitchen, and dining area, and a minimum two-night stay is required.

LOGE Alta Crystal

68317 Route 410; 360/663-2500; www.logecamps.com; $183-399

LOGE Alta Crystal offers comfortable rooms for groups of any size, including one-bedroom suites, a loft that can sleep up to six people, or a private cabin for a more secluded experience. Guests can also enjoy nearby hikes, free shuttle service to Crystal Mountain, and a heated pool and hot tub.

Enumclaw

GuestHouse Enumclaw

1000 Griffin Ave.; 360/825-4490; www.redlion.com; $119-185

The 40 rooms at GuestHouse Enumclaw are a bit outdated, but it's a good option if you want to save money. Its location in downtown Enumclaw makes it easy to walk around.

Rodeway Inn

1334 Roosevelt Ave. E.; 360/825-1626; www.rodewayinnenumclaw.com; $89-110

The 44 rooms at the Rodeway Inn are simple yet updated, and they all come with a balcony or sliding patio door. Guests can also enjoy the hotel's heated outdoor pool as well as ample RV parking and on-site laundry facilities.

INFORMATION AND SERVICES

Enumclaw Ranger Station

450 Roosevelt Avenue E., Enumclaw; 360/825-6585; www.fs.usda.gov; 8am-4:30pm Wed.-Fri.

Stop at the Enumclaw Ranger Station to get hiking and itinerary advice.

St. Elizabeth Hospital

1455 Battersby Ave., Enumclaw; 360/802-8800; www.vmfh.org

St. Elizabeth Hospital has a 24-hour emergency room, a family birth center, a walk-in clinic for labs, and radiology and diagnostic imaging services.

TRANSPORTATION

From Seattle, driving to the White River Entrance takes 1 hour 45 minutes (82 mi/132 km) via I-5 south and Route 410 east. Getting up to Sunrise (the main destination for most) takes an additional 45 minutes as you slowly climb up to Mount Rainier's highest drivable point.

From Enumclaw, Chinook Pass is about

1 hour (45 mi/72 km) east on Route 410. From Seattle, Crystal Mountain is about 2 hours (85 mi/137 km), reached by taking I-5, Route 410, and Crystal Mountain Boulevard. Chinook and Cayuse Passes are the only ways to connect the north side of Mount Rainier National Park and Enumclaw to Yakima and Eastern Washington. The roads can be heavily trafficked in the summer, as those who aren't visiting the park try to use this route before it's closed, which is often November-May.

Ohanapecosh Area

Ohanapecosh is in the park's southeast corner and is known for the scenic Ohanapecosh River and its old-growth forests, as you'll find western hemlocks and Douglas firs everywhere you look. This side of the park tends to be drier than the others, so camping is popular here. The 19-mi (30-km) Stevens Canyon Road that goes through it also provides numerous pullouts and photo ops. However, it's closed in the winter and only open about late May-early October.

You'll use the **Stevens Canyon Entrance** to enter this side of the park. Stop at the Grove of the Patriarchs parking lot just past the entrance station to use the restroom or park for nearby hikes. The visitor center itself is 5 mi (8 km) south of the park boundary on Route 123.

With a population of less than 300, **Packwood** is a tiny town but has a surprising number of places to eat and stay for its size. Packwood is 16 mi (26 km) south of Stevens Canyon Entrance, via US 12 and Route 123.

SIGHTS
In the Park
Stevens Canyon Road
While Stevens Canyon Road isn't the only route through this section of the park, it is the reason most people come. This scenic road winds 19 mi (30 km) from the Stevens Canyon Entrance to the Paradise section, and along the way you'll enjoy plenty of stunning pullouts. Some of the most popular stops are Box Canyon, Reflection Lakes, and Bench and Snow Lakes.

Grove of the Patriarchs
With a verdant forest floor and towering old-growth trees, the Grove of the Patriarchs is a popular destination. A little island in the center of the Ohanapecosh River is at the end of this 1.1-mi (1.7-km) round-trip self-guided nature trail, which winds its way through the forest on boardwalks, bridges, and dirt trails. Towering Douglas firs, silver firs, hemlocks, and western red cedars—some of which are hundreds of years old—line a loop trail on the island. **Note:** This area was affected by flooding and may be closed; verify plans prior to arrival.

HIKING
In the Park
Silver Falls
Distance: *3 mi (4.8 km) round-trip*
Duration: *1.5 hours*
Elevation gain: *600 ft (185 m)*
Difficulty: *easy/moderate*
Trailhead: *Ohanapecosh Campground*

Silver Falls is mostly shaded, a welcome relief on hot days at the park. This is a loop trail, so you can go either way, but clockwise will take you across a bridge over the beautiful Ohanapecosh River and continue up, following the river to reach the 95-ft-tall (29-m) Silver Falls. While it's tempting to only stop at the viewpoint at the bottom for pictures, continue up to get multiple vantage points as the trail ascends.

To get here from the Ohanapecosh Visitor Center, follow signs to the day use area for Ohanapecosh Campground and walk toward

White Pass Scenic Byway

White Pass Ski Area

Start: *Napavine*
End: *Naches*
Driving Distance: *125 mi (201 km)*
Driving Time: *2.5 hours*

White Pass Scenic Byway is much more than a beautiful drive (though it is that)—it's a recreation-packed adventure. The many stops along the way give you the chance to get out of the car and into nature. To learn more visit their website (https://whitepassbyway.com).

There are plenty of places to stop along the way. The following are some of the more scenic ones:

- **MP 18:** Enjoy camping, fishing, and swimming at **Mayfield Lake** (180 Beach Rd., Mossyrock; 360/985-2364; www.mytpu.org).

- **MP 67:** Elk sightings and a wide selection of antique shops are two of the most famous attractions at **Packwood.**

- **MP 87:** Winter sports enthusiasts love the **White Pass Ski Area** (48935 US 12, Naches; 509/672-3101; https://skiwhitepass.com) for skiing and snowboarding.

- **MP 90:** Those looking for waterfall views can't miss **Clear Creek Falls Viewpoint** (98937 Route 410, Naches).

- **MP 90:** **Rimrock Lake** (Rimrock; www.recreation.gov) is a paradise for water sports like boating and fishing.

1: Packwood Brewing Co. **2:** Hotel Packwood
3: Silver Falls

Carbon/Mowich Area

Carbon River

Although it receives fewer visitors than other areas of Mount Rainier National Park, the Carbon River and Mowich area, nestled in the park's northwest quadrant, offers a unique experience. Due to extensive flood damage to the Carbon River Road in 2006, the area is now only accessible by foot or bicycle.

The region is notable for having a temperate rain forest habitat, which benefits from heavy annual rainfall. The **Carbon Glacier** is one of its most striking features; the glacier drops to an elevation of 3,600 ft (1,100 m), lower than any other glacier in the 48 contiguous states.

The area is also home to **Mowich Lake,** the deepest and largest lake in the park. During the summer, the lake transforms into a popular spot for fishing and nonmotorized boating, providing a tranquil escape from the busier parts of the park.

HIKING

Popular hikes in the area include the **Carbon Glacier Trail,** a picturesque ascent that brings hikers near the massive glacier, and the **Mowich Lake Trail,** a starting point for many other treks and backpacking trips, including the well-known Wonderland Trail.

CAMPING

Although it's free to camp at **Mowich Campground** (360/569-2211; www.nps.gov; July-Oct.), the tricky part is it's first-come, first-served, with only ten sites. You'll need to have a backup plan if all sites are full; try a weekday or the end of the season for the best results. Campfires are not allowed, so bring your own stove to cook. The campground is located 9 mi (14 km) from the Carbon River Entrance, and you'll follow the Mowich Lake Trail to get to the campsites.

GETTING THERE

From Seattle, it takes 1 hour 45 minutes (63 mi/100 km) to get to the Carbon River Entrance via I-5, Route 18, Route 164, and Route 165 before turning left to Carbon River Road. The road ends at a small parking lot.

the Ohanapecosh River by the northwest corner of Loop B to get on the trail.

Shriner Peak

Distance: 8.5 mi (13.7 km) round-trip
Duration: 6 hours
Elevation gain: 3,434 ft (1,047 m)
Difficulty: moderate/strenuous
Trailhead: Route 123

For a more challenging hike, Shriner Peak will have you climbing uphill most of the time but reward you at the top with the old fire lookout and incredible views of the surrounding mountain range. This trail is primarily exposed and has minimal water sources, so bring your own and consider starting early in the morning or going in the cooler fall season.

From the Ohanapecosh Visitor Center, head north about 6 mi (10 km) on Route 123 until you see a brown hiking sign pointing to a trail into the woods. Park on the side of the road.

FOOD
Packwood
The Mountain Goat Coffee Company

105 Main St. E. #791; 360/494-5600; Facebook @MountainGoatCoffeeCo; 7am 5pm daily

You can't miss the giant coffee sign, complete with fake elk on the lawn, outside The Mountain Goat Coffee Company when you're looking for your morning java. This spot has a delicious selection of pastries and espresso drinks to help you start your day.

★ Packwood Brewing Co.

12298 US 12; www.packwoodbrewingco.com; 3pm-9pm Mon.-Thurs., 1pm-10pm Fri., noon-10pm Sat., noon-9pm Sun.; $5-20

Packwood Brewing Co. serves its beer in a historic building from 1933 and has creative twists on the names, such as Treeline IPA and Mountain Goat Coffee Porter. Fill up on tacos, quesadillas, and nachos after a day of visiting Mount Rainier.

Blue Spruce Saloon And Grill

13019 US 12; 360/494-5605; Facebook @Blue-Spruce-Saloon-and-Grill; 11am-11pm daily; $13-25

Blue Spruce Saloon and Grill has a dive-bar feel with a pool table and dim lighting, but it has a decent menu with options like a chicken or steak dinner and wraps and is a good place to get a quick meal.

Cruiser's Pizza

13028 US 12; 360/494-5400; www.cruiserspizza.com; 8am-9pm Mon.-Thurs., 8am-10pm Fri., 7am-10pm Sat., 7am-9pm Sun.; $23-34

Stop by Cruiser's Pizza after a day on the mountain for breadsticks and pizza, where you can make your own or choose from one of their combinations, such as the Packwood Special with pepperoni and cashews. It has a casual feel with plenty of seating indoors between tables and booths.

ACCOMMODATIONS
In the Park
Ohanapecosh Campground

Ohanapecosh Rd., Randle; 360/569-2211; www.recreation.gov; May-Oct.; $20

Ohanapecosh is one of the most-reserved campgrounds, as it tends to stay cooler than other areas of the park thanks to the dense forest surrounding it, so make your online reservations months in advance. There are 188 sites for both tent and RV camping, along with drinking water, and you'll be close to hikes such as the Grove of the Patriarchs and Silver Falls.

Packwood
Mountain View Lodge

13163 US 12; 360/494-5555; https://mtvlodge.com; $260-750

There are 22 basic but comfortable rooms available at Mountain View Lodge, including cabins, select rooms with kitchens or fireplaces, and single or double rooms. Large groups can book rooms next to each other, and guests can enjoy a lawn with picnic tables in the summer.

Packwood Lodge

13807 US 12; 360/496-5333; https://packwoodlodge. com; $119-219

The renovated Packwood Lodge has suites with kitchenettes, large guest rooms with king or double beds, and cabins with Jacuzzi tubs available. Located only 16 mi (26 km) from White Pass Ski Area and 9 mi (15 km) from the Stevens Canyon Entrance, this hotel is conveniently located.

★ Hotel Packwood

104 Main St. W.; 360/494-5431; www.packwoodwa. com; $296-483

The historic Hotel Packwood first opened its doors to guests in 1912 and had an upgrade in 2021. Each of the nine rooms is named after a local hiking route; five have private bathrooms, while the others are shared. A stunning wraparound terrace in an Old West design complements the hotel's two main floors. All guests must be 18 or older to stay here.

TRANSPORTATION

Getting to Packwood from Seattle will take about 2 hours 15 minutes (125 mi/200 km). Take I-5 south to exit 127 for Route 512 east, then follow Route 7 south to US 12 east. To get from Packwood to the Stevens Canyon Entrance, follow US 12 east for 13 mi (21 km).

Mount St. Helens

TOP EXPERIENCE

Mount St. Helens is one of the most awe-inspiring sights in Washington; thousands of people visit every year to see this active volcano. Although it hasn't had a large eruption in over 30 years, the devastation the 1980 eruption left behind is clearly visible—as is occasional steam rising out of the crater.

Today Mount St. Helens offers a unique opportunity to see the aftermath and ongoing recovery from the 1980 eruption. The Johnston Ridge Observatory has before-and-after pictures of the mountain, and visitors can learn how the area has come back to life over the years. A variety of hiking trails lead all over the volcano, so hikers can get up close to the destruction zones.

PARK INFORMATION
Entrances

There are three entrances to the park: the **west side, south side,** and **east side.** Most people visit the west side, which is easiest to get to from I-5 and has the Johnston Ridge Observatory. The south side is used for summiting Mount St. Helens and accessing Ape Caves. The east side is the least visited, as it's harder to reach and has minimal facilities.

Areas

The Johnston Ridge Observatory highlights the **west side,** offering the closest view of the volcano's crater and detailed information on the 1980 eruption. There are also various hikes in this area, as well as the Coldwater Ridge Visitor Center.

The **south side** features the Ape Caves Lava Tubes, one of North America's longest lava tube systems. People who want to summit the volcano also make their approach from here.

The **east side** of Mount St. Helens is the most remote area of the park, with few facilities or information. It's the farthest from Seattle, and the one-lane road is narrow.

Note that the three entrances don't connect to each other. You need to go back the way you came and around to the next one. That means a day trip around the entire mountain isn't possible, so pick one area you want to explore for the day, and stay overnight if you want to go to others.

Seasons and Weather

Mount St. Helens experiences a variety of weather throughout the year. The area transforms into a stunning **winter** scene with its

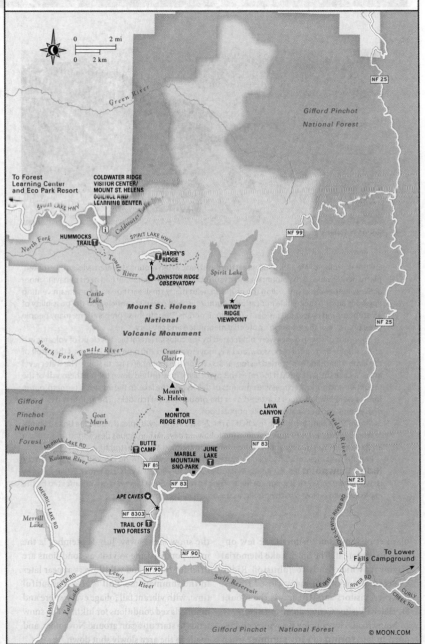

Mount St. Helens

0   2 mi
0   2 km

Green River

NF 25

Gifford Pinchot
National Forest

To Forest
Learning Center
and Eco Park Resort

COLDWATER RIDGE
VISITOR CENTER/
MOUNT ST. HELENS
SCIENCE AND
LEARNING CENTER

Spirit Lake Hwy

Coldwater Lake

SPIRIT LAKE HWY

NF 99

HUMMOCKS
TRAIL

North Fork

Toutle River

HARRY'S
RIDGE

Spirit Lake

JOHNSTON RIDGE
OBSERVATORY

Castle
Lake

Mount St. Helens

WINDY
RIDGE
VIEWPOINT

NF 25

National

Volcanic Monument

South Fork Toutle River

Crater
Glacier

Gifford

Pinchot

Mount
St. Helens

LAVA
CANYON

Muddy River

National

Goat
Marsh

MONITOR
RIDGE ROUTE

Forest

MERRILL LAKE RD

BUTTE
CAMP

NF 83

Kalama River

NF 81

MARBLE
MOUNTAIN
SNO-PARK

JUNE
LAKE

NF 25

NF 83

MERRILL LAKE RD

APE CAVES

NF 8303

Merrill
Lake

TRAIL OF
TWO FORESTS

RANDLE-LEWIS RIVER RD

NF 90

To Lower
Falls Campground

LEWIS RIVER RD

Yale Lake

NF 90

Lewis River

Swift Reservoir

LEWIS RIVER RD

CURLY CREEK RD

Gifford Pinchot National Forest

© MOON.COM

The 1980 Eruption of Mount St. Helens

Mount St. Helens' crater

On the morning of May 18, 1980, catastrophe struck when Mount St. Helens violently erupted, permanently altering the mountain and its surroundings. The mountain had been behaving more actively in the weeks preceding the eruption, with many small earthquakes and steam venting episodes among the telltale indications. Authorities and scientists anticipated the possibility of an eruption and evacuated residents from their homes. Despite these preparations, many people were unaware of the eruption's potential magnitude and severity.

Hundreds of square miles were obliterated by the colossal lateral blast. A cloud of volcanic ash and a smoldering mix of rock, snow, and ice, moving at up to 200 mph (322 kph), was the result of the largest landslide in recorded history at 8:32am on the mountain's north slope. The water level in Spirit Lake surged by 200 ft (60 m) as this pyroclastic flow rushed down the northern side of the mountain and deposited massive amounts of debris into the lake. In the instant aftermath, entire forests were leveled, trees scattered over the ground like matchsticks. The eruption destroyed ecosystems and decimated wildlife populations.

Mount St. Helens' ash plume reached 15 mi (24 km) in the sky. It spread across the United States, reaching Montana and even Canada in the following days. Ashen clouds descended upon urban areas, lowering air quality and wreaking havoc on farming and infrastructure.

For the best view of the volcano's crater, drive the winding 16-mi (26-km) road to **Windy Ridge Viewpoint** (Forest Road 99, Randle; 360/449-7800; www.fs.usda.gov). While the area is mainly barren, you'll see signs of life starting to rebuild. Spirit Lake was greatly affected by the explosion and is closed to the public, as the area is still regrowing.

blanket of snow, but visitors have few options to explore it. The Spirit Lake Memorial Highway, which leads to Johnston Ridge Observatory, is one of many closed routes; however, visitors can still access the Mount St. Helens Visitor Center at Silver Lake.

Many roads close during the winter and reopen in late **spring** to early **summer** when the snow melts away. July-September is the most popular time to visit, as conditions are drier for hiking and wildflowers appear later in the summertime. **Fall** is also a beautiful time, with vibrant fall foliage everywhere and more relaxed conditions for hiking. The snow tends to start up again around November, and roads in the area slowly shut down.

Fees

On the west side of the mountain, you'll need a **monument pass** ($8/person, under 16 free) to access the Johnston Ridge Observatory as well as any nearby hiking trails. Purchase your pass at the observatory upon arrival.

If visiting the east or south sides, you'll need a **Northwest Forest Pass** ($5/car or $30/year). You can buy day passes at self-service stations around the park, or look online to find the closest in-person vendor (www.fs.usda.gov).

Food and Accommodations

There is no food at Mount St. Helens, so bring a picnic lunch to the park. When you're ready for dinner, head out to Cougar on the south side for a small handful of restaurants or back west to Castle Rock near I-5 for some quick meal options.

There are minimal options for accommodations near the mountain, so it's best to either book a campsite or a hotel closer to Castle Rock.

Information
Coldwater Ridge Visitor Center

21000 Route 504, Castle Rock; 360/274-2131; www.fs.usda.gov; 10am-4pm daily May-Oct., 10am-4pm Sat.-Sun. Nov.-Apr.; $5/car winter, free spring-summer

Stop at the Coldwater Ridge Visitor Center to buy gifts and learn more about the mountain and its surrounding area.

Mount St. Helens Visitor Center

3029 Route 504, Castle Rock; 360/274-0962; https://parks.wa.gov; 9am-5pm daily summer, 9am-4pm Wed.-Sun. winter; $5 adult, $2.50 ages 7-17, free 6 and under, $15/family (2 adults plus any kids)

One of the first stops off I-5 on the way to the west side is the Mount St. Helens Visitor Center, and it's worth a visit to learn more about the volcano. A movie theater displays actual footage from the explosion, and plenty of exhibits explain the scientific parts of the eruption and how it changed the landscape.

WEST SIDE ACCESS

The west side is the most-visited area thanks to its multitude of hikes, places to visit, and Johnston Ridge Observatory. It's also the easiest and quickest spot to visit from I-5; Route 504/Spirit Lake Memorial Highway leads all the way to the observatory.

Sights
★ Johnston Ridge Observatory

Route 504, Toutle; 360/449-7883; www.fs.usda.gov; 10am-6pm daily May-Oct.; $8

Note: The road to the Observatory may be closed due to landslide damage; verify plans prior to arrival.

If you only stop at only one visitor center during your trip, make it the Johnston Ridge Observatory. Located at the end of Route 504, the hour-long drive from I-5 gives you peeks of increasingly dramatic views of the volcano, leading to one of the closest vantage points you can get to without hiking. Just a few miles from the crater, on the observatory's deck, visitors are often found mezmerized by the striking vista of the volcanic aftermath.

For those interested in a more immersive experience, free guided hikes (summer, first-come, first-served) lead visitors through the blast zone while providing informative insights into the landscape. Inside the observatory, explore a range of interactive exhibits and geological displays, including real-time seismograph readings and detailed accounts of the 1980 eruption. The observatory's theater shows a movie that vividly depicts the story of the mountain's eruption and subsequent recovery. Visitors can purchase snacks and drinks at a small food cart in the parking lot during the summer.

Forest Learning Center

17000 Route 504, Toutle; 206/539-3000; www.weyerhaeuser.com; 10am-4pm daily May-Oct.; free

Located inside the blast zone, the Forest Learning Center showcases what life was like before the eruption and then shows how recovery has been for the animals and forests in the area. Listen to stories from survivors who barely made it out alive, touch real lava rocks, and play on a playground. It's a fascinating perspective from the forest's point of view and talks about how Weyerhaeuser, a large lumber company, tried to salvage trees in the area.

Mount St. Helens Science and Learning Center

19000 Route 504, Toutle; 360/449-7883; www. mshinstitute.org; 10am-4pm Sat.-Sun. late Oct.-mid May; $8

The Mount St. Helens Science and Learning Center provides scientists' viewpoint on the eruption and subsequent recovery of nature. It's interesting to read exhibits explaining their take on the six disturbance zones created by the explosion and how they think life will recover in the future. The center is only open to the public during the winter when Johnston Ridge Observatory is closed, but in the summer it hosts a number of guided explorations and overnight camps (from $145/night).

Hiking

Hummocks Trail

Distance: *2.4 mi (3.9 km) round-trip*
Duration: *1 hour*
Elevation gain: *100 ft (30 m)*
Difficulty: *easy*
Trailhead: *Hummocks Trailhead*

Hummocks Trail is ideal for hikers of all ages, as it's a flat loop that goes through the hummocks, which are unusual hills the eruption created. Take your time to read the interpretive signs along the path, and keep an eye out for wildlife.

From Castle Rock, take Route 504 east for 43 mi (69 km), and turn right for the Johnston Ridge Visitor Center. Drive 2 mi (3 km) toward the visitor center and look for the trailhead on the right.

Harry's Ridge

Distance: *8.2 mi (13.2 km) round-trip*
Duration: *4.5 hours*
Elevation gain: *970 ft (295 m)*
Difficulty: *moderate*
Trailhead: *Johnston Ridge Observatory*

This is a more challenging yet highly rewarding hike, as you'll have views of the blast zone almost the entire way. Facing the mountain outside the observatory, follow signs for the trail to the left. It starts as a paved path and leads to switchbacks, and slowly continues upward. Late summer is one of the best times to visit, as parts are blanketed in huckleberries and wildflowers. You'll find an old weather station along the way and have views of both Mount St. Helens and Mount Adams as you climb.

Food and Accommodations

Eco Park Resort

14000 Route 504, milepost 24, Toutle; 360/274-7007; www.ecoparkresort.com; May-Oct.; $40-175

Eco Park Resort is the closest place you can stay to Mount St. Helens, only 28 mi (45 km) from the west side entrance. Choose from tent and RV campsites, cabins, and yurts, and enjoy hearty, home-cooked meals at their Backwoods Café before or after you visit Mount St. Helens.

Transportation

The west side of Mount St. Helens is about 2 hours 45 minutes from Seattle (155 mi/250 km). Take I-5 south to exit 63, and follow Route 504 east for 53 mi (85 km) to reach at the observatory.

SOUTH SIDE ACCESS

The mountain's south side had minimal damage from the eruption and is where climbers attempting to summit the volcano will start their journey. It's also popular for the Ape Caves lava tubes.

Sights

★ Ape Caves

Forest Road 8303, Toutle; 360/449-7800; www.fs.usda. gov; 9am-5pm daily May-Oct.; $5 rec. pass

Lava rushed down the southern slope of the mountain roughly 2,000 years ago. The molten center kept flowing even as the outer layer solidified, creating a lava tube with no solid substance inside. A logger found the cave in the 1950s; his friend and a group of young people called the Mount St. Helens Apes later explored it, giving it its distinctive name. The Ape Caves are the third-longest lava tube in North America, measuring around 13,000 ft (3,960 m), or over 2.4 mi (3.9 km), and consist of the Lower and Upper Caves.

Visitors in May-October need reservations, which can be made online (www.recreation. gov). One reservation is required per vehicle. Start your exploration at a set of stairs at the junction of the Lower and Upper Caves. You can do a self-guided tour of either from here.

If you choose the Upper Cave, a challenging 1.5-mi (2.4-km) hike awaits you — you'll see shifting lava tube formations, rock piles to climb over, and an 8-ft (2.5-m) lava fall that will test your agility. Skylight, a ceiling hole letting light in, and the Upper Entrance, indicated by a metal staircase, are natural features that contribute to the cave's allure.

The Lower Cave is more family-friendly, as it's only 0.7 mi (1.1 km) long and much easier to navigate. Most people start with this cave and then do the Upper Cave afterward if they feel up to it.

Inside, the temperature remains 42°F (6°C), with drippy ceilings and occasional puddles, so bring appropriate footwear, rain jackets, and flashlights with spare batteries. Pets are not allowed in the Ape Caves.

Hiking
June Lake
Distance: 2.9 mi (4.7 km) round-trip
Duration: 1.5 hours
Elevation gain: 445 ft (135 m)
Difficulty: easy
Trailhead: on Forest Road 83

June Lake is a great trail for families. This fairly flat hike goes through the forest and to June Lake with its crystal-clear waters and a 70-ft (21-m) waterfall that kids will love (although swimming isn't advisable).

To get here from I-5, take exit 21 for Woodland and drive 29 mi (47 km) east on Route 503, which turns into Forest Road 90; after 7 mi (11 km), turn left on Forest Road 83.

Drive this bumpy road for 7 mi (11 km) and turn left at the sign for the trailhead.

Lava Canyon
Distance: 5 mi (8 km) round-trip
Duration: 3 hours
Elevation gain: 1,600 ft (490 m)
Difficulty: moderate
Trailhead: end of Forest Road 83

Lava Canyon begins with a 0.3-mi (0.5-km) ADA-accessible trail with a waterfall viewpoint, but then the more challenging part begins. The route gets narrow and hugs the cliffs before leading to a 125-ft (38-m) suspension bridge with water rushing below it, which is the trail's highlight about 0.75 mi (1.2 km) in. Many people choose to turn around here, but you can continue deeper into the canyon, which includes going down a metal ladder and crossing the water while holding a cable. You'll then go on a loop to complete the trail.

To get here from I-5, take exit 21 and go east on Route 503 to Cougar (28 mi/45 km). Drive past the Swift Dam and turn left onto Forest Road 83, which ends at the trailhead (12 mi/19 km).

Butte Camp
Distance: 8 mi (12.9 km) round-trip
Duration: 5 hours
Elevation gain: 1,697 ft (517 m)
Difficulty: moderate
Trailhead: Merrill Lake Road

Beginning with a boulder field formed by an old lava flow, the Butte Camp hike continues into a verdant meadow rich with bear grass and wild strawberries. The trail then changes from a pine forest to a variety of dirt, pebbles, and roots. You'll reach Lower Butte Camp at 2.5 mi (4 km) and end at Upper Butte Camp at 4 mi (6.5 km), which gives you picturesque views of the mountain before you head back.

To get here from I-5, take exit 22 for Dike Access Road and turn left, followed by a left on E. Scott Avenue. Take the second exit at the traffic circle to Lewis River Road and proceed for 34 mi (55 km). Turn left on Forest Road 83 and drive 3 mi (5 km), turn left on Merrill

Climbing Mount St. Helens

Mount St. Helens, in contrast to the technical summit of Mount Rainier, attracts thousands annually because it's accessible for advanced hikers who are prepared for its mileage and elevation gain.

MONITOR RIDGE ROUTE

The most common path to the summit is the Monitor Ridge Route, starting from Climbers Bivouac trailhead on the south side (I-5 exit 22, then Lewis River Rd. to Forest Road 830 for 43 mi/69 km to the parking lot). This challenging yet nontechnical route climbs 4,500 ft (1,370 m) over 5 mi (8 km) to reach the crater rim at 8,328 ft (2,538 m). The first 2 mi (3 km) go through a forest before emerging onto the exposed mountainside. Here, climbers face 2 mi (3 km) of boulder fields, requiring careful navigation, followed by a final steep, rocky mile (1.6 km) to the summit.

No water sources are available along the way, so it's crucial to carry sufficient water and ample sun protection, as a large portion of the hike is devoid of shade. The round-trip hike generally takes 8-12 hours for those with sufficient conditioning. Once reaching the summit, hikers can enjoy a well-deserved rest and a once-in-a-lifetime view into the crater. However, it's vital to stay away from the rim, as fatalities have occurred over the years. This is especially true during the winter, when a giant cornice forms and gives a deceiving picture of where the edge is.

PERMITS

Climbing Mount St. Helens requires permits, the availability of which changes seasonally. In the peak climbing season, April 1-May 14, the daily limit is capped at 350 climbers. The limit goes down to 110 climbers daily May 15-October 31. Permits must be reserved in advance through recreation.gov; reservations open in March for climbs within that year.

However, in the off-peak season (November-March), the number of climbers is unlimited, and permits are free and self-issued at the trailhead. Regardless of season, each climber must carry their permit to show rangers who patrol the trail.

Before starting the climb, it's vital to sign in at the trailhead register. This is a critical safety measure, particularly since there's no cell service on the mountain. If climbing in the winter, make sure you have an ice axe and other winter gear to ensure a safer climb.

MOUNT ST. HELENS INSTITUTE

42218 NE Yale Bridge Rd., Amboy; 360/449-7883; www.mshinstitute.org/explore/guided-adventures; 10am-4pm Sat.-Sun.; from $288

If you're uncomfortable summiting Mount St. Helens by yourself, join one of the guided adventures with the Mount St. Helens Institute, where you can do a summit climb in winter or summer with experts. The company also offers other guided hikes with overnight camping stays and meals provided, if you're looking for a fun weekend adventure.

Lake Road, and continue for 3 mi (5 km) to the trailhead on the right.

Trail of Two Forests

Distance: *0.5 mi (0.8 km) round-trip*
Duration: *15 minutes*
Elevation gain: *50 ft (15 m)*
Difficulty: *easy*
Trailhead: *Forest Road 8303*

This wheelchair-friendly hike is more of a short stroll over boardwalks around two different forests that are 2,000 years apart in age. One of the forests has lava casts, which are tree imprints in old lava beds, and you can even crawl through one of the tree molds.

To get here from I-5, go east on Route 503 to Cougar (28 mi/45 km). Drive past the Swift Dam and turn left onto Forest Road 83, go 2 mi (3 km), and turn left onto Forest Road

8303, where the trail will be 0.5 mi (0.8 km) ahead on the left side.

Winter Sports
Marble Mountain Sno-Park
Forest Road 83; 360/449-7800; www.fs.usda.gov

On the southern end is Marble Mountain Sno-Park, perfect for winter sports enthusiasts. Visitors come here to go cross-country skiing, snowshoeing, hiking, and to begin Worm's Flow, the winter trail that leads to the volcano's summit. Winter visitors should be prepared with ice axes or crampons and aware that the mix of snow and wind can make for tough conditions. Check the Sno-Park and surrounding roads' conditions (www.fs.usda.gov) beforehand to ensure it's safe to visit.

To get here from Seattle, take I-5 south to exit 22 and go east on Route 503 (Lewis River Road), which turns into Forest Road 90. Continue until the junction with Forest Road 83. Turn left on Forest Road 83 and go 6 mi (10 km) to the parking lot.

Camping
Lower Falls Campground
Forest Road 90, turn right at the Pine Creek Visitor Center, Amboy; 509/395-3400; www.recreation.gov; May-Sept.; $15-35

Lower Falls Campground has 43 campsites for tents and RVs available to reserve, as well as drinking water and composting toilets. A big draw is it's near the Lewis River, which has plenty of shade and hiking trails to explore.

Transportation
Getting to the south side of Mount St. Helens from Seattle takes about 3 hours (180 mi/290 km). Take I-5 to exit 22 and follow Route 503 (Lewis River Road) east for about 50 mi (80 km).

CASTLE ROCK
Castle Rock sits in the shadow of Mount St. Helens. While it's not typically a destination to go to on its own, it's the local gateway and a convenient location to get food, stock up on groceries, and stay the night on the way to Mount St. Helens.

It takes about 1 hour 45 minutes (115 mi/185 km) to get here from Seattle via I-5 and exit 49.

Food
El Compadre
1289 Mt. St. Helens Way NE; 360/274-2265; https:// elcompadre.xyz; 11am-8pm Mon.-Thurs., 11am-9pm Fri.-Sat., noon-8pm Sun.; $12-18

This family-run business serves hearty Mexican meals made from scratch, such as sopitos with shredded beef and seafood burritos with salsa and sour cream. The colorful restaurant has a friendly atmosphere with plenty of table seating as well as a bar area.

★ Parker's Steakhouse and Brewery
1300 Mt. St. Helens Way NE; 360/967-2333; www. parkerssteakhouse.com; 1pm-8pm Tues.-Thurs., 1pm-9pm Fri.-Sat.; $14-25

Parker's Steakhouse and Brewery is a casual place to try local beer after a day on the mountain. You'll also find plenty of options to fill you up, such as Hawaiian ham steak topped with pineapple or the barbecue chicken and bacon sandwich.

Cascade Select Market
204 Cowlitz St. W.; 360/274-4143; www. cascadeselectmarket.com; 7am-10pm daily

You'll want to stop at Cascade Select Market at the beginning of your trip, as this large grocery store has a variety of groceries, including meat, produce, canned items, bread, and more.

Accommodations
★ Timberland Inn & Suites Castle Rock
1271 Mt. St. Helens Way NE; 360/274-6002; https:// timberlandinn.us; $104-199

Timberland Inn & Suites Castle Rock is a simple, no-frills hotel with 40 rooms, including queen and king rooms and family suites. They allow pets and have laundry facilities available, but the other amenities are minimal.

Silver Lake Resort

3201 Spirit Lake Hwy.; 360/274-6141; https://silverlakeresort.com; $154-200

Silver Lake Resort sits on the shores of Silver Lake and has seven tent sites, 19 RV sites, and five cabins, all equipped with fire pits. All guests have access to a camp store, boating and fishing, and restroom and shower facilities. Additionally, there's a small lodge with six rooms, and each room has a balcony you can fish from.

Mount Adams

Mount Rainier and Mount St. Helens get all the glory, while people tend to forget about Mount Adams. As a 4.5-hour drive (250 mi/400 km) from Seattle, it's not a day trip, but that doesn't mean it's not worth visiting. Originally named Klickitat, from the Indigenous Klickitat tribe who inhabited the area, it's the second-highest mountain in Washington at 12,280 ft (3,743 m)—and ideal for those who want to do summer hiking without the crowds.

PARK INFORMATION
Entrances

If you're visiting the south side of Mount Adams, **Trout Lake** will be the entrance you take. The town is about 30 minutes (10 mi/16 km) away from the base of the mountain, and you'll follow Mount Adams Road until you need to turn off for any hikes you might be doing.

If you're visiting the north side, you'll head south at Randle to Forest Road 23 until it turns into Mount Adams Road. This road goes down the west side of the mountain and eventually connects with Trout Lake. However, this road is closed during the winter.

MOUNT ADAMS WILDERNESS

www.fs.usda.gov; free with self-issued permit

The 47,000-acre (19,000-ha) Mount Adams Wilderness is home to the 18-mi-wide (29-km) volcano that is the largest by bulk in Washington. Those who wish to reach the peak of Mount Adams often use the South Climb route in this area, known for its challenging climbs.

The Mount Adams Wilderness is a joy for nature lovers who want a bit of solitude, with multiple activities such as backpacking, mountaineering, and hiking. Hikers will enjoy exploring a variety of terrains: open meadows, dense forests, glaciers, streams, and ancient lava flows.

The eastern portion of Mount Adams is within the Yakama Indian Reservation, and a considerable amount is off-limits to the public. Visitors should honor these boundaries and stick to the south and west side of the mountain.

Information
Mount Adams Ranger Station

2455 Route 141, Trout Lake; 509/395-3402; www.fs.usda.gov; 8am-4:30pm daily

Stop at the Mount Adams Ranger Station to get wilderness permits, information on trail conditions, and hiking recommendations.

Mt. Adams Chamber of Commerce

Route 14, milepost 65, 1 Heritage Plaza; 509/493-3630; www.mtadamschamber.com; 9am-3pm Tues.-Thurs., 9am-2pm Fri.-Sat., Mon.

Stop by the Chamber of Commerce before you head north to Trout Lake and Mount Adams to learn more about things to do in the area and hikes to go on.

1: Mount Adams 2: Trout Lake

Hiking

Mount Adams South Climb

Distance: *12 mi (19.3 km) round-trip*
Duration: *12 hours*
Elevation gain: *6,700 ft (2,050 m)*
Difficulty: *strenuous*
Trailhead: *Cold Creek Campground*

Many people prefer the South Climb because it requires the least technical expertise, but ice axes, hiking poles, crampons, or microspikes are still needed to summit. This isn't a hike to be rushed, so most climbers take two days to complete it. The trail starts in the forest and then becomes largely exposed for the rest of the way, so ample water and sun protection are necessary. Hikers will pass Lunch Counter around 4.5 mi (7.2 km) in, which is either a good resting stop or overnight camp. After that, continue onto Pikers Peak around 5 mi (8 km) in, where you'll encounter high winds and thin air that make breathing more difficult. This is a false summit, so you'll have less than a mile (1.6 km) for your final push to the top.

To get here, head north from Trout Lake onto Mount Adams Road to a V intersection, where you'll take a right onto Forest Road 23. Continue 1 mi (1.6 km) and then turn left on Forest Road 80, where you'll see a South Climb sign. Continue on this road to an intersection and turn right onto Forest Road 8040, past the Morrison Creek Campground, onto Forest Road 500 until you see the trailhead at the end by Cold Creek Campground.

Round the Mountain

Distance: *19.2 mi (30.9 km) round-trip*
Duration: *12 hours*
Elevation gain: *1,613 ft (492 m)*
Difficulty: *moderate/strenuous*
Trailhead: *Forest Road 285*

For those who want the mileage but not the elevation gain, head to the Round the Mountain trail, which follows part of the Pacific Crest Trail and crosses many others, such as the South Climb Trail, as it makes its way around the mountain. Contrary to the name, it doesn't go fully around Mount Adams but stops at the Yakama Indian Reservation, at which time hikers head back the way they came. Still, depending on the time of year, they'll get plenty of views of lakes, wildflowers, and often wildlife.

To get here, head north from Trout Lake on Mount Adams Road, and turn right onto Forest Road 82, following it for 6 mi (10 km). Turn left at Forest Road 285 (Bureau of Indian Affairs) and continue for 1 mi (1.6 km).

Crofton Butte

Distance: *4 mi (6.4 km) round-trip*
Duration: *2 hours*
Elevation gain: *600 ft (185 m)*
Difficulty: *easy/moderate*
Trailhead: *Crofton Ridge West trailhead*

Not all Mount Adams hikes have to be challenging, and Crofton Butte is an excellent example. You'll only gain 600 ft (180 m) in elevation as you make your way through fields of berries and flowers with views of Mount Adams and follow an area largely affected by wildfires several years ago.

To get here, head toward Trout Lake on Route 141 and turn right onto Mount Adams Road/Mount Adams Recreational Highway. Continue for 1.3 mi (2 km), then veer left at the fork onto Forest Road 23/Buck Creek Road. After 7.7 mi (12.4 km), turn right onto Forest Road 8031. Proceed for 0.5 mi (0.8 km), then turn right onto Forest Road 070/8031. Soon turn left onto Forest Road 060/8031 and follow it for 1.5 mi (2.4 km). Turn left onto Forest Road 020, marked for Crofton Butte Trail #73. Continue for 1.5 mi (2.4 km), then proceed straight onto Forest Road 050. Drive 1.5 mi (2.4 km) to the Crofton Ridge West trailhead on the left side of the road.

Climbing Mount Adams

The varied terrain of Mount Adams, with its glaciers, ridges, and snowfields, offers a wide variety of challenging summit routes. Skill in alpine climbing methods, accurate route finding, and effective use of climbing gear (such as crampons and ice axes) are required to complete these routes. The more difficult approaches, such as Adams Glacier or North

Lyman Glacier, require climbers to be well-prepared and aware of their particular skills to safely navigate complicated features like crevasses, ice falls, and granite headwalls.

Mount Adams is known for its highly unpredictable and rapidly changing weather, especially at elevations above 6,000 ft (1,800 m). Due to the increased risk of hypothermia and reduced visibility from frequent unexpected snowstorms, climbing becomes more challenging in the winter. To be safe, climbers must be well-prepared and make sound choices. They need to pay attention to weather advisories issued by the Northwest Weather and Avalanche Center and stay updated on the latest weather reports.

For those 16 and older, a **Mt. Adams Climbing Pass** is required to reach altitudes above 7,000 ft (2,130 m) on Mount Adams May 1-September 30. Climbers are required to obtain this pass ($20/person) on recreation.gov, regardless of whether they plan to summit. Visitors entering the Mount Adams Wilderness on their own need a free wilderness permit, which can be found at trailheads and Forest Service ranger stations. If you have a Mount Adams Climbing Pass, it also serves as your wilderness permit, so you don't need a separate one.

Alpine Ascents

109 W. Mercer St., Seattle; 206/378-1927; www. alpineascents.com; select 2-day trips June-July; $1,000
Alpine Ascents has been leading successful summits worldwide for many years, and they're a smart choice if you're considering climbing Mount Adams. Climbers learn the fundamentals of mountaineering over the course of two days, including how to use ice axes and crampons, how to travel and camp in the backcountry, how to move on snow, and how to self-arrest. The first night is camping overnight at the Lunch Counter, then the group wakes up early to begin the ascent. Some of the hike's necessities, such as breakfast, dinner, and tents, are supplied by Alpine Ascents, and they rent any other gear you may need. Climbers should be ready to carry a pack of 50-55 lbs (23-25 kg) or more when preparing to do this climb.

Camping

Camping is your best option for overnight stays in the Mount Adams area, unless you want a longer drive to stay at a hotel in Trout Lake.

Takhlakh Lake Campground

Takhlakh Loop Rd., Randle; 360/497-1100; www.fs.usda. gov; July-Sept.; $22-40
Takhlakh Lake Campground is a good base for hiking the area, as it's near several trailheads, and the campsites are well-shaded. There are 54 campsites but no drinking water is available. The first two weeks of July are first-come, first-served, then reservations are required for the remainder of summer.

Twin Falls Campground

Forest Road 90, Trout Lake; 509/395-3402; May-Sept.; free
Twin Falls only has five walk-in sites available, so get here early or on weekdays to snag a spot. You'll be near the Lewis River and Twin Falls Creek, making it a peaceful place to rest your head.

Transportation

To reach Trout Lake and the south side of the mountain from Seattle, take I-5 south, I-84 east, and exit 64 for Route 141 north, which takes about 4 hours (250 mi/400 km).

To reach the northwest side of the mountain from Seattle takes about 3 hours 45 minutes (150 mi/240 km) via I-5 south, Route 7 south, and US 12 east to Randle, then Route 131 south to continue onto Forest Road 23.

TROUT LAKE

With a population of 700, Trout Lake is the primary stop on the way to Mount Adams, just to the north. Camping is popular for those hiking around the mountain, but many people also want to sleep in a comfortable hotel bed and eat hot food at a restaurant, which the town is perfect for. If you don't mind driving back after a day of hiking, you'll get to experience what this small town has to offer.

Food

While there aren't a ton of options in Trout Lake, you will appreciate someone else cooking for you after a day on the mountain.

★ Mt. Adams Pizza

2291 Route 141; 509/496-4613; https://mt-adams-pizza. business.site; 4pm-8pm Thurs.-Sun.; $12-25

Order a pizza to split with your group at Mt. Adams Pizza, where you can sit in their small indoor area or on the outdoor patio to enjoy the sun. They have a variety of pizzas served on 14-in hand-tossed crusts, as well as salads and alcoholic and nonalcoholic beverages.

Station Café

2374 Route 141; 509/395-2211; Facebook @Station-Cafe-Espresso; 7:30am-7pm daily; $11-18

Refuel your body after a long day of hiking at the Station Café, which serves burgers and sandwiches for lunch and dinner as well as hearty breakfast options like pancakes and eggs. It's in a charming building with historical antiques on the wall, such as old license plates, and it doubles as a gas station.

Trout Lake Grocery

2383 Route 141; 509/395-2777; https://troutlake.org; 7:30am-7pm daily

If you're going camping, stop at Trout Lake Grocery to stock up on camping supplies, fuel, snacks, beer, ice, and much more. They also sell hunting and fishing licenses.

Accommodations

★ Trout Lake Valley Inn

2300 Route 141; 509/395-2300; www. troutlakevalleyinn.com; $135-145

Trout Lake Valley Inn has modern furniture with a log-cabin feel, and it offers free breakfast each morning as well as complimentary bikes during your stay. It also has a hot tub for relaxing after a long day.

Trout Lake Cozy Cabins

2291 Route 141; 509/395-2068; www. troutlakecozycabins.com; $149-179

Trout Lake Cozy Cabins give you privacy while being close to the base of Mount Adams. Choose from five private cabins that can sleep 2-6 people and have Jacuzzi tubs, partial kitchens, grills, and outdoor picnic tables.

Camping

Trout Lake Creek Campground

Forest Road 8810; 575/758-6200; www.fs.usda.gov; late May-late Oct.; free

Trout Lake Creek Campground is a small area with 17 first-come, first-served spots, and many people enjoy its proximity to Trout Lake. Visitors can fish off the dock (fishing license required) or hike the nearby Hoodoo Canyon Trail.

Transportation

Trout Lake is about a 4.5-hour drive (250 mi/400 km) from Seattle. To get here, take I-5 south to exit 27, follow Route 14 east for 16 mi (26 km), then turn left on Route 141 Alt, which turns into Route 141, and follow it for 20 mi (32 km) north.

Columbia River Gorge

Originating among the rugged Rocky

Mountains in British Columbia, Canada, the Columbia River flows majestically for 1,243 mi (2,000 km) to the Pacific Ocean. Along the way, it forms the boundary between the states of Washington and Oregon—and creates picturesque scenery.

The Columbia River Gorge, a 4,000-ft-deep (1,200-m) canyon that divides the two states, is at the river's southern end. The gorge is over 80 mi (130 km) long and full of beautiful waterfalls, historic landmarks, and small communities along the Historic Columbia River Highway.

Hood River, an hour east of Portland on the river's southern shore, is famous among windsurfers and kiteboarders. As you head north into Washington, Yakima's verdant valleys feed into the Yakima River, a

Highlights

Look for ★ to find recommended sights, activities, dining, and lodging.

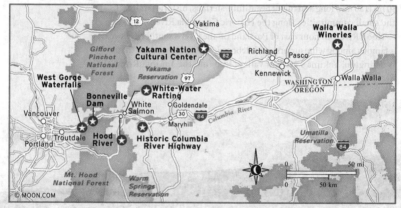

© MOON.COM

★ **Driving the Historic Columbia River Highway:** This scenic road along the river offers many waterfalls, historical sites, and viewpoints (page 388).

★ **Bonneville Dam:** This huge Columbia River dam is an impressive feat of engineering that plays a significant role in generating energy and managing the river (page 389).

★ **West Gorge Waterfalls:** This area of the Columbia River Gorge has a large portion of the state's waterfalls, making it easy to enjoy several in one trip (page 390).

★ **Hood River:** On the Oregon side of the Columbia River, Hood River is known for windsurfing, biking, and being a convenient base for Mount Hood (page 394).

★ **White-Water Rafting in White Salmon:** Get a thrill rafting down white-water rapids on the White Salmon River (page 404).

★ **Yakama Nation Cultural Center:** This museum, theater, and library share the Yakama tribe's story and how they shaped history in this area (page 415).

★ **Walla Walla Wineries:** With over 100 wineries in the region, Walla Walla is the top wine-tasting area in Washington for both locals and visitors (page 419).

major tributary of the Columbia River. Apple orchards, vineyards, and hop fields thrive here and have earned Yakima distinction as an agricultural wonder.

Continuing east, you'll find Walla Walla, a charming town with a thriving wine scene and an old-world feel. Historic sights and picturesque scenery dotted with vineyards make this area a popular choice for weekend getaways for residents and tourists alike.

ORIENTATION

From Seattle, it's about 3 hours via I-5 to Vancouver, Washington (where most people start their Columbia River Gorge journey), and then another 4 hours to Walla Walla, in the southeastern corner of the state.

I-84 parallels the Columbia River on the Oregon side, and US 30 runs alongside or near I-84 in parts. From Hood River to Yakima, I-82 is the primary route near the Tri-Cities. From Hood River directly to Walla Walla, or from Yakima to Walla Walla, US 12 is the main artery. On the Washington side of the Columbia River, Route 14 is a great smaller alternative to I-84.

Most sights are concentrated around Hood River, Yakima, and Walla Walla.

PLANNING YOUR TIME

On a Columbia River Gorge trip, allow at least **2-3 days** to fully see all the stops along the way. Although numerous bridges connect Washington and Oregon, many people prefer to pick one side instead of zigzagging back and forth. This can also save money, as some bridges have tolls. If you plan to add **Walla Walla** or **Yakima,** you'll want **an additional day for each** city so you'll have plenty of time to explore.

Most visitors begin their journey in Portland, Oregon, or Vancouver, Washington, and then head east along the Columbia River Gorge. Many small towns along the way are worth a stop, but you'll likely want to stay in the larger towns, such as Hood River and White Salmon, to have more access to food, gas, and lodging.

Summer tends to be the most crowded, so either book your hotels early or come during the spring or fall. **Spring** is the best time to visit the Columbia River Gorge if you want to see wildflowers. In winter, Hood River and the surrounding area can get heavy snow at times, so it's important to check road conditions ahead of time and bring chains if needed.

COLUMBIA RIVER GORGE
ITINERARY IDEAS

Itinerary Ideas

DAY 1

1 Start your day in Troutdale, Oregon, and visit the **Depot Rail Museum** to learn how railroads influenced the area.

2 Visit some of the Gorge's most beautiful waterfalls, such as **Elowah Falls** or **Latourell Falls.**

3 Head toward Hood River and enjoy pizza at **Solstice Wood Fire Pizza** for lunch.

4 On the Washington side of the river, stop at the **Stonehenge Memorial** in Maryhill before continuing east to Walla Walla.

5 In Walla Walla, check in to the **Marcus Whitman Hotel** and enjoy dinner at **Hattaway's on Alder.**

Columbia River Gorge and Washington Wine Country

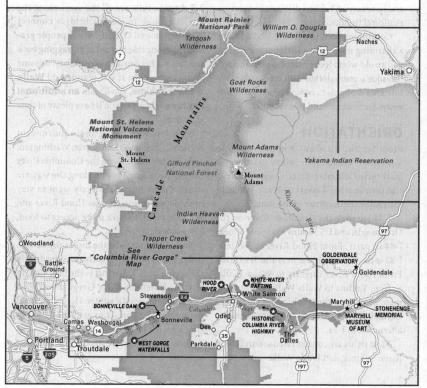

DAY 2

1 Start your day at **Carte Coffee** for coffee and pastries.

2 Dedicate your day to exploring Walla Walla's renowned wineries. Begin downtown with visits to **Seven Hills Winery** and **Kontos Cellars.**

3 For lunch, indulge in Italian flavors at **Passatempo Taverna.**

4 In the afternoon, explore south of town, such as **Amavi Cellars** and **Alton Wines,** enjoying the scenic vineyard views and exquisite wines.

5 Dine at **Hop Thief Taphouse and Kitchen** to end your day.

Previous: Columbia River Gorge; Elowah Falls; white-water kayaking.

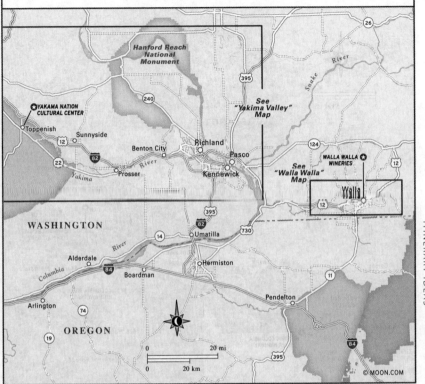

DAY 3

1 Set off toward Yakima and spend your morning exploring outdoor activities such as hiking the **Cowiche Canyon Uplands.**

2 Enjoy lunch at **Los Hernandez Tamales,** home of award-winning tamales.

3 Head to **Naches Heights Vineyard** for a tasting to start your Yakima wine experience, followed by **Treveri Cellars** for sparkling wines.

4 For dinner, head to **Cowiche Canyon Kitchen** for its farm-to-table fare.

Columbia River Gorge

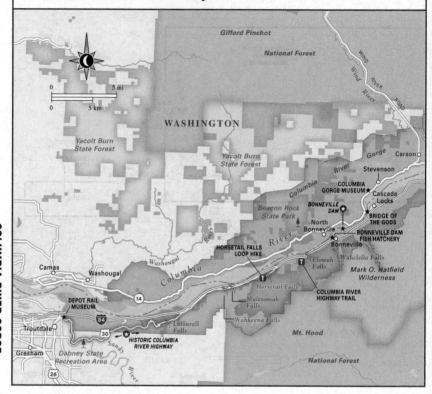

Oregon Side

The Oregon side of the Columbia River Gorge is rich in US history, as it was an essential part of the path Lewis and Clark took in 1805. The Historic Columbia River Highway (Route 30) between Troutdale and The Dalles was America's first planned scenic highway in 1913. Today only about one-third of the road is open to the public—I-84 runs parallel to it and is a quicker way to travel—but the open portion is one of the most beautiful sections. Driving Route 30 east of Troutdale, you'll pass by miles of hiking trails, stunning waterfalls, and infinite views. For people who like to get out of the car and into nature, the Oregon side of the river holds more appeal than its Washington counterpart, because of its proximity to so many waterfalls and hiking trails.

TROUTDALE, OREGON

While Troutdale has a population of over 16,000 and even its own airport, you'll likely only stop here if love fishing. With its proximity to the Columbia and Sandy Rivers, Troutdale is the place to fish in the area—you'll want to stay several days if that's your plan. There's also a small but charming historic downtown with a handful of restaurants.

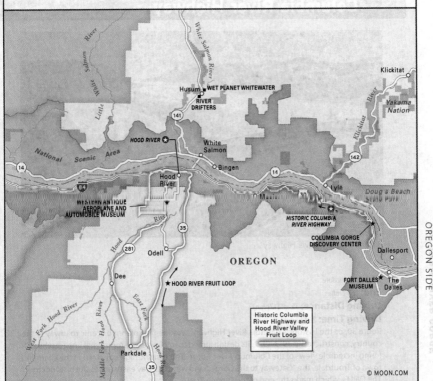

Historic Columbia
River Highway and
Hood River Valley
Fruit Loop

© MOON.COM

Sights

Depot Rail Museum

473 E. Historic Columbia River Hwy., Troutdale;
503/661-2164; www.troutdalehistory.org; 9am-3pm
Mon.-Thurs., 9am-5pm Fri.-Sun.; free

Troutdale became a thriving commercial center in 1882 when the railroad was built. The original depot burned down in 1907, but visitors can still view a historic railcar, photographs, and memorabilia from the era at the reconstructed depot.

Fishing

With its proximity to the Columbia and Sandy Rivers, the area is known for abundant stocks of salmon, steelhead, and trout. The best fishing seasons are summer and fall when the weather is dry and sunny, but you can fish year-round. You can catch more steelhead and other fish in the winter and spring, but if it gets too stormy, you might have to cancel your trip. Buy an Oregon **fishing license** online from the **Oregon Department of Fish & Wildlife** (https://myodfw.com; $23-93/person for 1-7 days for nonresidents).

Dabney State Recreation Area

Historic Columbia River Hwy., Corbett; 800/551-6949;
https://stateparks.oregon.gov; 6am-6pm daily; $5 day permit

Dabney State Recreation Area sits on the Sandy River and is popular for swimming, fishing, and boating throughout the year. Many people choose to fish from the

☆ Driving the Historic Columbia River Highway

Historic Columbia River Highway

Start: *Troutdale*
End: *The Dalles*
Driving Distance: *75 mi (121 km)*
Driving Time: *2-4 hours*

Route 30, or the Historic Columbia River Highway, was the first planned scenic roadway in the country, constructed in 1913-1922. Its design aimed to minimize environmental impact while offering incredible views of the Columbia River Gorge. This historic highway starts in the charming town of Troutdale, the "Gateway to the Gorge," and winds its way eastward to the historic city of The Dalles, which marks the end of the Oregon Trail.

The trip along this picturesque road can take 2-4 hours, depending on how often you stop to take in the scenery, which includes soaring cliffs, lush forests, and cascading waterfalls. The road's creative design has gentle curves, stone guardrails, and exquisitely built bridges that blend with the surrounding environment.

Over time, I-84 was built, cutting across part of the original highway; today most vehicles use I-84 through the Gorge when they have time constraints. However, there's still about 22 mi (35 km) of the old Route 30 you can drive on, with clearly marked signs along the way for hikes and waterfalls.

Among the several attractions in the area is Multnomah Falls, the tallest waterfall in Oregon, which drops an incredible 620 ft (190 m). Traveling further east, you'll see the fascinating Bonneville Dam and Fish Hatchery.

riverbanks, as no designated pier or fishing area exists. A boat launch is available for those who want to go further into the water.

Team Hookup

503/260-8285; https://teamhookupfishing.com; call for quote

An enthusiastic father-son duo runs Team Hookup, which hosts half-day and full-day guided fishing trips for Chinook and coho salmon using diverse techniques on the Columbia River and Pacific Ocean. They also lead trips in the Clackamas and Sandy Rivers, searching for winter and summer steelhead.

Food
Ristorante Di Pompello

177 E. Historic Columbia River Hwy., Troutdale;
503/667-2480; https://dipompello.com; 11am-10pm
daily; $18-24

Whether you're craving spaghetti and meatballs or seafood portofino, you can get authentic Italian food at Ristorante Di Pompello. It also has a wide selection of cocktails and wine, which you can enjoy on the small outdoor patio if you're early enough to snag a seat.

Le Petit Café

151 SW 257th Dr., Troutdale; 971/419-8391; www.
lepetitcafepdx.com; 8am-8pm daily; $10-20

Start your morning at Le Petit Café which many locals claim is the best coffee in town. This French bakery has plenty of freshly baked pastries you'll also want to buy, such as flaky pain au chocolat and savory macarons.

Accommodations
McMenamins Edgefield

2126 SW Halsey St., Troutdale; 503/669-8610; www.
mcmenamins.com; $45-166

McMenamins is known for restoring historic buildings and transforming them into beautiful resorts that pay homage to their history, and McMenamins Edgefield is no different. Built in 1911, this 74-acre (30-ha) property now has over 100 guestrooms, a soaking pool, a concert venue, a theater, craft studios, a golf course, and a spa. With multiple restaurants, a brewery, a winery, and a distillery to enjoy, there's no reason to leave the property if you want a relaxing weekend.

Information and Services
Legacy Mount Hood Medical Center

24800 SE Stark St., Gresham; 503/674-1122; www.
legacyhealth.org

This 115-bed hospital has an emergency room, a children's center, a behavioral health wing, and several specialty clinics.

Transportation

Troutdale is approximately 15 mi (24 km) east of Portland, via I-84 or Route 30. From Seattle, it takes about 3 hours (180 mi/290 km) to reach Troutdale via I-5 and US 84.

BONNEVILLE, OREGON

There isn't a lot to do in Bonneville, but it's worth stopping to see the iconic dam before continuing on your drive.

★ Bonneville Dam

Star Route, Cascade Locks; 541/374-8820; www.nwp.
usace.army.mil; 9am-5pm daily; free

As part of President Roosevelt's New Deal, the 1938 Bonneville Dam helped revitalize the Pacific Northwest by producing hydroelectric power, improving river navigation, and controlling flooding. The dam is accessible from both the Oregon and Washington sides of the river, with visitor centers on each end.

The five-story Bradford Island Visitor Center, situated on the dam's Oregon side, is packed with information about the dam's history. The top floor has an outdoor observation deck that allows visitors to get an up-close view of the dam. The fish ladder on the bottom floor is visible through an indoor viewing glass and can be reached from an outdoor walkway. You'll see various salmon here, particularly during late summer or early fall.

The Washington Shore Visitor Center (Dam Rd., North Bonneville, WA; 541/374-8820; 9am-5pm daily) may be just across the water, but you'll have to get back on I-84 east and take the Bridge of the Gods across the river, and then head west on Route 14 to reach it (about a 15-minute drive). You'll find similar exhibits about the dam, a fish viewing area, and an observation deck.

To get here, take exit 40 from I-84 in Bonneville and follow signs for the dam via NE Bonneville Way and Star Route to Dam Road (1.3 mi/2 2km).

Bonneville Dam Fish Hatchery

70543 NE Herman Loop, Cascade Locks; 541/374-
8393; https://myodfw.com; 7:30am-dusk daily; free

The Bonneville Dam Fish Hatchery, located 1 mi (1.6 km) south of the dam, is the largest in Oregon. The hatchery dates back to

☆ West Gorge Waterfalls

Multnomah Falls

If you're debating whether to drive the Washington or Oregon side of the Columbia River Gorge, the sheer number of waterfalls (over 70) along Oregon's historic Route 30 might persuade you. East of Troutdale, you'll find falls you can drive up to and others that take a bit of hiking but are worth the effort. The highest concentration of falls can be found on Route 30 between Corbett and Ainsworth State Park.

There's limited parking at the waterfalls, so taking the summertime **Sasquatch Shuttle** (47100 West Mill Rd., Corbett; 503/852-9092; https://sasquatchshuttle.com; 9:30am-5pm daily Memorial Day-Labor Day; $25-35) is a smart option if you don't want to deal with driving. This dog-friendly shuttle stops at six different viewpoints and waterfalls, giving you 15 minutes to look and take pictures at each. It's ideal for those who don't want to hike and instead want quick

1909 and was expanded in 1957 to address the loss in fish populations caused by dam building. During September and October you can see mature fall Chinook and coho salmon spawning. Stop by the hatchery's exhibit ponds to feed rainbow trout and see sturgeon that are more than 10 ft (3 m) long. You won't want to miss the 80-year-old, 500-lb (249-kg) sturgeon named Herman at the Sturgeon Viewing Center. You'll find a gift shop and informative displays around the building as well.

Transportation

Bonneville is 25 minutes (23 mi/37 km) east of Troutdale, reached by heading east on I-84.

CASCADE LOCKS, OREGON

Cascade Locks is a small town known for having the Bridge of the Gods, which connects Oregon and Washington, and has a handful of retaurants and hotels found along Wa Na Pa Street, the main street.

Sights
Bridge of the Gods

$3/car, free for pedestrians and bikes

Although multiple bridges cross the Columbia River, the 1,858-ft (566-m), steel truss Bridge of the Gods stands out among them. Built in 1926, it's an important vehicle crossing between Oregon's Cascade Locks and visits. However, the waterfalls tend to be the most powerful (from the melting snow) in late spring, which is before the shuttle season.

EASY-ACCESS WATERFALLS

- **Multnomah Falls:** At a stunning 620 ft (190 m) tall, Multnomah Falls is one of the most-visited places in the state, and it has multiple vantage points to get photos. A visitor center, gift shop, and restaurant are also available.

- **Horsetail Falls:** This is one of the easiest waterfalls to see with minimal effort, as you'll drive right by it on Route 30. You can also choose to park across the road and cross the highway to get a closer view of it.

- **Wahkeena Falls:** Named after the Yakama word for "most beautiful," this beautiful 242-ft (74 m) waterfall is two-tiered, and a path lets you get close to it for pictures.

WATERFALL HIKES

- **Horsetail Falls Loop Hike** (2.6 mi/4.2 km rt; 1.5 hours; 565 ft/172 m elevation gain): You'll pass by two waterfalls on this easy loop hike: first Horsetail Falls tumbling over a cliff, then some small switchbacks lead you up to Ponytail Falls. **Trailhead:** Take I-84 east from Troutdale for 18 mi (29 km) to exit 25 for US 30, where you'll find a small parking lot.

- **Elowah Falls** (2.1 mi/3.4 km rt; 1 hr; 340 ft/104 m elevation gain): This easy trail follows Gorge Trail 400 to Upper Elowah Falls Trail, a 213-ft (65-m) waterfall surrounded by rich lichen. **Trailhead:** From Troutdale, drive 18 mi (29 km) east on I-84, take exit 35, and follow NE Front-age Road for 2 mi (3 km).

- **Latourell Falls Loop** (2 mi/3.2 km rt; 1 hr; 639 ft/195 m elevation gain): This easy trail winds past several picturesque wooden bridges to a magnificent two-tiered waterfall that plunges over 200 ft (60 m) and is surrounded by dramatic basalt cliffs. **Trailhead:** Guy W. Talbot State Park

Washington's Stevenson and a famous Pacific Crest Trail landmark connecting the two states. Near the bridge, at approximately 110 ft (34 m) above sea level, the trail descends to its lowest point and links trekkers to the final leg of their lengthy ascent.

In 1927, aviator Charles Lindbergh gave the crowd a spectacular show as he skillfully flew the *Spirit of St. Louis* over and under the new bridge. Lindbergh's low flyover drew attention and gave the bridge's past a sense of mystery. The bridge became even more popular after the movie *Wild* came out in 2014. Based on Cheryl Strayed's memoir, the film highlighted the bridge's symbolic importance on the PCT.

Cascade Locks Marine Park

355 Wa Na Pa St., Cascade Locks; 541/374-8619; www portofcascadelocks.org; 6:30am-7:45pm daily; $10 parking

Cascade Locks Marine Park is an ideal place to take a break during a road trip, as there are picnic tables, restrooms, a beach, and a playground. Although it's no longer in use, the on-site train is also worth checking out—the first steam locomotive in the area—as is the **Cascade Locks Historical Museum** (541/203-0881; www.cascadelocksmuseum. org; 10am-5pm Thurs.-Mon. Mar.-Sept.; $6 adult, $3 ages 6-17, free 5 and under). The locks here are no longer in use, replaced by the Bonneville Dam, but you can still walk out onto Thunder Island to see remnants of the old ones. While you're at the park, check to see if **The Sternwheeler** (541/399-5029; www.sternwheeler.com; $40-100/person) is docked; it's a three-story paddle wheeler from 1983 that takes 1-2 hour cruises on the Columbia River.

Hiking
Eagle Creek to Punchbowl Falls
Distance: 4.2 mi (6.8 km) round-trip
Duration: 2 hours
Elevation gain: 450 ft (137 m)
Difficulty: easy
Trailhead: Eagle Creek Day Use Area

The entire Eagle Creek trail is almost 13 mi (21 km) long, but you can sample a portion of this popular trail. You'll walk through a lush forest for 2 mi (3 km) before taking a right to Lower Punch Bowl Trail, which leads to the beautiful Punchbowl Falls, where you might find people cooling off in the water during the summer. Get back on the trail to continue to the overlook to see the 35-ft (11-m) waterfall plunge into a large, bowl-shaped pool.

To get here from Troutdale, head east on I-84 for 24 mi (39 km) to Eagle Creek Day Use Area on the right.

Wahclella Falls
Distance: 1.9 mi (3 km) round-trip
Duration: 1.5 hours
Elevation gain: 308 ft (94 m)
Difficulty: easy
Trailhead: Yeon State Park

The Wahclella Falls trail leads through a narrow canyon that emerges at a small but beautiful waterfall by a bridge. You'll walk along a dense forest next to Tanner Creek before coming to the two-tiered waterfall that plunges 350 ft (107 m) into the pool. The bridge in front of it is a popular spot to get photos, but note that it can be icy in the winter and even into the spring.

From Troutdale, take I-84 east for 22 mi (35 km) to exit 40 and turn right to Yeon State Park; follow the sign to the trailhead on the right.

Food and Accommodations
Cascade Locks Ale House
500 Wa Na Pa St.; 541/645-5955; Facebook @cascadelocksalehouse; 8am-10:30pm Sat.-Sun., noon-7pm Thurs.-Sun., noon-4pm Mon.; $11-26

Cascade Locks Ale House feels like the place you go to catch up with friends after a long day, whether you're having a pint of Cascade Locks Pale Ale or eating a sweet and spicy Jamaican bacon pizza or cordon bleu sandwich for dinner. Check out their live music on the weekends.

Brigham Fish Market
681 Wa Na Pa St.; 541/374-9340; http://brighamfish. com; 11am-5:30pm Tues.-Thurs., 10am-6pm Fri.-Sun.; $15-23

You won't get fresher fish in the area than at Brigham Fish Market. The owners are a Native American family who use fishing methods passed down from their tribe to catch fish right from the Columbia River. You'll see the fish displayed on ice when you walk in and find tasty options like halibut and chips or a smoked salmon sandwich, which you can enjoy at an indoor table or take outside for a view of the river. You can also purchase fresh fish to go if you want to cook it yourself.

Columbia Gorge Inn
404 SW Wa Na Pa St.; 541/374-0015; https:// columbiagorgeinn.com; $107-161

The Columbia Gorge Inn is a simple but convenient place to stay on a trip through the Gorge, as their 40 rooms offer double, queen, and king options along with cable TV and free Wi-Fi. You'll be within walking distance of a handful of restaurants in Cascade Locks.

Cascade Motel
300 Forest Ln.; 541/374-8750; https:// cascadelocksmotel.com; $115-860

The Cascade Motel has been around since 1947 and is the last remaining motor court

1: Spinning Wheels Brewing Project 2: Solstice Wood Fire Pizza 3: Bridge of the Gods in Cascade Locks

in the Gorge area. It offers a variety of lodging options, from quaint cottages and roomy queen suites to 12 budget-friendly motel studios, with amenities like a fire pit and barbecue. It's set on 3 shaded acres (1 ha) only a few blocks from the main street.

Transportation

Cascade Locks is at exit 44 on I-84, about 26 mi (42 km) east of Troutdale or 7 minutes (5 mi/8 km) east of Bonneville.

★ HOOD RIVER, OREGON

As you drive east along I-84, the dense green forests start to lessen until you approach Hood River, a hip city full of farm-to-table restaurants, craft breweries, and boutique shops, with towering Mount Hood in the background. This picturesque town is a haven for windsurfing, kiteboarding, and sailing enthusiasts, due to its ideal location on the windy shores of the Columbia River. The charming downtown area also makes it a popular overnight stop.

Sights

Mount Hood Railroad

110 Railroad St.; 541/387-4000; www.mthoodrr.com; 11:30am departures Thurs.-Sat., specialty train times vary; $19-199

The Mount Hood Railroad is a historic and picturesque train that offers a one-of-a-kind way to see the beautiful Hood River Valley and the base of Mount Hood. Every season brings different rides, from 2-3 hour scenic tours through woodlands, orchards, and vineyards to themed ones like Halloween and the famous Christmas train, where Santa Claus will greet you.

Western Antique Aeroplane and Automobile Museum

1600 Air Museum Rd.; 541/308-1600; www.waaamuseum.org; 9am-5pm daily; $19 adult, $10 children

The Western Antique Aeroplane and Automobile Museum has over 150 vintage automobiles, motorbikes, and tractors on display, everything from early Model Ts to vintage muscle cars to one-of-a-kind treasures. There are also over 130 restored airplanes, including vintage biplanes, barnstormers, and military trainers from the height of aviation.

Scenic Drives

Hood River Fruit Loop

www.hoodriverfruitloop.com

This picturesque agricultural tour through Hood River Valley starts and ends in Hood

Mount Hood Railroad Depot

River. A well-marked 35-mi (56-km) loop takes visitors through the region's scenic agrarian landscapes, including lush orchards, rolling vineyards, rustic farms, and beautiful forests.

The loop only takes an hour without stopping, but you'll want to take your time and visit the family-run farms, fruit markets, vineyards, and cideries along the way. The route is dotted with places to buy fresh fruit, including cherries, apples, pears, peaches, and berries when they're in season. While you can do this drive any time of year, you'll get the most benefit in July-September, when fruit stands are open and full of freshly picked fruit.

Kiteboarding and Windsurfing

The wind along Hood River is strong and constant, because the temperature difference between the desert to the east and the Pacific Ocean to the west generates a natural wind tunnel effect in the Gorge. Thus Hood River is known as the Windsurfing Capital of the World. A windsurfer rides a board with an attached sail. Kitesurfing, also known as kiteboarding, combines elements of windsurfing, surfing, and paragliding; the rider holds a big, controllable kite to harness the strength of the wind and glide across the water. Gusts in Hood River can reach speeds far higher than the usual 15-25 mph (24-40 kph). Windsurfing and kitesurfing are year-round activities, although the best time is June-September, when the weather is hottest and the winds are most consistent.

Cascade Kiteboarding

Hood River Event Site, Portway Ave.; 541/392-1212; www.cascadekiteboarding.com; $375-675

If you're curious about kiteboarding but don't know where to start, Cascade Kiteboarding offers beginner lessons that teach all the basics you need. There's also advanced and self-sufficiency lessons if your aim is to be more independent on the kiteboard.

Wind Surf Express

502 N. 1st St.; 542/436-5454; www.windsurfexpress.com; from $250/day

If you already know how to windsurf, you can rent equipment from Wind Surf Express anywhere from one day to two weeks. They make it easy by delivering the gear to your hotel or vacation rental and will pick it up when you're done.

Sailing

Hood River is a popular sailing destination, given its consistent winds and stunning Columbia River Gorge landscape, and the region is ideal for sailors of all skill levels. The river's large width makes it a popular venue for sailing regattas and leisurely boat rides, with ample space for sailing maneuvers.

Columbia Gorge Sailing

Marina Boat Basin; 503/381-0660; www.columbiagorgesailing.com; 4pm and 6:30pm sailings various days mid-May-mid-Sept.; $300/up to 2 people, $75/extra person

Let someone else do the work for you—book a two-hour sailing cruise around the Columbia River and see some of the best spots along the way. Join the afternoon tour, or come for the sunset tour where you're encouraged to bring snacks and even champagne. Each tour leaves from a different dock in the Marina Boat Basin, so they'll let you know where to meet them.

Biking
Historic Columbia River Highway State Trail

Elowah Falls parking lot, Cascade Locks; 541/387-4010; https://stateparks.oregon.gov; $5 day permit

Separated into three disconnected paved sections along the original Route 30, the Historic Columbia River Highway State Trail winds along the Columbia River Gorge for 12 mi (19 km). From the Toothrock, Eagle Creek, and Bridge of the Gods trailheads, riders can easily reach the Bonneville segment, which links the John B. Yeon State Scenic Corridor to Cascade

Locks. From Starvation Creek State Park, visitors can reach the 6-mi (9.7-km) Mitchell Point segment, which provides views spanning Wyeth to Viento State Park. Beginning at the Mark O. Hatfield West and East trailheads, the 4.5-mi (7.2-km) Twin Tunnels segment travels downstream to Mosier, taking in river scenery and culminating at the historic Mosier Tunnels.

Hood River Mountain Bike Adventures

1813 Cascade Ave., Unit A; 503/705-3592; https:// bikehoodriver.com; 10am-5pm daily; tours $150-275, rentals $100-150/day

Check out some of the best mountain biking trails in the Gorge with Hood River Mountain Bike Adventures, where you can choose from half- or full-day guided tours for all skill levels. You can also rent a bike to hit the trails on your own.

Shopping
Doug's Hood River

101 Oak St.; 541/386-5787; https://dougshoodriver.com; 9am-6pm daily

Doug's Hood River is the place to stock up on clothing, from warm winter jackets to summer swimsuits. It also has all the gear you need for outdoor adventures, like skis, camping supplies, kiteboards, and much more.

Artifacts

202 Cascade Ave.; 541/716-1236; www. artifactsbookstore.com; 10am-6pm daily

When you're feeling adventurous about finding your next read, stop by Artifacts to choose from hundreds of random book titles. It's not the place to go looking for a specific title, but rather spend part of your afternoon browsing through books as you admire local art on the walls.

Laurel & Eddie

215 Oak St.; 541/490-5024; https://laurel-eddie.com; 10:30am-6pm Mon.-Sat., 11am-5pm Sun.

Laurel & Eddie has the latest women's fashion,

from athleisure to pajamas to seasonal dresses. The staff can help you with fittings to find the perfect size, and they have candles, jewelry, and more.

Breweries
Spinning Wheels Brewing Project

606 Oak St., Suite B; 541/716-1450; www. spinningwheelsbrewingproject.com; 4pm-8pm Sun.-Thurs., 4pm-10pm Fri.-Sat.

Follow the sound of records playing to find Spinning Wheels Brewing Project, which gets its name from the owner's love of both records and biking. Try their Shredipede Pale Ale and grab a seat on their outdoor (and dog-friendly) patio.

Ferment Brewing Company

403 Portway Ave.; 541/436-3499; https:// fermentbrewing.com; 11am-9pm Mon.-Fri., 10am-9pm Sat.-Sun; $12-21

Ferment Brewing Company has arguably one of the best views in town, on a second floor overlooking the Columbia River. They offer a large selection of beer, including barrel-aged beers and sours, ciders, wine, and mocktails. You can also order food to complement your drink, such as a small appetizer, salad, or sandwich.

Hood River Brewery Co.

101 4th St.; 541/705-7468; https://hoodriverbrewing. com; 2pm-8pm Mon., 2pm-8pm Wed.-Thurs., noon-9pm Fri.-Sun.

Hood River Brewing Co. is making a name for itself with beers like Waterfront Blonde Ale and Dog River IPA. Have a seat by their large corner windows to enjoy the sun, or come in the evening to listen to live music.

Food
Golden Goods

111 Oak St.; 541/436-3737; Instagram @goldengoodshr; 9am-3pm daily; $9-14

Vegans will rejoice when they see the menu at Golden Goods, where they make animal-free products taste amazing. Stop by for a chia parfait for a quick breakfast or get an eggplant pesto sandwich for lunch at this casual restaurant.

STOKED Roasters + Coffeehouse

603 Portway Ave., Unit 103; 541/436-0629; www. stokedroasters.com; 7:30am-4pm Mon.-Thurs., 7:30am-5pm Fri.-Sun.; $5-10

Start your morning at STOKED, a family-owned coffee shop that roasts its own signature blends. They always have creative seasonal coffee drinks to try, and you'll see locals greeting each other and then heading across the street to Waterfront Park for their morning walk.

★ Solstice Wood Fire Pizza

501 Portway Ave.; 541/436-0800; http:// solsticehoodriver.com; 11:30am-8pm Sun. and Wed.-Thurs., 11:30am-8:30pm Fri.-Sat.; $16-29

For a simple Margherita or something different like the spicy Hot Mama, Solstice's perfectly cooked wood-fired pizzas can't be beat. They focus on using local, seasonal ingredients in all their dishes, including their wide variety of salads. Order one of their innovative cocktails to enjoy while looking out at the waterfront from inside or the covered patio.

Celilo Restaurant and Bar

16 Oak St.; 541/386-5710; www.celilorestaurant.com; 5pm-9pm Tues.-Sat.; $17-39

Celilo perfectly represents the farm-to-table dining Hood River is famous for. They source locally as much as possible, whether it's the New York steak with red wine sauce, the house-made salmon patty, or the asparagus atop your fettucine. This is one of the best fine-dining places in the area, so make reservations.

Accommodations

Horsefeathers Boutique Hotel

115 State St.; 541/991-9998; www.horsefeathershotel. com; $349-999

Book a stay at the stylish Horsefeathers Boutique Hotel, which is on the edge of downtown and is one of the most convenient bases. Choose from four separate condominiums, each with its own kitchen, king-size bed, fireplace, and views of Hood River. You can easily explore the city from here before coming back to unwind on the balcony.

Westcliff Lodge

4070 Westcliff Dr.; 541/386-2992; https:// westclifflodge.com; $120-310

Westcliff Lodge is conveniently located near the Columbia River and offers 57 simple accommodations, some of which have scenic views. Choose from simple courtyard rooms, larger rooms with balconies, or even outdoor glamping. There's also a playground, outdoor fire pits, and barbecues, and several rooms are pet-friendly.

★ Columbia Gorge Hotel

4000 Westcliff Dr.; 541/386-5566; www. columbiagorgehotel.com; $124-453

The historic Columbia Gorge Hotel & Spa, with its 40 beautifully decorated guestrooms, provides a unique experience atop picturesque cliffs overlooking the Columbia River. Choose from accommodations with views of the tranquil gardens or the river for a peaceful stay. The hotel also offers luxurious treatments at Spa Remedease, classic cocktails at the Valentino Lounge (2pm-9pm Sun.-Thurs., 2pm-10pm Fri.-Sat.), and European food at the world-famous Simon's Cliffhouse Restaurant (7:30am-8pm daily; $22-41). Guests can also walk around the serene gardens and lush lawns and enjoy the beautiful on-site waterfall.

Information and Services

Providence Hood River Memorial Hospital

810 12th St.; 541/386-3911; www.providence.org

Stop by Providence Hood River Memorial Hospital for a 24/7 emergency room.

Transportation

Hood River is 20 minutes (20 mi/32 km) east of Cascade Locks via I-84 to exit 63.

THE DALLES, OREGON

Only 20 minutes east of Hood River sits The Dalles, the largest town along the river at 16,000 people. While it lacks the scenery that most of the Gorge has, it's a convenient place to stock up during a trip. It also tends to be a more affordable place to stay, with multiple chain hotels available as well as fast-food options for quick meals. Nevertheless, The Dalles has quite a bit of history to it, as shown in the Fort Dalles Museum and the historic downtown area full of local shops and restaurants.

Sights

Columbia Gorge Discovery Center

5000 Discovery Dr.; 541/296-8600; https:// gorgediscovery.org, 9am-5pm daily; $12 adult, $7 ages 6-16, $10 senior

The Columbia Gorge Discovery Center has two large wings with exhibits on the Ice Age, the dams found along the Columbia River, and the early settlers of The Dalles. Head outside to see historic wagons and cottages showing what life used to be like, and walk along the paved interpretive trail around the property for one of the best views of the Columbia River in the area.

Fort Dalles Museum

500 W. 15th & Garrison St.; 541/296-4547; https:// fortdallesmuseum.org; 10am-5pm daily Mar.-Oct.; $8 adult, $1 ages 7-17, $5 senior

One of the oldest museums in Oregon, the Fort Dalles Museum opened to the public in 1905. It features a traditional barn, historic homes filled with original artifacts such as clothing and furniture, and a building full of vintage cars. Constructed in 1856, the Surgeon's Quarters is the oldest structure within the museum and shows that era's local medical and military history. Visitors can take self-guided tours or join a free guided tour that lasts about an hour to get an in-depth history lesson.

Wineries

Sunshine Mill Winery

901 E. 2nd St.; 541/978-9588; www.sunshinemill.com; noon-6pm daily; tasting $20

The Sunshine Mill is an important part of the area's industrial history; it milled wheat for 130 years and had a Thomas Edison motor—the first building in the area to be electrified. The facility has since transformed into a winery with a variety of wines like pinot noir, malbec, and pinot gris, and a range of small plates like brie and artichoke dip. Seasonally, you can also experience a drive-up movie where wine and snacks are sold.

Food

Wild Brew

418 E. 2nd St.; Instagram @wild_brew_td; 7am-3pm Mon.-Sat.; $12-25

Located in the heart of downtown, Wild Brew is a cheerful place to get your morning brew, with big sunny windows and green plants throughout. If you stay until lunchtime, you can also order a pizza or a burger.

Cousins' Restaurant & Saloon

2114 W. 6th St.; 541/298-2771; https:// cousinsrestaurants.com; 6am-9pm daily; $13-30

No matter what you're craving—biscuits and gravy for breakfast, chicken fried steak for dinner—Cousins' has you covered. Fun decorations honor the area's farming past, including real tractors displayed throughout the eatery. You can also swing by the saloon if you're in the mood for a quick bite and a drink.

Casa El Mirador

1424 W. 2nd St.; 541/298-7388; www.casaelmirador. com; 11am-9pm daily; $14-25

Fill up on hearty servings of Mexican food such as tacos, enchiladas, or burritos at the colorful, casual Casa El Mirador. Their weekday happy hour (3pm-6pm) has discounts on drinks and appetizers.

1: Columbia Gorge Discovery Center 2: Fort Dalles Museum

Accommodations

Celilo Inn

3550 E. 2nd St.; 541/769 0001; https://celiloinn.com; $119-159

Celilo Inn may look like another roadside motel, but once inside, you'll find 46 rooms tastefully renovated with contemporary furnishings. These rooms are perfect for groups of all sizes, from solo travelers to families with children in the spacious two-bedroom suite. The view from most accommodations, which overlook the Columbia River, is even more stunning.

Information and Services

Adventist Health Columbia Gorge

1700 E 19th St.; 541/296-1111; https://mcmc.net

Adventist Health Columbia Gorge is a 47-bed hospital with an emergency room, childbirth center, and several other specialty areas such as behavioral health.

Transportation

The Dalles is about 20 minutes (21 mi/34 km) east of Hood River on I-84. To reach the downtown area, take exit 84.

Washington Side

While Oregon is the more popular side of the Gorge, the Washington side offers lush, green landscapes with thick forests in the western section. As you travel further east, the scenery shifts to rolling farmland. From Vancouver, you'll head east on Route 14 and follow it along the river.

VANCOUVER

Vancouver, Washington, sits just across the river from Portland, Oregon. Its history is connected to Fort Vancouver and the fur trade, but today this city provides a more relaxed atmosphere than lively Portland. Vancouver's waterfront has been beautifully restored to feature multiple waterfront eateries with stunning views across the Columbia River. Vancouver is an ideal place to stop and rest before going road-tripping east into the Columbia River Gorge.

Sights

Fort Vancouver National Historic Site

1001 E. 5th St.; 360/816-6230; www.nps.gov; 9am-4pm Tues.-Sat.; $10 day pass

Fort Vancouver was built in 1824 and was a vital fur trading station for the British Hudson's Bay Company, which relied on its riverside position for transportation and trade. The site became an important US military

station after it came under the Americans' control in 1846 as a result of the Oregon Boundary Treaty. The fort was further developed by the US Army and used as a supply depot throughout the Civil War and Indian War.

As military use of Fort Vancouver declined in the 20th century, preservation efforts ramped up, and in 1948 the fort was officially designated as a National Historic Site. The restored buildings now serve as a cultural center and museum where visitors can gain insight into the site's past and the dynamics between Indigenous people and European settlers.

The Chief Factor's House, fur store, and blacksmith's shop are just a few of the buildings that provide a look into the 19th-century fur trade. The nearby **Pearson Air Museum** (1115 E. 5th St.; 360/816-6232; www.nps.gov; 9am-4pm Tues.-Sat.) showcases the history of aviation in the Pacific Northwest through exhibits on early flight and antique aircraft. You can also visit the heritage garden that demonstrates historic horticulture techniques for cultivating crops to sustain the fort's inhabitants.

Hiking

Columbia River Renaissance Trail

Distance: 5 mi (8 km) one-way
Duration: 3.5 hours
Elevation gain: 10 ft (3 m)

Difficulty: *easy*

Trailhead: *Vancouver Waterfront Park*

While the Columbia River Renaissance Trail is a 10-mi (16-km) trip if you do the whole journey, many people walk part of it and then turn around. Most begin at the Vancouver Waterfront Park, but you can also start on the opposite end at Wintler Community Park and head west. Enjoy views of Portland and Mount Hood across the river as you stroll along this flat, paved trail that is wheelchair accessible. You'll come across numerous benches, picnic spaces, and playgrounds along the way.

Food

Relevant Coffee

1703 Main St., Suite A; 971/319-5773; http:// relevantcoffee.com; 7am-5pm daily

Relevant Coffee has a neighborhood coffee shop feel, where you'll see locals catching up before starting their day. It has a variety of espresso drinks like macchiatos or nitro cold brew in addition to savory French pastries and vegan cookies and muffins.

Twigs Bistro

801 Waterfront Way, Suite 103; 360/726-4011; www. twigsbistro.com; 11am-9pm Mon.-Wed., 11am-10pm Thurs., 11am-11pm Fri., 10:30am-11pm Sat., 10:30am-9pm Sun.; $29-46

Make a reservation at Twigs Bistro for one of the best waterfront dining experiences on the Columbia River. Enjoy indulging in options like truffle penne and wild mushroom shrimp risotto; they also have a small vegan menu available.

Loowit Brewing Company

507 Columbia St.; 360/566-2323; https:// loowitbrewing.com; noon-10pm Tues.-Thurs., 11am-10pm Fri.-Mon.; $13-19

This independent brewery is a fun place to watch the local game while enjoying a fried chicken sandwich or fresh fish and chips. Make sure to grab a pint of fresh beer, such as their flagship Shadow Shinobi IPA or German-style Corsair Kolsch.

Accommodations

The Heathman Lodge

7801 NE Greenwood Dr.; 360/254-3100; www. heathmanlodge.com; $138-280

The Heathman Lodge feels like you're in a luxurious log cabin with its rustic ambience with 182 guestrooms and 20 suites. Amenities include a hot tub, sauna, indoor pool, and state-of-the-art exercise equipment. The property has walking trails and a patio with a koi pond. Stop by **Hudson's Bar & Grill** (8am-2pm, 5pm-10pm Tues.-Sat., 8am-2pm, 5pm-9pm Sun.-Mon.; $19-46) for options like sweet potato gnocchi and duck or seared halibut.

Hotel Indigo Vancouver Downtown

550 Waterfront Way; 360/816-0058; www.ihg.com, $275-300

There are 138 boutique-style rooms at the Hotel Indigo Vancouver Waterfront, many of which have Columbia River views. The hotel is set on the Vancouver Waterfront Trail and provides free bike rentals for up to two hours. There are multiple options for when you get hungry, including fine dining at **El Gaucho** (4:30pm-9pm Tues.-Fri., 4pm-9pm Sat.), everything from egg Benedict to salmon dinner at **13 Coins** (7am-11pm Sun.-Thurs., 7am-2am Fri.-Sat.), drinks at the rooftop bar **Witness Tree** (4pm-10pm Tues.-Thurs., 4pm-10:30pm Fri.-Sat.), and espresso drinks at **13 Coins Coffee House** (7am-5pm Mon.-Sat., 7am-2pm Sun.).

Information and Services

Visit Vancouver

1501 E. Evergreen Blvd.; 360/816-6230; www. visitvancouverwa.com; 9am-5pm Tues.-Sat. summer, 9am-4pm Tues.-Sat. winter

Stop by Visit Vancouver's office to grab brochures on things to do in the area and get help creating a customized itinerary.

PeaceHealth Southwest Medical Center

400 NE Mother Joseph Pl.; 360/514-2000; www. peacehealth.org

This 450-bed hospital has an emergency

room, trauma center, cardiology center, and more.

Transportation

Vancouver is 2.5 hours (165 mi/265 km) from Seattle without traffic, reached by taking I-5 south. From Portland, Vancouver is a quick 15-minute (9 mi/14 km) drive north over the river on I-5.

CAMAS

Travel 14 mi (23 km) east of Vancouver and you'll come across the charming city of Camas. Known for its rich history rooted in the paper industry in the late 1800s, Camas has evolved into a picturesque small town with strong community ties. Despite often being overlooked on road trips, Camas is worth a stop for its beautifully restored historic downtown, full of locally owned stores, cozy coffee shops, and local eateries that give it a warm, inviting atmosphere.

Shopping
Bookish

335 NE 5th Ave.; 503/329-8449; www.itsbookish.com; 11am-5pm Tues.-Wed. and Fri.-Sat., noon-5pm Thurs.

Located in the heart of downtown, Bookish is an independent bookstore that carries the works of both popular and lesser-known authors. The children's area, complete with kids' cushions, is sure to be a hit with the little ones, and the warm, inviting atmosphere is ideal for a rainy day.

The Soap Chest

521 NE Everett St.; 360/834-1212; https://soapchest. com; 9:30am-5:00pm Mon.-Fri., 10am-5pm Sat.

The owner of The Soap Chest started making clean soaps from scratch with goat milk and herbs grown in her own garden after seeing a pattern of skin issues in her family. This cute shop has expanded to include lotion, bath bombs, salts, and more, so you'll want to stock up.

Food
Caffe Piccolo

400 NE 4th Ave.; 360/834-7044; www.caffe-piccolo. com; 7am-5pm Mon.-Fri., 8am-4pm Sat.-Sun.; $5-7

Caffe Piccolo is where locals go for morning coffee and quick breakfasts, like an egg croissant sandwich or vegetarian paninis for lunch. There's plenty of seating in the back, but the best seats are by the large windows where you can people-watch.

Nuestra Mesa

228 NE 4th Ave.; 360/210-5311; www. nuestramesacamas.com; 11:30am-9pm Mon.-Sat., 11am-8pm Sun.; $17-26

At Nuestra Mesa, you'll find tasty options like chile relleno and over a dozen tacos, such as avocado or spicy shrimp tacos. Larger groups can sit at one of the tables, while smaller parties can slide up to the bar for a Cadillac margarita while watching the game on TV.

Grains of Wrath Brewing

230 NE 5th Ave.; 360/210-5717; https://gowbeer.com; 11am-10pm daily; $12-18

Grains of Wrath is a fun, family-friendly place to grab dinner, with options like a tuna poke bowl, banh mi burger, and a small kids' menu. Its award-winning beers, like the Dystopia IPA and the Vienna Lager, are a must-try.

Accommodations
Camas Boutique Hotel

405 NE 4th Ave.; 360/834-5722; www. camasboutiquehotel.com; $139-209

With its charming European facade and furnishings, the Camas Boutique Hotel is one of the few options in town worth staying at. Built in 1911, this historic hotel is conveniently located in the middle of downtown Camas, making it easy to explore the neighborhood. There are 23 rooms; the ensuite ones have a private bathroom, while the European-style rooms will have you sharing with your neighbors.

Transportation

Head east on Route 14 for 15 minutes (14 mi/23 km) to get to Camas from Vancouver.

STEVENSON

Although Stevenson's population is well under 2,000, it's a convenient stop on Route 14 when you need a bite to eat. It's also home to the vast Beacon Rock State Park, if you're up for a hike.

Sights
Columbia Gorge Museum

990 SW Rock Creek Dr.; 509/427-8211; www.
columbiagorgemuseum.org; 10am-5pm daily; $6-10

Behind beautiful floor-to-ceiling windows, the Columbia Gorge Museum offers fantastic views of the Columbia River. Its extensive collection showcases Native American history, the Lewis and Clark expedition, and the growth of regional industries, including fishing, forestry, and river transportation. Two notable features are a working steam engine from an 1800s sawmill and a massive fish wheel measuring 37 ft (11 m) in diameter. The museum is also proud to have the most extensive rosary collection in the world.

Hiking
Beacon Rock State Park

34841 Route 14; 509/427-8265; https://parks.wa.gov; 8am-dusk daily; $10 day pass

Beacon Rock State Park is the area's most popular attraction and spans 4,500 acres (1,800 ha). Beacon Rock, a basalt plug that remains from the area's volcanic past, stands at 848 ft (258 m) and is its most distinctive feature. The park has more than 26 mi (42 km) of paths ideal for horseback riding, hiking, and mountain biking. You'll also find multiple places to camp, picnic, launch boats, and rock climb, and the park has 9,500 ft (2.9 km) of freshwater shoreline access. Learn about the park's natural and human history, starting with the Ice Age floods, at the Doetsch day use area, which has an interpretive route that is 1.2 mi (1.9 km) long and wheelchair accessible.

Food
Bigfoot Coffee Roasters

91 2nd St.; 509/774-7167; www.bigfootcoffeeroasters.
com; 7am-4pm Mon.-Fri., 8am-4pm Sat.-Sun.

Just behind a Chevron station is this unique coffee shop, so you can recharge your body and car at the same time. You can tell the difference in their coffee as they use organic, fair-trade beans sourced from all over the world. Sit down at one of their indoor tables with a latte, a muffin, or quiche before you hit the road again.

Red Bluff Tap House

256 2nd St.; 509/427-4979; http://redblufftaphouse.
com; 11:30am-8:30pm Mon.-Tues. and Thurs., 8am-9pm Fri.-Sat., 8am-8:30pm Sun.; $14-18

The Red Bluff Tap House is a family-friendly gastropub with brick-lined walls, a full bar, and an inviting patio. Its menu includes options like the Shoulda Gouda Woulda burger topped with melted gouda and bacon jam or fish tacos with a spicy jalapeño chimichurri. You'll also find over a dozen beers from Pacific Northwest breweries on tap.

El Rio Texicantina

193 2nd St.; 509/427-4479; www.elriotexicantina.com; 4pm-8pm Mon.-Tues. and Thurs., 4pm-11pm Fri., noon-11pm Sat., noon-8pm Sun.; $16-23

Columbia quesadillas with chipotle sour cream and blue corn enchiladas suizas are just two of the unique Mexican foods served at El Rio Texicantina. The restaurant has a lively vibe with weekly events like music bingo and karaoke, which is perfect for those who want to linger a bit longer with their margaritas.

Accommodations
Hotel Stevenson

77 South West Russell Ave.; 509/219-5009; www.
hotelstevenson.com; $138-216

Built in 1909 as the Colonial Hotel, this building was renovated in 2020 to restore its original purpose as an upscale boutique hotel. While the 12 rooms are fairly simple and amenities limited, it has **77 Cork & Tap Bistro** (3pm-7pm Wed.-Fri., noon-7pm Sat.), where you can get small bites like hummus and local wine and beer.

Skamania Lodge

1131 SW Skamania Lodge Way; 509/314-4177; www. skamania.com; $219-471

Get away to the picturesque Skamania Lodge in a lush forest setting. The main lodge has 244 rooms, plus options for glamping and the one-of-a-kind Treehouse Village, where you can stay in life-size treehouses. The lodge has amenities including a full fitness center, an indoor swimming pool, indoor and outdoor hot tubs, and a spa. Outdoors, there are several nature walks, a nine-hole golf course, an 18-hole mini-golf course, a ziplining course, and tennis, basketball, and volleyball courts. The **Cascade Dining Room** (7am-9pm daily; $15-50) has dishes like chorizo hash for breakfast or seafood risotto for dinner.

Transportation

From Camas, take Route 14 east for 40 minutes (31 mi/50 km) to reach Stevenson.

WHITE SALMON

Across the Columbia River from Hood River, White Salmon is a smaller town but with equal outdoor adventures. Kayaking and white-water rafting along the White Salmon River are among the most popular activities. White Salmon has a handful of restaurants and a few accommodation options, but it lacks the diversity of restaurants and hotels and the charm of Hood River. There's a small downtown area where most of these are clustered around a few blocks.

★ White-Water Rafting and Kayaking
River Drifters

856 Route 141; 800/972-0430; https://riverdrifters.net; Apr.-Oct.; $65-165

The White Salmon River has some of the best white-water rafting in the area, and River Drifters has been taking people of all skill levels out on the waters for decades. Choose from a guided half-day or a full day if you're

feeling adventurous. No experience is necessary, as the staff will teach basic strokes to any newcomers.

Wet Planet Whitewater

860 Route 141; 509/493-8989; https:// wetplanetwhitewater.com; June-Sept.; $155-165

Wet Planet Whitewater offers both whitewater rafting and kayaking classes and day trips, as well as programs for kids. For a longer experience, book one of their multiday river rafting trips ($1,495-2,295/person), which include meals and the necessary camping gear.

Food
Pixán Taqueria & Cantina

216 E. Jewett Blvd.; 509/281-3054; www.pixantacos. com; 4pm-9pm Tues.-Sun.; $7-27

Pixan Taqueria & Cantina puts a twist on Mexican food like corn truffle popcorn or specialty tacos like salmon with avocado mousse, in addition to classics like chips and guacamole. They also have an extensive bar menu, and you'll be lucky to grab a table outdoors on a sunny day.

Everybody's Brewing

177 E. Jewett Blvd.; 509/637-2774; https:// everybodysbrewing.com; 11:30am-9pm daily; $11-19

While neighboring Hood River may have its share of breweries, this side of the river has Everybody's Brewing. Try the citrusy Early Riser IPA in their large tasting room, or order from their extensive food menu that includes vegan nachos, sweet chili wings, and other pub classics.

Accommodations
Inn of the White Salmon

172 W. Jewett Blvd.; 509/493-2335; www. innofthewhitesalmon.com; $129-312

The Inn of the White Salmon is one of the few places to stay in town. While it's basic, it does the trick if you're looking for affordable overnight accommodation. They have a 22 rooms, from standard queens to family suites with bunk beds.

Transportation
White Salmon is 30 minutes (22 mi/35 km) east of Stevenson via Route 14.

MARYHILL
While Maryhill's current population is about 50, it was originally established with high hopes. In 1907 Samuel Hill bought some property in what is now Maryhill to establish a Quaker farming community. Though the agricultural community didn't thrive, he did manage to build the Maryhill Museum of Art. Despite being planned as a house, in 1926 it was dedicated as a museum, and today it houses one of the most varied art collections in the region. Hill also built the Stonehenge replica, one of Maryhill's main attractions. While the town itself doesn't have much outside these two attractions, they're worth the stop.

Sights
Maryhill Museum of Art
35 Maryhill Museum Dr, Goldendale, 509/773-3733; www.maryhillmuseum.org; 10am-5pm daily Mar. 15-Nov. 15; $16 adult, $5 youth

Located on the magnificent cliffs of the Columbia River Gorge, the Maryhill Museum of Art is an isolated site. Originally designed

as Samuel Hill's mansion, the building opened to the public in 1926, dedicated to the celebration of art, history, and culture. The museum's collection is extensive and varied, including works by European artists, relics from Native American cultures, sculptures by Rodin, and much more.

One of the permanent collections features numerous items from Queen Marie of Romania. She was Sam Hill's friend and, after her visit to the museum, donated more than 100 items from her personal collection. These included paintings, Russian icons, manuscripts, jewels, and a copy of her coronation crown from 1923.

Stonehenge Memorial
3 mi (5 km) east of Maryhill Museum, Goldendale; 509/773-3733; www.maryhillmuseum.org; 7am-dusk; free

In 1918 the Stonehenge Memorial was built as the first World War I monument in the nation. It is a moving tribute to the local soldiers who died in the conflict. Inspired by his incorrect assumption that the original Stonehenge's function was a sacrificial site, Samuel Hill built this copy to show how the senseless death toll of the war was similar to ancient sacrifices. This meticulous re-creation

Stonehenge Memorial

faithfully reproduces the layout and proportions of the original English monument. Hill was buried in a crypt at the base of the monument, which visitors can see today.

Wineries
Waving Tree Winery & Vineyards

123 Maryhill Hwy., Goldendale; 509/773-6552; https://wavingtreewine.com; 10am-5pm daily; tasting $20-30

Waving Tree Winery is a family-operated vineyard featuring 18 varietals, including Italian favorites like Sangiovese, Barbera, and Nebbiolo, Rhone varietals such as Syrah and Grenache, and unique sweet wines like orange muscat. It's open for tastings by appointment only and has a small tasting room with antique wooden furniture plus outdoor lawn seating when it's dry out.

Transportation

Maryhill is about 45 minutes (39 mi/63 km) east of White Salmon and reached by taking Route 14.

GOLDENDALE

Founded in 1872, Goldendale quickly became the county seat and an important center for transportation, agriculture, and trade because of its proximity to the Columbia River. The Goldendale Observatory, a prominent public American observatory, also had a significant impact on the town's growth and development. The downtown area has a variety of restaurants, shops, banks, and more, but the observatory is the main draw.

While several hotels are available, most people stay closer to the Gorge or continue north to the Tri-Cities for overnight lodging. Goldendale is about 7 mi (11 km) north of the Columbia River, so people tend to stop here either for the observatory or on their way to Yakima, about 70 mi (110 km) north.

Sights
Goldendale Observatory

602 Observatory Dr., Goldendale; 509/773-3141; www.goldendaleobservatory.com; appointments only, 2pm-4pm and 7pm-10pm Fri.-Sun. Oct.-Mar., 3pm-5pm and 9pm-midnight Thurs.-Sun. Apr.-Sep.; $10 Discover Pass to park, museum free

Constructed in 1973, the Goldendale Observatory is known for its large telescopes that are open to the public. Set atop a hill in Goldendale Observatory State Park, this educational institution offers afternoon solar viewings and nighttime sky explorations. You'll learn about the sun during the afternoon program, while the coveted nighttime program lets you see galaxies, planets, and more through their giant telescope. Both are free to attend, but you'll need to reserve your spot in advance on their website.

Food
Pete's Pizza Pub

340 E. Collins St., Goldendale; 509/281-2772; https://petespizzapub.com; 4pm-9pm Wed.-Thurs., 2pm-9pm Fri.-Sat.; $15-34

Stop by Pete's Pizza Pub for a hearty pie, with creative options like the Meat Lovers Lane or the vegetarian Roger Rabbit. They also have hot sandwiches, salads, and local beer on draft in this casual restaurant with comfortable booths and bright-red walls.

Bake My Day Café

118 W. Main St.; 509/773-0403; Facebook @BakeMyDayWA; 8am-3pm Mon.-Thurs., 9am-2pm Sun.; $6-14

Bake My Day Café is an affordable spot to grab breakfast, such as biscuits and gravy or a Monte Cristo sandwich for lunch, while enjoying local photography that lines the walls. They also have plenty of quick treats to grab, like donuts or cupcakes, in addition to espresso drinks.

Transportation

Goldendale is approximately 55 minutes (46 mi/74 km) east of White Salmon. Take Route 14 east for 34 mi (55 km) then exit at Goldendale Goodnoe Hills Road/Hoctor Road and drive north on US 97 for 7 mi (11 km).

Yakima Valley

The Yakima Valley has become a popular weekend getaway, as it's a major player in Washington's wine production, with more than 120 vineyards. The Yakima Valley is also the country's leading producer of hops, accounting for more than 75 percent of the nation's total hops output. Many Washingtonians come to Yakima for a weekend of wine- or beer-tasting and enjoying the frequently warm weather for outdoor activities like hiking or biking.

There are dozens of chain hotels just off I-82, making it a convenient base for a weekend of exploring the region. Downtown Yakima has plenty of restaurants and bars within walking distance, but many of the wineries are found miles away in the vineyards.

YAKIMA

With a population of 96,000, Yakima has transformed over the years from a small pioneer town to the epicenter of the Yakima Valley. The historic downtown is bustling with a variety of restaurants and shops, and you'll find larger chain restaurants and stores on the outskirts as well. The Yakima River borders the east and north parts of downtown, adding to the town's beauty.

TOP EXPERIENCE

Wineries

Not only are the rich soils of Yakima Valley essential to the region's reputation as a leading wine producer, but they're also full of small, family-run vineyards that attract people wanting an intimate wine-tasting experience. In these more personal settings, guests can better understand the stories that went into making each bottle of wine. The wineries are scattered throughout the valley, so you'll need a car to visit them all.

Naches Heights Vineyard

1853 Weikel Rd., Yakima; 509/945-4062; www. nhvwines.com; 11am, 12:30pm, 2pm; tour and tasting $30

The land at Naches Heights Vineyard has been in the family for over 75 years, and the vineyard spans 8 acres (3 ha), producing grapes like pinot gris, Albarino, and Gruner Veltliner. You'll enjoy sipping wine in the cozy house-turned-tasting room or outside on the lawn. If you have time, book a tour with the owner, who'll walk you through the vineyards and explain the wine you're drinking in more depth.

Freehand Cellars

420 Windy Point Dr., Wapato; 509/866-4664; www. freehandcellars.com; noon-5pm Sun.-Thurs., noon-6pm Fri.-Sat.; tasting $18

Thanks to the stunning architecture of the building and the land it sits on, you'll likely want to stay past your tasting at Freeland Cellars. Either by the fireplace or outdoors with a view of Mount Adams, you'll love trying their single-varietal wines like cabernet Sauvignon.

Treveri Cellars

71 Gangl Rd., Wapato; 509/877-0925; www. trevericellars.com; noon-7pm Mon.-Thurs., noon-9pm Fri.-Sat., 10am-6pm Sun.; free

While there are many wineries in the area, Treveri Cellars stands out as a sparkling-wine house. This family-owned winery uses the traditional method to make fruit-forward varietal sparkling wines, such as Gewürztraminer. Their large winery has plenty of places to sit and taste, from the terrace beneath umbrellas to a luxurious indoor space with plush chairs.

Farms and Orchards
Washington Fruit Place

1209 Pecks Canyon Rd., Yakima; 509/966-1275; https:// fruitplace.com; 10am-4pm Mon.-Sat., noon-5pm Sun.

Yakima Valley

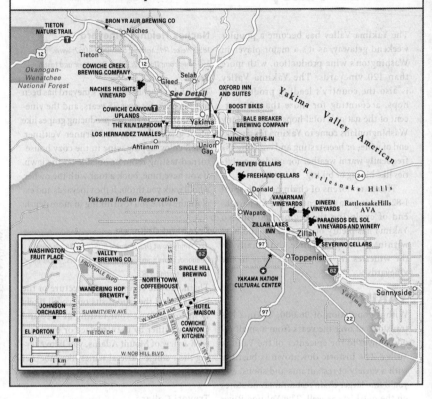

You'll find plenty of roadside fruit stands in the valley, but picking your own is even more fun. Washington Fruit Place lets you go into the orchards to pick seasonal fruit such as cherries. They also have a large gift shop to buy even more local goods like jam.

Johnson Orchards

4906 Summitview Ave., Yakima; 509/966-7479; www. johnsonorchardsfruit.com; 9am-4pm Tues.-Sat.

Johnson Orchards has been around since 1904 and has a seasonal selection of fruits including cherries in summer and apricots, plums, pears, apples, and more into late summer, all ready to purchase at their fruit stand. Stop by the 1916 warehouse for their famous baked

goods, as well as candles, coffee, lavender products, and beer and cider.

Hiking
Tieton Nature Trail

Distance: *6.8 mi (10.9 km) round-trip*
Duration: *3.5 hours*
Elevation gain: *300 ft (91 m)*
Difficulty: *easy/moderate*
Trailhead: *Oak Creek Wildlife Recreation Area*

Cross a bridge and go through the elk fence, where you'll follow the river through flatlands and bushes in a largely unshaded area. You'll reach a suspension bridge about 2 mi (3 km) in, which is the highlight for many hikers. You can continue at this point to see an array of

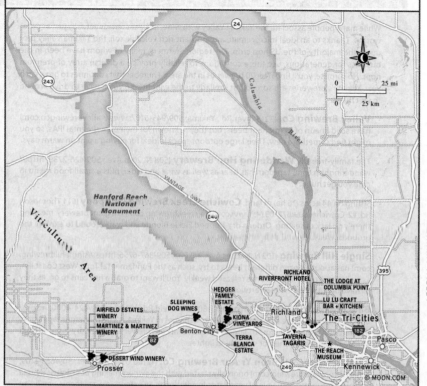

different plants, including colorful springtime wildflowers or vibrant fall foliage, or turn back for a shorter hike. If you continue, you'll reach a peninsula with stunning views of the Tieton River Canyon. Rattlesnakes are prevalent in this area, so keep an eye out for them as you walk.

To get here from Yakima, travel west on US 12 for about 4 mi (6.5 km) past the Naches stoplight to the junction with Route 410. Turn left to continue on US 12 and head southwest for 2 mi (3 km) to arrive at the parking lot for Oak Creek Wildlife Recreation Area. The trail is across the street.

Cowiche Canyon Uplands

Distance: *3.3 mi (5.3 km)*

Duration: *1.5 hours*
Elevation gain: *288 ft (88 m)*
Difficulty: *easy*
Trailhead: *Cowiche Canyon Preserve*

Cowiche Canyon Preserve has over 20 mi (32 km) of trails to explore, but you can do a shorter 3-mi (5-km) one on the Cowiche Canyon Uplands Trail. It's good for beginners and has plenty of views of the surrounding valley—sunrise and sunset are particularly good times to visit.

To get here from downtown Yakima, head west on Englewood Avenue for about 5 mi (8 km) then turn right on N. 80th Avenue. You'll then take a left on Scenic Drive and soon see a parking lot on the right.

The Center of American Hops Production

While many people associate the Yakima Valley with wine, its beer scene is actually just as noteworthy. Thanks to an ideal microclimate and nutrient-rich volcanic soil, the Yakima Valley produces the majority of the US hop crop. The region's farmers, many of whom have been in the business for generations, use these conditions to reliably provide a diverse array of premium hops. No surprise, you'll find over 20 breweries in the area, a number that continues to grow each year. Yakima's breweries are spread out similarly to the wineries, so you'll have to drive around to visit them.

- **Valley Brewing Co.** (3215 River Rd., Yakima; 509/945-5107; www.valleybrewingco.com) has a solid lineup of permanent beers, but they're known for their experimental IPAs, so you might find something new. Their large outdoor space is ideal for having a pint on warm days.

- The family-friendly **Wandering Hop Brewery** (508 N. 20th Ave.; 509/426-2739; http://wanderinghop.com) taproom has beer as well as wine and cider, plus a small food menu in case you get hungry.

- Sitting on 44 acres (18 ha) of land, **Cowiche Creek Brewing Company** (514 Thompson Rd. #2, Cowiche; 509/678-0324; www.cowichecreekbrewing.com) is a giant brewery, meaning there's no lack of seating. Order a dry-hopped Fickle Blonde and walk around to explore the grounds. Well-behaved dogs are welcome.

- **Single Hill Brewing** (102 N. Naches Ave., Yakima; 509/367-6756; https://singlehillbrewing.com) has about a dozen different beers to try, such as the Fundamental Tone West Coast IPA, as well as two experimental ones released weekly. You'll want to grab a few cans to go, as they all have beautifully designed artwork.

- **Bale Breaker Brewing Company** (1801 Birchfield Rd., Yakima; 509/424-4000; https://balebreaker.com) is one of the more well-known names in Yakima. It's on numerous taps across the state and is the state's fourth-largest independent craft brewery. Try their dry-hopped Field 41 Pale Ale or crisp pilsner for something lighter.

- Welsh for "hill of gold," **Bron Yr Aur Brewing Co.** (12160 US 12, Naches; 509/653-1109; https://bronyraurbrewing.com) originally started with the owners making beer-infused pizza and grew into a brewery several years later. In addition to an extensive pizza menu, you'll also find their selection of core beers, such as the Beaver Deceiver Cream Ale, which has won half a dozen awards over the years.

- **The Kiln Taproom** (815 S. 72nd Ave., Yakima; 509/426-2865; www.thekilntaproom.com) has over 30 beers on tap from around the Pacific Northwest. In addition to pizza, sandwiches, and salads, they also have an indoor play area for kids as well as a large, dog-friendly outdoor backyard.

Biking

The Cowiche Canyon Trail System is a 13-mi (21-km) network of trails spread out over 900 acres (365 ha) for mountain bikers of all skill levels. Most trails are short, so riders can easily combine multiple trails or add extra loops to increase their mileage. Spring and fall are particularly popular times, as wildflowers, fall foliage, and mild temperatures draw people from all over.

Boost Bikes

4040 Terrace Heights Dr., Suite #120, Yakima; 509/823-7064; https://eboostbikes.com; 10am-6pm daily; $40-80/hour, $25-100/daily

Whether you want to cruise around downtown Yakima or hit a trail in the mountains, Boost Bikes rents ebikes that fit your needs. They also rent adult and kid scooters.

1: vineyards in Yakima 2: trail in Cowiche Canyon

Food
North Town Coffeehouse

32 N. Front St., Yakima; 509/895-7600; www.
northtowncoffee.com; 8am-8pm daily

Visit North Town Coffeehouse if you're looking for a unique place to grab your morning coffee. Their establishment has transformed the old Yakima train depot into a charming spot for a croissant and espresso.

★ Cowiche Canyon Kitchen

202 E. Yakima Ave., Yakima; 509/457-2007; www.
cowichecanyon.com; 11am-8pm Mon.-Thurs., 11am-9pm
Fri.-Sat.; $16-48

Cowiche Canyon Kitchen, one of the best places to eat in Yakima, has a beautiful, well-lit interior and the Icehouse Bar, which is famous for its craft cocktails. The upscale restaurant's diverse menu includes everything from steak frites to tortilla soup, and with a no-reservations policy, expect a wait on the weekends, as it's one of the more sought-after dinner spots in town.

Los Hernandez Tamales

6411 W. Nob Hill Blvd., Yakima; 509/367-6480; www.
loshernandeztamales.com; 11am-6pm Sun.-Fri., 10am-
7pm Sat.; $10-12

You won't find fresher tamales in Yakima Valley than at Los Hernandez Tamales, where they mill their own masa and hand-make every tamal. They take advantage of the region's fresh produce and use it in their James Beard Award-winning tamales, such as asparagus and peperjack cheese. Go early at lunchtime, as there's often a long line, and indoor seating is limited.

HopTown Wood-Fired Pizza

2560 Donald Wapato Rd., Wapato; 509/952-4414;
https://hoptownpizza.com; 4pm-8pm Wed.-Thurs.,
11:30am-8pm Fri.-Sat., 11:30am-5pm Sun.; $13-20

HopTown does wood-fired pizza well, whether you get the Just Cheese Please or the vegetarian HopTown Harvest. They also have a variety of salads, soups, and local beer and wine available. Choose from tables inside or seats on their covered porch.

Miner's Drive-In

2415 S. 1st St., Yakima; 509/457-8194; Facebook
@Miners-Drive-In-Restaurant; 8am-1am Sun.-Thurs.,
8am-2am Fri.-Sat.; $4-10

One of the area's most classic places to eat is Miner's Drive-In, which has been serving hungry customers since 1948. You won't leave hungry, as they have huge portions of burgers, fries, and milkshakes. Many people enjoy the drive-in aspect and have their order brought out to their car, while others prefer to head inside the large restaurant to eat.

Accommodations
★ Hotel Maison

321 E. Yakima Ave., Yakima; 509/571-1900; www.hilton.
com; $183-304

Hotel Maison is one of the more exquisite places to stay in town, as this 1911 boutique hotel has 36 charming rooms with either two queen beds or a spacious king bed. They also have a fitness center, offer a European breakfast, and are close to numerous shops and restaurants.

Oxford Inn and Suites

1701 E. Yakima Ave., Yakima; 509/457-9000; www.
oxfordsuitesyakima.com; $114-199

Oxford Suites Yakima sits right next to the Yakima River, so book a riverside room with a balcony. You can enjoy the walking trail next to the river, the pool, or the fitness center for some activity. There's 108 guestrooms and complimentary breakfast each morning, and the Riverside Bistro serves dinner and drinks.

Transportation

Yakima is about 2.5 hours (160 mi/260 km) from Seattle, via I-90 east and I-82 south. From Goldendale, Yakima is about 1 hour 15 minutes (70 mi/113 km), reached by taking US 97 north and I-82 west.

1: Teapot Dome Service Station 2: Rattlesnake Hills wineries map 3: Los Hernandez Tamales

RATTLESNAKE HILLS

The rich soils and mild climate of the Rattlesnake Hills are ideal for cultivating world-class wine grapes, and the area is known for growing 40 grape varieties, most of which are red (such as merlot and cabernet Sauvignon). Since the first vines were planted here in 1968, the Rattlesnake Hills have grown into an essential part of the Washington winemaking. Located just 20 mi (32 km) south of Yakima on I-84, the town of Zillah is home to the majority of the Rattlesnake Hills' vineyards, making it an easy day trip.

Sights
Teapot Dome Service Station

117 1st Ave., Zillah; 509/829-5151; www.cityofzillah.us

An intriguing example of novelty architecture, the Teapot Dome Service Station was conceived out of the Teapot Dome Scandal the early 1920s. Under President Warren G. Harding, Secretary of the Interior Albert B. Fall secretly leased government oil deposits at Teapot Dome, Wyoming, for personal kickbacks. Fall's was the first conviction at the cabinet level. In 1922, with this political controversy serving as a backdrop, Jack Ainsworth built a gas station as a humorous satire and protest. The teapot-shaped station, with a concrete spout and a sheet-metal handle, closed in 2006 but is worth a visit to see the exterior.

Wineries
Severino Cellars

1717 1st Ave., Zillah; 509/829-3800; www.severinocellars.com; 10am-4pm Mon.-Tues., 10am-3pm Wed., 10am-6pm Thurs.-Sat., noon-6pm Sun.; tasting $18-28

Conveniently just off I-82, Severino Cellars is in a charmingly restored farmhouse that's over a century old. They have a variety of wines to enjoy, such as a fruity rosé and a crisp Viognier.

VanArnam Vineyards

1305 Gilbert Rd., Zillah; 509/829-1540; www.vanarnamvineyards.com; noon-4pm Mon.-Thurs., noon-6pm Fri.-Sat., noon-5pm Sun.; tasting free

Sip a glass of malbec while taking in the scenery at VanArnam Vineyards, situated on a picturesque 40-acre (16-ha) property. When you get hungry, order from the menu at **Tin Roof Grill** (noon-5pm Sat.-Sun; $15-30), and visit during the summer to catch one of the many concerts they host.

Paradisos del Sol Vineyards and Winery

3230 Highland Dr., Zillah; 509/829-9000; https://paradisosdelsol.com; 11am-6pm daily; tasting $20

Vineyard del Sol has a much more casual feel than some other wineries in the area—more like you're tasting in someone's home, complete with a private garden. You can talk to the family that owns the winery, and they let you taste their small-batch wine, such as a sangiovese. You can also tour four different vineyards with their master winegrower (daily except Sat.; $20/person).

Dineen Vineyards

2980 Gilbert Rd., Zillah; 509/829-6897; https://dineenvineyards.com; usually 9am-5pm daily; tasting $15

Dineen Vineyards has approximately 100 acres (40 ha) of land to grow Bordeaux varietals, from which they make about a dozen wines. The family has been in agriculture for generations, and the black 1950 Chevrolet on the property is a replica of the owner's father's first truck from when they lived on a farm. Visiting hours change by season, so check their website or call them for the most current hours.

Food
Scott's Fuel Yard

314 1st Ave., Zillah; 509/829-1368; Facebook @Scotts-Fuel-Yard; 6am-3:30pm Mon.-Fri., 7am-2:30pm Sat., 8am-2pm Sun.

Half the fun of getting your mocha at Scott's Fuel Yard is taking pictures of the outside—there's a vintage yellow truck and tons of other decorations around. The inside is a cozy coffee shop with various furniture, although many choose to sit on the porch on sunny days. They have pastries like cinnamon rolls in addition to a full espresso menu.

The ChopHouse at The Old Warehouse

705 Railroad Ave., Zillah; 509/314-6266; www. theoldwarehousezillah.com; 11am-8pm Tues.-Wed., 11am-9pm Thurs., 11am-10pm Fri., 11am-midnight Sat.; $16-35

The Old Warehouse always has something going on, whether it's their Saturday auctions or live music in the evenings. You'll notice the original wood beams and brick walls from when it was a fruit warehouse, and its menu features options like pan-seared salmon or country fried steak with mashed potatoes.

El Porton

4808 Tieton Dr., Yakima; 509/965-5422; www. elportonyakima.com; 11am-9pm Sun.-Thurs., 11am-10pm Sat.-Sun.; $14-25

You'll get large portions of classics like tostadas, burritos, enchiladas, quesadillas, and more at El Porton, where they pride themselves on making everything from scratch. The colorful restaurant is simple but a good place to stop after a day of venturing around Zillah.

Accommodations

Many people choose to stay in nearby Yakima instead, as there are more lodging options.

Zillah Lakes Inn

701 Fountain Blvd., Zillah; 509/581-0522; www. zillahlakesinn.com; $173-270

Zillah Lakes Inn is a beautiful place to relax at the end of the day, as it sits next to several small lakes and a four-hole golf course. This pet-friendly hotel also encourages checking out the 2 mi (3 km) of walking trails nearby. They have six lakeside rooms available for the best views and plenty of outdoor seating and fire pits to enjoy at night.

Transportation

Rattlesnake Hills is about 23 minutes (20 mi/32 km) south of Yakima via I-82 east.

TOPPENISH

Toppenish is part of the Yakama Indian Reservation, where the various tribes of the Yakama Nation reside. It stands out for the dozens of historic murals depicting the town's history. The current count is 80, and a new one is added every year in the downtown area. Visit the Toppenish Chamber of Commerce's website (www.visittoppenish. com) to find out about the murals and their locations. At the Yakama Nation Cultural Center, visitors can get an in-depth look at how the Yakama tribe shaped history in the area.

Sights

★ Yakama Nation Cultural Center

100 Spiel-yi Loop; 509/865-2800; www. yakamamuseum.com; 9am-6pm Mon.-Fri, 9am-5pm Sat.-Sun.; $5

You'll want to spend an hour or so at the Yakama Nation Cultural Center, which is dedicated to preserving and showcasing the heritage of the Yakama people. It has a gift shop and theater, but its 12,000-sq-ft (1,115-sq-m) museum is where it really shines. Visitors can scan QR codes to learn the pronunciation of words in the native language. You'll see examples of early 20th-century homes and artifacts and learn the history of the Yakama Treaty—the tribe ceded over 15,000 sq mi (39,000 sq km), which formed the current Yakima Valley.

Northern Pacific Railway Museum Toppenish

10 Asotin Ave.; 509/865-1911; https://nprymuseum.org; 10am-4pm Tues.-Sat., May 1-Oct. 15; $3-5

Locomotives, cars, and a 1911 depot are on display at the Northern Pacific Railway Museum, which provides fascinating insight into rail history. The museum also includes a freight room with old trucks and maintenance tools, a refurbished passenger waiting area with authentic railroad uniforms, North Coast Limited china, and multiple freight cars outside.

Food

El Charrito Toppenish

120 E. Toppenish Ave.; 509/865-7707; 10am-10pm daily; $9-18

There are numerous Mexican places in Toppenish, and El Charrito is a good option for a quick meal. It has the typical menu of fajitas, burritos, and quesadillas, as well as tamales and tostadas, and has a fast-food restaurant feel to it, with a digital menu at the counter that you order from.

Bamboo Thai

13 E. Toppenish Ave.; 509/314-6498; Facebook @BambooThai509; 11am-8:30pm Mon.-Fri., noon-8:30pm Sat.; $10-25

If you're craving something other than Mexican food, Bamboo Thai offers Thai fried rice, curries, and more. The simple restaurant also offers Thai salads, pho, and other soups to round out their menu.

Transportation

Toppenish is 20 mi (32 km) south of Yakima; take I-82 east to exit 50.

PROSSER

Prosser is a charming area known for its vibrant wine-tasting scene. Numerous wineries surround the area, and there are an impressive number of restaurants for such a small town.

Wineries

Airfield Estates Winery

60 Merlot Dr.; 509/203-7646; www.airfieldwines.com; 11am-5pm daily; tasting $15

From its humble beginnings as a WWII Army Air Corps training site, Airfield Estates has grown into a renowned vineyard since planting its first crop of wine grapes in 1968. It has an impressive 830 acres (336 ha) of vineyards growing more than 20 varieties. The winery's name and storage space are derived from the property's aviation history, and the tasting room resembles an airplane hangar. Try their Old Vine Cabernet Sauvignon or the Blanc de Noirs sparkling wine.

Martinez & Martinez Winery

357 Port Ave., Suite G; 509/786-2392; www.martinezwine.com; 11am-6pm Sun.-Thurs., 11am-5pm Fri.-Sat.; tasting $25

Cabernet Sauvignon is the house specialty at Martinez & Martinez Winery, where grapes are handpicked from vineyards, including Alder Ridge and their own estate. After an early start working in California vineyards, the founder created what is now Washington's second Hispanic-owned winery; the establishment features a stunning tasting room and grounds for visitors to taste wine.

Desert Wind Winery

2258 Wine Country Rd.; 509/786-7277; www.desertwindwinery.com; 11am-5pm Sun.-Wed., 11am-7pm Thurs.-Sat.; tasting $15

Most of the vines at Desert Wind Winery are over 20 years old, and the most notable varieties include Syrah, chardonnay, and merlot. Tasting flights and wine by the glass are available, and you can try limited-edition wines on request. Located in a beautiful Southwestern-style building, the tasting room offers comfortable couches and umbrella-covered outdoor patio areas that welcome pets.

Food

Horse Heaven Hills Brewery

1118 Meade Ave., Prosser; 509/781-6400; www.horseheavensaloonprosser.com; 3pm-8pm Tues.-Fri., noon-8pm Sat., 1pm-5pm Sun.; $15-36

While Prosser is prominently wine country, beer also has a place in it. Horse Heaven Hills Brewery serves about half a dozen beers, including the Stallion Stout and Honey Girl, and has a food menu with options like burgers, all-day breakfast, and cod and chips. It has a fun equestrian theme to it, with pictures of horses all over the walls.

Neighbor's BBQ

1115 Grant Ave., Prosser; 509/778-4165; https://neighborsbbq.com; 10:30am-3pm Wed.-Sat.; $11-23

Your mouth will water as soon as you get out

of the car at Neighbor's BBQ, as they specialize in Texas barbecue. Their smoker makes delicious meals like smoked chicken salad sandwiches, pork belly, and more. You can take it to go, as the restaurant operates out of a small house with minimal seating.

Accommodations

Most people tend to visit Prosser for a day trip and use Yakima be their base.

Inn at Desert Wind

2258 Wine Country Rd., Prosser; 509/786-7277; www.
desertwindwinery.com/inn; $277-323
If you plan on wine-tasting at Desert Wind Winery, book one of the four luxurious rooms above the winery for a convenient stay. These Southwest-style rooms have gas fireplaces, balconies with a view of the Yakima River, hardwood floors, and lavish beds. In addition to wine-tasting, an on-site restaurant is open for lunch through dinner.

Transportation

Prosser is on the edge of Yakima Valley, about 50 minutes (50 mi/80 km) south of Yakima via I-82.

THE TRI-CITIES

Kennewick, Pasco, and Richland make up the Tri-Cities, located at the point where the Yakima, Snake, and Columbia Rivers meet. The area wasn't much until the Hanford plant was constructed near Richland during World War II to produce plutonium for nuclear weapons. It became an essential part of the Manhattan Project and brought thousands of people to work and live in the Tri-Cities. The site is now known as Hanford Reach and is a national monument where visitors can explore and take plant tours. Of the three cities, Richland has the biggest draws for visitors and is where you'll likely spend most of your time. You'll find wineries west of Richland, on the slopes of Red Mountain.

Sights

REACH Museum

1943 Columbia Park Trail, Richland; 509/943-4100;
https://visitthereach.us; 10am-4:30pm Tues.-Sat.; $12
adult, $6 students and seniors
Visiting the REACH Museum is a great way to learn about the Hanford site's significant role in WWII and the Cold War. It also shows the Columbia River's agricultural development, demonstrating how irrigation transformed dry areas into thriving farmland.

In addition to its exhibits, the museum offers free, 45-minute guided tours to see the Hanford site and the B Reactor National Historic Landmark up close and personal. In April-November, the Manhattan Project National Historical Park facilities at Hanford are open to the public for free tours provided by the United States Department of Energy

TOP EXPERIENCE

Wineries

About 12 mi (19 km) west of Richland, the slopes of **Red Mountain** face south, which is excellent for ripening grapes, and the soil is rich in calcium carbonate and has a high pH, which stresses the plants and increases the flavor concentration in the grapes. The region's hot days and cool nights result in grapes with well-balanced development of sugars and acids, which is necessary for producing complex wines. Minimal rainfall means irrigation can be precise, which in turn encourages the production of smaller berries packed with taste. Red Mountain has become renowned for its robust red wines with complexity, intensity, and structure.

Kiona Vineyards

44612 N. Sunset Rd., Benton City; 509/588-6716;
https://kionawine.com; noon-5pm daily; tasting $20
Kiona Vineyards was the first to recognize Red Mountain's potential for premium wine production and planted the first vineyards here in 1976. Years later, they have a unique

building carved into a hill with a large tasting room overlooking the vineyards, where you can taste wine like their Syrah.

Hedges Family Estate

53511 N. Sunset Rd., Benton City; 509/588-3155; https://hedgesfamilyestate.com; 11am-5pm Wed.-Sun.; tasting $25-35

At Hedges Family Estate, you'll feel like you stepped into a French vineyard. This exquisite home resembles a chateau, complete with beautifully manicured grounds. You'll understand why once you learn that the owners are from Champagne, France, and they'll delight you with a mix of reds, including their cabernet Sauvignon.

Terra Blanca Estate

34715 Demoss Rd., Benton City; 509/588-6082; https://terrablanca.com; 10am-5pm daily; tasting $30

Terra Blanca Winery and Estate Vineyard specializes in red wine varietals, notably merlot and Syrah. A Tuscan-style tasting area overlooks the beautiful vineyards and the winery's unique barrel caves.

Sleeping Dog Wines

45804 N. Whitmore PR NW., Benton City; 509/460-2886; https://sleepingdogwines.com; 11am-5pm Fri.-Sun. Apr.-Nov.; tasting free

A small-batch winery that produces 300 cases yearly, Sleeping Dog Wines is named after friendly Jett, who will welcome you when you visit. The owners are involved in every step of the production process. Wines like the Pound Puppy (a blend of Syrah, merlot, cabernet Sauvignon, Carménère, and malbec) and the Faux Paw (a blend of petit verdot and petit Syrah) have names that fit the theme.

Food

Atomic Ale Brewpub & Eatery

1015 Lee Blvd., Richland; 509/946-5465; https:// atomicalebrewpub.com; 11am-8pm Sun. and Tues.-Thurs., 11am-9pm Fri.-Sat.; $14-27

Atomic Ale Brewpub & Eatery was the first brewpub in Tri-Cities and specializes in wood-fired pizza but also has options like sandwiches and salads. It has an assortment of beer on tap, such as Atomic Amber, and weekly events like musical bingo each week that you can enjoy under the unique green ceiling.

★ Lu Lu Craft Bar + Kitchen

606 Columbia Point Dr., Richland; 509/778-5117; https://lulucraftbar.com; 11am-8pm Mon.-Tues., 11am-9pm Wed.-Thurs., 11am-9:30pm Fri., 9:30am-9:30pm Sat., 9:30am-8pm Sun.; $15-40

Lu Lu Craft Bar + Kitchen offers waterfront seating for farm-to-table dining with fresh, local ingredients. Their extensive menu includes options like creamy garlic shrimp risotto or a green chili cheeseburger, and custom cocktails are available from their bar. You can also sit outside on the patio for a view of the water.

Taverna Tagaris

844 Tulip Ln., Richland; 509/628-0020; www. tagariswines.com; 11:30am-8pm Tues.-Thurs., 11:30am-9pm Fri.-Sat.; $15-55

Taverna Tagaris emphasizes tapas to share, or you can get your own entrée such as grilled meats and flatbread. With dozens of reds and whites, their wine list is even more vast than their menu. They have extensive seating, indoors in the elegant restaurant or alfresco under the string lights.

Accommodations

Richland Riverfront Hotel

50 Comstock St., Richland; 509/946-4661; www. choicehotels.com; $108-264

The Tri-Cities has mainly chain hotels, but the Riverfront Hotel is one of the better ones, located right by the Columbia River. It's a dog-friendly hotel with 136 various rooms, from queen beds up to family rooms for larger groups.

★ The Lodge at Columbia Point

530 Columbia Point Dr., Richland; 509/713-7423; https://lodgeatcolumbiapoint.com; $179-359

As the only 4-star hotel in the area, The Lodge

at Columbia Point is the most luxurious place to stay with its Columbia River views and 82 guestrooms. In addition to the outdoor pool, guests can use the free bike rentals to explore the nearby waterfront trail. They also have an on-site restaurant where you can get decadent weekend brunch or enjoy fresh seafood for dinner.

Transportation

The Tri-Cities are about 1 hour 15 minutes (77 mi/124 km) southeast of Yakima via I-82 east.

Walla Walla

Missionaries and settlers journeying along the Oregon Trail began arriving in Walla Walla in the early 19th century, marking the beginning of the city's transformation into a key trading and agricultural hub. With the arrival of a slew of prospectors spurred on by the region's gold rush, the population and economy of the area grew further. Walla Walla's rich soil also made it a perfect location for farming.

Walla Walla is currently home to 34,000 people and is renowned for its sophisticated wine scene. With more than 120 wineries, it has the highest concentration of wineries in the state, and locals often come here for a wine-tasting weekend. Its ideal climate and soil can grow a wide range of grapes, resulting in wines of exceptional quality. Wine lovers come to Walla Walla for the small tasting rooms, the vineyard excursions, and the chance to talk to the winemakers.

Walla Walla's small-town friendliness and cultural riches captivate visitors beyond the grapes. The downtown district has historic architecture and an extensive choice of shops, restaurants, and nightlife venues. Music festivals, theatrical shows, and art walks highlight local talent, making the city a center for the arts. Whitman College and other nearby educational institutions contribute to the town's vibrant intellectual scene.

SIGHTS
Fort Walla Walla Museum

755 NE Myra Rd.; 509/525-7703; www.fwwm.org; 10am-4pm daily; $10 adult, $5 child, $2 student and senior

The 17-building Fort Walla Walla Museum replicates a pioneer community from the 19th century. It features well-maintained gardens and five spacious exhibit rooms housing thousands of artifacts. Beginning with a remarkable stagecoach exhibit, this vast museum takes visitors through Walla Walla's history. Exhibits include a 33-mule team working a wheat field, the earliest locomotive in Washington state, and stories from the Oregon Trail. Visitors can also enter a replica of a cell from the Washington State Penitentiary.

Whitman Mission

328 Whitman Mission Rd.; 509/522-6360; www.nps.gov; 9am-4pm Thurs.-Sat.; free

Marcus and Narcissa Whitman founded the mission in the 1830s to provide medical treatment but also bring Christianity to Indigenous people. A large portion of the Cayuse tribe died in 1847 after settlers exposed them to measles, which they had no immunity to. Believing it was intentional poisoning, members of the Cayuse tribe murdered multiple missionaries, including the Whitmans, and the Cayuse War broke out.

Today the Whitman Mission National Historic Site delves into the narrative of the Cayuse and missionaries' interactions. The site's educational displays and programs explore the viewpoints of both European settlers and the Cayuse people.

TOP EXPERIENCE

★ WINERIES

With more than 120 wineries dotting its scenic terrain, Walla Walla Valley has become

Walla Walla

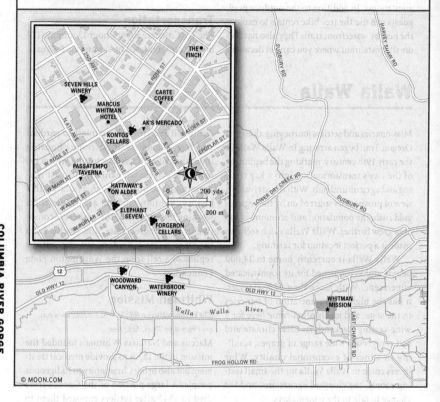

THE FINCH

SEVEN HILLS WINERY

CARTE COFFEE

MARCUS WHITMAN HOTEL

AK'S MERCADO

KONTOS CELLARS

PASSATEMPO TAVERNA

HATTAWAY'S ON ALDER

ELEPHANT SEVEN

FORGERON CELLARS

N 2ND AVE

E ROSE ST

N 4TH AVE

W ROSE ST

W MAIN ST

W ALDER ST

W POPLAR ST

S 3RD AVE

S 2ND AVE

E ALDER ST

EPOPLAR ST

S 1ST AVE

HARVEY SHAW RD

SUDBURY RD

LOWER DRY CREEK RD

SUDBURY RD

0   200 yds
0   200 m

WOODWARD CANYON

WATERBROOK WINERY

WHITMAN MISSION

OLD HWY 12

OLD HWY 12

Walla   Walla   River

FROG HOLLOW RD

LAST CHANCE RD

12

© MOON.COM

a renowned wine region since its 1984 classification as an AVA. It can be challenging to decide where to go with such a wide variety. There are several regions, so some people stick to wineries all in one area. Others might want to try specific types of wine and seek out those wineries. A great way to decide where to go is to talk to the locals—they all have favorites and are happy to share.

Downtown

Going wine-tasting downtown is convenient because you can walk a few blocks around Main Street to several dozen wine shops without needing to drive anywhere. It's also easy to grab lunch or a snack at a local restaurant in between. The trade-offs are they can be a bit more expensive for tastings, and you don't get the vineyard feel of other wineries in the valley. The downtown n central has historic architecture and an extensive choice of shops, restaurants, and nightlife, plus a lot of local talent, mak

Seven Hills Winery

212 N. 3rd Ave.; 509/529-7198; www.sevenhillswinery.com; 10am-5pm daily; tasting $30

Seven Hills Winery has an elegant brick building where you can watch wine being made in the back room. They offer regular and reserve tastings as well as private tastings and lunch with the winemaker, where you can try wines like their petit verdot.

Elephant Seven

134 W. Poplar St.; www.elephantsevenwine.com; 11am-5pm Fri.-Sun., winter by appointment only; tasting $15

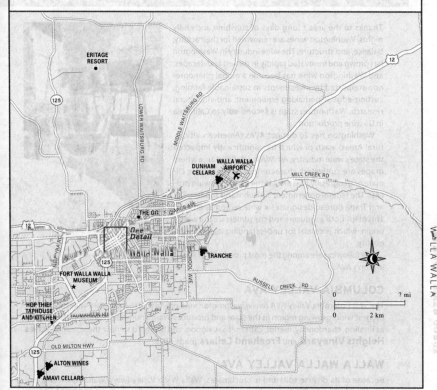

Elephant Seven stands out for its focus on small-batch wines in its modern, sleek tasting room. They use the valley's ability to produce expressive and complex wines by focusing on varietals like Syrah and grenache.

Forgeron Cellars

33 W. Birch St.; 509/522-9463; www.forgeroncellars.com; noon-5pm Thurs.-Sun.; tasting $20

Forgeron Cellars' name comes from the French word for "blacksmith," chosen to honor the winery's location in a historic blacksmith shop in downtown Walla Walla and symbolize the craftsmanship involved in winemaking. The winery serves wines like cabernet Sauvignon and cabernet Franc, among others.

Kontos Cellars

10 N. 2nd Ave.; 509/204-2141; www.kontoscellars.com; 11am-6pm Sun.-Thurs., 11am-6:30pm Fri.-Sat.; tasting $30

Owned by a father-and-son team whose roots in Walla Walla go back six generations, Kontos Cellars focuses on producing limited-production red wines. Their cabernet Sauvignon and merlot are favorites, but they also serve whites and sparkling wines. Reservations are recommended, whether you want to sit indoors, upstairs in their loft with a group, or on the outdoor patio.

The Airport

After serving as an airbase during WWII, the Walla Walla Airport District has transformed

All About Washington Wine

Thanks to the area's long days of sunshine and chilly nights, Washington wines are renowned for their acidity, balance, and structure. The wine industry in Washington has grown and innovated rapidly in the last few decades, and Washington wine has become a global phenomenon supported by investments in sustainable farming, cutting-edge winemaking equipment, and viticultural research. Washington state is second only to California in US wine production.

Washington has 20 distinct AVAs (American Viticultural Areas), each of which has significantly impacted the state's wine industry. An AVA is a defined area where grapes are cultivated, characterized by the unique climate or geography that affects the grape-growing process. The federal government's Alcohol and Tobacco Tax and Trade Bureau designates a wine region as an AVA. This helps both producers and consumers track a wine's origin, which is crucial for understanding its flavor and quality.

wine-tasting

The following are among the most prominent of Washington's AVAs:

COLUMBIA VALLEY AVA

The vast Columbia Valley AVA (www.washingtonwine.org/resource/columbia-valley-ava) is the biggest wine-growing region in the state and produces a large number of grape varieties, such as Riesling, chardonnay, merlot, cabernet Sauvignon, and Syrah. To sample these, visit **Naches Heights Vineyard** and **Freehand Cellars** (page 407).

WALLA WALLA VALLEY AVA

Because of its diverse soils and microclimates, Walla Walla Valley (www.wallawallawine.com) produces full-bodied red wines, focusing on Syrah and cabernet Sauvignon. **Elephant Seven** (page 420) and **Amavi Cellars** (page 423) are good examples of these.

YAKIMA VALLEY AVA

Nearly half of Washington's wine production comes from Yakima Valley (https://yakimavalleywinecountry.com), the state's oldest AVA. The region has diverse varietals, including merlot, cabernet Sauvignon, chardonnay, and Riesling, among other wines. You can visit **Terra Blanca Estate** or **Sleeping Dog Wines** to try these (page 418).

into a thriving wine community. Historic buildings and old hangars have been imaginatively converted into vineyards, tasting rooms, and production hubs. The wineries are all conveniently located near one another, so visitors can easily explore a wide variety of wines, only 4 mi (6.5 km) east of the downtown area.

Dunham Cellars

150 E. Boeing Ave.; 509/529-4685; www.dunhamcellars.com; 11am-4pm daily; tasting $20

Housed in a beautifully restored airplane hangar from World War II, Dunham Cellars provides a unique setting for wine-tasting. Among the many acclaimed wines produced by the estate are the Bordeaux-style blend Trutina and the red table wine Three Legged Red.

Tranche

705 Berney Dr.; 509-526-3500; www.tranche.wine; 1pm-5pm Thurs.-Mon.; tasting $20

On gorgeous grounds with picturesque views, Tranche Winery has an array of varietals, including Rhône and Bordeaux blends. In April-October, they provide vineyard tours on top of the regular tastings. Check out their evening concert lineup to catch live music.

West of Town

Stopping at one of the west side wineries can be a nice welcome to the Walla Walla region. Many of these are on Old Highway 12, which runs parallel to US 12.

Waterbrook Winery

10518 US 12, Walla Walla; 509-522-1262; https:// waterbrook.com; 11am-5pm Tues.-Thurs., 11am-6pm Fri. Sun.; tasting $10-15

Situated on a tranquil 49-acre (20 ha) estate, Waterbrook Winery has been in business since 1984. It produces a wide range of wines, from Sangiovese rosé and pinot gris to several alcohol-free options. The vineyard's menu reflects its dedication to farm-to-table principles in dishes made with fresh, in-season vegetables grown in the vineyard's own garden. Visitors are encouraged to relax by the pond or take a walk along the path on the grounds. Its stylish tasting area has high-top tables and high ceilings.

Woodward Canyon

11920 Old Hwy. 12, Lowden; 509-525-4129; www. woodwardcanyon.com; 10am-5pm daily; tasting $20

Woodward Canyon is the second-oldest winery in the Walla Walla Valley, and it's been in the family since 1981. Tastings are in a restored 1870s farmhouse, where guests can experience the estate's signature cabernet Sauvignon and other varieties. While you're there, be sure to look through the labels; they feature a range of artworks created by local artists.

South of Town

The south side of Walla Walla tends to have some of the newer wineries, and many are grouped together so it's easy to visit a few at a time.

Amavi Cellars

3796 Peppers Bridge Rd., Walla Walla; 509-525-3541; www.amavicellars.com; 11am-5pm daily; tasting $20

Whether you're lounging on the patio or peering through the telescope indoors, Amavi Cellars' estate provides incredible views of the Blue Mountains. Both settings are perfect for sipping a glass of their Semillon or Stone Valley Syrah, and guests are welcome to use the communal guitar hanging inside if they want to sing a song or two. The beautiful tasting room has plenty of places to sit, with the best being next to the large windows overlooking the valley.

Alton Wines

3783 Peppers Bridge Rd., Walla Walla; 509-720-7136; www.altonwines.com; 11am-4:30pm Fri-Sun; tasting $30

The elegant tasting area at Alton Wines has floor-to-ceiling windows that allow visitors to take in spectacular views of the surrounding mountains and Pepper Bridge vineyards. The winery produces a variety of wines, but its malbec and chardonnay are particularly noteworthy.

FOOD

Carte Coffee

8 N. Colville St., Walla Walla, 509-393-9999; https:// cartecoffee.com; 7:30am-4pm daily

Carte Coffee started as a coffee food truck and now has its own establishment in downtown Walla Walla. Its friendly baristas are happy to make your regular espresso drink or help you find a new one, and they also have an assortment of pastries.

★ AK's Mercado

21 E. Main St., Walla Walla; 509-572-0728; www. andraeskitchen.com; 11am-9pm Mon., 11am-9pm Thurs., 11am-10pm Fri., 10am-10pm Sat., 10am-9pm Sun.; $13-17

From its modest beginnings as a hot dog and taco stand at a gas station, AK's Mercado has grown into a trendy setting for locals and visitors alike, boasting a two-story location with a bar in downtown Walla Walla. Daily tortilla preparation and the innovative use of the same corn in brewing their distinctive AK's Mercado Lager highlight the importance of freshness. Street tacos and a wide variety of mezcal are two of the menu's standout items.

Hattaway's on Alder

125 W. Alder St., Walla Walla; 509/525-4433; www. hattawaysonalder.com; 4pm-8pm Mon.-Wed., 4pm-9pm Thurs.-Sun.; $14-33

Hattaway's on Alder blends the Northwest with Southern charm in dishes like chicken and grits and clams and sausage. To complement your dinner, there is an extensive wine list with more than 100 varieties. The chic dining room is perfect for a special night.

Passatempo Taverna

215 W. Main St., Walla Walla; 509/876-8822; www. passatempowallawalla.com; 4pm-9:30pm Thurs.-Mon.; $15-55

Passatempo Taverna has a cozy atmosphere with dim lighting, perfect for romantic evenings or special occasions. The ever-changing drink list and menu showcase seasonal delicacies like winter squash pizza and mushroom conchiglie made with the freshest ingredients. Passatempo has a complete bar with inventive cocktails to complement the menu's rotation. Reservations are suggested.

Hop Thief Taphouse and Kitchen

795 SE Sydnee Ln., College Place; 509/593-5150; https://hopthieftaphouse.com; 11am-10pm Sun.-Thurs., 11am-11pm Fri.-Sat.; $6-13

Hop Thief is a self-pour taphouse—you pour your own beer, cider, wine, kombucha, or nitro coffee from their selection and only pay for that amount. The food menu includes pizza, burgers, salads, and tacos, and the place has an energetic vibe to it, especially on game days when local teams are on the numerous TVs.

ACCOMMODATIONS

★ Eritage Resort

1319 Bergevin Springs Rd., Walla Walla; 833/374-8243; www.eritageresort.com; $309-399

Just 10 minutes north of the city center, Eritage Resort provides a serene retreat into luxury, perfect for a getaway. With 20 beautiful suites and a restaurant that uses only products grown or produced in the area, Eritage is the ideal place to unwind. Choose a room with a balcony and a lake view to sip your coffee while listening to the birds. Guests can relax at an outdoor saltwater pool or go paddleboarding on Lake Sienna.

The FINCH

325 E. Main St., Walla Walla, 509/956-4994; www. finchwallawalla.com; $85-350

The FINCH is a boutique hotel situated just one block from Walla Walla's downtown, providing an ideal home base for exploring the surrounding area. Each of the 80 rooms is tastefully decorated by local artists. There is a courtyard, spacious outdoor seating areas, and a wood-burning fireplace, as well as other outdoor entertainment options such as giant Jenga and cornhole.

The GG

922 Bonsella St., Walla Walla; 425/647-8245; https://theggwallawalla.com; $450-600

The GG exemplifies high-end living and flair with its room furnishings and varied collections that include Northwest art and vintage Louis Vuitton trunks. Housed in a renovated building from 1909, this inn offers five unique rooms, each with a delicate touch that provides European elegance.

Marcus Whitman Hotel

6 W. Rose St., Walla Walla; 509/525-2200; https://marcuswhitmanhotel.com; $111-359

Standing tall over Walla Walla's downtown, the Marcus Whitman Hotel was built in 1928 and combines modern grandeur with the

1: Seven Hills Winery 2: AK's Mercado 3: Eritage Resort

grace of the Roaring Twenties. This is one of the top hotels in town and has a variety of 133 rooms and suites, each with high-quality linens and modern decor. Guests can choose between the historic 10-story tower and the smaller, more modern rooms in the contemporary wing. The hotel's restaurants highlight the area's abundant agriculture and world-famous Walla Walla wines.

TRANSPORTATION
Getting There
Walla Walla is 4.5 hours (260 mi/418 km)

southwest of Seattle via I-90, I-82, and I-182. From the Tri-Cities, Walla Walla is 1 hour (57 mi/92 km) away, reached by taking US 12 east. From Maryhill, Walla Walla is 2 hours 15 minutes (141 mi/227 km) away, via I-84, US 730, and US 12.

Getting Around
There are daily flights between the **Walla Walla Regional Airport** (ALW, 45 Terminal Loop; 509/525-3100; www.wallawallaairport.com) and Seattle, where you can catch connecting flights.

Eastern Washington

Eastern Washington might not get the crowds of the state's western side, but its expansive farmlands, impressive geological formations, and rolling hills are just as captivating. The eastern side is ideal in summer for enjoying warmer temperatures at one of the many lakes, whether boating or relaxing shoreside. And with fewer people here, you're more likely to get the camping spot you want, plus hiking trails are usually less congested.

The region's most popular attraction is the Grand Coulee Dam, one of the world's largest concrete structures, which plays a key role in generating hydropower. The dam's construction created Lake Roosevelt and Banks Lake, two large lakes popular for camping and water sports. To the south, Sun Lakes-Dry Falls State Park shows off a different era

Highlights

Look for ★ to find recommended sights, activities, dining, and lodging.

★ **Wild Horse Renewable Energy Center:** Explore the power of wind and solar energy through tours at Wild Horse, which highlights sustainable practices in the Columbia River Gorge (page 433).

★ **Gorge Amphitheatre:** Enjoy a concert with a view at this outdoor venue set against the Columbia River (page 434).

★ **Grand Coulee Dam:** This engineering marvel also gives insights into America's hydropower history, with a nightly laser light show (page 437).

★ **Sun Lakes-Dry Falls State Park:** See Ice Age remnants and hike around the landscape of what was once the world's largest waterfall (page 438).

★ **Spokane River Centennial Trail:** Follow this paved path that connects parks and historical sites, ideal for biking, walking, and enjoying river views (page 445).

★ **Palouse Falls:** This striking waterfall within a rugged canyon has serene viewpoints and trails showcasing Washington's dramatic landscapes (page 446).

of nature—a time when a colossal Ice Age waterfall dominated the landscape. Trekking through this park feels like walking through history.

Near the border of Idaho is Spokane, Washington's second-biggest city, a favorite among road-trippers for its many hotels, restaurants, and stores, which are notably absent in other areas of Eastern Washington. Spokane also has historical sites, a vibrant art scene, and lush parks throughout the city.

Hot summers and severe winters contribute to the region's thriving agricultural industry, which is known for its exceptional crop diversity. Hiking, biking, fishing, and boating on the many lakes and rivers are just a few reasons people visit during spring and summer.

ORIENTATION

The major routes in Eastern Washington are I-90, which runs east-west, connecting Seattle to Spokane through the Cascade Mountains, and **US 395,** which travels north-south.

PLANNING YOUR TIME

Eastern Washington is large, and its major sights and activities are spread out, so it's best to spend a **minimum of three days**, if not a week, exploring everything it offers. With a **week,** you can spend a full day at the Grand Coulee Dam, enjoy a few days around Roosevelt Lake, and end by exploring Spokane for several days. If you're on a shorter trip, pick a few sights in the same general area to see, such as the Ginkgo Petrified Forest State Park and Wild Horse Renewable Energy Center.

From Seattle, it's at least a **4-hour drive** to reach the eastern part of the state. That means you'll have to purposely plan this trip out; you likely won't be driving through on the way to somewhere else.

There isn't a great central base for this trip. Spokane is the region's largest city, but it's at the far eastern end of the state—several hours away from any day-trip destination. Spending the night at different locations as you move around is easier. You'll need your own vehicle when you visit, as attractions are hours apart, and the only connecting public transportation is in Spokane.

In Eastern Washington, **summers** are hot, regularly reaching high 80s-mid-90s°F (29-35°C). The region's arid landscapes mean there's often little natural shade, so visitors must plan on using sun protection and staying hydrated during these warmer months. Winters can be quite cold, with temperatures frequently dropping below freezing. Daytime highs in the coldest months often range 20-30°F (-6 to -1°C).

Mountain passes and roads may close due to ice and snow in the winter. Routes like Snoqualmie Pass on I-90 frequently close or require tire chains during heavy snowfall and icy conditions. It is essential to check road conditions and weather forecasts before traveling in the winter.

Previous: Palouse Falls; Wild Horse Renewable Energy Center; Grand Coulee Dam.

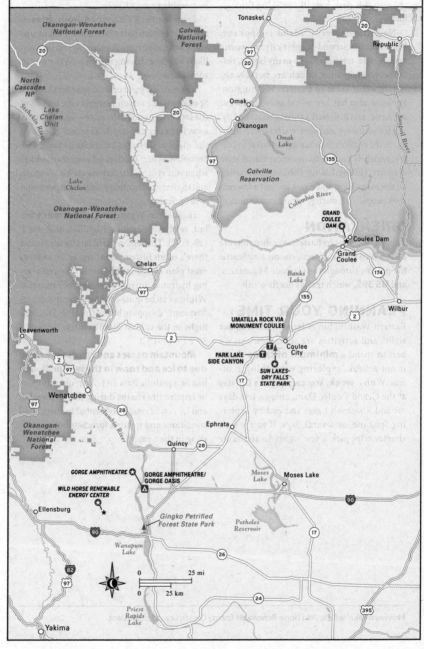

Eastern Washington

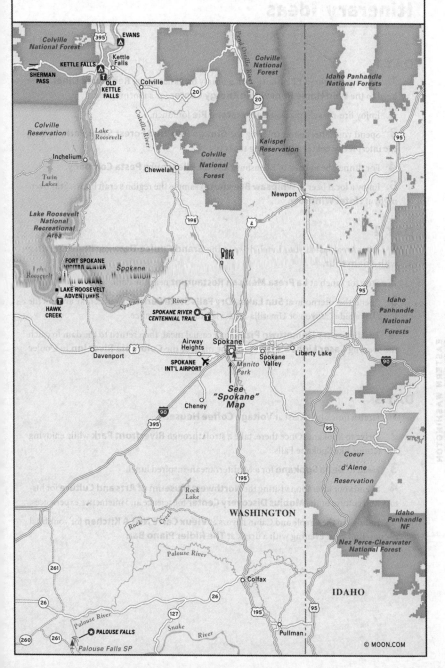

© MOON.COM

Itinerary Ideas

DAY 1

1 Begin your trip in Ellensburg with a hearty breakfast at the **Red Horse Diner.** Then head to the **Wild Horse Renewable Energy Center** for a morning tour.

2 Enjoy fire-roasted pizza at **Cornerstone Pie** for lunch.

3 Spend your afternoon exploring the **Ginkgo Petrified Forest State Park,** visiting the interpretive center and walking the trails.

4 For dinner, head back to Ellensburg and the **Ellensburg Pasta Company.**

5 Enjoy a local beer at **Whipsaw Brewing** to sample the region's craft brews. Stay overnight at **Hotel Windrow.**

DAY 2

1 After breakfast at your hotel, drive to the **Grand Coulee Dam** and begin exploring with a **dam tour.**

2 Stop for lunch at **La Presa Mexican Restaurant** near the dam.

3 Spend the afternoon at **Sun Lakes-Dry Falls State Park** for a quick hike around the Park Lake Side Canyon or Umatilla Rock via Monument Coulee.

4 For dinner, try **Hometown Pizza** for a casual meal, then return to the dam to catch the evening **Laser Light Show.** Spend the night at the **Columbia River Inn** in Coulee Dam.

DAY 3

1 Grab a quick breakfast at **Voltage Coffee House.**

2 Drive to Spokane. Once there, take a stroll through **Riverfront Park** while enjoying attractions like Spokane Falls.

3 Head to **Baba Spokane** for a Mediterranean-inspired lunch.

4 Spend your afternoon visiting the **Northwest Museum of Arts and Culture** for history and culture or the **Mobius Discovery Center** for science and interactive experiences.

5 Indulge in the Creole and Cajun flavors at **Vieux Carré NOLA Kitchen** for your final dinner. End your evening with a drink at **The Ridler Piano Bar.**

Ellensburg and Central Columbia Valley

Ellensburg is a stark contrast from hilly, lush western Washington—once you get over the mountain pass, you'll be greeted by flatlands and expansive open spaces. As the home of Central Washington University, Ellensburg has a population of about 20,000 and a college-town vibe, where students fill the bars on weekends.

Intrinsic to the town's identity is the Ellensburg Rodeo, one of the nation's oldest, which brings in visitors from far and wide. The rodeo celebrates the Central Columbia Valley's agricultural heritage, in addition to Ellensburg's ties to cowboy culture,

ELLENSBURG

Sights

★ **Wild Horse Renewable Energy Center**

25905 Vantage Hwy., Ellensburg; 509/964-7815; www. pse.com; 9am-5pm daily Apr.-Oct.; free

You'll notice dozens of wind turbines as you drive on I-90; the area's 149 turbines can generate up to 273 megawatts of electricity. The visitor center at Wild Horse Renewable Energy Center, 16 mi (26 km) east of Ellensburg, has exhibits explaining the process. For a more interactive experience, join a free tour (10am and 2pm daily) to walk the area and see the blade, gearbox, and more up close.

Festivals and Events

Ellensburg Rodeo

609 N. Main St., Ellensburg; 800/637-2444; https:// ellensburgrodeo.com; Labor Day weekend; $21-58

Since 1923, the Ellensburg Rodeo has been an integral part of the local community and a major attraction on the professional rodeo circuit, making it one of the oldest rodeos in Washington state. On Labor Day weekend, participants gather for bull riding, steer wrestling, team roping, and barrel racing,

among other traditional Western competitions. Rodeo competitors from all over the country are here to earn points and prizes to help them climb the national rankings. The rodeo also features a parade, the Ellensburg Rodeo Royal Court Pageant, and a variety of entertainment performances throughout the weekend.

Breweries

Whipsaw Brewing

704 N. Wenas St. Ellensburg; 509/900-3111; www. whipsawbrewing.com; 4pm-8pm Mon.-Tues., 3pm-9pm Wed.-Thurs., noon-9pm Fri.-Sun.

After a day of exploring Ellensburg, relax at Whipsaw Brewing, inside or on their patio. They have about a dozen beers on tap, such as their refreshing Buzz on Blackberry Wheat and juicy Hacksaw Hazy IPA, and events like trivia night. While food isn't offered, they encourage you to bring in takeout from nearby restaurants.

Food

Ellensburg Pasta Company

600 N. Main St., Ellensburg; 509/933-3330; https:// ellensburgpasta.com; 11am-9pm Mon.-Sat.; $12-35

Ellensburg Pasta Company has a welcoming atmosphere with delicious Italian dishes, such as pastas, chicken parmesan, steaks, and seafood, and a large kids' menu. Twice a month, their Fresh Sheet menu uses only local ingredients in their specials.

★ **Red Horse Diner**

1518 W. University Way, Ellensburg; 509/925-1956; Facebook @redhorsediner; 7am-9:30pm Sun.-Thurs., 7am-10pm Fri.-Sat.; $14-25

Located in an old gas station, the Red Horse Diner has retained the retro vibe with gas pumps outside and vintage signs inside. You'll find the typical diner food options here, including appetizers like chili cheese fries and entrées like burgers and wraps.

Cornerstone Pie

307 E. 5th Ave., Ellensburg; 509/933-3600; www. cornerstonepie.com; noon-8pm Sun.-Thurs., noon-9pm Fri.-Sat.; $10-26

Cornerstone Pizza serves quality fire-roasted pizza in their dining room or outside on the patio while you listen to live music. A newer addition is The Loft, a quaint bar area.

Accommodations

★ Hotel Windrow

502 N. Main St., Ellensburg; 509/962-8000; https:// hotelwindrow.com; $118-539

Hotel Windrow has 59 modern rooms and suites, all pet-friendly. The boutique hotel features an on-site fitness center and the **Elk Kitchen + Wine Bar** (8am-10am and 6pm-8pm Tues.-Sat., 8am-10am Sun.; $9-15). It's conveniently located in downtown Ellensburg, near many other restaurants, bars, and shops.

Icon Inn

1720 S. Canyon Rd.; 509/540-3113; www.icon-inn.com; $175-229

A quaint, 15-room hotel with the feel of an intimate bed-and-breakfast, the Icon Inn allows you to slip in without talking to anyone, thanks to a contactless check-in process and digital room key. Each room is unique, with a mix of local photographs and art, and many rooms have a gas fireplace.

Transportation

Ellensburg is about 107 mi (172 km) southeast from Seattle via I-90; the drive takes around 1 hour 45 minutes.

★ GORGE AMPHITHEATRE

754 Silica Rd. NW, Quincy; 509/785-6262; www. gorgeamphitheatre.com; price varies by show

Nothing signifies the arrival of summer more than attending a concert at the iconic Gorge Amphitheatre, an outdoor venue with the scenic backdrop of the Columbia River Gorge. With a capacity of 27,500, it hosts a variety of music artists throughout the season. Many attendees choose to stay at one of the Gorge's campsites to enjoy the warm weather and be close to the venue.

Food

Most campers bring their own food, but if you do want to eat out, you'll need to venture 9 mi (14 km) east to George for some quick food options.

Tendrils Restaurant

344 Silica Rd. NW, Quincy; 509/787-8000; https:// sageclifferesortandspa.com; 9am-2pm and 5pm-9pm daily; $28-78

Tendrils Restaurant at the Sagecliffe Resort and Spa is the only option near the Gorge Amphitheatre. You'll need a reservation, as you'll be fighting for spots with the resort guests. Their menu includes options like hazelnut-crusted chicken and the spicy black-bean veggie burger with sriracha aioli.

Accommodations

Gorge Amphitheatre Campground

754 Silica Rd. NW, Quincy; 509/785-6262; www. gorgecamping.com; $100-1,865

Camping at the Gorge ranges from standard tent sites to glamping. All have access to showers, slow but available Wi-Fi, water refill stations, and portable toilets. The more expensive sites have more room and are typically closer to the walking path to the venue. Book your campsite as soon as you get your concert tickets, as sites are limited.

Gorge Oasis Campground

754 Silica Rd. NW, Quincy; 509/785-6262; www. gorgecamping.com; $100-2,465

For those who prefer glamping, Gorge Oasis has a variety of beautiful canvas tents complete with comfortable beds, tables, rugs, and chairs. Most tents fit up to two people, while

1: Gingko Petrified Forest State Park **2:** Whipsaw Brewing **3:** Gorge Amphitheatre

select ones can sleep up to four guests. You'll have access to air-conditioned restrooms and showers.

Transportation

The Gorge is about 45 minutes east of Ellensburg; take I-90 east for 34 mi (55 km), take exit 144, and follow Silica Road NW for 7 mi (11 km).

GINKGO PETRIFIED FOREST STATE PARK

630 Ginkgo Ave., Vantage; 509/856-2290; https:// parks.wa.gov; 6:30am-dusk daily summer, 8am-dusk daily winter; $10 Discover Pass

The petrified gingko trees at this state park shed light on the slow transformation of wood into stone. Volcanic ash and sediment covered fallen trees, which blocked oxygen and prevented decay. Over millions of years, water rich in silica seeped through the buried wood and displaced the organic matter, gradually turning it into stone.

This gingko species is indigenous to China, which suggests that the climate and ecosystems of Eastern Washington were very different in the past. Petrified gingko, walnut, oak, and other trees give us a glimpse of the wide diversity of organisms that have lived in the area. The Ginkgo Petrified Forest Interpretive Trails have a mix of short and long trails, with a wheelchair-accessible 0.25-mi-long

(0.4-km) paved loop showcasing petrified tree specimens.

The state park is 30 minutes (30 mi/48 km) east of Ellensburg via I-90.

Sights and Recreation

Ginkgo Petrified Forest Interpretive Center

10am-5pm daily mid-May-late Sept., 10am-5pm Fri.-Sun. Oct.-early May; free

It's helpful to first stop at the Ginkgo Petrified Forest Interpretive Center to learn about petrification and see petrified wood specimens up close. Interactive displays show how the environment has changed over time, and a ranger is always on hand for questions. Make sure to step outside, where you can walk on top of a vast cliff face shaped by Ice Age floods and take in the stunning view of the Columbia River below.

Ginkgo Petrified Forest Interpretive Trail

Distance: *3 mi (4.8 km) round-trip*
Duration: *1.5 hours*
Elevation gain: *200 ft (60 m)*
Difficulty: *easy*
Trailhead: *Ginkgo Petrified Forest Interpretive Center*

This loop goes around the park's perimeter, passing sagebrush and ancient stone trees. The area is largely uncovered, so it can be warm during summer.

Grand Coulee Dam Region

As you leave Eastern Washington's expansive, flat fields, the terrain starts to change, revealing the spectacular volcanic formations and aftermath of Ice Age floods that characterize this region. As you get closer to Grand Coulee, you'll see the dam, the biggest electric power-producing facility in the United States. The dam has changed the environment and people's lives, in addition to its major impacts on irrigation and flood control. You'll find nearby towns like Coulee Dam, Electric

City, and Grand Coulee to call your base for outdoor activities and food.

GRAND COULEE AND COULEE DAM

Although similar in name, Grand Coulee and Coulee Dam are two different cities. Grand Coulee is the main city southwest of the dam, while Coulee Dam is northeast of it. You'll drive through Grand Coulee when coming from Ellensburg and other cities to the south.

Access Coulee Dam by driving over a bridge crossing the Columbia River just north of the dam.

★ Grand Coulee Dam

Route 155, Coulee Dam; 509/633-9265; www.usbr.gov; 8:30am-5pm daily; free

A symbol of the New Deal period, the Grand Coulee Dam divided the Columbia River to establish Lake Roosevelt and Banks Lake. Built to regulate floods and facilitate irrigation, the dam quickly became an essential generator of hydroelectric power, aiding the area's agricultural and industrial growth.

At 5,223 ft (1,592 m) long and 550 ft (168 m) tall, with a capacity of 6,809 megawatts, the Grand Coulee is the tallest dam in the Columbia River Basin—and the largest hydroelectric power producer in the United States. Due to its remote location, it doesn't get as many visitors as other state attractions, but seeing this stunning engineering marvel is worth a detour.

The visitor center, which looks like a giant generator rotor, has exhibits explaining how the dam affected early settlers and Native Americans, as well as how the dam controls floods.

From the city of Grand Coulee, take Route 155 north for 2 mi (3 km) to the visitor center.

Tours

Grand Coulee Dam, Coulee Dam; 509/633-9265; www. usbr.gov; 9am, 11am, 1:30pm, 3:30pm daily late May-late Oct.; free

First-come, first-served tours last 1 hour and take you to one of the power plants and then to the top of the dam. A van drives you to the different locations, and you can't bring any bags, so leave everything besides cameras in your car.

Laser Light Show

10pm nightly May-July, 9:30pm nightly Aug., 8:30pm nightly Sept.; free

The half-hour "One River, Many Voices" laser light show is a fun way to spend the evening, especially since there isn't much nightlife in the area. You'll be outside to watch a story play out in the sky in the form of lasers while narration from local tribes booms over the speakers. The Bureau of Reclamation worked with local tribes to talk about the dam's cultural effects, such as losing a salmon fishery, and included voices from people who helped create the dam.

Food

La Presa Mexican Restaurant

515 E. Grand Coulee Ave., Grand Coulee; 509/633-3173; Facebook @La-Presa-Mexican-Restaurant-Grand-Coulee-WA; 11am-9pm Mon.-Sat.; $11-28

Casual, brightly colored La Presa has an extensive menu, including beef, chicken, and vegetarian options for burritos, enchiladas, tostadas, and more.

Hometown Pizza

212 Bridgeport Hwy., Grand Coulee; 509/633-3393; https://hometownpizza.com; 11am-8pm Tues.-Sat.; $9-24

Despite its name, Hometown Pizza also serves sub sandwiches, pasta, hamburgers, and wraps. The inside is sparse, but the large menu makes it easy to satisfy groups with different cravings.

★ Voltage Coffee House

140 Spokane Way, Grand Coulee; 509/631-2035; www. voltagecoffeehouse.com; 6:30am-2:30pm Mon.-Sat., 7:30am-2:30pm Sun.

Voltage Coffee House's name gives a nod to the nearby dam, and the ample seating encourages visitors to take their time and socialize. They serve a variety of breakfast pastries in addition to salads and sandwiches.

Accommodations

★ Columbia River Inn

10 Lincoln Ave., Grand Coulee; 509/633-2100; https:// columbiariverinn.com; $107-275

Right across from Grand Coulee Dam, the Columbia River Inn has one of the best views of it, even from the outdoor hot tub. Their 36 rooms range from queen-size to a two-bedroom apartment. Amenities include an outdoor pool (open seasonally) and sauna.

Grand Coulee Center Lodge

404 Spokane Way, Grand Coulee; 509/633-2860; https://grandcouleecenterlodge.com; $77-208

Grand Coulee Center Lodge is only 2 mi (3 km) south of Grand Coulee Dam and is a convenient base for walking around the area where most of the restaurants are. It has 32 basic rooms with queen and king beds, and some have kitchens.

Transportation

To get to Grand Coulee from Ellensburg (2 hours, 120 mi/193 km), head east on I-90, take exit 151 for Ephrata Soap Lake/Route 283, and continue north on Routes 283, 17, and 155 following Banks Lake to Grand Coulee. From Seattle to Grand Coulee, you'll be on I-90 for an additional 90 mi (145 km), with a total travel time of 3 hours 45 minutes (228 mi/367 km).

★ SUN LAKES-DRY FALLS STATE PARK

34875 Park Lake Rd. NE, Coulee City; 509/632-5583; https://parks.wa.gov; $10 Discover Pass

Sun Lakes-Dry Falls State Park has over 4,000 acres (1,600 ha) of picturesque basalt cliffs, deep coulees, and the remnants of what was once one of the largest waterfalls on Earth. Dry Falls, the park's centerpiece, is a spectacular 3.5-mi-wide (5.5-km) chasm with a drop exceeding 400 ft (120 m). This geological phenomenon was formed approximately 15,000-20,000 years ago, during the last Ice Age, when the Missoula Floods carved out the landscape. Experts estimate Dry Falls was 10 times larger than Niagara Falls.

The park offers various outdoor activities, including 15 mi (24 km) of hiking trails and numerous lakes for boaters to fish on, plus 150 campsites. Several hotels are also nearby.

Dry Falls Visitor Center (35661 Route 17 North, Coulee City; 509/632-5214; https://parks.wa.gov; 10am-4pm Thurs.-Mon. summer, 10am-4pm Fri.-Sun. winter; free) has exhibits telling the story of the floods thousands of years ago and their impact on the surrounding area.

Hiking

Park Lake Side Canyon

Distance: *6 mi (9.7 km) round-trip*
Duration: *3 hours*
Elevation gain: *350 ft (107 m)*
Difficulty: *easy*
Trailhead: *parking lot for Umatilla Rock Trail*

Sun Lakes-Dry Falls State Park

The Park Lake Side Canyon is a great trail if you want mileage without too much incline. The first mile (1.6 km) is generally flat, then you climb through sagebrush and past stunning basalt cliffs, which give the impression of being in a high desert. You'll get a good sense of how varied the routes can be on this side of the mountains. Long pants or gaiters are recommended in this area due to the sagebrush and basalt.

From the Dry Falls Visitors Center, head south on Route 17 and turn east at milepost 92.5 toward Sun Lakes State Park. Proceed for 1 mi (1.6 km), then turn left toward Deep Lake. Drive 1 mi (1.6 km) and then turn left onto a dirt road to Perch and Dry Falls Lakes. Follow for 0.4 mi (0.6 km) to the parking area.

Umatilla Rock via Monument Coulee
Distance: 5 mi round-trip
Duration: 2.5 hours
Elevation gain: 100 ft (30 m)
Difficulty: easy
Trailhead: Umatilla Rock Trail

The hike around Umatilla Rock goes beneath Dry Falls, giving you a close-up look at the results of the Ice Age floods. The loop starts at Monument Coulee and has minimal elevation gain—but also no shade or water, so you'll need to prepare in advance.

From the Dry Falls Visitors Center, head south on Route 17, and turn east at milepost 92.5 toward Sun Lakes State Park. Proceed for 1 mi (1.6 km), then turn left toward Deep Lake. Drive 1 mi (1.6 km) and then turn left onto a dirt road to Perch and Dry Falls Lakes. Follow for 0.4 mi (0.6 km) to the parking area

Fishing

Fishing is abundant on Banks Lake, which is more than 27 mi (43 km) long. Largemouth and smallmouth bass, whitefish, lingcod, sunfish, kokanee, perch, crappie, and sturgeon are some of the game fish that the lake is famous for. While you can try your hand at fishing from the shore, you'll have a better chance of catching something by renting a boat and going out onto the lake.

Coulee Playland
401 Coulee Blvd., Electric City; 509/633-2671; https:// couleeplayland.com; call to reserve boats or gear (no set hours); boat rentals $100-450
Coulee Playland rents pontoon boats, Sea Rays, and fishing boats from 2 hours to all day, and you don't need a boater's license. They also have a vast selection of fishing gear.

Camping
34875 Park Lake Rd. NE, Coulee City; 509/632-5583; https://parks.wa.gov; $32
Sun Lakes-Dry Falls State Park has 96 tent and 41 full hook-up campsites, with multiple restrooms and showers. Reservations are necessary in the summer. The site can be windy, so bring reinforcements for your tent.

Transportation
Sun Lakes-Dry Falls State Park is 40 minutes (36 mi/58 km) southwest of Grand Coulee Dam via Route 155, US 2, and Route 17.

LAKE ROOSEVELT NATIONAL RECREATIONAL AREA
1008 Crest Dr., Hunter; 509/754-7800; www.nps.gov; free entry, $8 boat launch fee
Grand Coulee Dam created the enormous Lake Roosevelt, which is contained inside the Lake Roosevelt National Recreation Area. With a length of over 150 mi (240 km), this lake is popular for water sports, camping, and fishing. Key towns along the lake include Inchelium and Kettle Falls, which have several restaurants.

Sights
Fort Spokane
44150 District Office Lane N., Davenport; Memorial Day-Labor Day 11am-3pm Fri.-Sun.
Strategically located at the junction of the Spokane and Columbia Rivers, Fort Spokane was established in 1890 and served as a military base until 1898. It was repurposed as a boarding school for Native American children until 1914, then transformed into a sanatorium for Native Americans to receive

tuberculosis treatment; the government abandoned the location in 1929.

The National Park Service took ownership in 1960 and established the visitor center showcasing the fort's evolution over the years. Four of the original structures remain: the stable, powder magazine, reservoir, and guardhouse.

Scenic Drive

If you want to see a more extensive section of this region, this 140-mi (225-km), 3-hour loop goes along the lake, into the mountains, and through forests. Starting in Inchelium, drive north via Inchelium Kettle Falls Road and Route 20, where you'll cross the river to Kettle Falls, a town named for the waterfalls that were a significant fishing site for Native American tribes until the construction of the Grand Coulee Dam flooded the area. From Kettle Falls, take Route 20 west for 26 mi (42 km), ascending Sherman Pass, the highest mountain pass (5,575 ft/1,700 m) open year-round in Washington state.

After crossing Sherman Pass, the route descends for 17 mi (27 km) into the town of Republic. With a rich mining history, the town today serves as a gateway to outdoor adventures in the surrounding areas. To complete the loop back to Inchelium, head south on Route 21 for 36 mi (58 km), then turn east on Bridge Creek Road for 27 mi (43 km) to Inchelium.

Hiking

Hawk Creek Trail

Distance: 4.5 mi (7.2 km) round-trip
Duration: 2.5 hours
Elevation gain: 900 ft (275 m)
Difficulty: easy/moderate
Trailhead: Hawk Creek Campground parking lot, at the kiosk

Winter and spring are the best times to hike Hawk Creek, as water levels are low enough to walk along the beaches. Look for a fisherman's trail from the parking lot, follow that to an old road, and continue until you see the beaches of Lake Roosevelt. You'll pass through a mix of forest and open land alongside the lake.

To get here from I-90, take exit 277 onto US 2, and continue west for 48 mi (77 km) to the Telford rest stop, just past Davenport. Turn right onto Telford Road and go north for 4.5 mi (7 km) to the Miles Creston Road junction. Turn right onto Miles Creston Road; the sign for Hawk Creek Campground is about 6.5 mi (10 km) ahead on your left, then it's 1 mi (1.6 km) to the parking area.

Old Kettle Falls Trail

Distance: 2.6 mi (4.2 km) round-trip
Duration: 1 hour
Elevation gain: none
Difficulty: easy
Trailhead: Ranger station at Kettle Falls Campground

This scenic trail passes wetlands rich in birdlife and through the remnants of old homesteads. When the dam was built and Lake Roosevelt created, eleven communities were submerged beneath the reservoir's waters. The town of Kettle Falls moved to the higher land where it is today.

To get here from Kettle Falls, head west on Route 20/US 395 for 2.2 mi (3.5 km), then left onto Boise Road. After 1.6 mi (2.5 km), there is a fork in the road; keep to the right for the campground and park by the ranger station.

Boating and Fishing

Lake Roosevelt National Recreation Area has 22 public boat launches, making it easy to find a spot to get onto the water. The lake is home to over 30 species, including white sturgeon, rainbow trout, kokanee salmon, and yellow perch. Water levels vary throughout the year, and not all launches may be open, so check with the **Bureau of Reclamation** (800/824-4916) ahead of time.

Boat launch passes are required at all times for every launch within the recreation area. The weekly pass is $8 for seven consecutive days of access from the purchase date; buy it online (https://pay.gov) before arriving at the park. The annual pass ($45) remains valid through December 31 of the year it's issued. The annual pass must be purchased in person, such as at local hardware stores.

Fishing at Lake Roosevelt is a popular activity, and everyone needs a valid **fishing license,** which can be purchased from the Washington Department of Fish and Wildlife (WDFW), through authorized dealers like sporting goods stores and some grocery stores, or online (https://wdfw.wa.gov). Short-term, seasonal, and annual licenses are available.

Additionally, anglers fishing close to or from **tribal reservation shores** must check for any extra **permit** requirements. Specifically, fishing near the Colville Reservation's shoreline requires calling the Confederated Tribes of the Colville Reservation (509/634-3110) to understand their licensing needs, which ensures compliance and respect for local regulations.

Lake Roosevelt Adventures

1250 Marina Dr., Davenport; 509/725-7229; http:// lakerooseveltadventures.com; 9am-6pm daily; boat rentals $250-700

If you don't have a boat, you can rent a 22-ft (8-m) Princecraft pontoon that seats 12 people or a Starcraft for up to 7 people (half-day, full-day, or 24-hour rental available). Lake Roosevelt Adventures also rents houseboats (3 night min.; $1,945-9,345 for 6-12 people).

Camping

There are several dozen campgrounds around Lake Roosevelt, with options for standard tent camping, groups, and boat-ins. Standard and group campsites require a reservation, and all sites are reservable May 1-September 30.

Evans Campground

1949 Route 25 N., Evans; 509/754-7889; www. recreation.gov; Jan. 1-Sept. 30; $11.50-23

Evans Campground, 10 mi (16 km) north of Kettle Falls on the lake's east shore, is one of the more popular sites in the summer, so you'll need to make an early reservation several months in advance to get one of the 43 spots. It has a boat launch, group sites, and a day use area with a swimming beach. There are vault toilets year-round and seasonal flush toilets.

Kettle Falls Campground

1368 Kettle Park Rd., Kettle Falls; 509/754-7889; www. recreation.gov; Jan. 1-Sept. 30; $11.50-23

A forested spot open to tents and RVs along the lake, Kettle Falls Campground has trailer parking and a boat launch, with 74 total sites. While there isn't a camp store, the town of Kettle Falls is only a few miles away.

Transportation

From Spokane, Fort Spokane is about a 1-hour (60-mi/97-km) drive via I-90 west, US 2 west, and Route 25 north. Kettle Falls is 1.5 hours (80 mi/130 km) north of Spokane, via US 395 north. Kettle Falls is about 2 hours (110 mi/177 km) northeast of Grand Coulee, via Route 174 east, US 2 east, and Route 25 north.

Spokane

Vibrant, charming Spokane is the second-largest city in Washington. Spokane Falls, in the middle of town, is a focal point for the Spokane River, which naturally divides the city's historic center. The Centennial Trail alongside the river is popular with locals for daily walks and bike rides. The dynamic downtown district has an abundance of restaurants, shops, and nightlife.

SIGHTS
Riverfront Park

507 N. Howard St.; 509/625-6600; https://my.spokanecity.org

Riverfront Park is known as the center of Spokane and sprawls over 100 acres (40 ha) along the Spokane River. Spokane successfully hosted the 1974 World's Fair here, the smallest city to do so at the time, attracting millions of global visitors. To this day, the park has remained a vibrant community space.

Majestic Spokane Falls is visible from suspension bridges, and from the **Numerica SkyRide gondola** (11am-7pm Sun.-Thurs., 11am-8pm Fri.-Sat.; $9-13), which glides high above the river for a different viewpoint. Looff Carrousel (11am-7pm Sun.-Thurs., 11am-8pm Fri.-Sat.; $3.25) is a 1909 classic carousel that has been meticulously restored.

The park also houses playgrounds, numerous walking and biking trails, and the iconic Red Wagon, a large-scale Radio Flyer replica that's a slide. The Spokane Pavilion, an outdoor amphitheater added in 2020, hosts summer concerts.

Manito Park

1702 S. Grand Blvd.; 509/625-6200; www.manitopark.org; 8am-8pm daily Apr.-Oct., 8am-3:30pm daily Nov.-Mar.; free

Manito Park is a stunning 90-acre (36-ha) park designed in 1904 by the Olmsted brothers, who also created Central Park in New York. The area was originally a zoo, which closed during the Great Depression, and visitors can still see parts of the old zoo. The park has diverse themed gardens, including the European-inspired Duncan Garden, the serene Nishinomiya Tsutakawa Japanese Garden, and the vibrant Joel E. Ferris Perennial Garden, alongside the Gaiser Conservatory.

Other attractions include two children's playgrounds, Mirror Pond for waterfowl watching, the seasonal **Park Bench Café** (8am-7pm daily summer), and Loop Drive and Bridge, which allows you to drive through the park for stunning views of the Rose Garden and surrounding areas. Spring is when you'll find the flowers in bloom, while vibrant foliage covers the park in the fall.

Northwest Museum of Arts and Culture

2316 W. 1st Ave.; 509/456-3931; www.northwestmuseum.org; 10am-5pm Tues.-Sun.; $8-12

Inaugurated in 1916, the Northwest Museum of Arts and Culture (MAC) is distinguished as one of the five Smithsonian affiliates in Washington state. It features over one million pieces, including an impressive array of documents, pictures, fine arts, historical artifacts, and cultural objects from Europe, the Americas, and Asia. It has the largest global exhibit of Plateau Indian arts and artifacts. Visitors can also walk through the 1898 Campbell House, a sprawling 13,000-sq-ft (1,208-sq-m) estate that shows what Spokane life was like in the early 1900s.

Mobius Discovery Center

331 N. Post St.; 509/321-7121; https://mobiusdiscoverycenter.org; 10am-5pm Wed.-Sat., 11am-5pm Sun.; $11-12

Mobius Discovery Center is a fun way for kids to get out their energy while learning. Hands-on exhibits include experimenting with different bubble sizes, a pretend eye clinic and grocery store, an art studio, and a toddler-only play area.

Spokane

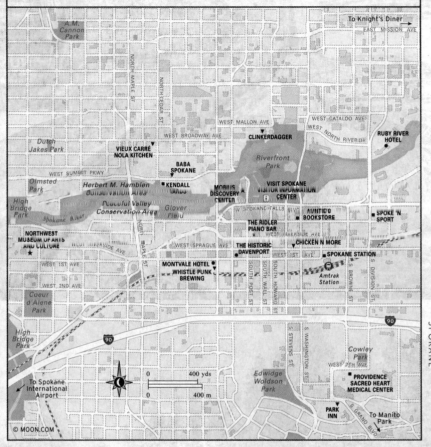

NIGHTLIFE

Park Inn

103 W. 9th Ave.; 509/624-8111; www.parkinnspokane. com; 11am-11pm Mon.-Thurs., 8am-1am Fri.-Sat., 8am-11pm Sun.; $14-25

Stop at the Park Inn for a family-friendly dining experience, from pizza to burgers. There's a full bar, sports on the TVs, and pinball and arcade games.

The Ridler Piano Bar

718 W. Riverside Ave.; 509/822-7938; https:// ridlerpiano.bar; 6pm-2am Fri.-Sat.; $5-11

The Ridler Piano Bar has dueling pianos on weekends that encourage audience participation, so you can request and sing along with your favorite songs. They play a wide range of genres and have a full bar with light snacks available.

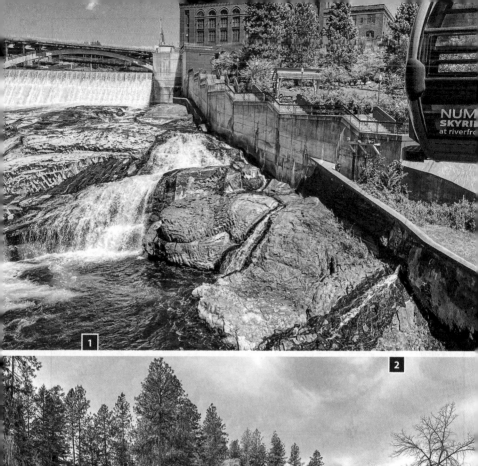

Whistle Punk Brewing

122 S. Monroe St. #4007; 509/315-4465; www.
whistlepunkbrewing.com; 3pm-9pm Mon.-Thurs., 1pm-
10pm Fri.-Sat., 1pm-7pm Sun.

A father-son team runs Whistle Punk Brewing and has a rotating tap list, such as the sour Apricot Crumble or the Helles Lager. They also have cider, wine, and nonalcoholic drinks, and food can be delivered from **Heritage Bar and Kitchen** (509/863-9235; www. heritagebarandkitchen.com; $9-14) next door.

FESTIVALS AND EVENTS

Hoopfest

downtown (various locations); 509/624-2414; www.
spokanehoopfest.net; last weekend in June; free

Every June, downtown Spokane buzzes with energy as it hosts Hoopfest, the largest outdoor 3 on 3 basketball tournament globally. The city streets transform into a sprawling basketball arena, with temporary courts occupying numerous city blocks to accommodate thousands of teams from around the country. Hoopfest has divisions for youth, elite, and wheelchair athletes, creating an inclusive atmosphere. The festival also has interactive kiosks, food booths, and live sports demonstrations.

Spokane Lilac Festival

various locations; 509/535-4554; https://
spokanelilacfestival.org; mid-May; free

To celebrate the arrival of blooming spring lilacs, the Spokane Floral Society and the Associated Garden Clubs started this event in 1938 as a small parade and flower exhibit. Since then, it's grown into a weeklong festival that kicks off with an art exhibition featuring local artists and a golf competition co-hosted with the nearby air force base. A beer festival showcases local breweries, and there's a classic car show with vehicles from all eras. The week ends with the largest armed forces torchlight parade in the United States, which has

---

1: view of the Spokane River from the Numerica SkyRide gondola **2:** Manito Park

military units, bands, and floats and attracts more than 150,000 people annually.

SHOPPING

Kendall Yards

1335 W. Summit Pkwy.; 509/321-5888; www.
kendallyards.com

Once a hub for the Great Northern Railway's rail yards, Kendall Yards has transformed into a contemporary neighborhood with residential spaces and a vibrant local business scene. Set along the northern banks of the Spokane River, this dynamic community features a diverse mix of restaurants, boutique stores, art galleries, cozy coffee shops, wine bars, and beer-tasting rooms. Rich green spaces like the Centennial Trail wind through the neighborhood and encourage visitors to linger.

Auntie's Bookstore

402 W. Main Ave., 509/838-0206; www.auntiesbooks.
com; 9am-7pm Sun.-Thurs., 9am-9pm Fri.-Sat.

Auntie's Bookstore has a giant selection of books, whether you're looking for new ones from your favorite author or a harder-to-find used book. The store holds regular book readings and signings, and also carries novelty items, greeting cards, and shirts.

RECREATION

TOP EXPERIENCE

★ Spokane River Centennial Trail

Spanning 37 mi (60 km) from Riverside State Park to the Idaho border, the Spokane River Centennial Trail was created to celebrate Washington state's 100th birthday. Built along decommissioned railway lines, repurposed roadways, and reclaimed timber company territories, this scenic trail is a great way to explore of the area by bike or on foot. At its western end, the trail integrates with Riverside State Park's extensive network, allowing hikers and cyclists to discover the allure of Deep Creek Canyon's formations.

Key points of interest along the trail

☆ Palouse Falls

Palouse Falls

Palouse Falls, the official waterfall of Washington, plunges 198 ft (60 m) into a canyon carved out by the Palouse River. Located in the southeastern part of the state, this natural wonder may require a bit of travel to reach but is well worth a visit. The falls are housed in 94-acre (38-ha) **Palouse Falls State Park** (506/646-3229; https://parks.wa.gov; 6:30am-dusk daily summer, 8am-dusk daily winter; $10 Discover Pass), where you can enjoy scenic overlooks and spots for picnicking and experience one of Washington's darkest skies for stargazing.

Hiking down into the canyon itself is not allowed, but 2 mi (3 km) of trail within Palouse Falls State Park provides several vantage points for capturing the beauty of the waterfall. Give yourself at least 2-3 hours to explore the park and its trails, including the Fryxell Overlook for the best view of the falls. The park tends to attract crowds on weekends, and with limited parking available, arriving early or on a weekday is recommended. Plan your trip carefully—the park lacks cell phone service and the nearest amenities are 38 mi (61 km) away in Dayton. Since there aren't many food options nearby, bring a picnic. For those looking for a treat, a shaved ice stand is available on weekends April-October. The park also restricts access for RVs and trailers.

GETTING THERE

The picturesque 2-hour drive to Palouse Falls State Park makes it an easy day trip from Spokane, or you could also take a detour from Ellensburg on the way to Spokane. From Spokane, start out westbound on I-90, take exit 221, and follow Route 261 south until you reach Palouse Falls Road, which leads directly to the park. To get here from Ellensburg, it's about a 2-hour 15-minute drive (130 mi/209 km). Take I-90 east for 126 mi (203 km) to Route 26 east, then take a left on Palouse Falls Road. Follow this road for 6 mi (10 km).

include the Horse Slaughter Camp monument, commemorating an 1858 tragedy where Colonel George Wright slaughtered 800 horses in an effort to weaken the resistance of the Spokane, Palouse, and Coeur d'Alene tribes, and the Denny Ashlock Bridge, which leads to Arbor Crest Winery (4705 N. Fruit Hill Rd.; 509/927-9463; www.arborcrest.com; noon-5pm daily; tastings $20/person) (formerly the Royal Newton Riblet Mansion). Before bridges were built, Antoine Plante's ferry served as the only means of crossing the river in this area. Historical plaques and interpretive signage along the trail explain the ferry's role in transportation and trade along the Spokane River during the 1850s.

Spoke 'N Sport

212 N. Division St.; 509/838-8842; www. spokensportinc.net; 10am-6pm Mon.-Fri., 10am-5pm Sat., 11am-4pm Sun.; $30-100/day

Spoke 'N Sport's location right next to the Centennial Trail makes it easy to get out and explore Spokane on wheels. The shop has a variety of bike rental options, including mountain and road bikes and kid trailers, all of which come with helmets. Their staff is happy to give you suggestions on where to ride, and car racks are available if you need to transport the bike.

FOOD

Clinkerdagger

621 W. Mallon Ave. 11/915/5 28-5988) www.clinkerdagger. com; 11:30am-9pm Mon.-Thurs., 11:30am-10pm Fri.-Sat., 3pm-9pm Sun.; $16-45

Clinkerdagger, situated in the historic Flour Mill area, has built a reputation over four decades for its fresh seafood, prime rib, and comprehensive wine selection. Its rustic decor and picturesque views of downtown Spokane and the Spokane River make it an ideal place for dining.

Chicken-N-More

414 1/2 W. Sprague Ave.; 509/838-5071; https:// chicken-n-more.com; 11am-8pm Mon.-Fri., noon-8pm Sat.; $8-37

Indulge in Southern cuisine at Chicken-N-More, which features a wide selection of chicken, ribs, and fish meals as well as BBQ beef brisket sandwiches. Complement your meal with sides like hushpuppies, or satisfy your sweet tooth with homemade desserts like sweet potato pie and peach cobbler. The restaurant is narrow with only a handful of tables, so getting takeout might be the best option.

Baba Spokane

1242 W. Summit Pkwy.; 509/443-4410; https:// eatgoodgroup.com; 3pm-9pm Mon.-Thurs., 10am-10pm Fri.-Sun.; $15-32

Baba Spokane is known for its dishes influenced by Middle Eastern, Mediterranean, and Asian flavors, such as chicken skewers, lamb kebabs, and Israeli salad. They also host a happy hour twice daily (3pm-5pm and 8pm-closing), when food and drinks start at $5. Large windows and lots of natural light make for a cheerful, casual setting.

★ Knight's Diner

2909 N. Market St.; 509/319-2247; Facebook @knightsdinerspokane; 6:30am-2pm Mon.-Sat., 8am-2pm Sun.; $12-18

Knight's Diner is a fun eating experience set in a restored 1906 railroad dining car full of tables and booths. It's known for its generous helpings of comfort food classics, from biscuits and gravy to Monte Cristo sandwiches.

Vieux Carré NOLA Kitchen

1403 W. Broadway Ave.; 509/495-1400; https:// vieuxcarrespokane.com; 11am-10pm Mon.-Thurs., 11am-11pm Fri.-Sat., 9am-9pm Sun.; $18-32

Vieux Carré NOLA Kitchen draws inspiration from New Orleans's French Quarter with authentic Cajun and Creole dishes. The menu is full of Southern favorites like po'boys, gumbo, jambalaya, and beignets.

ACCOMMODATIONS

Montvale Hotel

1005 W. 1st Ave.; 509/624-1518; https:// montvalespokane.com; $132-293

Established in 1899, the Montvale Hotel holds the title of Spokane's oldest boutique hotel. The 36 rooms are uniquely decorated with original art and antique wood. Situated in the heart of the entertainment district, theaters and restaurants are just a short walk away. The hotel also offers guests complimentary bike rentals.

★ The Historic Davenport

10 S. Post St.; 509/455-8888; www. davenporthotelcollection.com; $186-479

One of the finest places to stay is the Historic Davenport Hotel, which has been a Spokane landmark since its opening in 1914 and has hosted many famous people, such as John F. Kennedy, Bing Crosby, and Johnny Cash, and dignitaries in its 284 rooms throughout the years. Its grand design includes a stunning lobby, marble throughout the hotel, a pool, and a spa.

Ruby River Hotel

700 N. Division St.; 509/326-5577; https:// rubyriverhotelspokane.com; $116-399

Situated on 8 scenic acres (3 ha) on the north side of the Spokane River, the Ruby River Hotel has 241 guest rooms and suites that welcome both families and dogs. It has seasonal outdoor pools, a playground, and a full-service restaurant with patio seating overlooking the river.

INFORMATION AND SERVICES

Visit Spokane Visitor Information Center

620 W. Spokane Falls Blvd.; 509/747-3230; www. visitspokane.com; noon-4pm Mon.-Thurs., 10am-5pm Fri.-Sun.

Stop by Visit Spokane at Riverfront Park to get information on the area and pick up brochures.

Providence Sacred Heart Medical Center

101 W. 8th Ave.; 509/474-3131; www.providence.org

Providence Sacred Heart Medical Center has an emergency room and transplant center and is the only Level IV NICU and Level II Pediatric Trauma Center east of the Cascades.

TRANSPORTATION

Car

It's about 4 hours (280 mi/451 km) to drive from Seattle to Spokane; take I-90 east the entire way. From Ellensburg, driving to Spokane via I-90 takes 2.5 hours (173 mi/278 km). Grand Coulee is 1.5 hours (85 mi/137 km) from Spokane, via Route 174, US 2, and I-90.

Bus

Greyhound has about a dozen buses per day from various spots in downtown Seattle to the Spokane Station (221 W. 1st Ave.; 800/231-2222; www.greyhound.com; $40-50/person). The trip takes 5-8 hours, depending on how many stops the bus makes.

Train

Amtrak has one direct train daily from King Street Station in Seattle to the Spokane Amtrak Station (221 W. 1st Ave.; www.amtrak. com; $47-87/person) and takes about 7.5 hours.

Air

The **Spokane International Airport** (9000 W. Airport Dr.; 509/455-6455; https:// spokaneairports.net) has several dozen flights each day between Seattle and Spokane, as well as around the country. The flight between Seattle and Spokane is approximately 1 hour.

Background

The Landscape

GEOGRAPHY AND CLIMATE
Seattle

Seattle's geography is defined by stunning natural settings and distinctive topography. Two prominent hills, Queen Anne Hill and Capitol Hill, provide beautiful panoramas and are characteristic of the city's steep landscape, which is defined by its location between Puget Sound to the west and Lake Washington to the east. To the west, you'll see the majestic Olympic Mountains, while to the east is the Cascade Range.

Among the many bays, inlets, and rivers that make up Seattle's vast waterfront is Puget Sound's Elliott Bay.

Contrary to what many visitors think, it isn't always raining in Seattle. In reality, October-May often has overcast skies with intermittent rain showers, but it doesn't usually pour all day. The city receives about 38 in (1 m) of rain annually, almost half of that in November-January. Winter temperatures average 45-50°F (7-10°C) with frequent rain showers and occasional snow. Spring starts transitioning into dry, warmer weather and less frequent rain. Summer sees an average high temperature of 77°F (25°C) in August, though temperatures can occasionally soar above 85°F (29°C).

Olympic Peninsula and the Coast

Northwestern Washington is home to the diverse Olympic Peninsula, bordered to the west by the Pacific Ocean, to the north by the Strait of Juan de Fuca, and the east by Puget Sound. The towering Olympic Mountains like 7,980-ft (2,432 m) Mount Olympus characterize the peninsula. The temperate Hoh and Quinault rain forests, situated on the western slopes of these mountains, are defined by thick, moss-covered vegetation and heavy rainfall. Rocky outcrops, hidden coves, and sandy beaches dot the coast, while Olympic National Park safeguards enormous stretches of wildness inland.

From its southern border with Oregon to its northern tip at the Strait of Juan de Fuca, the Washington coast is a varied and vibrant region. Long sandy beaches like Ocean Shores and Long Beach contrast with rocky cliffs like Cape Flattery, which have spectacular sea stacks and tide pools. The Quinault, Queets, and Hoh Rivers, among others, form estuaries along the coast as they empty into the Pacific Ocean from the Olympic Mountains, providing abundant habitats for a wide variety

of animals. Seaside towns like Aberdeen, Westport, and La Push provide easy access to natural beauty, such as the untouched beaches of Olympic National Park's coastal strip.

The Olympic Peninsula receives about 140 in (3.6 m) of rain annually, which creates lush, verdant landscapes. The rainy season extends November-April, marked by frequent showers. Winter temperatures on the peninsula are typically 40-50°F (4-10°C). Higher elevations, such as Hurricane Ridge and Mount Olympus, experience 30-35 ft (9-11 m) of snow each year. The abundant rainfall supports the temperate rain forests on the peninsula, where dense canopies and moss-covered trees thrive. In the summer, the Olympic Peninsula enjoys high temperatures around 70°F (21°C).

The coast also experiences heavy rainfall, about 100 in (2.5 m) per year. Coastal towns like Long Beach and Ocean Shores often see dramatic winter storms rolling off the Pacific Ocean. These areas can be particularly windy in the spring, making them ideal for kite flying. In July-September, the temperature warms up (around 70°F/21°C in August), with more frequent sunny days. Don't let the morning fog fool you—many mornings start with heavy fog that clears up completely by midday.

San Juan Islands and North Puget Sound

There are more than 170 islands in the San Juans, although most of them are uninhabited. Hilly landscapes, rocky coastlines, and verdant woods define the three main islands: San Juan, Orcas, and Lopez. Diverse landscapes, including farmland, dense forests, and dramatic coastal cliffs, make up these islands. Orcas and seals are among many marine species that thrive around the smaller islets that dot the Salish Sea. Bays, inlets, and harbors line the landscape, providing protected waterways perfect for kayaking and boating.

The San Juan Islands experience a mild

maritime climate year-round. Winters are cool and wet, with average highs of 40-50°F (4-10°C) and occasional snow. Spring temperatures range 50-60°F (10-16°C), with decreasing rain showers. Summer is the driest period and averages 65-75°F (18-24°C), occasionally over 80°F (27°C). Fall returns to cooler temperatures, 50-60°F (10-16°C), and frequent rain showers. The unique location creates a rain shadow effect, which gives it less rainfall than nearby mainland areas.

The Cascades

The Cascade Range stretches from the southern part of British Columbia, Canada, to Northern California and is characterized by varied topography, including deep valleys, dense woodlands, and soaring peaks. Mount Adams towers over the southern part of the state, while its neighbors Mount St. Helens and Mount Rainier sit north of it. By the Canadian border, Mount Baker is one of the world's snowiest locations. Nearby, the North Cascades are known for rugged peaks and dramatic scenery. The Skagit and Yakima Rivers and alpine lakes like Lake Chelan are also part of the range. You'll find dense woods of Douglas fir, western hemlock, and cedar at lower levels.

The Cascades' varying elevations experience a wide range of temperatures. In winter, lower elevations see highs of 30-40°F, while higher elevations such as Paradise at Mount Rainier are much colder, often below freezing (0°C), with significant snowfall that can last until July. Spring brings gradual warming, with temperatures of 40-60°F (4-16°C) at lower elevations, while higher elevations, like those in the North Cascades, often remain snow-covered until late May. Summer sees the most significant temperature variation; lower elevations enjoy highs of 70°-80°F (21-27°C), occasionally reaching above 90°F, while higher elevations are cooler, 50-70°F (10-21°C). Fall in the lower elevations averages 50-60°F (10-16°C), and higher elevations are 30-50°F (-1 to 10°C), as the region transitions to winter.

Columbia River Gorge and Wine Country

The Columbia River naturally divides Washington and Oregon and creates the stunning Columbia River Gorge. Waterfalls dot this region's forested slopes and cliff faces. The Missoula Floods, which occurred around 15,000 years ago during the last Ice Age, primarily shaped the gorge. These massive outbursts from glacial Lake Missoula swept across the region. Since then, continual erosion and shaping by the Columbia River over time formed the Gorge's present shape.

Walla Walla wine country's verdant valleys and rolling hills are at the eastern end of the Gorge. The unique microclimate and rich volcanic soil here are perfect for growing grapes, which makes for world-class wine.

The weather varies in the Columbia River Gorge. On the western end near Vancouver, October-May have overcast days and regular rain. June-September, the weather shifts to dry and sunny, with high temperatures around 80°F (27°C). Further east toward White Salmon, there is noticeably less precipitation fall-spring, and June-September bring warmer weather, with highs up to 100°F (38°C). Spring and summer also have strong wind, which is ideal for kiteboarding and windsurfing. Winter months bring snow and ice, with temperatures around 30°F (-1°C).

Eastern Washington

From the rich valleys and forests of the Palouse and Spokane regions to the Columbia Basin's dry plains and rolling hills, the landscape varies in Eastern Washington. Because it's located in the Cascade Range's rain shadow, this region gets less Pacific Ocean moisture and receives far less precipitation, less than 10 in (25 cm) annually, but is also known for agriculture. Because of its sloped hills and rich, loamy soil, the Palouse is ideal for growing wheat and legumes. The Blue Mountains and the Rocky Mountain foothills are also in the eastern part of the state. Major rivers like the Columbia, Snake, and Spokane Rivers provide essential water for farming.

Eastern Washington experiences a wide range of weather conditions throughout the year. In towns like Ellensburg, October-May typically bring cold temperatures with occasional rain and snow showers, and temperatures can drop below freezing (0°C). As it gradually warms in spring, Ellensburg has highs of 60-70°F (16-21°C) by late May. June-September, expect mostly sunny skies and warm temperatures, often reaching 80-90°F (27-32°C), and occasionally above 100°F (38°C).

In Spokane, winters are cold and snowy, with temperatures of 20-30°F (-7 to -1°C). Spring brings milder weather, gradually climbing to 60-70°F (16-21°C). Summers in Spokane are hot and dry, with temperatures typically 80-90°F (27-32°C), occasionally surpassing 100°F (38°C). The region also experiences summer thunderstorms. Fall becomes cooler with increasing precipitation.

ENVIRONMENTAL ISSUES

Washington is seeing the effects of climate change, which is **changing weather patterns** and endangering ecosystems. The snowfall in mountainous locations is decreasing because temperatures are rising. This snowpack is critical for the summer water supply to agriculture, electricity, and salmon habitats. More intense winter downpours and longer summer droughts are examples of altered precipitation patterns. Climate changes impact migration patterns, reproductive cycles, and ecological dynamics, which in turn disturb local flora and animals.

Wildfires have been ravaging the landscape with increasing frequency and intensity in recent years, especially in the drier, hotter parts of central and Eastern Washington. The effects of climate change include a prolonged fire season and more destructive wildfires. Beyond destruction of homes and infrastructure, wildfires pose a grave threat to human health and the environment. The smoke they generate, even when miles away, significantly deteriorates air quality, posing serious risks to respiratory health.

A combination of variables, including climate change, is causing **salmon populations** to decline in Washington. When river and stream water temperatures rise, salmon endure difficult and sometimes fatal phases of their lives. River flows are disrupted by changing precipitation patterns, which impact salmon migration and breeding environments. Dams change river ecosystems and obstruct migration pathways. To rehabilitate and maintain salmon populations—vital to the state's ecological well-being and economy—conservation efforts are centering on repairing habitats, enhancing fish passage, and mitigating the impacts of climate change.

Plants and Animals

Because of its diverse landscapes and temperatures, Washington is home to a wide variety of plant and animal species. Washington's ecosystems range from dry plains to temperate rain forests, and numerous native plant species and animals live here.

FORESTS

The Cascade Mountains are home to a rare deciduous conifer known as a **larch,** which transforms into a brilliant gold before dropping its needles, creating a magnificent autumn show. This transformation lasts only 2-3 weeks in late September and early October, making for a brief but stunning spectacle.

Lush woods and temperate rain forests thrive in parts of the Cascade Range from the region's mild temperatures and heavy rainfall. The terrain is dominated by towering **Douglas firs** of over 250 ft (76 m) and **western hemlocks** of up to 200 ft (61 m). The decay-resistant wood of **western red**

cedars, which can reach heights of over 200 ft (61 m), makes them an attractive addition to lowland forests. The Olympic Peninsula is home to some of the tallest **Sitka spruce** trees in the world. These majestic trees thrive in wet coastal environments and can reach heights of 300 ft (91 m). The Hoh and Quinault rain forests are perfect settings for these magnificent trees.

The variety of tree species in the Cascades changes as elevation increases. Mixed conifer forests are found at lower elevations. Woodlands move from subalpine to alpine zones as you climb higher. There are more subalpine firs, mountain hemlocks, and Pacific silver firs, which can grow to 150 ft (45 m) and flourish in the cool, damp climate typical of higher altitudes. Trees such as subalpine larch and whitebark pine can thrive in the windy and snowy alpine meadows and scant krummholz woods found in the highest levels of the Cascades.

East of the Cascade Range, where it's considerably drier, woodlands and grasslands are the defining features. The most common trees in central and Eastern Washington are ponderosa pines, which can be 230 ft tall (70 m) and have thick bark that protects them from fires. In stark contrast to the thick woods in the west, these scant pines typically rise tall across the terrain. In riparian areas around rivers and streams, cottonwoods and willows thrive.

FLOWERS AND PLANTS

In the spring and summer, Washington's trails attract hikers and nature lovers for the vivid wildflower displays. Lupine, Indian paintbrush, avalanche lilies, and bear grass are common ones that brighten landscapes. June-August is usually the peak for wildflowers, but it varies by elevation and location. The higher alpine meadows of Mount Rainier National Park and the North Cascades display their floral brilliance later in the season.

Rhododendrons

The official state flower of Washington, the rhododendron, can flourish in a wide variety of habitats across the state. However, it's most at home in the temperate woods west of the Cascade Mountains. These colorful bushes thrive in the damp, acidic soil typical of coastal woodlands and other shady places. One species that stands out is the Pacific rhododendron, or *Rhododendron macrophyllum*, with enormous, spectacular flowers that can be any shade from pink to deep purple. Blossoms usually appear in April-June. The Washington Park Arboretum in Seattle is a prime location to see extensive collections of rhododendrons.

MARINE LIFE

The waters of Washington provide a home to a diversified and active marine life. Along with larger mammals like whales and sea lions, the coast is teeming with many smaller species in its kelp forests and intertidal zones.

Orcas

Killer whales, or orcas, are common in these seas, especially the southern resident pods that frequent Puget Sound and the San Juan Islands waters. These highly intelligent marine mammals are apex predators vital to the aquatic ecosystem. The best time to see orcas in this region is May-September, when they are most active and visible, although the resident pods can be spotted year-round.

Other Whales

Minke, humpback, and gray whales are common sights as they pass through on their annual migrations. Gray whales migrate north in March-May and south in October-December. Humpback whales are commonly seen May-October, while minke whales can be spotted in summer.

Fish

Lingcod, rockfish, and halibut are just a few of the many fish species inhabiting the coastal waters and playing an essential role in the marine food chain as well as the local fishing economy. Salmon, including Chinook, coho, and sockeye, can be found in Washington's rivers and in coastal waters. These iconic fish are particularly significant in the cultural heritage of the Pacific Northwest, symbolizing the region's natural bounty and resilience.

Sea Otters

Despite being on the brink of extinction not long ago, sea otters are now a common sight as they forage on kelp beds. By eating sea urchins, which would otherwise overgraze the kelp, these animals keep kelp forest ecosystems healthy.

Sea Lions

California and Steller sea lions are often observed sunbathing on docks or rocky coastlines, while harbor seals can be found all across Puget Sound, watching humans curiously.

Dungeness Crab

Dungeness crab is a highly prized catch in Washington's coastal waters, known for its sweet, tender meat and significant role in the local seafood industry. These crabs are commonly found in the sandy and muddy bottoms of Puget Sound, the Strait of Juan de Fuca, and coastal waters off the Pacific Ocean. Other species, such as red rock and tanner crabs, are also prevalent in Washington's waters.

Tide Pools

Sea stars, anemones, and a variety of shellfish, such as mussels and barnacles, inhabit the tide pools that line rocky shorelines. Coastal waters are also home to a wide variety of seabirds, including cormorants, puffins, and murres.

Oysters and Clams

The state's coastal waters and estuaries are prime habitats for oyster and clam populations, with Pacific oysters and Manila clams being particularly common. Recreational harvesting is popular at designated public beaches, especially during low tide.

LAND ANIMALS

Black Bears

Black bears are commonly found in the dense forests west of the Cascade Range. These bears are generally smaller than grizzly bears, averaging 200-300 pounds (90-130 kg), and more adaptable to different habitats.

Grizzly Bears

A smaller population of grizzly bears, bigger than black bears and weighing 400-600 pounds (180-275 kg), is found primarily within the North Cascades. There's thought to be only 10 remaining grizzly bears, so they're very rare to see.

Elk

The Olympic Peninsula is home to the Roosevelt elk, the largest subspecies of North American elk, known for its impressive size and majestic antlers. The eastern part of Washington is home to the Rocky Mountain elk.

Cougars

Cougars, also known as mountain lions or pumas, roam these forests and many parts of the state. While they generally keep to themselves and stay hidden, sightings have been on the rise in recent years.

Mountain Goats

The rugged hillsides are frequently traversed by mountain goats, characterized by their thick coats and modified hooves. They are primarily found in the Cascade Range and the Olympic Mountains, typically at elevations of 4,000-8,000 ft (1,200-2,400 m).

Smaller Mammals

Marmots, including the Olympic marmot—a species unique to the Olympic Mountains—and black-tailed deer also call this territory home. Smaller mammals, including foxes, raccoons, and various rodent species, are also found in the Cascades.

Mule Deer

The wildlife east of the Cascade Range is adapted to the arid climate. Mule deer are well-suited to the open grasslands and sagebrush plains.

BIRDS

Common coastal and wetland species include waterfowl, bald eagles, and herons. The great blue heron is a common sight along Columbia River and Puget Sound beaches—look for its enormous wingspan and blue-gray plumage. It's common to see bald eagles hunting fish in coastal areas, especially near the San Juan Islands and the Skagit River.

Birds such as the marbled murrelet, varied thrush, and northern spotted owl inhabit Washington's woodlands and hilly terrain.

A key indicator species for old-growth forests, the northern spotted owl is mainly found in the Cascade Range and the Olympic Peninsula. The little seabird known as the marbled murrelet flies to the ocean to feed, yet it builds its nests on the tall branches of old-growth trees. In the state's damp coniferous forests, you can hear the mournful singing of the varied thrush and admire its stunning orange and black plumage.

A large portion of Washington's bird variety is migrating birds. The state is along the Pacific Flyway, a significant north-south migration path for birds such as sandhill cranes, snow geese, and tundra swans. During their lengthy migrations, these birds frequently stop in the Skagit Valley and the Columbia Basin to feed and rest.

History

EARLY HISTORY

The Indigenous peoples of Washington profoundly influenced the state's early history. Tribes like the Coast Salish, Yakama, and Chinook created thriving cultures long before Europeans arrived. Utilizing the rich natural resources, these Indigenous communities fished for salmon in rivers, collected shellfish from the shore, and hunted wildlife in the woods. Their villages were highly structured, and the shared living quarters were enormous, ornately built longhouses. The Pacific Northwest had extensive trading networks for products such as shells, dried salmon, and woven baskets.

Evidence shows the area has been inhabited for more than 12,000 years. The Kennewick Man is a well-preserved skeleton discovered along the Columbia River in 1996. Radiocarbon dating established that the bones are over 9,000 years old. One of the most important archaeological finds in the state is the ancient Ozette town site on the Olympic Peninsula. A mudslide buried this Makah city around 500 years ago, and it was only

unearthed in the 1970s. Thousands of items, including fishing gear, baskets, and wooden tools, were preserved, providing priceless insights into the daily life and intricate craftsmanship of the Makah people.

The Europeans' arrival had devastating effects on the Native American communities in Washington. Indigenous populations were decimated by epidemics of introduced diseases like smallpox, measles, and influenza, to which they lacked immunity. The arrival of trading posts and settler communities displaced Indigenous peoples from their land, which in turn altered their subsistence practices and ways of life. Violent confrontations and forced relocations followed because of settlers' disputes over resources and land. The colonists' repeated breaches of unfairly negotiated treaties severely isolated Native American tribes and undermined their social and cultural institutions.

EXPLORERS ARRIVE

Although there were several earlier efforts, Spanish navigators were the first documented

Europeans to reach the area that is now Washington. Bruno de Heceta claimed the northwest coast for Spain in 1775 after leading an expedition down the coast. Once reaching the mouth of the Columbia River, his crew noted its potential as a site for future trade and expeditions. The Spanish missions marked the beginning of European invasions into Indigenous lands and prepared the way for future European discoveries.

Russian explorers set out into the Pacific Northwest in the late 18th century to map potential land and sea routes, with an eye on extending their fur-trading activities in Alaska. One objective was to determine the feasibility of a land bridge linking Russia to Alaska and possibly farther south. Russian expeditions along the Washington coast were small despite their extensive network of Alaskan trading posts and towns.

The Americans and British significantly advanced the exploration and mapping of Washington. European interest in the region was further piqued in 1778 when British Captain James Cook traveled around the coast of Washington. Captain George Vancouver's 1792 voyage mapped out Puget Sound and its surroundings in great detail, laying the groundwork for future trade and population. The exploration of Vancouver firmly established the British government's claims to the Pacific Northwest.

The American explorers Lewis and Clark played a crucial role in expanding American interests in Washington. In 1805, they reached the Pacific Ocean on an expedition ordered by President Thomas Jefferson to investigate the recently acquired western lands and to establish American settlements there. Their journey provided valuable insights into the Native inhabitants, natural resources, and topography of the Columbia River Basin. The subsequent arrival of American fur traders and residents further solidified American interests, paving the way for eventual statehood. The stage was set for a new era of rivalry and strife between the US and British explorers

over Washington's abundant riches and advantageous sites.

EARLY SETTLERS

The fur trade greatly impacted the early settlers of Washington state. In 1825 the Hudson's Bay Company built Fort Vancouver in what is now Vancouver, Washington; it served as the center of the company's Pacific Northwest activities. Many trappers, merchants, and settlers came to the area because Fort Vancouver was an important supply and commercial center. The fort played a crucial role in the region's early economic development by serving as a trading post for Indigenous and European settlers and encouraging the expansion of agriculture.

The Donation Land Claim Act of 1850 also encouraged people to settle in Washington. Under this law, American settlers could farm land in the Oregon Territory—which included today's Washington—for four years before they could claim it (320 acres/130 ha for individual settlers, 640 acres/260 ha for married couples). This policy drew thousands of settlers in search of better possibilities and land ownership. Land conflicts and resource competitiveness escalated as a result of the inflow, leading to higher tensions with Native American groups.

One notable conflict during this period was the Pig War of 1859, a boundary dispute between the United States and Britain over the San Juan Islands. The dispute was triggered when American settler Lyman Cutlar shot a pig belonging to the Hudson's Bay Company that was rooting in his garden. This seemingly minor incident escalated as both American and British authorities dispatched military forces to the islands. For several months, troops from both sides faced off, though no actual combat occurred. After lengthy talks and arbitration, the matter was finally resolved in 1872 when German Kaiser Wilhelm I sided with the US. The ruling ceded the San Juan Islands to the US and set the border across the Haro Strait.

GROWTH OF A NEW STATE

In its original 1848 formation, the Oregon Territory included what is now Oregon, Washington, Idaho, and portions of Wyoming and Montana. Population growth and northern settlement expansion made it abundantly evident that the enormous land needed to be split for better administration.

In 1853, the northern portion of the Oregon Territory was officially named the Washington Territory, which included Washington state and portions of what are now Idaho and Montana, then home to about 4,000 people. The growing population necessitated a new government to oversee the many new residents. Olympia was the original territorial capital and is still Washington's state capital.

Economic opportunities in forestry, fishing, and mining encouraged the population to continue growing, accelerating the campaign for statehood in the following decades. Washington Territory's population had grown substantially by the late 1880s, reaching over 350,000. Washington was formally admitted to the Union as the 42nd state on November 11, 1889.

PRESENT DAY

Present-day companies like Amazon, Boeing, and Microsoft have made Washington a center for economic growth and technical innovation. During the last half-century, these companies have been instrumental in developing the state's economy, culture, and international standing.

Boeing—which began operations in Seattle in 1916—grew substantially during and after WWII, eventually becoming the biggest aerospace firm in the world. Numerous Boeing manufacturing plants and corporate headquarters can be found around the state, with a concentration in the Puget Sound region.

Initially established in Albuquerque in 1975 by Paul Allen and Bill Gates, Microsoft moved its headquarters to Redmond, Washington, in 1979. Microsoft has since become a global powerhouse in personal computing and the broader IT industry. The area's influx of talent has fostered a thriving tech environment in metro Seattle, in large part due to Microsoft's contributions.

In 1994 Jeff Bezos launched an online book shop based in a Bellevue, Washington, garage. Over the years, Amazon has grown into an e-commerce and tech giant. Downtown Seattle is home to Amazon's headquarters, where real estate values have risen, and the number of jobs has increased by tens of thousands due to the company's fast expansion.

A number of other large companies have had a significant impact on Washington's economy. The Seattle-based coffeehouse chain Starbucks has expanded since 1971 to become a worldwide phenomenon. Costco, the membership warehouse chain, has its headquarters in Issaquah and operates on a global scale. Redmond-based Nintendo of America has a huge impact on the video game business.

People and Culture

NATIVE AMERICAN CULTURE

Look at a map of Washington and you'll see the impact of Native Americans—names such as Puyallup, Tacoma, and Seattle. However, just 92,000 Native Americans call Washington home today, or 1.2 percent of the state's population. There are 29 officially recognized tribes in Washington, each with a unique history, language, and cultural practices.

There are 29 reservations in the state, which are areas reserved for Indigenous peoples. Located in south-central Washington, the Yakama Nation Reservation is the largest reservation at approximately 2,000 sq mi (5,200 sq km). Less than half of Native

Americans live on reservations; the rest reside in urban and rural areas around Washington.

There are various places around the state to learn more about Native American culture. Neah Bay's Makah Cultural and Research Center showcases the Makah people's long and storied maritime past, and the Ozette archeological site has artifacts on display. The Seattle Burke Museum houses extensive collections and exhibits relating to natural history and Indigenous Northwest coastal civilizations. The Yakama Nation Cultural Center, located near Toppenish, has hundreds of artifacts from tribes in that area.

THE ARTS
Literature

Many well-known American poets and novelists were born and raised in Seattle. Richard Hugo is among the most prominent; his poems frequently depict scenes from the Northwest and its inhabitants. Many writers have been inspired by Hugo's poetry, which is profoundly tied to the landscape and character of the region. Hugo also established Hugo House, a literary center in Seattle, where a thriving literary community is nurtured through seminars, readings, and events, providing a welcoming environment for writers and readers to connect.

Tom Robbins was born in Seattle; his unusual and inventive novels include *Even Cowgirls Get the Blues* and *Jitterbug Perfume*. Native American novelist Sherman Alexie has become a significant player in the city's literary scene. *The Absolutely True Diary of a Part-Time Indian* and *The Lone Ranger and Tonto Fistfight in Heaven* are two of his works that delve into Native American identity and life in the Pacific Northwest.

Popular literature with deep ties to Washington is also strongly identified with Seattle. Set in the sleepy town of Concrete, *This Boy's Life* is a moving book by Tobias Wolff that details his troubled youth. The story paints a vivid picture of perseverance and coming-of-age in a rural environment and was eventually made into a movie.

A significant piece by David Guterson is *Snow Falling on Cedars*, which is set in the Puget Sound area. Love, loss, and racial discrimination are the central themes of this story of a village that has just emerged from the shadow of WWII. The book has become a classic in modern literature due to its vivid descriptions of the area's landscapes and the complexities of its socioeconomic problems.

The many literary festivals, writing programs, and independent bookstores that dot Seattle contribute to its thriving literary scene. One of the most cherished bookstores in town, Elliott Bay Book Company, often brings in authors from all over the country for readings and other events.

Music

Seattle's rich musical history has had a major impact on American music. Jimi Hendrix, whose groundbreaking guitar work and electric concerts shook up rock music in the '60s, is arguably the most famous Seattleite. MoPOP in Seattle celebrates Hendrix's impact and includes a significant memorabilia collection.

The city is also famous for being the birthplace of grunge music, which came into popularity in the '80s and '90s. Some of the most influential grunge bands emerged from Seattle, including Soundgarden, Alice in Chains, Pearl Jam, and of course Nirvana. Their album *Nevermind* made lead singer Kurt Cobain an icon in his own right. The Crocodile and Sub Pop record labels were key in bringing several area grunge bands to fame.

The iconic Seattleite Quincy Jones has made an everlasting impression on jazz, pop, and film scores as a composer, conductor, and producer. For over 60 years, Jones has collaborated with countless legendary musicians and hugely influenced modern music.

Essentials

Transportation

AIR

Seattle-Tacoma International Airport (SEA; 17801 International Blvd.; 206/787-3000; www.portseattle.org) is the state's main airport, located 13 mi (21 km) south of downtown Seattle. It's home to over 30 airlines that provide local and international flights, and it serves over 50 million passengers every year. The airport has a stellar reputation for supporting Pacific Northwest-based businesses and eateries rather than national chains. Sign up for **SEA Spot Saver** (www.portseattle.

org/SEAspotsaver) to be assigned a time to go through security and skip the lengthy lines.

Paine Field Airport (PAE; 3220 100th Street SW, Everett; 425/388-5125; www.painefield.com) is located about 23 mi (37 km) north of downtown Seattle and serves as a regional airport; with only a few gates, it's a more intimate travel experience. Paine Field hosts a few major airlines, providing primarily domestic flights to destinations around the western part of the country.

Tri-Cities Airport (PSC; 3601 N 20th Ave.; 509/547-6352; www.flytricities.com) is in Pasco and is the largest airport in the state's southeastern region. It hosts several major airlines and mainly has domestic flights to the western half of the United States. Tri-Cities Airport is a 2 hour 45 minute drive (214 mi/344 km) from Seattle.

Airport Transportation
The **Link** light rail (www.soundtransit.org; $3/one-way, $4.50-7/day pass) provides quick access between Seattle-Tacoma International Airport, downtown Seattle, and north Seattle. Trains run every 8-15 minutes 5am-1am weekdays and Saturdays, and 6am-midnight Sundays. Tickets ($3/one-way) can be purchased from on-site ticket machines with credit cards or contactless cards at electronic fare readers. Several taxi companies and rideshare services are also available at the airport.

TRAIN
Amtrak (800/872-7245; www.amtrak.com) operates several key routes through Seattle. The Cascades route travels along the I-5 corridor, connecting Vancouver, British Columbia, and Eugene, Oregon, with stops in Seattle and Portland as well as other cities in between. The Empire Builder route spans from Seattle to Chicago, passing through Spokane, Glacier National Park, and the Rocky Mountains. The Coast Starlight route extends between Seattle

and Los Angeles, with various stops along the I-5 corridor.

BUS
Greyhound (800/231-2222; www.greyhound.com) provides extensive bus service across Washington State. Key routes include stops in major cities such as Seattle, Tacoma, Olympia, and Bellingham along the I-5 corridor. In addition to these, Greyhound also serves Eastern Washington, with stops in cities like Spokane, Yakima, and Walla Walla.

FlixBus (855/626-8585; www.flixbus.com) is another alternative for bus travel. Along the I-5 corridor, its stops include Seattle, Tacoma, Olympia, and Bellingham. It also goes to select cities in Eastern Washington, such as Yakima and Spokane, and other states, like Oregon.

FERRY
Washington state has several ferry systems that provide essential transportation across its waterways.

Washington State Ferries
The **Washington State Ferry System** (https://wsdot.wa.gov) has the most extensive fleet in the United States, with 21 boats transporting millions of passengers and vehicles across Puget Sound each year. These ferries have a wide range in size and capacity; the largest can carry 2,500 people and 200 vehicles. There are 20 ports in Puget Sound and the San Juan Islands serviced by the fleet, providing vital transit connections for residents and visitors. Popular routes include Seattle to Bainbridge Island, Fauntleroy to Vashon Island, Edmonds to Kingston, Mukilteo to Clinton, and Anacortes to the San Juan Islands.

Other Ferries
Other ferries in the state include the **Black Ball Ferry Line** (360/457-4491; www.

cohoferry.com) and the **Victoria Clipper** (800/888-2535; www.clippervacations.com). The Black Ball Ferry Line operates the *MV Coho*, which runs up to four sailings daily between Port Angeles and Victoria, British Columbia, for passengers and vehicles. The Victoria Clipper offers passenger-only service between Seattle and Victoria. This high-speed ferry operates daily year-round.

CAR

A car is the best way to explore Washington, as many parts are hard to reach without one. Public transportation is reliable around major cities like Seattle and along the I-5 corridor, but you will need a car to get to other areas, such as hikes or national parks. There's a significant reduction in public transportation options once you head east over the Cascade Mountains, so it's best to have your own car to get to your destination.

In November-March, plan on snow and ice over the mountain passes, notably I-90 and US 2. These close down regularly when the weather gets too poor. Check the **WSDOT** website (www.wsdot.org) for the most current conditions in the mountain passes. Even when the passes are open, chains are often required to drive over them, so get yours before you start your trip.

Major Highways

Washington state borders the Canadian province of British Columbia to the north, Oregon to the south, and Idaho to the east.

I-5 begins at the Canadian border in Blaine, Washington, and runs south through Oregon and California before ending at the Mexican border.

I-90 runs east-west across the state, connecting Seattle with Spokane before continuing to Idaho and ending in Boston.

US 2 starts in Everett and travels east-west across Washington, reaching the Idaho state line, and continues across the country to Maine.

US 101 runs in a loop around the Olympic Peninsula, connecting Olympia, Port Angeles,

and the Pacific Coast, before extending south through Oregon and California.

US 97 runs north-south through Eastern Washington and Oregon, continuing until Northern California.

Route 20, known as the North Cascades Highway, runs east-west, from the Olympic Peninsula near Port Townsend, through North Cascades National Park, and to the Idaho state line.

Tolls

Washington state has several major toll bridges that help manage traffic congestion and fund infrastructure maintenance. The **Route 520 Bridge,** also known as the Evergreen Point Floating Bridge, has tolls of $1.25-6.50, varying by time of day and payment method. The **Route 99 Tunnel,** which replaced the Alaskan Way Viaduct, charges $1.20-4.70. The **Tacoma Narrows Bridge** on Route 16 has tolls of $1.50-6.50, depending on the type of vehicle and payment method. There are no toll booths on these bridges, so you pay when you receive a bill by mail if you take your own car, or the rental company will add the fares to your total at the end of your trip. To learn more about tolls, visit the WSDOT website (https://wsdot.wa.gov). For an easy way to pay tolls, create an account on Good To Go! (www.mygoodtogo.com) so you can pay for them online instead of being billed each time in the mail.

Car and RV Rentals

Car rental companies are in and around Seattle, but the **Seattle-Tacoma International Airport** (SEA, 17801 International Blvd.; 206/787-5388; https://portseattle.org) is the most accessible place to get rentals if you fly there. All car rental companies are off-site at the Sea-Tac Rental Car Facility, which you can reach through a free shuttle service that runs 24/7 from the airport terminal. Major rental companies like Alamo, Avis, Budget, Dollar, Enterprise, Hertz, National, and Thrifty operate from this facility.

Ridesharing Services

Ridesharing services like **Uber** and **Lyft** are primarily available in Washington's major urban areas, including Seattle, Tacoma, Bellevue, Spokane, and Olympia, with coverage extending to nearby suburbs and communities. However, many small towns have a taxi service of some sort.

Electric-Vehicle Charging Stations

Washington state has almost 2,000 public electric vehicle charging stations across various networks, such as EVgo, ChargePoint, and Tesla. These charging stations can be found throughout the state, including in many rural locations. You can use the **ChargeHub app** (https://chargehub.com) or **West Coast Green Highway** (www.westcoastgreenhighway.com) to find charging stations.

BIKE

Bikers in Washington state follow the same laws and regulations as drivers of motor vehicles, including keeping to the right side of the road, signaling, and stopping for pedestrians. All parts of a road, bike lane, or sidewalk are open to bikers unless otherwise stated in a local ordinance. Helmets aren't a statewide requirement but a smart choice for everyone. Seattle, Tacoma, Bellevue, and the counties of Pierce, Spokane, and King require helmets for residents of all ages. When riding at night, bikers must have a white front light and a red rear reflector or light. Additionally, when passing other bikes or pedestrians, it is recommended that you employ audible signals.

The **Washington State Department of Transportation** (https://wsdot.wa.gov) has more information on rules, bike routes, and maps. The **Seattle Department of Transportation** (www.seattle.gov/transportation/projects-and-programs/programs/bike-program) also has detailed bike maps and resources specifically for Seattle, including bike lanes, trails, and bike parking locations.

Recreation

Washington's plethora of outdoor activities is one of the state's biggest draws. During winter, skiers and snowboarders flock to the Cascade Mountains and destinations like Stevens Pass and Crystal Mountain. As soon as the weather warms up, these mountains become utopia for hikers, bikers, and campers. Locations such as Westport and the San Juan Islands along the Pacific coast attract tourists who come for fishing, whale-watching, and beachcombing. Water sports enthusiasts love the state's many rivers and lakes, like the Columbia River and Lake Washington, perfect for canoeing, kayaking, and fishing.

PUBLIC LANDS

Almost half of Washington is public land. Some larger landowner agencies are the US Forest Service, Bureau of Land Management, National Park Service, and Bureau of Indian Affairs.

National Parks

Washington state is home to three national parks, each offering unique natural attractions. **Mount Rainier National Park** (www.nps.gov/mora) is known for its iconic 14,411-ft (4,392-m) volcanic peak, extensive wildflower meadows, and countless hiking trails. **Olympic National Park** (www.nps.gov/olym) includes lush temperate rain forests, a rugged Pacific coastline, and the glaciated peaks of the Olympic Mountains. **North Cascades National Park** (www.nps.gov/noca) has dramatic alpine scenery, featuring jagged peaks, pristine lakes, and over 300 glaciers.

The **entry fees** for Mount Rainier and Olympic National Parks are $30/vehicle for a **seven-day pass,** $25/motorcycle, and $15/ pedestrian or biker for a seven-day period. Purchase a pass in advance on **recreation.gov** or in person at the entrance booth. There is no entrance fee to North Cascades National Park.

State Parks

Washington has over 140 state parks, covering diverse landscapes from marine parks and heritage sites to historic parks and ocean beaches. Some are small, but others, like Whidbey Island's Deception Pass and Orcas Island's Moran State Park, are several thousand acres.

History buffs will love Fort Ebey, Fort Worden, and Fort Flagler with their old military fortifications. Cape Disappointment is home to lighthouses and beautiful ocean views, while Deception Pass is known for its stunning bridge and tidal currents. The magnificent Palouse Falls, inland in Palouse Falls State Park, is a 198-ft-tall (60-m) cascade that thunders down a steep canyon.

To visit Washington State Parks, you'll need a **Discover Pass** ($30/year, $10/day pass). Purchase your pass in person at bigger parks or online (www.discoverpass.wa.gov). The pass is also valid for parking at state parks and lands managed by the Washington Department of Fish and Wildlife (WDFW) and the Department of Natural Resources (DNR).

Forest Service Lands

You'll need a **Northwest Forest Pass** ($30/ year, $5/day pass) to access Forest Service lands in Washington state. Purchase a pass online (www.fs.usda.gov), at Forest Service offices, and from various local vendors. The pass is required for parking at many trailheads and recreation sites within national forests.

HIKING

Hiking is a favorite outdoor activity in Washington, with trails available for every skill level. On the state's western side, most trails are accessible year-round, if wet during the winter. High-elevation trails are in the Cascades and Olympic Mountains are typically snow-free June-October. Trails in Eastern Washington are also accessible during these months, but temperatures can reach triple digits (38°C and up) during peak summer months. Popular hiking spots near Seattle and destinations like Mount Rainier, the North Cascades, and the Olympic Peninsula experience heavy traffic in the summer, with parking lots filling up by 8am, so it's best to arrive early.

If you plan on hiking in Washington in the summer, keep yourself updated on wildfire conditions. Wildfires can create unhealthy air quality and obscure scenic views The **Washington State Department of Natural Resources** (www.dnr.wa.gov) has the latest information on wildfires.

Additionally, car break-ins are common around trailheads off I-90 and Mountain Loop Highway, so never leave anything visible in your vehicle, and always take your possessions with you.

For the most up-to-date hiking information, visit the **Washington Trails Association** website (www.wta.org). The WTA's hiking guides include content written by local hiking experts with mileage, elevation gain, and other important facts to plan for. It also has trail reports from users that can inform you about current conditions.

BIKING

Thanks to a variety of programs and improvements to bicycle infrastructure, Washington has become known as a bike-friendly state. The Washington Bikes Act, enacted in 2017, is incorporating bike lanes and pedestrian routes into transportation plans. Significant progress has been made in cities like Seattle, where more than 4 percent of workers opt to ride their bike to the office. Several biking events, including the Emerald City Bike Ride and the Seattle to Portland (STP) ride, take place in Seattle, which has a network of protected bike lanes and bike-sharing programs,

FISHING AND HUNTING

The Washington **Department of Fish and Wildlife** (https://wdfw.wa.gov) is the main source for the latest rules, regulations, and information on seasonal opportunities and closures. Anglers in Washington can use the free Fish Washington app to find the latest fishing regulations for all bodies of water in Washington, maps, tidal predictions for marine waters, and more.

Fishing Licenses

In Washington, anglers age 15 and over are required to have a fishing license. Purchase your license online through the **Washington Department of Fish and Wildlife** (https://wdfw.wa.gov/licenses/fishing) or at local retailers. Licenses for residents start at $11/day or $30/year and vary depending on where you're fishing. The cost for nonresidents begins at $20/day or $60/year.

Hunting Licenses

Washington offers excellent hunting opportunities, particularly in the eastern and central regions, for game such as waterfowl, deer, and elk. Annual hunting licenses start at $45 for residents and $184 for nonresidents, with additional costs for specific tags.

In Washington, you can hunt at any age, but you'll need to take a hunter education course if you were born after January 1, 1972; register for it on the **WDFW website** (https://wdfw.wa.gov). A current hunting license and any other applicable tags, permits, or stamps must be always carried by every hunter. At WDFW check stations, hunters may be asked to display any game they have taken. Licenses can be purchased via the **Washington Department of Fish and Wildlife website** (https://wdfw.wa.gov), by calling 360/902-2464, or from various dealers throughout the state. Note that purchasing online or by phone may result in a 7-10-day wait for license delivery, so plan accordingly.

CAMPING

There are abundant campgrounds throughout the state. **Washington State Parks** (www.parks.state.wa.us) has sites with amenities like showers, flush toilets, and electrical hookups. Some parks also feature cabins and yurts with electricity and heating. Campsite fees range $20-50 for tent or RV sites and $45-80 for cabins and yurts. Reservations can be made up to nine months in advance through the **Washington State Parks website** (www.washington.goingtocamp.com). Popular sites, especially along the coast and near lakes, tend to book up quickly during summer.

The **US Forest Service** (www.fs.usda.gov) also manages numerous campgrounds in Washington, often in more remote locations. These campgrounds have fewer amenities, such as vault toilets and potable water. The usually have fewer campsites and are on rural roads. Fees generally range $10-25 per night, and reservations can be made six months in advance through **recreation.gov.**

Campfire bans may be in effect during the summer, particularly mid-late summer, to prevent human-caused wildfires and ensure campers' safety. Always check for current fire restrictions before your trip and plan accordingly.

WATER SPORTS
Kayaking, Canoeing, and Stand-Up Paddleboarding

Rivers, coastal seas, and alpine lakes in Washington are perfect for kayaking, canoeing, and stand-up paddleboarding. Each individual on board a boat, even in a paddle craft, is required by Washington law to have their own personal flotation device. While adults are not required to wear life jackets, they are strongly advised for safety reasons. At all times while the boat is in motion, children under the age of 12 must wear a life jacket that the United States Coast Guard has authorized.

Boating

A **Washington State Boater Education Card,** which can be obtained by completing a boating safety course recognized by

Washington State Parks (https://parks.wa.gov), is required for operating a boat with 15 horsepower or greater. This card ($10) can be purchased online or from authorized course providers. Visitors from other states do not require a card if their boating trip is shorter than 60 days.

White-Water Rafting

There are excellent white-water rafting options along Washington's many rivers. On the Wenatchee River near Leavenworth, you'll find the exhilarating Class III and IV rapids that thrill-seekers want.

WINTER SPORTS

While Seattle locals get excited the few times a year it snows in the city, you'll have to head to the mountains for the majority of snow. Mount Rainier is a popular

snowshoeing and cross-country skiing destination, particularly in the Paradise area. Stevens Pass and Snoqualmie Pass have skiing, snowboarding, snow tubing, and sledding opportunities. Another popular site is the Methow Valley, home to one of North America's biggest networks of cross-country ski trails.

Recreation Passes and Fees

A **Sno-Park permit** is required to park at popular trailheads for cross-country skiing and snowshoeing on Washington state federally managed properties November-April. You can buy these passes at local stores or online (https://parks.wa.gov; $25/day, $50/season). There are no pay stations at most Sno-Parks, so you'll need to get a pass in advance.

Travel Tips

ENTRY REQUIREMENTS

By law, air travelers from other countries must provide a valid passport and proof of return transit before entering the United States. With an e-passport, citizens of **Visa Waiver Program** (VWP) nations can enter the United States visa-free for up to 90 days. Travelers from non-VWP nations require a valid passport and a tourist visa. For specific country requirements and travel advisories, visit the **US Department of State website** (https://state.gov).

ACCESS FOR TRAVELERS WITH DISABILITIES

Travelers with disabilities will find many restaurants and attractions in larger cities to be accommodating, with wheelchair-accessible ramps or elevators. However, facilities may be limited at outdoor activities or historical sites, and some may not have ramps or paved walkways.

Anyone with a permanent disability, such as a vision impairment, can use the **Access Pass** (https://store.usgs.gov/access-pass) to enjoy complimentary access to federal recreation sites for the rest of their life, regardless of age. National parks, monuments, historic sites, leisure areas, and wildlife refuges are just a few places this pass grants admission to.

Washington Trails Association (www.wta.org) has helpful filters you can use when searching for a hike, including wheelchair-friendly trails.

LGBTQ+ TRAVELERS

Washington State is great for LGBTQ+ tourists because of its liberal attitude and welcoming policies toward the LGBTQ+ community. Cities like Tacoma and Seattle have thriving LGBTQ+ neighborhoods and annual festivals like Seattle Pride. When it comes to housing, jobs, and public spaces, Washington state has extensive anti-discrimination legislation that safeguards people based on their gender identity and sexual orientation. Same-sex marriage has been lawful since 2012.

Seattle's **LGBTQ+ Center** (www.gayclty. org) is an excellent resource for events happening in the area. Promoting LGBTQ+ equity in all areas of state government is the objective of the **Washington State LGBTQ Commission** (https://lgbtq.wa.gov).

TRAVELERS OF COLOR

About 67 percent of Washington citizens identify as white, although Seattle has significant Asian, Black, Hispanic, and Native American communities. The Yakima Valley is one of several areas in Washington that has a large Latino or Hispanic population—nearly half of the region's residents identify as such—and the rich cultural diversity that this brings.

Many groups in Washington promote racial equality and justice. The **Asian Counseling and Referral Service** (https://acrs.org) and the **Urban League of Metropolitan Seattle** (https://urban league.org) both work to strengthen minority communities via advocacy, education, and community-building programs. Native American and Hispanic communities in Washington are also supported by the **Governor's Office of Indian Affairs** (https://goia.wa.gov) and the **Washington State Commission on Hispanic Affairs** (www.cha.wa.gov). In 2022, Washington reported 652 hate crime offenses, with 63 percent being racially motivated. Black individuals are the most frequently targeted in race-related hate crimes, accounting for the majority of incidents.

SENIOR TRAVELERS

Washington welcomes elderly travelers and has a range of services and amenities designed specifically for them. Wheelchair-accessible paths and guided tours are accessible in many tourist spots. Seniors can save money on the state's public transportation networks, including buses and ferries, through discounted fares. **Age Friendly Seattle** (https://seattle. gov/agefriendly) has an extensive directory of senior-friendly places to visit and discounts available at local businesses.

SOLO TRAVELERS

While traveling alone in Washington is usually safe, there are also plenty of options to join tours or groups for socialization and increased safety. Solo travelers can meet locals and see Seattle's top sights on guided walking tours, culinary tours, and cultural excursions. Adventurers can sign up for guided kayaking trips, whale-watching expeditions, and group treks. In addition, hostels are great places for solitary travelers to meet like-minded people and participate in group activities. There are multiple hiking groups on Facebook if you feel like joining someone, like Women Who Hike Washington.

TRAVELING WITH CHILDREN

Washington is a great place to take kids on vacation. There is no shortage of outdoor activities, from tide-pooling and beachcombing to kid-friendly hiking paths in parks like Olympic and Mount Rainier. Discounts are provided for children at many museums and attractions, and in the summer, walks in state parks are often led by park rangers. While most accommodations, restaurants, and even breweries are family-friendly, some of the more upscale ones may have age restrictions, so call before you go.

Health and Safety

EMERGENCY SERVICES

Call 911 anywhere in Washington for assistance if you run into an emergency.

Most midsize or large towns have hospitals with emergency rooms open 24 hours. If you're in a small town, you might have to go to urgent care; otherwise, you might have to drive to the next biggest city with a hospital.

BACKCOUNTRY SAFETY

The varied and frequently difficult terrain in Washington's backcountry makes safety an essential concern for anyone venturing out into it. Get yourself outfitted in appropriate footwear, weather-appropriate clothing, a trustworthy map, a compass or GPS device, and a fully charged cell phone or satellite communication device. Always make sure you have the **ten essentials**: a map, sunscreen, insulating clothing, light, emergency shelter, food, water, tools for repairs, and first-aid supplies.

Before you hit the route, get a feel for the trail conditions, the predicted weather, and the likelihood of dangers like avalanches and wildlife. To be extra safe, tell someone when you're going somewhere and when you anticipate to come back. You can also consider getting a personal locating beacon (PLB).

You also need to know and follow the **Leave No Trace** principles. These include staying on well-defined routes, camping in approved locations, and removing all your garbage. To prevent waterborne infections, treat or filter water sources before drinking them. In addition, you should be familiar with basic first-aid procedures and always have an emergency kit to deal with injuries, unexpected weather changes, or becoming lost.

WILDLIFE
Snakes

Washington is home to the western rattlesnake, the only venomous snake found in the region. These snakes are primarily located in the dry, eastern parts of the state, particularly in the shrub-steppe and pine forest areas. While their venom is potent, bites are rare and usually occur when the snake is accidentally provoked. Western rattlesnakes will let out a warning rattle when threatened, but otherwise they prefer to remain silent.

Ticks

Ticks can be a concern when hiking and camping, particularly the western black-legged tick and the American dog tick, which can transmit diseases such as Lyme disease, anaplasmosis, and Rocky Mountain spotted fever. These ticks are commonly found in grassy, brushy, and wooded areas, especially in the western regions and lower elevations. To reduce the risk of tick bites, use repellents containing DEET, wear long sleeves and pants, and perform thorough tick checks after spending time outdoors. If a tick is found, remove it promptly with tweezers and clean the area.

Cougars

Cougars, also known as mountain lions or pumas, have an estimated population of 2,100-2,400 in the state. Over the past century, there have only been 20 reported attacks, as cougars tend to keep to themselves in remote areas. While these encounters are rare, it's important to know how to stay safe if you do have one.

Traveling in groups and keeping kids close can help you avoid interactions with cougars. Cougars tend to avoid larger groups and target smaller individuals. Cougars are most active between dawn and dusk, so stay attentive and do not use headphones while you're out and about. If you encounter a cougar, never run; instead, stand your ground, make yourself appear larger, and make loud noises to scare the animal away. Maintain eye contact and back away slowly without turning your back. Carrying bear spray can also be a useful precaution.

In the extremely unlikely case that you are attacked, retaliate aggressively using any objects at your disposal, with a focus on the cougar's eyes and face.

Bears

Black bears and grizzly bears both call Washington state home. Black bears are far more prevalent; an estimated 25,000-30,000 occupy the state's forests, mountains, and coastlines. Fewer than 20 grizzly bears are known to inhabit the North Cascades and the northeastern region of Washington, making them extremely rare.

Hikers can lessen the likelihood of being startled by bears by making a lot of noise—talking, clapping, or even utilizing bear bells. Be extra careful near food sources like berry bushes, hike in groups, and stick to marked trails. Always maintain your distance from bears, and never get too close to cubs because their mother is always nearby. When camping, make sure to store all food, trash, and scented goods in bear canisters away from your campsite. Never store food in your tent or cook near your sleeping area, and always clean up completely after meals.

If you meet a bear while hiking, stay calm and do not run. Running can trigger the bear's chase instinct. Instead, speak calmly and firmly, and wave your arms slowly to help the bear recognize you as a human. Avoid direct eye contact, which can be taken as a threat, and slowly back away, ensuring the bear has an escape route. Stand your ground if the bear shows signs of aggression, such as making huffing noises, swatting the ground, or charging. Make yourself look larger by raising your arms or opening your jacket, and make loud noises by yelling or banging objects. If the bear continues to approach, use bear spray if you have it, aiming for the bear's face.

In the rare event of a black bear attack, fight back aggressively using any available objects. Black bears are more likely to be scared off by resistance. For a grizzly bear, play dead by lying flat on your stomach, covering your neck with your hands, and spreading your legs so it's more difficult for the bear to turn you over. Stay there still until the bear completely leaves.

WILDFIRES

Wildfires are becoming more of a concern during the summer as the years go on. Washington has its share of wildfires but also gets smoky skies and poor air quality from fires to the north in British Columbia and south in Oregon and California. Fires typically start at the end of June and can go until the end of September, so you should have a backup plan for outdoor activities during this time.

You can stay updated on fire conditions in real time by downloading the **AirQualityWA** or **AirNow** apps.

Resources

Suggested Reading

Bentley, Judy, and Craig Romano. *Hiking Washington's History*. Seattle: University of Washington Press, 2021. This guidebook covers 44 hikes across Washington and includes historical narratives with full-color trail maps.

Hill, Craig. *Moon Washington Hiking: Best Hikes plus Beer, Bites, and Campgrounds Nearby*. Berkeley: Avalon Travel, 2021. Discover the best hikes across Washington, featuring diverse trails from easy lakeside walks to challenging mountain hikes, complete with detailed descriptions, maps, and tips on nearby breweries, local eateries, and camping spots.

Miller, Marli B. *Roadside Geology of Washington*. Missoula: Mountain Press, 2017. Learn about the geological features of Washington, including the state's volcanoes, earthquakes, landslide risks, and historic Ice Age floods, along with insights into its diverse rock formations and geologic features along more than 40 highways.

Morgan, Murray. *Skid Road: An Informal Portrait of Seattle*. Seattle: University of Washington Press, 2018. Read an engaging portrait of Seattle's first century, tracing its history from a timber town to a dynamic city, highlighting colorful citizens, significant events, and the constant theme of change.

Ritter, Harry. *Washington's History: The People, Land, and Events of the Far Northwest.*

Seattle: University of Washington Press, 2018. Delve into the Northwest's captivating history and its people through 55 vignettes that highlight the diverse individuals who shaped the Evergreen State, from Native peoples and explorers to contemporary technological innovators.

Steelquist, Robert. *The Northwest Coastal Explorer: Your Guide to the Places, Plants, and Animals of the Pacific Coast*. Portland: Timber Press, 2016. Explore the marine life of Oregon, Washington, and British Columbia with vibrant illustrations, informative profiles of plants and animals—including tips on locating them—and a getaway guide featuring the best weekend trips.

Stienstra, Tom. *Moon Washington Camping: The Complete Guide to Tent and RV Camping*. Berkeley: Avalon Travel, 2020. Explore Washington's great outdoors with a range of campsites, from family-friendly car camping to secluded hike-ins, complete with ratings, amenities, recreation highlights, maps, and expert advice.

Williams, David B. *Seattle Walks: Discovering History and Nature in the City*. Seattle: University of Washington Press, 2017. Discover Seattle's walkability through diverse trails and sidewalks that blend history and architecture, offering scenic views, hidden gems, and architectural treasures while showcasing how nature intertwines with the urban landscape.

Internet Resources

The Seattle Times
www.seattletimes.com
This Seattle-based daily newspaper covers local and regional news, politics, business, sports, entertainment, and lifestyle.

Seattle Post-Intelligencer
www.seattlepi.com
This Seattle-based daily newspaper provides in-depth coverage of local news, politics, business, technology, sports, and entertainment, with a focus on the Seattle metropolitan area and the broader Pacific Northwest region.

The Stranger
www.thestranger.com
This Seattle-based alternative weekly is known for its edgy and opinionated take on news, arts, and entertainment in Seattle and the broader Puget Sound area.

Washington Trails Association
www.wta.org
The Washington Trails Association provides detailed information on hiking trails, trail conditions, and outdoor recreation in the state, offering resources such as trail guides, trip reports, and maps.

National Park Service
www.nps.gov
Explore national parks, historic sites, and outdoor recreational sites with resources such as park maps, closure information, and visiting hours.

US Forest Service
www.fs.usda.gov
Find information on hiking, camping, wildlife viewing, forest management, and current conditions in national forests managed by the Forest Service.

State of Washington Tourism
https://stateofwatourism.com
Find travel guides, itineraries, and tips for exploring Washington through the state's tourism board.

Washington Department of Transportation
https://wsdot.wa.gov
Access real-time traffic updates, road conditions, and transportation services across the state provided by the Washington Department of Transportation.

Washington Department of Fish and Wildlife
https://wdfw.wa.gov
Get information on fishing, hunting, wildlife viewing, habitat conservation, species management, and licensing.

Visit Kitsap
www.visitkitsap.com
Discover the Kitsap Peninsula with guides on where to stay, dine, and explore, along with information on local events and attractions.

Lake Chelan
www.lakechelan.com
Plan your visit to Lake Chelan with resources on accommodations, dining, outdoor activities, and seasonal events.

Visit Long Beach Peninsula
www.visitlongbeachpeninsula.com
Explore the Long Beach Peninsula with tips on dining, lodging, beach activities, and local festivals.

Olympic Peninsula
https://olympicpeninsula.org

Find comprehensive travel information for the Olympic Peninsula, including places to stay, Olympic National Park itineraries, and road trip ideas.

Visit San Juans
www.visitsanjuans.com

Learn about the San Juan Islands with guides on accommodations, dining, outdoor recreation, and local events.

Visit Seattle
https://visitseattle.org

Access travel guides, event calendars, neighborhood highlights, and recommendations for dining and attractions in Seattle.

Visit Spokane
www.visitspokane.com

Explore Spokane with information on hotels, restaurants, events, and things to do, along with travel tips and itineraries.

Visit Tacoma
https://visittacoma.com

Discover Tacoma's attractions, dining options, accommodations, and events with detailed travel guides and recommendations.

Port of Seattle
www.portseattle.org

Learn about the Port of Seattle's services, including cruise information, airport updates, and port facilities, along with travel tips and visitor guides.

Washington Wine Directory
www.washingtonwine.org

Explore Washington's wine country with a directory of wineries, tasting rooms, wine events, and touring tips

Washington Brewers Guild
www.washingtonbrewersguild.org

Discover Washington's craft beer scene with information on local breweries, beer events, and advocacy efforts supporting the state's brewing industry.

Index

List of Maps

Photo Credits

MAP SYMBOLS

≡≡≡ Expressway	○ City/Town	ⓘ Information Center	♠ Park
▬▬ Primary Road	◉ State Capital		♢ Golf Course
═══ Secondary Road	⊛ National Capital	Ⓟ Parking Area	✦ Unique Feature
▭▭▭ Unpaved Road		♙ Church	
---- Trail	◍ Highlight	♠ Winery/Vineyard	⌇ Waterfall
···· Ferry	★ Point of Interest		▲ Camping
┄┄┄ Railroad	• Accommodation	Ⓣ Trailhead	▲ Mountain
▨▨▨ Pedestrian Walkway	▼ Restaurant/Bar	Ⓣ Train Station	✗ Ski Area
▭▭▭ Stairs	■ Other Location	✈ Airport	⬭ Glacier
		✗ Airfield	

CONVERSION TABLES

°C = (°F - 32) / 1.8
°F = (°C x 1.8) + 32

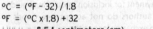

1 foot = 0.304 meters (m)
1 yard = 0.914 meters
1 mile = 1.6093 kilometers (km)
1 km = 0.6214 miles
1 fathom = 1.8288 m
1 chain = 20.1168 m
1 furlong = 201.168 m
1 acre = 0.4047 hectares
1 sq km = 100 hectares
1 sq mile = 2.59 square km
1 ounce = 28.35 grams
1 pound = 0.4536 kilograms
1 short ton = 0.90718 metric ton
1 short ton = 2,000 pounds
1 long ton = 1.016 metric tons
1 long ton = 2,240 pounds
1 metric ton = 1,000 kilograms
1 quart = 0.94635 liters
1 US gallon = 3.7854 liters
1 Imperial gallon = 4.5459 liters
1 nautical mile = 1.852 km

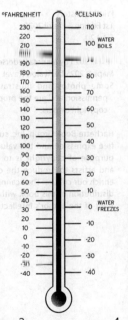

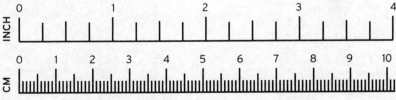

MOON WASHINGTON STATE
Avalon Travel
Hachette Book Group, Inc.
555 12th Street, 18th Floor
Oakland, CA 94607, USA
www.moon.com

Editor: Rachael Sablik
Managing Editor: Courtney Packard
Copy Editor: Matthew Hoover
Graphics and Production Coordinator: Darren Alessi
Cover Design: Toni Tajima
Interior Design: Avalon Travel
Map Editor: Karin Dahl
Cartographers: Abby Whelan, Karin Dahl
Proofreader: Brett Keener
Indexer: Rachel Kuhn

ISBN-13: 979-8-88647-086-4

Printing History
1st Edition — April 2025
5 4 3 2 1

Front cover photo: boardwalk at Cape Flattery ©
Amit Basu Photography / Getty Images
Back cover photo: Mount Rainier in the dusk ©
Michal Balada | Dreamstime.com

Printed in China by APS